Serbia

the Bradt Travel Guide

Laurence Mitchell

edition
5

www.bradtguides.com

Bradt Travel Guides Ltd, UK
The Globe Pequot Press Inc, USA

May 2018

Subotica: a prominent Hungarian character and distinctive secessionist architecture set this town in the far north as a place apart

Novi Sad: known for its history of scholarship and culture, this elegant city has long been referred to as the 'Serbian Athens'
pages 230–53

'Šargan Eight' Railway: encompassing numerous switchbacks, tunnels and bridges in just a few kilometres, this railway at Mokra Gora is an exhilarating ride
pages 309–11

Studenica Monastery: in a country full of exquisite Orthodox monasteries, this remote 12th-century jewel is one of the best for architecture and location
pages 316–17

CROATIA

BOSNIA - HERZEGOVINA

MONTENEGRO

ADRIATIC SEA

Subotica
Senta
Sombor
Bečej
A1
Vrbas
Bačka Palanka
Novi Sad
Fruška Gora Hills
Sremska Mitrovica
Ruma
Šabac
Drina
Sava
Loznica
Valjevo
Tara National Park
Užice
Zlatibor
Priboj
Zlatar
Prijepolje
Studenica

N

Bradt

KEY
Capital city	■
Other city	●
Main town	○
Other town	○
Main road	
Other road	
Railway	
National/nature park	––––
International boundary	–·–·–
Province boundary	

0   50km
0   50 miles

Belgrade: Serbia's relaxed capital has a plethora of cafés and restaurants, a vibrant atmosphere and the best nightlife in southeast Europe
pages 99–180

Vršac: delightful town near the Romanian border with charming Hapsburg architecture and a historic wine-making tradition
pages 286–91

Golubac Fortress: this photogenic 13th-century Hungarian fortress is one of the highlights of the River Danube route
pages 188–9

Niš: despite its industrial past, Serbia's third city has plenty of character, with an Ottoman fortress, lively cafés and stunning countryside
pages 348–62

Rock formations of Đavolja Varoš: a remote site near the Kosovo border, the otherworldly rock formations of 'Devil's Town' are a sight to behold
pages 378–9

Novi Pazar: with an animated bazaar and mosques aplenty, the Raška town of Novi Pazar has a distinctly Turkish vibe
pages 321–6

Kikinda

Zrenjanin

Danube

Deliblatska Pešcara

Vršac

Zemun

BELGRADE

Pančevo

Smederevo

A1

Požarevac

Danube

Kladovo

ROMANIA

Homoljske Planina

Đerdap National Park

Negotin

Smed Planka

Velika Morava

Bor

Kragujevac

Jagodina

Zaječar

Paraćin

A1

Čačak

Kraljevo

Kruševac

Knjaževac

Stara Planina

Niš

Kopaonik National Park

Prokupje

Pirot

Novi Pazar

Kosovska Mitrovica

Leskovac

BULGARIA

Pec

KOSOVO

Pristina

Vranje

Đakovica

Urosevac

Prizren

Serbia
Don't
miss...

Belgrade
Strategically placed at the confluence of the Sava and Danube rivers, Serbia's capital has embraced its position at a cultural and historical crossroads with an undeniable *joie de vivre*; shown here is the view from Savamala over the water
(VN/S) pages 99–179

Niš region
Ideal for cycling and hiking, the rugged landscape of the Niš region is home to several precipitous peaks, such as Babin Zub in the Stara Planina range
(TON) pages 348–62

Monasteries

Often hidden in remote valleys, the monasteries of Serbia are a highlight of any trip; shown here, Studenica Monastery, established in the 12th century and one of the holiest places in Serbia

(DB/ANTOS)
pages 316–17

Subotica

An overwhelming feature of this culturally Hungarian town, the middle European secessionist architecture demonstrates a flair for gaudy elegance and colourful grandeur

(MM/S) pages 268–77

Novi Sad

Renowned as a cultural and scholastic centre and nicknamed the 'Serbian Athens', this elegant and lively city contains stunning Baroque buildings and the oldest theatre in the country

(NS/D) pages 230–53

Serbia in colour

top left Elegant façades line Belgrade's famous Knez Mihailova Street (DB/ANTOS) pages 152 & 154–5

above left Belgraders can often be found playing chess in Kalemegdan Park in the early evening (LM) pages 147–8

above right The Savamala waterfront area, earmarked for large-scale development in the near future, is the best place to see artistic graffiti in Belgrade (LM) page 151

below At one time separate from Belgrade and under Habsburg control, Zemun offers a quiet escape from the city (DB/ANTOS) pages 161–5

below left   The quintessential example of the romantic ruin, Golubac Fortress is a majestic site along the banks of the Danube at the head of the Đerdap Gorge (BJ/ANTOS) page 188

bottom left   An unusual memorial constructed by the Turks as a warning to all who would oppose them, the grotesque Skull Tower (Ćele kula) in Niš elicits a macabre sense of fascination (TON) pages 358–9

below right   Smederevo Fortress is remarkable for the sheer scale of its impressive defences and the extent of its preservation (LM) pages 181–7

AUTHOR

Laurence Mitchell has, at various times, taught English in Sudan, surveyed historic farm buildings in Norfolk, pushed a pen in a local government office and worked as a geography teacher. Travel has been an important part of his life ever since his first tentative steps overseas in the 1970s, well before the term 'backpacker' was invented. These days, he works as a freelance travel writer and photographer and has contributed to publications that include

Geographical, hidden europe, Walk and *Discover Britain* as well as writing walking guides and several guidebooks for Bradt. With a particular penchant for forgotten places, border zones and territories in transition, he makes regular forays to such places from his home base in Norfolk. He has been visiting Serbia since it was part of the former Yugoslavia and Tito was in charge. Laurence is a member of the British Guild of Travel Writers and the Outdoor Writers and Photographers Guild. His blog can be found at **w** eastofelveden.wordpress.com and photography website at **w** laurencemitchell.com.

AUTHOR'S STORY

I first passed through the country that now calls itself Serbia back in the 1970s when it was still part of Tito's Yugoslavia. I was hitchhiking to India, so although the country seemed interesting, I was determined to push on eastwards without stopping for long. A decade later, a tourist boom started to bring hundreds of thousands of sun-seekers to Yugoslavia's Adriatic shores but I missed out on this too.

Before I knew it, Tito had died and dreadful events were starting to unravel in the region. I watched the television news horrified as the Balkans imploded in savage civil war and the Yugoslav federation fragmented and fell apart in bloody chaos.

When peace finally came I was curious to see what remained, so I travelled around the region visiting each of the six countries that used to comprise Yugoslavia. It soon became clear that although there was a renewed interest in newly independent states like Croatia and Slovenia, Serbia still remained well off the radar for most travellers. It was plagued with a wholly negative image, a legacy of the 1990s wars that was hard to shake. My personal experience did not tally with this, as I knew that most of its citizens were a far cry from the villainous war criminals they were often portrayed as. At that time there was little travel advice available other than antiquated guides to Yugoslavia that were written in the 1980s. It was time, I thought, that someone addressed this matter.

The Serbs I met when I was researching the guidebook generally provided one of two reactions: most were delighted that I was taking an interest in putting them back on the map; a few thought I was completely mad. I will leave it up to you to make up your own mind.

PUBLISHER'S FOREWORD   *Hilary Bradt*

Serbia's reputation has shifted from association with war in the Balkans to being a significant tourist hot spot. Belgrade's nightlife attracts an increasing number of young people, but I first became enthused when a birding friend turned up with a Serbian birdwatcher's T-shirt, and regaled me with descriptions of the untouched countryside and helpful people. Once again, Laurence Mitchell has more than done the country justice. His detailed descriptions of hotels and restaurants, and his ability to 'paint the picture', ensure that travellers who venture to this destination will not be disappointed.

Fifth edition published September 2017
First published 2005
Bradt Travel Guides Ltd
IDC House, The Vale, Chalfont St Peter, Bucks SL9 9RZ, England
w bradtguides.com
Print edition published in the USA by The Globe Pequot Press Inc,
PO Box 480, Guilford, Connecticut 06437-0480

Text copyright © 2017 Laurence Mitchell
Maps copyright © 2017 Bradt Travel Guides Ltd, includes map data © OpenStreetMap contributors
Photographs copyright © 2017 Individual photographers (see below)
Project Managers: Anna Moores, Laura Pidgley and Edward Alexander
Cover research: Pepi Bluck, Perfect Picture

ISBN: 978 1 78477 056 3 (print)
e-ISBN: 978 1 78477 512 4 (e-pub)
e-ISBN: 978 1 78477 413 4 (mobi)

British Library Cataloguing in Publication Data
A catalogue record for this book is available from the British Library

Photographs Alamy: saturno dona' (sd/A); Archive National Tourism Organisation of Serbia: B Jovanovic (BJ/ANTOS), D Bosnic (DB/ANTOS); Dreamstime: Joyfull (J/D), Nikolai Sorokin (NS/D); Getty Images: Katarina Stefanovic (KS/G); Laurence Mitchell (LM); Shutterstock: Angelaoblak (A/S), Andrej Antic (AA/S), Alberto Loyo (AL/S), Aleksandar Todorovic (AT/S), Bojan Milinkov (BM/S), fernando sanchez (fs/S), Karel Bartik (KB/S), mandritoiu (m/S), Mikhail Markovskiy (MM/S), Pecold (P/S), Tomasz Wozniak (TW/S), Vladimir Nenezic (VZ/S); Subotica Tourist Organization (STO); SuperStock (SS); Tourism Organisation of Niš (TON)

Front cover Boats on a lake near Ovčar-Kablar Gorge (KS/G)
Title page Haystacks are a common sight throughout rural Serbia (DB/ANTOS); Mileševa Monastery in southwest Serbia (DB/ANTOS); Folk dancers in Sremski Karlovci (DB/ANTOS)
Back cover Performers at the Dragačevo Music Festival (sd/A); Manasija Monastery in the Resava Valley (AA/S)

Maps David McCutcheon FBCart.S

Typeset by Ian Spick, Bradt Travel Guides
Production managed by Jellyfish Print Solutions; printed in India
Digital conversion by w dataworks.co.in

Acknowledgements

As always, I would like to thank the team at Bradt Travel Guides for their help and encouragement with the earlier versions of the guide and for the opportunity to update the book for this edition. Thanks especially go to Rachel Fielding, Anna Moores, Laura Pidgley and Edward Alexander, who project managed this edition, as well as to everyone else who aided and abetted the earlier editions of the guide.

For this fifth edition, I would like to thank Ivana Dukčević Budja, Miša and Saša Kolić and their families, Bojan and Vesna Stanislavjević, and Dragan Simić for their help and friendship in Serbia, and I am particularly grateful to Dragan for his conscientious work in keeping the birding information up to date. Thanks are also due to correspondents Snežana Bulatović, Ragab van den Hoek, Peter Chovanec, Michael Upton, Cecilia Keaveney and Branislav Mitić who all made useful contributions to this new edition.

ATTENTION WILDLIFE ENTHUSIASTS

For more on wildlife in Serbia, why not check out Bradt's *Central and Eastern European Wildlife*? Visit **w** bradtguides.com/shop for a 10% discount on all our titles.

FEEDBACK REQUEST AND UPDATES WEBSITE

At Bradt Travel Guides we're aware that guidebooks start to go out of date on the day they're published – and that you, our readers, are out there in the field doing research of your own. You'll find out before us when a fine new family-run hotel opens or a favourite restaurant changes hands and goes downhill. So why not write and tell us about your experiences? Contact us on ☏ 01753 893444 or **e** info@bradtguides.com. We will forward emails to the author who may post updates on the Bradt website at **w** bradtupdates.com/serbia. Alternatively you can add a review of the book to **w** bradtguides.com or Amazon.

Contents

LIST OF MAPS

Introduction

It is over 12 years since the publication of the first edition of this guide and much has changed in Serbia during that time. Back in 2005, the country was still officially part of a federation with Montenegro, a neighbour that went its own way in 2006. This was the last of several breakaways from the country that used to be known as Yugoslavia, after Slovenia, Croatia, Bosnia and Herzegovina and Macedonia had all chosen to declare their independence in the 1990s. Serbia's final territorial blow – long anticipated but painful nevertheless – came in 2008 when Kosovo unilaterally declared independence.

In just a few short years, the country has lost both a federal partner and a former territory. Given this, you might assume that Serbia's appeal as a tourist destination has made little progress since. You would be quite wrong. The country has, in fact, become increasingly tourist-friendly over the past few years, not that it was 'unfriendly' in the first place. New signs in English have gone up all over Belgrade and the main cities to point the way to the main sites of interest; tourist offices have opened their doors around the country to dispense information and friendly advice; new hotels have been built, old ones have been restored and refurbished, and there have also been exciting initiatives for village tourism, vineyard tours and long-distance cycling routes. At last, you feel that Serbia is no longer selling itself short and that there is a new enthusiasm for welcoming foreign visitors alongside a national pride in showing what the country has to offer.

Tourism has been a slow burn since the cessation of hostilities at the turn of the millennium. At the beginning there was just a trickle of adventurous types, but word has slowly started to spread that Serbia is a destination well worth visiting. Over the past few years, more and more foreign visitors have come for the EXIT festival, held in July each year at Novi Sad, as well as to the frenetic beer-swilling brass-band fest at Guča in August. Most have gone away suitably impressed and surprised by what they found. Belgrade's thriving nightlife and vibrant café culture has also become well known in recent years but most visitors do not bargain for such a welcoming reception nor expect to find such attractive countryside. What also comes as a surprise is the sheer variety of landscapes in what is a relatively small country. The flat northern plains of Vojvodina could hardly be a greater contrast to the lofty Kopaonik plateau in the south or the mountainous forests of Tara in the west.

With a long and colourful history that stretches back as far as the early medieval period, and indeed to the Roman occupation long before that, Serbian culture is rich and varied: a unique hybrid that is westward-looking but with echoes of an Ottoman past. The long period of Turkish rule has left its mark on the food, music and language of the country, as have influences from Austria and Hungary to the north. While a Habsburg city like Novi Sad, a place resolutely part of the central European milieu, lies just an hour's drive north of Belgrade, travelling to the south of the country brings the visitor to very different places like Novi Pazar, where the Turkish influence remains strong and the skyline bristles with minarets.

Belgrade itself, the largest city in the region, may not be the most elegant of capitals, but it has a vitality undiminished by its years of isolation. These days, it is a vibrant, sophisticated city where tradition and modernity comfortably coexist – a dynamic capital with museums, galleries and nightlife equal to anywhere in the region. Smaller university cities like Novi Sad and Niš have their own individual appeal too, as do many of Serbia's smaller country towns.

In a landscape punctuated by river valleys, gorges and rolling hills, nature lovers are well provided for. National parks such as Mount Tara in the west, Fruška Gora in the north and Đerdap Gorge in the east are ideally situated for outdoor activities such as hiking, cycling and birdwatching, while Zlatibor and the southern mountain resort of Kopaonik offer winter skiing.

Thankfully, Serbia's bad-boy image and demonised reputation are now seen as a thing of the past. Even a casual observation reveals a country keen to take its rightful place in wider European society. In 2011, following the country's placement on the White Schengen List, Serbians were finally allowed visa-free travel inside the EU bloc. For the first time in decades – since they were all 'Yugoslavs' in fact – Serbians were able to freely travel to the countries that surrounded them. The year 2012 brought further progress when the country was awarded full EU candidate status. Things are definitely looking up for Serbia these days, so don't delay: get there as soon as you can.

NOTE ABOUT MAPS

Several maps use grid lines to allow easy location of sites. Map grid references are listed in square brackets after listings in the text, with page number followed by grid number, eg: [156 C3].

FOLLOW US

Use #serbia to share your adventures using this guide with us. We'd love to hear from you.

- BradtTravelGuides
- @BradtGuides & @eastofelveden
- @bradtguides
- bradtguides

Part One

GENERAL INFORMATION

Location In the central part of the Balkan Peninsula of southeast Europe, with Hungary to the north, Romania to the northeast, Bulgaria to the southeast, Albania and Macedonia to the south, Bosnia and Herzegovina to the west, Montenegro in the southwest and Croatia to the northwest. Kosovo, unrecognised by Serbia as an independent republic, also lies to the south.

Status Republic, formerly part of a loose union with Montenegro, which voted for full independence in 2006. Kosovo declared unilateral independence in 2008.

Size 77,474km^2

Climate A temperate, continental climate, with warm summers up to 30°C and snowy winters down to −5°C, colder in mountain areas

Longest river The Danube (588km), flowing west to east through Serbia

Highest peak Midžor (2,169m)

Population 7,041,600 (2016 estimate excluding Kosovo). 83% Serbs, 4% Hungarians, 2% Bosniaks, and Romanians, Croatians, Bulgarians, Roma and Vlachs among a total of 37 minority groups.

Government Parliamentary democracy

Capital Belgrade (metropolitan population approximately 1.65 million)

Other major cities and towns Novi Sad (280,000), Niš (260,000), Kragujevac (180,000), Subotica (100,000)

Language The official language is Serbian, which is written in both the Cyrillic and Latin alphabets

Religion The main religion is Serbian Orthodox with Catholic, Protestant and Muslim minorities

Weights and measures Metric system

Time GMT+1

Currency Serbian dinar (1 dinar = 100 para)

Exchange rate £1 = 138din, US$1 = 109din, €1 = 121din (June 2017)

International telephone code +381

Electricity 220 volts AC, 50Hz. Round, two-pin sockets.

Public holidays 1 January (New Year), 7 January (Orthodox Christmas), 14 January (Orthodox New Year), 15 February (Constitution Day), 1–2 May (Labour Days), Orthodox Easter is variable, 11 November (Armistice Day)

Flag Red, blue and white horizontal stripes with Serbian coat of arms

UPDATES WEBSITE

You can post your comments and recommendations, and read the latest feedback and updates from other readers online at **w** bradtupdates.com/serbia.

1

Background Information

GEOGRAPHY AND CLIMATE

GEOGRAPHY With a surface area of 77,474km², Serbia is roughly the same size as Portugal or Austria, although Americans might prefer to compare it to the states of Maine or Kentucky. Even combined with newly independent Kosovo and neighbouring Montenegro, Serbia occupies a mere 2.1% of the European land mass. This makes it a relatively small country, only about one-third of the size of the former Yugoslavia. Nevertheless, it does hold an important central position in eastern Europe, having an over 2,000km-long border with a total of eight independent countries. One of these, Kosovo, was until recently considered to be an autonomous province within Serbia, while another, Montenegro, was formerly combined with Serbia as part of a loose federation. Almost a quarter of the population live in the capital, Belgrade. Throughout most of the rest of the country, Serbia's population is distributed fairly evenly with an average population density of 99.5 people per km².

Serbia lies at the crossroads of Europe, both politically and geographically, and its river valleys provide the fastest link for international roads and railway connections between western and central Europe, on one side, and Asia Minor and the Middle East on the other. These roads follow the course of the River Velika Morava, which joins with the western Zapadna Morava to lead to the city of Niš before following the valley of the southern Morava to lead the way to Thessaloniki. Joining the Morava at Niš, the valley of the River Nišava leads east to Sofia and Istanbul.

Serbia's rivers belong to three separate drainage systems: those of the Adriatic, the Black Sea and the Aegean. Three of the country's rivers are navigable but by far the most important is the Danube, which passes for 588km across Serbia as part of its 2,857km, eight-country journey to its mouth at the Black Sea. At Belgrade, the Danube, which enters Vojvodina from Hungary in the north and defines the border with Croatia as far south as Bačka Palanka, is joined by its major tributary, the River Sava, while just north of the capital in Vojvodina, the River Tisa flows into the Danube on the stretch between Belgrade and Novi Sad. Most of southern Serbia is drained by another Danube offshoot, the Morava River, which flows north to meet the Danube near Smederevo east of Belgrade.

The northern province of Vojvodina, north of the River Danube, is mostly flat arable land, with the exception of the 80km-long, forest-covered Fruška Gora range that hugs the south bank of the Danube, just to the south of Novi Sad. The highest point here is Crveni čot, which rises to 539m. The flat lands that make up most of northern Serbia belong to the Pannonian Plain and its rim: Mačva, the Sava Valley, the Morava Valley, Stig and the Negotin marshes. Another feature of this region is large expanses of remnant sand dunes, most notably the Deliblato Sands, which stretch in a crescent northeast to southeast in the southern part of the Banat close to Belgrade.

South of the River Danube, the east of the country has limestone ranges and basins, with older mountains and hills further south near the Bulgarian border. To the southwest, beyond the rolling hills of the Šumadija (forested area) of central Serbia, lies the Sandžak, a transition zone both culturally and topographically, which forms the border region with Bosnia and Herzegovina, and Montenegro. South of here, the landscape becomes increasingly mountainous as it approaches the Kosovo frontier.

The southern two-thirds of Serbia are ringed by mountains: the Dinaric Alps to the west, the Šar and Prokletije ranges to the south in Kosovo, and the Stara Planina to the east. Generally, the highest relief is in the Kopaonik region of the south close to the border with Kosovo and in the Stara Planina range of the southeast where Serbia's highest peak Midžor (2,169m) is found right on the border with Bulgaria.

Much of Serbia's intensive agriculture takes place in the flat and fertile Pannonian Plain, formerly an inland sea, which covers a vast tract of Vojvodina. Other regions in which large-scale, mechanised agriculture takes place include parts of the Kruševac and Leskovac districts of the south. In areas like the Šumadija, southwest of Belgrade, fruit production and viniculture replace pure arable farming, while forestry, cattle and sheep farming take place in the more rugged, mountainous regions of Zlatibor, Rudnik, Stara Planina and Kopaonik. Overall, 55% of Serbia is arable land and 27% forest.

CLIMATE The climate is moderate continental, with four distinct seasons. The average air temperature in Belgrade is 11.9°C. Autumn is longer than spring, often with extended periods of warm, sunny, anti-cyclonic weather; in contrast, spring is often short and rainy. Winter is not especially harsh by eastern European standards, with only an average of 21 days annually below 0°C. The average temperature in January is 0.4°C making it the coldest month of the year. Summers generally begin abruptly, with July and August being the hottest months overall, having average temperatures of 21.7°C and 21.3°C respectively. A characteristic wind of the region, known as the *košava*, sometimes blows from the southeast in autumn and winter bringing fair and dry weather. Usually this occurs when there is high pressure to the northeast over Ukraine in combination with low pressure over the Adriatic. Belgrade has an average 139 days of precipitation per annum (including 27 days of snow), which is most intense in the months of May and June and at its least in February. The country as a whole receives an average precipitation of between 600mm and 800mm annually in the plains – about the same as that of southeast England – and between 800mm and 1,200mm in highland regions.

NATURAL HISTORY AND CONSERVATION

With a wide range of habitats, Serbia offers more ecological diversity than other similar-sized countries in the region such as Hungary or Bulgaria. For such a small country, there is an unusually large number of species, some of which are endemic to Serbia. Broadly speaking, Serbia has six main habitat-zones that can be categorised as high montane rocky areas, coniferous forests, sub-Mediterranean and southern European forest (mainly deciduous), upland Mediterranean vegetation, steppe and wooded steppe.

Serbia has a rich and varied fauna, with nearly 80% of European bird species being recorded in the country as either breeding or on migration; it is also home to 66% of Europe's mammals, butterflies and insects and 50% of its freshwater fish. Of its plant communities, 9% are found only in the Balkans and 2% solely in Serbia itself.

Together with Montenegro, Serbia is home to 4,300 species of plant, 2% of the world's total number (while only having 0.035% of the total global land mass), and of these 400 are endemic. These include rare Balkan trees such as the pines *munika* and *molika*, and the endemic spruce *omorika* (Serbian spruce) that was discovered only 100 years ago by the Serbian botanist Josif Pančić. Many of the plants that grow wild in Serbia are valued for their medicinal properties and are still widely used by some rural communities.

Serbia's fauna is similarly rich. Over 90 species of mammals are present, with several mammals that are scarce elsewhere in Europe finding a haven here. There are at least 110 species of freshwater fish, with 14 subspecies that are found only in the region; seven fish species are listed on Europe's Red List. Compared with Britain, which has only 12 different species of reptile and amphibian, Serbia has 70 species of reptile alone, a much greater number than in either Romania or Bulgaria.

With plentiful forest to provide ideal habitat, countless species of fungi are found in Serbia, including over 100 species mentioned in the European Red List. Species such as the royal cep (*Boletus regius*), considered as one of the most threatened in the world, has much of its distribution within Serbia's borders. Rarities aside, Serbia is actually the world's greatest exporter of edible cep species, and mushroom picking is an important source of income for many rural families. Serbia's forests also provide a rich habitat for other species of fungi that have been identified as having important medicinal properties in the treatment of cancer, one example being *Ganoderma applanatum*. There is currently great concern that the ecological damage caused by the hostilities of 1999 has yet to reveal the true scale of the damage done to Serbia's fungi, as highly toxic substances inevitably permeate any fungi population. What seems certain is that the economic hardships suffered by the economy will necessitate more clear-cutting of Serbia's forests in the future, thus removing valuable natural habitat.

BIRDS Over 356 different species of bird have been recorded in Serbia, a large number of which pass through on passage to their breeding grounds in northern Europe. Many others (239 species) find suitable habitat for summer breeding in the country, while some species migrate from the north to winter in Serbia. Among the breeding birds, there are 103 species that are considered to be of European Conservation Concern (SPECs) and this includes five species that are of global concern: ferruginous duck, imperial eagle, lesser kestrel, great bustard and corncrake. Serbia also has a significant proportion of the European populations of relatively scarce birds such as saker falcon, little bittern, purple heron, scops owl, and middle-spotted and Syrian woodpeckers.

The Pannonian Plain of Vojvodina offers wetland areas that are attractive to many species of birds, particularly waders. Among these, Zasavica, Koviljska-Petrovaridinski Rit, Obedska and Carska Bara all provide valuable habitat. In the Carska Bara area alone, birds recorded include pygmy cormorant (*Phalacrocorax pygmeus*), bittern (*Botaurus stellaris*), little bittern (*Ixobrychus minutus*), night heron (*Nycticorax nycticorax*), squacco heron (*Ardeola ralloides*), great white egret (*Egretta alba*), purple heron (*Ardea purpurea*), spoonbill (*Platalea leucorodia*), ferruginous duck (*Aythya nyroca*), white-tailed eagle (*Haliaeetus albicilla*), bee-eater (*Merops apiaster*), common redstart (*Phoenicurus phoenicurus*), Savi's warbler (*Locustella luscinioides*) and lesser grey shrike (*Lanius minor*).

Away from the wetlands, the Deliblato Sands (*Deliblatska Peščara*) zone to the east of Belgrade, which supports spacious steppe woodland, scrub, conifer plantations and arable, provides a further specialised habitat, with notable steppe birds such as saker falcon (*Falco cherrug*) and the rare raptor, the imperial eagle (*Aquila heliaca*).

A diverse and interesting selection of birds is also found to the south of Belgrade, where the landscape transforms into more mountainous terrain. Birds of prey, in particular, are well represented. In the southwest, the Uvac and Mileševka Griffon Vulture Sanctuary is noteworthy as one of the best places in the central Balkans for watching raptors. The national parks such as Kopaonik in the south, Tara in the west and Đerdap (Iron Gates) in the east, close to the Romanian border, are equally rewarding, as are some of the gorges like Ovčar-Kaplar, Zlot, Sićevo and Jerma. Raptors of particular interest in these mountainous areas include short-toed eagle (*Circaetus gallicus*), long-legged buzzard (*Buteo rufinus*) and griffon vulture (*Gyps fulvus*), while smaller birds of note include red-rumped swallow (*Hirundo daurica*), wallcreeper (*Tichodroma muraria*), rock thrush (*Monticola saxatilis*), shore lark (*Eremorphila alpestris*), sombre tit (*Parus lugubris*), lesser grey shrike (*Lanius minor*), woodchat shrike (*Lanius senator*), red-backed shrike (*Lanius collurio*), cirl bunting (*Emberiza cirlus*), rock bunting (*Emberiza cia*), black-headed bunting (*Emberiza melanocephala*), Ortolan bunting (*Emberiza hortulana*), barred warbler (*Sylvia nisoria*), subalpine warbler (*Sylvia cantillans*), Bonelli's warbler (*Phylloscopus bonelli*), nutcracker (*Nucifraga caryocatactes*), alpine chough (*Pyrrhocorax graculus*), pallid swift (*Apus pallidus*), Spanish sparrow (*Passer hispaniolensis*) and rock sparrow (*Petronia petronia*).

Additional information on the relative abundance of breeding birds in Serbia may be found at w fatbirder.com/links_geo/europe/serbia.html. A useful website with regard to birds in Serbia is w birdwatchserbia.rs; another concerning birds, conservation and Serbian nature, is w 10000birds.com/tag/serbia. For more precise information on the practical aspects of birding in Serbia, see box, pages 8–10.

Those who would like to be more involved in bird conservation in Serbia might wish to contact **Bird Study and Protection Society of Serbia/BirdLife Serbia** (e *sekretar@pticesrbije.rs;* ℳ *@BirdLifeSerbia;* w *pticesrbije.rs*), which was established in 1989. A quarter of a century later, BSPSS is an active and committed organisation that carefully maintains a network of active members throughout the country, focusing on bird and habitat conservation and on increasing knowledge about birds in Serbia at local, regional and national levels. BSPSS publishes two magazines each year: an issue of the scientific magazine *Ciconia* and two issues of *Detlić*, a magazine for bird and nature lovers. The Serbian-language version of most of these can be found on their webpage.

CONSERVATION A large number of the species found in Serbia are protected by European and international law, or are included in the Red List of endangered species. Serbian law itself protects a total of 380 plants, 490 animals and 100 types of fungus.

NATURE RESERVES There are four national parks, all in upland areas (Tara, Fruška Gora, Đerdap and Kopaonik), which provide some degree of protection, together with three wetland regions that are protected by the International Ramsar

Convention (Lake Ludaš, Obedska Bara and Carska Bara). Serbia now has a total of ten Ramsar sites in the country: eight are found in the lowlands of Vojvodina, while the remaining two are in the mountain plateau of Pešter in the southwest and at Vlasina Lake in the southeast.

Tara National Park The Tara National Park covers about 20,000ha at an altitude between 250m and 1,500m. It is located in a bend of the Drina River in a mountainous region of western Serbia that includes the Tara and Zvijezda ranges, and was given national park status in 1981. This national park consists of a group of mountain peaks and deep gorges, the most striking being the Drina Gorge. Karst caves and pits are also a feature of the landscape. Three-quarters of the park is covered by forest, mostly coniferous, and Tara is home to a rare endemic species of tree, the Serbian spruce (*Picea omorika*), which is under state protection, and an endemic insect, the Pančić locust.

Fruška Gora National Park The Fruška Gora National Park in Vojvodina covers over 10,000ha of low hills that stretch east to west above the flat, low Pannonian Plain. Meadows, orchards, grain fields and vineyards cover the lower slopes while, above 300m, dense deciduous forests dominate, with maple and white oaks in addition to the greatest concentration of lime (linden) trees in Europe. More than 1,400 species of flora are found within the park boundaries, including over two-dozen species of orchid and many hundred species of medicinal herbs. Two hundred species of bird are found in the area, with elusive rarities like imperial eagle (*Aquila heliaca*) among a variety of raptors; woodpeckers, too, are well represented. Other fauna includes rare mammals like wildcat, badger, pine marten and wild boar, as well as several species of bat.

Ðerdap (Iron Gates) National Park The Ðerdap (Iron Gates) National Park lies in eastern Serbia, on the border with Romania, covering some 63,680ha. The natural phenomenon that the park is centred upon is the Ðerdap Gorge, the longest and deepest gorge in Europe. The gorge, better known as the Iron Gates, which stretches for a distance of around 100km, is actually composed of a whole series of gorges: Golubačka Klisura, Gospođin Vir, Kazanska Klisura and Sipska Klisura. The terrain and the favourable climate here have made this an important area for tertiary flora and fauna. As well as being rich and diverse, the Ðerdap flora is notable for its distinct relict character, with species that include bear-hazel bush, small nettle, walnut, lilac, silver linden and Montpellier maple. The fauna has relict qualities too, and includes brown bear, lynx, wolf and jackal. Golden eagle (*Aquila chrysaetos*), black stork (*Ciconia nigra*) and eagle owl (*Bubo bubo*) are among the many bird species present.

Kopaonik National Park Kopaonik National Park in south-central Serbia consists of nearly 12,000ha in the high plateau area of the mountainous region delimited by the valleys of the Ibar, Jošanica, Toplica and Brzeća rivers. Away from the more disturbed environs of the ski resort, this park is one of the most important centres of biodiversity in the whole of the Balkans, with 91 endemic and 82 sub-endemic species to its credit. Of a total of 1,500 species of flora, three endemic species are worth mentioning – Kopaonik houseleek, Kopaonik violet and Pančić cuckoo flower – while noteworthy among the avifauna are golden eagle (*Aquila chrysaetos*) and crossbill (*Loyia curvirostra*). The rare viviparous lizard also thrives on the mountain's higher slopes.

Dragan Simić, bird blogger and guide (e birdingserbia@gmail.com; > @albicilla66;
BirdingBalkansAndBeyond)

Updating something that has seen only minor changes since the first edition of this guide in 2005, I want to reflect on changes in the birdwatching scene in Serbia. To a foreign visitor, the most obvious change is an increased number of eBird users. eBird.org is the largest geo-referenced bird observation database in the world, but before I dive into a wealth of observations revealing the best birds and birding sites, I should say that the biggest number of Serbian eBird users live in Belgrade, followed by northern Vojvodina province, so the choice of these hot spots is somewhat biased towards those regions. From a different perspective, if the area is hardly visited by local birders, it often means that it is inconveniently far from main roads and hard to get to.

1. KOMPEZACIONI BAZEN Having said that, the dominant eBird site, with 205 birds eBird-reported by a single observer, Ivan Medenica, is in the southeast at the Kompezacioni bazen (compensation pool) in his home town of **Pirot**, 75km east of Niš (towards Bulgaria), where the valley forms a significant migration corridor and the bird fauna has a distinct Mediterranean flavour. Of 238 species in total, local birds include citrine wagtail, tawny pipit, in some years rosy starling, barred and eastern olivaceous warbler, red-rumped swallow, lesser grey shrike, alpine swift, Mediterranean gull, rough-legged buzzard, glossy ibis, and even Dalmatian pelican and Slavonian grebe.

2. DANUBE IN BELGRADE The Danube in Belgrade comes as a high second with 197 species shared between several nearby hot spots: Beljarica and Kozara floodplains, Reva Lake, Veliko Ratno Island, Ušće Park and Dorćolski kej riverbanks. At the waters around Veliko Ratno Island (126 eBirded species), as seen from Ušće Park and Dorćolski kej riverbanks, the main season is winter and local specialities include ferruginous duck, greater scaup, velvet scoter, long-tailed duck, common merganser, red-breasted merganser, smew, red-throated diver, black-throated diver, as well as the year-round birds such as pygmy cormorant and the white-tailed eagle (breeding on Veliko Ratno Island). Find out more about this area in the Belgrade chapter.

3. BARANDA FISH FARM With 193 species eBirded at the time of writing, in third place is the Baranda fish farm, about 40km north of Belgrade. Baranda is the centrepiece of the fish-farm triangle and several hot spots around the villages of Čenta, Baranda and Sakule and this area offers probably the best wetland birding near Belgrade. In some years, Spanish sparrows were reported breeding inside white storks' nests in Sakule. Other birds of the triangle are reed bunting, bluethroat, Savi's and common grasshopper warbler, Eurasian penduline tit, bearded reedling, red-backed and lesser grey shrikes (in winter replaced by great grey shrike), Eurasian hoopoe, European bee-eater, little owl, breeding whiskered tern (plus black- and white-winged terns on migration), 22 species of waders, common crane on migration (mostly in March and November), black-crowned night heron, glossy ibis, Eurasian spoonbill, wintering greater-spotted eagle and, in some years, irruptions of rosy starlings. Find out more about this area in the Belgrade chapter.

4. LABUDOVO OKNO This is an up-to-3km-wide section of the Danube with eight hot spots and 159 eBirded species. It is protected as a Special Nature Reserve and Ramsar site and is located some 80km east of Belgrade, mostly between the villages of Dubovac and Ram. Labudovo okno is an important stopover site and wintering area that attracts the largest congregations of waterbirds anywhere in the country. In winter, local specialities include huge flocks of greater white-fronted and greylag geese, with a few taiga bean geese among them, red-crested pochard, ferruginous duck, common goldeneye, smew, common merganser, black-throated diver and greater-spotted eagle; in spring joined by spotted crake, Caspian, black- and white-winged terns (on migration only), breeding whiskered tern, European turtle dove and colourful European bee-eater; while year-round species include white-tailed eagle and long-legged buzzard.

5. RUSANDA NATURE PARK In fifth place is the Rusanda Nature Park, with 150 species eBirded at the time of writing, by the village and spa of Melenci, about 90km north of Belgrade, or 80km east of Novi Sad. Rusanda is the name of a salt lake, a protected area of special importance for migrating waders, of which some 27 species were reported here, including red-necked phalarope, sanderling, dunlin, etc. Other birds of Rusanda are meadow and rare red-throated pipit, icterine warbler, Eurasian penduline tit, lesser grey shrike, breeding red-footed falcon and little and long-eared owls.

6. NOVI KNEŽEVAC FISH FARM With 135 eBirded species, Novi Kneževac fish farm comes next. It lies 130km north of Novi Sad. This is a private property and permission to enter is necessary. Species to look out for are water rail and little crake, European bee-eater, breeding European rollers and red-footed falcons, sedge, marsh and Savi's warblers, Eurasian reed warbler, great reed warbler and bluethroat.

7. SLANO KOPOVO NATURE RESERVE AND RAMSAR SITE This is a saline marsh near the town of Novi Bečej, 65km northeast of Novi Sad and 120km north of Belgrade. It has 135 eBirded species so far and is of special importance for migrating common cranes (up to 20,000 birds) and wintering geese (taiga bean goose, greater and lesser white-fronted goose, greylag goose and red-breasted goose). Other species to look for include short-eared owl and red-footed falcon.

8. KOVILJSKO-PETROVARADINSKI RIT NATURE RESERVE This reserve stretches along both banks of the Danube between the towns of Petrovaradin and Kovilj. With 129 eBirded species, it is a seasonally inundated floodplain area with ponds, reedbeds and forest – a place to look for ferruginous duck, black and white storks, purple heron, black-crowned night heron, white-tailed eagle, little crake, whiskered tern and European bee-eater; also middle-spotted, Syrian, black- and grey-headed woodpeckers.

9. TEMERIN Sewage ponds in the town of Temerin about 20km north of Novi Sad have 121 eBirded species, such as common quail, grey partridge, spotted crake, Eurasian stone curlew, great snipe, red-necked phalarope, bearded reedling, Eurasian penduline tit, willow and wood warblers, common chiffchaff, sedge warbler, Eurasian and great reed warblers, Savi's warbler, meadow and tree pipits and reed and corn buntings.

continued overleaf

Background Information NATURAL HISTORY AND CONSERVATION

1

10. KARAJUKIĆA BUNARI PEAT BOG Finally, Karajukića Bunari peat bog and Ramsar site, together with surrounding steppe pasture in the Pešter plateau – the largest karst area of Serbia that straddles the border with Montenegro, 230km west of Niš, 320km southwest from Belgrade. Being so far from urban centres, with 118 eBirded species, this area stands out thanks mainly to just one birder – Vladan Vučković. Mouth-watering species here include common merganser, glossy ibis, Eurasian griffon, short-toed eagle, Montagu's harrier, long-legged buzzard, water rail, spotted and little crakes, 21 species of waders, lesser grey and woodchat shrikes, horned lark, common rock thrush, tawny, meadow and red-throated pipits and ortolan and corn buntings.

Uvac and Mileševka Griffon Vulture Sanctuary

The Uvac and Mileševka Griffon Vulture Sanctuary, 255km southwest of Belgrade in the Zlatibor region is, as its name implies, a refuge for the now-endangered griffon vulture (*Gyps fulvus*). The sanctuary offers an opportunity to observe griffon vultures sitting on their nests and roost ledges before they launch themselves into the morning thermals.

Carska Bara

Of the wetland areas designated for protection by the International Ramsar Convention, that of Carska Bara stands out in particular. This 1,767ha reserve is situated southwest of Zrenjanin, in the middle of the Banat region, between the Tisa and Begej rivers. It is actually a complex of various wetland ecosystems – lakes, swamps, meadows and willow and white poplar forest – that is mostly used for recreational purposes like sports fishing.

Lake Ludaš

Lake Ludaš (*Ludaško Jezero*) lies further north, 12km east of the town of Subotica and near the Hungarian border. This 593ha reserve is one of the few remaining natural lakes of the Pannonian Plain and is important for its breeding birds, which include black-necked grebe (*Podiceps nigricolis*), purple heron (*Ardea purpurea*), squacco heron (*Ardeola ralloides*) and little bittern (*Ixybrychus minutus*). It is also an important feeding station for migratory birds on passage.

Obedska Bara

Obedska Bara, another of the Ramsar Convention sites, lies 50km west of Belgrade. The site is important for threatened breeding bird species including little egret (*Egretta garzetta*), night heron (*Nycticorax nycticorax*), little bittern (*Ixobrychus minutus*), black stork (*Ciconia nigra*) and white stork (*Ciconia ciconia*), spoonbill (*Platalea leucorodia*), white-tailed eagle (*Haliaeetus albicilla*), lesser-spotted eagle (*Aquila pomarina*), honey buzzard (*Pernis apivorus*), river warbler (*Locustella fluviatilis*) and middle-spotted woodpecker (*Dendrocopos medius*). The site also includes rare insects, fish, reptiles, amphibians and mammals, as well as rare and relict water lilies.

Zasavica

Zasavica, another protected reserve near Sremska Mitrovica, is also very important for its 200 plant species and 120 bird species, 80 of which breed in the area.

ECOLOGICAL DAMAGE Despite the valuable conservation work carried out in the above locations, the lack of chemicals used in farming practices and a generally good environmental record for much of Serbia's industry, there is concern in some quarters about the amount of ecological damage wrought by the NATO air raids of 1999. In particular, the Serbian Institute for Nature Protection points at the way NATO attacked non-military targets such as industrial complexes, refineries and nuclear research centres during the hostilities. It demonstrates how rivers, the Danube in particular, were heavily polluted due to leakages from stricken industrial complexes along its banks and gives evidence of how some national parks became targets themselves, how depleted uranium was widely used in warheads, and how so-called 'smart' bombs were often far from clever. Naturally, these are controversial and emotive issues, and accusations that foreign visitors should at least keep in mind.

HISTORY

EARLY SETTLEMENT The first evidence of settlement in the area that is now Serbia comes from Lepenski Vir on the Danube, close to the Romanian border. This site, only recently discovered in 1985, is the oldest known Neolithic site in Europe and dates from around the 7th millennium BC. From what remains, it appears to have been a reasonably developed civilisation, and strange life-size stone sculptures have been found here that appear to represent fish-headed men. No doubt these early settlers took advantage of the river's plentiful fish supply and so the figures may represent some form of fish divinity totem, although nothing else resembling these sculptures has been found elsewhere in the Balkans or Danube delta.

The region entered the Iron Age when Illyrian tribes from the west colonised the Balkan Peninsula during the 6th century, together with Thracian settlers who came from the east. These groups were followed shortly, in the 4th century BC, by Celts from the north. The Illyrians were skilled manufacturers of iron implements and weapons, and held some degree of trade with the Greek city states further south. The arrival of the Romans resulted in their being subdued by the greater number and superior military power of the new invaders. The Romans, with their well-trained and disciplined troops, continued to expand their empire deeper into the Balkans, incorporating the Illyrians into their army as they marched inexorably on. Finally in AD9, under the rule of Emperor Tiberius, the Roman Empire formally annexed all of the Illyrian territories.

The Romans made their mark on the region in typical fashion, building roads and constructing garrisons for their troops. They conquered the Celtic fortress at Singidunum, which had been built on a hill overlooking the confluence of the Sava and Danube rivers, a settlement that, after many more invasions, would go on to become Serbia's capital, Belgrade. Similarly, they developed the fortress at Taurunum nearby at modern-day Zemun and built a bridge over the Sava to connect the two. Singidunum became an important crossroads for the empire, linking the Roman provinces of Moesia, Dacia, Pannonia and Dalmatia, while a military road – a *Via Militaris* – passed through from west to east, from Sirmium (now Sremska Mitrovica) through Singidunum to Viminacium (Kostolac) and on to Byzantium.

Three centuries later, with the emergence of a rival empire to the east, the Roman Emperor Diocletian was forced to divide the territory into two halves, so that in AD395, the eastern half – that which roughly corresponds to modern-day Serbia, Montenegro, Macedonia, Bulgaria and Greece – found themselves under the influence of Byzantium. Singidunum had now become a border town on the edge of the eastern empire, an unfortunate location in geopolitical terms that would have some bearing on its later misfortunes. This division into two opposing empires created a political and cultural fault line whose effect is still felt today as one of the crucial factors in Balkan discord: in the west, corresponding to present-day Croatia and Bosnia and Herzegovina, they looked to Rome, so the inhabitants of this region became Roman Catholic by and large and made use of a Latin alphabet; to the east of the line the focus of power was Constantinople – present-day Istanbul – which resulted in the population of this region becoming Orthodox Christian and learning to use a Cyrillic script.

THE ARRIVAL OF THE SERBS As the Roman Empire finally disintegrated in the 5th century AD, Barbarian raiders started to appear – Huns, Goths and Avars from the central Asian steppe. It was also about this time that the Slavs started to arrive. Their first appearances in the region were as raiders, but by the beginning of the 7th century they were starting to settle in considerable number. The first Slavs had been undifferentiated in terms of the ethnic divisions of today, but by the time they started to colonise the Balkans they could be recognised as two distinct groups according to the route of their migration into the region. The Slavs who would later become the Croats, that occupied the western territories, migrated from lands they had established in southern Poland, while the other group, the proto-Serbs, made their home in the lands that lay to the south of the Danube, having moved from an area that is now the Czech Republic where they had been briefly settled. These two tribes already had, and would continue to have, closely entwined histories: quarrelsome cousins who then, as now, spoke an almost identical language. It was these Slavic tribes, together with the Romanised pastoralists, the Vlachs (page 40), that displaced or absorbed the Illyrians, Greeks, Thracians, Romans and Dacians living in the western Balkan region at the time. Just a small coastal enclave of Illyrian language and culture managed to survive the influx intact. This enclave would later delineate the boundaries of what is now Albania.

THE FIRST SERBIAN KINGDOM As the Croatian tribes settled the territories of the Adriatic littoral, a region they still populate today, the Serbs occupied an area they termed Raška, which is now often referred to by its Turkish name of Sandžak. This territory gave the Serbs the name of 'Rascians', by which they were known for several centuries. Raška was not the whole extent of their settlement, and other lands settled by Serbs at this time included tracts of present-day Montenegro, Herzegovina and southern Dalmatia.

The Serbs came under the influence of Orthodox missionaries from Constantinople, in the same way that Rome proselytised Croats in Dalmatia, but it was not until the late 9th century that the Serbian *župans* (patriarchs) fully accepted Christianity and Serbs as a whole started to relinquish their paganism. The first three centuries of Serb presence in the Balkans were characterised by conflict, with constant power struggles taking place between competing local princes. The first Serbian kingdom emerged in present-day Montenegro in the early 11th century when Stefan Vojislav set up the vassal state of Duklja and began to bring Serbian tribes under his control after renouncing his allegiance to Constantinople and pronouncing himself in favour of Rome. This state expanded to incorporate much of the territory of present-day Montenegro, Herzegovina and Albania, and in 1077, Zeta, as it had come to be known, became a kingdom under the auspices of Rome, with a Catholic ruler, Constantine Bodin, at the helm. After Bodin's death, the kingdom plunged into civil war and power shifted northwest to Raška. It was here that Serbia's first dynasty was founded in the 1160s under Stefan Nemanja – a 200-year dynasty that would go on to exert enormous military power as the fledgling Serbian state consolidated and expanded its territories within the Balkans.

THE NEMANJIĆ DYNASTY The next two centuries are often looked upon as Serbia's golden age and above all as the period when the Serbs' sense of national consciousness was forged, first by a pride in unhindered military success, then later by the bitter tears of defeat at Kosovo. This period of Serbian history has always been looked upon with great affection and self-esteem by Serbs, and with good reason: before the Nemanjić era, the Serbs were just a loose association of tribes; by the end of this period they shared a common identity, a national spirit and a sense of destiny that would sustain them through the difficult years to come. This was also the era when Serbia's close association with the Orthodox Church was at its peak. The Nemanjić dynasty brought a stability and confidence that nurtured the sense of Serbian statehood. It was also during this period that parts of Kosovo came under Nemanjić tutelage and became another component of the Serbian milieu.

Stefan Nemanja was succeeded by his middle son, also called Stefan, while his youngest son, Rastko, entered a monastery and took the name of Sava. Stefan became embroiled in a feud with his elder brother Vukan, who sought papal support for his claim to the crown. The Hungarian Catholic king Imre invaded and placed Vukan on the throne. The kingdom became Catholic for a brief spell but returned to Orthodoxy in 1204 when King Imre died, and Stefan regained the throne from his brother.

The feud between the brothers was reconciled when Sava returned from Mt Athos in Greece with the mortal remains of their father, Stefan Nemanja, who would soon be venerated as Simeon, the first Serbian saint, and his body buried at Studenica, where he remains to this day. Sava was a clever diplomat and this was just one of many remarkable achievements.

In 1217, Sava sent an emissary to Pope Honorius III asking for his blessing and for 'the royal wreath' for his brother Stefan. The Pope acceded to Sava's wishes and King Stefan came to be known from now on as Stefan Prvovenčani, 'Stefan the First Crowned'. This was a tremendous boost for the Serbian monarchy, as to receive the papal blessing was the medieval equivalent of international recognition. Sava's work was still unfinished: having dealt with the Catholic Church in Rome, he now turned his attention to the Byzantines. In 1219, he visited the exiled Byzantine emperor Theodore I Lascaris in Nicaea and secured autocephaly (self-appointing autonomous status) for the Serbian Orthodox Church. Naturally, the first archbishop to be appointed was Sava himself. Like his father before him, Sava went on to be canonised after his death in 1236.

Many other members of the Nemanjić dynasty chose the priesthood as an alternative, or reclusive conclusion, to their reign. As well as Stefan Nemanja choosing to end his days at Mt Athos as a monk, his son Stefan the First Crowned also died there. Following this tradition, Stefan Prvovenčani's son and successor Radoslav chose to abdicate after six years on the throne and died as a monk named John. The unique religious identity that the Serbs had by now claimed for themselves expressed itself in other ways than just a royal propensity for the priesthood. The most obvious expression of this was the extent of church building that took place throughout the kingdom. Serbian monasteries that date from the golden age of Nemanjić rule include Đurđevi Stupovi near modern-day Novi Pazar, Studenica and Hilandar on Mt Athos.

The next generation of Serbian kings – Radoslav, Vladislav and Uroš I – were altogether less impressive and marked a period of stagnation in the state. These leaders were far more dependent on neighbouring states like Hungary, Bulgaria and Byzantium than the earlier kings had been. However, when Uroš I's son Dragutin married a Hungarian princess and abdicated to become a monk in favour of his younger brother Milutin, the Hungarian king Ladislaus IV handed over lands in northeastern Bosnia, together with the regions of Srem and Mačva and the city of Belgrade, all of which became part of the Serbian state for the first time. Under Milutin (who later became King Uroš II) Serbia grew in strength, mainly through his many diplomatic marriages (he was married five times, to Hungarian, Bulgarian and Byzantine princesses). Uroš II (Milutin) went on to build a large number of churches, some of which remain as the finest examples of medieval Serbian architecture: the Gračanica Monastery in Kosovo, the St Archangel Church in Jerusalem and the cathedral in the Hilandar Monastery on Mt Athos. Milutin was succeeded by his son Stefan 'Dečanski' (who became Uroš III) who expanded Serbian territory east as far as Niš, and south to include parts of Macedonia, and went on to build the Visoki Dečani Monastery in Metohija, thereby earning his monastic soubriquet.

It was Stefan Dečanski's son Dušan, born in 1307, who would go on to become the most powerful of all the Nemanjić kings, although he engineered his own succession in something of an unorthodox manner. Dušan seized power from his father and had him incarcerated in the fortified town of Zvečan, and in 1331 Dušan was crowned as King of Serbia shortly after his father had been strangled on his own orders. Stefan Dečanski was buried in Visoki Dečani, the monastery he had started to build, and whose work was continued by his patricidal son. Dušan would go on to be recognised as the greatest of the Serbian monarchs but, unlike his father who was to become celebrated as a saint at his Dečani Monastery resting place, he would never be canonised due to the part he played in his father's death. Dušan's rule (as Uroš IV) was celebrated chiefly for two achievements. Firstly, there was the short-lived empire that he expanded quite spectacularly in just a few short years. Secondly, there was the legal code he introduced in 1349 that gave his name the epithet 'the lawgiver'. The legal code dealt partly with religious matters but was also devoted to the most common crimes of the day like bribery, theft and forgery. The punishments it meted out were severe – cruel even – but no worse than anywhere else in Europe in the medieval period.

By the time of Stefan Dušan's death in 1355, the Serbian kingdom had expanded considerably from what it had been just 200 years before. Now, the Serbian Empire stretched from the Danube south as far as the Peloponnese, and Serbian armies stood at the gates of Salonica, poised to expand their empire further east towards Constantinople. At this stage, Serbia's territory included Macedonia, all of Bulgaria and parts of northern Greece – the most powerful nation in the Balkans. But with the death of Stefan Dušan came a sudden and drastic decline of the nation's fortune. Quarrels divided the empire when two brothers, Vukašin and Jovan Uglješa, feudal landowners from Macedonia, tried to usurp power from Stefan Uroš V, Dušan's rightful but weak successor. Vukašin was declared king under the nominal sovereignty of Stefan Uroš V, and ruled in the south before being killed along with his brother at the Battle on the Marica River in 1371. Stefan Uroš V died soon after in the same year and, with no sons to his name, this was effectively the end of the Nemanjić dynasty.

After the Battle on the Marica River, that which was left of Serbian lands was divided up between a number of feudal landlords. It was around this time that Lazar Hrebeljanović, who claimed kinship to the Nemanjić clan, started to come into view. Prince Lazar had lands in central Serbia and parts of Kosovo and, after expanding his territories by seizing land on the Bosnian border, was starting to emerge as one of the most powerful of the lords that ruled over Serbian territories. He also had great support from the Church who viewed Lazar as a suitable leader for restoring the Serbian kingdom to its former glory. The Church also thought that Lazar would be able to reconcile the Serbian Church with the Orthodox patriarchy

Although the Battle on the Marica River of 1371 was probably a greater military defeat, and the event that most significantly led the way for Turkish subjugation of the Serbs, it was the events of St Vitus's Day 1389 at Kosovo Polje in Kosovo that held and still holds the greatest sway on the Serbian psyche. It is hard to think of a parallel European example, in which a specific military defeat is taken as such a defining moment in a nation's history. For Serbs, the failure to hold back the Turkish tide at Kosovo Polje was a noble defeat, something which is considered both a tragedy and a source of national pride, the misfortune of an overwhelmed nation bravely defending its freedom.

The night before the battle Prince Lazar is said to have been visited by an angel and offered the choice between an earthly or a heavenly kingdom, a choice that would result in victory or defeat on the battlefield. Lazar opted for martyrdom and holy salvation for his people, which explains why Lazar, St Vitus's Day (15 June in the Julian calendar, now celebrated on 28 June) and the very soil of Kosovo itself hold so much significance for Serbs.

There are few hard facts about what really happened on the battlefield. It is true that numerous epic poems were composed later on praising the valour of those taking part but this is myth-making rather than any detached first-hand account. What is certain is that on the Serbian side the main contingents were led by Prince Lazar and his son-in-law Vuk Branković, along with Bosnians under the command of Vlatko Vuković. There were probably mercenaries involved too, on both sides of the lines.

As the events of the day unfolded, Sultan Murad met his fate, supposedly stabbed by Miloš Obilić, a Serbian warrior who had posed as a deserter in order to get into his tent. Lazar, who did not perish on the battlefield itself, was captured and executed by the Turks, while Vuk Branković, Vlatko Vuković and Bayezid, Murad's son, all managed to survive the carnage. Vuk Branković was later condemned by many as a traitor to Lazar and the Serb cause.

Losses were undoubtedly very heavy on both sides but probably more disastrous for the Serbs who had lost much of their political elite. However, the notion that the defeat was the death knell of the medieval Serbian state is not wholly accurate. For a start, the Turks did little to consolidate their victory: almost as soon as the battle was over they retreated to Adrianople (modern-day Edirne), their capital at that time, to crown Bayezid as the new sultan, and it would be another 70 years before they pushed north in earnest. What is also in doubt was whether or not it was such a clear-cut defeat. Some initial reports from Kosovo seem to have celebrated the battle as a victory against the Turks rather than the other way round. Whatever the facts, what has had far more bearing on the Battle of Kosovo's place in Serbian consciousness is the myth and legend that followed the event to give it metaphysical meaning – the epic poems that celebrate the battle and the need for sacrifice, and the promotion of Lazar as a cult figure.

in Constantinople, which had broken relations with the Serbian Orthodox Church on the occasion of Dušan's coronation. Lazar achieved this reconciliation and as his power grew started to consider himself as 'the ruler of all Serbs'. This was not quite correct, of course, but it did demonstrate the scope of his ambition.

With none of Stefan Dušan's successors able to maintain the impetus that he had set up during his reign, coupled with sudden, violent advances of the Turks from the south, disaster was on the horizon. The empire's swift demise led the way to a catastrophic downfall that is still remembered today as Serbia's darkest hour. In 1389, Prince Lazar grouped together the nation's forces for a last-ditch attempt to repel the advancing Turks at the Battle of Kosovo (see box, page 15). To say that this was nothing more than a decisive battle is to underestimate its continuing importance in the Serbian psyche. In many ways, the defeat at Kosovo Polje (Field of Blackbirds) was a defining moment in Serbian nationhood. The battle was not completely one-sided – the Turkish sultan perished on the battlefield, along with many Turkish troops – but the defeat marked a turning point for a state that was already in decline.

OTTOMAN RULE A large-scale Serb migration north to Hungary and west to the Adriatic began soon after the defeat at the Battle on the Marica River and continued with the loss at the Battle of Kosovo in 1389. An unstable period followed, with a shrinking nation that was ruled jointly by Prince Lazar's son, Despot Stefan Lazarević, and his cousin, Đurađ Branković, who moved the capital to the new fortified town of Smederevo on the Danube. The final collapse came in 1459, when Smederevo fell into Turkish hands. This resulted in a much larger northern migration.

Fear of the Ottomans was tangible enough and, as the Ottoman Empire was a strict Islamic theocracy, religious persecution was rife. The sultan handed over large tracts of Serbian land to Muslim knights and some Serbs converted to avoid subjugation as serfs or *rayah*. Many did not, however, and the Turks took tens of thousands of Christian Serbs into slavery, dragging many of them from their lands to serve Ottoman masters in Constantinople. The Turks targeted the Serbian aristocracy in particular, determined to wipe out the *župan* social elite that headed the *zadruge* (loose family groups that associated as clans). Many left the urban centres where they had previously lived, preferring to withdraw to the mountains where they could eke out a living by cattle breeding and farming.

What was resented more than anything else under Turkish rule was the ongoing recruitment and increasing power of the Janissaries. Originally, the Janissaries were Muslim converts who had been forcibly taken from Christian families when they were children to be trained as the elite troops of the Ottomans. Although they began as a military instrument of the sultan's will, with time the Janissaries became a powerful and self-determining elite that protected its own power and influence with quite spectacular savagery and cruelty. They imposed taxes and exploited the peasantry to such a degree that they ended up being more hated than the Turks themselves.

Belgrade itself did not finally succumb until 1521, when it was besieged and burnt down by Sultan Suleiman the Magnificent. It remained in Turkish hands until 1717 when it was conquered once more, by Prince Eugene of Savoy.

Over the next few centuries there were many Serbian uprisings against Turkish rule, some more effective than others. In 1594, during the Austrian–Turkish War (1593–1606), an insurrection was staged in the Banat region north of the Danube, a region now in Vojvodina province. The Turkish sultan responded by skinning alive and hanging the Serbian patriarch, Teodor, before bringing the relics of St Sava to Vračar near Belgrade to be burned because the figure of St Sava had adorned so many of the rebel flags. This desecration was considered to be an unimaginably sacrilegious act by all Serbs, and even by many Muslims equally devoted to the saint who had something of a reputation as a miracle worker.

During the war between Turkey and the Holy Alliance (1683–90), Austria, Poland and Venice incited the Serbs to rebel once more. Insurrection spread throughout the western Balkans from Montenegro to the Danube basin but the Austrians soon withdrew their support. As the Austrians withdrew from Serbia, they invited the Serbs to travel north with them, to live alongside them in their territories. For many Serbs, this was the lesser of two evils, and faced with choosing between certain Turkish vengeance and a life in a Christian, albeit Catholic, imperialist state, many chose the latter. Large areas of southern Serbia were depopulated as a result of this and the Turks used the opportunity to proselytise Raška (the Turkish *Sandžak*), Kosovo and Metohija, and parts of Macedonia. This widespread conversion explains much of Serbia's present-day religious demographic.

Shortly after this mass movement north, another important episode took place when Serbia territories became the battleground for another Austrian–Turkish war launched by Prince Eugene of Savoy in 1716. Once again, the Serbs sided with Austria and, after a peace treaty was signed in Požarevac, Turkey lost control of its possessions in northern Serbia and the Danube basin, as well as in northern Bosnia, parts of Dalmatia and the Peloponnese.

SERBIAN UPRISING By the turn of the 19th century, the Ottoman leadership was corrupt, profligate and in decline, and the Janissaries, who originally had been selected and trained by the Turks, had become an unruly and self-perpetuating elite that were a law unto themselves. As the years of Turkish domination progressed, small-scale resistance to Ottoman rule, and especially to the Janissaries and the *spajis* – Turkish cavalry units of similarly rapacious character – started to emerge. This came in the form of rebel bands called *hajduci* (singular: *hajduk*). These had started to form in the 15th century but became far more numerous and troublesome during the later years of Turkish domination. The name translates literally as 'brigands' or 'outlaws' but the *hajduci* of Ottoman Serbia are more popularly viewed as guerrillas or Robin Hood-type folklore heroes – bandits with a political agenda.

ST VITUS'S DAY – 28 JUNE

St Vitus's Day, in Serbian known as Vidovdan, is a Serbian Orthodox religious holiday held on 28 June each year. The date is central to Serbian culture as it commemorates the day in 1389 when Prince Lazar died at the Battle of Kosovo whilst defending Serbia against the invading army of the Ottoman Empire. Either by accident or design – probably a mixture of both – the same date has many more resonances in Serbian history as the list below demonstrates.

Battle of Kosovo	1389
Assassination of Archduke Franz Ferdinand by Gavrilo Princip	1914
Treaty of Versailles signed	1919
Constitution of Kingdom of Serbs, Croats and Slovenes proclaimed	1921
Yugoslavia expelled from Cominform for 'abandoning Marxist theory', marking the final split between Tito and the Soviet Union	1948
Milošević makes Gazimestan speech at the Kosovo Polje battle site on the 600th anniversary of the Battle of Kosovo	1989
Milošević deported to The Hague ICTY for trial	2001
Montenegro joins UN as independent country	2006
Inaugural meeting of Community Assembly of Kosovo and Metohija	2008

1

It was the actions of the *hajduci* that inspired the first larger-scale rebellion against the Turks in the **First National Uprising** of 1804.

This, the first of two national revolts, was headed by a cattle-herder and trader from the Šumadija region called Đorđe Petrović, commonly known as Karađorđe (Black George) because of his dark complexion and short temper. The rebellion started early in 1804, when Janissaries executed up to 150 Serbian local leaders or *kneze* in an operation they termed 'The Cutting Down of the Chiefs'. This action was viewed as a pre-emptive strike against those who were plotting against them but all it really achieved was to precipitate a widespread rebellion. Karađorđe was elected leader and the rebels soon liberated most of the Belgrade *pashalik* (district) from Janissary control. At first, the Serbs were joined by many Muslims, who suffered as much from the excesses of the *dahis* – the Janissary commanders – as anyone else, but this co-operation turned to bloodshed when it became clear that the Serbs were rebelling not just against Janissary tyranny but against all aspects of Turkish rule. Under Karađorđe, the Serbs demanded complete autonomy, which so alarmed the Turkish rulers that they set up an Ottoman army to fight them. By now, the rebels had made contacts with semi-independent Montenegro and had sent a delegation to Russia to seek assistance.

The Ottoman army was beaten soundly at Ivankovac in August 1805, and, after two years of fighting, Belgrade was liberated on 8 January 1806. Karađorđe, with his army of about 25,000 rebels found the city in ruins. It was soon rebuilt and went on to become the capital of the territories that made up newly liberated Serbia. A fledgling Serbian government (the Praviteljstvujušči Sovjet) had its first assembly there in 1807; by 1811, the first ministries had been set up.

By the end of 1806, the Russians too had joined the fight on the Serbian side. This support encouraged the Serbs to fight on to try and reclaim more of their past territories. However, within a few weeks, the Russians had signed a treaty with the Turks and their short-lived support fell away. Fighting resumed between the Turks and the Serbs in 1809, who again received a moderate amount of help from the Russians. But once again, this was not going to be long-lived as Russia was soon going to need all of its military might in its own territories due to the sudden appearance of Napoleon Bonaparte and his armies in the Russian homeland.

A short time afterwards, the Russians and Turks signed another peace treaty together, which specified that Serbia would return to Ottoman rule on the condition that amnesty be given to all participants in the insurrection. This was rejected outright by the Serbs, and Karađorđe, along with thousands of others, fled north across the Danube to safety in the Habsburg provinces. The Turks, never ones to forgive and forget, soon took vengeance: hundreds of villages were sacked, and thousands of Serbs, particularly women and children, were taken into slavery. In 1813, the city of Belgrade, which had enjoyed just a few years of freedom, was conquered once again by the Turks.

The **Second National Uprising** of 1815 was led by Miloš Obrenović, a veteran of the first campaign, who, after the first rebellion's failure, rather than fleeing north with Karađorđe had tried to make a deal with the Turks instead. Although the Turks offered Obrenović a local position of limited power, it soon became clear that such a deal was untenable. In 1814, one of Karađorđe's former commanders attempted to start up a fresh rebellion but this was soon quelled. However, in the wake of the brutal reprisals that followed, new plans were hatched for another, more ambitious, uprising. This attempt was far more successful, and by mid-July 1815, Obrenović's rebels had succeeded in liberating most of the Belgrade *pashalik*.

The Turks were more wary this time, influenced by events abroad: Napoleon had just been defeated at Waterloo, and they were concerned that the Russians, now free from the threat of French invasion, might join the fight on the part of the Serbs. Consequently they were willing to do a deal with Obrenović. Obrenović was undoubtedly a brave commander in battle but, unlike Karađorđe, he was also skilled in the art of diplomacy, and this helped in his negotiations with the Turks. He negotiated for the Belgrade *pashalik* to become autonomous to the extent that the Turks would remain only in the towns and forts of the province, and that only Serbian chiefs would have the right to collect taxes from now on. As he sought these concessions he cleverly managed to undermine the power of the Turks in other ways, such as in encouraging Serbs from the south to move to Belgrade, which resulted in many Turks being obliged to sell their houses and land at prices far below their real worth.

In 1817, Karađorđe sneaked back into Serbia, but Obrenović, doubting the former commander's motives, had him murdered by his agents. Karađorđe's head was duly stuffed and sent to the sultan – an act prompting the beginning of a feud between the two families that would last for almost 100 years.

Miloš Obrenović turned out to be as avaricious as the Turks when it came to tax collecting, and his increasingly oppressive rule prompted seven uprisings against him

'BLACK GEORGE'

Đorđe Petrović, better known as Karađorđe – 'Black George' – was a colourful figure who could best be described as brave, determined and uncompromisingly violent. He was born in the village of Viševci in 1768 and worked in his youth as a cattle-herder. In 1787, after killing a Turk, he fled to Habsburg Austria to join the army where he served with distinction against the Turks. At the end of the Austro-Turkish war in 1791, he returned to Serbia to settle in Topola where he traded in livestock and participated in occasional *hajduk* forays against the Ottoman invaders. He was elected leader of the Serb insurgents at Orašac in February 1804 and quickly instigated the events that led to the First National Uprising of that year. This was initially a great success but, with the Russian withdrawal from the fray in 1812, Karađorđe felt obliged to flee once again to Habsburg Austria. He travelled on to Bessarabia (now Moldova) where he encountered Filiki Eteria, a Greek secret society dedicated to liberating all Christians from Turkish rule. He re-entered Serbia in June 1817 on a forged passport but was dead within the month, murdered by the command of Miloš Obrenović, leader of the Second National Uprising and founder of a dynasty that would become rival to Karađorđe's.

Karađorđe was not averse to murdering members of his own family on occasion as a means of setting an example to his followers. Early in the campaign, he had his stepfather killed for refusing to stop fighting when a tactical withdrawal had been ordered; later on, he had his brother hanged on a charge of rape, and suspended the body from the gate of his house as a warning to others. Despite, or perhaps because of, this violent streak, Karađorđe went on to found a royal dynasty, a remarkable achievement for an illiterate herdsman of peasant stock. There are those that accuse Karađorđe of cowardice, saying that he should not have fled when the Turks got the better of him; others would contest that he was merely making a tactical withdrawal to regroup his forces before renewing his campaign, and that he was a warrior not a diplomat and so would brook no negotiations with the enemy.

between 1815 and 1830. Nevertheless, it was a progressive and prosperous time for the capital. Many new buildings were constructed in Belgrade during this period: Princess Ljubica's *konak*, the cathedral and the king's palace complex at Topčider. Great scholars and educators also emerged during this period, like Dositej Obradović, who became minister of education and opened the Great School, the country's first institution of higher education, and Vuk Karadžić who collected epic poems, developed the Cyrillic alphabet for modern Serbia and single-handedly reformed the Serbian language. Influenced by these innovators, Belgrade soon became a centre for literary activity: in 1831 the first printing press was opened, and in 1837, the first bookshop. Soon after, newspapers would be printed in the city for the first time. It was a rapid advance from Ottoman stagnation and, from the 1830s onwards, Serbia started to develop an identity that was more akin to central European society than to that of a peripheral province of a flagging empire. The days of foreign rule were numbered. Belgrade's familiar minarets started to disappear as mosques were taken down following the Turkish exodus. Ottoman soldiers left Belgrade for the last time on 18 April 1867. The Principality of Serbia received full international recognition at the Congress of Berlin in 1878 and the Kingdom of Serbia was proclaimed four years later.

THE BALKAN WARS OF THE EARLY 20TH CENTURY Serbia in the latter part of the 19th century was ruled by a dynasty descended from Miloš Obrenović, with the exception of Prince Aleksandar Karađorđević who reigned from 1842–58 and was the son of Karađorđe. A *coup d'état* in 1903 brought Karađorđe's grandson to the throne with the title of King Petar I. Petar had received a European education, and had been influenced by liberal ideas, especially those of John Stuart Mill. He introduced a democratic constitution and initiated a period of parliamentary government that encouraged political freedom.

This new-found political freedom was interrupted by the outbreak of liberation wars in the region, and the whole of the Balkans underwent rapid change as new Balkan states were created in the vacuum left by the Turks. With full backing from King Petar I, the League for the Liberation of the Balkans from Turkey was set up, in which Bulgaria, Greece, Serbia and Montenegro all co-operated to drive the Turks from the region. The **First Balkan War** of 1912 was short and successful and forced the Turks to concede both Macedonia and Kosovo to Serbia. However, the new allies soon fell out over Macedonia, and Bulgaria attacked both Greece and Serbia in its attempt to claim sole possession. This led to the **Second Balkan War** of 1913, in which Romania entered the fray on the side of Greece, Serbia and Montenegro. The war ended in the same year with the Treaty of Bucharest, an agreement that was unsatisfactory on all sides, especially to the Slavs of Macedonia who now found themselves divided. Serbia, though, came out of it reasonably well, having acquired western Macedonia as part of the settlement.

By 1914, Turkish domination in the region had finally ended for good but now there were fresh problems of national sovereignty to deal with. Bosnia and Herzegovina had been part of the Ottoman Empire but was governed by Austria since its annexation in 1908. Discontent here caused a number of pan-Slavic movements to agitate for union with Serbia, something that greatly worried the Austrians. The assassination of the Austrian prince, Archduke Franz Ferdinand, in Sarajevo on 28 June 1914 gave the Austrians the excuse they needed to attack Serbia, first politically, then militarily. The assassin had been Gavrilo Princip, a Bosnian Serb and member of the 'Black Hand' and 'Young Bosnian' nationalist movements. The Serbian government had no connection with Princip or his co-assassins but in July the Austrians invaded regardless, after first having imposed an impossible ultimatum. This single Bosnian incident had immediate repercussions in a Europe that was already embroiled in territorial disputes and military allegiances: World War I had begun.

WORLD WAR I The Serbs fiercely defended their country from the Austrian invasion but after several major victories they were eventually overpowered by the joint forces of Austria-Hungary, Germany and Bulgaria. The army had to withdraw from its national territory by marching across the Albanian mountains in winter to the Adriatic, suffering dreadful losses along the way. What was left of the army regrouped on the island of Corfu before returning to fight on the Salonica (Thessaloniki) front alongside the other forces of the Entente – Britain, France, Russia, Italy and the United States. Even on the horrific scale normally expected of World War I casualty figures, the Serbian losses were appalling. By the end of the war Serbia had lost 1,264,000 of its men: 28% of its pre-war population of 4,529,000, and 58% of its total male population. Such a devastating loss could never be fully recovered from.

As war ended and eastern Europe reshaped itself, Serbia became incorporated as just one component in a greater South Slav nation. On 1 December 1918, the Kingdom of Serbs, Croats and Slovenes came into existence, which united the territories of these three republics along with Bosnia and Herzegovina and Macedonia. This short-lived federation would become the blueprint for the future Yugoslavia.

THE YUGOSLAV STATE OF THE INTER-WAR YEARS 1918–39 The post-World War I state had come into existence, under Western supervision, as a monarchy headed by Prince Aleksandar Karađorđević. Inevitably, having a Serbian monarch in power soon led to accusations of Serbian dominance. When the constituent states of the new kingdom met to draw up a constitution in 1921, the Croats, led by Stjepan Radić, refused to vote on any of the proposals and returned to Zagreb. As a result, a very centralist constitution favoured by the Serbs was drawn up: the Croat withdrawal had merely exacerbated matters and made the new constitution more Belgrade-centred than it might have been had the Croats participated. Radić was assassinated along with several other Croatian Peasants' Party (CPP) members in the Belgrade parliament building on 20 June 1928 by Puniša Račić, a pro-Serbian Montenegrin deputy. Radić did not die immediately but was left for dead and perished a short time later as a result of his stomach wounds. In January of the following year, Aleksandar (now King Aleksandar after the death of his father King Petar I), perturbed by the attempts to promulgate a workable constitution, banned all political parties, dissolved parliament and imposed a Royal Dictatorship, renaming the country Jugoslavija (Yugoslavia). In Serbian, jug means south, and so this new name simply meant 'land of the South Slavs' – a term that carried none of the baggage of traditional Serb–Croat rivalry.

The Royal Dictatorship was an unmitigated disaster, which solved none of the existing problems as it failed to bring any Croats into positions of responsibility. Instead, many Croats, frustrated by their lack of power, were now joining an underground nationalist movement led by a lawyer, Ante Pavelić. This organisation, coined the Ustaša, had fascist leanings and its supporters wanted to rid themselves of the Serbian king in any way possible. King Aleksandar I was assassinated on a visit to France in 1934 by a member of VMRO, an extreme nationalist organisation in Bulgaria that had close links with the Ustaša. VMRO had plans to annex lands along the southern and eastern Yugoslav borders and sympathised with the Ustaša cause, which had its own territorial aspirations.

Aleksandar's son, Prince Petar, was just ten years old at the time of his father's death and so authority passed instead to the assassinated king's brother, Prince

Pavle (Paul). Under Pavle, ever fearful of more Ustaša-style killings, anti-separatist repression was rife, which further exacerbated the rift between the Croats and a Serbian monarchy that favoured its own.

At around the same time another political force was emerging in Yugoslavia – the Communist Party – a political force that had already succeeded in uniting the Soviet Union, a vastly more disparate nation, earlier in the century. The unifying appeal of communism was undeniable: the party won a number of seats in the early municipal elections in both Serbian Belgrade and Croatian Zagreb but they were forbidden to enter parliament being proscribed, along with trade unions, from the national government. This denial of power drove the Yugoslav Communist Party further underground, where it regrouped and forged links with the Soviet Union. A leader eventually emerged in the form of Josip Broz, who had been imprisoned for his beliefs but had worked in Moscow with the Third International on his release (pages 24–5). In 1939, Josip Broz was elected chairman of the Yugoslav Communist Party. Later to be better known simply as Tito, Josip Broz would go on to play a crucial role in uniting the resistance against Nazi occupation before modelling the country's destiny in the post-war years that followed.

WORLD WAR II At the outbreak of World War II, Yugoslavia found itself surrounded by hostile countries. Hitler was pressuring Yugoslavia to join the Axis powers so, after a brief period of neutrality, the regent, Prince Pavle, decided to align his government with the Nazis. This prompted rebellion from many quarters, with massive protests in Belgrade on 27 March 1941. A group of air force officers, supported by the communists, arrested Prince Pavle and replaced him on the throne with Prince Petar, who was still a teenager. The reaction from Berlin was to bomb Belgrade, which the Nazis carried out with great ferocity on 6 April 1941. This was followed by a land invasion of both German and Italian forces. Petar, now King Petar II, fled with his government to exile in London. Belgrade was occupied just a few days later on 12 April.

The country was divided up between the Axis powers. Germany took most of Slovenia, Italy annexed Montenegro and the Adriatic coast, while Bulgaria occupied much of Macedonia. Meanwhile, Croatia and Bosnia and Herzegovina combined to become a Nazi puppet state, called the Independent State of Croatia (NDH), with the head of the Ustaša fascists, Ante Pavelić, a natural choice as its leader. Serbia was occupied by German troops, apart from its northern territories, which were annexed by Axis Hungarians, and parts of eastern and southern Serbia by Bulgaria. Kosovo and Metohija was mostly annexed by Albania, which at that time was being sponsored by fascist Italy. Croatia's autonomous territory was enlarged and the regime adopted an extreme policy of racial purification, a repugnant and peculiarly Balkan feature of war that would reappear half a century later during the break-up of Yugoslavia. Over two million Serbs lived in this territory at the time, together with many other minorities like Roma. Enthused by the Nazi model, the Independent State of Croatia established extermination camps where they committed genocide on 750,000 Serbs, Jews and Roma over the next three years. Such were the excesses of the Ustaša that even some Nazis baulked at the zeal with which their Ustaša compatriots went about their murderous handiwork.

The lust for genocide displayed by the Ustaša, and the presence of a ruthless German occupation force, prompted Serbian resistance on a large scale. Two very different resistance groups emerged. One of these was the Chetniks, who were pro-Serbian but devoutly royalist and anti-communist, and headed by Colonel Dragoljub 'Draža' Mihailović. The Chetniks were supported by King Petar's government in exile in London. The other resistance group – the Partisans – was pro-communist and led by Josip Broz Tito. Most Ustaša were Croats, but by no means all, and many Croats chose to join the resistance struggle, particularly later on in the war. The Partisans, in particular, would draw fighters from all over Yugoslavia, even if the bulk of their support was Serbian. The Partisans, after all, had a post-war agenda that went beyond simply liberating the country from the Nazis and returning to the previous status quo.

The first Chetnik acts of resistance to occupation met with savage reprisals from the Nazis, which led to an extended period of relative inactivity in which Mihailović tried to accommodate the Germans, although he stopped short of active collaboration. In contrast, the Partisans under Tito's leadership fought an all-out struggle and, despite suffering dreadful losses, went on to have far more success. Many non-communists joined the struggle on the Partisan side once it became clear that their opposition was more effective than that of the Chetniks. The Partisan and Chetnik leaderships met up several times in the early years of the war but on each occasion Mihailović rejected any idea of joint resistance. Inevitably, this led to an armed struggle between the two resistance armies: a Chetnik–Partisan civil war broke out between the two factions in November 1941 and lasted until liberation in October 1944. With the Croatian Ustaša as a common enemy of both, this led to a three-way struggle, another depressingly common feature in Yugoslavia's history that would emerge again later in Bosnia and Herzegovina in the 1990s.

Despite the distraction of internecine warfare with the Chetniks, Tito's Partisans continued to harass the Germans during 1942 and 1943. They were often on the run from the Nazis' far superior military machine: at one time, forced to retreat from Croatia into the mountains of Bosnia and Montenegro; then later, obliged to undergo a spectacular withdrawal along the Sutjeska Valley, carrying their wounded along with them. In the areas that they successfully liberated they set up pockets of de facto government, the AVNOJ, which although a direct challenge to the royalist government in exile, received great local support in areas freshly liberated from Axis control.

A British military mission under Brigadier Fitzroy Maclean was sent in September 1943 to support Tito's Partisans. The British had always wanted to encourage anti-Nazi resistance in the Balkans but initially it had been a matter of debate which of the two factions they should support. At first, influenced no doubt by the presence of the Yugoslav king in London, and a general distaste for communism, the British had supported the Chetniks, but after a meeting with other Allies at Tehran they decided to withdraw all support for Mihailović and to provide material aid to Tito instead. This additional support greatly helped the Partisan cause and considerable advances were soon made. There was an attempt to kill Tito at his island headquarters at Vis, but this was thwarted and the Partisans proceeded to systematically force the Axis armies out of the Balkans during the early months of 1944.

With the end of the war in sight, Tito saw the necessity for making plans for the future. Always a shrewd leader, he knew that when liberation came there would immediately be an internal struggle for political dominance in the post-war nation. He fully understood that there were two possible endgames: either his preferred communism, or the return of King Petar from London and royalist rule. He met secretly with Churchill, and then flew immediately afterwards to Moscow to meet with the Soviet leadership. The outcome of this second meeting was to invite Soviet troops into Yugoslavia so that they could participate in the inevitable liberation that would soon come about.

The Partisans, together with Soviet Red Army units, entered Belgrade on 22 October 1944. By early spring of the following year they were in full control of all Yugoslav territory. Yugoslavia was liberated from Nazi rule but the human cost

1

had been appalling: in just five years, nearly one-tenth of the nation's population, an estimated 1,700,000 Yugoslavs, had perished, in combat, in reprisals or in the concentration camps that targeted not only Jews but also Serbs, Roma and many others who did not fit in with the notion of an Aryan 'master race'. In a few short years, Belgrade had run the whole gamut of political fortune. It had at first been neutral, then briefly pro-Alliance before being bombed comprehensively by the Germans; it was then occupied by the Nazis for three years before being bombed yet again, this time by Allied forces. When Tito's Partisans and their communist supporters marched into the capital that autumn day in 1944, perhaps its citizens had every right to be a little sceptical about any sort of lasting peace.

TITO'S YUGOSLAVIA Tito reached an agreement with King Petar's government in exile in which he was given temporary authority as a leader. By the end of 1945, elections were held throughout the country. The Communist Party, which was still technically illegal, stood as the People's Front and won 90% of the vote for the Federal Council. Such a landslide victory resulted in royalist members of Tito's provisional government resigning, while the king remained in exile and Mihailović was executed, along with many Chetniks and other opponents considered troublesome.

JOSIP BROZ TITO

Tito was born Josip Broz in 1892 in Kumrovec, northwest Croatia, then part of the Austro-Hungarian Empire. He was the seventh child of Franjo and Marija Broz; his mother, a Slovene and his father, a Croat. His first job at age 15 was as a locksmith's apprentice. In 1910 he joined both the Union of Metallurgy Workers and the Social Democratic Party of Croatia and Slavonia, both of which contributed to developing his political awareness. From the autumn of 1913, Tito served in the military and at the outbreak of World War I was sent to Ruma in Vojvodina.

During his time in the Austro-Hungarian army he was arrested and briefly imprisoned in Petrovaradin Fortress for distributing anti-war propaganda. He was subsequently released and sent to fight against the Russians. In 1915, he was badly injured by a grenade from a Russian howitzer at Bukovina. After months in a Russian prison hospital, Tito was sent to a work camp in the Urals where he was arrested again in 1917 for organising demonstrations of prisoners of war. He later escaped from the camp and went to join the demonstrations in St Petersburg of July of that year. Here he was arrested once more and locked up in the city's Petropavlovsk Fortress for three weeks before being sent to a prison camp in Kongur from where he escaped to enlist in the Red Army at Omsk. In the spring of 1918 he applied for membership of the Russian Communist Party.

After his wartime adventures in revolutionary Russia, Tito returned home to become a member of the Yugoslavian Communist Party in 1920. In 1928, he led street demonstrations against the authorities following the assassination of the Croat deputies in the parliament building in Belgrade. He was arrested in August 1928 after bombs had been discovered in his apartment, and spent the years 1928–34 in prison, a term which coincided with the establishment of the Royal Dictatorship of King Aleksandar I. On his release, he became a member of the Central Committee in the Political Bureau of the Yugoslavian Communist Party, then in exile in Vienna, adopting the nickname 'Tito' for the first time. He travelled to the Soviet Union again in 1935 to work for the Balkan section of Comintern and returned to Yugoslavia in 1937, having been selected by Stalin to be the new

Socialist Yugoslavia was established as a federal state made up of six republics – Serbia, Croatia, Bosnia and Herzegovina, Macedonia, Slovenia and Montenegro – together with two autonomous regions within Serbia itself – Vojvodina and Kosovo-Metohija. A Soviet-style constitution was drawn up as Tito immediately instigated a number of reforms. Industries were nationalised, large estates were confiscated and redistributed, there were currency reforms, and the first Five Year Plan, emphasising the need to develop Yugoslavia's industrial base, was started. At this stage, Yugoslavia was still closely linked with the Cominform, the Soviet-controlled organisation of east European communist states. This membership guaranteed financial aid for the country with its pro-Soviet policies. However, things changed quite dramatically in 1948, when, because of his differences with Stalin, Tito severed his links with the Soviet Union. Already he had begun to develop his own ideas about how the country's foreign policy should operate, and had resisted Soviet pressure on several important issues. Yugoslavia was expelled from the Cominform and there followed a tense period when it seemed quite likely that the Soviet Union would invade Yugoslavia in order to bring it into line. Tito refused to waver, however, even when the Soviets started to shell the country from its 'friendly' satellite states of Bulgaria and Albania.

secretary-general of the still-outlawed Yugoslavian Communist Party (Stalin had had Milan Gorkić, the previous incumbent, assassinated in Moscow in that same year). Tito officially took up the post in 1939. World War II came and, following the alignment of the Yugoslav crown with the Nazis in 1941, Tito called for armed resistance. Between 1941 and 1945 he was the chief commander of the National Liberation Army, better known as the Partisans, and became entrenched in the bitter, three-way war between Partisans, Nazis (both German and Croatian Ustaša) and royalist Chetniks.

After victory finally came in 1945, Tito became both prime minister and minister of foreign affairs of the new communist republic. He followed the hard-line Soviet example for a while but in 1948, after a serious rift with Stalin, he decided that Yugoslavia should follow its own path and started to develop ideas for a non-aligned version of socialism. In 1961, along with Egypt's Gamal Abdel Nasser and India's Jawarhalal Nehru, he co-founded the Non-aligned Movement. Tito became president of Yugoslavia on 13 January 1953; on 7 April 1963 he was named 'president for life', which he remained until his death in May 1980.

Tito died in a clinic in Ljubljana, Slovenia, on 4 May 1980. His funeral was a spectacular and solemn occasion that drew world leaders of every political persuasion. In Western eyes, Tito's greatest strength was his ability to maintain unity throughout the country and hold the various factions together. Following his death, the glue that held the federation together seemed to start becoming unstuck and within ten years ethnic divisions and conflict had grown to the extent that civil war was inevitable. Tito's admirers would say that it was his political genius and powerful personality that held Yugoslavia together for so long; his critics would declare that it was by manipulation and political repression. The real truth is, no doubt, somewhere between the two.

His grave is at the mausoleum in south Belgrade called 'The House of Flowers' (Kuća cveća) although there is no longer a guard of honour and it does not receive the silent, awestruck lines of pilgrims that it used to.

1

Having rejected Stalin's hard-line and inflexible brand of communism, Tito went it alone with his own vision of socialism. He instigated a federal system, which gave each of the constituent republics individual autonomy for its internal affairs. Another innovation, introduced in 1950, was the introduction of self-managing workers' councils in industry, with producers' councils operating on a regional level.

Although Tito himself was no stranger to odd bouts of autocracy, especially during his early years in power, his brand of socialism was generally far more democratic than that practised throughout the rest of eastern Europe. Tito felt that he had much to offer other non-aligned countries that did not embrace the full-on communism of the Soviet Union. In 1961, the First Conference of Non-aligned Countries was hosted by Belgrade. With continued reforms, and a determinedly non-aligned approach, Tito steered Yugoslavia into becoming a reasonably prosperous and liberal state, which reached its zenith in the 1960s and 1970s. There were a few problems along the way, as Tito did not always quite receive the unfailing support he would have liked – as in many other parts of Europe, there were widespread student riots in 1968 – but overall, he was a respected leader who was genuinely popular with most of his own people and, from the viewpoint of the Western democracies, a preferable choice to any hard-line alternative. Much of his popularity was down to his persuasive powers of unification, and perhaps his greatest achievement of all was to successfully unite Yugoslavia's diverse population in a post-war climate in which the scars of ethnic conflict were still fresh. This unification would not be permanent, however; it would not be long before the wounds and violent memories of World War II would be resurrected in many people's minds.

TITO'S DEATH AND ITS AFTERMATH 1980–91 When Tito died in May 1980, many commentators predicted imminent economic collapse. Tito had achieved much on the strength of his personal charisma and his skill in dealing with problems of nationalism. Before his death, he had laid down conditions for a power-sharing leadership that would ensure the survival of the federation and avoid the emergence of any dictator-like figures. The presidential authority was to change yearly from one republic to the next thus avoiding concentrating power in any particular region.

The predictions came true: within five years Yugoslavia had accumulated a massive foreign debt, had 60% inflation and was suffering from high unemployment throughout the republic. Membership of the Communist Party started to decline and many critics were arguing for modernisation and liberalisation of the economy. The Party, without Tito at the helm, was starting to become something of a behemoth that could only respond to criticism by clamping down on such dissidents.

Ironically, this same period of economic decline and political stagnation was also Yugoslavia's heyday as a tourist destination. Tourism, along with large loans from Western banks, became a lifeline for the Yugoslav economy. As package-tour operators searched for alternative destinations to Spain, Italy and Greece, Yugoslavia became increasingly popular, and by the 1980s millions of northern European tourists were coming each summer to Yugoslavia's Adriatic coast to swim, sunbathe and enjoy bargain prices. The income from this did much to prop up Yugoslavia's flagging economy but it was not enough in itself.

At the same time as this economic decline, regionalist dissatisfactions were starting to emerge once again. Some Croats were suspicious of what seemed to them a Serbian dominance in Yugoslav politics. The Slovenes, too, were starting to resent being dragged down economically by central government – Slovenia had always been one of the most prosperous republics of the federation, and a region which looked more to central Europe than to the Balkans. Most worrying

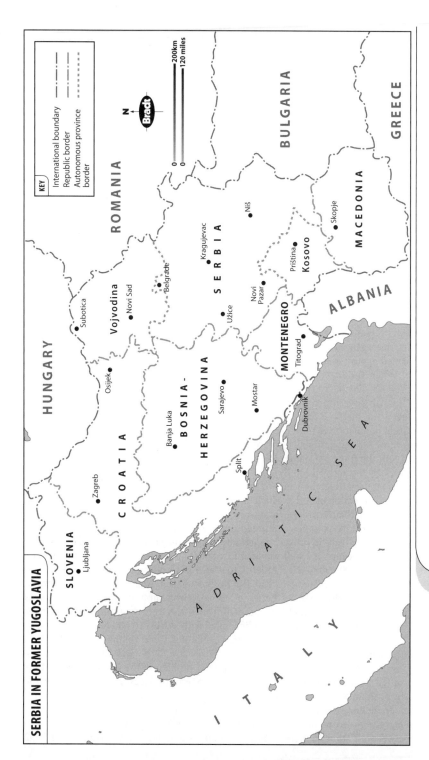

SERBIA IN FORMER YUGOSLAVIA

KEY
International boundary
Republic border
Autonomous province border

200km
120 miles

N

HUNGARY

ROMANIA

BULGARIA

GREECE

SLOVENIA
Ljubljana

CROATIA

Zagreb

Osijek

Subotica

Vojvodina
Novi Sad

Belgrade

SERBIA

Kragujevac

Niš

Kosovo
Priština

MACEDONIA
Skopje

BOSNIA - HERZEGOVINA

Banja Luka

Sarajevo

Mostar

Split

Užice

Novi Pazar

MONTENEGRO
Titograd

ALBANIA

Dubrovnik

ADRIATIC SEA

ITALY

was the situation developing in Kosovo-Metohija, Yugoslavia's poorest and most-overlooked province, where the Albanian majority had been demanding autonomy for many years. With Tito dead, and a growing dissatisfaction with federalism, the seeds of secession were planted for the full-scale civil war that would tear the country apart in the 1990s.

THE BREAK-UP OF YUGOSLAVIA 1991–2000 By 1991, the tensions between the six republics had grown to crisis point. Slovenia was the first to withdraw from the federation, after fighting a brief war of independence in which there was limited bloodshed. This was followed by Croatia, which still had a sizeable Serb minority living in the Krajina and Slavonia regions of the country. Many Serbs within Croatia did not initially want their area to secede and become part of a 'Greater Serbia' but the election of Croatian nationalist Franjo Tuđman in 1990 brought in a new constitution that proclaimed that ethnic Serbs would become a 'national minority' rather than a 'constituent nation' within an independent Croatia. The Serb population had already been radicalised by state television propaganda and the branding of Tuđman as little more than a born-again Ustaša. Serb nationalists further manipulated these fears by publicising false reports of the planned slaughter of ethnic Serbs. In April 1991, the Serbs within the self-declared RSK (Republic of Serbian Krajina) areas of Croatia made their bid for secession. How much of this was locally motivated and how much down to encouragement and manipulation by the Serbian leader Slobodan Milošević and his plans for a 'Greater Serbia' is open to debate. Serb nationalists in the Krajina region began taking control of their own areas, confronting Croatian officials with armed opposition and occupying Croatian government property.

When Tuđman declared independence in July 1991, the Serbian-dominated JNA (Yugoslav People's Army) moved in to intervene, ostensibly to mediate between the Croatian government forces and the Serb rebels but, hardly surprisingly, heavily favouring the Serb cause. Tuđman made a speech on 19 October calling for the Croat population to mobilise against what he termed 'Greater Serbian imperialism'. By now Serbian nationalist paramilitary groups like Arkan's 'Tigers' had also started to join the fray as Croatian towns such as Vukovar and Osijek came under heavy attack by the Serbian-led JNA.

In January 1992, the Vance Peace Plan proclaimed UN-controlled (UNPA) zones for the protection of Serbs, which brought an end to the heaviest violence, although sporadic Serbian artillery forays on Croatian cities and incursions by Croatian forces into UNPA zones continued until 1995. As a result, the Serbs in Croatia continued to leave in droves, sometimes because they had been burned out of their homes or because of a well-founded fear of the consequences if they remained. By 1995, over 200,000 Serbs had left Croatian soil to become refugees in Serbia. A similar number of Croatians had also been displaced. Actual numbers are hard to verify due to discrepancies between Serbian, Croatian and international sources but what is without doubt is that dreadful atrocities were committed by both sides during the hostilities and the conflict ended with at least 10,000 dead.

A parallel crisis had developed in Bosnia and Herzegovina by 1992. With a mixed population of Catholic Croats, Orthodox Serbs and Muslim Bosniaks, Bosnia and Herzegovina had its own special problems. The Croats and Muslims wanted to secede from the federation (although not necessarily together), while the Bosnian Serbs wanted to remain tied to Belgrade. Bosnia and Herzegovina's independence was recognised internationally in 1992, much to the chagrin of the Belgrade government who feared for the future of Serbs in Bosnia. Fighting raged between all three factions – Serbs, Croatians and Bosniaks – from April 1992 until the signing of the Dayton Peace Accord in November 1995. Bosnia was an even bloodier and more savage conflict than Croatia and 'Bosnia' and became a sort of byword for medieval-style butchery, treachery and heinous deeds. New terms like 'safe haven' and 'ethnic cleansing' became common parlance as the rest of the world watched the terrible events unfold on their television sets. Much – perhaps most – of the blame was laid firmly at the door of the Bosnian Serbs, both the VRS (Army of Republika Srpska) and the various Serb paramilitary groups that supported them. These were undoubtedly responsible for many dreadful acts but it is undeniable that all three factions acted disgracefully at times, scorning the usual rules of engagement to fight in a manner that sometimes resembled a medieval war fought with 20th-century weaponry. One particular action that would haunt Serbia in the future was at the UN-protected so-called 'safe haven' of Srebrenica where at least 8,000 Bosniak men were killed by the VRS under the control of Ratko Mladić in July 1995. This, and a catalogue of other war crimes, would have a great influence on the political future of post-war Serbia and its standing abroad.

With Macedonia newly independent as well, it left just two of the former republics – Serbia and Montenegro – to constitute what was by now a severely eroded Yugoslavia. Belgrade was still unwilling to let go of the idea of federation and announced, in April 1992, the establishment of the new Federal Republic of Yugoslavia, a creation made up of these two remaining countries, which from now on would each have their own president and legislature.

Even a new Yugoslavia composed of just two republics was fraught with difficulties, and in 1998, Kosovo, the region which everyone expected trouble to emerge from, erupted into violence. The cause of the disunity here was just as predicted: Serbia still had Kosovo, which remained an autonomous province with a majority Albanian population that wanted full independence from its masters. Given its history, its ethnic make-up, its years of neglect and the degree of ethnic violence that was emerging from every corner of the Balkans, it was only a matter of time before bloodshed spilled over into Kosovo. In 1998 the Kosovo Liberation Army (KLA), supported by many of the ethnic majority Albanians, came out in open rebellion against Serbian rule. President Milošević sent in Serbian troops to quell the uprising and, as the Serbs became embroiled in civil war in Kosovo, international pressure grew in demanding that he withdraw. NATO attempted to bring the two sides together in peace talks in early 1999. Representatives of the KLA signed a deal in Paris on 18 March, but the Serbs chose to boycott the event. Finally, NATO launched air strikes against Serbia on 24 March 1999. On 3 June 1999, Milošević accepted a peace plan brought by EU and Russian envoys that required withdrawal of all forces from Kosovo and the entry of an international peacekeeping force under UN mandate. Serbian forces started to leave the province a week later, and NATO halted the bombardment of Serbian territory on 9 June. Russian peacekeepers entered Kosovo for the first time on 11 June, and a day later, NATO troops crossed the border.

Slobodan Milošević had already been active in Serbian politics for some time, having been president since 1989. There had been protests against him in 1996 because of his rejection of opposition victories in municipal elections. Reeling from the failure of the Kosovo campaign and the humiliation of NATO bombing, the Serbs were becoming increasingly disenchanted with Milošević and what they perceived as bullyboy tactics. In April 2000, more than 100,000 Serbs assembled in central Belgrade to listen to opposition leaders call for early general elections: a defiant act which prompted Milošević to set presidential, parliamentary and local

THE RISE AND FALL OF SLOBODAN MILOŠEVIĆ

Slobodan Milošević was born in Požarevac, Serbia (then Yugoslavia), of Montenegrin parents on 20 August 1941. His first career was as a banker with the Beogradska banka, with whom he served as their official representative in New York for a while. He had joined the Communist Party when he was 18 years old and gave up banking to enter politics full time in 1981 when he took over as head of the local communist organisation in Belgrade. He emerged as a leading force in Yugoslav politics in September 1987 when he replaced Ivan Stambolić as party leader in the Serbian section of the League of Communists of Yugoslavia. He went on to be elected president of Serbia by the National Assembly in May 1989 and a month later, on the 600th anniversary of the Serbian defeat at the Battle of Kosovo, gave a rousing speech to a huge crowd at Kosovo Polje, in which he promised the Kosovo Serbs his protection and full support. As president, Milošević presided over the transformation of the League of Communists into the Socialist Party of Serbia in July 1990, and the adoption of a new Serbian constitution in September of that year. The new constitution provided for the direct election of a president with increased powers. In December 1990, it was Milošević who went on to win the presidency. The new constitution also abolished Kosovo's autonomous status, a move that pleased the Serb minority who lived there but which enraged many Albanians.

Milošević's rise to power coincided with the growth of nationalism that followed the collapse of communism throughout eastern Europe. In Yugoslavia, part of this nationalism could, no doubt, be attributed to Milošević's centralist tendencies that created a fear of Serb domination in the other republics. When Croatia and Bosnia and Herzegovina (along with Slovenia and Macedonia) seceded from the federation, the Serb minorities in both of these former Yugoslav republics called for self-determination to remain part of what was, by now, a Yugoslavia with a mainly Serb population. Civil war soon broke out in both Croatia and Bosnia and Herzegovina. The Serb cause was supported politically and militarily by the Yugoslav government during this period and Milošević sent Yugoslav Federal Army troops into action in both countries to assist the Serb militias fighting to unite their portions of Bosnia and Croatia with Serbia to form a 'Greater Serbia'.

Under Milošević, Yugoslavia had been suffering from trade sanctions imposed by the United Nations since 1992. By agreeing to sign the Dayton peace agreement in November 1995, and withdrawing his active support for the Bosnian Serbs, Milošević got the sanctions lifted. But his troubles were not yet over. Student demonstrations broke out in the winter of 1996, following reports of fraud in local elections. This badly damaged his reputation at home. In June 1997, when the constitution of Serbia prevented him from being president for the third time, Milošević assumed the presidency of the Yugoslav Federation (by now just Serbia and Montenegro remained anyway).

Following its loss of autonomy in 1990, the situation in Kosovo deteriorated throughout the 1990s as Albanian separatists sought independence in the face of increasing state repression. In February 1998, Milošević ordered Yugoslav military forces into Kosovo to join local Serbian police as part of a hard-line crackdown on the separatists. A succession of violent encounters between Serbian police and Albanian Kosovars culminated in full-scale civil war in the province. Hundreds of ethnic Albanians were killed and hundreds of thousands more left the province as refugees to Albania, Montenegro or Macedonia. In the brutal cycle of war, the Kosovo Serb population continued to suffer too as reprisals were taken out against them. Western support was firmly on the side of the Albanian population and Milošević was threatened with military attack if he did not withdraw his forces from the province. The subsequent NATO air strikes increased his popularity to some extent but he was eventually forced to pull out.

On 27 May 1999, Milošević was indicted for war crimes and crimes against humanity in Kosovo. Following the elections in September 2000, Milošević's rejection of a first-round opposition victory led to mass demonstrations in Belgrade on 5 October and the complete collapse of his authority as opposition leader, Vojislav Koštunica, took office as Yugoslav president the following day.

Milošević was arrested on 1 April 2001 on charges of abuse of power and corruption and later on 28 June was handed over to the United Nations International Criminal Tribunal to face his war crimes charges. After his transfer, the original charges were upgraded by adding charges of genocide in Bosnia, as well as further war crimes in Croatia. The trial began in The Hague on 12 February 2002 with Milošević providing his own defence while at the same time refusing to recognise the court's jurisdiction. The trial continued, seemingly *ad infinitum*, for four years, continually delayed by his call for witnesses and extended periods of illness. The prosecution case was to try and prove that Milošević had command responsibility in Croatia and Bosnia, at least de facto, as holding the post of Serbian president at the time means that, technically, he was formally not in charge. Although Milošević was widely vilified abroad he still had some support in Serbia: some critics of the tribunal argued that the trial was just a showcase to justify the bombing actions of NATO in 1999 and the thinly disguised US sponsorship of Albanian terrorists/freedom fighters such as the KLA.

Before Milošević's trial managed to reach a conclusion, he was found dead in his cell on 11 March 2006, almost five years after his arrival at The Hague and with just 50 hours of testimony left before the trial's conclusion. Autopsies revealed that he had died of a heart attack – he had long suffered from heart problems and high blood pressure. Reactions to his death were mixed: some detractors were furious that he had gone to his grave unpunished, while supporters blamed the actions of the tribunal for what had happened. His supporters suggested that his death was brought about by his captors either deliberately or through neglect (Milošević himself had expressed fears that he was being poisoned and a request for treatment at a Russian heart surgery centre had been turned down). In contrast to this, others have proposed that he may have deliberately taken drugs to worsen his heart condition in order to allow a passage to Russia and possible escape.

His funeral was held in his home town of Požarevac after a farewell ceremony in Belgrade that was attended by thousands. The return of the body to Serbia aroused a considerable amount of controversy, which is perhaps appropriate for an autocrat who seemed to thrive on notoriety.

Whatever the reality of his crimes, portraying Slobodan Milošević as a straightforward nationalist is probably to do him a disservice. During the war in Bosnia and in the period immediately after Dayton he was often criticised by genuine hard-line nationalists like Vojislav Šešelj, and it was not until 1998 that Šešelj and his Radical Party agreed to join in a coalition with him. What is without doubt is that Milošević's personality was that of a highly stubborn traditionalist. He was also quite manifestly a skilled manipulator who was able to put a nationalist 'spin' on events whenever it suited him politically.

elections for September of that year. Opposition candidate Vojislav Koštunica won by 48.22% to 40.23%, but a second round was called as neither candidate had an absolute majority. Koštunica's supporters accused the federal election commission of fraud and rejected the result. This rejection set in motion a campaign of strikes and civil disobedience that finally forced Milošević to relinquish power. On 6 October, he conceded defeat and Koštunica was sworn in as Yugoslav president the following day.

SERBIAN POLITICS POST-MILOŠEVIĆ

In January 2001, three months after Milošević's involuntary step down from power, the Serbian Parliament overwhelmingly approved a reform government headed by Zoran Đinđić, head of the Democratic Party. A rift soon started to develop in the second half of 2001 between Prime Minister Đinđić, a keen reformer, and the new president Vojislav Koštunica, a conservative who had been in favour of Milošević going on trial in Belgrade, rather than The Hague as Đinđić had wanted. In August 2001, Koštunica's Democratic Party of Serbia (DSS) pulled out of the government in protest over alleged corruption charges and, in the June of the following year, all 45 deputies belonging to Koštunica's party walked out of parliament as protest at the prime minister's decision to replace 21 of the party's members for absenteeism.

In February 2002, under pressure from the UN, the country changed its name from Yugoslavia to Serbia and Montenegro, although by now, Montenegro, having been persuaded by the EU to forgo independence for the time being, was a somewhat reluctant partner in a loose federation with its larger neighbour. A precondition of this was that there would be a vote in 2006 on the future of the combined state.

In March 2003, Zoran Đinđić was assassinated in Belgrade while stepping out of his car. The assassin was allegedly Zvezdan Jovanović, a Kosovo Serb policeman who had served in the Yugoslav wars of the 1990s, but those behind the murder have yet to be positively identified. Organised crime syndicates, Albanian separatists and even revenge-seeking Milošević supporters have all been suggested as prime suspects. The heavily implicated crime leader Ulemek, a former Milošević supporter and 'Red Berets' paramilitary fighter, has since been sentenced to 40 years for other offences that include murder and attempted murder.

To replace Đinđić, Zoran Živković was appointed as the new Serbian prime minister on 18 March 2003. In the aftermath of the assassination the government imposed a 42-day state of emergency and a crackdown on organised crime designated 'Operation Sword'. Twelve thousand people were arrested as a result, not just as suspects in the assassination but also in connection with other murders, kidnappings and drug-related crimes. At the same time, the remains of Ivan Stambolić, the former Serbian president who went missing in August 2000, were found and charges were made against, among others, Slobodan Milošević, his wife Mirjana Marković and the 'Zemun Clan' leader Milorad 'Legija' Ulemek.

Serbia had been without a president since Milan Milutinović's term finished in December 2002. Serbian Parliament Speaker, Nataša Mičić, stepped in as acting president and two attempts were made to elect a new president in 2002 but both were declared invalid because voter turnout failed to reach the required 50%. A third attempt on 16 November 2003 failed yet again, largely due to a boycott by opposition parties.

Parliamentary elections took place in December 2003, in which the Democratic Party of Serbia emerged as the largest of the democratic parties and Koštunica was elected prime minister in March 2004 to head a minority government. The election of the new president took place in June 2004. Because of repeated low turnouts of the past the 50% minimum was abolished – after three previous attempts it was essential that one be elected this time. In the first round, on 13 June, the largest share of the vote went to Tomislav Nikolić for the Radical Party and Boris Tadić for the Democratic Party, with the government's DSS candidate, Dragan Maršićanin, only coming in at fourth place. The biggest surprise perhaps was Bogoljub Karić, Serbia's wealthiest businessman, who won nearly 20% of the vote and came in at third place. All the early polls suggested that it would be the Radical candidate who would win but in the end it was Boris Tadić, the former minister for defence, who received the support of both the government and Bogoljub Karić to win with 53.2% of the vote. He was sworn in as president in July 2004.

Following his election, Tadić impressed many with his progressive outlook and willingness to acknowledge the wrongs of the past, although others, both nationalist and pro-European, condemned him for making too many compromises. His representation of Serbia at the Srebrenica memorial ceremony in Bosnia and Herzegovina in July 2005 was welcomed by many abroad as a positive step forwards, although this same act was criticised by some at home who wanted the same compassion to be shown towards Serb victims who also died in Bosnia. Tadić's attendance came just after video evidence of the Srebrenica massacre had been shown at the Milošević trial in The Hague. The video had shown Serb 'Scorpion' paramilitary soldiers being blessed by an Orthodox priest before callously executing four young captives in civilian clothes. The video, which found its way on to Serbian television, caused a public outrage and the government quickly arrested some of the soldiers identified by the video. It was hard to remain in denial about mass killings in Bosnia after such flagrant evidence, although there would always be some hard-line nationalists who would manage to do this.

Slobodan Milošević's death in March 2006 and his subsequent burial at his home town of Požarevac caused another stir but in many ways it brought closure and signalled the end of an era. The EU, meanwhile, were putting pressure on Serbia to deliver Ratko Mladić and Radovan Karadžić to The Hague on charges of genocide, believing them both to be taking refuge somewhere in Serbia. A deadline of 1 May issued by Chief UN Prosecutor Carla del Ponte for the handover of Mladić was passed and preliminary talks for Serbia's proposed entry into the European Union were called off.

On 21 May of the same year, Montenegro held a referendum on whether or not to end its union with Serbia. The result was 55.5% in favour, marginally above the 55% required for independence. On 3 June 2006, the Montenegrin parliament declared itself independent of the State Union of Serbia and Montenegro and two days later the National Assembly of Serbia declared Serbia as successor to the state union. To consolidate matters, Serbia held a two-day referendum on 28–29 October 2006 to ratify a new constitution that would replace the previous one written during the Milošević period.

Over the space of just three years Belgrade had been capital of three separate state entities: Yugoslavia, then Serbia and Montenegro, and finally Serbia. But what actually constituted Serbia was still not yet fixed, geographically or politically: there was still the question of Kosovo. In November 2006, a final decision on the future of the province was delayed by UN envoy to Kosovo Martti Ahtisaari until after the Serbian elections of January 2007 as the international community did not want to encourage a pro-nationalist vote. This frustrated the Kosovar Albanians, as did the new Serbian constitution drawn up by Prime Minister Vojislav Koštunica that proclaimed that Kosovo should remain an inalienable part of Serbia.

Parliamentary elections were held on 21 January 2007 in which the nationalist Radicals emerged with the most votes even though they were unable to form a government. This prompted coalition discussions between the pro-Western democratic parties who came in as runners-up.

In spring 2007, Martti Ahtisaari submitted a plan to the UN Security Council that gave Kosovo supervised independence. Objections to this plan were raised by both Russia and Serbia but what may have been seen as inevitable happened on 17 February 2008 when Kosovo unilaterally proclaimed independence from Serbia at a meeting of the Kosovo Assembly in Priština that was boycotted by all 11 deputies representing the Serb minority. Boris Tadić had been re-elected as president and sworn in on 15 February 2008, just two days before Kosovo's independence declaration. Although remaining largely pro-Western, Tadić asserted that Serbia would never be able to recognise an independent Kosovo. The declaration was immediately declared null and void by the Serbian National Assembly in Belgrade but accepted by the US, UK and much of western Europe. It was opposed by Russia, China, Spain, Greece, Romania and Brazil among others. At the end of 2009, Kosovo's independence was recognised by only about 33% of sovereign UN countries, although accepted by 22 out of 27 European Union states and 24 out of 28 NATO members.

In July 2008, Radovan Karadžić was arrested in New Belgrade where, heavily disguised with a voluminous beard, he had been practising alternative medicine for some time right under the noses of the authorities (he had also written several volumes of poetry during the years that he had been a fugitive from justice). Karadžić was promptly dispatched to The Hague to face trial for war crimes against Bosnian Muslim and Croat civilians during the 1992–95 Bosnian War. Trial proceedings began in October 2009, although Karadžić refused to enter a plea, dismissing the court as a 'court of NATO'. In November 2009, the court forcibly imposed a lawyer on him and in response Karadžić filed a motion challenging the legitimacy of the court. A verdict was finally arrived at in March 2016 that found Karadžić criminally responsible for the Srebrenica genocide, sentencing him to 40 years' imprisonment.

In May 2011, Ratko Mladić, the last of the former military leaders wanted for crimes against humanity and genocide, was arrested and extradited to The Hague, an action that was regarded as essential for Serbia to progress towards eventual EU membership. An initial hearing was made in June 2011, and after several delays the trial formerly opened in May 2012 with Mladić refusing to enter a plea, declaring it a 'Satanic court'. The trial has since dragged on for several more years, with Mladić refusing to testify at the parallel Karadžić trial. At the time of writing a verdict had still not been announced, although the prosecutors were suggesting that anything less than a life sentence would be an insult to his victims.

The general election of May 2012 brought about a change in government with the election of Tomislav Nikolić, co-founder and former leader of the Serbian Progressive Party, as president. Nikolić, who once admitted that he would rather align with Russia than join the EU, appears to have softened his views on Europe in recent years, declaring upon winning the election that Serbia would 'not stray from its European path'. Nikolić's success is widely attributed to his bringing large numbers of former Radical Party voters to his newly founded and more centrist Serbian Progressive Party, a party that also attracted liberal voters dissatisfied with Tadić's reign as president.

In 2012, the then minister of defence Aleksandar Vučić took over from Nikolić as leader of the Serbian Progressive Party. Vučić went on to replace the Socialist Party's Ivica Dačić as prime minister in 2014, leading the way for a more pro-Russian stance whilst still courting good relations with the European Union. In July 2015, invited by the Bosnian government, Vučić attended the annual Srebrenica Genocide Memorial to pay his respects but was greeted by an angry crowd hurling bottles and abuse – an act of reconciliation that seriously misfired. During the 2015–16 European migrant crisis, Vučić strongly supported the policies of Germany's Angela Merkel and pledged to take in migrants and not hinder their passage and build fences as some neighbouring countries had done. Serbia's humanitarian stance during the crisis – and indeed the generosity of many of its people – has been praised by many observers critical of the more right-wing, anti-immigrant position taken by existing EU-member countries like Hungary. Vučić won the presidential election in April 2017 with a majority of 55%. Following the election and accusations of electoral fraud, large-scale protests took place in front of the Serbian National Assembly in Belgrade and in several other Serbian cities over the weeks that followed.

ECONOMY

Serbia's economy is slowly making a recovery after years of sanctions, war and inner turmoil. The serious problems started around 1991 when secession by Croatia, Slovenia and Macedonia meant that Serbia had to radically rethink its economic framework, which previously had been centrally planned with the focus of power in the capital. With secession came the loss of much of its manufacturing base that had favoured Croatia and Slovenia; the revenue from package tourism, too – enormously important to the pre-war Yugoslav economy – had come mostly from the Adriatic region of Croatia but, with the advent of war, tourism ceased to be a reality anywhere in the region for many years. Fortunately, the Vojvodina region continued to be the most productive agricultural region in the whole of the Balkans, and raw materials were still being unearthed from the coal mines in the southeast and the mineral mines of Kosovo. Nevertheless, the unhappy break-up of the Yugoslav federation meant that Serbia's economy soon became deficient in terms of raw materials, manufacturing base and a market for its goods. Successive wars and sanctions compounded the problem until a point in the mid 1990s when inflation reached the world's highest-ever figure – a staggering 600,000% – that eclipsed even that of pre-war Germany (see box, page 37). Serbia, shunned by most of the world, had reached a point where some of its people were living in conditions of almost Third World-style poverty. Many of those that could leave – the young and well educated – did so, which left a skills shortage that further inflamed the situation. Finally, when popular protest finally brought the regime of Slobodan Milošević to its knees in late 2000, the widespread protest was fuelled as much by dissatisfaction with the dire shape of the economy as it was by political and ideological rejections of Milošević's plans for a Greater Serbia.

The coalition government that followed Milošević inherited an economy shattered by war and nearly a decade of sanctions. The Serbian government has since taken several bold economic decisions: stabilising the dinar, streamlining the tax system and reforming the banking sector. In 2001, Serbia, then still the FRY, became eligible for interest-free loans from the World Bank and a credit of US$540 million was authorised to contribute towards political, economic and social reforms. In 2003, the European Union granted €242 million in aid to Serbia and Montenegro, €229 million of which was destined for Serbia. By 2006, economic growth was 6.3%, a marked improvement on the earlier years of the decade. However, problems of high unemployment (20%), a high export deficit and considerable debt (US$12.2 billion in 2006) remained. With corruption and organised crime steadily on the wane, foreign investment slowly increasing and more stable government in power, the current mood is one of quiet optimism. A 2008 estimate put Serbia's GDP growth at 6.1%, maintaining the trend of two years earlier, and inflation was a manageable 6.8%. According to a 2009 estimate, unemployment had reduced to 13% and the foreign debt was down to US$11.4 billion – still very high but clearly an improvement. Nevertheless, GDP per capita was still only 35% of the EU average by 2011, a little higher than Bosnia and Herzegovina (30%) and Albania (30%), but considerably lower than its other neighbours Croatia (61%), Hungary (66%) and Romania (49%).

An optimistic outlook for Serbia's economy is partially dependent on its joining the European Union at some stage in the future. Preliminary talks regarding this were suspended in 2006 because of Serbia's failure to deliver war criminal Ratko Mladić to the United Nations International Tribunal in The Hague. It was hoped that the arrest of Radovan Karadžić in 2008 would help unblock the road to EU membership but the bloc said that to advance Serbia's pending application, Ratko Mladić, The Hague tribunal's most wanted man, must also be arrested and handed over. However, as part of the Stabilisation and Association Agreement (SAA) signed by Serbia in April 2008, it was agreed by EU ministers that Serbia, along with Macedonia and Montenegro, would be allowed visa-travel inside the EU bloc from 19 December 2009 when Serbia was placed on the White Schengen List. Ratko Mladić was finally arrested by Serbian special police forces in Lazarevo, Vojvodina, on 26 May 2011 and extradited to The Hague on the 31st of that month. His trial continues. Serbia finally attained full candidate status on 1 March 2012 and negotiations for membership commenced in January 2014.

PEOPLE

The population of Serbia is surprisingly varied in its ethnicity. Even the briefest look at the country's demography reveals that Serbia today is anything but a homogeneous population, with Serbs, according to the last census, representing a little over 83% of the total population, Hungarians 4% and a diverse mix of Romanians, Croats, Bulgarians, Bosniaks, Ruthenians, Slovaks, Vlachs (see box, page 40), Roma and others making up the remaining 13%. Notwithstanding this, the Serbs are the most populous group across the country, apart from those parts of Vojvodina that have a large Hungarian or Romanian element. It is interesting to note that at the last census in 2011 only 0.3% of the population claimed to be 'Yugoslavs' whereas the 1991 and 2002 figures were 4.1% and 1.1% respectively.

SERBS The origins of the Serbs (and the Croats) are unclear. One school of thought states that the Slavs were a group of tribes living in the Carpathian Mountains region, close to what is now the Romanian–Ukrainian border, and that they were driven from these lands by raiding Avars and Bulgars. Others contend that the Slavs came from the Caucasus region and were escaping from the clutches of an Iranian elite. Evidence for this second theory is supported by the records of Greek geographers who wrote, in the 2nd century AD, of an Iranian tribe called the *Serbi* or *Serboi* living on the banks of the River Don, but Professor John Fine, a foremost historian on the region, suggests that even if the first Serbs and Croats were actually Iranian, the Iranians quickly became assimilated into a society that was clearly Slavic, despite the non-Slavic origins of its ruling class. Whatever their true origin, the Slavs, unlike the other raiding tribes, came to stay; they settled in the territories depopulated by warfare and clung tenaciously to their new-found lands.

Differentiation took place as some tribes occupied the lands along the Adriatic littoral, to become the Croats, while others filled the niche available in the depopulated lands below the Danube. The two tribes had much in common, particularly in their unique social organisation: both Serbs and Croats lived as large, extended family groups (*zadruge*) governed by a patriarch or chieftain (*župan*). The Serbs especially, would maintain this unique form of social organisation, even during the long, oppressive years of Turkish domination.

To understand what constitutes the Serbian character, it is probably best to consider the way that Serbs see themselves. Proud, generous, strong-willed and brave are all adjectives that few Serbs would find argument with and it is undeniable that the Serbian character is strongly individualistic with an enormous love for home, family and nation. As for racial stereotypes, the so-called 'victim' mentality that Serbs are said to suffer from is undoubtedly more the result of years of isolation than any generic, deeply embedded psychological trait.

Rebecca West was clearly a great fan of the Serbs and writes fondly of them in *Black Lamb and Grey Falcon*, her epic pre-war journey through Yugoslavia. Unlike the Croats, whom she considered to be caught at odds between their inner Slavic souls and outward Western aspirations, she repeatedly observed that Serbs were proud, honest and completely in touch with their warrior roots. She quotes (in French) from a book by the Serbian author, Mičić:

La ciel serbe est couleur d'azur	The Serb sky is the colour of azure
Au dedans est assis un vrai dieu serbe	Inside which sits a true Serb god
Entouré des anges serbes aux voix pures	Surrounded by pure-voiced Serb angels
Qui chantent la gloire de leur race superbe	Who sing the glory of their superb race

ALBANIANS The Albanians, who make up the great bulk of the population in Kosovo and Metohija, are a non-Slavic people descended from the ancient Illyrians who speak an Indo-European language that has developed from Illyrian. The date of their appearance in medieval Serbia is a matter of contention but there is little doubt that by the 15th century, when Ottoman advances drove many Christian Serbs north to safety, many land-hungry Albanians moved in to fill the void and colonised much of Kosovo and Metohija.

Serbian–Albanian relations were not always so fractious if we are to believe Rebecca West in her reflections in *Black Lamb and Grey Falcon*. She remarks that, 'We noted again the liking that most Serbs now feel for the Albanians, who during the Turkish occupation were their most constant tormentors', although perhaps she is a little too ingenuous in her estimation of Serb forgiveness. Such forgiveness has never featured very strongly in Balkan history, whatever the ethnicity of the offended group.

ROMA The Roma in Serbia arrived in the Balkans sometime around the 10th century after a slow migration west from India. Throughout their history in the region they have remained, for the most part, outside mainstream culture, having little bearing on political and social systems of the countries they lived in, regardless of whether they were feudal, socialist or capitalist. Persecution and racial discrimination has always been a feature of life for eastern Europe's Roma but this turned to genocide during World War II when Nazis and Ustaša collaborated in their murder.

Serbia's Roma population are no worse off than their kinsmen in other parts of eastern Europe. That, however, is not saying very much. Like Roma everywhere they are a disadvantaged and disenfranchised section of the population who live beyond the reaches of any state aid, such that may exist. A limited number have become integrated into Serb society to follow professional careers but for the most part Serbia's Roma live in poor conditions eking out an existence at society's fringes. Few Roma get to enjoy the benefit of a full state education (unlike other minorities in Serbia, Roma children are not taught in their native language); consequently, many are illiterate. With many suffering from the diseases and poor health that are associated with substandard living conditions it is hardly surprising that average life expectancy is well below the national average.

The former Yugoslavia had one of the largest Roma populations in eastern Europe with an estimated 1981 population of 850,000. Life was marginally better in the pre-war period before the break-up of the federation. Under the Yugoslavian constitution, Roma had, theoretically at least, an equal status with other ethnic groups in the federation. In practice, things were not so equitable, but at least they were recognised as being a constituent people of the republic. Since the break-up, Roma have become even more disadvantaged, suffering greater discrimination in employment, social services and education, as well as having to endure the privations of the Western trade embargo that affected them disproportionately.

In recent years, many Roma have migrated from rural poverty to Serbian cities for a better life that rarely materialises. Many of them have had no choice but to move, and a large number of Roma have arrived as refugees in central and northern Serbia as a result of ethnic cleansing in Kosovo. In Serbia, the Kosovar Roma, who may number as many as 30,000, are considered to be internally displaced people rather than bona fide refugees, which excludes them from many basic rights and benefits. In neighbouring Montenegro, they have fared better and been afforded true refugee status.

To see the depressing makeshift huts that line the railway tracks leading into Belgrade's central station, or to visit 'Bangladesh', the disused pig farm outside Novi Sad that has served as home to a Roma community of 200 for the past 35 years, is to witness conditions that bring to mind Third-World shanty towns or Brazilian *favelas*, and serves as a reminder of their position at the bottom of the social heap. But, despite their lowly status, and the rising incidence of racist violence against them, Roma are grudgingly admired in some quarters. In particular, they are lauded for their skill as musicians, and Roma wedding bands always have plenty of work. Some musicians of Roma descent, like trumpet player Boban Marković and his son Marko, have gone on to become household names with a reputation that extends beyond national boundaries.

OTHER MINORITIES Vojvodina has more minorities than any other Serbian province, with a total of 37 ethnic groups represented. The minorities in Vojvodina are far less visible than Kosovar Albanians or Roma and are generally fully integrated into mainstream Serbian society even though many of them still maintain their own traditions. The most numerous of these groups are the Hungarians, who make up about 4% of Serbia's total population and over 14% of that of Vojvodina, and who constitute a large proportion of the citizens in northern towns like Sombor and Subotica. The Hungarian influence in these northern towns is quite palpable, with the Hungarian language widely spoken and prevalent in newspapers, advertisements and street signs. The architecture, music and food of northern Vojvodina are also heavily influenced by Hungarian culture. Of the other minorities in Vojvodina, ethnic Romanians are numerous in the northeastern villages of the Banat, as are Slovakians, Croatians and Ruthenians in other parts of the province. Hungarian, Romanian and Slovakian are taught as the first language in some of the schools of this region, along with Serbian. Other minorities in this most ethnically diverse part of the country include Germans, Montenegrins and Ukrainians.

REFUGEES AND THE INTERNALLY DISPLACED One of the realities of life in post-Milošević Serbia is the large number of refugees that remain in the country as a result of ethnic persecution or conflict. Depending on the source of the data, there are estimated to be between 350,000 and 800,000 refugees and internally displaced persons (IDPs) living in camps or makeshift accommodation throughout Serbia. The refugees originate from former Serbian enclaves in Croatia like Krajina or Slavonia, or from non-Serbian parts of Bosnia and Herzegovina, while the internally displaced persons are either ethnic Serbs or Roma from Kosovo-Metohija. Many of these arrived in Serbia with just the clothes on their back, and despite a limited amount of state and foreign aid have often found it difficult to adapt to their new circumstances. Often this is as much to do with cultural differences as it is a consequence of the trauma they have already suffered. In some cases, refugee Serbs, such as rural Krajina farmers, find that they have little in common with the communities they find themselves in, and that acceptance by their host communities, who themselves have suffered economically as a result of sanctions and war, is often begrudging. This is especially true of displaced Roma from Kosovo.

According to a 2001 census carried out by the Serbian Commissariat for Refugees in co-operation with the UNHCR, the majority of the refugees (63%) are from Croatia, with a smaller and declining percentage from Bosnia and Herzegovina (36%) as some refugees start to return to their homes there. In both cases, about 60% of refugees and IDPs have opted for integration into the State Union of Serbia and Montenegro (existing as two separate countries – Serbia and Montenegro – since 2006). Within Serbia there are over 400 registered collective centres that accommodate over 30,000 people, two-thirds of which are refugees and the rest, IDPs from Kosovo-Metohija. At least another 10,000 live in unregistered collective centres, while many more live with relatives and friends. The greatest numbers of

1

THE VLACHS

Although there is some controversy about their origins, the most commonly held view is that the Vlachs are a Romanised pre-Slavic group who survived the Slavic onslaught in the Balkans during the 6th century AD. With the arrival of the Serbs, first as raiders, then later as settlers, they took to the hills or migrated to the Balkan fringes. These nomadic clansmen moved around the Balkans in the wake of the rise of urban centres. The Vlachs with their large herds of sheep, goats and cattle would service the cities, driving their flocks over long distances whilst taking advantage of seasonal grazing lands along the way. In Roman times they provided cheese to many parts of the empire. The Latin tongue they developed over the centuries of doing this became preserved as Vlachs took to more mountainous areas during subsequent Slavic invasions. Centuries later, the Vlachs were practising transhumance over vast areas, spurred on by the Byzantine taxation system, which was far easier to evade when constantly moving. Later colonisation encouraged the Vlachs to maintain this way of life when the Turks persuaded them to keep to their nomadic lifestyle as the expanding Ottoman cities of the Balkans had great demand for the cheese, milk, wool and leather they provided.

Despite many being later assimilated by the Serbs and taking up their language and culture, many others kept true to their traditions, speaking a Latin-based language that is close to modern Romanian. Modern-day Vlachs in Serbia are generally integrated into mainstream society and seem little different from ordinary Serbs although they still retain elements of their language and tradition.

The most populous enclaves of Vlachs (or Vlasi as they are known in Serbia) today are the villages of the Homolje Mountains in the east, near to the Romanian border, but even in this region they do not form a majority. The southern, or Aromanian, Vlachs that live in Kosovo, Macedonia and Montenegro appear to be a separate group without any Romanian ties. The writer, Noel Malcolm, in his book *A Short History of Kosovo*, puts forward the somewhat controversial theory that both of the Latinised tribes – Romanians and Vlachs – have their origins in Kosovo and adopted their northern territories after a gradual northerly migration. It is hard to establish how many genuine Vlachs there are in Serbia today: in a 1948 census, nearly 100,000 declared themselves to be Vlachs but this number dwindled to a third of this by 1954, and to a negligible 1,369 by 1961. This decline probably reflects a lack of ethnical commitment more than other factors like migration. Clearly, many had recovered their Vlach identity by the 2002 census when 39,953 registered themselves as such (reduced again to 35,330 in the 2011 census). Many Vlachs in eastern Serbia today spend much of their adult life working abroad in Austria and Germany. Many invest their foreign earnings by constructing large, kitsch houses in their home villages, houses that remain largely empty apart from brief summer holiday visits. One of the several annual events celebrated by the Vlachs is the 'Slatina gathering', which takes place in a village close to the industrial town of Bor every year.

refugees are housed in Belgrade, Vojvodina and in the municipalities of Loznica and Šabac in western Serbia. Most of those displaced from Kosovo-Metohija have become spread right across Serbia, in Belgrade, Kraljevo, Kragujevac, Niš, Smederevo, Kruševac, Leskovac, Vranje and Kuršumlija.

In many ways the IDPs are the worst off, because as they originate from within Serbia's previous national boundaries, which included Kosovo-Metohija, they do not qualify as bona fide refugees. Consequently, they receive little of the meagre state and foreign aid that is available to refugees from beyond Serbia's borders.

Another important demographic factor that needs to be considered is the large-scale exodus of many of Serbia's young professionals to Europe, Australia and North America during the 1990s, which has resulted in a skills shortage in the country, particularly in areas like health and education.

LANGUAGE

Standard Serbian is one of the eastern variants of the Central-South Slavic language that was previously referred to as Serbo-Croat; Croatian is a western variant of the same. It is an Indo-European language that is closely related to other Slavic languages like Russian, Czech or Polish, although modern Serbian, because of the long Ottoman occupation of the region, also contains a considerable number of words of Turkish origin. The Serbian language, which is based on the Shtokavian dialect, is spoken primarily in Serbia and in the Republika Srpska of Bosnia and Herzegovina, in addition to Serb communities abroad in cities such as Chicago, Melbourne and Toronto.

Serbian, in its written form, uses both a Latin and a Cyrillic alphabet of 25 consonants and five vowels, the Latin form being adjusted by the use of standardised diacritical accents to render it phonetically accurate. The Cyrillic alphabet is based upon an earlier form that was first devised by St Cyril in the 9th century, later to be refined by St Kliment at Ohrid, Macedonia. Cyrillic may look intimidating at first, but given the ubiquitous nature of Cyrillic signs on display it soon becomes familiar enough, at least in its upper-case form. Using either alphabet, written Serbian is completely phonetic, with none of the unvoiced letters or variants in pronunciation that confound foreign students of English. Foreign names are also transcribed phonetically, so that well-known English names can appear unfamiliar when they are seen in their Serbian form, such as Džon Mejdžor for John Major, or Đordž W Buš for a certain former US president. The Cyrillic alphabet is still widely used throughout Serbia (perhaps a little less in Vojvodina where Latin-script Hungarian is common) and has enjoyed something of a revival since the break-up of Yugoslavia and the rise of Serbian nationalism, with the use of Cyrillic serving as a clear way of distinguishing Serbian from closely related Croatian and Bosnian that use only the Latin alphabet. For information on pronunciation and a brief vocabulary, together with a comparison of the Cyrillic and Latin alphabets, see *Appendix 1*, page 380. For those who would like to learn the language there is a free online Serbian tutorial at w http://skolasrpskog.com.

Under Tito, Russian was the main foreign language taught in Yugoslav schools but that has long been replaced by English, a language that most under 30s know at least a little of. This secondary-school tuition, coupled with the influence of growing up on a diet of Western rock music and Hollywood movies, has resulted in many young Serbs, in Belgrade especially, having an impressively fluent command of the English language. German is also quite widely spoken or understood in some quarters, often by older Serbs who learned it while working abroad in Germany or Austria.

Minorities such as the Hungarians and Romanians in Vojvodina generally learn to speak, write and read in their own native languages as well as in Serbian. Most of Serbia's Roma community speak their own Roma language among themselves, although there is so much variation between dialects spoken in different parts of Serbia that they may be mutually unintelligible. Although Roma does have a written form, very few Roma speakers are able to read or write in this language even though they may be fully literate in Serbian.

RELIGION

The majority religion in Serbia is Orthodox Christianity, with an ethnic Slav Muslim majority in the Sandžak/Raška region of southwest Serbia. There are also Catholic (mostly Croatian and Bunjevci) and Protestant (mainly Hungarian) minorities in the north of the country.

Serbia started to become Christian in the 7th century with the encouragement of Byzantine missionaries and, although some pockets of paganism resisted for longer, most of the country was Christian by about AD790. For the next 200 years, religious influence fluctuated between Rome and Constantinople until 1054, when the Eastern Orthodox Church finally broke with Rome over the issues of the primacy of the Pope and the language of the creed. For the next 165 years, all of Serbia's archbishops were appointed by the Patriarchate of Constantinople, but in 1219 the Serbian Orthodox Church separated from the Eastern Orthodox Church when Stefan Nemanja's youngest son Sava succeeded in negotiating with Constantinople for autocephalous status. Sava, who was later canonised like his father before him, became the first archbishop of this newly established Church.

SERBIAN MONASTERIES The period of the Nemanjić dynasty saw a proliferation of church and monastery building as successive rulers sought to mark their time in power with new construction projects. Many of Serbia's most noteworthy religious buildings date from this 'golden age' in the years before Ottoman subjugation, from the late 12th century to the early 1400s. The monastic churches that were built during this period represent some of the finest achievements of the Byzantine era, both in terms of the architecture itself and the richly coloured decorative frescoes they contain within.

King Stefan Nemanja was responsible for the building of the Monastery of Studenica in the latter part of the 12th century. His son Stefan the First Crowned was responsible for the construction of Žiča in 1208, which became the seat of the newly established Serbian Archbishopric, while the Monastery of Mileševa was founded by King Vladislav in 1234 to become one of the most important Serbian spiritual centres in the 13th century. During the reign of King Stefan Uroš I (1243–76), the centre of the Serbian Church was moved to the Church of the Holy Apostles at Peć, which was completed about 1250, because it was considered that Peć was not only closer to the centre of the Serbian state but it was also less vulnerable to raids from the north. King Uroš I also founded the Monastery of Sopoćani close to the source of the Raška River. Several members of the Nemanjić family were buried in the monastery, including Stefan the First Crowned, under the gaze of some of the finest medieval frescoes.

Gračanica, perhaps the most spiritually important of Serbia's surviving medieval churches, was founded by King Milutin Nemanja close to what is now Priština in present-day Kosovo, while his son, King Stefan Uroš III, went on to initiate work on the Church of the Ascension at Dečani south of Peć, alongside his own son and heir, Stefan Dušan, who oversaw its completion. Both monasteries could be described as the jewel in the crown of medieval Serbian architecture: Gračanica for its grace; Dečani for its imposing form as well as its wealth of medieval paintings. Later monasteries belong to the so-called Morava style. Before perishing at the

Battle of Kosovo, Prince Lazar built Ravanica in 1370, where his body still rests today; he also founded Ljubostinja in 1388, together with his wife Princess Milica, who entered the monastery after Lazar's defeat the following year. The Monastery of Manasija with its massive defensive towers and walls was founded by Despot Stefan Lazarević between 1407 and 1418.

CULTURE

NATIONAL FOLKLORE There are many facets of Orthodox religious practice that are central to Serbian culture even for individuals who are not especially religious. One of the most important of these is the custom of celebrating *slava*, a practice which may also be encountered in Montenegro, Macedonia, Bulgaria and Croatia, although it is most commonly associated with Serbs. *Slava*, which might best be translated as meaning 'praise' or 'glory', is the celebration of a patron saint. Each family celebrates its own saint, who is considered to be its protector. A particular *slava* is inherited from father to son and the occasion brings families together as each household, in sharing the same *slava*, is obliged to celebrate the event together. In special cases, such as migration abroad, family members may stage the event separately but as a rule it takes place under one roof, that of the family patriarch.

During a *slava* the family home is open to anyone who wishes to drop by. It is considered untraditional to actually invite guests outside the family, but visitors are welcomed if they come of their own free will. To be turned away from a Serbian home during a *slava* is unheard of as this would bring disgrace to the household. The Krsna *slava* ritual involves the breaking of bread and the lighting of a candle by a priest. A prayer is said over the *koljivo* – ground cooked wheat – the third of the three ingredients central to the *slava* ceremony (the Serbs have a thing about the number three). Incense is burned and everyone present is blessed with holy water before the priest blesses and cuts the bread in the sign of the cross. The bread is then rotated by the family patriarch, his godfather and the priest before everyone assembled sits down for a meal. Of the various saints' days, the most commonly celebrated are those of St Nicholas (Nikoljdan) on 19 December, St George (Đurđevdan) on 6 May, St John the Baptist (Jovanjdan) on 20 January and St Archangel Michael (Aranđelovdan) on 21 November.

The custom of *slava* is believed to date back to the late 9th century when Serbs were first Christianised. It is thought that each of the Serb tribes adopted its collective saint protector around this time and this is borne out by *slava* variations according to geographical regions. Another commonly held belief, which does not necessarily contradict this, is that the custom of *slava* is a remnant from pre-Christian paganism and that *slava* was a syncretic adaptation in which the qualities of the old Serbian gods found sustenance in the personalities of the new Christian saints. Occasionally, a new *slava* is adopted when it is believed that a particular saint has facilitated deliverance from an affliction such as an illness, in response to prayer.

As well as individuals and families, various communities such as villages, cities, organisations, political parties, institutions and professions, can have their own *slava*. Belgrade's *slava* is on Ascension Day, which takes place on a Thursday, 40 days after Easter each year.

Christmas is celebrated in a different way from the West. Orthodox Christmas Eve falls two weeks later than its Western counterpart, on 6 January, its date according to the Gregorian calendar. Tradition dictates that early on Christmas Eve morning the head of the family should go to a forest to cut *badnjak*, a young oak sapling, which is then brought to church to be blessed by a priest. The sapling is then stripped of its branches and burned in the family fireplace. Rather like the burning of a yule log in Britain, this is clearly a ritual that has pagan origins. These days, with many Serbs living in cities at some distance from the nearest forest, the ritual is remembered by the Church dispensing the oaks themselves. The floor of the church, and sometimes the home, is covered with straw to remind of the stable where Jesus Christ was born. The Christmas meal usually consists of roast piglet and the sweet ground wheat *koljivo*, but the most important item on the table is *česnica*, a special loaf that contains a coin. Whoever gets the coin is considered to be especially lucky for the forthcoming year. Presents are not distributed at Christmas as in the West but are given instead on the *slava* of St Nicholas on 19 December. Under communist rule it became more traditional to give presents on New Year's Day, which follows shortly after.

Easter is probably a more important event in the Orthodox calendar and a time when even many non-believers attend church for midnight mass on the night of Good Friday. Again, the timing of the Gregorian calendar means that it usually takes place later than Easter in western Europe. On this night, attendance of the mass is accompanied by much jollity afterwards and the drinking of *šljivovica*.

The painting of eggs is another Serbian Easter custom that still survives, especially in Vojvodina, and which takes place the week before Easter. During this week whole families become engaged in painting hard-boiled eggs red and sometimes decorating them, although this is a later tradition. The painting of the eggs symbolises the renewal of life and one egg remains on the family altarpiece throughout the coming year. The red colouration is thought to frighten away the devil.

NATIONAL COSTUME Little evidence remains today of the varied styles of national dress once worn in different parts of Serbia, although Belgrade's Ethnological Museum has an excellent collection that is well worth seeing. Some Muslim women in the Sandžak region of southwest Serbia wear distinctive *hijab*-style dress, although this comes from a religious adherence to dressing modestly rather than any form of national costume. Further north, in Vojvodina, some older Slovak women still regularly wear the headscarf, pleated skirt and embroidered apron that is their national dress. All across Serbia, as elsewhere in eastern Europe, many older women wear headscarves, regardless of religion.

In rural areas of central Serbia, some older men still adopt the *šajkača*, the narrow, black or grey cap that used to be worn right across the country by Orthodox Serbs. This headgear is now making something of a comeback and its retro-style is favoured by some Serb nationalists, who tend to wear their *šajkača* at a rakish tilt. In contrast, *opanak*, the traditional Serb shoes with turned-up toe, are now only sported by self-conscious waiters in national restaurants.

ART AND ARCHITECTURE
Serbian religious art and architecture
The fine Christian art produced in the period of Nemanjić rule represents the apex of artistic achievement in medieval Serbia – an era of great creativity that might be compared to the Italian Renaissance that was yet to come. The monasteries built during this golden age were deliberately located in inaccessible spots around the country. Part of the reason for this was defensive, but it was also important to ensure that the monks who lived in them were able to follow a purely contemplative life away from all worldly distractions. With the arrival of the Turks in the first half of the 15th century, many of these monasteries were either converted into mosques or completely demolished, as the biblical scenes displayed in the lush frescoes offended the Ottoman sensibility with its Muslim proscription on representing the human image. Consequently, many

frescoes were simply plastered over to hide the offending images; in many cases this plaster remained firmly in place until restoration was possible in the 19th and 20th centuries after the final withdrawal of the Ottomans had taken place.

As with all Orthodox churches, Serbian churches differ in layout from those of the Catholic and Protestant faith. Instead of a nave or choir, there is a naos, a central area for worship that might be of a square or round plan, which is usually topped by a dome, a symbolic representation of Heaven above. The congregation always stands for the liturgy – there are no seats – and the central, public part of the church is separated from the apse by means of an iconostasis, a tall screen, usually made of wood that is decorated with elaborate carving and numerous icons of the saints. What characterises the Orthodox Church, in particular the medieval Serbian Orthodox Church, is the use of frescoes to decorate the walls. These are far more than ornamental flourishes; they are there to show the congregation the heavenly kingdom that they can aspire to, to bring to life the Gospels and the lives of the saints for what would formerly have been an almost entirely illiterate congregation.

In medieval Serbia the art of fresco painting was developed to a high art form, but there were strict conventions that had to be adhered to. The images portrayed were considered to be representations of Christ's manifestation on Earth and so there was little scope for wild experimentation. However, regional stylistic differences did develop over time, both in the style of architecture and in the visual art on the walls.

The earlier Serbian monastery churches were built in what is now referred to as the **Raška School**. This style, seen in the early Nemanjić monasteries, takes its name from Raš, the capital of the early Serbian kingdom. During this period, the Serbian Church was distancing itself from Byzantium and starting to lean more to the West, which explains the undeniable Romanesque influences that can be seen in the monasteries that were built at this time. The Romanesque influence is apparent in features such as animal and floral decoration around portals, and scenes such as nativities or *pietás* carved in high relief in the lunettes above doors and windows. A good example of this East–West fusion of styles is the fresco of *The Crucifixion* at Studenica, in which the iconography is clearly Byzantine yet the rendering of the head of Christ, with eyes closed and head on one side, recalls the work of painters of the Pisan School. The Studenica paintings are impressive but a lighter and more personal style had developed by the time the frescoes of Mileševa were laid out.

These were done under the patronage of King Vladislav, whose portrait appears in the narthex of the monastery church. The paintings here are highly varied: the head of the *Virgin of the Annunciation* is delicate and tender, like an Italian Renaissance portrait, while the angel's head from the scene of *The Resurrection* reflects a more Eastern influence. Possibly the best of all of the religious art of this period comes from Sopoćani. Some of the works from here, like *The Dormition of the Virgin*, are particularly striking because of the large number of figures represented in the painting and the elaborate detail of the architectural background in the scenes.

The Raška churches, which were always stone-built, although they were sometimes faced in marble, characteristically have no aisles, but just a central apse with side transepts below a raised dome. The most prominent examples of the Raška style that still survive today are, in chronological order: Studenica, built in 1209, Žiča (1219), Mileševa (1237), Morača (1252), Peć (1263), Sopoćani (1265), Gradac (1275) and Arilje (1295).

The continued expansion of Serbia under King Milutin in the late 13th century led to new architectural influences. From the late 13th century until the defeat by the Turks in 1389, a new style flourished: the **Serbo-Byzantine School**. This style reintroduced some of the Byzantine features that had been neglected by the Raška School. The cruciform shape was replaced with a cross-in-square plan; cupolas were introduced around domes; external sculpting was spurned; façades utilised coloured bricks and stones to create a striped effect – the overall effect was much more oriental in appearance than before. The frescoes of the Serbo-Byzantine School portrayed a broader choice of subject matter and adopted a more narrative style, depicting figures in mythical landscapes, the lives of saints and Serbian royalty in addition to the more familiar scenes from the Gospels. By the early years of the 14th century a new realism had crept in that suggested that painters might be using life models from the neighbourhood as a basis for their portraiture.

It was also at about this time that painters started to put their name to their handiwork. One of the most important painters from this period, who worked on a whole series of King Milutin's projects between about 1295 and 1310, was a man called Astrapas, whose best work appears in the church of Bogdorica Ljeviška at Prizren. The most extensive frescoes from this period are found at Gračanica and Dečani in Kosovo. At times, quality is sacrificed for sheer abundance: at Dečani, for example, there are a total of 46 scenes from *Genesis*, 43 from *The Passion* cycle, 26 from *The Last Judgement,* and a *Calendar* with a scene for every day of the year. Existing churches of the Serbo-Byzantine School include Gračanica, built in 1320, and Dečani (1350), both in Kosovo.

The death of King Stefan Dušan in 1355 heralded the start of a decline in Serbia's fortunes, while the momentous defeat at the Battle of Kosovo in 1389 brought about a Serbian retreat northwards to the relative safety of the Morava Valley. This withdrawal gave birth to another architectural style – the **Morava School** – that combined elements of both of the two previous schools. Churches kept their domes and multiple cupolas and their striped brickwork, but animal and vegetable motifs, that echoed the style of the Raška School, were added in low relief on windows and doors. The Morava churches were tall and quite large but, overall, were simpler and less ostentatious than their antecedents. The painting style had now been developed to reflect the influence of both previous schools, combining Raška-style restraint with Serbo-Byzantine dynamism. The colouring is naturalistic, and the compositions are elegant, often with architectural backgrounds; the figures, tall and imposing with refined faces. This new style was intimate and tender, very much at odds with the realities of the day, as if there had been a conscious effort to take the human spirit beyond the reaches of the terror that lay at Serbia's door. The principal churches of the Morava School were built over a relatively short period of time: Ravanica (built in 1377), Rudenica (1403–10), Ljubostina (1405), Manasija (1407–18) and Kalenić (1413).

The Ottoman advance northwards announced an end to monastery-building in Serbia as the country came under Muslim rule but later, in the 16th century, new monasteries started to emerge in the Fruška Gora hills in Habsburg-controlled Vojvodina. These monasteries, the most famous of which are Krušedol, Hopovo and Vrdnik, were built with a strong sense of nostalgia for Serbia's earlier golden age, and display features from all of the previous schools in their design.

Art in the Ottoman era With the Muslim injunction on representation of the human figure, many of the skills developed by the medieval fresco painters were soon lost to history. The Ottomans imported architects and builders from Turkey to build mosques or convert existing churches. Unfortunately, many of these collapsed with disuse, or were destroyed outright, when the Turks finally came to leave. Ottoman rule left its imprint in later Serbian architectural style when, in the early 19th century, many Turkish-style *konaks* were built in Belgrade. However, most of those which made it to the next century were destroyed in the Nazi bombings of 1941.

Art in the 18th and 19th centuries

The churches that were built in the early 18th century were influenced by an Eastern Baroque tradition but by around 1750 Western influences were starting to feature once more. From the end of the 18th century to the 1880s, Serbian art was closely tied to that of Vienna. The art of portrait painting, which had started to become popular in the previous century, was in the ascendant, and although the work of the Viennese masters was closely studied, artists like Arsa Teodorović and Konstantin Danil succeeded in infusing Viennese Classicism with a distinctive Serbian character. As the 19th century developed, a Romanticist tendency appeared in Serbian art. Serbian Romanticism went on to reach its peak in the work of Đura Jakšić who was influenced by the use of chiaroscuro in paintings by artists such as Rembrandt. Up until the late 19th century, landscape had always played a subordinate role in Serbian artwork but it was during this Romantic period that paintings with pure landscape themes started to appear, usually as a digression by portrait painters such as Steva Todorović and Novalk Radonović.

After 1870, a generation of painters educated in Munich heralded a new phase in Serbian art, one in which pure landscape was accepted as an independent art form. Influenced by a range of ideas from various European schools, still lifes and village scenes now became respectable subject matter. Two prominent artists from this time, both Munich-trained, were Miloš Tenković and Đorđe Krstić.

By the end of the 19th century, Serbia was striving to establish itself as an equal member among sovereign European states. Many artists were forced to compromise their artistic sensibility with the requirements of patrons who wished to glorify Serbia's history in the eyes of Europe. For this, large, pompous paintings showing idealised scenes from Serbia's past were required, which gave birth to patriotic canvases such as *The Great Serbian Migration 1690* by Pavle Jovanović (1896) and *The Entry of Tsar Dušan into Dubrovnik* by Marko Murat (1900).

Modern art

From 1900 until the end of World War I, painters like Milan Milanović and Branko Popović were under the spell of French Impressionism, but in the years that followed Serbian art became heavily influenced by a wider range of styles. Artists like Nadežda Petrović became acquainted with the work of painters like Van Gogh, Munch and Kandinsky, and subsequent artists such as Veljko Stanojević, Milan Konjović and Ignjat Job experimented with the genres of Constructivism, Cubism and Surrealism. By the 1930s, a new form of Expressionism had emerged that concerned itself more with regional identity and ethnicity, an example being Petar Lubarda's painting *The Gusle Player* (1935), which depicts a peasant musician playing a folk instrument.

After 1945, many of the new tendencies that were emerging on both sides of the Atlantic in the 1950s – neo-Surrealism, action painting, etc – had their counterparts in Tito's Yugoslavia, even if they were a little self-conscious and unoriginal at times. As elsewhere in post-war eastern Europe, much creativity was constrained by the requirements of Socialist Realism, which did not always make for great art. Following the split with the Soviet Union, politically driven art became less of a compulsion and artists were free to explore the abstract. By about 1970, Conceptual art had become an important new direction in Belgrade and Novi Sad.

Because of Tito's post-war split with Stalin's Soviet Union, the tradition of Socialist Realist **sculpture**, so abundant elsewhere in the Communist bloc in the

1950s and 1960s, is not particularly well represented in Serbia, although there are a number of imposing military monuments scattered throughout the country, the most notable being the war memorial at Avala by Ivan Meštrović. Croatian-born Meštrović (1883–1962) was heavily influenced by the Vienna secession movement and met Rodin at the turn of the century while studying in Paris. He developed an epic style that was very much his own and went on to produce some of Yugoslavia's most memorable monuments, the most notable Serbian examples beyond that at Avala being the *Gratitude to France* and *Messenger of Victory* monuments that stand in Belgrade's Kalemegdan Park.

LITERATURE
Poetry The oral tradition has always been strong in Serbia: in World War I, a Serbian general roused his troops into action by speaking of the Emperor Dušan; in World War II, some Partisan groups took an oath of loyalty identical to the one Karađorđe used for his troops at the time of the First National Uprising. Since the time of the defeat at Kosovo Polje in 1389, Serbian heroic poetry has been an oral tradition in which epic poems are memorised and handed down from one generation to the next. This remained an oral tradition until Vuk Karadžić, the great Serbian philologist and scholar, collected many of the epic poems and transcribed them to paper in the 19th century. The rich and lyrical works collected by Karadžić soon attracted considerable attention from devotees of the Romantic movement. Serbian epic poetry was translated into English, French and German, and both Goethe and Walter Scott were sufficiently enthused to translate the same classic work called *Hasanaginica*.

The themes of these poems mostly concern heroic battles, bravery, morality and the exploits of Serbian monarchs. Naturally, many of them are based upon the Battle of Kosovo. These are not written as a cycle but as separate poems that observe the battle from different viewpoints, which, when read together, have a cohesive quality. Other poems deal with Prince Marko, a heroic figure with a magic horse, animal cunning and a prodigious thirst for wine, who manages to kill numerous Turks on the battlefield and outwit those who escape his sword. Later heroic poems deal with the Serbian uprisings and the activities of the *hajduk* outlaws, and even with events from World Wars I and II. Much of the poetry, however, deals with themes of nationhood and belonging:

> Whoever is a Serb and Serbian born,
> Serbian his blood and his lineage,
> Who has come not to fight at Kosovo,
> By his own hand shall he bring forth nothing:
> Neither golden wine nor fine white meat,
> There shall be no harvest from his lands
> Nor in his house children of his blood.
> While his race lives, they shall waste away.

The popularity of Vuk Karadžić's translations and the introduction of Belgrade's first printing press in the mid 19th century encouraged Serbia to develop its own tradition in literature. During this period, the indefatigable Karadžić translated the *New Testament*, the Montenegrin bishop and poet Njegoš published *The Mountain Wreath*, and poems by the Romanticist Branko Radičević were printed, together with the philological treatise *The War for the Serbian Language and Orthography* by Đuro Daničić. In the wake of this literary renaissance, a new generation of poets started to appear, the most notable being Jovan Jovanović Zmaj (1833–1904) who went on to leave a massive legacy of literature that incorporated a wide range of themes and genres.

The Serbian novel The modern Serbian novel began with Borislav Stanković (1867–1927), who explored the contradictions of man's spiritual and sensory life in his 1910 work *The Tainted Blood*. This was the first Serbian novel to receive praise in its foreign translations. A little later, in the period between the wars, Expressionism appeared as an avant-garde movement in literature, just as it had done so in painting and music, when *The Manifesto of the Expressionist School* by Stanislav Vinaver was published in 1920.

Following World War II, the narrative form of the novel, which has always been important in Serbian literature given its oral traditions and epic poetry, was developed and perfected by Ivo Andrić (1892–1975), a Yugoslav of Bosnian Croat descent who lived in Belgrade most of his later life. To this day, Andrić remains probably the most famous writer from the former Yugoslavia. His most famous works are those of the trilogy published in 1945: *The Bridge on the Drina*, *The Travnik Chronicle* and *The Spinster*. By the time Andrić received the Nobel Prize in Literature in 1961, he had become the most commonly translated Serbian-language writer ever. A contemporary of Andrić, who dealt with similar themes but especially in the struggle between opposing principles, and between authority and the individual, was Mehmed 'Meša' Selimović (1910–82), a Bosnian Muslim by birth who explicitly claimed to be Serb by ethnicity. Selimović's novels, *Death and the Dervish* (1966) and *The Fortress* (1970), both deal with these themes in a historical framework; in the first case in the form of a narrative about a Muslim cleric in the 18th century, and in the second, from the viewpoint of an educated man in the 17th century.

From the 1960s onwards, many Serbian writers became as preoccupied with the form of their work as they were with the content. Experimentation continued with varying success: novelists like Bora Ćosić (born 1932) baffled many readers with his constant interplay of construction and deconstruction in his massive novel *The Tutors*. Others, like Borislav Pekić (1930–92) and Danilo Kiš (1935–89), were more successful, Kiš in particular with his 1976 novel about the Stalinist purges, *A Tomb for Boris Davidović*, which brought him international acclaim for his skilful interweaving of fiction and documentation. Another writer from this period was Croatia-born Slobodan Selenić (1933–95) who became Belgrade's Poet Laureate. Selenić's major work *Fathers and Forefathers* is firmly of the psychological conflict/inner monologue school, and spans 50 years of Belgrade life as it covers the fortunes of an Anglo-Serb family and more generally the 20th-century struggles of the Serbian people.

Perhaps the most groundbreaking and innovative of all of the post-war Serbian novelists is Milorad Pavić (1929–2009), whose most famous work *Dictionary of the Khazars* (1984) has been widely acclaimed by critics both at home and abroad. This novel, which is not really a dictionary or a historically faithful tract on the Khazars, is quite unique and recognised by many as a postmodern masterpiece. In this 'dictionary', Pavić challenges the usual temporal sequence of the narrative by making a random order reading of the text possible, even desirable. The text, which claims to be a reprint of the surviving fragments of a 1691 dictionary, purports to offer parallel sources from three civilisations and three religions – Christian, Muslim and Jewish – that give an interwoven account of the Khazars, an ancient people about which very little is known. The allure of the text is its interplay between knowledge and fantasy, and the real and the possible, and the non-linear narrative allows the reader to follow numerous, labyrinthine hyper-textual links

1

between the three accounts at whim. The book works as a type of mystery novel that seeks to answer two questions: to which religion did the Khazars convert, and why at regular intervals do representatives of the three religions come together to try and solve this first question?

The twist is that the first question cannot be answered as clues in the text point to each of the religions believing that it alone was the one ultimately chosen by the Khazars. The coming together of the representatives ends in destruction, and the search for synthesis is seen to be a utopian pipe dream. On one level at least, the *Dictionary of the Khazars* can be seen as an allegorical account of Serbian (and Yugoslav) history and the necessity of simultaneously looking at the past from different perspectives. The *Dictionary* makes the case for the postmodern contention that, like the polemicists of the Khazar accounts, attempts at synthesis inevitably lead to destruction as no single 'meta-narrative' – Khazar religion or unified Yugoslavia – will suffice.

More recent works by Pavić that have been translated into English include *Last Love in Constantinople: A Tarot Novel for Divination* (1993) and *The Inner Side of the Wind, or the Novel of Hero and Leander* (1998), both of which utilise unorthodox, non-linear narrative forms (the latter can be read either front to back or back to front). Another work, *Landscape Painted in Tea*, mixes the traditional form of the novel with that of a crossword puzzle while in *Unique Item* the reader has a choice of 100 different endings. In his own words he states:

> I have tried my best to eliminate or to destroy the beginning and the end of my novels. *The Inner Side of the Wind*, for example, has two beginnings. You start reading this book from the side you want. In the *Dictionary of the Khazars* you can start with whatever story you want. But writing it, you have to keep in mind that every entry has to be read before and after every other entry in the book. I managed to avoid, at least until now, the old way of reading, which means reading from the classical beginning to the classical end.

Milorad Pavić died on 30 November 2009 aged 80. More on the author can be read at **w** khazars.com.

CINEMA The first motion picture ever shown in Serbia was in a Belgrade café called 'At the Golden Cross' on 6 June 1896. This was just six months after the first demonstration of moving pictures in Paris. The first permanent cinema was opened in 1909 in Belgrade at, appropriately enough, the city's Hotel Paris. By World War I there were 30 permanent cinemas in Serbia, together with many other travelling ones.

The early films were all of French origin but in the autumn of 1911 Svetozar Botorić, the owner of the Paris Picture Theatre, engaged a French cameraman to make the first Serbian feature film *Karađorđe*, a historical drama about the life of the leader of the First National Uprising. Other works soon followed but production came to a halt with the outbreak of World War I. In the 1920s, several film companies set up in Belgrade to create newsreel and documentary films as well as a few feature films. The most ambitious and successful of the films made before World War II was the 1932 production of *With Faith in God* directed by Mihajlo Popović.

From the end of World War II right up until 1991, the Yugoslavian film industry was centralised in Belgrade with Serbia being responsible for at least 50% of the output in the Yugoslav federation. From 1953 onwards several films were made in co-production with foreign countries like Austria and Norway, and the first colour feature was made in 1957. Throughout the 1960s, Serbian film was dominated by the work of Aleksandar Petrović, who won the Grand Prix at the International

Film Festival at Cannes for his 1967 film *I Met Some Happy Gypsies Too*. A new generation of younger film directors started to appear in the middle of the 1970s, like Goran Paskaljević *The Beach Guard in Winter* (1976), and *The Dog Who Liked Trains* (1977) and Slobodan Sijan *Who's That Singin' Over There?* (1980).

With the disintegration of the former Yugoslavia, Serbian cinema suffered less than the other republics as it had been operating more or less independently for some time. Despite war and sanctions, film production was not halted, and new directors started to emerge alongside an older generation that was still directing films like *The Origin of the Forgery* (director Dragan Krešoja, 1991) and *Tito and Me* (Goran Marković, 1992). Ironically, it was at about this time that, despite its international pariah status, Serbian cinema was starting to receive plaudits from the foreign film community for the quality of its productions. One director who would go on to develop this international reputation made a great impact around this time with a film called *Time of the Gypsies* (1989). This was Emir Kusturica, who won Best Director at the Cannes Film Festival in 1989 and Best Foreign Film at Sweden's Guldbagge Awards (see box, pages 52–3).

In more recent years, *The Optimists* (2006) by Goran Paskaljević has been a well-received black comedy, while *The Wounds* (1998) by Srđan Dragojević explored Belgrade gangster culture. Goran Paskaljević's earlier *A Midwinter Night's Dream* (2004) caused a considerable amount of controversy in Serbia because of its criticism of Serbian nationalism in Yugoslav wars of the 1990s. In a somewhat different vein, the 2009 film *Ordinary People*, the directorial debut of Vladimir Perišić, tells the story of a young soldier faced with the task of executing enemy prisoners during the Balkan war and the psychological wounds that ensue.

MUSIC

Folk music Serbia has a rich and varied folk music culture that draws influences from as far away as Hungary and Turkey and beyond. Much of this is still relatively unknown to the outside world, as Serbia's musical traditions have not received as much attention as other eastern European countries like Bulgaria or Romania.

Geography plays some part in explaining the prevailing influences. In the far north of Vojvodina, Hungarian traditions are strong: many of the songs are sung in Hungarian and instruments like cimbaloms and *tamburica* are used alongside the more traditional violin and accordion. In the Šumadija region of central Serbia, a popular instrument is the *frula*, a small recorder-like flute. There is even a *frula* festival devoted solely to this instrument in July in the village of Prislonica near Čačak. In Kosovo, a musical tradition akin to that of the Ghegs in northern Albania predominates, with the widespread use of bagpipes, hand drums and clarinets. A popular dance throughout the country is the *kolo*, a village circle dance which is a great leveller and allows participants from all walks of life – young and old, educated and unschooled, male and female – to take part.

Traditional music is currently enjoying something of a renaissance in Serbia and it is starting to reach wider audiences now that go-ahead recording companies like B-92 are recording both established performers and new talent, and releasing their CDs internationally. Artists that are beginning to get an international reputation include Lajko Felix, an ethnic Hungarian violinist from Subotica; singer Svetlana Spajić-Latinović from western Serbia; Bokan Stanković, a bagpipes player from eastern Serbia; Earth-Wheel-Sky Ensemble, a Roma group from Vojvodina led by Olah Vince; and Kal, a Roma group from the Belgrade suburbs who play traditional music with a modern rock attitude. All of these have toured throughout Europe but still remain close to their musical roots.

Roma music Serbia's Roma community have had an enormous effect on the development and propagation of music styles throughout the country. Roma, undaunted by mere tradition and unfettered by the attentions of the folk-music police, have always been musical magpies and regularly perform a seamless repertoire that is a happy hybrid of traditional dance tunes from all over the region, as well as pop tunes, nationalist anthems, film music and even television commercials. One Roma artist who managed to achieve some degree of international acclaim was Šaban Bajramović, a crack-voiced crooner from Niš. Army deserter, prisoner, gambler, actor and singer, Bajramović's career followed a colourful, if wobbly, trajectory since he first emerged from dismal poverty in southern Serbia. His smoky voice possessed a cracked, anguished tone that made accolades like 'King of the Balkan Blues' seem perfectly reasonable. With his white suit and gold teeth, he became an influential artist at home and abroad although, in fairness, he probably never received anything like the credit he truly deserved. A songwriter as well as an

THE CINEMA OF EMIR KUSTURICA

Emir Kusturica made his first feature-length debut with the much-acclaimed *Do You Remember Dolly Bell?* (1981), which won the Golden Lion award at that year's Venice Film Festival. This was followed by *When Father Was Away on Business* (1985), which enjoyed great success in Yugoslavia and earned a Palme d'Or at Cannes as well as being nominated for Best Foreign Film at the American Academy Awards. His first really big international success, however, was with *Time of the Gypsies* (1989). The film, originally titled *Dom za vešanje* (*A House for Hanging*), is remarkable for its use of non-professional actors, its Roma-inspired musical soundtrack (music by Goran Bregović) and for having its dialogue in the Roma language throughout. The film 'reads' like a magical realist novel: a sad, joyous, helter-skelter of a film with humour, pathos and romance all jumbled together with elements of Surrealism. It combines elements of road movie, gangster film, romantic comedy and rites of passage, 'feel good' classic, as if Fellini and the Coen brothers both had a hand in its making.

With this and subsequent films like *Black Cat, White Cat* (1998), Kusturica was both applauded and reviled for his portrayal of Roma as picaresque characters. Kusturica was inspired to make *Time of the Gypsies* after reading an article about Roma involvement in child trafficking, one of the subplots of the film. He describes it as follows ... 'the film is just like the typical suit of a Gypsy. Under his shirt he wears three T-shirts of different colours, his trousers seem to come from another planet ... It is a film where everything mixes ... The cinema being pulled about between video, television, music, literature, it can only have a strange form.'

The Roma theme was taken up again in 1998 with *Black Cat, White Cat* (*Crna mačka, beli mačor*), which once more was full of larger-than-life characters and was, if anything, even more chaotic than *Time of the Gypsies*, with wonderful surreal images like that of a brass band tied up in a tree playing their instruments, and a pig attempting to eat a rusting Yugo.

Between the making of these two films, Kusturica worked on his most ambitious, and most controversial project yet, *Underground* (1996) – a film that attempted to encapsulate the history of Yugoslavia (and in particular that of Serbia) in the period 1941–92. Although this was, once again, a spectacular roller-coaster of a movie, it would be fair to say that it was not entirely successful and the plot gets a little lost near the end. Again he had his critics. This time he was accused of influential singer, Bajramović was allegedly responsible for composing the famous Roma anthem 'Djelem, Djelem' along with many other popular songs. As well as music he flirted with the world of cinema and worked with both Emir Kusturica and Goran Bregović, although he accused the latter of purloining his material to reshape it and claim it as his own in his film scores. Ironically, and perhaps inevitably, his life ended once more back in poverty in Niš where, following a spell of ill health, he died of a heart attack in June 2008 aged 72. His reputation was such that even *The Times* carried an obituary and Serbian president Boris Tadić attended his funeral along with 10,000 mourners. A memorial statue to him stands by the river in Niš opposite the Turkish fortress (page 361).

Brass-band music Some aspects of Roma music have become semi-respectable of late, particularly the brass-band music that has been developed by musicians in the villages of Serbia's southeast and which has encouraged a plethora of non-Roma

being an apologist for Serbia's excesses in the Balkan conflicts of the early 1990s. Kusturica, a Bosnian Muslim by birth (although he would probably say Yugoslav), left Sarajevo for Belgrade at the beginning of the siege of that city. Many could not forgive him for what they saw as jumping ship.

His films have also been hugely influential in their music, which has always been composed and recorded by either Goran Bregović or by himself and his No Smoking Orchestra (he started out as a bass player in a rock band, while Bregović was a guitarist in another Yugoslav group). Several tunes from his films will be familiar to any Serbia visitor: the beautiful Roma anthem 'Ederlezi', and 'Mesečina' and 'Wedding Čoček' from *Underground* – tunes that are always requested of brass bands at Serbian weddings.

His 2004 release, *Life is a Miracle* (*Život Je Čudo*), was based on a story centred upon the Mokra Gora railway in the Zlatibor region of western Serbia. He followed this in 2006 with a documentary on the Argentine football legend Maradona that featured a soundtrack by Manu Chao. His next venture, *Promise Me This* (*Zavet*), was premiered at the 2007 Cannes Film Festival where he had served as president of the jury in 2005. Kusturica's most recent films are *Words with Gods* (2014) and *On the Milky Road* (2016).

Since January 2008, Kusturica has presided over his own Küstendorf Film Festival in his purpose-built mountain village of Drvengrad in western Serbia (page 312). His most recent venture, across the Bosnian border in Višegrad, Republika Srpska, involves another grand project similar to Drvengrad at Mokra Gora, with the construction of a stone-built settlement called Kamengrad ('stone town', also referred to as 'Andrićgrad') close to the Ottoman bridge that is the centrepiece of Ivo Andrić's *Bridge over the Drina* story at Višegrad. Kamengrad, partly financed by the Republika Srpska government as a future tourist development, is also earmarked for future use as a film set for an adaptation of Andrić's novel.

On Đurđevdan (St George's Day) in 2005, Kusturica formally converted to the Orthodox Church, taking the Christian name Nemanja. This was seen by many as a final betrayal of his Muslim roots. Kusturica answered his critics by saying that his father had been an atheist who had described himself as a Serb. Although his family had been Muslims for 250 years or so, they had originally been Orthodox and only converted to survive the Turkish occupation.

Ceca was born Svetlana Veličković in Žitorađa, southeast Serbia, in 1973. She began singing at the age of nine and by the time she was 14 had achieved considerable national success. By the time her third album was released she was the third-best-selling female folk artist in Yugoslavia. At around the age of 18 Ceca underwent a radical change of image and by 1992 had been transformed from a girl-next-door folkie with a bubble-perm into a sultry beauty with a gravity-defying cleavage and a clinging dress split to the hip. The new image did no harm at all and she continued to go from success to success, selling even more records and headlining sell-out live shows. She soon became the best-known musical artist in the whole Balkan region, a standing she still keeps today, despite having suffered a few downturns in her career.

Her life and career have often been highly controversial. During the 1990s she had dalliances with a few minor gangsters before she met up with and married the man who was to be the greatest love of her life, Željko Ražnatović, aka 'Arkan', international gangster and leader of the 'Tigers' paramilitary group, who was viewed as a picaresque hero by some and a heinous war criminal by others – it depended on your viewpoint. Their marriage in 1995 was a very expensive, high-profile affair that had echoes of both *Cinderella* and *Gone with the Wind*: for Ceca and Arkan's many admirers it was a modern-day Balkan fairy tale. A convoy of 40 cars drove the 300km from Belgrade to Ceca's home town of Žitorađa so that Arkan could shoot an apple off the roof of her parents' house – a traditional way of claiming a bride – and before the ceremony Ceca was fitted with a golden slipper by the best man. Their happiness would last only five years, as Arkan had as many enemies as he had supporters and was assassinated in Belgrade in 2000. Ceca went into a period of mourning for 18 months following this, and, to this day, she remains, officially at least, single and wedded to his memory.

Ceca herself has fallen foul of the law on occasion. She was arrested in March 2003 and detained for four months during the clampdown that followed the assassination of Prime Minister Zoran Đinđić. The accusations of her association with the Zemun clan were never proved and she was eventually cleared of all charges. In 2011, she was sentenced to one year of house arrest and fined €1.5 million after pleading guilty to charges of embezzlement of football player transfer fees at FK Obilić and illegal possession of 11 machine guns that she claimed had belonged to her deceased husband.

As a performer, Ceca's preference has always been for spectacular one-off concerts rather than wide-ranging tours. One of her largest was in 2002 at FC Red Star Belgrade's 'Marakana' stadium, which had an estimated 100,000 attending. This was eclipsed in June 2006 at Ušće in Belgrade where around 150,000 are said to have attended but her largest audience ever was at the Orthodox New Year's celebration on 13 January 2007 in Belgrade, when she joined other artists like Riblja Čorba and Rambo Amadeus in an all-night performance that had an estimated 350,000 attending. Her popularity in recent years seems to be undiminished: a concert at Ušće in 2013 for her 40th birthday, in which she sang a total of 47 songs over 4 hours, brought an estimated crowd of 170,000. In 2014, Ceca appeared at the Guča Festival for the first time. In 2016, she released her 16th album *Autogram* (English: *Autograph*).

imitators in its wake. The annual Guča Trumpet Festival (see box, page 302) is a showcase for these, and the venue where now-famous Roma performers like Boban Marković first made their name. The most popular style played by these bands is called *čoček*, a fast 2/4 dance that is performed better when lubricated with a few glasses of *šljivovica*.

Although village brass bands have always been popular in rural Serbia the popularity of the films of Emir Kusturica, like *Underground* and *Time of the Gypsies* with their brass-band soundtracks, has brought about an enormous revival of interest in the form and introduced a crossover influence between the Roma bands and ethnic Serb musicians. Prior to 1990, most Serb bands would try to shun any Roma influence but, increasingly, they are now embracing it. Nowadays, there are ethnic Serb bands from Šumadija playing a very Roma-influenced repertoire, while ensembles of non-Slav brass players from as far away as Toronto or New York are producing *čoček* music that is authentic enough to be warmly applauded at Guča.

Turbo-folk music Unlike the Roma tradition, other musical experiments that have fused Serbia's folk music with other forms have not always been successful. In the Milošević years, a new musical hybrid raised its ugly head to attain large-scale popularity. This was so-called turbo-folk, a noisy dance music characterised by deeply sentimental lyrics sung by pneumatic, scantily clad young women to sugary folk tunes backed by industrial-strength techno rhythms. If the mere idea of this sounds bad, then the reality is worse. Imagine The Prodigy performing 'Edelweiss' with a Julie Andrews vocal, then throw in the worst sentimental excesses of bad country and western to complete the picture. In the wild, wartime days of the 1990s, the jackhammer rhythms of turbo-folk provided a soundtrack for the 'live today–die tomorrow' lifestyles of Belgrade's shady underworld of racketeers, hoodlums, gunrunners, gangsters, hard-line nationalists and paramilitary Rambo figures. The spirit of turbo-folk is that of a sort of Balkan version of gangster rap – but without the rap. One of the most famous singers in the turbo-folk tradition is Svetlana Ražnatović, better known to her fans as Ceca, the widow of paramilitary leader Željko 'Arkan' Ražnatović. Although she is equally famous for her marriage, her good looks and dodgy business associates, she is actually a talented singer. Ceca is still enormously popular in Serbia but has moved away from turbo-folk and on to a more sophisticated repertoire in recent years (see box opposite).

Pop-folk Over the past decade or so turbo-folk has softened considerably and incorporated more pop and electronic elements into the mix. The new music is most usually referred to as pop-folk, and the first singer to become successful in this genre was **Indira Radić**, who became the best-selling Serbian singer in the years between 2003 and 2005. Introducing a modicum of gay content in her songs and music videos – something that would have been ill-thought of just a decade earlier – Radić also went on to become something of a gay icon. Other well-known pop-folk singers who made the successful transition from turbo-folk include **Viki Miljković**, **Stojanka Novaković Stoja**, **Saša Matić** and **Seka Aleksić**, who is sometimes referred to as 'The Princess of Pop-Folk'. Although a genre dominated by female stars, a few male singers have also emerged, most notably **Aca Lukas**, a controversial figure with a troubled criminal past.

Rock music In the field of Serbian rock music there is perhaps less cause for excitement. During the 1970s and 1980s Yugoslavia produced many competent, if somewhat derivative, rock groups whose musical influences clearly came from the

TURBO-FOLK – WORTHY FUSION OR MUSICAL NIGHTMARE?

Turbo-folk emerged as the sound of 1990s Serbia as an unholy fusion of nationalist folk tunes and techno dance music: an unlikely meeting of Western pop culture, traditional values, state-controlled media and criminality. The term turbo-folk was coined in the late 1980s by the rock musician Rambo Amadeus, who used it jokingly to describe his own melange of styles and influences, although the term was re-employed in the early 1990s to describe a new musical style that was altogether different. Turbo-folk's genesis was partly down to Slobodan Milošević's firm grip on the media during that period. Those in power recognised what they termed newly composed folk music (*novokomponvana narodna muzika*) or 'neo-folk' was more in keeping with the new order than Western rock music. Neo-folk fused traditional musical styles with new lyrics and modern arrangements and, like country and western, to which it could be comfortably compared, songs about patriotism and national pride were the order of the day. Songs with anti-communist and royalist themes, dating from World War II and firmly underground during Tito's socialist era, were resurrected and new ones were written along the same lines.

Turbo-folk was the natural development of this, adapting already existing commercial forms and combining them with neo-folk using the latest technology. Turbo-folk appropriated images of a consumer lifestyle, beats from Western dance music and traditional Serbian folk tunes. Unlike the obvious agitprop of neo-folk, turbo-folk was escapist and all about love and romance. Turbo-folk videos, which were shown endlessly on TV Pink and TV Palma during the 1990s, celebrated the glamour of the criminal elite, with beautiful, scantily clad women and a spirit of defiant optimism. Perhaps because of this, it was popular with all factions rather than just the Serbs and its strains could be heard thumping from the trenches of both sides.

The phenomenon of turbo-folk has been described by some commentators as 'porno-nationalism', which is probably taking things a little too far. However, the message that turbo-folk gave was certainly not at odds with the viewpoint of ultra-nationalists in the 1990s, or with the get-rich-quick philosophy of the gangsters who profited during this period. In recent years, turbo-folk has faded away a little but it has certainly not died. It could be argued that modern-day turbo-folk, particularly as promoted by artists like Ceca, has moved on from its 1990s' prototype and now carries a far less nationalistic subtext and higher production values. It remains popular with the *dizelasi* (so-called because of their taste for Diesel clothing), the urban skinhead youth who favour its macho values and, ironically, it is also becoming increasingly popular with club-goers in Croatia and Bosnia.

other side of the Atlantic. With sanctions, war in Croatia, Bosnia and Kosovo, and then the final indignity of NATO bombing, it is easy to see why a nation's youth might wish to look beyond the usual fertile ground of American rock and MTV for its influences. This is not to say that Western-influenced pop music stopped dead in its tracks in the 1990s, as since that time some highly individualistic (and politically attuned) groups like Darkwood Dub and Eyesburn have emerged, as well as Celtic music oddities like the Orthodox Celts, Belgrade's answer to The Pogues. One quirky rock artist who has been making music since the 1980s is Rambo Amadeus, a Belgrade-based, Montenegrin-born singer-songwriter whose outspoken anti-war stance during the 1990s earned him a television ban in Serbia for a while. Never one to merely churn out the expected, his concerts tend to be a mixture of musical improvisation and humour. Rambo Amadeus's work is satirical, wide-ranging and highly original, and he is sometimes compared by fans to artists like Frank Zappa and Captain Beefheart.

Despite such home-grown talent, there remains a large audience for foreign – mostly British and American – acts although, thankfully, enthusiasm for boy bands is largely absent from the scene. Performers as diverse as Madonna, David Byrne, Tom Jones, ZZ Top and Kraftwerk have all performed in Belgrade in recent years.

Jazz Serbia has a small but enthusiastic jazz scene that rarely ventures beyond the city limits of Belgrade, Novi Sad or Niš. That being said, the standard of musicianship is usually very good and it is well worth attending one of Belgrade's jazz clubs if you are not allergic to cigarette smoke or late nights. One of the best-known Serbian jazz artists of all time is **Duško Gojković**, a trumpeter, composer and arranger who started performing in the 1950s, recording and playing with international artists such as Sonny Rollins, Stan Getz and Dizzy Gillespie. A more contemporary jazz artist who attempts to combine jazz and traditional music in a sort of Balkan jazz-folk fusion is saxophonist Jovan Maljoković. Another fusion artist in a very different vein is Boris Kovač from Novi Sad. What he and his musicians play is not folk, jazz or rock but something akin to Balkan tango, a highly theatrical chamber music that Kovač likens to a palm court orchestra playing a gig on the night before the apocalypse.

SPORT Serbia is passionate about sport, especially football, basketball and tennis, and while its artists, writers and musicians may be relatively unknown outside the country of their birth, the same cannot be said for its sports personalities. Over the past 15 years or so a number of Serbian sports stars have become internationally well known.

In **football**, there is plenty of talent to choose from currently playing in the English Premier League: Manchester City defender Aleksandar Kolarov, Liverpool and Hull's Lazar Marković, Chelsea's Nemanja Matić, and Southampton midfielder Dušan Tadić. Even better known perhaps are the now-retired Nemanja Vidić, the former Manchester United defender and captain, who was born in Užice, and Branislav Ivanović, who formerly played for Chelsea FC.

However, it is probably in the field of **tennis** that Serbia receives the most attention for its sporting prowess. Female stars include Jelena Janković, former World No 1 (No 50 in 2017); Ana Ivanović, also former World No 1 who retired in 2017; and Jelena Dokić, World No 4 back in 2002, who retired from the game in 2014. A little further back in time in 1991, Novi Sad-born Monica Seleš was World No 1. As for male tennis players, Viktor Troicki is currently World No 35 (2017), having been ranked No 12 in 2011, while Janko Tipsarević was World No 8 in 2012 and Nenad Zimonjić World No 1 doubles player in 2008.

The biggest tennis star without a doubt has to be Novak Đoković (spelled Djokovic in the international press), current World No 2, winner of 12 Grand Slam titles: the Australian Open in 2008, 2011, 2012, 2013, 2015 and 2016, the US Open in 2011 and 2015, Wimbledon in 2011, 2014 and 2015 and the French Open in 2016. Having also won numerous other tournaments and awards such as Best Male Tennis Player ESPY Award (2012) and ATP World Player of the Year (2011, 2012, 2014 and 2015), he has become a household name throughout the world and, with his good-natured, humorous personality, a worthy ambassador for his country.

In 2007, he founded the Novak Djokovic Foundation, whose mission is to help children from disadvantaged communities, and in 2015 was appointed a UNICEF Goodwill Ambassador.

Basketball is another highly popular sport in Serbia and throughout the Balkan region, a sport well suited to a nation whose people are among the tallest in the world in terms of average height (Montenegro is the tallest). Two of the major teams in the domestic league bear the same name as established Belgrade football teams – Crvena Zvezda (Red Star) and Partizan. The Serbian national team coached by former Yugoslav and Serbia basketball hero Aleksandar Đorđević is currently ranked third in the world and won a silver medal at the 2016 Rio Olympics.

2

Practical Information

WHEN TO VISIT

Serbia has a climate similar to the rest of southeast Europe, although it rarely gets as hot as Greece during the summer months or as cold as Romania in winter. Unless a skiing vacation is planned, winter is not a good time to visit: it will be cold and wet, perhaps snowing, and many of Serbia's less expensive hotels have inadequate heating. The summer months are rarely oppressively hot, although it can become quite sticky in Belgrade during the dog days of August.

Generally speaking, the best time to visit is anytime between late spring and early autumn. Depending on personal interests, it is a good idea to try and make your visit coincide with particular events that are taking place throughout the country, ie: for music fans this might be during the EXIT Festival (pop and rock) that is held in Novi Sad during July, the Dragačevo Trumpet Festival (Gypsy brass bands) that takes place at Guča in western Serbia every August, or the Belgrade Music Festival BEMUS (classical) that is hosted by the capital in October. Alternatively, you may wish to time your visit to coincide with religious and cultural celebrations like Orthodox Easter, which can be an enjoyable time to visit. Overall, May, June and September are probably the most perfect months, although May and June are also marginally the wettest. In the countryside, early to mid-October can be a delight, still reasonably warm but with golden autumn colours, and this is a superb time for energetic outdoor activities like walking or cycling. Hotel accommodation and public transport can be at a premium at certain times of year like Easter, New Year or during the EXIT festival in Novi Sad in July or the Belgrade Book Fair in October, but as a rule this presents few problems. The one thing that you can be certain of, for the time being at least, is that wherever you go and whenever you choose to visit Serbia, it is unlikely to be overrun with tourists. Enjoy this while it lasts.

PUBLIC HOLIDAYS AND FESTIVALS

1 January	New Year's Day
7 January	Orthodox Christmas Day
14 January	Orthodox New Year
15 February	Constitution Day
March–April	Orthodox Easter
2018	Good Friday, 6 April–Easter Monday, 9 April
2019	Good Friday, 26 April–Easter Monday, 29 April
2020	Good Friday, 17 April–Easter Monday, 20 April
1 & 2 May	Labour Days

The following are also considered to be holidays but are working days:

27 January	St Sava's Day
9 May	Victory Day
28 June	St Vitus's Day

Individual towns and cities have their own *slava* day, which is treated as a holiday. The most commonly celebrated *slava*s are those of St Nicholas (Nikoljdan) on 19 December, St George (Đurđevdan) on 6 May, St John the Baptist (Jovanjdan) on 20 January and St Archangel Michael (Aranđelovdan) on 21 November. Đurđevdan is of particular importance to Serbia's Roma and Vlach communities and St Vitus's Day on 28 June, being the anniversary of the Battle of Kosovo, is a meaningful date for many Serbs, especially those with strong nationalist concerns.

In rural areas, country fairs are held during traditional feast days (*zavetina*) at certain times of year, the most popular time being at Whitsun and on Ascension Day (Spasovdan), which occurs 40 days after Easter.

HIGHLIGHTS

Serbia has always been overlooked by visitors to the southeastern Europe region; this was even the case during the heyday of Yugoslav tourism in the 1970s and 1980s. It is difficult to understand why this is, as the country has plenty to offer: a fascinating, although admittedly not beautiful, capital city that boasts a rich cultural life, with excellent restaurants and nightlife; quiet, rural market towns that still cling to traditional ways; and a countryside that is characterised by lush green hills and forested mountains, with age-old monasteries hidden away in remote valleys. Perhaps the current lack of foreign visitors should be seen as an advantage as, in this case, low tourist numbers equate to low prices. Although not as cheap as it was a few years back, Serbia remains one of the least expensive countries in Europe, apart from hotel prices, which tend to be about average for the region. The people are friendly; the food is good, wholesome and organic for the most part, due to the lack of fertilisers and pesticides used. Public transport connections are reasonable too, although a car is useful for visiting more out-of-the-way places like some of the monasteries. Compared with other destinations in the same region, Serbia is currently untouched by the crowds, high prices and indifferent service that are starting to characterise parts of the Adriatic coast. Put simply, now is a great time to visit.

Belgrade is worth at least a couple of days if your interests are cultural and historical; if you are of a more hedonistic persuasion then you will need longer, as Belgrade has one of the best restaurant, nightclub and music scenes in all of southeast Europe. Much the same can be said of Novi Sad, which offers a slightly more refined and second-city version, although the city can easily be visited as a long day trip from the capital. Other Serbia highlights might include a trip along the Danube to see Golubac Castle, the archaeological finds at Lepenski Vir and the Iron Gates at Đerdap. Further options might be a monastery tour to see some of Serbia's hidden gems like Studenica or Manasija; a tour of some Hungarian minority towns in Vojvodina like Subotica with its ornate secessionist architecture or Sremski Karlovci with its splendid Habsburg buildings; or hiking among the forested hills of Zlatibor and Kopaonik national parks. Railway enthusiasts will enjoy taking part in one of Belgrade's summer steam excursions or travelling along the intriguing 'Šargan Eight' line. In the south, the cities of Novi Pazar and Niš have a reasonable amount to see and both can serve as good bases for visiting the hinterland. Old Turkish towns like Pirot or Vranje are also worthy of a day's visit. As an alternative to touring the country, there is also much to be said for basing oneself in Belgrade for the duration of a visit, especially if it is a fairly short one – Serbia is not a large country and many places of interest can be reached by travelling just a few hours from the capital.

SUGGESTED ITINERARIES

The suggested itineraries below are for visitors with a general interest in the country and its culture. They all assume that Belgrade is the start and end point of any such visit. If your interests are more specific – music, monasteries or wildlife for example – then you will need to adapt and plan accordingly in order to get the full benefit of the time that you have in the country.

ONE WEEK A week in Serbia is enough time to explore the capital Belgrade, make a visit to the second city Novi Sad and still have a few days left over to take in some attractive Vojvodina towns like Subotica or Sremski Karlovci. Alternatively, after visiting Belgrade and perhaps day tripping to Novi Sad, you could spend two or three days exploring some of the more easily visited monasteries of central Serbia like Žiča, Ljubostina or Manasija.

TWO WEEKS A fortnight affords far more flexibility. After Belgrade and Novi Sad, a short circular tour of Vojvodina to the north could take in some of its towns like Sombor, Subotica, Vršac and Sremski Karlovci before returning to the capital and then venturing east along the River Danube to visit Golubac Fortress and Lepenski Vir. Or instead, after returning to Belgrade, make a circular tour of either southeast Serbia, taking in destinations such as Kruševac, Niš, Sokobanja and Zaječar, or alternatively, head to west and southwest Serbia, visiting the Tara National Park, Zlatibor and the Sandžak region around Novi Pazar.

THREE WEEKS With three full weeks at your disposal, it is possible to see quite a lot of Serbia. As well as Belgrade, this could include parts of Vojvodina as above, and then incorporate a sweeping circular tour that takes in much of Serbia's south. Places to include on such an itinerary might include the city of Niš, the unusual rock formations at Đavolja Varoš, the Kopaonik area, Novi Pazar, the central Serbian town of Kraljevo and some of the monasteries of Šumadija. It might also be possible to squeeze in a visit to the west of the country, visiting either the Tara National Park or the Zlatibor region where you could take a trip on the Mokra Gora railway. Another alternative might be to venture all the way east along the River Danube to Kladovo after returning to Belgrade from Vojvodina. From Kladovo, head south through the little-visited east Serbian towns of Zaječar and Knjaževac to reach Niš before heading back to Belgrade.

To get a full impression of all of Serbia's markedly distinctive regions – Vojvodina, the Danube, southeast and southwest – would realistically require a full month.

TOURIST INFORMATION

The **National Tourist Organisation of Serbia** (NTOS) have their headquarters at Čika Ljubina 8, 11000 Belgrade (✆ 011 6557 100; e office@serbia.travel) and an information centre at Makedonska 22 in Belgrade (✆ 011 6557 127; e info@serbia. travel). They also have an informative website at w serbia.travel.

In Belgrade, the main branch of the **Tourist Organisation of Belgrade** (TOB) is at Trg Republike 5 (✆ 2635 622), with another branch at International Arrivals at

2

Belgrade Nikola Tesla Airport (☎ *2097 828*), and another at the main railway station (☎ *3612 732*). For more details, see their website w tob.rs.

Many regional towns and cities have their own tourist office and/or information websites, which are referred to in the appropriate chapter. These are normally helpful and courteous, answering enquiries and offering a range of maps and illustrated booklets.

TOUR OPERATORS

For the time being, there is a limited choice of organised tours that visit Serbia although quite a few include it as part of a Danube cruise or multi-country itinerary.

Aside from Kutrubes Travel, the only other US-based tours presently on offer are Danube River Cruises that take in Belgrade as a port of call.

UK

Balkan Holidays Ltd Sofia Hse, 19 Conduit St, London W1S 2BH; ☎ 0845 130 1115 (local rate) for brochure request, ☎ 020 7543 5555 for reservations; e res@balkanholidays.co.uk; w balkanholidays.co.uk. Balkan Holidays offer Zagreb-based tours that take in Belgrade & Novi Sad as part of their itinerary.

Cosmos Tours and Cruises Wren Court, 17 London Rd, Bromley, Kent BR1 1DE; ☎ (booking hotline) 0800 668 1365; w cosmostoursandcruises.co.uk. Cosmos has a Danube River cruise that passes through Belgrade between Bucharest & Prague. Also a 13-day Balkan & Transylvania tour that takes in Belgrade & Novi Sad.

Exodus Travelopia, TUI Travel Hse, Crawley Business Quarter, Fleming Way, Crawley RH10 9QL; ☎ 020 8772 3829; e sales@exodus.co.uk; w exodus.co.uk. Exodus has a 9-day Gem of the Balkans tour that includes monastery visits, vineyards & the Šargan Eight train ride; also an 11-day Balkan Explorer tour that visits Albania & Macedonia in addition to Serbia.

Explore! Nelson Hse, 55 Victoria Rd, Farnborough, Hants GU14 7PA; ☎ 01252 883916; e sales@explore.co.uk; w explore.co.uk. Offers an 8-day Highlights of Serbia tour as well as a 12-day Journey Through The Balkans & a 12-day Former Yugoslavia Rail Adventure tours that take in Serbia.

Intrepid 4th floor, Piano Hse, 9 Brighton Terrace, Brixton, London SW9 8DJ; ☎ 0808 274 5111; e ask@intrepidtravel.com; w intrepidtravel. com. An Australian company with a British office offering several tours visiting Serbia as part of a larger Balkan or central Europe itinerary.

Noble Caledonia 2 Chester Close, Belgravia, London SW1X 7BE; ☎ 020 7752 0000; e info@ noble-caledonia.co.uk; w noble-caledonia.co.uk. Runs a number of eastern Europe river cruises that pass through Serbia by way of the Sava & Danube rivers.

ReadyClickandGo.com 18 The Crescent, High Wycombe, Bucks HP13 6JY; ☎ 01494 461234; e tara@readyclickandgo.com; w readyclickandgo.com. Private Belgrade-based day tours.

Regent Holidays ☎ 020 7666 1244; e regent@ regent-holidays.co.uk; w regent-holidays.co.uk. Organises city breaks to Belgrade throughout the year as well as twin-centre, fly-drive & cultural tours.

Responsibletravel.com ☎ 01273 823700; e rosy@responsibletravel.com; w responsibletravel.com. This established company, dedicated to giving its clients experiences rather than just tours, can provide Danube cycling trips, small group tours in Serbia, & cultural & motorcycle tours in southeastern Europe that include Serbia in its itinerary.

Travel the Unknown Riverbank Hse, 1 Putney Bridge Approach, London SW6 3BQ; ☎ 020 7183 6371; e enquiries@traveltheunknown.com; w traveltheunknown.com. See ad, 1st colour section. This small company offers several guided tours to Serbia including an 8-day hiking & cycling tour of southeast Serbia, a 4-day Belgrade city tour, a 6-day culinary tour & a 7-day tour of the Danube & southern Serbia (Devil's Town & the Danube).

Travelsphere Compass Hse, Rockingham Rd, Market Harborough, Leics LE16 7QD; ☎ 01858 898138; e enquiries@travelsphere.co.uk; w travelsphere.co.uk. Offers a 12-day Danube cruise through Serbia finishing in Bucharest, & a 14-day Balkan Peninsula tour that begins in Sarajevo, ends at Zagreb & spends 3 days in Serbia.

Tucan Travel 316 Uxbridge Rd, Acton, London; ☎ 0800 804 8435, 020 8896 1600; e adventures@tucantravel.com; w tucantravel.com. A number of this adventure overland company's tours pass through or spend some time in Serbia, although all have multi-country itineraries.

Undiscovered Destinations PO Box 746, North Tyneside NE29 1EG; ☎ 0191 296 2674; e info@undiscovered-destinations.com; w undiscovered-destinations.com. Tours to Serbia in conjunction with Bosnia & Herzegovina & Montenegro.

Viking River Cruises Nelsons Hse, 83 Wimbledon Park Side, London SW19 5LP; ☎ 0800 319 6660; e info@vikingrivers.com; w vikingrivercruises.co.uk. Offers 11-day Danube River cruises that sail between Budapest & Bucharest, stopping in Belgrade.

US

Avalon Waterways 5301 South Federal Circle, Littleton, CO 80123; ☎ (toll free) +1 877 797 8791; w avalonwaterways.com. Has several multi-country cruises along the Danube through Serbia.

Grand Circle Travel 347 Congress St, Boston, MA 02210; ☎ +1 800 221 2610; e online@gct.com; w gct.com. Offers 13-day river trips from Mar to Nov that dock at Belgrade & a 28-day Grand European cruise between Amsterdam & the Black Sea that also visits Belgrade.

Explore! 1853 Embarcadero, Suite 2c, Oakland, CA 94606; ☎ (toll free) +1 800 715 1746; e tripinfo@exploreworldwide.com; w exploreworldwide.com. Offers the same options as their UK counterpart (see opposite).

Kutrubes Travel 328 Tremont St, Boston, MA 02116; ☎ (toll free) +1 800 878 8566, 617 426 5668; e adventures@kutrubestravel.com; w kutrubestravel.com. Organises a 20-day Balkan Odyssey tour that takes in all the countries of the Balkans. Kutrubes Travel can also arrange individualised custom tours.

Uniworld River Cruises Uniworld Plaza, 17323 Ventura Bd, Los Angeles, CA 91316; ☎ +1 800 733 7820, 818 382 7820; e info@uniworld.com; w uniworld.com. Offers various cruises along the Danube that pass through Serbia & visit Belgrade & Novi Sad.

CANADA

Tripcentral Hamilton City Centre, 77 James St N, Unit 230, Hamilton, Ontario L8R 2K3; ☎ (toll free) +1 800 665 4981; e enquiry@tripcentral.ca; w tripcentral.ca. Organises a variety of cruises along the Danube of 11–25 days' duration.

SERBIA

ACE Adventure Brace Ignjatović 17/37/1, 18000 Niš; m 064 2476 311; e info@ace-adventurecentre.com; w ace-adventurecentre.com. ACE offers a broad range of hiking & cycling trips of 2–7 days' duration in the mountains of southeast Serbia & elsewhere in the country. Several standard packages are available, such as a 7-day hiking trip in southeast Serbia that includes hiking to the highest peaks of the Stara Planina & Suva Planina ranges, & a cycling tour along the River Danube that entails cycling some of the more attractive stretches between Belgrade & Kladovo. Also walking & gourmand tours of west Serbia. All tours are fully supported & include HB in a 3-star hotel, lunches, transportation from Belgrade, bicycle use & the service of guides. Some self-guided options also available. ACE also offers a range of kayaking, rafting & snowshoeing itineraries & can tailor bespoke tours to customers' requirements.

Argus Tours Balkanska 51, 11000 Belgrade; ☎ 011 3617 660; e office@argus.co.rs; w argus.co.rs. Arranges 3- & 4-day programmes in Belgrade, 5-day tours of rural Serbia & visits to Serbian spas & resorts like Tara & Zlatibor.

Astra Travel Svetozara Markovića 4, 11000 Belgrade; ☎ 011 2622 104, 2622 105; e astraoffice@astratravel.rs; w www.astratravel.rs. Organises a variety of tours & ski packages.

Equestrian Adventure Serbia Kamenica, 34205 Bare; ☎ 034 539 328; m 064 3885 199; e reservation@reiten-in-serbia.com; w equestrianadventure-serbia.org. Guided 8-day summer horse tours of the wooded countryside of Šumadija with transfers from Belgrade. Suitable for intermediate riders prepared to spend 5–7hrs a day on a horse. Accommodation in village guesthouses, mountain lodges & 1 night's camping.

Glob Metropoliten Tours Makenzijeva 26, 11000 Belgrade; ☎ 011 2430 852, 2430 899; e glob@metropoliten.com; w travelserbiabelgrade.com. Offers a variety of full-day excursions in addition to 2-day & week-long tours of Serbia.

GO2 Serbia Gračanička 11, 11000 Belgrade; ☎ 011 3284 323; e office@go2serbia.net; w go2serbia.net. Monastery tours, Danube wine tours & excursions to Sremska Mitrovica in addition to Belgrade sightseeing tours & guided pub crawls.

Intertours Poenkareova 20, 11000 Belgrade; ☎ 011 2098 000, 2762 139, 2763 447; e inter-bg@ infosky.net, inter-it@tiscali.it; w intertours.co.rs. Intertours can organise Belgrade sightseeing tours & Danube cruises.

Kon Tiki Travel Bulevar Arsenija Čarnojevića 54a, 11070 New Belgrade; ☎ 011 2098 000; e info@ kontiki.rs; w kontiki.rs. Kon Tiki can book hotels & transport & offer skiing packages at Kopaonik.

Magelan Corporation Pašićeva 7, 21000 Novi Sad; ☎ 021 6624 823, 4724 088; e incoming@ magelan.rs; w magelan.rs, incoming.magelan.rs. Offers a wide range of services & tours, from 1-day Fruška Gora excursions to 8-day tours of Serbia that include 'Serbia for Beginners' & 'Beautiful Serbia'. Further options include a 12-day gastronomy tour of Serbia & an 8-day 'Route of Roman Emperors' tour. They also organise dental tourism packages to Novi Sad & longer tours that include Montenegro, Croatia & Macedonia. Magelan also provide birdwatching tours to west Serbia & sites in Vojvodina such as the Carska Bara wetlands, Obedska Bara, Deliblato Sands & Fruška Gora.

Panacomp Bulevar Cara Lazara 96, 21000 Novi Sad; ☎ 021 466 075; e info@panacomp.net; w panacomp.net. Offers a range of tours through Serbia & Vojvodina from 2 to 9 days along with some village tourism options. Also all-inclusive Music & Gastronomy packages to the Guča region.

Panoramic Serbia Bulevar Mihaila Pupina 10z/ IV, 11070 New Belgrade; ☎ 011 3119 727; e info@ panoramic-serbia.com; w panoramic-serbia. com. Various eco & cultural tours, medical tourism & services – transfers, local guides, transport & special programmes – for tailor-made tours.

Rubicon Travel Vojvode Stepe 146, 11000 Belgrade; ☎ 011 4141 511; e info@rubicontravel. rs; w rubicontravel.rs. A wide range of tours offered, including monastery visits, Guča & EXIT festivals, & food tours.

Serbiain Vuka Karadžića 9, 11000 Belgrade; ☎ 011 3284 323; w serbiain.com. Serbiain, a member of the Eurojet travel company, specialises in incoming tourism & offers various tours that include spas, Belgrade city breaks & day trips to the Roman site of Viminacium.

Serbian Heritage Tours S Nikolajevića 5, 11050 Belgrade; m 065 2410 746; e serbian.heritage. tours@gmail.com; w serbianheritagetours. com. Private cultural tours led by knowledgeable heritage interpreter that explore Belgrade & beyond, aimed at solo travellers, parties of friends & business travellers.

Serbian Travel System Vukice Mitrović, 11000 Belgrade; ☎ 011 2449 275; e office@serbian-travel-system.com; w sts.co.rs. Guided tours through all regions of Serbia, monastery tours & bus & walking tours in Belgrade.

RED TAPE

Nationals from UN member states that do not have diplomatic relations require visas to enter Serbia, however, most foreign visitors do not require visas for a short stay in the country. Passport-holders of the following countries may stay in Serbia for a period up to 90 days without the requirement of a visa: Andorra, Argentina, Australia, Austria, Belgium, Bolivia, Canada, Chile, Costa Rica, Croatia, Cuba, Cyprus, Czech Republic, Denmark, Estonia, Finland, France, Germany, Greece, Hungary, Iceland, Ireland, Israel, Italy, Japan, Latvia, Liechtenstein, Lithuania, Luxembourg, Mexico, Monaco, Netherlands, New Zealand, Norway, Poland, Portugal, San Marino, Seychelles, Singapore, Slovakia, Slovenia, Spain, Sweden, Switzerland, Tunisia, United Kingdom, United States of America and Vatican City.

Those from the following countries may stay in Serbia for up to 90 days without a visa if they are in possession of a diplomatic passport: Armenia, Azerbaijan, China, Ecuador, Egypt, Georgia, Guinea, Kyrgyzstan, Malta, Mongolia, North Korea, Peru, Russian Federation, South Korea, Tajikistan, Turkmenistan and Vietnam.

The following are granted 30 days' visa-free stay in Serbia: Albania, Belarus, Bosnia and Herzegovina, Bulgaria, Macedonia (60 days), Pakistan (diplomatic passports) and Turkey (for diplomatic, special and official passports only). For those requiring a visa, an application should be made at one of Serbia's foreign embassies where the applicant will be required to produce a valid passport, a letter of introduction (this can be organised through a Serbian tourist agency or a business contact), a return ticket, proof of funds and evidence of medical cover for the duration of the stay.

Funds in excess of €5,000 should be declared on arrival in the country as, in theory at least, failure to do this could result in confiscation on leaving Serbia.

THE KOSOVO BORDER STAMP ISSUE Following Kosovo's unilateral declaration of independence in 2008 there was initially a great deal of uncertainty regarding the border crossing from Kosovo into Serbia. Because Serbia did not recognise the new republic, it was reported that on some occasions Serbian guards had not allowed travellers to travel into Serbia from Kosovo unless they had begun their journey in Serbia in the first place. A little while after the declared independence, the Kosovan authorities started stamping passports with a 'Republic of Kosovo' stamp, which did not help matters. Although this remains a grey area, partially dependent on the whims of the border guards, it is safest to assume that it will not be possible to cross the border from Kosovo into Serbia unless you originally began your journey in Serbia (and therefore have a Serbian entrance stamp) and are returning directly. So in short, travel Serbia–Kosovo–Serbia should present no problem but something like Serbia–Kosovo–Macedonia–Serbia might be problematic due to the absence of a Serbia exit stamp. For the same reason, travellers wishing to travel Serbia–Kosovo–Montenegro–Serbia are advised to make a short detour back into Serbia at the Zubin Potok border rather than going directly to Montenegro from Peč. The Kosovan–Serbian border is not regarded as an official entrance point by the Serbian authorities, and the lack of a Serbian exit stamp in your passport if leaving Kosovo for a third country may also cause problems for future Serbia visits.

Of course, the situation might change for better or worse in the future, so check the British FCO website (**w** *fco.gov.uk*) or equivalent to make sure.

REGISTRATION WITH POLICE All foreigners visiting Serbia are obliged to be registered with the police within 24 hours. This is normally done automatically by hotels on checking in. You will be registered anew each time you change hotels and given a registration card when you check out. If you are staying somewhere privately, or camping, then you are supposed to register with the police within 12 hours of arrival and to report any subsequent change of address within 24 hours. This seems to be a mere formality but, in theory at least, you may be asked to provide the necessary registration documents when you leave Serbia. In practice, this never seems to happen but it is best to be prepared.

EMBASSIES

The Ministry of Foreign Affairs of the Republic of Serbia has a full list of Serbian embassies abroad at **w** mfa.gov.rs/en/embassies/serbian-diplomatic-missions/serbian-embassies whilst there's a downloadable PDF file of foreign embassies in Serbia available from the Ministry of Foreign Affairs of the Republic of Serbia's website: **w** mfa.gov.rs/diplomatic_list.pdf.

BY AIR Several airlines serve Belgrade directly. These include the national carrier Air Serbia, Aeroflot, Air France, Alitalia, Austrian Airlines, Eurowings, Lufthansa, Malev, Montenegro, Olympic Airways Swiss, Tarom, Turkish Airlines and Wizz Air. At Belgrade's Nikola Tesla Airport, Terminal 2 deals with all international traffic, while domestic flights use Terminal 1. Although Belgrade handles virtually all of Serbia's international traffic, Niš's Constantine the Great Airport currently receives a limited number of international flights and this is likely to increase in the future.

Belgrade Nikola Tesla Airport information: \ *011 2094 444 (flight information), 2094 000 (switchboard);* w *beg.aero).*

For international flights, Belgrade Nikola Tesla Airport charges all adult passengers a **departure tax** of €16.50, although this should be included in the ticket price.

From the UK British Airways no longer flies to Belgrade as the service was terminated in 2010 due to unprofitability. There are, however, daily direct flights to Belgrade from Heathrow every day with **Air Serbia** (w *airserbia.com*), with flights that leave Heathrow in the early afternoon to conveniently arrive in Belgrade by late afternoon. The return flight leaves mid morning to arrive at Heathrow around midday. The best price is about £220 return including tax, although it may be difficult to get this price during busy holiday periods or at short notice.

The other direct flight alternative from the UK is to fly to Belgrade with **Wizz Air** (w *wizzair.com*) from Luton Airport, which has return flights as low as £70 (extra for baggage) if booked well in advance. Wizz Air flights leave Luton early evening three to four times a week. These arrive in Belgrade around midnight, which is not convenient although hotel transfers from the airport can be pre-booked in advance. The return flights to Luton leave Belgrade late afternoon to arrive in London early evening. An indirect option that might save a little money is to combine a cheap budget airline flight with a train or bus journey through to Serbia, for example, by taking a cut-price **Ryanair** (w *ryanair.com*) flight to Trieste in Italy, Timişoara in Romania or Budapest in Hungary, and then continuing the journey by train or bus. It is unlikely that great savings will be made by doing this, especially if sleepers need to be booked, but it is a good way of seeing more of the region. Another option is to use **easyJet** (w *easyjet.com*) flights to Budapest and Ljubljana, both of which have good, reasonably cheap rail and road connections with Belgrade.

From Europe Air Serbia has direct flights that connect Belgrade with Amsterdam, Athens, Banja Luka, Berlin, Brussels, Copenhagen, Düsseldorf, Frankfurt, Gothenburg, Hamburg, Hanover, Istanbul, Kiev, Larnaca, Ljubljana, London Malta, Munich, Moscow, Paris, Prague, Sarajevo, Skopje, Sofia, St Petersburg, Stockholm, Trieste, Vienna, Warsaw and Zurich. The best connected of these are Paris and Zurich with around 15 flights a week. There are also several flights a day from Belgrade to Podgorica and Tivat in Montenegro with Air Serbia and Montenegro Airlines. There are also limited services to the Middle East and North Africa, with Beirut, Cairo, Tel Aviv, Tripoli and Tunis all being served by Air Serbia.

From the United States There are no direct flights between Belgrade and the United States so it is necessary to find a connecting flight in one of the European hubs like London, Paris or Amsterdam. Air Serbia offer code-share flights to New York with a change of planes and a layover at Berlin airport.

BY TRAIN To travel all the way to Serbia by train from Britain requires time, money and planning. It is actually cheaper to fly, but the following may appeal to rail buffs. The first stage is to take the 10.24 Eurostar from London St Pancras to Paris Gare du Nord, arriving at 13.47. This costs from £58 return. At Paris Gare du Nord you then walk to the nearby Gare de l'Est and take the TGV to Munich Hauptbahnhof that leaves at 15.55 and arrives there at 21.36. From Munich, you can then travel overnight on the 'Kalman Imre' sleeper train that leaves Munich at 23.35 and arrives at Budapest Keleti station at 09.24 the following morning. This train has a choice of two- and three-bed sleeping compartments or four- and six-berth couchette cars. Leaving Budapest, you can then take the 'Avala' that leaves Keleti station at 12.05 to arrive in Belgrade at 20.15. This whole journey can cost as little as £140 one-way, £260 return in second class if booked well in advance. The normal fare is, of course, far more. Tickets for the daytime trains can be booked online at **w** raileurope.co.uk, while sleeper and couchette tickets can be purchased at **w** bahn.de. Booking by phone, you can telephone Deutsche Bahn's UK office (**** *0871 880 8066;* **w** *bahn. co.uk*) or European Rail (**** *020 7619 1083;* **w** *europeanrail.com*), although the latter charges a hefty booking fee. Train reservations out of Belgrade station can be made at the Wasteels agency at the station.

A swifter alternative is to travel by rail to Serbia from somewhere rather nearer, perhaps in combination with a low-budget flight. Belgrade can be reached directly by train from all of the surrounding countries, as well as some beyond. From Zagreb the journey takes around 6 hours. From Venice via Zagreb the overnight journey to Belgrade takes around 16 hours and requires a change and a 2-hour stopover in the early hours of the morning. Direct services are also available from Ljubljana, which take around 9 hours.

Rail connections are also good with Budapest to the north, and go via Novi Sad, Subotica and the Hungarian border at Horgoš, although the journey time at around 7 hours is not really long enough to be convenient for an overnighter. Direct routes also exist between Greece, Romania, Turkey, Macedonia and Bulgaria and Belgrade, although the railway route between Sarajevo and Belgrade is rather circuitous and it is generally better to travel between Bosnia and Herzegovina and Serbia by bus. From Montenegro, there is a convenient overnight service between Bar and Belgrade by way of the Montenegrin capital, Podgorica, however, this journey is really better done during the daytime in order to make the most of the stunning scenery along the way.

Full details of all **European train times** may be found at **w** bahn.hafas.de. For Serbian railway services, look at **w** serbianrailways.com.

BY BUS There are direct bus routes to Serbia from all over western and northern Europe. For the longer journeys, given the cost, time and discomfort involved, flying is probably a more attractive option. Eurolines, which in Serbia are operated by the Lasta bus company (**w** *lasta.rs*), run services between Serbia and Austria, Benelux, Bosnia and Herzegovina (and Republika Srbska), Croatia, Czech Republic, Denmark, France, Germany, Greece, Hungary, Macedonia, Slovakia, Slovenia, Sweden and Switzerland. Another company, Srbija Tours International (*Lička 3, Belgrade;* **** *011 7619 576, 7614 545, 3065 496;* **e** *office@srbija-tours.com;* **w** *srbija-tours.com*), operates services to various destinations in Germany and Italy.

From the UK The Eurolines service from London to Belgrade requires a change of bus and a lengthy layover at Frankfurt. Coaches leave late morning throughout the year, arriving in Belgrade in the early morning of the third day. The services take around 42 hours in all and cost from £130 one-way, £250 return with a small reduction for youth and senior concessions.

Eurolines bookings: ✆ 0871 781 8181 08.00–20.00 Monday–Friday, or online at w eurolines.co.uk.

From France
Paris–Belgrade: 5 weekly
Lyon–Belgrade: twice weekly

From Benelux
Amsterdam–Belgrade: twice weekly

From neighbouring former-Yugoslavian countries
A range of private bus companies operate in addition to Lasta.
Banja Luka–Belgrade: 6 services daily
Sarajevo–Belgrade: daily
Ljubljana–Belgrade: 2 daily
Zagreb–Belgrade: 5 daily
Dubrovnik–Belgrade: daily
Split–Belgrade: twice daily

International bus tickets
These can be booked at various agents in the country of origin. Find them in:

🚌 **Croatia** At 'Otisak Tours', Put Plokite 57, Split; ✆ (021) 524 852
🚌 **France** At the Eurolines bus station which in Paris is found at 28 Av Général de Gaulle; ✆ (01) 49 72 51 51, (01) 49 72 51 66
🚌 **Slovenia** At 'Kompas-Hertz', Celoveska 206, Ljubljana; ✆ (061) 573 532

The Lasta head office in Belgrade is at Železnička 2 (✆ *011 625 740*). For other international services that operate from Belgrade bus station contact BAS Turist (*Železnička 4;* ✆ *011 6658 759, 2627 146, 2622 526, 2180 377;* w *www.bas.rs*). Some of the Eurolines international services may be reserved online (w *eurolines.com*) for a small reservation fee.

BY FERRY Serbia is landlocked but a frequent ferry service operates between Ancona and Bari in southern Italy and Bar in Montenegro from where trains and buses are available to continue through to Serbia.

BY CAR With Serbia's landlocked position, surrounded by a total of eight other countries, it is little surprise that there are many options available if you are driving your own vehicle. From Hungary, there are **crossing points** at Bački Beg, Bajmok, Đala, Horgoš and Kelebija, and from Romania at Đerdap, Kaluđerovo, Srpska Crnja and Vatin. From Bulgaria, crossings exist at Gradina, Mokranje, Ribarci, Strezimirovci and Vrška Čuka, and from Macedonia at Globočica, Preševo and Prohor Pčinjski. Croatian border crossings are at Bačka Palanka, Batrovci, Bezdan, Bogojevo, Ljuba, Neština, Odžaci, Šid and Sot, while land crossings across to Bosnia and Herzegovina are at Badovinci, Bajina Bašta, Kotroman, Ljubovija, Loznica, Mali Zvornik, Sremska Rača, Trbušnica and Uvac. There are also border crossings between Albania and Kosovo at Čafa Prušit and Vrbinca and at Đeneral Janković between Kosovo and Macedonia. All of the crossings listed are open around the clock.

Insurance policies from countries that have signed the Vehicle Insurance Convention are fully valid, but citizens of other countries must purchase an **insurance policy** when entering Serbia. Green Card cover can be issued for drivers of the following countries: Albania, Andorra, Austria, Belgium, Bosnia and Herzegovina, Bulgaria, Croatia, Cyprus, Czech Republic, Denmark, Finland, France, Germany, Greece, Hungary, Iceland, Ireland, Italy, Luxembourg, Macedonia, Moldova, Netherlands, Norway, Portugal, Romania, Slovakia, Spain, Sweden, Switzerland, Tunisia, Turkey and the United Kingdom. Drivers who have insurance policies issued in countries other than these will be required to purchase a short-term insurance policy on entry. Whatever your country of origin, it may be hard persuading immigration officials that a particular policy from any of these countries is valid for Serbia (it should state it clearly on your document, or you should have a covering letter) and they may try and insist that you purchase compulsory insurance anyway.

On entering Serbia drivers with foreign registration plates have to pay motorway road tolls at a higher premium. Tolls, which work out about €10 per 100km, are paid on the following roads: from Novi Sad to Belgrade on the E-75, from Novi Sad to Subotica on the E-75, for the section of the E-75 from Belgrade to Niš, for the E-75 from Niš to Leskovac, and on the E-70 from Belgrade to Šid, on the Croatian border. These tolls may be paid in either Serbian dinars or euros.

In the case of breakdown or emergency, the roadside service of the **Automobile and Motorists Association of Serbia – AMSS** (*Ruzveltova 18, Belgrade;* \ *011 3331 100, 3331 200;* w *amss.rs*) – is available for assistance and the towing or transport of damaged vehicles (*24hr breakdown* \ *1987*). If a vehicle with foreign licence plates is abandoned, it should be reported to the local AMSS unit so that a certificate may be released. Similarly, if a foreign tourist enters Serbia driving a vehicle with damaged bodywork, they should receive a certificate from the officials at the border crossing that clearly evaluates the extent of the damage. In the case of a traffic accident, the **traffic police** (*Saobraćajna policija*) should be summoned (\ *192*), who will then issue an accident report.

BY RIVER TRANSPORT Sadly, no international public river transport currently plies the Danube, Tisa or Sava waterways, although many international cruises transit Serbia *en route* to the Black Sea. For those willing to paddle their own canoe, one interesting but challenging option would be to join in the **Tour International Danubien** (w *tour-international-danubien.org*) that takes place every year along the River Danube, and which traverses Serbia as part of a 2,080km kayak journey from Ingolstadt, Germany, to Silistra, Bulgaria. The tour leaves Germany in late June and arrives in Serbia at Apatin at the end of July before taking a further 16 days to cross the country. Daily stages are between 40km and 65km long, allowing plenty of time for sightseeing in the towns passed by. The Canoe Federation of Serbia organises the tour within Serbia's boundaries and provides camping and free food along the way – ideal for a cheap, albeit highly energetic, holiday. It is also possible to canoe just sections of the route and there may even be a chance of finding a place in someone else's canoe for part of the tour. (*For information in Serbia,* \ *011 3541 145;* e *kajakss@eu.net.*)

HEALTH   *with Dr Felicity Nicholson*

Medical treatment is available free to UK residents on production of a UK passport if you are a UK resident. If you are a UK resident but not a UK national, you will need a certificate of insurance from HM Revenue and Customs Centre for non-residents. However, taking out health insurance is highly recommended. Hospital treatment, some dental and medical treatment should be free, but you will have to pay for prescribed medication. With good insurance you may prefer to use a private clinic. Many doctors who work in private clinics will have been educated abroad and thus able to speak English – a great comfort in times of illness. Also, the standard of care in most private clinics is reasonably high. Some medications may not be as freely available as at home, so it is important that the visitor brings along a sufficient supply of any necessary medication that they are dependent upon.

On the whole, Serbia is a healthy place; the greatest health danger that visitors are likely to encounter is probably an unacceptable degree of passive smoking in public places. Most food in Serbia is hygienically prepared and meat is rarely served very rare, which minimises the risk of picking up parasites and developing intestinal complaints. Tap water is generally perfectly safe for consumption. However, it is always best to drink bottled water if you can to avoid any unnecessary upset stomachs. Some of the homemade liquor that may be offered to the visitor in parts of rural Serbia should be treated with caution but to refuse it outright might appear rude.

There has been concern in some circles about the use of depleted uranium in Kosovo and Serbia during the recent conflicts. There is some evidence that its use leads to a greater incidence of leukaemia and other cancers. Whatever the reality of this is for the people who live there, visitors who visit Serbia for a short period have absolutely nothing to fear.

IMMUNISATIONS The following immunisations are recommended, depending on the nature of a visit. In all cases, these are of low to moderate risk and some really only apply to extended visits to more remote areas of the country. If you are planning an extended stay, it is wise to visit your doctor or a reputable travel clinic at least four weeks before travel.

Routinely you should be up to date with tetanus, diphtheria and polio, which is now given as an all-in-one vaccine (Revaxis) that lasts for ten years. **Hepatitis A** vaccine (eg: Havrix Monodose, Avaxim) is also recommended as standard. A single dose gives protection for a year. This can be extended for up to 25 years by having a follow-up booster dose of vaccine.

Other vaccines that may be recommended depending on the length and nature of your trip are rabies and hepatitis B. The latter two vaccines are composed of three doses, so ensure that you leave plenty of time.

Hepatitis B This is acquired through risky behaviour, such as body piercing, tattooing, in places where needles may be re-used or not sterilised properly. It may also be acquired through unsafe sex, or through medical treatment through inadequately sterilised needles or syringes. Prevention is always better than cure, but carrying a small pack of needles and syringes can be very useful. For those aged 16 or over a shorter course of the vaccination comprises three doses over a minimum of 21 days. Longer courses have to be used for those under 16, requiring a minimum of two months to complete.

Hepatitis B is always recommended when working in medical settings and also with children.

Rabies Serbia is classed as a high-risk rabies country and so rabies vaccination is ideally recommended for everyone, but is imperative for anyone working with animals. The virus can be transmitted through the saliva of any mammal through a bite, a scratch or lick on skin – you don't need to have an obvious open wound. Dogs are the most likely source in Serbia. If you are exposed, wash the wound immediately with soap and water, scrubbing for a good 10–15 minutes and go straight to medical help.

If you have not had a vaccine before you have an exposure, then you may need a blood product called rabies immunoglobulin (RIG), which is put around the wound and includes five doses of vaccine over about a month. RIG is very expensive, but more importantly, it is not readily available and crucial that it is given, especially if you have been bitten or scratched. If you have had three doses of vaccine before you go (given ideally over 28 days but 21 will do if time is short), then you no longer need RIG. Instead you will just need to get a couple of doses of vaccine given ideally three days apart following an exposure. For people who are immunosuppressed, more post-exposure doses of vaccine are likely to be recommended. Contrary to popular belief, rabies vaccine is safe and relatively painless to have.

Tick-borne encephalitis Travellers wishing to visit more rural parts of Serbia from late spring to autumn should take precautions against tick-borne encephalitis. This disease, as the name suggests, is spread by the bites of ticks that live in long grass and the branches of overhanging trees. Wearing long trousers tucked into socks and boots, hats and applying repellents can all help. Likewise, checking for ticks after forays into grassy areas is sensible. Remember to check the head and in particular behind the ears in children. Any ticks should be carefully removed as soon as possible (see box below). Medical help should always be sought as soon as possible even if the tick is safely removed. Tick encephalitis vaccine (Ticovac) is available in the UK and is safe and effective. It can be used from one year upwards (Ticovac Junior). Two doses should be given ideally a month apart but can be as short as two weeks if time is short. A third dose should be given five–12 months later if there is continued exposure. However, taking the preventative measures described above is also very important. Go to a doctor as soon as possible if you have been bitten by a tick (whether or not you have been vaccinated) as tick immunoglobulin may be needed for treatment. Antibiotics will not work against this viral disease so prevention and precautions are important.

TRAVEL CLINICS AND HEALTH INFORMATION A full list of current travel clinic websites worldwide is available on **w** istm.org. For other journey preparation

TICK REMOVAL

Ticks should ideally be removed as soon as possible as leaving them on the body increases the chance of infection. They should be removed with special tick tweezers that can be bought in good travel shops. Failing that you can use your fingernails by grasping the tick as close to your body as possible and pulling steadily and firmly away at right angles to your skin. The tick will then come away complete as long as you do not jerk or twist. If possible douse the wound with alcohol (any spirit will do) or iodine. Irritants (eg: Olbas oil) or lit cigarettes are to be discouraged since they can cause the ticks to regurgitate and therefore increase the risk of disease. It is best to get a travelling companion to check you for ticks and if you are travelling with small children remember to check their heads, and particularly behind the ears. An area of spreading redness around the bite site, or a rash or fever coming on a few days or more after the bite, should stimulate a trip to the doctor.

information, consult **w** travelhealthpro.org.uk (UK) or **w** wwwnc.cdc.gov/travel/ (US). Information about various medications may be found on **w** netdoctor.co.uk/travel. All advice found online should be used in conjunction with expert advice received prior to or during travel.

SAFETY

Serbia's oft-perceived image as a lawless, rather dangerous sort of place is far from the truth. The reality is in fact very different and visitors have nothing to fear. Even Serbia's largest city Belgrade feels very safe indeed when compared with London, Paris or New York. In fact, it seems the sort of city where anyone – young or old, male or female – can walk around safely at any time of day or night. The British disease of aggressive binge drinking does not appear to exist here; instead, the streets are calm and civilised, even late at night, with well-behaved young people crowding the pavements or drinking coffee at outdoor tables. If this all sounds too good to be true, the statistics bear it out: robbery and violent crime *are* rare, which is not to say that visitors should be complacent as opportunist thieves exist everywhere, and perhaps should be expected in a country that has suffered continual economic hardship for such a long period. As in any city, you should avoid seemingly deserted streets and parks late at night. As long as you keep away from large public demonstrations, and avoid the few unfortunate areas where there are obvious ethnic tensions, Serbia is very safe indeed.

In rural areas care should be taken to avoid tick bites (page 71) and walkers should be aware of the possible presence of poisonous snakes when hiking in hilly areas – the long-nosed adder (*Vipera ammodytes*), a small snake that is relatively common in some areas, is particularly venomous although the risk of accidentally stepping on one is very slight.

WOMEN TRAVELLERS

Although domestic violence against women is sadly a reality in some parts of Serbia, foreign women undergo no particular risks in visiting the country – the majority of Serbian men are courteous in the extreme. Sexual harassment is not completely unknown but it is by no means commonplace. It is probably true to state that women visitors are at a lower risk of sexual assault or rape here than they are back home in northern Europe.

GAY TRAVELLERS

Unfortunately, many Serbian men, especially young macho ones, have a rather unenlightened view of homosexuals, in particular, gay men. The situation is slowly improving but it is wise to remember that there have been numerous cases of openly gay men being attacked in the street, especially late at night whilst leaving clubs. The caveat of no 'open displays of affection between same-sex couples' is a sensible one as emotions seem to run high when those more conservative members of Serbian society are confronted with a sexuality that differs from their own (see also pages 93–4).

TRAVELLING WITH CHILDREN

There is little difficulty in travelling with children in Serbia, providing parents can be reasonably flexible and resourceful in their outlook. As everywhere in Europe,

Despite independence in 2006, the war in the region has had a lasting effect on the people of Serbia. Whilst care for the disabled is not as good as it is in other European countries, people are aware of the need to look after those who suffered in the recent conflict.

PLANNING AND BOOKING There are few specialist travel agencies running trips to Serbia.

GETTING THERE AND AWAY There are fully accessible facilities available at the Nikola Tesla Airport in Belgrade. For smaller airports in other cities it is worth checking beforehand to ensure that they have similar facilities to those in the capital available for wheelchair-bound travellers.

ACCOMMODATION There are a number of wheelchair-accessible hotels in Serbia such as the **Zira Hotel** (*Belgrade 35, Ruzveltova 11000, Belgrade;* 011 3314 800; e *reservations@zirahotels.com*) (page 119).

SIGHTSEEING Serbia has a mixture of old and new buildings. Getting around the historical sites may be difficult for those in wheelchairs, an example of this being the World Heritage Site at Gamzigrad–Felix Romuliana; a fortified Roman palace.

In Belgrade, the road surfaces are uneven and in many parts of the city there is a lack of pavements. Crossing the road can be particularly hazardous. As in many European cities, drivers don't always adhere to the rules of the road. Some of the shopping centres offer disabled facilities, with lifts and accessible toilets.

Unfortunately, the public transport system is rather outdated and often overcrowded so it is always worth checking beforehand if you are unable to board buses unaided.

TRAVEL INSURANCE AND HEALTH FACILITIES There are a few specialised companies that deal with travel to Serbia. A number of operators deal with pre-existing medical conditions such as **Insure For All** (0800 082 1265; w *insureforall.com*). You can also get quotes for travel insurance for pre-existing conditions from many of the larger insurance companies.

If you need hospital treatment, the Bel-Medic hospital in Belgrade has full wheelchair access. However, there may be limited access at hospitals in other parts of the region.

FURTHER INFORMATION A good website for further information on planning and booking any accessible holiday is w access-able.com, which provides many tips and links to travel resources worldwide.

The Tourist Organisation of Belgrade provides further information for travellers wishing to go there (w *tob.co.rs/eng*).

Practical Information   TRAVELLING WITH CHILDREN

2

children are generally well provided for, although with city pavements often blocked by carelessly parked cars access for buggies and pushchairs may not always be ideal. Restaurants and cafés are generally welcoming of children but there may not be any high chairs available. They may well be smoky too and in the warmer months sitting outside may be the preferred option. Most towns and cities are reasonably well provided with facilities like children's playgrounds. Pharmacies can be found almost everywhere and so finding children's medicines should not present a problem, although it is probably safer to bring along enough medication to last for the duration of your visit. Virtually all hotels and guesthouses are able to provide cots and additional beds for children as necessary, and many hotels of mid-range category and above are able to provide child minders on request.

WHAT TO TAKE

A visit to Serbia does not require the same sort of preparation as a trip to the Amazon rainforest but a few hard-to-find items may prove useful. Any personal medication should be brought along, as it may be imprudent to assume that a supply will be readily available in Serbia. Spectacle-wearers will probably not need reminding that they should bring along a spare pair, and their own prescription sunglasses, essential in the summer glare. A pocket torch (flashlight) is always a good idea too, although power cuts are no longer a feature of Serbian life. A plug adaptor (two-prong, round-pin) will enable you to use your own electrical devices whilst in the country, and, in considering such devices, a portable laptop computer or iPod-type device is probably the most useful in terms of size-to-satisfaction ratio. American 110-volt electrical devices will require an adaptor to use the 220-volt European current.

Although foreign bank-friendly ATMs are widespread these days, it is always best to back up plastic with a reasonable supply of cash too – euros preferably, but dollars or sterling will suffice – although it is usually possible to find a working ATM in even the smallest of towns.

Insect repellent is a good idea as mosquitoes can sometimes be a pain in summer, even in Belgrade. Kalemegdan Park can be particularly bad around dusk on a warm summer's night and the use of a repellent with a high DEET content is a wise precaution.

As for clothing, be prepared for cold in winter, early spring and late autumn, and anticipate the possibility of rain, even in the summer months, by bringing along a waterproof jacket or an umbrella.

MONEY AND BUDGETING

CURRENCY The official monetary unit of Serbia is the **dinar**, which is usually abbreviated as 'din' and has the international currency code of RSD in exchange transactions. As of June 2017, there were around 138 dinar to the pound sterling, around 122 to the euro, and around 109 to the US dollar. In recent years, the Serbian dinar has become a reasonably stable currency thanks to its pegging to the euro. This is fine for those living in the eurozone but not necessarily such good news for those with sterling or dollars in their pockets. Thankfully, the hyperinflation of the 1990s is a thing of the past, and it is no longer necessary to push along wheelbarrows of multiple-zeroed banknotes in order to make a simple purchase (see box, page 37).

The Serbian dinar is divided into 100 **para**, although these are no longer used. Banknotes come in denominations of 10, 20, 50, 100, 200, 1,000 and 5,000din; coins are 1, 2, 5, 10 and 20din. Some of the older notes and coins say 'Yugoslavia' instead of 'Serbia' but otherwise they are almost identical in design. Foreign nationals may take a maximum of 120,000din in or out of the country. It is hard to exchange Serbian dinars outside the country although it may be possible in some of the banks in Szeged, just across the Hungarian border, or with money changers in towns like Timișoara in Romania that are close to the Serbian border. Serbian dinars also serve as an acceptable second currency in parts of the Republika Srpska entity of Bosnia and Herzegovina.

Exchange rates vary very little between **banks** and **exchange offices** (*menjačnica*) so it is not really worthwhile shopping around. As well as the usual manned outlets, in Belgrade and the other large cities there are also money-exchange machines that accept euros, dollars or pounds sterling; you are required to feed your notes into the machine, which will then, hopefully, provide the correct equivalent in Serbian dinars.

Serbia is much less a **cash** economy than it was just a few years ago and electronic banking has caught on to the extent that many goods and services can now be bought using plastic. Foreign exchange of cash can be performed at banks and post offices throughout the country, as well as at numerous small exchange offices where the transaction is usually quicker. The euro usually gets the best rate. There is no black market. **Travellers' cheques**, these days very much a thing of the past, are becoming increasingly hard to change: branches of Raiffeisenbank or Komercijalna banka are probably the best bet, but beware of high commission charges. For Eurocheques, branches of ProCredit banka are probably the best bet. Neither personal nor travellers' cheques can normally be exchanged for goods in shops, so credit or debit cards make far more sense.

Banks are generally **open** from 08.00 to 19.00 on weekdays and from 08.00 to 15.00 Saturdays. In Belgrade, some banks and post offices are also open on Sundays, one being the Komercijalna banka at Trg Nikole Pašića 2 (✆ *011 3234 087*), which is open from 08.00 to 20.00 on Saturdays, and from 09.00 to 15.00 on Sundays and holidays.

Visa is the most widely accepted **credit card**, closely followed by MasterCard, and cash can be withdrawn from ATMs bearing these symbols, as well as cash advances being given in banks throughout the country. Maestro and Electron debit cards may also be used where the symbol is displayed. American Express and Diners Club are not so well accepted, although they may be used in payment for goods in some shops, top hotels and car-rental agencies. It is worth remembering that, even for the payment of goods with MasterCard, you will need to know your PIN code.

Electronic banking is moving swiftly forwards in Serbia but it is inevitable that there may be some hiccups: occasionally ATMs may not recognise foreign cards and, in a worst-case scenario, may even swallow your card. To be on the safe side, it is probably wise to carry more than one type of card if at all possible; say, two different credit cards – Visa and MasterCard – as well as a debit card.

Emergency help numbers for credit cards: Visa (✆ *011 3011 550*); MasterCard (✆ *011 3010 160*); Diners Club (✆ *011 3440 622*); American Express card holders may be able to receive help from the emergency service of Komercijalna banka (✆ *011 3080 115*).

For those arriving by plane, there is an ATM at the arrivals hall (downstairs) of Belgrade's Nikola Tesla Airport, which will accept Visa, Visa Electron, Visa Plus, MasterCard, Maestro and Cirrus cards.

The best way to arrange a fast **transfer of funds** from abroad is to make use of the services of Western Union Serbia (w *wu.co.rs*). Whatever currency your money is sent in, you will receive it in euros. All Serbian banks are members of SWIFT, and so another alternative is to open a bank account in Serbia then arrange for a transfer. A SWIFT transfer will take between two and seven business days to come through.

BUDGETING Serbia remains a relatively inexpensive country; a little cheaper than its immediate neighbours Bosnia and Herzegovina, Croatia and Slovenia, and noticeably less pricey than Montenegro. On any reckoning, Serbia offers pretty good value:

food, drink and transport are all very reasonably priced, although some consumer items like clothing can appear relatively expensive. Accommodation is not quite such a bargain, although this too is rarely prohibitively expensive and the situation is actually improving, especially in the larger cities. Serbia is rapidly emerging from a tradition of faceless hotels that were not required to compete against each other. Although bargains do exist, on the whole, many of the remaining state-run Serbian hotels can seem a little overpriced considering what they have to offer in terms of facilities and service. This situation is changing as more private hotels come on to the market, although these mostly tend to be in the middle or upper price bracket. Although accommodation costs will take up a large proportion of any daily budget, outside Belgrade it is usually perfectly possible to get by on less than €60 a day or less. Travelling with a partner or friend helps to keep the cost down, as double rooms tend to cost around 1½ times that of a single rather than double the price.

For some idea of costs, a meal with wine, depending on the exclusiveness of the establishment, will cost between 800din and 2,500din; an espresso coffee, 80–140din; a beer, 120–180din. A bus journey of 100km will cost about 450din, the equivalent train journey cheaper (and slower) at about 300din. Food bought at green markets – fruit, vegetables, dairy produce and meat – is generally very inexpensive for such high quality. For items like clothes and household goods, the many Chinese shops that are found around the country offer excellent value for money.

In cafés and run-of-the-mill restaurants, it is customary to round up the total rather than adding a percentage. In smarter establishments, 10% would be considered more than adequate. It is not necessary to tip taxi drivers although, naturally, any gratuity offered will be gladly accepted.

GETTING AROUND

BY BUS This is the most popular and practical means of getting around the country. There are services between most towns and, from Belgrade in particular, there are frequent departures to even far-flung parts of the country. Most towns of any size have a purpose-built bus station that will have left-luggage and snack facilities. Timetables of departures and arrivals are shown on large boards, usually in Cyrillic. Tickets can be bought in advance from booths inside the bus station and on some routes they can sell out quickly, particularly during public holidays. Buses that run between major centres like Belgrade, Novi Sad or Niš are so frequent that it is often unnecessary to buy a ticket in advance, although the caveat about holidays still applies. Buses are usually quite comfortable with reasonable legroom, and seat reservations are honoured, but additional standing passengers are often taken on board once a journey is in progress and some buses can become uncomfortably crowded and stiflingly hot in summer.

Many larger bus stations will sell you a *peronska karta* with your ticket – either a platform ticket or a token for a turnstile. This generally adds 30–70din to the total ticket price. It is also possible to buy a *peronska karta* only and then go through and choose your own bus, paying the driver or conductor. This will give you more flexibility on busy routes as, generally, the ticket counter will just sell you a ticket on the next bus available. Sometimes, particularly if the bus is due to leave, they just sell you a platform ticket anyway and let you sort it out on the bus.

In most of Serbia, especially the north, there is usually a small charge of around 40–70din to put your luggage in the storage compartment of the bus. The conductor or driver will do this for you and give you a ticket in exchange.

Contact details and information on regional bus companies is supplied in the relevant guide chapters.

BY TRAIN Trains are an alternative on some routes, although the Serbian railway network has deteriorated over the past two decades as a result of poor maintenance, lack of investment, management–trade union clashes and war damage. In 2006, Serbian Railways received a loan of €60 million from the European Bank for Reconstruction and Development but this was invested in freight traffic rather than improving passenger services.

In practical terms, trains are cheaper than the bus option but they are usually slower and more prone to breakdown. For comparison, while there are about 30 buses a day from Belgrade to Novi Sad, by train there is more limited choice of only nine services, although in this case the journey time is about the same as the bus. Between Belgrade and Niš there are 20 buses a day that take around 3 hours to make the journey compared with eight trains that take between 4 hours and 5½ hours. Serbian trains do come into their own on longer journeys, such as the overnight services to neighbouring capitals like Sofia or Bucharest, or the wonderfully scenic journey down to the coast at Bar in Montenegro. Sleepers should be booked as far in advance as possible.

Overall, trains are a good way to travel if you are not in any great hurry. The common perception is that Serbian trains generally leave on time but arrive at their destinations late. Certainly, they are a good way to meet people, especially on longer trips.

Information on train services can be gathered from Serbian Railways (*Železnice Srbije, Nemanjina 6, 11000 Belgrade;* \ *011 3602 899;* e *medijacentar@srbrail.rs;* w *serbianrailways.com*), or from individual railway stations. There is a useful online timetable at w srbvoz.rs/eng.

⋙ Belgrade \011 636 493, 641 488 (from 06.00 to 22.00), 011 629 400, 645 822 (24hr service), 011 688 722 (for car train & sleeping cars)

⋙ Niš \018 364 625, 369 786
⋙ Novi Sad \021 443 178
⋙ Subotica \024 555 606

BY CAR Rental cars are available in towns and cities throughout the country, although Belgrade and Novi Sad have the widest choice of agencies – see individual chapters for details. Driving is reasonably straightforward, and takes place on the right – mostly. Most main roads are in reasonable condition, although minor roads in the countryside can be in quite poor repair with pot-holes and loose stones. Because of the preponderance of blind corners and the occasional speed-crazed local, driving at night in rural areas can sometimes prove to be a nerve-racking experience that is probably best avoided.

In order to drive in Serbia you must have an international driver's licence and a Green Card (international insurance). The wearing of seat belts is compulsory and traffic police are keen to impose fines for failing to do this, as they are for any infringements of the speed limit. Foreign licence plates are more likely to attain the attention of traffic police who can be quite zealous in their work. Spot penalties for minor infractions are about 2,000din. The speed limit is 120km/h (75mph) on highways, 100km/h (62mph) on secondary roads and 60km/h (37mph) in built-up areas. For vehicles with a trailer the limit is 80km/h. There are many speed cameras and traffic police to check on this. The police have radar guns and use them enthusiastically to catch speeding drivers, especially at city limits. The maximum permissible amount of alcohol in the blood is 0.05% (0.5g/litre). Children under 12 (and adults 'affected by alcohol') are not permitted to sit in the front seat next to the driver. Foreign cars must bear the appropriate country designation sticker, which unfortunately will single it out for special attention from the police, and from petty thieves when it is parked. Petrol (gasoline) is fairly expensive at around 145din (€1.16) a litre for premium and unleaded, and 155din (€1.22) for diesel. Auto gas is also available at a limited number of outlets for around 80din per litre. Petrol stations along main roads and in cities are usually open 24 hours a day.

Road conditions vary throughout Serbia but are generally worse in the south of the country.

Road tolls are charged on the major trunk roads; foreign-registered cars pay a premium, about 2½ times more than nationals – see page 69 for details.

The **Automobile and Motorists Association of Serbia** (*AMSS; Ruzveltova 18, Zvezdara, 11000 Belgrade;* \ *011 3331 200;* e *info@amss.org.rs;* w *amss.org.rs*), forwards details on traffic information and road conditions on a daily basis to other European motor organisations, and the AMSS International Alarm and Information Centre at the same address can supply traffic information and other information on touring. For help on the road, dialling 1987 will summon the road assistance service of the AMSS. To summon the traffic police in the case of accident, dial 192.

BY BICYCLE Cycling in Serbia definitely offers great potential, particularly if main roads are avoided (see box opposite). Cycling in central Belgrade itself is not very enjoyable due to heavy traffic, cobbled streets, tramlines and unheeding drivers but even here there are places where leisure cycling is highly popular and where purpose-built tracks make it both safe and enjoyable – see the Belgrade chapter for details. Cycling across the country along the River Danube has become increasingly popular in recent years (see box, page 183), especially with cyclists from Germany.

Mountain biking While mountain biking is on the increase domestically, few foreign visitors come specifically to Serbia in pursuit of off-road trails. The most fruitful areas for mountain biking are probably the hill trails of Fruška Gora close to Novi Sad and the Tara National Park.

Fruška Gora has a long tradition of hiking and a wealth of well-marked trails. Trails vary from as short as 3.5km to the 103km-long 'Ultra Marathon'. For the past ten–15 years there has been a regular **mountain biking marathon** held here in May. These follow slight variations of the hiking marathon held the week before, with Small (31km), Medium (54km) and Big (81km – a killer!) marathons to choose from. The same well-marked trails can be ridden year-round of course. This is serious and demanding mountain biking, certainly not for the uninitiated, which involves a great deal of strenuous climbing and descending. Those looking for something less demanding might be better off sticking to the quiet tarmac roads that run along the ridge of the range and occasionally descend to the monasteries that punctuate the wooded hills here.

The **Tara National Park** is the only area in Serbia where trails have been specifically mapped out for mountain bikers (they serve for hikers too but were originally compiled by bikers). A map showing the various biking trails in this beautiful mountainous park can be obtained from Tara NP information centres.

Helpful mountain-biking websites include w freebiking.org (Serbian only), which has the useful **Freebiking Atlas** (w *freebiking.org/Atlas/atlas.html*) and w ciklonaut.com (Serbian only).

CITY TRANSPORT Local **bus** transport serves all urban areas throughout the country, with additional trolleybus and tram services operating in some of the larger towns and cities. There is usually a flat fare for any journey along a particular

Dutch biker Ivo Miesen, who cycled through Serbia from the Hungarian border to the Montenegrin coast, offers the following advice:

I started cycling just north of the Yugoslav–Hungarian border, in the town of Szeged. From Novi Sad to Smederevo I followed the Danube Valley, then diagonally through Serbia and Montenegro to the Durmitor Mountains; and from the Durmitor Mountains through the valley of the Žeta to Podgorica. With the benefit of hindsight, I would not take the Novi Sad–Belgrade main road again, and Belgrade is only to be cycled in when it's really necessary. It would have been better if I had gone directly south after crossing the border between Szeged and Subotica. Another option for those with less time would be to go south from Novi Sad and stick close to the Bosnian border.

I used a variety of maps. For planning, I used the Freytag & Berndt *Yugoslavia and Macedonia* map at 1:500,000. This map lacks detail. Slightly better is the *Serbija* map of the AMCC at 1:535,000. It gives a little more detail, and lots of altitude information in its colour schedules. This was the main map for my trip. The *Novi Sad & Vojvodina* map at 1:270,000 is hardly better than the AMCC map. All of the maps are unreliable and conflicting. Not all of the roads on the map exist; sometimes the information is outdated; sometimes roads not yet built are shown.

I used a standard touring bike, a Koga Miyata Alloy Randonneur. Being nine years old, and having suffered many blows, it was to be its last trip. For tyres, I used Swallow City Marathon 35-622 at the front and Michelin Tracer 32-622 at the back. As a spare, I took a Panaracer Tour Guard 32-622. The gearing was standard, with 28-38-50 front rings and a 12/28 seven-speed cassette. Both rear racks and lowriders were by Tubus, with two large Karrimor panniers at the rear and two Karrimor Universals (30l) at the front. A Karrimor barbag and a standard sports bag on top of the rear rack completed the luggage. Since the weather in April can be both mild and cold, I took full winter kit, as well as summer clothes. I also took a large duffel bag and a transport bag for my bike. The estimated combined weight of the bike and luggage was between 40kg and 45kg.

In the Danube Valley and the lower mountain ranges, I either camped wild or stayed with local friends. In the mountain ranges, the opportunities for wild camping were limited, as most flat land was already in use. Wild camping is not very well known among the local population, so it can be hard to get permission to camp on somebody's land.

Before I set out, I did not know what to expect. So I prepared for the worst, deliberately not taking anything with me that might arouse unnecessary interest. None of these precautions were needed. There were no safety issues resulting from the various wars in the region. Serbia was spared from ground war, so the danger of landmines is negligible. There might be stray bombs near some bombed sites, so don't dash through the undergrowth in those places. Traffic safety depends on the region. I regard the Novi Sad–Belgrade main road and the city of Belgrade as unsafe in regards to traffic. Elsewhere it's OK.

In mid-April the weather was a bit wet and cold. I guess that May/June and September/October would be the best months for the region.

Practical Information GETTING AROUND

2

route. Routes can be hard to decipher at times: often they are only given in Cyrillic, or they rely on obscure landmarks to denote the route that only a local would know. More often still, bus routes are not written down at all and exist only inside the minds of the driver and local passengers. It is always best to ask fellow passengers: state your preferred destination clearly and confirm this with the driver when you enter the vehicle. Depending on the size of the vehicle, you pay the driver on entry or, as is sometimes the case in articulated trolleybuses, you pay a conductor at a little counter in the rear part of the vehicle. Fares are invariably cheap.

Sometimes it is easier to take a **taxi**, which can be easily found in almost any Serbian town. Apart from the sharks that haunt the airport and railway stations in Belgrade, taxi drivers are usually honest and helpful, although you should always agree on a price at the outset if there is no obvious sign of a meter.

MAPS A useful map to have is the pocket-size *Autoatlas-Srbija i Crna Gora/Beograd* published by M@gic M@p, which contains a useful 1:880,000 Serbia–Montenegro map, good for route planning, together with a detailed city map at 1:20,000 and a gazetteer for both. The 1:500,000 Gizi Map of Serbia and Montenegro with an inset map of central Belgrade is a good overall map of the country, as is the Freytag & Berndt 1:500,000 map of Serbia, Montenegro and Macedonia.

The Planplus online road atlas (**w** *planplus.rs*) is an excellent resource for those with a laptop or smartphone.

ACCOMMODATION

The **hotel** situation in Serbia is similar to that of other eastern European countries surfacing from long years of indifferent state control. In the recent past, one of the main troubles with the Serbian hotel industry was the lack of choice outside the ubiquitous, mid-price, state-owned range. In the smaller towns there are usually just one or two of this type of hotel, with a few motels strung along the trunk roads to complement them. The situation is fast improving, however, especially in Belgrade and larger cities like Novi Sad and Niš, and in recent years quite a number of state-run properties have been taken into private ownership to be fully refurbished, or new luxury hotels have been built. In some cases though, especially in smaller towns, the old hotels have been closed down without anywhere to replace them and you need to look a little harder to find somewhere to stay.

Despite an encouraging improvement of late, some old-style Serbian hotels can still be characterised as large, concrete landmarks in which charm and personality have been sacrificed for size and space. With cavernous restaurants that serve institutional food, and dark bars that often have a men's-club atmosphere, they can seem more geared up to the needs of business conventions rather than individual travellers. But, on the plus side, they are always clean and, because they are invariably large, it is nearly always possible to find a room without a reservation, although singles can sometimes be elusive.

Prices vary, but can range from quite good value for money to seriously overpriced (for price codes, see inside front cover). Generally speaking, it is hard to find anywhere for less than €20 single or €30 double. A residence tax of around 130din a day applies to all hotel rates, which is sometimes, but not always, included in the price quoted. A television set nearly always comes as standard, even in the cheapest places, and these are usually wired for satellite or cable channels. Check-out time is usually at noon.

Breakfast is usually included, and will normally consist of a combination of bread, jam, ham and eggs – especially eggs. Although coffee or tea will be offered, this may well mean a tepid infusion of herbs or a milky beverage that contains only homeopathic quantities of coffee. If you hanker for something more familiar – a cappuccino, an espresso or a pot of English breakfast tea – then you will probably be charged extra. This, of course, applies just to some of the old-style state-run establishments: most of the new breed of hotels serve excellent breakfasts with a wide choice of things to eat.

The star system is only a rough indicator of quality, and in some cases can seem purely academic. There are even instances where single-star hotels outshine those bearing three. With four or five stars, things start to become more predictable – and far more expensive. A good rule of thumb, for state-run hotels at least, is to knock off a star to get some idea of the western European equivalent. Most motels in Serbia do not tend to use the star system at all.

Although the middle ground is generally well served, there tend to be few decent budget options or pensions for the more impecunious traveller other than the hostels that are now quite numerous in Belgrade, Novi Sad and Niš. Hopefully this will change in the future as more independently financed hotels are set up, and as more people offer private accommodation in their homes. For the time being, signs that offer SOBE – a room in a private house – are quite rare in Serbia, as the tradition has not yet caught on in the same way as it has on the Adriatic coast of Croatia or at resorts like Ohrid in Macedonia. The most likely places to find private *sobe* are resorts and destinations popular with holidaying Serbians like the Zlatibor region. **Village tourism** is a phenomenon that will probably become more popular in the next few years and private accommodation in towns and villages can sometimes be booked through the office of the local tourist organisation – those in Donji Milanovac, Knić and Zlatibor are particularly well geared-up for this. A useful list of households and contact advice can be found on the Visit Serbia website (w *visitserbia.org*) under the 'Village tourism' option.

At the time of writing, although some of Serbia's state hotels were undergoing restoration as a result of being taken into private ownership, quite a number seemed to be permanently closed awaiting potential buyers. This inevitably means that there will be both improved standards and increased prices in the future. A useful resource for finding hotels throughout Serbia is the accommodation search engine on the w serbia.travel site. The more international accommodation booking sites like w booking.com and w hotels.com are also a useful resource.

Outside Belgrade, Novi Sad and Niš, there are few **hostels** in Serbia that offer cheap, dormitory-style accommodation. The capital is a different matter, and over the past few years dozens of privately owned city-centre hostels have opened up to offer inexpensive beds to young travellers. City **apartments** have blossomed too, and sites like w booking.com have many of these on offer at prices comparable to those of hotel rooms in the larger cities. Official **campsites** in Serbia are relatively rare. Where they do exist they are usually places with cabins and caravans that have limited space for tents. They are generally open from May to October. Further information on camping in Serbia may be found at the website of the **Camping Association of Serbia** (*Makedonska 22/II, 11000 Belgrade;* ✆ *011 3240 406;* e *info@ camping.rs;* w *camping.rs*), which has details of all official Serbian campsites in English.

Wild camping is possible although not widely practised. It is best to be out of sight of a road and/or ask a landowner's permission to erect a tent.

EATING AND DRINKING

DINING OUT Serbian cuisine is similar to that of other Balkan countries, with a few specialities that it can claim for its own. The long Ottoman occupation clearly had some influence, especially in the wide range of grilled meats available. In fact, Serbs enjoy eating meat in as many ways as they can think of cooking it. This passion for animal flesh is reflected in a cuisine that, whilst both tasty and wholesome, can be daunting for vegetarians and health-food aficionados.

Although there are hints of the Mediterranean in the cooking, most Serbian food is on the heavy side with a tendency towards greasiness. This is not the whole picture, of course. While meat is enjoyed in quantity at every possible opportunity, so are fresh vegetables, and, in a country where fresh, unadulterated produce is still a fact of life – fertilisers and pesticides are rarely used – it is possible, with a little careful selection, to eat well whatever one's personal dietary tastes might be. If you are vegetarian then you will need to declare, '*Ja sam vegetarijanac*' if you are a man, or '*Ja sam vegetarijanka*' if female. It's probably better to be more specific and say, '*Ne jedem meso*' – 'I don't eat meat' – perhaps adding, '*Ne jedem pileće meso, ribu ni šunku*' – 'I don't eat chicken, fish or ham' – just to be on the safe side.

The problem with eating out in Serbia is often a matter of understanding exactly what is on offer, as menus are often written in Cyrillic and hard to decipher. There is also the phenomenon of overly optimistic menu-writing in which the items listed merely reflect the chef's familiarity with sophisticated cuisine rather than his ability or willingness to produce it.

A typical meal might consist of *kajmak* – a sort of salty, cream-cheese spread unique to Serbia – with bread to start, then a grilled meat like *ćevapčići* with a salad. Fresh fruit is as likely to conclude a meal as any sweet dish. While wine is often chosen to accompany a meal, something stronger like a glass or two of *šljivovica* might well precede it as a high-octane aperitif. For many Serbians, lunch (*ručak*) is the main meal of the day, followed by something a bit lighter for dinner (*večera*). Most restaurants in Serbia tend to be open between noon and 23.00, although opening (and closing) hours are not always slavishly adhered to.

As well as 'national food', foreign and international cuisine is also available in some of the larger towns and cities. Italian food is especially popular, as evidenced by the numerous pizza and pasta restaurants even in small towns throughout the country. More exotic cuisine like Indian, Mexican or Thai can generally be found only in Belgrade. So-called 'national food' is itself fairly variable and shows an undeniable Hungarian influence in Vojvodina in the north of the country.

For starter courses, smoked meats are a popular choice, with *dalmatinski pršut*, a lightly smoked ham, or *užički pršut*, a hard, smoked beef, frequently offered on menus. Another meat preserve, *pihtije*, a dish of jellied pork or duck with garlic, tastes much better than you might imagine. A dip that can be spread on bread in the same way as *kajmak* is *ajvar*, spiced peppers and aubergine, which are chopped and seasoned with vinegar, oil and garlic. Although there are proprietary brands of *ajvar* available, the very best is that which is produced in thousands of rural Serbian kitchens each autumn at the end of the pepper season.

For the main course, the most popular meat dishes are *pljeskavica* (meat patties, usually a mixture of pork, beef and lamb, sprinkled with spices, then grilled and served with onion), *ražnjići* (shish kebabs of pork or veal), *ćevapčići* (spiced minced meat kebabs), *leskovački čevapčići* (kebab with peppers), *mešano meso* (mixed grill), *karađorđeva snicla* ('Black George's schnitzel'), *medaljoni* (veal steak), *ćulbastija* (grilled veal or pork), *prasetina na ražnju* (spit-roast suckling pig), *jagnjetina na ražnju* (spit-roast lamb), *jagnjeće pečenje* (roast lamb), *kapama* (lamb stew), *kolenica* (leg of suckling pig) and *kobasice* (sausages). Other Serbian dishes combine meat with vegetables, as

in *sarma* (minced beef or pork mixed with rice and stuffed inside pickled cabbage leaves), *podvarak* (roast meat with sauerkraut), *punjene tikvice* (courgettes stuffed with meat and rice), *đuveč* (pork cutlets baked with spiced stewed peppers, courgettes, tomatoes and rice) and *punjene paprike* (peppers stuffed with minced meat and rice).

Accompaniments to the above might include a *šopska salata* (chopped tomatoes, onions and cucumber with grated white cheese), a *mešana salata* (mixed salad – rather variable) or a *srpska salata* (tomatoes, onions, peppers and parsley); alternatively, you might choose something cooked like *pečenje paprike* (roast peppers).

Fish (*riba*) dishes can be very good but generally are far more expensive, as fish has to be brought a considerable distance from the coast. There are some restaurants where you make your selection from specimens swimming around in a large tank, which introduces a personal touch to the proceedings that not everyone is comfortable with.

As well as seafood, freshwater fish are widely available too, and just as popular, especially *pastrmka* (trout) and *šaran* (carp). One tasty freshwater fish dish that appears on menus throughout the north of Serbia is *alaska čorba i riblji paprikaš*, a

DROP THE DONKEY CHEESE

In December 2012, a story emerged in the British media that tennis star Novak Đoković was intent on buying up the entire world supply of *pule* – donkey cheese – a Serbian speciality. The production of *pule*, as you might imagine, is not the most straightforward of processes and consequently the cheese, as well as being among the most unlikely, was also the world's most expensive. The story – reported in such heavyweight journals as the *Daily Telegraph* and the *Daily Mail* – suggested that he was keen to secure enough to supply a chain of restaurants he was opening up in Serbia. The cheese, produced by just a single supplier, a donkey farm in Zasavica, west Serbia, takes 25 litres of donkey milk to make a single kilogram and costs around €1,000 a kilo. The same farm offers equally expensive donkey milk baths to women with a Cleopatra fixation.

The story soon turned out to be not so much inaccurate as untrue: the Zasavica farm had merely left a sample with the manager of Đoković's father's restaurant in Belgrade; the rest was made up by journalists. Although it remains possible that *pule* may be sold in the Đoković restaurant chain sometime in the future – the Serbian star admits to being quite interested in the cheese – there is still plenty available for other cheese fanciers with money in their pockets.

fiery-red fish stew that incorporates vast quantities of paprika pepper. Traditionally, this is a festive dish prepared out of doors in large cauldrons over camp fires but it is also available as a standard menu item in many restaurants, especially in Vojvodina.

For dessert, if you still have room after battling through a typical Serbian culinary onslaught, there is usually a choice of seasonal fruit, along with less healthy options like *doboš torta*, a Hungarian-style cake, or *baklava*, a flaky pastry filled with nuts and oozing syrup. All you need now is a *Turska kafa*, another *šljivovica* and perhaps a good lie down.

SNACK FOOD Some of the tastiest food in Serbia is the snack food that is sold on the street and from bakeries. Apart from the ubiquitous *pljeskavica*, *senvić* and hamburger outlets, there are also many small hole-in-the-wall establishments that sell *burek* (cheese or meat pies, sometimes with apple to cut the grease a bit; with cheese is *burek sa sirom*, with meat, *burek sa mesom*; they are also made with

SERBIAN WINE ROUTES

Serbia has several distinct wine-producing regions, all of which are worth a visit for wine aficionados. Cellar visits and tastings may be organised through local tourist offices or directly by contacting the winery.

PALIĆ In the far north of Serbia close to Subotica, the moderate climate and sandy soils of this region are suitable for Italian and Rhine Riesling and Chardonnay white varieties as well as Muscats and Semillion. Red varieties include Merlot, Frankova, red Burgundy and Cabernet. There are several wine cellars close to Subotica/Palić that may be visited. These include **Čoka Winery** (*Segedinski 80, Subotica;* \024 546 555), established 1903, the **WOW Winery** (*Josipa Kolumba 33, Palić;* \024 603 001) and **Vinski Dvor** (*Horgoški put 221, Hajdukovo, Subotica;* \024 754 762; e *vinskidvor@ suonline.net;* w *vinskidvor.com*) producing Chardonnay, Riesling, Pinot Blanc and Kevdinka wines. Vinski Dvor also has two restaurants and its own 32-room hotel.

FRUŠKA GORA The slopes of the Fruška Gora in Srem are home to 60 wine cellars. The specialities here are sweet varieties like Bermet and Ausbruch and strong aromatic wines like Neoplanta as well as Riesling and Chardonnay. Sremski Karlovci has several cellars that may be visited, such as the **Živanović Cellar** (*Mitropolita Stratimirovića 86b;* \021 881 071; e *muzpcela@eunet.rs*) and **Dulka Cellar** (*Poštanska 8;* \021 881 797; e *dulka@eunet.rs;* w *dulka-vinarija.com*). Other wineries can be found at nearby villages like Irig, Neštin, Erdevik and Banoštor, where there is the **Vinarija Bononija** (*Svetozara Markovića 3;* \021 879 032; e *ims467414@eunet.rs*).

VRŠAC Also in Vojvodina, in the Banat region of the east, Vršac has an ancient tradition of viticulture that is said to go back to Dacian and Roman times and which was further developed under Austro-Hungarian rule. The German settlers that came to the region following the end of Ottoman rule brought Rhine grape varieties with them and villages like Gudurica close to Vršac became famous for their wine production. This is mostly a white grape region with native varieties that include Župljanka, Rkatsiteli and Kreaca as well as Rhine and Italian Riesling, Chardonnay and Pinot Blanc. Cellars to visit here include **Vršački Vinogradi** (*Svetosavski trg, Vršac;* \013 822 088; e *marketing@vvinogradi.co.rs;* w *vvinogradi.co.rs*).

potatoes, *krompiruša* – very heavy and filling – or with mushrooms, *pečurke*). *Burek*, which is of Turkish origin, is often eaten with yoghurt, and is more usually on sale in the mornings. Other popular snack choices are *gibanica* (a sort of cheese and egg pie baked with filo pastry), *zeljanica* (similar to *gibanica* but with chard leaves, rather like the Greek dish *spanakópita*), a mouth-watering, flaky sour cherry strudel called *pita sa višnjama* and sometimes a range of mini pizzas. All of these are cheap and delicious, and an excellent choice for breakfast or a snack; servings are generous, so they can be quite filling.

SWEETS AND PASTRIES Sweet tooths are well catered for in Serbia. Many *poslastičarnica* (confectioners) offer table service and fresh coffee, together with a tantalising selection of delicious cakes (*torta*) and pastries (*kolač*) to choose from: the strudels (*štrudla*) in particular, are to die (but not diet) for. *Štrudla sa jabukama* is apple strudel, and *štrudla sa višnjama* is filled with sour cherries. Ice cream (*sladoled*)

SMEDEREVO This winemaking region between the Danube and Velika Morava rivers is best known for its native white grape variety of Smederevka, which is often blended with Riesling, Semillion and white Burgundy. Red wines such as Gamay are also produced here. The **Mali Podrum Radovanović Cellar** (*Dositijeva 10, Krnjevo;* 026 821 085; e *podrumradovanovic@neobee.net;* w *podrumradovanovic. rs*) just outside Smederevo can accommodate groups of up to 50 for wine samplings.

NEGOTIN Winemaking is long-established in this eastern region, possibly going back as early as the 3rd century AD. With an ideal climate and sandy soils, this was once Serbia's biggest wine region and large quantities were exported from here to Austria, Germany, Russia and France. Native grape varieties from this region include the red Prokupac and Bagrina, which produces a gold-coloured white wine. The region is known for its unique *pimnice* (stone and wood wine cellars). The *pimnice* of the village of Rajac, constructed between the mid 18th century and the 1930s, were dug at least 2m deep into the ground to prevent temperature fluctuation. Of the 316 that once stood, only around 60 survive. The **Bogdanović Cellar** in Rajac village (019 422 867, 531 724) can accommodate up to 40 visitors.

ALEKSANDROVAC Aleksandrovac, surrounded by vineyards of the Župa wine region, just south of Serbia's central Šumadija region, is another 'wine capital'. The main varieties here are Tamjanika, a straw-yellow grape with a characteristic Muscat taste and smell, and Prokupac, a 1,000-year-old ruby-coloured cultivar that produces a distinctive red wine. Riesling grapes are also grown. One of the most important and long-established vineyards in this region is that of the **Ivanović Winery** (*18 Avgust 10, Aleksandrovac;* m *063 528 246;* e *kontakt@ivanovicvino.com;* w *ivanovicvino.com*), which has a large cellar at the family home in Aleksandrovac. Cellar tours can be arranged between 12.00 and 20.00 on weekdays and 12.00–17.00 on weekends.

Other wine regions in Serbia include **Oplenac**, just south of Belgrade, and **Knjaževac** in southeast Serbia.

is as popular as it is in Italy and is available in just as many flavours from numerous street-corner *poslastičarnica*. Another Serbian favourite is pancakes (*palačinke*); most towns have at least one dedicated *palačinkanica* that offers pancakes with a range of inventive sweet and savoury fillings. However, all of these calorific treats belong to imported central European or Italian traditions (Turkish in the case of *baklava*); the only dessert that is exclusively Serbian and does not owe anything to foreign cuisine is the luxury version of a country dish called *žito*, a kind of creamed wheat porridge that is flavoured with almonds, nuts and raisins and served with whipped cream.

HOT BEVERAGES Traditionally coffee means strong and thick Turkish coffee (*Turska kafa*), although many Serbs, like the Greeks, prefer to believe that they invented the drink themselves. Sugar is added at the beginning of the brew and so it is customary to specify the amount of sweetening that you require. If you do not specify then it will invariably come medium sweet (*sredina*), although with foreigners they quite often let you add your own to taste. The relative proximity to Italy has meant that most establishments now have espresso machines and so even a *kafana* in a small provincial town can usually conjure up a convincing *espresso* or *cappuccino*. It is probably best not to ask for an *americano* as this will just lead to confusion. As well as the real thing, instant coffee in the form of Nescafé is also available, although decaffeinated coffee, a concept not really understood in this part of the world, is hard to find. Tea (*čaj*) is also available but it is usually fairly weak and insipid. For tea with milk, ask for *sa mlekom*, with lemon, *sa limunom*. Speciality and herb teas are also popular and some city cafés have a good selection of these.

ALCOHOLIC DRINKS Most Serbian wines are drinkable and some are actually very good. The best are probably the white wines (*belo vino*) that come from the Sremski Karlovci region in Vojvodina, but Serbia has a range of wines that come from various grape-producing regions such as Vršac and Negotin. Some red wines (*crno vino*) also come from Montenegro. Wine can be bought in restaurants and cafés by the bottle, by the glass or in carafes of various sizes. In a supermarket, a bottle of decent domestic wine will cost something in the order of 200–600din; in a restaurant, maybe double this.

Serbians are proud of their wines but probably more enthusiastic about the range of alcoholic spirits they produce. Experimentation with these products can be something of an adventure. *Šljivovica* is a sort of brandy traditionally made from plums, but *rakija*, which is normally a spirit made from grapes, tends to be used as a generic term for any sort of strong liquor. *Konjak* is, as its name implies, cognac, and *lozovača*, another form of grape brandy. There are proprietary brands of all of these spirits available at low prices, as well as home-distilled versions of the same that range from palatably fruity to downright dangerous. For Serbian home brewers, there is a sort of unwritten kudos attached to distilling a spirit so high in alcohol content that it is better suited to paint removal purposes rather than as a refreshment offering for unsuspecting foreigners. An annual *šljivovica* festival takes place in the small town of Kolvinj near Novi Sad, which boasts a wide range of home-produced spirits made from various fruits and vegetables. Attend it at your peril.

At least beer (*pivo*), both draught and bottled, is always an alternative. The most popular domestic brand is Jelen, but MB, BIP (Beogradska Industrija Pivara), BG (Beogradsko Pivo), Weifert and Montenegrin Nikšićko are also widely available; Karlovačko brand is not recommended. German-style draught beer is also frequently on sale and often heavily advertised. Imported bottled beers like Amstel, Heineken, Slovenian Laško and Efes from Turkey, some of which – to my taste at least – seem inferior to many of the domestic brands on offer, are always more expensive, and their popularity seems to owe more to their being a trendy tipple than anything to do with flavour.

NON-ALCOHOLIC DRINKS Besides the usual Fanta, Sprite and Coca-Cola, a wide range of bottled fruit drinks are available, as well as the real thing in season. *Sok od pomorandže* is orange juice; *sok od jagode*, strawberry, and *sok od jabuka*, apple juice. Bitter lemon is also widely available and for my money far more thirst-quenching than the other carbonated drinks. Although tap water is generally safe to drink, mineral water (*mineralna voda*) is easy to find.

SHOPPING

Shops in Serbia are normally open 08.00–20.00 Monday to Friday, 08.00–15.00 on Saturdays and closed on Sundays. There is often a long lunch break from noon until mid afternoon. Grocery stores keep longer hours: usually 06.30–20.00 in the week, 06.30–18.00 on Saturdays and 07.00–11.00 on Sundays. Many supermarkets stay open longer than this, until late in the evening. It may come as a surprise to some that there is no lack of consumer goods, as supermarkets stock most of the items that you might expect to find at home.

The best place to buy souvenirs is, without a doubt, Belgrade. Leather goods, needlework and embroidered textiles are all good value. Lace can be a good deal too, especially when bought in the countryside; the quality is usually very good. Some food items, like smoked sausages and chocolates, are inexpensive and make good gifts, as do bottles of *šljivovica* or Vojvodina wine (although, of course, there is the perennial problem of carrying liquids in airplanes). For more traditional souvenirs like handicrafts, the best place to look is in one of the capital's souvenir emporiums (pages 139–40). Fans of naive art and folk pottery may wish to visit the villages where these are produced, such as Jagodina south of Belgrade, or Kovačica in the Banat. However, it is unlikely that the goods on sale will be that much cheaper, even at the point of origin.

ARTS AND ENTERTAINMENT

Belgrade is very much the cultural capital when it comes to the arts, although Novi Sad has a thriving scene too, particularly in music and theatre, as does Niš to a lesser extent. All manner of musical events – folk, rock, world music, jazz and classical – take place in the capital throughout the year, at a variety of venues that range from small clubs and theatres to the cavernous halls of the Sava Centar. In October each year the capital is host to BEMUS, a classical music festival, while the annual **Belgrade Guitar Arts Festival** that takes place in April (February in recent years) has attracted internationally famous names like John Williams in the past.

Belgrade is not always the centre of Serbia's musical universe, however: **EXIT**, the country's largest rock and pop event, which is held each July, actually takes place just outside Novi Sad, in the environs of the Petrovaradin fortress by the Danube. Not to be outdone by this, the city of Niš makes use of its Ottoman fortress as the location for **Nišomnia**, its own version of the same. Numerous folk-music events take place throughout the country in the summer months; most of these are small, local affairs, with the obvious exception being the massive, and very hectic, **Dragačevo Trumpet Festival** (or **Guča**) that is held in central Serbia in August.

2

Both Belgrade and Novi Sad have an enthusiastic **theatrical scene** that stages productions by both classical and contemporary writers. As for films, the latest Hollywood blockbusters hit the screens of the capital and Serbia's larger cities shortly after their release. Belgrade is very much the focus of Serbia's domestic **film industry** and the city plays host to **FEST**, a regionally important film festival, for ten days each February. The visual arts best represented in Belgrade, where, as well as occasional retrospectives by established artists, many exhibitions of new work are staged throughout the year.

Further details can be found in the appropriate chapters and an up-to-date list of cultural events is available at w serbia.travel.

PHOTOGRAPHY

Beware of unwittingly taking photographs of military installations. Also, photographing any obvious war damage does not always go down well with the authorities or with proud civilians.

Digital photographers should ensure that they have enough memory cards for their visit, or at least a laptop to download on to, but this is not a real problem as memory cards are available in the major towns and cities. More importantly, do not forget to bring an adaptor to recharge digital camera batteries.

MEDIA AND COMMUNICATIONS

NEWSPAPERS AND MAGAZINES Serbia's biggest-selling daily newspaper is *Večernje Novosti* (think British *Daily Mail*), closely followed by *Blic*. These Belgrade-based dailies are probably the most influential in the country, if not the most serious. *Kurir* is another tabloid that has a growing circulation thanks to its unashamed sensationalism. The oldest and probably most prestigious of the printed media is the 100-year-old *Politika*. This was the flagship of serious journalism before the collapse of communism, and later became a mouthpiece for Milošević's propaganda. After Milošević was ousted, the newspaper drew closer to Kostunica's opposition. Currently it is owned by the German WAZ group. Another well-regarded daily is *Danas*, a newspaper that began publication in 1997, only to be closed down for a short period by government decree a year after its launch. Since the Milošević era it has re-emerged as a left-leaning serious publication that eschews entertainment gossip and sensationalism. Perhaps because of this, its circulation is in decline.

All of the above newspapers are in Serbian only, although *Blic* does have an English-language digest on the web at w blic.rs. It is usually possible to find day-old copies of some of the international press like *The Times* or *NY Times International Edition*, and possibly French, Italian and German newspapers too, in the bookshops and postcard booths along Knez Mihailova in Belgrade.

A few English-language or bilingual publications have emerged in the past few years. *Belgrade Insight* (w belgradeinsight.com) is a fortnightly newspaper that focuses on Serbian news, culture and politics. *BelGuest* (w belguest.rs) is an excellent bilingual magazine for visitors to Belgrade, with beautifully illustrated features that cover the whole of Serbia along with Belgrade listings. It is published four times a year. *Welcome to Belgrade* magazine is also printed four times a year, is available from branches of the Tourist Organisation of Belgrade and consists mostly of listings. Another useful monthly magazine in Belgrade, along the lines of London's *Time Out*, is *Yellow Cab* (w yc.rs). It is mostly in Serbian, with a little English content, but has comprehensive up-to-date listings for events in the capital.

TELEVISION Serbia's state television network, RTS, was considered so powerful during the Milošević years that its headquarters became a target for NATO bombers in the 'war of propaganda', an action that was subsequently condemned by Amnesty International as a war crime. For some years following the Milošević period RTS held a smaller share of the media than before, with the independent RTV Pink being placed as the most popular television channel. In response, RTS launched a digital channel in 2008 following the investment of millions of euros in new technology. RTS digital was in place in time for Belgrade's 2008 Eurovision Song Contest that subsequently became the most-watched television event ever broadcast in Serbia with an audience of over 4½ million.

RTV Pink, which has since been demoted to second place in Serbian broadcasting, used to be characterised by brash and noisy programming that favoured loud music, scantily clad dancers and vapid soap operas. It was through RTV Pink that turbo-folk first came to the attention of the Serbian public, pumped out as a glitzy patriotic sop to the masses during the troubled years of sanctions, civil war and isolation. These days it is somewhat tamer, with chat shows, reality television, the latest Hollywood blockbusters and even *The Simpsons* on its schedules.

RTV Pink has, at times, strayed beyond the boundaries of good taste to broadcast content that could by any standards be considered offensive. It has been accused of promoting a culture of stereotypes and intolerance, continuing the tradition it began while maintaining the previous regime by offering a false image of reality and Serbian society. In 2003, RTV Pink broadcasted a prime-time 'entertainment' show called *It Cannot Hurt*, which promoted a very misogynistic outlook in which women were depicted as being little more than sex objects, with constant reference being made to the necessity for their being submissive to men. Following these broadcasts, a law suit was filed on 20 November 2003 to the Second District Court in Belgrade signed by 55 women NGOs and other individuals. This was the first court proceeding to be filed according to a new law on public information, which sanctions hate speech in article No 38. Shortly after, on 10 December, the International Day of Human Rights, posters appeared around Belgrade declaring, 'Yes it hurts, because violence starts with insults.'

Controversial broadcasting is sometimes less a case of political correctness and more a matter of copyright. In 2004, one independent television channel, Enigma, found itself in trouble with the authorities when it broadcast a pirated version of *The Lord of the Rings: The Two Towers* just weeks after its European premiere. What was truly scandalous was the poor quality of the tape: it had been videotaped directly from a cinema screen.

In contrast to the chauvinism and old-regime leanings of some of the other independents, TV B92 is an independent television station that grew out of a radio station, B2-92, which was very critical of the old regime. Although it does not have anything like the market share of RTV or Pink TV, B92 wields a disproportionate amount of influence thanks to its perceived integrity and the international respect it earned for its anti-Milošević stance during the late 1990s (see box, page 90). In 2006, TV B92 increased its ratings dramatically by hosting the Serbian version of *Big Brother* (*Veliki Brat*), although this move towards commercialisation was heavily criticised by its old faithful. It also has the licence for the Serbian market for Formula 1 and UEFA Champions League football. B92 launched a 24-hour news cable network in 2008.

Other Serbian television channels include Prva, TV Košava, Happy TV (for children) and TV Avala. TV Košava, a broadcasting company that takes its name from the characteristic autumn and winter wind of the region, and which was formerly in the ownership of Milošević's daughter Marija, is not to be confused with TV Kosova,

Practical Information **MEDIA AND COMMUNICATIONS**

2

Radio B92 started life in May 1989 as a temporary student radio station. It was not long before it made an impact with its unusual mix of music and independent news reporting. Over the next few years B92 was shut down four times by the authorities for its role in the opposition movement. The first time was in 1991 when B92 disc jockeys encouraged people out on to the streets to take part in demonstrations against Milošević's regime. In 1993, they joined forces with seven other Serbian stations to form the Association of Independent Electronic Media (ANEM). By 1996, when even larger anti-Milošević demonstrations were hitting the streets, B92 had expanded beyond radio programmes to publishing and CD production, had launched Belgrade's first internet service provider, Opennet, and had even set up its own cultural centre, Cinema Rex. B92 was closed for the second time in December 1996, which prompted it to switch its news bulletins to its website. Because of its high profile, it was allowed to broadcast again after only two days, the result of much national and international pressure.

In April 1999, extensive NATO air raids on Serbia resulted in a massive clampdown from a government that would brook no dissent. B92's name and broadcasting frequency, together with its premises, were hijacked by the regime. In order to disseminate information about the domestic situation in Serbia to the world at large it was necessary to put full reliance on the internet, which allowed B92 journalists to tell the truth as they saw it, without the mask of state censorship, but with the fear that all independent journalists felt in the face of the state-sanctioned violence against them. Soon the website was attracting over one million hits a day.

The radio station was back on the air in August 1999, this time as B2-92, using a borrowed frequency and premises. They branched out briefly into television production before being closed for the fourth and final time in May 2000. This was the signal that drove them firmly underground and a guerrilla-like existence of secret premises that changed almost daily. Radio and television productions were sent to other ANEM members around the country by way of satellite, and radio stations just over the border in Bosnia and Romania were used for transmissions.

Instead of folding under pressure, B92 diversified even further, promoting two concert tours around Serbia that encouraged voting in the forthcoming autumn elections. The resulting turnout led to a victory for the democratic parties, widespread anti-regime protests and the long-awaited downfall of Milošević on 5 October of that year. On that same momentous day, B92 TV started broadcasting for the first time alongside its sister radio station.

With the return of democracy B92 continues to play a key role in ANEM, which now has a total of 58 radio and 37 television stations across Serbia, Montenegro and Kosovo. One of ANEM's bravest initiatives is to launch the Truth, Responsibility and Reconciliation project, which aims to acknowledge and lay open the horrors of the previous decade by means of television and radio programmes and international conferences, and to move Serbia forward into a new era of peace, tolerance and cultural richness.

For a more detailed history of B92 and its role during the Milošević period, consult Matthew Collin's book, *This is Serbia Calling: Rock 'n' Roll Radio and Belgrade's Underground Resistance* (Serpent's Tail, 2001).

an Albanian-language channel that is owned by the German Bertelsmann group. Each region of the country also has its own local channel; Vojvodina has two – RTV1 and RTV2. Serbia also has a large number of cable-television companies, and high-definition television was launched in 2009 with the RTS HD channel, which has been available throughout the country since 2012.

RADIO There are over 1,000 private radio stations throughout Serbia, a number that is probably way beyond the optimum for a relatively small country. As well as the two stations on state-run RTS Radio, prominent broadcasters are:

Art Radio On FM 88MHz
Radio 021 From Novi Sad on 92.2MHz
Radio B92 With live news radio on Real Audio & MP3 on FM 92.5MHz

Radio Barajevo On FM 105.9MHz
Radio Index From Belgrade on 88.9MHz
Radio Jat On FM 90.2MHz

INTERNET With broadband now widely available, and most hotels and many cafés offering free Wi-Fi these days, internet cafés are now mostly unnecessary and consequently hard to find.

Internet addresses It is worth noting that since 2010, virtually all Serbian internet addresses have changed their country suffix from *.co.yu* to *.co.rs* or *.rs*. The web addresses in this edition have been updated accordingly.

Internet news and information sources
ANEM w anem.rs
B92 w b92.net
Balkananalysis.com w balkanalysis.com
BalkanInsight.com w balkaninsight.com
BETA w beta.rs
Institute for War & Peace Reporting w iwpr.net
Tanjug w tanjug.rs

Internet providers
BeoTelNet w beotel.rs
BitsYUNet w bits.rs
EUnet w eunet.rs
InfoSky w infosky.net
MTS w mts.rs
Nadlanu w nadlanu.com
Orion w oriontelekom.rs
PostaNet w postanet.rs
VeratNet w verat.net

TELEPHONES Halo telephone cards can be bought from post offices and kiosks. They work in the more modern Orange phones, which have an 'i' button that can be pressed to change foreign-language settings. Calls can also be made directly from post offices, where you are directed to a booth and pay for the call when you have finished. The code for dialling abroad from Serbia is 00; you then dial the country code then the city and the recipient's number. To phone Serbia from abroad, you must first dial the international access code (which is usually 00), then 381 for Serbia; then you dial the city code (11 in the case of Belgrade) and the number. **International calls** can be made from Orange kiosks using a telephone card, or from telephone centres at post offices, which are usually open until fairly late at night. Making international calls from hotels is invariably very expensive and best avoided.

Mobile-phone users with roaming contracts and dual-, tri- or quad-band phones can use their phones throughout Serbia. This can prove expensive and so if you need to make a lot of local calls it is a good idea to purchase a local SIM card for your mobile phone. These can be bought at many city outlets. All mobile-phone numbers in Serbia begin with 06 (commonly 063 for Telenor, 064 for MTS; recently Telenor have also added 062, and MTS, 065; VIP Mobile numbers begin with 060 and 061).

2

City codes
Belgrade ☏(0)11
Novi Sad ☏(0)21
Niš ☏(0)18

Important phone numbers
Police ☏192
Fire Department ☏193
Ambulance ☏194

Serbian online telephone book
w yellowpages.rs
w 11811.rs

POST Post offices are open 08.00–20.00 weekdays, 08.00–15.00 Saturdays. In Belgrade, some may be open on Sundays. The cost of sending a postcard to elsewhere in Europe is 40din. Letters cost 70din for up to 20g and then the tariff increases to 170din up to 100g. Post from Serbia to the United Kingdom takes between five days and a week. All of the major express courier companies like DHL and FedEx have offices in Belgrade.

The basic ZIP code for Belgrade is 11000. For a list of mail couriers in Belgrade, see page 143.

BUSINESS

Many Serbian entrepreneurs are keen to develop business links overseas, especially with western Europe. After years of feeling that they were out in the cold, there is a begrudging confidence that things might finally be moving forwards economically and that burgeoning Serbian business interests will have a chance to play in the international field. It has not been easy: whereas most eastern European countries have experienced teething pangs in converting a communist state monopoly to a free-market economy, Serbia has had civil war and economic sanctions to deal with as well. There are still vestiges of the old way of doing things and, despite ongoing privatisation, a lingering feeling that good service is not a commodity in itself. But this is changing rapidly, as state ownership of many enterprises is privatised and foreign companies start to move in. While it would be foolhardy to claim that the business climate of the 1990s, where corruption and nepotism counted for more than business skills and hard work, has changed completely, by and large, doing business in Serbia today is little different from anywhere else in eastern Europe. Serbian entrepreneurs like to take their time, and to impress: business in Serbia is often conducted over a large shared meal or, more likely, after it; inevitably, the host will pick up the bill.

- The Serbian Chamber of Commerce and Industry has lots of useful advice for businesses wishing to invest in Serbia at w pks.rs.
- Information on facts and figures, regional data, and rules and regulations that affect businesses in Serbia are available at w invest-in-serbia.com.

CULTURAL ETIQUETTE

Perhaps it should go without saying that any discussion of politics in Serbia may well invite argument from some quarter. Anything regarding Kosovo, in particular, is a very tricky topic. Opinion is frequently divided in Serbian politics, but rarely are the arguments in clear-cut opposition. Rather, there are many grey areas, and to disapprove of the past Milošević regime is not the same thing as condoning the NATO bombing. This is not to say that discussions of politics should be avoided

– that would be impossible anywhere in the Balkans – but simply that it is best to have an open mind and listen, and to offer opinions only when they are asked for. Serbians are only too aware of the problems facing their country, and do not take warmly to foreign smart alecs who claim to know all the answers. The same might be said of conversations about Serbian football teams too.

Serbians take a pride in their reputation for hospitality and will defend it to a fault. When paying the bill in a restaurant it is customary for the host to pay the whole bill. This is done regardless of the host's financial standing, and in most circumstances foreigner visitors are automatically considered to be guests. Often the bill is paid surreptitiously to avoid protest. The idea of breaking a bill down so individuals can pay for their own share of food and drink is unheard of. Similarly, if you are invited to have something to eat or drink, even if it is just a cup of coffee, it is always best to accept graciously. To refuse something proffered in this way can cause offence as it may give the impression that you are behaving in a haughty manner.

Eating and drinking is a serious business in Serbia, as is the conversation and toasting that punctuates a meal. When sharing a toast with someone it is imperative that you look into their eyes as you do this. To avoid eye contact is considered disrespectful or, at best, weak.

Dress should be conservative and respectful when visiting churches, monasteries or mosques; no shorts, short skirts or flip-flops.

GAY SERBIA Homosexuality is tolerated, officially at least, but open displays of same-sex affection could well provoke a hostile reaction. The gay scene in Belgrade is extremely discreet, to say the least – so discreet that there is hardly any visible 'scene' at all. This is hardly surprising: as elsewhere in the Balkans, the general attitude is fairly unenlightened, with many viewing homosexuality as distinctly un-Serbian and a form of aberrant behaviour that is imported from the West. Such social pressures oblige most gays and lesbians in Serbia to lead a double life but thankfully things are starting to change slowly.

A Gay and Lesbian Pride march in 2001 ended in bloodshed when crowds of skinheads, nationalists and members of Obraz, an Orthodox religious group, attacked lesbians and gay men taking part in the march. The police were criticised for appearing to stand by and let it happen. The attack was subsequently condemned by Amnesty International as a human rights violation. Similarly, another march planned in 2003 had to be called off for fear of attacks. In September 2009, further plans for a Gay Pride march had to be abandoned when the police authorities refused to guarantee the safety of the participants, telling the organisers that they must move the march from the city centre. The Pride 2009 organisers subsequently filed a complaint in the Constitutional Court but the ban on the march was regarded with glee by nationalist and right-wing elements who said it was a defeat for 'Satanists' and 'infidels'. Perhaps disingenuously, Belgrade Pride organisers had also called on the Serbian Orthodox Church for support: their response was that they could not be seen to encourage the event, labelling it a 'shame parade of Sodom and Gomorrah'. A Pride march went ahead in Belgrade 2010 but, predictably perhaps, this was attacked by right-wing groups and subsequent clashes with police left more than 100 injured. As a result, the event was banned in 2011. The going-ahead of the planned 2012 Pride March was seen by some as a test of Serbia's pledge to respect human rights regarding its eventual European Union membership. However, this march was also banned, ostensibly over security concerns, although there was undoubtedly pressure from Serbia's Orthodox Church too. The ban was criticised by Thorbjoern Jagland, Secretary General of the Council of Europe, who expressed surprise and disappointment that the march had been banned yet again, declaring, 'Serbia should be in a position to safeguard such an event, which is commonplace in modern democracies.'

In 2014, the planned Gay Pride march finally went ahead after its four-year hiatus. Compared with the violence that marred former marches this went off peacefully, although in truth there were five times more police in attendance than actual participants. Local media streamed the event live, a handful of ministers and the Belgrade mayor joined the march in solidarity, and the Albania building was lit up in rainbow lights to celebrate the event – marked progress had clearly been made. Marches in the following years continued to take place peacefully, albeit with a large protective police presence.

Useful websites
w **gay-serbia.com**
w **belgrade-gay.com**

INTERACTING WITH LOCAL PEOPLE

Many of Serbia's younger generation speak and understand English, but a few words of Serbian will always be well received. Older people may speak German or French instead. Indeed, in poorer parts of the country like southern Serbia, German speakers are quite plentiful as so many of them worked abroad as *Gastarbeiter* (guest workers) when they were younger. Away from the cities it may be harder to find people who share a common language but with hand gestures, patience and a dictionary or phrasebook, it is always possible to communicate at least on a rudimentary level.

If you are staying with a Serbian host, any offers of cash will probably be swept aside, but small gifts of a non-monetary nature will be gladly accepted. Suitable gifts might be books, flowers, foreign magazines or clothing items like T-shirts with foreign logos. Business cards, family photographs and postcards of home are always appreciated.

Although they will probably just expect you, as a foreigner, to shake hands, most Serbians will be impressed if you adopt their custom of planting three kisses on alternating cheeks, a practice that takes place both between men and between women. However, this is a custom that takes place mainly between family members and close friends and so it may be best to let them initiate you into this to spare any potential embarrassment. The number three is of great significance to Serbs. One Serbian expression goes, 'God helps three times', and even the national tourist organisation has used 'Three times love' as their slogan in the past.

Nicotine and caffeine are the twin fuels of Serbian youth culture, with alcohol sitting firmly in third place. In Serbia, tobacco smoking is less of a habit and more a way of life, as is the frequent consumption of strong coffee. Non-smokers will just have to grin and bear it, although the situation is slowly improving.

TRAVELLING POSITIVELY

Several charities work in Serbia doing their best to alleviate the suffering of refugees and displaced people. Serbia's Roma community, given the straitened circumstances in which they often find themselves, are frequently targeted as being an especially deserving cause. **Save the Children UK** (*1 St John's Lane, London EC1M 4AR;* \ *+44 (0)20 7012 6400;* w *savethechildren.org.uk*) has been active in Serbia since 1993.

Trish MacCurrach

We fell in love with our village because of the horses. Rush hour is the sound of horses and carts clattering off to the fields and back again in the evening. The streets are lined with mulberry trees, the elders sit on shady benches in the evening air discussing the news. We have a village swimming pool and a lake, which at the right times of the year is full of migrating birds. Gliding through the reeds in our canoe, listening to the bitterns booming, fully compensates for any minor difficulties of choosing such an unlikely place for our holiday home.

Buying a village house in Serbia is not difficult. It requires perseverance and patience and if you find the right person to help you they will lead you like a child through the procedure quite painlessly. There are many village houses to choose from at very reasonable prices and you could have the privilege of being the only foreigner in the community. First, find your house. Older village houses in northern Serbia come in different sizes but similar styles. Most will have an orchard and a small farmyard, well and long drop. It quite possibly won't have inside facilities for bathing or cooking.

You will need a good translator who knows her/his way round the bureaucracy, a solicitor and lots of patience. The buyer does a lot of the running around, doing searches, registering things and endlessly waiting for stamps from different departments. Lots of coffee and passive smoking got us through it. When we had agreed our price, drunk a toast in *rakija* and shaken on it, our seller went directly on to the internet to print off a contract. We all signed it and then we took it to our solicitor who changed it 'just a little'.

As soon as you arrive at your new home, the word will get out and workmen will be queuing to offer their services as plumbers, carpenters and sellers of rat poison. We were fortunate to have a friend who became our master of works. He visited the project most days during the renovation period. Don't expect things to work in the way you are used to. Getting a quote for anything is difficult, there is a habit of saving money so door handles and lavatory parts, eg: small but vital gadgets, quickly break. Styles, materials and methods are different, lots to watch out for and things to learn. What your plumber thinks is a beautiful bathroom may not be quite what you had in mind.

Don't be daunted. Serbian communities are hospitable and friendly. The culture is rich in music, history and art. The soil is deep and the food is wonderfully rustic, yet everything is available if you want something unusual. The language is a killer but poetic and enormously satisfying when you find you can make yourself understood.

Formerly they were most active in emergency aid and rehabilitation work but since 2003 have focused mainly on development activities, most notably in working with local Roma NGOs to improve educational achievement for Roma children. **SOS Children's Villages** (*SOS-Kinderdorf International, Representative Office Kraljevo, Prvomajska 46a, 36103 Kraljevo, Serbia;* +381 (0)11 344 722; e *office@sos-kraljevo. org;* w *soschildrensvillages.org.uk*) works in Novi Sad and Kraljevo supporting disadvantaged children by running creative free-time activities, while **Care International UK** (*9th floor, 89 Albert Embankment, London SE1 7TP;* +44 (0)20 7091 6000; e *info@careinternational.org;* w *careinternational.org.uk*) works in Serbia to prevent human trafficking and support peace-building activities.

In contrast to the above charities, the US-based **BLAGO Fund** (e *info@srpskoblago.org*; w *srpskoblago.org*) concerns itself primarily with Serbia's cultural heritage, especially its Orthodox churches and monasteries. The BLAGO Fund state that their mission is to preserve and promote Serbian treasures that tie together past, present and future. One of their current projects is to save the frescoes of Mileševa Monastery, which are in urgent need of conservation. They receive considerable patronage from the Serbian Orthodox Church and the Serbian diaspora overseas, particularly in the United States. Donations can be made to BLAGO Fund Inc, PO Box 60245, Palo Alto, CA 94306, USA, or paid by credit card using PayPal online.

Those who would prefer to help Serbian birdlife might be interested in the activities of the **Bird Study and Protection Society of Serbia** (☎ *+381 (0)21 6318 343*; e *sekretar@pticesrbije.rs*; w *pticesrbije.rs*), which was established in 1989 and is an active and committed organisation that carefully maintains a network of active members throughout the country, focusing on bird and habitat conservation and on increasing knowledge about birds in Serbia. More information can be found on their website (see also page 6).

OTHER PRACTICALITIES

Serbia is 1 hour ahead of GMT and, in spring, adds an hour on for summer time, the same as the UK. **Public toilets** are uncommon but may be found at markets and bus or train stations; the facilities in cafés or restaurants are usually a much better bet. There is usually a small charge made for the privilege but this does not guarantee cleanliness. Men's and women's facilities are often marked in Cyrillic, with М, МУШКИ, Muški for men, and Ж, ЖЕНСКИ, or Ž, Ženski for women. **Electrical power** is 220 volts, 50Hz. Plug sockets are the standard European two-prong, round-pin type. Power cuts are rare these days.

Part Two

THE GUIDE

3

Belgrade Београд

Telephone code 011

The first thing anyone will tell you about Serbia's capital is that it does not live up to its name – Belgrade, or Beograd (the 'White City'), is anything but white. Rather, it is mostly a utilitarian grey, the colour of concrete, which looks its dreary worst under a leaden, winter sky and only marginally more cheerful in spring sunshine. This stereotypical Eastern-bloc greyness is deceptive though, because although the grim monoliths of New Belgrade's high-rises and the Roma shanty town that clings haphazardly alongside the railway tracks do their best to dispirit the first-time visitor, the city has far more to offer than these initial impressions might suggest.

For a start, there is Belgrade Fortress perched high above the town, overlooking the confluence of the Sava and Danube rivers. The 18th-century fortress is impressive enough but it is Kalemegdan Park, the ample green space of parkland and gardens that surrounds the fortress, which holds most year-round appeal for Belgrade's citizens. The view from Kalemegdan Park gives a clue to the way the city's history has unfolded by virtue of its geographical position. Belgrade's singular geography has been both a blessing and a curse; its strategic vantage point at the confluence of two great rivers and its position as a sort of crossroads between northern and southern Europe have led to it being attacked, sacked, plundered and bombed numerous times during its long history – at least 20 times in fact. The city lies at a political and cultural tectonic boundary, at a point where, historically, civilisations, cultures and religions have collided and clashed for over a millennium with furious upheavals: Christianity and Islam; Austro-Hungarians and Turks; the Catholic and Orthodox schism; the westward-looking Croats and eastward-facing Serbs; communism and free markets. Even today, Belgraders who live in Novi Beograd (New Belgrade) or Zemun joke about some fellow citizens across the water being 'Turks', as if the city is still divided by some invisible cultural fault line.

Nudging the park to the south and east is Stari Grad, the Old City, with its cathedral, secessionist buildings and a few, and now sadly rare, Ottoman remnants. Running through the elegant streets that lead down to the city's more prosaic commercial centre is pedestrianised Knez Mihailova (alternatively called Kneza Mihaila) – a constant stream of humanity, particularly in the evening when Belgrade's younger citizens take their place in the Balkan equivalent of the *korso*, the southeast European evening promenade.

Such is the cosy and intimate scale of this older part of Belgrade that it is only when you reach the splendid Art Nouveau edifice of the Hotel Moscow on busy, traffic-laden Terazije at the bottom end of Knez Mihailova, having passed Trg Republike (Republic Square) and Studentski trg (Students' Square) along the way, are you reminded that you are in a large capital city; a city that has, perhaps inevitably given its recent history, become a little battered and careworn in places. However, those expecting to find a bomb-damaged, war-ravaged city on its uppers may be disappointed – despite the extensive damage done by the NATO bombing of 1999, little physical evidence remains of this today. Similarly, the mood on the streets is upbeat. To those in the know, Belgrade is party city; a calm, dignified party that shows style, finesse and an undeniable *joie de vivre*.

In recent years Belgrade has shifted considerably from its stereotyped image of Eastern-bloc greyness. Proposed new developments along the waterfront in Savamala, still in the planning stage at the time of writing, look set to show a far more modern and dynamic face of the city to the world. With new ultra-modern high-rise buildings and dramatical redevelopment, Belgrade should certainly look very different when seen from confluence of the Sava and Danube rivers in a few years time. How such a project will influence developments in the rest of the city remains to be seen. What is certain is that – whatever happens – the city's soul should remain intact. Nevertheless, some might argue that it is the juxtaposition of a unique natural setting coupled with the thick patina of history that is displayed in the well-worn and occasionally down-at-heel face that Belgrade shows to the world are precisely that which give the city its unique character.

HISTORY

The first evidence of settlement comes from Zemun, across the Danube from Old Belgrade. At Zemun, formerly a separate town but now effectively a Belgrade suburb, archaeological evidence has been found to suggest that the banks of the Danube were first settled here about 7,000 years ago. The Celts were the first to colonise the opposite bank, on a bluff overlooking the confluence of the Danube and Sava rivers, founding the settlement of Singidunum in the 3rd century BC. The next to come were the Romans, who arrived in the 1st century AD and remained for the best part of the next 400 years. With their typical flair for disciplined road-building, the Romans provided the route and some of the foundations for present-day Knez Mihailova, Belgrade's first and, in the hearts of its citizenry at least, still most important thoroughfare.

Huns, Goths and Avars took turns at occupying the city before the Serbs arrived to make Belgrade their capital in 1403, having fled their southern territories after a momentous defeat at the hands of the Turks at the Battle of Kosovo in 1389. The Serbian occupation continued for the next century or so until the ever-advancing Ottomans captured the city from the Hungarians in 1521, in whose hands it remained until 1842 when a final Turkish withdrawal allowed it to become the capital of a newly liberated Serbia. Later, as the first of several regional federations was formed, Belgrade became the capital of the short-lived Kingdom of Serbs, Croats and Slovenes created at the end of World War I. With the establishment of the larger, and far more ambitious, federation of Tito's socialist Yugoslavia at the end of World War II, it was only natural that Belgrade should become the new capital. Even as late as the end of World War II Belgrade was still a relatively small country town, and a great deal of that which remains is, in fact, a pragmatic, if not always aesthetically pleasing, response to the appalling devastation unleashed by Nazi bombers during 1941. Much of what you see today is the result of this post-war reconstruction: a very necessary response to the widespread homelessness and migration to the city in the years that followed the creation of the new socialist state.

GETTING THERE AND AWAY

BY AIR Belgrade's Nikola Tesla Airport (*code: BEG; for flight information,* ☎ *2094 444, for general information,* ☎ *2094 000;* w *beg.aero*) lies 20km west of the city. After passing through immigration you enter the arrivals hall that has money exchange, several ATMs and a tourist information counter. Waiting for you both inside the arrivals hall and outside in the car park will be any number of taxi drivers, all delighted to be of service. However, it is probably best not to entrust any of these freelance knights of the road with the responsibility of taking you into town as the taxi syndicate that operates out of the airport is something of a racket and, like many other airport-based operations the world over, it serves as a poor ambassador for the profession. Taxis are fairly priced in Belgrade, even cheap; but not here. The airport taxi drivers may conjure a price of anything up to €40 to go into town, depending on how malleable you appear to be; the real cost should be something more like €15–20 for the 30-minute journey. Better then, to walk straight past them and catch either city bus 72, which leaves every 20–30 minutes from outside the main terminal building and terminates at Zeleni venac close to Terazije and Knez Mihailova [114 D7], or the A1 minibus that departs every 20 minutes from 07.00 to 19.00, with later services at 19.30 and 20.30, which will take you to Hotel Slavija at Trg Slavija downtown [103 E5], stopping in Novi Beograd and the railway station [102 D4] (probably the most useful stop for most of Belgrade's hotels) along the way. The city bus costs just 150din, the A1 minibus, 300din. If you have too much luggage to consider this, and really do require a taxi, then you can get the tourist information counter at the arrivals hall to organise a legitimate one for you. These have set fares to different zones of the city and from the airport to Stari Grad should be around €18.

Getting a taxi to take you from the city centre to the airport for a fair price is far easier. Once again, you could take the minibus that leaves hourly from Trg Slavija in front of the Hotel Slavija at 03.20 and then every 20 minutes from 06.20 until mid evening. The airport's departures lounge possesses all of the services that you might expect and a last chance to buy a souvenir bottle of *šljivovica* or that essential *Best of Ceca* CD. Happily, the 'No Smoking' signs plastered all over the airport terminal's walls are finally starting to be taken seriously.

Airline offices

✈ **Aegean** [114 D5] Knez Mihailova 30/IV; ☏3284 781

✈ **Aeroflot** [114 D5] Knez Mihailova 30/III; ☏3286 071

✈ **Air Serbia** [102 A4] Bulevar Umetnosti, New Belgrade; ☏3112 123

✈ **Alitalia** [114 D5] Knez Mihailova 30/II; ☏3245 000

✈ **Austrian Airlines** [103 E4] Terazije 3/III; ☏3248 077

✈ **Belavia** [114 D5] Knez Mihailova 30; ☏2185 616

✈ **easyJet** Nikola Tesla Airport Terminal 2; ☏2094 863

✈ **Emirates** [102 A5] Jurija Gagarina 12, New Belgrade; ☏0800 190 561

✈ **flydubai** [114 D5] Knez Mihailova 30/III; ☏3282 271

✈ **Lot** [114 C6] Topličin venac 19-21; ☏2028 047

✈ **Lufthansa** [103 E4] Terazije 3/VII; ☏3034 944

✈ **Montenegro Airways** [114 D6] Knez Mihailova 23/I; ☏2621 122

✈ **Norwegian** Nikola Tesla Airport Terminal 2; ☏2094 863

✈ **Pegasus** Nikola Tesla Airport Terminal 2; ☏2286 400

✈ **Qatar** [114 D5] Knez Mihailova 30/III; ☏7859 007

✈ **Swiss** [103 E4] Terazije 3/III; ☏3030 140

✈ **Tarom** Nikola Tesla Airport Terminal 2; ☏2286 400

✈ **Turkish** [114 D5] Knez Mihailova 30/V; ☏3036 195

✈ **Wizz Air** Nikola Tesla Airport Terminal 1; ☏0900 232 321

BY BUS AND RAIL Arriving by train or bus brings you right into the city centre itself, as the **main railway station** (Železnička Stanica Beograd) [102 D4] and the **central**

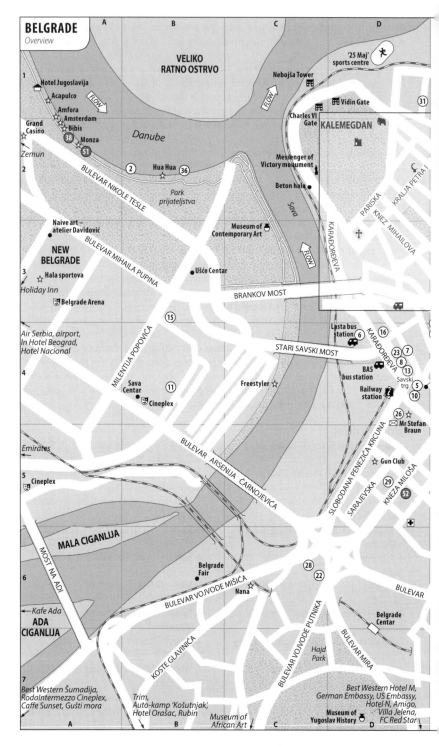

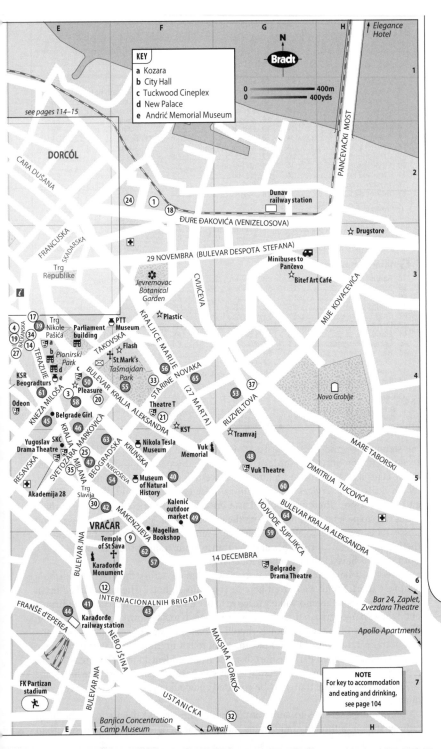

KEY
- **a** Kozara
- **b** City Hall
- **c** Tuckwood Cineplex
- **d** New Palace
- **e** Andrić Memorial Museum

N

Bradt

0 _____ 400m
0 _____ 400yds

↑ Elegance Hotel

see pages 114–15

DORĆOL

CARA DUŠANA

FRANCUSKA
SKADARSKA

Trg
Republike

ℹ

24 1 18

ĐURE ĐAKOVIĆA (VENIZELOSOVA)

Dunav railway station

☆ Drugstore

29 NOVEMBRA (BULEVAR DESPOTA STEFANA)

Minibuses to Pančevo

☆ Bitef Art Café

CVIJIĆEVA

✿ Jevremovac Botanical Garden

☆ Plastic

KRALJICE MARIJE

MIJE KOVAČEVIĆA

17 39 Trg Nikole Pašića
4
19 34
27 14

TERAZIJE

BAĆANSKA

Parliament building

a
b Pionirski Park
c
d
e

🖂 PTT Museum

TAKOVSKA

☆ Flash
✝ ☆ St Mark's
Tašmajdan Park

56

STARINE NOVAKA (27 MARTA)

65

37

53

Novo Groblje

KSR Beogradturs

61 50 Pleasure
3 58
20

Odeon

45 ● Belgrade Girl

KNEZA MILOŠA

Theatre T
21

☆ KST

RUZVELTOVA

☆ Tramvaj

MARE TABORSKI

46

Yugoslav Drama Theatre

SKC

KRALJA MILANA

SVETOZARA MARKOVIĆA

25
35 47

63

BEOGRADSKA

KRUNSKA

NJEGOŠEVA

⚜ Nikola Tesla Museum

Vuk Memorial

48 ☺ Vuk Theatre

60

DIMITRIJA TUCOVIĆA

RESAVSKA

✚ Akademija 28

54

Trg Slavija

⚜ Museum of Natural History

40

Kalenić outdoor market 49

BULEVAR KRALJA ALEKSANDRA

VOJVODE ŠUPLJIKCA

64

59

✚

30 42

MAKENZIJEVA

VRAČAR

9 Magellan Bookshop

Temple of St Sava ✝

62
57

14 DECEMBRA

☺ Belgrade Drama Theatre

BULEVAR JNA

Karađorđe Monument

12

41 44 Karađorđe railway station

43

INTERNACIONALNIH BRIGADA

MAKSIMA GORKOG

FRANŠE d'EPEREA

NEBOJŠINA

Bar 24, Zaplet, Zvezdara Theatre

Apollo Apartments

FK Partizan stadium
🏃

BULEVAR JNA

USTANIČKA

32

Banjica Concentration Camp Museum

Diwali

NOTE
For key to accommodation and eating and drinking, see page 104

BELGRADE Overview
For listings, see pages 113–32

🛏 Where to stay

1	Allure Caramel......F2	14	Hotel Moskva......E4	27	Prag......E4
2	ArkaBarka......B2	15	Hyatt Regency......B3	28	Radisson Blu
3	Belgrade Eye......E4	16	Jasmin......D4		Old Mill......C6
4	Beograd......E4	17	Kasina......E3	29	Rex......D5
5	BG City......D4	18	King......F2	30	Slavija......E5
6	Bristol......D4	19	Life Design......E4		Slavija Garni.......(see 30)
7	Centar......D4	20	Manga......E4	31	Spirit......D1
8	Central Station......D4	21	Metropol Palace......F4	32	Srbija......G7
9	Chillton......F6	22	Mint......C6	33	Taš......F4
10	City Center......D4	23	Mr President......D4	34	Vila Terazije......E4
11	Crowne Plaza......B4	24	Nevski......F2	35	Villa Manjež......E5
12	Crystal......E6	25	Park......E5	36	Yachting Club Kej......B2
13	Downtown......D4	26	Pošta......D4	37	Zira......G4

Off map

Apollo......H7	Elegance......H1	Nacional......A4
Auto-kamp 'Košutnjak'......B7	Holiday Inn......A3	Orašac......B7
Best Western Hotel M........D7	Hotel N......D7	Trim......B7
Best Western Šumadija......A7	In Hotel Beograd......A4	Villa Jelena......D7

✖ Where to eat and drink

38	Bahus......A2	49	Kalenić......F5		Steak House
39	Burrito Madre......E3	50	Kantina......E4		'El Toro'......(see 45)
40	Bukowski Bar......F5	51	Keops......A2	60	Tabor......G5
41	Byblos......E6	52	Lava Bar......D5	61	The Three Carrots......E4
42	Casa......E5	53	Lorenzo i	62	Trandafilović......F6
43	Đorđe......F6		Kakalamba......G4	63	Whatever@
44	Franš......E6	54	Lovac......E5		The Corner......E5
45	Greenet Panorama......E4	55	Madera......F4	64	Zaplet......G5
46	Hari's Creperie......E4	56	Makao......F4	65	Zorba......F4
	Hotel Moskva......(see 14)	57	Orač......F6		
47	Jump Café......E5	58	Resava......E4		
48	Kafana Pavle Korčagin......G5	59	Square......G6		

Off map

Amigo......D7	Diwali......F7	Rubin......B7
Caffe Sunset......A7	Gušti mora......A7	

bus station (Beogradska Autobuska Stanica, БАС in Cyrillic) [102 D4] lie next door to each other on busy Karađorđeva, one of Belgrade's main thoroughfares. Adjacent to the central bus station, just a little to the west, lies the **Lasta bus station** [102 D4], which deals with services to destinations fairly close to Belgrade like Smederevo and Mladenovac. There is another Lasta bus station at the edge of the city where buses stop to pick up passengers. Both the railway station and the central bus station possess a *garderoba* – a left-luggage office – and currency-exchange facilities, and there is also a small tourist office at the entrance to the train station (⏱ *09.00–22.00*). Both stations have exchange offices for changing cash.

Unless you have elected to stay in New Belgrade across the river, it will be a relatively short, uphill walk from here to your chosen hotel. The taxis parked up in front of the stations are more likely to agree to use their meter than those at the airport but if they do not agree to this, then it is easy enough to flag down one that is passing. The fare to any of the central hotels should be no more than €3–4. Alternatively, any one of trams number 2, 11 or 13 passing right to left in front of the station will take you up to Kalemegdan Park, a short distance from Studentski trg. The fare is 100din if you pay the driver or considerably less if you have a BusPlus pass (see box, page 107). Be aware that the tram may be crowded and could be a trial if you are carrying much luggage.

International services to and from Serbia terminate and depart from the main railway station, although some trains may stop at Beograd Centar and suburban stations such as Dunav as well. Through tickets may be bought on services to Zagreb, Budapest, Ljubljana, Thessaloniki, Skopje and Bucharest, or even to more far-flung destinations like Moscow or Istanbul. The main domestic line runs north to Subotica in Vojvodina, and south into Montenegro, to Bar on the Adriatic coast.

Depending on the time of day, the railway station sometimes has a slightly deserted feel to it. The bus station is altogether livelier and handles far more domestic traffic. Generally, there are more buses than trains running to any given destination, and the bus network is considerably more wide-ranging anyway, serving every corner of Serbia. In addition, there are international buses, mainly used by migrant workers, which run as far as Germany and Istanbul. As a general rule, trains are slower but cheaper than buses.

For information and reservations:

🚌 **Central (BAS) bus station (БАС)** [102 D4] Železnička 4; ☎ 2636 299; w www.bas.co.rs
🚌 **Lasta bus station** [102 D4] Železnička bb; ☎ 3206 922; w lasta.rs

🚌 **Railway station** [102 D4] Savski trg 2; ☎ 3602 899

GETTING AROUND

Belgrade has a comprehensive bus, trolleybus and tram network, which is cheap but invariably crowded at rush hour. Belgrade does not have a metro system, although one was planned back in the 1990s and an underground station, now a white elephant, was actually built by the Vuk monument (see box, page 106) and now serves as a station on the Beovoz local train network. Whatever form of city transport you use, do not neglect to swipe your pass or, if you have bought a ticket from the driver, ensure that it gets cancelled in the machine on board or you will run the risk of having to pay a hefty fine if caught. Public transport starts early in the morning – around 04.30 – but stops running quite early too, at about 23.30. After this time, there is a limited night bus service until 03.00 from Trg Republike [115 E6] and Trg Slavija [103 E5]. For ticketing purposes, the wider Belgrade urban area is divided into four zones. Tickets bought from drivers cost 150din for zones 1 and 2, 300din for three zones and 400din for all four zones. It works out much cheaper to get hold of a **BusPlus Pass** (see box, page 107), even if using public transport just a few times.

Unfortunately there are few facilities for disabled travellers on Belgrade's public transport system at present. Only trolley number 22 and trams number 7, 12 and 13 are currently fully accessible.

BUSES These have the most extensive coverage, plying every corner of the city on both sides of the Sava River. One particularly useful service is the route that runs between Zeleni venac by McDonald's [114 D7], just down from the Hotel Moscow, and New Belgrade. Buses number 15, 84 and 706 run from here across the River Sava and along Bulevar Nikole Tesle to reach the waterfront at the Hotel Jugoslavija and Zemun, an area rich in floating cafés and restaurants. Other useful bus routes include number 31 from Studentski trg to Bulevar JNA (St Sava's Church), numbers 15, 84, 704E and 706 from Zeleni venac to Hotel Jugoslavija and Zemun, number 72 between Zeleni venac and Nikola Tesla Airport, and bus 1A that plies between Zeleni venac and Ada Ciganlija.

TROLLEYBUSES These are more limited and run mostly between Stari Grad, Trg Slavija and the southwest of the city. One useful route is that which connects Trg Slavija with Kalemegdan: trolleybus numbers 19, 21, 22 and 29. Another is number 41 between Studentski trg and Bulevar Mira. Trolleybuses do not operate in New Belgrade.

TRAMS Trams trundle along a few well-placed routes that link the city centre with Stari Grad. There are also a couple of routes that delve into the city's southern extremities (tram number 3 terminates near Rakovica Monastery). A single line crosses the Sava into New Belgrade: tram 7L from Tašmajdan Park to Jurija Gagarina and Buvlja pijaca. One of the most useful routes for visitors is the tram service that runs between the Old Town and the bus and railway stations – the aforementioned numbers 2, 11 and 13. A lot of the cranky old trams that used to run in the city have been replaced in recent years with much quieter modern ones. A route that is useful for sightseeing purposes if nothing else is tram number 2, which takes about an hour to run in a circle around the Old Town and central Belgrade.

TAXIS For many, taxis are a better option. Not only are they fairly cheap but their appeal is strengthened with the knowledge that, with the exception of a few airport-based operators, cab drivers in Belgrade are usually honest and helpful. With a meter start of 170din and a rate of 65din per kilometre in the daytime and 85din per kilometre at night (between 22.00 and 06.00) and on Sundays and public holidays, a typical fare for a short city ride is in the order of 350–500din. Waiting time is 750din per hour. A genuine registered taxi can be recognised by a clear plastic sign on the roof, a functioning meter and a sticker in the window displaying its rates. A discount is sometimes offered if taxis are called by phone. Dependable companies which may be called up are:

Alfa ☏19807		**NBA** ☏3185 777	
Alo ☏3564 555		**Palma** ☏3162 020	
Beogradski ☏19801		**Pink** ☏19803	
Beotaxi ☏19999		**Plavi** ☏3553 324	
Lux ☏3033 123		**Zeleni** ☏3246 008	
Naksi ☏2157 668		**Žuti (Yellow)** ☏19802	

Since February 2012, BusPlus passes have been in use in Belgrade. These work like London Transport Oyster cards and can be used on all Belgrade public transport in the city – buses, trams, trolleybuses and Beovoz trains. They should be scanned at the machines by the doors on entering, where the amount of credit remaining will be indicated on the display.

Three types are available: personalised plastic cards with the user's name and photo, plastic cards without personal information and smart paper cards. The first type is a prepaid pass aimed at city commuters. The second type costs 250din and any amount of credit can be added to them at a booth – they last for three years. This non-personalised plastic card works as a 'pay as you go' smart card. It can be used for journeys up to 90 minutes (89din within zones 1 and 2, 179din for three zones and 269din in all four zones), but should be validated upon every entry into a vehicle within the journey period. The third type of card is a paper non-personalised smart card that can be charged just once for one-, three- or five-day validity, costing 280din, 720din and 1,100din respectively. It is valid from the moment it is charged and expires once the period of validity is exhausted. Either of the last two is suitable for foreign visitors to the city. A fourth option is to buy an electronic ticket but only users of the MTS mobile network can use this.

TRAINS Beovoz (w *beovoz.rs*) is a limited commuter rail service that links towns close to Belgrade to the city centre by way of stations at Zemun, Novi Beograd, Nova Železnička Beograd Centar (near Hajd Park), Karađorđev Park and Beograd-Dunav by Pančevački, most on the south bank of the Danube. There are six Beovoz city railway lines in total that extend as far north as Stara Pazova and as far south as Mladenovac and Valjevo, as well as connecting the city with Pančevo to the northeast and Zemun to the northwest. Belgrade's main railway station is not part of this network although it is expected that Beograd Centar will eventually become Belgrade's main station when the Savamala area is developed in the future.

CAR RENTAL Within Belgrade itself, secure parking can be a headache and not all hotels have their own car park. Parking is zoned in the city – red, yellow and green – with red being the most limited in time allowed. In the green zone you may pay for up to 3 hours' parking, in the red, just 1 hour. Tickets may be bought from kiosks in all three zones, or from a meter in the red zone.

Most of the services below can be pre-booked online.

🚗 **Auto-Rent** Nikola Tesla Airport; ☎ 2286 388; m 063 349 341; w carrental.co.rs. Also rent cars with drivers as well as self-drive.

🚗 **Avaco** [103 G5] Trmska 7; ☎ 2433 797 (*08.00–16.00*); m 064 1845 555 (*24hr*); e avacodoo@gmail.com; w avaco.rs. Their office is located off Bulevar Revolucije, with cars from around €30 per day for long-term hire, more for shorter periods. Min age is 21, requiring at least 2 documents with photo & a deposit of €500–1,000.

🚗 **Avis** w avis.rs. Pivljanina Baje 43/6; ☎ 3676 644, & Nikola Tesla Airport; ☎ 2097 064

🚗 **Budget** w budget.rs. Branches at Hotel Hyatt Regency, Milentija Popovića 5; ☎ 2137 703, 3113 050, & Nikola Tesla Airport; ☎ 2286 361, 2094 959

🚗 **Europcar** w europcar.com. Bulevar Dr Zorana Đinđića 59; ☎ 3015 004, & Nikola Tesla Airport; ☎ 2289 028

🚗 **Hertz** w hertz.rs. Vladimira Popovića 6; ☎ 2028 200, & Nikola Tesla Airport; ☎ 2286 017

Belgrade Београд   GETTING AROUND

3

🚗 **Master** [103 E5] At Hotel Slavija Lux; 📞2449 657; w mastercar.rs
🚗 **Mobil & Auto** Nikola Tesla Airport; 📞2286 363; m 065 3233 910; e mobilauto@yahoo.com;

w rent-a-car.rs. Rent a range of vehicles both with & without driver.
🚗 **Sixt** Nikola Tesla Airport; 📞2286 356; e aerodrom@sixt.rs; w sixt.rs

CYCLING As a rule, central Belgrade is not a great place for bicycles, as the combination of cobbled streets, tramlines and unheeding drivers makes cycling more of a trial than a pleasure. There are other places in the city, however, where leisure cycling is highly popular and where purpose-built tracks make it both safe and enjoyable. Such areas include the 8km track that borders the lake at Ada Ciganlija, parts of Kalemegdan Park, Košutnjak Park, and the promenades that run along the Sava and Danube riverfronts.

Belgrade has 35km of official bicycle paths that stretch along two routes. Route A goes from the marina at the waterfront at Dorćol along the east bank of the Sava River to Ada Ciganlija. Route B follows a circuit of New Belgrade between Hotel Jugoslavija and Blok 45 to the south. Route A connects with Route B at Brankovo most, where there is now a bicycle lift to carry bikes up from the river cycleway to the higher level of the bridge.

Bicycle hire is available at several places along these designated paths: by the Hotel Jugoslavija in New Belgrade [102 A1], a little further on at the beginning of Zemun, in Dorćol by the '25 Maj' sports centre [102 D1], and on Ada Ciganlija at the east end of the lake near the causeway. Some hostels also have bicycles to rent.

Guided **bicycle tours** of the city are also available from local tour operators (pages 109–12).

TOURIST INFORMATION

The main branch of the **Tourist Organisation of Belgrade (TOB)** is at Knez Mihailova 5 [114 D6] (📞 2635 622, 2635 343; e bginfo.knezmihailova@tob.rs; w tob.rs; ⏰ 09.00–19.00 daily), with another branch at the main railway station [102 D4], which has a useful exchange office next door (📞 3612 732; e bginfo.stanica@tob.rs; ⏰ 07.00–13.30 Mon–Sat, closed Sun) and at Nikola Tesla Airport (📞 2097 828; e info-aerodrom@serbia.travel; ⏰ 09.00–21.30 daily). All of these can issue city maps, hotel listings and copies of English-language magazines about Belgrade, as well as advise on current events.

For further information on places beyond the capital, the **National Tourist Organisation of Serbia (NTOS)** have tourist information centres at Trg Republike 5 [114 D6] (📞 3282 712; e info@serbia.travel; w serbia.travel; ⏰ 10.00–21.00 Mon–Fri, 10.00–18.00 Sat/Sun), and Makedonska 22 [115 F6] (📞 6557 127; ⏰ 09.00–17.00 Mon–Fri, closed Sat/Sun).

MAPS AND GUIDES One of the most useful city maps is the Belgrade map in the pocket-sized *Beograd – plana grad*, published by Magic Map (w magicmap. rs) at 1:20,000 scale, which shows public transport routes, parking zones and the city suburbs. Another good map is the *Beograd* city map 1:20,000, published by Intersistem Cartography. Both of these are readily available at the postcard kiosks and bookshops along Knez Mihailova. The Tourist Organisation of Belgrade produce their own 1:20,000 city map based on the Intersistem map, which shows museums, churches and other tourist sights, together with an inset city transport map, and this is perfectly adequate for most purposes. The Planplus online road atlas (w planplus.rs) is another excellent resource that can be sourced online.

The TOB, and some bookshops, might sell the *Belgrade Tourist Guide* by Ljubica Corović, which was last updated in 2011. Although this has little in the way of practicalities it serves as a useful guide to Belgrade's historical landmarks.

LOCAL TOUR OPERATORS

The **Tourist Organisation of Belgrade** (**w** *tob.rs*) offer a range of good-value, guided city sightseeing tours including daily open-top bus tours run by Lasta Travel & Tourism and BS Tours (**w** *bstours.rs*). They can also reserve places on other tours of the city that include underground Belgrade, the dungeons of Belgrade Fortress, Princess Ljubica's residence, tours of the Savamala creative district and out-of-city visits to Avala Tower. Bookings should be made at the TOB tourist information centre at Knez Mihailova 5 [114 D6]. TOB also organise 2-hour group visits to the Royal Compound at Dedinje on weekends between April and November.

For the purchase of tickets, both the ticket office at **BAS**, the central bus station [102 D4] (\ *2636 299*; ⊕ *05.30–22.00*) and **Turist Biro Lasta** opposite at Milovana Milovanovića 1 (\ *6642 473*; **w** *lastatravel.rs*; ⊕ *07.30–20.00 Mon–Fri, 08.00–16.00 Sat*) sell bus tickets.

Train information and tickets may be obtained from the English-speaking staff at **KSR Beogradturs**, Milovana Milovanovića 5 [102 D4] (\ *6641 258*), avoiding the crush and possible communication difficulties at the station itself. They do not charge commission.

Association of Tourist Guides [115 F7] Dečanska 8; \ 3230 566; **e** guides.serbia@gmail. com; **w** guides-serbia.com. This is a collective of trained multi-lingual guides who can guide you around the fortress or further afield in the city & beyond.

Belgrade Free Tour [115 E6] **m** 061 6197 476; **e** belgradefreetour@gmail.com; **w** belgradefreetour.com. This operator offers 2 free daily walking tours that leave from Trg Republike at 10.30 & 14.00 – no reservation is necessary. The same operator also provides a number of short €10 tours that need to be pre-booked.

Belgrade Walking Tours [115 E6] **m** 066 5091 793; **e** belgradewalkingtours.com; **w** belgradewalkingtours.com. Offer free walking tours daily, starting at Trg Republike at 11.00 & 16.00.

Fly Orient [115 E5] Beogradska 37; \ 3035 632, 3035 633; **e** info@flyorient.rs; **w** flyorient. rs. This company runs half-day sightseeing tours & UndergroundBelgrade tours that visit some of the caves & tunnels that run underneath the city. Prices are available on request.

Glob Metropoliten Tours [115 E5] Makenzijeva 26; \ 2662 211, 2430 899; **e** glob@metropoliten. com; **w** metropoliten.com. Excursions include Belgrade musical w/ends & walking tours of the city. They can also arrange tickets & car hire.

GO2serbia [114 B5] Gračanička 11; \ 3248 323; **m** 062 605 089; **e** office@go2serbia.net; **w** go2serbia.net. Part of the Eurojet Travel Agency, GO2 run Belgrade Underground tours 4 times a week, guide-led pub crawls every night, bohemian evenings on Mon, Fri & Sat, & sightseeing walks every day at 10.00. Also boat sightseeing tours in summer.

iBikeBelgrade [114 A7] Brace Krsmanović 5; **m** 066 9008 386; **e** info@ibikebelgrade.com; **w** ibikebelgrade.com. Highly rated guided bicycle tours of Belgrade led by a Dutch expat dedicated to promoting cycling in Belgrade. Tours last 3–4hrs, run 1 May–31 Oct & cost €22 pp, bicycle provided. The meeting point is at the iBikeBelgrade shop at Brace Krsmanović near Brankov Bridge.

Jolly Travel [115 F6] Makedonska 5; \ 3220 130; **e** info@jolly.rs; **w** jolly.rs. Jolly Travel mainly deals with domestic travel needs but they can arrange tours for visitors in Belgrade & beyond, assist with car hire & booking airline tickets.

Serbian Heritage Tours **m** 065 2410 746; **e** serbian.heritage.tours@gmail.com; **w** serbianheritagetours.com. Heritage tours of the city given by a knowledgeable, licensed tour guide who can guide in English, Spanish & Italian. A number of tours to choose from, walking or with private transport, from 2hrs' duration to full-day

Belgrade Београд LOCAL TOUR OPERATORS

3

JANUARY–FEBRUARY

FEST – International Film Festival (w *fest.rs*) Held from the last Friday in February through the first week in March. The festival is a showcase for the latest releases in world cinema.

BEOWINE An international wine festival held at the same time as the **International Fair of Tourism** (w *beogradskisajamturizma.rs*) at Belgrade Fair (w *sajam.rs*).

MARCH

Spring exhibition of Udruženje Likovni Umetnika Sbije (ULUS) (w *ulus.rs*) Association of Fine Artists of Serbia at Cvijeta Zuzorić Art Pavilion in March–April (with another autumn exhibition taking place in November).

Guitar Art Festival (w *gaf.rs*) Features a range of soloists and guitar ensembles and is held at Sava Centar, Dom Omladine and Foundation of Ilija M Kolarac. Check the website for exact dates.

APRIL

Belgrade Dance Festival (w *belgradedancefestival.com*) International festival of modern and classical dance that takes place in late March and early April.

The Belgrade Marathon (w *bgdmarathon.org*) Takes place in the second half of the month.

MAY

International Festival of New Music 'Ring, Ring' (w *ringring.rs*) Takes place over a period of two weeks at Rex Cultural Centre and other venues highlighting jazz, folk and avant-garde music.

International Platform of Composers (IPCS) In the second half of May at the Studentski Kulturni Centar (SKC), Students' Cultural Centre.

Museum Night (w *nocmuzeja.rs*) In the middle of May, this nationwide event features museums and galleries presented to the public in new ways, with concerts, performances, thematic exhibitions and permanent museum exhibitions taking place at unorthodox times.

JUNE

Mikser Festival (w *festival.mikser.rs*) An annual themed festival of creative arts events held mostly in the Savamala neighbourhood.

International Theatrical Belgrade Adventure (TIBA) (w *tibafestival.com*) A children's drama festival held at various Belgrade theatres in June for ten days.

Choirs among Frescoes A series of events that features sacred choral music is usually held at the Fresco Gallery in June–July.

Kalemegdan Twilights (w *beogradskatvrdjava.co.rs*) A series of performances of popular classical music that are held from June to July in Kalemegdan Park, on the plateau in front of the Belgrade City Institute for the Protection of Cultural Monuments.

JULY

Pantomime Festival (w *festmono-pan.org.rs*) Held at 'Pinokio' puppet theatre at the beginning of the month.

BELEF (w *belef.org*) Belgrade's summer festival of theatre, contemporary dance, visual arts and music held every year at various venues around the city between the end of May and mid-August. Outdoor venues such as Kalemegdan Park and the Sava and Danube riverbanks are utilised for performances as well as theatres and larger venues such as Dom Omladine and the Sava Centar.

AUGUST
Belgrade Beer Festival (w *belgradebeerfest.com*) Held in mid-August at Friendship Park (Park prijateljstva) in Novi Beograd. As well as a huge range of beers to sample there is a music stage where live performances by Serbian and international bands can be seen throughout the night. Other events such as beer-drinking competitions also take place. This festival grows bigger each year and currently attracts up to 500,000 visitors over five days.

SEPTEMBER
BITEF Belgrade International Theatre Festival (w *bitef.rs*) An international festival of drama that takes place at several of Belgrade's theatres over a period of about 15 days.

OCTOBER–DECEMBER
Belgrade Jazz Festival (w *bjf.rs*) Usually takes place in late October at Dom Omladine (w *domomladine.org*) and the Sava Centar.
BEMUS Belgrade Music Festival (w *bemus.rs*) An international musical event of ensembles and soloists from around the world. This takes place in the second half of October; the main emphasis is on classical and contemporary music but there is some 'world' music too. BEMUS is staged at the Sava Centar, the Foundation of Ilija M Kolarac, and other theatres across the city.
Joy of Europe or International Meeting of Children of Europe (w *joyofeurope.rs*) An international children's event, held in the first week of October, which promotes socialising and shared artistic creativity between children from all over Europe. It takes place at the Children's Cultural Centre of Belgrade, at Ada Ciganlija, the Sava Centar and various galleries around the city.
October Salon (w *oktobarskisalon.org*) Promotes the most recent significant achievements in the field of fine and applied arts and design. Held at Cvijeta Zuzorić art pavilion in Kalemegdan Park and at various ULUS (Association of Fine Artists of Serbia) galleries such as Zvono, Artget and the Faculty of Fine Arts.
Belgrade Book Fair (w *sajamknjiga.rs*) An international event of book publishing and booksellers held at Sajam fairground from the end of October to the beginning of November.
Belgrade Fashion Week (w *belgradefashionweek.com*) At several locations around the city from late October to early November, this is an opportunity for Serbian designers to show off their latest styles.
New Year's Eve A major event in Belgrade, with numerous free concerts taking place at various squares throughout the city. A mini carnival is held on Svetogorska and Makedonska on the afternoon of New Year's Day.

tours. Also layover tours for those with little time in the city.

Smile & Ride [103 E6] Krušedolska 13/1; m 065 9934 455; e info@rentascooterbelgrade.com; w rentascooterbelgrade.com. Guided scooter tours of Belgrade between Apr & Oct that leave from in front of St Sava Temple. Also City Relax tours on summer w/ends that take in beaches of Ada Ciganlija.

RIVER PLEASURE CRUISES River services between Belgrade and other Serbian towns used to run in the past and there is some hope that pleasure cruises may restart in the next year or two.

The **Tourist Organisation of Belgrade** has information on a number of local river cruises during the summer months. A regular 90-minute river sightseeing cruise leaves from the Yachting Club Kej [102 B2] at Ušće bb each day at 18.00 and 20.00. The tour costs 800din adults, 400din children. Reservations are necessary (m *064 8251 120, 064 8251 150*), or ask at the TOB office.

Donau Ships [102 A1] Dunavski kej (near Hotel Jugoslavija); m 069 1995 959; e office@donauships.com; w donauships.com. Provide a regular daily 100min cruise on the Stevanske Livade between Apr & Oct. Also dinner cruises along the Danube & Sava rivers on the boat *Trajan*.

RAILWAY LEISURE TRIPS During the summer months, one-day excursions with the *Romantika* steam train take place between Belgrade and Sremski Karlovci. Tickets can be booked at the railway station [102 D4] (✆ *3602 899;* w *zeleznicesrbije.com*) at desk number 19, or at any branch of **KSR Beogradturs Agency** [102 D4] (*Nemanjina 4/14;* ✆ *3620 839*) and **Želturist Travel Agency** [103 E4] next to Hotel Beograd at Balkanska 52–54 (✆ *6683 058, 6683 046*), next to Hotel Beograd.

The famous and luxurious '**Blue Train**', formerly used by Tito for entertaining foreign dignitaries, is available for hire for excursions too, but only by special contract.

🏠 WHERE TO STAY

HOTELS Although a few of Belgrade's hotels remain in state ownership, many more privately owned ones have opened for business in recent years. At the higher end of the market, the majority are geared more towards expense account-funded business conventions than to the tastes of foreign tourists but these are, at least, invariably spacious and comfortable.

The new privately funded hotels that have opened up in the city are welcome additions to Belgrade's hotel stock and hopefully, in the future, a few more mid-range options will swell the ranks. In addition, some of the older state-run hotels have been taken into private ownership and undergone renovation.

There is a degree of overlap between the mid-range and budget categories listed below. The stars awarded in each category should be taken with a pinch of salt, especially at the bottom end of the market, although the categorisation tends to be applied much more rigidly with the privately owned hotels.

As a rule, budget travellers are not particularly well catered for in regards to hotels, although there have been an enormous number of hostels with dormitory accommodation opening up for business in the last few years. There are also many private apartments available for short or long stays that may be booked online using accommodation websites like w booking.com.

During busy periods such as high summer and New Year budget-priced hotel rooms can be hard to find, and it is usually safer to book well ahead. Solo travellers suffer from the disadvantage that single rooms are sometimes small and cramped, often less than half the size of a double but inevitably more than half the price.

There is small residency tax to pay of around €1 that cheaper hotels tend to include in the quoted price but more expensive ones usually do not. Although accommodation must be paid for in dinars, prices are often quoted in euros to avoid amending rates according to fluctuations in the dinar. Virtually all three-star hotels and above will accept credit cards for payment.

The hotels below are listed according to price and facilities offered rather than strictly by star category. For **mid-range** options, the enormous three-star Hotel Jugoslavija on the south bank of the River Danube in New Belgrade is currently functioning solely as a top-flight casino, although a new hotel with 33-storey twin towers managed by the luxury Kempinski chain is planned for the future following massive investment by Alpe-Adria Hotels. The Jugoslavija used to be a five-star hotel during Yugoslavia's heyday and was the place of choice for guests as distinguished as Tina Turner, Queen Elizabeth II, Richard Nixon and Buzz Aldrin. However, such illustrious history did not prevent NATO from bombing it in 1999, destroying the swimming pool, conference hall and some of the rooms. The Chinese Embassy nearby was also famously hit in the same raid.

Budget hotels are a shrinking category. In recent years, some of the state-owned hotels that formerly belonged in this category have been closed down for refurbishment. If, and when, they reopen for business they will no doubt be more expensive to stay in than before.

GUESTHOUSES, APARTMENTS AND B&BS This is a growth area for accommodation in Belgrade, and a good option for those looking for something slightly different. Breakfast is provided at some but not all guesthouses and bed and breakfasts; see individual listings below for details.

HOSTELS Not so very long ago, there was very little in this category but in recent years a large number of hostels have opened to offer a wide choice of cheap-and-cheerful accommodation for those who do not crave too much privacy. Most of these offer similar facilities: dorm beds, kitchens, internet access, luggage storage and lockers. Generally there is no curfew, which may be seen as an advantage or disadvantage depending on how well you sleep. It should be noted that some of the establishments below may only be open seasonally and advance bookings are a good idea anyway.

New hostels are opening all the time in Belgrade and this list is by no means exhaustive. Internet sites such as w hostels.com, w hostelworld.com, w hostelz. com or w hostelbookers.com should be able to provide further options. Most of those mentioned below can also be pre-booked online using these same websites.

For ease of reference, all accommodation has been listed by location: for listings in the Old Town, see map, pages 114–15; for listings in central Belgrade, New Belgrade and the surrounding area, see map, pages 102–3, unless otherwise noted.

OLD TOWN
Luxury

🏠 **Evropa** **** [115 E7] (7 suites, 2 rooms) Sremska 1; ☎ 3626 017; e office@hotelevropa.rs; w hotelevropa.rs. With a perfect location convenient for Knez Mihailova & Terazije, this elegant converted building has just 9 luxurious rooms & suites, all tastefully furnished. The suites & rooms are themed as capital cities such as 'London', 'Paris' or 'Moscow' & come with a 5-star price tag. Free use of spa centre. €€€€€

🏠 **Belgrade Art Hotel** **** [114 D6] (50 rooms, 6 suites) Knez Mihailova 27; ☎ 3312 000; e info@belgradearthotel; w belgradearthotel.

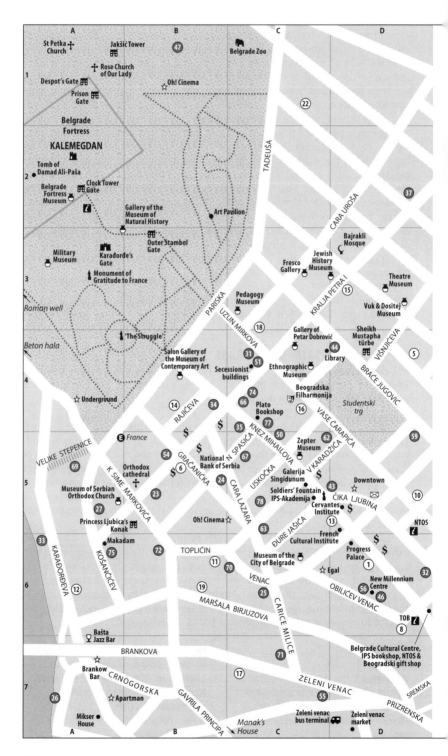

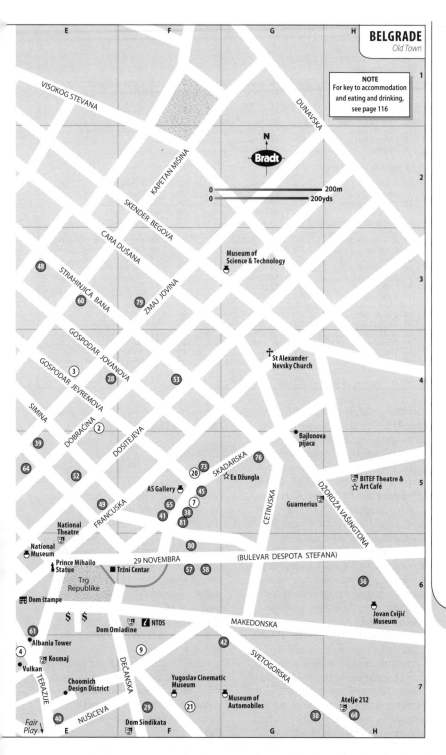

NOTE
For key to accommodation
and eating and drinking,
see page 116

0 _____ 200m
0 _____ 200yds

N

Bradt

VISOKOG STEVANA

DUNAVSKA

KAPETAN MIŠINA

SKENDER BEGOVA

CARA DUŠANA

Museum of
Science & Technology

48

STRAHINJIĆA BANA

60

79

ZMAJ JOVINA

St Alexander
Nevsky Church

GOSPODAR JOVANOVA

GOSPODAR JEVREMOVA

3

28

53

SIMINA

DOBRAČINA

2

DOSITEJEVA

Bajlonova
pijaca

39

64

52

20   73

76

SKADARSKA

☆ Ex Džungla

BITEF Theatre &
☆ Art Café

AS Gallery

45

CETINJSKA

DŽORDŽA VAŠINGTONA

49

FRANCUSKA

65

41

7

38

81

Guarnerius

National
Theatre

80

National
Museum

29 NOVEMBRA

(BULEVAR DESPOTA STEFANA)

Prince Mihailo
Statue

Tržni Centar

57   58

Trg
Republike

36

Dom štampe

$ $

Jovan Cvijić
Museum

61

Dom Omladine

NTOS

MAKEDONSKA

Albania Tower

4

Kosmaj

9

42

Vulkan

SVETOGORSKA

TERAZIJE

Choomich
Design District

DECANSKA

Yugoslav Cinematic
Museum

Atelje 212

40

29

21

Museum of
Automobiles

68

Fair
Play

NUŠIĆEVA

Dom Sindikata

30

115

🏠 **Where to stay**

❌ **Where to eat and drink**

com. Ideally situated on the Old Town's pedestrian thoroughfare, this newish business hotel has all the amenties you might expect of a modern 4-star hotel. Meeting & conference rooms, sauna & fitness centre. Many rooms have views down to busy Knez Mihailova below. €€€€€–€€€€

🏠 **Square Nine** ***** [114 C4] (34 rooms, 11 suites) Studentski trg 9; 🕾 3333 500; e info@squarenine.rs; w squarenine.rs. Very conveniently situated in the heart of the Old Town, this boutique luxury hotel, opened in 2011, has very stylish rooms. Brazilian hardwood fittings & limestone bathrooms with deep tubs & rain showers. Vintage furnishings, cashmere throws & electronically controlled lights & curtains. €€€€€–€€€€

🏠 **Townhouse 27** **** [114 B6] (21 rooms, 1 suite) Maršala Birjuzova 56; 🕾 2022 900; e hotel@townhouse27.com; w townhouse27. com. A boutique hotel in the centre of the Old Town on a quiet street close to Trg Republike. Modern minimalist design enhanced with photographs, sculpture & *objets d'art*. All rooms & apartments are non-smoking with minibar,

espresso machine, satellite TV, AC & anti-allergy bed linen. €€€€€–€€€€

Upmarket

✳ 🏠 **Le Petit Piaf** *** [115 F5] (13 rooms, 5 suites) Skadarska 34; 🕾 3035 252; e reservations@ petitpiaf.com; w petitpiaf.com. Le Petit Piaf is a privately owned central hotel situated in the heart of Skadarlija behind the house of the writer & painter Đura Jakšić. The 3 stars do not do justice to the hotel's true status as, in many ways, the facilities & service are superior to some of those awarded 4 stars. All rooms & suites have cable TV, internet access, direct phone lines & AC. W/end discounts (€€€) on all room types. €€€€

🏠 **Majestic** **** [114 D6] (76 rooms) Obilićev venac 28; 🕾 3285 777; e office@ majestic.rs; w majestic.rs. The Majestic enjoys an excellent, central location just off pedestrian-only Knez Mihailova & close to a concentration of bars, clubs & restaurants. The Majestic has a restaurant, a coffee shop, a summer terrace & garage. Discounted rates (€€€) at w/ends. €€€€

🏠 **Palace** **** [114 B6] (71 rooms, 15 suites) Topličin venac 23; 📞 2185 585, 2184 485; e office@palacehotel.co.rs; w palacehotel.co.rs. This is another of the older city-centre hotels, in this case dating back to the 1920s. The Palace has an elegant façade, which is brightly lit at night, & 2 restaurants (the 'Classic' in the lobby, & the 'Belgrade Panorama' on the 6th floor, which offers excellent city views) as well as a bar, exchange office, casino, garage with car wash service & all standard business facilities. The hotel has been privatised, with most rooms now refurbished or renovated. €€€ (suites €€€€)

🏠 **Srbija Garni** **** [114 C7] (32 rooms, 3 suites) Brankova 13–15; 📞 2633 323; e office@hotelsrbijagarni.com; w hotelsrbijagarni.com. A newish central hotel, opened in 2012, with neat, stylish rooms, modern furniture, cable TV, AC, Wi-Fi & minibar. Non-smoking rooms available. Free parking & bar on 1st floor. €€€€–€€€

Mid-range

🏠 **Royal** ** [114 D3] (105 rooms) Kralja Petra I 56; 📞 2626 426; e bookin@hotelroyal.rs; w hotelroyal.rs. This is actually Belgrade's oldest existing hotel, dating from 1886. The hotel has a superb location on a quiet street that runs across the top of Knez Mihailova, close to many restaurants & bars, museums, Kalemegdan Park & Belgrade's solitary mosque. The Royal has its own inexpensive restaurant, lobby bar & exchange facilities. This decent economy choice was closed for refurbishment at the time of writing but should be reopened by the time of publication. €€€

🏠 **Union** *** [115 F7] (54 rooms, 6 suites) Kosovska 11; 📞 3248 022, 3248 172; e office@hotelunionbelgrade.com; w hotelunionbelgrade.com. 5mins' walk from Trg Republike & the Serbian Parliament, this is a comfortable, well-kept hotel with helpful, obliging staff. The Union was renovated a few years back & passed into private ownership. The larger dbls are particularly pleasant & represent very good value. All rooms have cable TV, & free internet access is available on request. The hotel's restaurant has live music some nights. Parking is available. A 30% discount is offered at w/ends. €€€

Guesthouses, apartments and B&Bs

🏠 **Villa Kalemegdan** [114 C1] (6 suites) Strahinjića bana 7; 📞 2637 856; e reservation@villakalemegdan.com; w villakalemegdan.com. Elegant luxury suites on this famous Old Town street of bars & cafés. B/fast provided. €€€€

🏠 **City Code** [115 E4] (6 apts) Dobračina 26; 📞 3037 200; e office@citycode.rs; w citycode.rs. Central & close to Strahinjića bana, so ideal for city slickers. Luxury apartments with 24hr room service & b/fast. More apartments at Čika Ljubina 10 & in Zemun. €€€€–€€€

🏠 **Rezime Crown** [114 D5] (10 apts) Knez Mihailova 33; 📞 3282 404, 2627 471; e rezimecrown1@gmail.com. Apartments in a 19th-century Old Town building. B/fast provided. €€€€–€€€

🏠 **Travelling Actor** [115 F5] (5 rooms) Gospodar Jevremova 65; 📞 3234 156; e actor@sezampro.rs; w travellingactor.rs. In the heart of Skadarlija, this small guesthouse has cosy rooms with cable TV, minibar & AC. Restaurant in basement. €€€€–€€€

🏠 **Rezime Diamond** [114 B4] (12 rooms) Rajićeva 16; 📞 3348 044. Nicely decorated apartment suites near Kalemegdan Park. B/fast provided. €€€

Hostels

🏠 **Crossroad** [115 E4] (2 rooms) Gospodar Jeveremova 41; 📞 2637 570; e office@crossroad-hostel.com; w crossroad-hostel.com. Nice clean apartment hostel with just 2 rooms that can serve as sgl, dbl or trpl rooms. €€

🏠 **Hedonist Hostel** [114 D4] Simina 7; 📞 3284 798; e office@hedonisthostelbelgrade.com; w hedonisthostelbelgrade.com. With a great location near Studentski Park, this is on the ground floor of an attractive old house. Dorms of various sizes & a large common area, kitchen & garden. Friendly staff organise theme nights & BBQs. A good place for cyclists to stay. €

🏠 **Hostel Che** [114 B5] Kraja Petra 1 8, apt 7; 📞 2637 793; e hostelchehostel@gmail.com; w hostelchehostel.com. A centrally located hostel that comes highly rated by many; range of private rooms & 4- & 6-bed dorms. Free b/fast & free 4th night in dorm rooms. €

🏠 **Montmartre** [115 F7] Nušićeva 17/2; 📞 3224 157; e montmartrehostel@gmail.com. A friendly hostel inspired by French art & culture, with well-equipped kitchen & an excellent central location. B/fast included. Dorms & private dbl room (€€). €

🏠 **Olive** [114 D5] Vase Čarapića 3/38; 📱 064 2611 484; e olivehostelbgd@gmail.com.

A small hostel with an excellent location by the National Theatre. With entrance next door to the Grand Café on Trg Republike, this could not be more central. 6-bed dorm, room with bunk bed & private dbl. €

🏠 **PopArt** [114 A6] Karađorđeva 69/2; ☎2185 908. A stylish new hostel close to the bus station with pop art on the walls & themed dorms – Jim Morrison, Andy Warhol, etc – & 1 dbl room. €

🏠 **Star** [114 C3] (6 rooms) Cara Uroša 37; ☎2184 104; e hostel_star@yahoo.com. This hostel receives consistently good reports. It is located in a 1st-floor flat in a wonderfully central location close to the Pedagogy Museum & Kalemegdan Park, with 4- & 6-bed dormitories & dbl & trpl rooms available. No b/fast, but free tea & coffee, & free, fast internet access. €

CENTRAL BELGRADE
Luxury
🏠 **Allure Caramel** ★★★★ [103 F2] (17 rooms) Venizelosova (Đure Đakovića) 31; ☎3349 572; e reservations@allurecaramelhotel.com; w allurecaramelhotel.com. Formerly known as Admiral Club, this rebranded boutique hotel in a converted Neoclassical Dorćol villa has elegant rooms & suites with Baroque-style furniture & modern facilities. Restaurant & aperitif bar, fast internet access in each room & business & conference facilities. €€€€€

🏠 **Metropol Palace** ★★★★★ [103 F4] (199 rooms, 40 suites) Bulevar kralja Aleksandra 69; ☎3333 100; w metropolpalace.com. Formerly the Metropol Hotel, this was reopened as a luxury 5-star hotel in 2012. Rooms are stylish & come with free internet, minibar, desk, armchair & marble bathroom. Suites have separate office facilities with distinct living & sleeping areas. Greek restaurant & elegant lobby bar. €€€€€

🏠 **Radisson Blu Old Mill** ★★★★ [102 C6] (236 rooms & suites) Bulevar Vojvode Mišića 15; ☎6357 457; e reservations.belgrade@radissonblu.com; w radissonblu.com. Part of the Radisson Blu franchise, this has all you might expect: a range of modern, well-appointed executive, business-class &' standard' rooms all with minibar, AC & Wi-Fi. The more expensive rooms come with desks, coffee machines & free newspapers. B/fast not included with standard rooms. Discounts for advance bookings. €€€€€–€€€€

Upmarket
🏠 **Crystal** ★★★★ [103 E6] (44 rooms) Internacionalnih Brigada 9; ☎7151 000; e info@crystalhotel.rs; w crystalhotel-belgrade.rs. South of the centre in Vračar close to St Sava's Church, this elegant new boutique hotel has comfortable, well-equipped rooms & suites with cable TV, queen-size beds, internet access & minibar. Modern restaurant serving French & Mediterranean cuisine. €€€€

✳🏠 **Hotel Moskva** ★★★★ [103 E4] (124 rooms) Terazije 20; ☎3642 069; e info@hotelhotelmoskva.rs; w hotelmoskva.rs. Right in the heart of the city, the Hotel Moskva is actually one of Belgrade's most beautiful buildings with a very attractive Art Nouveau façade & lots of period charm. This well-appointed hotel, built in 1906 & reconstructed in 1973, is one of central Belgrade's better-known landmarks. There are genuine antiques in some of the rooms, while others are rather more prosaically furnished. The lobby is deceptively small, but the rest of the hotel is airy & spacious with high ceilings. Restaurant, aperitif bar, banquet hall, patisserie, business lounge, limited parking. There is an atmospheric coffee shop at street level with a delicious choice of cakes. €€€€

🏠 **Life Design** ★★★★ [103 E4] (46 rooms, 6 suites) Balkanska 18; ☎3534 300, 3534 328; e reservations@lifedesignhotel.rs; w lifedesignhotel.rs. A new city-centre state-of-the-art hotel that oozes style & elegance. Spacious, minimalist rooms & what it claims to be the 'best breakfast in the city'. €€€€

🏠 **Mr President** ★★★★ [102 D4] (50 rooms, 10 suites, 1 penthouse) Karađorđeva 75; ☎3602 222; e sales@belgradehotelsgroup.com; w hotelmrpresident.com. Note the 'Mr', this is Serbia's first Design Hotel, opened in 2007 virtually opposite the bus station, a rather incongruous location for such an expensive hotel. Each room has a portrait of an American president (with Tito gracing the penthouse) & there is plenty of contemporary artwork about the place, including a bar that has a Mt Rushmore sculpture that looks a little like Crosby, Stills, Nash & Young carved into stone. There is a Serbian version of Mt Rushmore too. All rooms come with a 'maxi bar' that has over 80 types of food & drink, satellite TV, Wi-Fi & a fully equipped bathroom. €€€€

🏠 **Slavija Garni** ★★★ [103 E5] (80 rooms, 12 suites) Svetog Save 2; ☎3084 800; e office@slavijahotel.com; w www.slavijahotel.com. Located

1km south of the city centre & railway station, towering over the thunderous traffic circling Trg Slavija & looking more like an office block than a place to sleep, this high-rise hotel has restaurants, piano bar, fitness centre, garage & casino. Non-smoking rooms on higher floors. €€€€

🏠 **Taš** *** [103 F4] (13 rooms, 2 suites) Beogradska 71; 📞4142 050; e hoteltash011@gmail.com; w hoteltash.com. Located to the east of Tašmajdan Park, this small hotel was fully refurbished & reopened as a boutique hotel in 2012. Economy & business rooms with cable TV, AC. Minibar, internet access & free international phone calls. Sauna, 2 swimming pools, gym & spa facilities. Restaurant & nightclub. Bright, pleasant rooms, some with good views. €€€€

🏠 **Zira** **** [103 G4] (119 rooms, 8 suites) Ruzveltova 35; 📞3314 800; e reception@zirahotels.com; w zirahotels.com. With direct access to Zira shopping mall but some way from the Old Town, this high-tech hotel is probably of more interest to business visitors than tourists. All rooms are non-smoking. Business centre, free international phone calls & internet access, fitness centre & ample underground parking. €€€€

🏠 **Nevski** **** [103 F2] (10 rooms, 30 suites) Venizelovsova 24a; 📞3229 722; e reservations@hotelnevski.com; w hotelnevski.com. Another newish hotel, opened in 2010, this one mostly consists of nicely furnished, roomy suites. Good-value promotional winter rates. €€€€–€€€

🏠 **Prag** **** [103 E4] (82 rooms) Kraljice Natalije (Narodnog fronta) 27; 📞3214 444; e office@hotelprag.rs; w hotelprag.co.rs. Located in a small street halfway up the hill between the station & the Old Town, the recently renovated Prag has its own restaurant, exchange office & bar. Rooms come with AC & cable TV. Wi-Fi access in the lobby. €€€€–€€€

Mid-range

🏠 **BG City Hotel** **** [102 D4] (87 rooms) Savski trg 7; 📞3600 700; e reservations@bigcityhotel.com; w bgcityhotel.com. Very convenient for the bus & railway stations, this hotel occupies an attractive Neoclassical building that was renovated in 2009. Large, well-equipped rooms offering good value for money. €€€

🏠 **Kasina** *** [103 E3] (97 rooms, 5 apts) Terazije 25; 📞3235 575, 3235 576; e booking@hotelkasina.rs; w hotelkasina.rs. The Kasina has a

very central location, close to Balkan & Moskva on Terazije, one of Belgrade's busiest thoroughfares. The sgl rooms are quite small but the dbls are better value. The hotel has a good bar & pavement café serving beer from its own small brewery. No private parking. Most rooms have been renovated but there are a few unrenovated rooms at a lower rate available. There are also a few well-renovated apartments. €€€

🏠 **Mint** **** [102 C6] (22 rooms) Kvanerska 4, Senjak; 📞4113 311; e reservations@hotelmint.rs; w hotelmint.rs. On the edge of the suburb of Senjak, 2km south of the city centre, close to Hajd Park, this modern boutique hotel has spacious comfortable rooms with natural light, all with Wi-Fi, cable TV, AC, minibar & bath. Good b/fast included. €€€

🏠 **Park** *** [103 E5] (120 rooms) Njegoševa 2; 📞4146 800, 4146 801; e reception@hotelparkbeograd.rs; w hotelparkbeograd.rs. The Park lies about 1km from the city centre, within walking distance of the Belgrade Palace, the Student Cultural Centre, & the Nikola Tesla & Natural History museums, in a street full of designer cafés & bars. Fully renovated, some of the lower rooms may be noisy due to rush-hour traffic. The hotel has its own restaurants, bar & garage. €€€

🏠 **Pošta** *** [102 D4] (32 rooms) Savska 3; 📞3614 260. Refurbished & reopened in 2011, this hotel close to the railway station continues to offer good value & friendly service. €€€

🏠 **Rex** *** [102 D5] (89 rooms, 4 suites) Sarajevska 37; 📞3611 862, 3611 949; e info@hotelrex-belgrade.com; w hotelrex-belgrade.com. Another of the small concentration close to the railway station, this hotel was formerly known as the 'Turist' & originally more geared towards businessmen than tourists, despite the name. Facilities include restaurant, coffee bar with terrace, conference hall & parking. €€€

🏠 **Srbija** *** [103 G7] (283 rooms, 18 suites) Ustanička 127c; 📞3044 003; e office@hotelsrbija.com; w hotelsrbija.com. This is a large high-rise hotel, 4km from the city centre, which caters mostly for businessmen. It has a restaurant, a bar, parking, disabled facilities, conference hall & non-smokers' rooms. €€€

🏠 **Vila Terazije** *** [103 E4] (12 rooms, 1 apt) Prizrenska 1; 📞3610 100; e info@vilaterazije.rs; w vilaterazije.rs. Very central, this small budget hotel offers good-value, spacious rooms right in the heart of the action. Wi-Fi, AC & modern bathrooms. €€€

Budget

🏠 **Beograd** ** [102 E4] (71 rooms) Balkanska 52; ☎2645 199. A cheap hotel located near the railway station, the Beograd is one of the city's more basic hotels & its noisy, shabby rooms could really do with renovation. It has a restaurant & bar. €€

🏠 **Bristol** ** [102 D4] Karađorđeva 50; ☎2631 895; e bristol@vudedinje.com; w vudedinje.mod. gov.rs. Close to the bus station, with a restaurant & bar, this is a fairly basic but acceptable budget choice. Old-fashioned rooms are a little noisy with the passing traffic on Karađorđeva but on the plus side they are quite spacious. Good old-fashioned bar. €€

🏠 **Slavija** ** [103 E5] (168 rooms, 2 suites) Svetog Save 1–9; ☎3084 800; e office@ slavijahotel.com; w www.slavijahotel.com. This hotel is the poor relation of the Slavija Garni. Still, at least it has plenty of rooms in a crisis. €€

Guesthouses, apartments and B&Bs

🏠 **Apollo** [103 H7] (41 apts) Subotička 23; m 063 430 294; e office@apollo011.in.rs; w apollo011.in.rs. Apartments in a new building in Zvezdara, with bedroom, kitchen, bathroom & balcony. All rooms come with cable TV, internet access & telephone. €€€

🏠 **Villa Manjež** [103 E5] (4 rooms, 2 suites) Svetozara Markovića 49; ☎3621 111; e office@ manjez.rs; w manjez.rs. A quiet, newly built place in the city centre with room service available from its attached national restaurant. B/fast not included. €€€

Hostels

🏠 **Belgrade Eye** [103 E4] (11 beds) Krunska 6b; ☎3346 423; e hostelbegradeeye@gmail. com; w hostelbelgradeeye.com. Pleasant well-organised hostel located in central Belgrade close to the Serbian Parliament & Tašmajdan Park. With 1 6-bed dormitory, 1 dbl & 1 trpl room. Large common room, luggage lockers, kitchen, laundry service, cable TV & free coffee. Lower prices in winter apart from New Year. €

🏠 **Centar** [102 D4] (9 rooms) Gavrila Principa 46a; ☎7619 686; e info@hostelcentar.com; w hostelcentar.com. A clean & tidy 3-storey hostel

conveniently located close to the bus & railway stations. Dbls (€€) & trpls as well as dorms. €

🏠 **Central Station** [102 D4] (13 rooms) Karađorđeva 87; ☎6685 067, 6685 069; e office@ hostelcentralstation.com; w hostelcentralstation. com. Another hostel close to the bus & railway stations, this looks unprepossessing from the outside but is reasonable enough within. Dorms & 9 twin-bed rooms available (€€). €

🏠 **Chillton** [103 F6] (3 dorms, 2 rooms) Katanićeva 7; ☎3441 826; e chilltonhostel@gmail. com; w chilltonhostel.com. Some distance from the Old Town near St Sava's in Vračar. Dorms, dbl (€€) & trpl rooms, AC. €

🏠 **City Center** [102 D4] (58 rooms) Savski trg 7; ☎6644 055; e info@cityhostel.rs; w hostelcitycenterbelgrade.hostel.com. A large hostel that was formerly a budget hotel close to the stations with dbls (€€), trpls, dorms & suites (€€). Separate male & female bathrooms. Some rooms have their own shower. €

🏠 **Downtown** [102 D4] (18 beds) Karađorđeva 91/7; ☎6687 217; e downtownbelgrade@yahoo. com; w downtownbelgradehostel.com. Close to the bus & train stations. 2 dormitories with 6 or 8 beds & 2 dbls (€€) with shared bathroom. B/fast included. €

🏠 **Jasmin** [102 D4] Karađorđeva 69/2; ☎2184 411; e office@hostelbelgradejasmin.com; w hostelbelgradejasmin.com. A newish hostel located almost directly across from the bus station. Fully AC with sgl, dbl, 3-, 4-, 6- & 8-bed rooms. Discount for students. €

🏠 **King** [103 F2] (3 rooms) Venizelosova 58; m 065 5551 847; e hostelkingbelgrade@yahoo. com; w hostel-king.com. 1 twin & 2 8-bed mixed dorms. €

🏠 **Manga** [103 E4] (4 rooms) Resavska 7; ☎3243 877; e fun@mangahostel.com; w mangahostel.com. Comfortable, friendly hostel in city centre with 1 sgl room (€€) & 3 dorms. €

🏠 **Spirit** [102 D1] Braće Baruh 20b; ☎2920 055; e office@sprithostel.com; w spirithostel. com. A popular & highly rated hostel in Dorćol not far from Kalemegdan Park. Clean & well run, with dorms & sgl room & dbl-bed apartment. €

NEW BELGRADE, ZEMUN AND AROUND

Luxury

🏠 **Crowne Plaza** ***** [102 B4] (17 rooms, 10 suites) Vladimira Popovića 10;

✆ 2204 004; e begcp.frontdesk@ihg.com; w ihg.com. Formerly the Hotel Continental, this large hotel tends to be mostly used by business visitors attending conferences. Spacious modern rooms & excellent facilities that include a fitness centre with pool & various spa treatments. €€€€€

⌂ **Holiday Inn** **** [102 A3] (140 rooms) Španskih boraca 74; ✆3100 000; e info@hibelgrade.rs; w holidayinn.com. This large, modern hotel in New Belgrade belongs to the international chain & is aimed squarely at business travellers with business centre, various conference & meeting rooms. €€€€€

⌂ **Hyatt Regency** ***** [102 B3] (302 rooms & suites) Milentija Popovića 5; ✆3011 234; e belgrade.regency@hyatt.com; w belgrade.regency.hyatt.com. This is close to the Continental, 1km from the city centre in New Belgrade, next to the Sava Congress Centre, a modern concert & conference venue. Used by embassies for visiting VIPs, as well as by visiting businessmen & discerning tourists, the Hyatt interior welcomes you into a massive marble lobby area that resembles a Classical temple. The rooms are spacious & elegant, with excellent views of the city from the upper floors, while the service is just the right balance between friendly & formal. The Hyatt has a good restaurant & a large relaxed tea room with excellent cakes. Other facilities include business centre, solarium, fitness centre with swimming pool, disabled facilities. B/fast is not included in the basic price but Serbian, American & continental varieties are all available with plentiful fresh juice & foreign newspapers. Rooms cost slightly less for sgl occupancy; also various suites – Diplomatic, Executive, Regency, etc, with prices on request. €€€€€

⌂ **In Hotel Beograd** **** [102 A4] (187 rooms) Bulevar Arsenija Čarnojevića 56; ✆3105 300, 3105 355; e frontoffice@inhotel-belgrade.rs; w inhotel-belgrade.rs. A large hotel in New Belgrade built in 2006, situated 4km from the city centre & 9km from the airport. Also 28 suites, 3 conference halls, leisure & fitness clubs. €€€€€

⌂ **Villa Jelena** **** [102 D7] (10 rooms) Generala Sturma 1a; ✆3066 509; e club@vila-jelena.com; w vila-jelena.com. Located in Dedinje south of the centre, this stylish hotel in a converted Neoclassical villa reflects its wealthy suburban surroundings. Elegant spacious rooms, with queen-size beds, marble bathrooms, internet access, cable or wireless TV & DVD player. Restaurant offering Serbian, Mediterranean & macrobiotic food. €€€€€

⌂ **Zlatnik** ***** [162 A1] (27 rooms, 4 suites) Dobanovačka 95, Zemun; ✆3167 515; e office@hotelzlatnik.com; w hotelzlatnik.com. Zlatnik is a privately owned hotel located in Zemun, 7km from Belgrade city centre. This modern hotel has 2 restaurants – national & seafood, both of which are highly rated – a conference hall & business centre, a gift shop & an aperitif bar. All rooms have AC, cable TV, internet access & safe-deposit boxes. Both garage parking & non-smoking rooms are also available. Most credit cards are accepted. €€€€€

Upmarket

⌂ **Best Western Hotel M** **** [102 D7] (173 rooms) Bulevar oslobođenja (formerly JNA) 56a; ✆3090 401, 3090 402; e office@hotel-m.com; w hotel-m.com. About 4km from the city centre, in a wooded residential area close to the FC Red Star football stadium; this is, perhaps, best suited to business travellers & those travelling in groups or with their own transport. This modern, comfortable hotel, near the quiet upmarket Dedinje area, joined the Best Western group in 2000 when it was completely overhauled & renovated. Facilities include conference halls, nightclub, restaurant, aperitif bar, free parking facilities & hair salon. €€€€

⌂ **Best Western Šumadija** **** [102 A7] (98 rooms, 6 apts) Šumadijski trg 8; ✆3054 100; e office@hotelsumadija.com; w hotelsumadija.com. This is another 4-star choice located well away from the city centre at Banovo Brdo, halfway between Ada Ciganlija & Košutnjak, 7km from the city centre but just 2km from Sajam fairground. With 3 conference rooms & a business centre, the hotel, which is part of the Best Western group, is more geared to business visitors than it is to tourists. All rooms are well appointed, with satellite TV, minibar, AC & internet access. W/end rates are about 20% lower. €€€€

⌂ **Tulip Inn Putnik** *** [162 B4] (84 rooms, 12 suites) Palmira Toljatija 9; ✆2259 999; e info@tulipinnputnikbelgrade.com; w tulipinnputnikbelgrade.com. A good-value, well-equipped business hotel in New Belgrade, 4km from the city centre, this 1972 Putnik hotel was fully renovated in 2010 & reopened as the

Tulip Inn. All rooms with Wi-Fi, desk, minibar & AC. Restaurant, café-bar & exchange office, & plenty of space for parking. Special-discount w/end deals available €€€€–€€€

Mid-range

⌂ **Bali Paradizo** **** [162 A2] (28 rooms, 5 apts) Ugrinovački put 72, Zemun; ☏ 3170 860; e hotel@bali.rs; w bali.rs. This pleasant hotel is a long way from the action but might suit business visitors or those with their own transport. Spa centre & swimming pool. €€€

⌂ **Elegance** *** [103 H1] (43 rooms, 3 suites) Zrenjaninski put 98a; ☏ 2075 000; e office@ hotelelegance.rs; w hotelelegance.rs. A business hotel at the city's outskirts. Decent, simply furnished rooms with AC, satellite TV & internet connection. Rooms for non-smokers. Good value but inconveniently located. €€€

⌂ **Hotel N** ** [102 D7] (108 rooms) Bilećka 57; ☏ 3972 183; e office@hotel-n.rs; w hotel-n. rs. At 5km from the centre, in the quiet suburb of Voždovac, this is a long way out. With its own restaurant, parking & coffee shop, & decent modern rooms. Discounts for large groups. €€€

⌂ **Lav** ** [162 A1] (29 rooms, 2 apts) Cara Dušana 240, Zemun; ☏ 3163 289; e reception@ hotellav.co.rs; w hotellav.co.rs. A modern budget choice in Zemun, 7km from the city centre with its own restaurant & private parking. Restaurant, conference facilities & free 24hr internet access. €€€

⌂ **Orašac** *** [102 B7] (7 rooms, 6 suites) Luke Vojvodića 25; ☏ 2561 090; e orasac.hotel@ gmail.com; w hotelorasac.co.rs. A small new hotel 12km south of the city centre in Rakovica close to Košutnjak Park. Lower rates at w/ends. €€€

⌂ **Skala** *** [162 B2] (14 rooms, 2 suites) Bežanijska 3, Zemun; ☏ 3075 032; e rezervacije@ hotelskala.rs; w hotelskala.rs. Located in Zemun, this small hotel is privately run, with quiet, well-furnished rooms grouped around a covered courtyard. It has its own restaurant & garage. All rooms have satellite TV, minibar & AC. €€€

Budget

⌂ **Imperium** *** [162 A3] (10 rooms) Partizanska 19a, Zemun; ☏ 3164 773. This is a small new guesthouse in Zemun with just 9 dbl rooms & 1 sgl. It is 6km from Belgrade city centre, close to Zemun-Novi Grad railway station & the motorway north & west. €€

⌂ **Nacional** ** [102 A4] (65 rooms) Auto put 5; ☏ 2601 122, 2601 156; e recepcija@nacional-bgd.com; w nacional-bgd.com. Located 8km from the city centre on the highway, & reasonable value for those with their own transport. The Nacional boasts a restaurant, aperitif bar & conference hall. There is parking for guests. €€

⌂ **Trim** ** [102 B7] (33 rooms, 1 apt) Kneza Višeslava 72; ☏ 3540 669, 3540 670; e info@ trimhotel.rs; w trimhotel.rs. In Košutnjak, 9km from the city centre. Conference hall, restaurant, parking, TV, minibar. €€

Guesthouses, apartments and B&Bs

⌂ **Vila Zemun** [162 C1] (10 rooms) Fruškogorska 1, Zemun; ☏ 2191 778; m 062 661 414; e office@vilazemun.com; w vilazemun.com. Close to the river in Zemun. All rooms with TV, minibar, AC & internet access. No b/fast provided, but free tea & coffee. €€€

Hostels

⌂ **Yachting Club Kej** [102 B2] (9 twin rooms) Ušće bb; m 064 8251 103; e kontakt@klubkej. com; w klubkej.com. Another floating hostel on the Danube River with clean twin-bedded cabins. There is a restaurant & a catamaran for evening booze cruises provided for guests. €€

⌂ **ArkaBarka** [102 B2] (8 rooms) Ušće bb, Blok 14; m 064 9253 507; e arkabarkahostel@gmail. com; w arkabarka.net. This colourfully painted floating hostel on the Danube River is moored in a tranquil spot surrounded by trees. There is also a pleasant bar on board. Dbl (€€) & trpl rooms are available, as well as dorms. €

CAMPING There is nowhere to pitch a tent anywhere near the city centre, although you may wish to consider the following:

⋏ **Auto-kamp 'Košutnjak'** [102 B7] Kneza Višeslava 17; ☏ 3555 127; e office@ kampkosutnjak.rs; w kampkosutnjak.rs. This is close to Topčider Park, to the south of the city centre. The site is in a pleasant, leafy suburb & has plentiful sports facilities. They do not have places for tents but have bungalows available. €€

⋏ **Dunav** [162 A1] Batajnički put, Zemun;

2199 072; e campdunav@amkjedinstvo.rs; w campdunav.com. This is the nearest campsite outside the city & is 12km northwest of the city centre. They charge 450din to camp, 400din for a car & 350din to be connected to an electricity supply. They also have bungalows to rent. €

✖ WHERE TO EAT AND DRINK

> We ate too large a lunch, as is apt to be one's habit in Belgrade, if one is man enough to stand up to peasant food made luxurious by urban lavishness of supply and a Turkish tradition of subtle and positive flavour.
>
> Rebecca West, *Black Lamb and Grey Falcon*

Belgrade abounds with restaurants, cafés and bars for all tastes and pockets. Cheapest and most plentiful are the ubiquitous fast-food places, where, although the produce may be familiar in some – McDonald's and the like – there are many more that demonstrate a particularly Balkan slant on what constitutes fast food: *čevapčići, burek, pljeskavica*, etc. In contrast, restaurants serving slow food – and they can sometimes be very slow – can be considered as serving either Serbian or foreign cuisine, only occasionally both. Most of the 'foreign' cuisine is actually Italian, although these days Belgrade does boast culinary representatives from all over the globe. It should be noted that the smarter restaurants, especially those of the Serbian, 'national cuisine' variety, are considered more as suitable venues for a fine evening out than merely as places to take the necessary calories on board; after all, that is what fast food is for. With large family groups enjoying quality time eating, drinking, talking, smoking and singing together, restaurants are seen as places to linger, let your hair down and enjoy life.

Despite the Serbian fixation for meat, vegetarians need not despair even if they cannot expect too much in the way of variety. Reliable standbys like *gibanica, srpska* or *šopska* salad are nearly always available. Dedicated non-smokers, on the other hand, may find life difficult: in the tobacco-friendly world of Belgrade's restaurants, the air is often smog-thick with plumes of Marlboro Lite. The concept of passive smoking has yet to catch on in the Balkans, where non-smokers are considered to be a touch eccentric. Thanks to new laws passed in 2012, restaurants are now obliged to indicate smoking and non-smoking areas but this has yet to be taken very seriously. Smarter restaurants will often have clearly marked non-smoking tables, although these are often located immediately next door to others where smoking is permitted. At least in summer you can usually sit outside.

Restaurants tend to be clustered in certain areas of the city, as do the café-bars. In the Old Town, many cafés, bars and restaurants line the pedestrian thoroughfare of Knez Mihailova, as well as the side streets that lead off from it. In particular, Obilićev venac, by the Metropol Hotel, has almost totally given itself over to trendy theme-bars, the haunt of young folk mostly, and the place to be seen sipping your cappuccino. Many of the bars also serve light snacks: pancakes, sandwiches, ice creams and the like. For heavier fare, there is a dense concentration of Serbian 'national' restaurants running all the way along the short length of Skadarska, although this area is much busier during the summer months than the rest of the year. Similarly, the lines of boat restaurants moored along the Danube and Sava tend to be most active when nights are warm and at their shortest. Generally speaking, they open relatively late and stay open until the early hours. The small 'bohemian' enclave of Skadarlija lies within the limits of the Old Town but has such a concentration of restaurants and cafés that it is listed here separately. A little further afield, and a pleasant choice for a summer's

3

evening, is the neighbouring town of Zemun with its own dense concentration of fish restaurants lining the river frontage there.

In the business-oriented part of the city, restaurants are more spread out and generally more geared to the lunchtime trade, although there are notable exceptions to this. Even here, there are pockets of activity that lure people out in the evening, an example being the concentration of stylish café-bars along Njegoševa close to the Park Hotel.

Another up-and-coming area with regard to restaurants and cafés, mainly of the fairly smart variety that attract a slightly older crowd, is the recently developed complex on the Savamala waterfront at Beton hala just north of Brankov Bridge. Several stylish places have opened here since 2011 and no doubt will continue to do so in the future as this area gains in popularity.

Belgrade has a bewildering number of **café-bars** that range from extremely upmarket, with luxurious furniture and gleaming Italian espresso machines, to bohemian fly-by-night places. The Old Town area especially is chock-a-block with places to drink coffee, or something stronger, and watch the world go by. The Savamala district down by the waterside is still up and coming, but already highly popular with young people at weekends. At the upmarket end of the scale is the concentration of cafés, bars and clubs along Strahinjića bana, a street popularly known as 'Silicone Valley' due to the hordes of supposedly surgically enhanced young women that are said to frequent the area at night. The name is a bit of a misnomer, as the vast majority of Belgrade's women have no need for cosmetic surgery and would probably not choose it even if they could afford it. Then again, there are always 'sponsors' who might wish to fashion their image of the 'perfect woman' by way of a credit card and a scalpel (see box, page 134).

As stated elsewhere, the boundary between what defines a place as a bar, a café, a restaurant or a nightclub is a blurred one – some institutions may serve as all four. By the same token, a 'pub' is not usually the same as one might expect in the UK.

For listings located in the Old Town, see map, pages 114–15; for listings located in the city centre and elsewhere, see map, pages 102–3, unless otherwise noted.

RESTAURANTS Most restaurants are open 7 days a week but some may close earlier on Sun evenings.

Old Town

✗ **Daka** [115 H6] Đure Daničića 4; ✆ 3341 347; ⏰ 10.00–23.00. Not to be confused with 'Dačo', this is an exclusive restaurant with a lovely garden. It is located through an entrance opposite the junction with Šafarikova. €€€€

✗ **Kalemegdanska terasa** [114 B1] Belgrade Fortress, Mali Kalemegdan 7; ✆ 3283 011, 3282 727; w kalemegdanskaterasa.com; ⏰ noon–01.00. This is a fine, & fairly pricey, restaurant serving international cuisine for those who like to surround themselves with history while they eat. Situated just behind Belgrade Zoo, there are superb views of both the Danube & Sava rivers from here, & so it is undeniably a romantic spot. This restaurant has a fairly strict dress code,

ie: no shorts & sandals. Live music is provided some nights. €€€€

✗ **Beogradska panorama** [114 B6] 6th floor of Hotel Palace, Topličin venac 23; ✆ 2185 585; ⏰ 19.00–01.00. As you might expect, there is an excellent city view from up here. International & Serbian cuisine. €€€

✗ **Cantina de Frida** [114 A6] Beton hala, Karađorđeva 2–4; ✆ 2181 107; w cantinadefrida. com. In the new Beton hala development facing the river, this is a smart, brightly painted Spanish/Mexican café-bar with a Frida Kahlo theme. Tapas, asados & salsa dips, ideally shared with friends. Live music most nights. €€€

✗ **Dorian Gray** [114 D2] Kralja Petra I 87–89; ✆ 2634 151; ⏰ 09.00–01.00; w doriangray.rs. This is a posh café-restaurant at the upper end of 'Silicone Valley'. With a stylish Art Nouveau interior, balcony & patio, & an international menu, it is popular with Belgrade's expat community. €€€

✘ **Fish & Bar** [115 E5] Braće Jugović 3; 3281 701. A modern & stylish fish restaurant that specialises in promptly served meals of pre-prepared fish – the acceptable face of fast food. The fish is admirably fresh & they also have decent salads & a wide choice of wines; also a non-smoking section. There is another branch near Kalenić Market at Njegoševa 82 (2434 256) & 2 more in New Belgrade at the Ušće shopping centre on Bulevar Mihaila Pupina 4 (3129 582) & at Tržni Centar, Jurija Gagarina 16 (2203 860). €€€

✘ **Klub književnika** [115 E5] Francuska 7; 2627 931, 2187 777; w klubknjizevnika.rs; noon–01.00. This place, The Writers' Club, is an institution that dates back to the Tito era when Belgrade's government-approved literati would meet here to discuss metaphors over *kajmak* & glasses of *šljivovica*. The entrance to this grand stucco mansion is through a gate on the street that has a plaque next to it that reads: 'Association of Literary Translators of Serbia'. The main dining room is downstairs but there is also a large summer garden. White-jacketed waiters help to complete the impression of a bygone age. No literary credentials required. €€€

✘ **Peking** [114 C5] Vuka Karadžića 2; 281 931; w peking.co.rs; 11.00–23.00 Mon–Sat. Not surprisingly, the Peking is a Chinese restaurant, ideal for those hankering to order their food by numbers. As well as Chinese specialities like pork in sweet & sour sauce, it also serves Serbian dishes. €€€

✘ **Trattoria Campania** [114 B6] Kneza Sime Markovića 10; 3115 531; noon–22.00 Mon, 10.00–23.30 Tue–Thu, 10.00–midnight Fri, 11.00–midnight Sat, noon–23.00 Sun. Housed in an old building close to the Saborna Church & Princess Ljubica's mansion, the food here is genuine Italian cuisine, with good pizzas & an interesting range of regional dishes. €€€

✘ **Vuk** [114 C5] Vuka Karadžića 12; 2629 761; 09.00–23.00. Good, if rather pricey, grilled meats on a pleasant, breezy summer terrace just off Knez Mihailova. €€€

✘ **Brankovina** [114 C4] Uzun Mirkova; 2622 189. Cosy Old Town restaurant just off Knez Mihailova with Serbian national cuisine & illustrated English menu. €€

✘ **Kolarac** [114 C5] Knez Mihailova 46; 638 972; 09.00–23.30. Many meaty Serbian choices

at reasonable prices are available in this old-fashioned restaurant favoured by locals & family groups. Good value & good, solid food, also a good place to stop for a beer at the outside tables. €€

✘ **Little Bay** [115 E5] Dositejeva 9a; 3284 163; w littlebay.co.uk; 11.00–01.00. A Belgrade version of the London chain with interesting fusion of cuisine & highly idiosyncratic décor. The daily menu offers a fairly limited choice of options but the food is excellent & the price a bargain for such good quality. The faux-opera house interior is charming & there is live classical music most nights. Understandably, Little Bay gets very busy at w/ends. €€

✘ **Manufaktura** [114 B5] Kralja Petra I 13–15; 2180 044; w restoran-manufaktura. rs; 11.00–01.00. A well-located Old Town restaurant that offers authentic Balkan food & wine in atmospheric surroundings at very reasonable prices. Live music some nights. €€

✘ **Ottimo** [114 D5] Studentski trg 10; 3286 454; w restoranottimo.rs; 10.00–midnight. A small Italian restaurant with a good range of pasta, meat, fish & antipasto dishes, a pleasant atmosphere & good service. The outside raised dining area next to the park is decorated in the style of a rural Italian home. €€

✘ **Stepenice Velike** [114 A5] Stepenice 6; 2634 124; w velikestepenice.com; 09.00–midnight Sun–Thu, 09.00–01.00 Fri/Sat. Near the top of the old steps (*velike stepenice*) that lead steeply up from Karađorđeva, this restaurant has a good selection of Italian-style meat dishes, pasta, salads & pizzas, as well as superb views from its balcony. There's also a music bar with live performers (small cover charge). €€

✘ **Srpska Kafana** [115 H7] Svetogorska 25; 3247 197; w srpskakafana.rs; 07.00–23.00. A traditional Serbian *kafana* with friendly waiters, wooden cartwheel chandeliers & good, honest home-cooked food at modest prices. €€–€

✳ ✘ **'?' (Znak pitanja) Kafana** [114 B5] Kralja Petra I 6; 2635 421; 08.00–midnight daily. The story goes that the Question Mark Inn was once named 'By the Cathedral' (for obvious reasons: the Orthodox Cathedral is directly opposite the restaurant). The religious authorities decided that such an association with a common hostelry was highly blasphemous & so the proprietor was ordered to remove the sign immediately. Instead of taking the sign down, he merely covered it with a large question mark & somehow this new interrogative appellation stuck. The '?' is actually one of very few 19th-century buildings still standing in the city but, instead of being a museum piece, it remains an authentic local restaurant, refreshingly un-themed & without a hint of pretence. Very popular with foreign visitors these days, there is an English-language menu & the food, the usual range of Serbian grilled meat & salads, is filling, wholesome & encouragingly cheap. It is a good place for a beer or a decanter of wine too. €€–€

✗ **McDonald's** [114 C7] Brankova plato; ☎ 2638 249; ⏰ 07.00–02.00. This is one of a dozen or so McDonald's in Belgrade, & this branch sits on a terrace above Zeleni venac, the terminus for many of the city's bus routes. There is a much larger branch nearby on Terazije. €

✗ **Orao** [115 F6] 29 Novembra (Bulevar despota Stefana) 28; ☎ 3228 836; w orao-pizza.co.rs; ⏰ offers 24hr service. This pizzeria provides a wide range of both national & Italian dishes that are good value & come with prompt service. The outside terrace, however, is extremely noisy with the constant stream of heavy traffic thundering down this major thoroughfare. There are 3 other branches spread around the city centre. €

✳️✗ **Proleće** [114 C5] Vuka Karadžića 11; ☎ 2635 436; ⏰ 10.00–23.00. This down-to-earth national restaurant close to Knez Mihailova has low prices, friendly service & decent grilled meat & home-cooked Serbian staples. €

✗ **Walter** [115 F3] Strahinjića bana 57; ☎ 3300 002; w walter.rs; ⏰ 08.00–23.30. One of 4 branches in the city, Walter's speciality is genuine *Sarajevska ćevapi*, although it also sells a range of traditional Serbian grill dishes. €

Skadarlija

✗ **Chez Tristan** [115 F5] Skadarska 34; ☎ 3035 252; w petitpiaf.com; ⏰ noon–midnight. This small, elegant restaurant belongs to Le Petit Piaf Hotel & exudes a calm modernity when compared with most of the other restaurants in the vicinity. There is a good range of international dishes, expertly cooked, & a large wine list. Special musically themed evenings are sometimes staged here. €€€

✗ **Dva Jelena** [115 F5] Skadarska 32; ☎ 3234 885; w dvajelena.rs; ⏰ 11.00–01.00. One of many 'national cuisine' restaurants on this street, the 'Two Deer' is an institution that dates back to

1832. With 2 large, smoky dining halls that can cater for large groups, this restaurant is often the location for the 'folklore evening' attended by visiting tour groups. Like all Skadarlija restaurants, it is a tad overpriced – you pay for the atmosphere & the musical accompaniment – but the Two Deer is really not 'too dear' for what you get: the food is wholesome & filling & the choice of wine is good. €€

✗ **Guli** [115 F5] Skadarska 13; ☎ 3237 204; w guli.rs; ⏰ noon–00.30. This is a small Italian place with its own pizza oven, a vaulted roof & bench seating. Authentic pizzas are served on wooden platters. €€

✗ **Ima dana** [115 F5] Skadarska 38; ☎ 3234 422; w restoran-imadana.rs; ⏰ 09.00–01.00. Ima dana is a 4-star national restaurant & perhaps the most exclusive of the choices on this street, with 2 restaurant halls & a covered terrace. A wide selection of appetisers is available, along with popular national dishes like *karađorđeva šnicla*. €€

✗ **Šešir moj** [115 F5] Skadarska 21; ☎ 3228 750; ⏰ 11.00–midnight. Certainly the most attention-grabbing restaurant of this street with a fantastic floral display around the entrance, Šešir moj, which means 'My Hat' (look at the sign) offers more in the way of vegetarian choice than most others in Skadarlija. €€

✗ **Tri Šešira** (Three hats) [115 F5] Skadarska 29; ☎ 3247 501; w trisesira.rs; ⏰ 11.00–01.00. This large, 4-star restaurant, one of the most popular along this street, is probably also one of the best here. House specialities include *sarma*, stuffed pickled cabbage leaves, & *proja*, corn bread. There is also live music, of course. €€

✗ **Velika Skadarlija** [115 G5] Cetinjska 17; ☎ 3342 230; w restoranvelikaskadarlija.com; ⏰ 09.00–01.00. At the bottom of Skardalija, on the corner, with a large dining hall that is often popular with wedding parties. €€

✗ **Zlatan Bokal** [115 F5] Skadarska 26; ☎ 3234 834; ⏰ 11.00–01.00. Another good choice on this street that has a pleasant raised outdoor terrace for summer dining. €€

Central Belgrade

✗ **Tabor** [103 G5] Bulevar kralja Aleksandra 348; ☎ 2412 464; w restorantabor.com; ⏰ noon–02.00. Tabor is a 4-star restaurant that serves both Serbian & international food & puts on live music for its diners. €€€€

✕ Casa [103 E5] Makenzijeva 24; ✆ 2421 554; w casarestoran.com; ⏰ noon–midnight. Casa is an elegant restaurant, located in a refined 19th-century house, which offers dishes from a variety of Italian regions. €€€

✕ Lovac [103 E5] Alekse Nenadovića 19; ✆ 2436 128; w restoranlovac.rs; ⏰ 09.00–01.00. A long-established restaurant close to Nikola Tesla & Natural History museums that specialises in game dishes like venison with chestnut purée & 'hunters' sausages'. Meat dishes are served at the table on hot charcoal grills. €€€

✕ Madera [103 F4] Bulevar kralja Aleksandra 43; ✆ 3231 332, 3247 148; w maderarestoran. com; ⏰ 10.00–01.00. Elegant, smart Art Deco-style restaurant with a large, circular garden terrace that overlooks Tašmajdan Park. Wide range of Serbian & international meat & fish dishes; extensive wine list. €€€

✕ Resava [103 E4] Resavska 24; ✆ 3233 192; ⏰ noon–midnight. This is another high-class Italian restaurant. €€€

✕ Steak House 'El Toro' [103 E4] Masarikova 5; ✆ 3612 429; w eltoro.rs; ⏰ noon–23.00. As the name suggests, Argentine meat-dominated cuisine. €€€

✕ Whatever@The Corner [103 E5] Beogradska 37; ✆ 3236 470; w nacosku.rs; ⏰ 11.00–23.00 Mon–Sat, noon–18.00 Sun. An interesting modern restaurant with quirky Mediterranean & oriental dishes like Vietnamese salad, beef stir fry & sole provençale. €€€

✕ Zaplet [103 G5] Kajmakčalanska 2; ✆ 2404 142; w zaplet.rs; ⏰ 09.00–midnight Tue–Sun. Directly opposite Café Sq in Vračar district, this fashionable, elegant restaurant has a modern, imaginative menu that combines elements of both Serbian & Mediterranean cuisine. Some good, inventive vegetarian dishes too. €€€

✻ ✕ Lorenzo i Kakalamba [103 G4] Cvijićeva 110; ✆ 3295 351; w lk.rs; ⏰ noon–midnight. This very quirky restaurant has all sorts of eccentric touches to its interior décor. The speciality here is a sort of Florentine–Pirot hybrid, mixing Serbian & Italian influences. Very popular, so best to book at w/ends. €€€–€€

✕ Byblos [103 E6] Nebojšina 6; ✆ 2441 938; w byblos.rs; ⏰ noon–01.00. Close to the Slavija roundabout, Byblos is a Lebanese restaurant that specialises in mezze dishes. €€

✕ Hari's Creperie [103 E4] Kraljice Marije 8; ✆ 3345 145; ⏰ 08.00–midnight. True to its name, the predominant dishes on offer are pancakes with a wide choice of savoury or sweet fillings. €€

✕ Makao [103 F4] Starine Novaka 7a; ✆ 3236 631; w makao-bg.com; ⏰ 14.00–23.00. Close to Tašmajdan Park, this pleasant restaurant serves dim sum & a wide range of excellent Chinese food. The ambience is good & the prices are very reasonable. They have opened other branches at Šafarikova 11 (✆ 3224 733), at Pere Velimirovića 74 (✆ 2682 777) & in Zemun at Prve pruge 8 (✆ 3192 931). €€

✕ Trandafilović [103 F6] Ugao Mutapove I Makenzijeva; m 065 3402 020; w bistrotrandafilovic.com; ⏰ 08.00–midnight. This city restaurant, within walking distance of St Sava's Church & Kalenić Market, specialises in Serbian national cuisine & attracts many well-known Belgraders, politicians & lawyers. The leafy garden, an excellent place to be in summer, is shaded by an old oak tree that is protected by law. €€

✕ Zorba [103 F4] Kraljice Marije; ✆ 337 6547; ⏰ 11.00–midnight. Zorba is a small Greek taverna with very reasonable prices. €€

✕ Kafana Pavle Korčagin [103 G5] Ćirila i Metodija 2a; ✆ 2401 980; w kafanapavlekorcagin. rs; ⏰ 07.30–01.00 Mon–Fri, 10.00–01.00 Sat, 11.00–23.00 Sun. This is a little hard to find, tucked away down an alleyway behind the Vuk Theatre a little way off Bulevar kralja Aleksandra. Fairly standard Serbian food served in a charmingly cosy but slightly chaotic interior that serves as a playful shrine to Tito & old Yugoslavia. Old records, posters & framed photos all help to promote the 'Yugostalgia' theme. Live music some nights. €€–€

✕ Kalenić [103 F5] Mileševska (Save Kovačevića) 2; ✆ 2450 666; ⏰ 08.00–midnight. As its name suggests, this national restaurant is located close to Kalenić Market on the corner with Maksima Gorkog. There is a large dining hall with wood panelling inside, as well as some tables on a terrace facing the street. Kalenić comes recommended by many for its traditional Serbian cooking. €€–€

✕ Burrito Madre [103 E3] Terazije 27; ✆ 3037 450; w burritomadre.com; ⏰ 09.00–01.00. With 2 more branches at Karađorđeva 65 & Bulevar kralja Aleksandra 54, this offers custom-made burritos using the freshest of ingredients. €

✕ Kantina [103 E4] Bulevar kralja Aleksandra 26; ✆ 3341 484; w kantina.rs; ⏰ 08.00–22.00

Mon–Sat, 10.00–18.00 Sun. On the corner with Resavska opposite Tašmajdan Park, this popular, fast-moving place offers a dazzling range of traditional dishes at rock-bottom prices from a self-selection counter. €

✗ Orač [103 F6] Makenzijeva (Maršala Tolbuhina) 81; ☎ 2430 885; ⏰ 09.00–midnight. On the corner of Makenzijeva & Mutapova at Vračar, this is a Serbian grill restaurant with very reasonable prices. €

Elsewhere in the city

✗ Đorđe [103 F6] Moravska 10; ☎ 3441 422; w restorandjordje.rs; ⏰ 09.00–midnight Mon– Sat, 10.00–18.00 Sun. Đorđe is a smart restaurant in the well-to-do suburb of Dedinje that serves a wide range of international dishes. Good selection of wines from Serbia & beyond. €€€€

✗ Franš [103 E6] Bulevar oslobođenja 18a; ☎ 2641 944; w frans.rs; ⏰ 09.00–midnight. A smart restaurant with a summer garden that serves international cuisine, mostly French & Italian. Despite its unenviable location beside one of the city's major thoroughfares, the restaurant is very popular & so it is always best to book at least a day ahead. €€€€

✗ Gušti mora [102 A7] Radnička 27; ☎ 3551 268; w gustimora.com; ⏰ noon–midnight. An excellent fish restaurant on the main road opposite Ada Ciganlija that serves a wide selection of grilled fish, risottos & soups. €€€

✗ Rubin [102 B7] Kneza Višeslava 29; ☎ 3510 987; ⏰ 10.00–23.00. On top of the hill in Košutnjak, it is probably worth coming here for the view alone. €€€

✗ Diwali [103 F7] Ljubićka 1b; ☎ 3446 235; w diwali.rs; ⏰ 11.00–23.00 Tue–Sun. Well away from the city centre, close to the Indian Embassy in the suburb of Dušanovac, this stylish restaurant, formerly known as Maharajah, serves the sort of mouth-watering northern Indian food that is familiar to British taste buds. Despite an awkward location, this restaurant is a very worthwhile target for curry addicts. €€€–€€

✗ Amigo [102 D7] Mladena Stojanovića 2a; ☎ 2663 366; ⏰ 09.00–midnight. This is a Mexican-style restaurant in the Dedinje area. €€

New Belgrade and Zemun

✗ Bahus [102 A2] Bulevar Nikole Tesle; ☎ 3015 082, 3015 083; w bahus.co.rs; ⏰ 10.00–01.00. A smart, expensive floating restaurant close to the

Hotel Jugoslavija that is air-conditioned in summer & heated in winter. The emphasis is on fresh fish. Bahus refers to the Greek god of indulgence rather than any pre-war German school of art. €€€€

✗ Bella Napoli [162 C1] Zmaj Jovina 35, Zemun; ☎ 2198 162; w bellanapoli.rs; ⏰ noon–midnight. A cosy Italian restaurant a little way in from the Zemun waterfront with fish, meat & salads as well as pizza & homemade pasta dishes. €€€

✗ Campo de Fiori [162 B1] Njegoševa 35, Zemun; ☎ 3169 006; w campo.rs; ⏰ noon– midnight. Not to be confused with another Italian restaurant of the same name in Skadarlija, this is a delightful trattoria with authentic-tasting Italian food including 15 types of pizza located on a quiet street in Zemun away from the waterfront. €€€

✗ Reka [162 B1] Kej oslobođenja 73b, Zemun; ☎ 2611 625; w reka.co.rs. A popular Zemun restaurant with fish, national & international dishes that has a convivial friendly atmosphere. There is live music every night (small cover charge) & usually dancing too. €€€

✗ Šaran [162 B1] Kej oslobođenja 53, Zemun; ☎ 2618 235; w saran.co.rs; ⏰ 15.00–23.00 Mon, noon–01.00 Tue–Sat, noon–23.00 Sun. Šaran (meaning 'carp') is considered to be one of the best fish restaurants along the waterfront in Zemun. Live music. €€€

✗ Salaš 034 [162 B1] Sinđelićeva 34; ☎ 2190 324; m 065 2190 324; w restoransalas034.com; ⏰ 13.00–midnight. A restaurant in a traditionally decorated period house in Zemun, away from the river on the cobbled street that leads to Gardoš tower. The speciality here is Vojvodina cuisine. In the English-language menu you can find dishes such as 'Herdsman's spit' & 'Mulligan of rabbit'. €€€–€€

✗ Danubius [162 C1] Kej oslobođenja 39, Zemun; ☎ 3750 099; w restorandanubius.com; ⏰ 09.00–01.00 Sun–Thu, 09.00–02.30 Fri/Sat. This waterfront café-restaurant in Zemun serves *riblja čorba* (fish soup), fish & grilled meats, all at very reasonable prices. There are several similar restaurants close by that also serve fish dishes in a riverside setting. €€

✗ New Marinero [162 D2] Kej oslobođenja 11a, Zemun; ☎ 2195 095; w newmarinero.rs; ⏰ 09.00–midnight Mon–Sat, 10.00–18.00 Sun. A floating restaurant on the Danube waterfront at Zemun that has live music most nights. €€

✗ Perper Lux [162 B4] Omladinskih brigada

18a, Novi Beograd; ☎2606 046; ⏰ noon–01.00. Perper is considered by some aficionados to produce the best grilled meat in Belgrade. Try *leskovačka mućkalica* – spicy grilled pork with vegetables. Live music. €

✗ **Venecija** [162 C2] Kej oslobođenja 6, Zemun; **m** 064 3635 220; **w** venecijarestoran.rs; ⏰ 09.00–23.00. This is an unpretentious riverside *kafana* in Zemun, with a large terrace & very reasonable prices. €

BARS AND CAFÉS
Old Town

🍺 **Apropo** [114 B5] Cara Lazara 10; ☎2625 839; **w** www.apropro.co.rs; ⏰ 10.00–20.00 Mon–Fri, 11.00–16.00 Sat. A cosy bookshop & tearoom with Wi-Fi.

🍺 **Berliner** [114 A7] Braće Krsmanović 6–8, Savamala; ⏰ 13.00–01.00. With the motto 'Ich bin ein Berliner', this is a beer hall in an old railway warehouse. Bewildering choice of beers (more than 50!) & food like chicken wings & sausages. Live music.

🍺 **Black Turtle Pub V** [115 G7] Svetogorska 14; ☎3239 263; **w** theblackturtle.com; ⏰ 09.00–midnight Sun–Thu, 09.00–01.00 Fri/Sat. An English-style pub near the Atelije 212 theatre that brews its own beer, this has retro features like Wild West swing doors, heavy wooden furniture, a bar with hand pumps & dense cigarette smoke. A good choice of beers includes stout, pils, weissbier & Belgian-type flavoured brews. There are other branches at Kosančićev venac 30 [114 A5], Gospodar Jovanova 56 [115 E4] & Dečanska 2 [115 F7].

🍺 **Café Theatre** [114 D6] Trg Republike 3; ☎2621 373. Right next to the square by the museum, this is highly convenient for Old Town sightseers. A little expensive for what it is – hardly surprising given its prime position. Good coffee, cakes & ice cream.

🍺 **Choco Caffe** [114 B4] Knez Mihailova 49; **m** 064 8382 050; **w** chococaffe.com; ⏰ 08.00–midnight Sun–Thu, 08.00–01.00 Fri–Sat. A pavement café near the top of Knez Mihailova, with another branch at Obilićev venac, this has all manner of sumptuous sweets made from mixing fruit & Belgian chocolate.

🍺 **Coffee Dream** [114 C4] Nikole Spašića 2; ☎ 2620 552; **w** coffeedream.rs; ⏰ 09.00–midnight. One of over a dozen branches of this highly popular coffee chain, this one on the corner

of Knez Mihailova is perfectly placed for watching the world – or at least Belgrade – go by.

🍺 **Hanan** [115 G7] Svetogorska 2; ☎3345 304; ⏰ noon–22.00. A small Lebanese café-restaurant serving delicious Lebanese sweets like *baklava*, as well as savouries like *shwarma, tabbouleh* & *fattoush*.

🍺 **Hot Spot Café** [114 D4] Studentski trg 21; ☎2639 205; ⏰ 10.00–midnight Mon–Sat. This light, airy café at the northwest end of Studentski trg has window stools with views over the park, tables & chairs near the bar & a comfortable sofa area at the back. Plenty of coffees, teas, beers & cocktails to choose from & a limited selection of food.

🍺 **Jazz Café** [114 D6] Obilićev venac 19; ☎3282 380; ⏰ 09.00–02.00. As the name says, the musical focus is jazz in this relaxed hangout, which has modern art on the walls & wooden benches to sit on. A good variety of iced teas & non-alcoholic *mojitos* available. Occasionally, live music is staged here.

✴ 🍺 **Kandahar** [115 E3] Strahinjića bana 48; ☎2910 311; ⏰ 08.00–late. A café with an oriental theme along the upper reaches of Silicone Valley. More laid-back than most around here, Kandahar has carved wooden partitions, low tables & chairs & an Arabian tent ambience. There are a variety of flavoured teas to choose from, made with a mix of leaves, seeds & petals rather than teabags. There is proper Turkish coffee too, served with pieces of rose-flavoured *lokum*.

🍺 **Leila** [114 C4] Gospodar Jevremova 6; **m** 065 3247 258; **w** leila.rs; ⏰ 09.00–01.00. A curiosity, this place has a twin function as both a snug café-bar & a record shop that promotes occasional low-key musical events. Be careful not to spill your beer on the vinyl as it doesn't come cheap.

🍺 **Mamma's Biscuit House** [115 F4] Strahinjića bana 72; ☎3283 805; **w** mammasbiscuit.rs; ⏰ 09.00–01.00. Not that many biscuits, despite the name, but a wide selection of absolutely delicious (& highly calorific) tortes & cakes as well as the usual coffees & teas. In warm weather, the small outside terrace provides welcome relief from the smoky interior.

🍺 **OK.no** [114 D6] Obilićev venac 17; ☎2629 072; ⏰ 07.00–02.00. Next door to the Jazz Café, this establishment is a real curiosity with its mining nostalgia theme. Even the doors on to the street have pickaxes for handles &, once inside, the extensiveness of the coal-mine theme becomes apparent, with faux ventilation ducts & pit props, miners' lamps hanging from the ceiling, & tools suspended on the walls. There is a sitting area outside too, although here the mining theme is not really apparent. There is a wide range of beers, juices, coffees & cocktails to choose from. Also on this street are Jazz Café & many more.

Pastis [114 E3] Strahinjića bana 52b; ✆ 3288 188; ⏰ 08.00–00.30. A trendy coffee bar (on a very trendy street) styled as a French bistro.

Snežana [114 C4] Knez Mihailova 50; ✆ 2635 706; **w** snezana.rs; ⏰ 09.00–midnight Mon–Sat, 11.00–midnight Sun. This café-bar on the corner of Knez Mihailova & Kralja Petra I, next to Tribeca, serves a range of pizzas, cakes & ice creams.

Supermarket Deli [114 C6] Topličin venac 19–21; ✆ 2028 008; **w** supermarket.rs; ⏰ 08.00–midnight Mon–Fri, 09.00–midnight Sat/Sun. Serving as both a delicatessen & a café, this is a good choice for b/fast.

Tribeca [114 C4] Kralja Petra I 20; ✆ 3285 656; ⏰ 09.00–02.00 Mon–Sat, 10.00–02.00 Sun. Next door to Snežana with its own patio deck & a smart stylish interior that perhaps tries a bit too hard. Menu has a range of interesting fusion dishes that combine various international cuisines.

Via del Gusto [114 C4] Knez Mihailova 48; ✆ 3288 200; **w** viadelgusto.rs; ⏰ 08.00–midnight Sun–Fri, 08.00–01.00 Sat. They have a pizza oven & a pancake ring in the front window but many people come here for a take-away pastry or to sit outside with a coffee. Light French, Italian & Greek dishes & good sweet & savoury pancakes.

♀ **Optimist** [115 F6] 29 Novembra 22; ✆ 3373 467; ⏰ 08.00–04.00. One of the closest things Belgrade has to being a 'pub' in the British sense: usually packed; cheap draught beer & a good atmosphere.

♀ **Rakia Bar** [115 E5] Dobračina 5; ✆ 3286 119; **w** rakiabar.com; ⏰ 09.00–midnight Mon–Fri, 09.00–02.00 w/ends. As its name suggests, a tiny bar dedicated to *rakija* – over 100 different types in fact. Evening '*rakija* tours' visiting 3 different locations also leave from here; reservations should be made 24hrs in advance.

♀ **Sports Pub** [114 C5] Nikole Spašića 1; ✆ 4090 409; ⏰ 08.00–01.00 Sun–Thu, 08.00–03.00 Fri/Sat. Large Old Town bar that has walls covered with football shirts & sports memorabilia, & numerous screens showing a variety of football matches. Good choice of draught & bottled beers

as well as a menu that offers typical beer-hall food like hot dogs & chicken wings.

☀ ♀ **U Podrumu** [114 A6] Kosančićev venac 20; ✆ 2630 272; ⏰ 11.00–23.00. On a quiet street away from the crowds on Knez Mihailova, this café-wine bar's nicest feature is its tables out on the street – a great place to relax & watch the world go by. There is also an art gallery.

☀ ♀ **World Travellers' Club** (Udruženje svetskih putnika) [115 F6] 29 Novembra (Bulevar despota Stefana) 7; ✆ 3242 303; ⏰ 13.00–midnight Mon–Fri, 15.00–midnight Sat/Sun. This curious place is in a basement more or less opposite the Optimist pub. The name is a wry joke as the club, also known as the Federal Association of Globetrotters, originated in the hard years of the Milošević era when all most Belgraders could do was dream of travel. Now it attracts a slightly older arty crowd. The interior is decorated with a collection of miscellaneous bric-a-brac, photographs & international memorabilia. Outside in the narrow cobbled yard area are ferns & a water feature. Ring the doorbell & speak into the door phone to be let in.

Central Belgrade

Greenet Panorama [103 E4] Masarikova 5; ✆ 3618 533; **w** greenet.rs; ⏰ 07.00–23.00 Mon–Sat, 09.00–23.30 Sun. Near the entrance to the 'Beograd anka' building, with an excellent choice of coffees, this place is always busy with office workers. A take-away service is available; also, a good choice of cakes, pizzas & pasta dishes. There are 10 branches altogether in the city, including 1 at Nušićeva 4 [115 E7] (✆ 3238 474) in the Old Town.

Jump Café [103 E5] Njegoševa 10; ✆ 3239 860; ⏰ 08.00–01.00 Mon–Sat, 10.00–01.00 Sun. Jump is just one of several smart designer cafés along this street by the Hotel Park.

♀ **Bukowski Bar** [103 F5] Kičevska 6; ✆ 2436 796. A small, intimate bar close to the Vuk monument.

♀ **Lava Bar** [102 D5] Kneza Miloša 77; ✆ 3610 525; ⏰ 10.00–01.00. In the city centre, close to various embassies, this stylish lounge bar has good wines, Mediterranean food, a relaxed atmosphere & a summer garden.

The Three Carrots [103 E4] Knez Miloša 16; ✆ 2683 748; **w** threecarrots.co.rs; ⏰ 08.00–midnight. An Irish pub, & Belgrade's 1st Hibernian representative. Its name apparently derives from an error in translation, as it was originally intended to be something to do with shamrocks. The Three Carrots has a vaguely faux-Paddy décor, with musical instruments & old wireless sets on the bare brick walls, a nice marble floor, & an upstairs area directly above the bar. The interior is wooden & darkish: quite atmospheric, if not strictly Irish. The pub is frequented by the city's young crowd as well as by expats & embassy staff. A wide range of whiskies & liqueurs are available, as well, of course, as draught Guinness, which costs about the same as it does in central Dublin.

New Belgrade and Zemun
🖥 **Caffe Codex** [162 C2] Gospodska 15; 🖂 3731 437. No-nonsense café-bar between the river & Glavna on pedestrianised Gospodska.

GRABBING A QUICK BITE

Snack bars and take-aways are everywhere throughout the city with similar prices and quality. A few usefully located ones are indicated below.

In the Old Town at Kolarčeva 6–8, between the Albania tower and Trg Republike, is **Pekara Toma** [115 E6] (🖂 2636 343; w pekaratoma.rs). This Belgrade institution, which has several other branches around the city, is open 24 hours a day and sells pizza slices, cakes, croissants and 20 different types of sandwich. There are a few stand-up tables to eat at outside but most come here to grab something to eat on the hoof. Next door is a pancake place also open 24 hours a day. Another counter sells take-away pizza slices nearby on the corner by the Hotel Evropa. Just downhill from here at the entrance of the pedestrian tunnel on Zeleni venac are several popular places selling burek, pita, pancakes and sandwiches. For more upmarket (and slightly more expensive) bakery products – artisan breads, rolls, croissants, pretzels, cakes, etc – **Hleb i Kifle** (w hlebikifle.rs) has 33 branches throughout the city – there is a handy one at Knez Mihailova 34 [114 D5].

A very popular place for Middle Eastern take-away food is the **Tel Aviv Hummus House** [114 C7] (🖂 2632 224) at Carice Milice 3, close to the junction with Brankovo near the local bus station – there always seem to be queues here, day and night. Lebanese take-away shwarma (šawarma) and bakery goods can be had from **Hanan** [115 G7] at Njegoševa 31.

Pancakes or palačinke, with both sweet and savoury fillings, are very much a Belgrade thing. Quite an elegant place to sample them is the floating raft **Keops** [102 A2] (w keops.rs) on Dunavski kej in New Belgrade close to the Hotel Jugoslavija, which claims to have 150 different flavours.

Good **ice cream** is available everywhere throughout the city in a huge variety of flavours – there are usually stalls doing brisk business along Knez Mihailova. Another very tempting place for take-away ice cream is the small outlet that is located close to the **Kandahar** [115 E3] on Strahinjića bana.

For **cakes**, the pastry shop in the central **Hotel Moskva** [103 E4] is highly recommended with its staggering range of cream-rich torte. Another excellent place for coffee and cake is **Mamma's Biscuit House** [114 F4] on Strahinjića bana, although it can get rather smoky inside if it is too cold to sit out on the terrace. **Balkan Baklava** [114 C6] at Carice Milice 15 (🖂 2633 575) has a superb selection of take-away Turkish baklava to choose from.

In Zemun, there are a couple of fast-food places at the market place and on Karađorđev Square next to McDonald's. Nearby, at the Glavna junction with Gospodska, is the **Skroz Dobra bakery** [162 B2] and another branch of **Hleb i Kifle** [162 B2].

3

🍺 **Caffe Dalton** [162 B2] Glavna 13a, Zemun; m 065 3160 785. A decent café with outdoor seating in the town centre.

Elsewhere in the city
🍺 **Caffe Sunset** [102 A7] Ada Ciganlija lok 9; m 063 8073 210; w sunset.rs. This large outdoor café is close to the beach on the eastern shore of the lake at Ada Ciganlija & is very busy on summer w/ends.

🍺 **Square** [103 G6] Vojvode Šupljikca (Žarka Zrenjanina) 32; ✆ 3830 038; ⏰ 09.00–02.00. A café situated, as the name says, on a square. This particular square, just off Bulevar Aleksandra, is in a pleasant residential area between the Vračar & Zvezdara neighbourhoods of the city. The same square also hosts a bakery, a quality fast-food take-away & a fashionable restaurant (see *Zaplet*).

ENTERTAINMENT AND NIGHTLIFE

Belgrade offers some of the best nightlife in southeastern Europe, with a constantly changing, finger-on-the-pulse club scene that is sufficiently hip to attract international performers and DJs. Despite the privations of recent years, and low wages that make clubbing expensive for locals, the Serbian capacity for nightlife remains legendary. Dispense with any notions of a dreary, retrograde city locked into a grey, post-Yugoslav recession; Belgrade is up there with the best of them. In fact, it is much better than most.

The focus for nightlife is spread throughout the city: much of the activity takes place on boats and rafts (*splavovi*) moored along the Danube and Sava. There is also a dance club located on one of the beaches of Ratno Ostrvo (Great War Island), a short ferry ride from New Belgrade, where you have the opportunity to dance in the sand underneath the stars. Other pockets of nightlife lie closer to the Old Town, near the top of Knez Mihailova, at the top end of Kneza Miloša and along Resava. Another area of the Old Town that is busy at night is Strahinjića bana – the so-called 'Silicone Valley': a long street of fancy cafés, bars and clubs that has become highly fashionable over the past few years.

Note that there is a certain amount of crossover between the listings for cafés, bars and clubs: some restaurants have live music and double as night-time hot spots and so there is not always a clear division, although the opening hours should give a clue as to how lively they become at night. With such a constantly evolving scene, venues come and go in terms of popularity. Make enquiries about which places are currently in vogue.

☆ **Bitef Art Café** [103 G3] Mitoploita Petra 8; m 063 594 294; w bitefartcafe.rs; ⏰ 19.00–04.00. Formerly a club in a converted church near Bajloni Market, this is now located in Palilula near Pančevački Bridge. Hosts theme nights & a variety of live music that ranges from house music to rock bands at w/ends. The musical mix ensures a mixed crowd of all ages.

☆ **Brankow Bar** [114 A7] Crnogorska 12; m 069 8300 777; w brankow.com; ⏰ Wed–Sat 21.00–04.00. A bar & nightspot in a converted building near Brankov Bridge that attracts a slightly older well-dressed & well-heeled crowd.

☆ **Drugstore** [103 H3] Bulevar despota Stefana 115; m 063 8287 928; ⏰ 23.00–10.00. Very post-industrial in character – techno

& electronic music in a darkly lit former slaughterhouse.

☆ **Ex Džungla** [115 G5] Skadarska 40c; m 064 1883 251; ⏰ 22.00–03.00. Also known as Crazy Horse, this is the only club in the Skadarlija restaurant district.

☆ **Flash** [103 F4] Aberdareva 1b; ✆ 3340 671; ⏰ 23.00–05.00. This place, formerly 'Bus', close to Tašmajdan Park has grown up around a red London double-decker bus, which now serves as the DJ's station. Surprisingly, the music played is not necessarily 'garage'. The bus is usually crowded & at its most lively on w/end nights.

☆ **KST (Klub studenata tehnike)** [103 F4] Bulevar kralja Aleksandra 73; ✆ 3218 391; w kst. org.rs; ⏰ 23.00–03.00. As its name implies, this is a student club, with cheap drinks & a youthful clientele. The music is hard-edged metal & punk. Live bands perform here frequently.

☆ **Mr Stefan Braun** [102 D4] Nemanjina 4, 9th floor; m 065 5566 456; ⏰ 23.00–06.00. This fashionable place, hidden away on the 9th floor in a high-rise office block, is highly rated for its charged atmosphere, its young crowd, loud techno music & high-spirited bar staff. Currently it is one of the city's most popular night-time venues & gets very crowded at w/ends.

☆ **Nana** [102 C6] Koste Glavinića 1; m 060 5050 662. This club in Senjak does not get going until very late, but then it continues until dawn or after.

☆ **Oh! Cinema** In winter, at Gračanicka 18 [114 C5]; ☎627 059, in summer, at Mali Kalemegdan [114 B1]; ☎3281 177; ⏰ 23.00–05.00 (summer). Note the 2 different locations: at Gračanicka, it is in a hall decorated with cinema posters; at the fortress, on an outside terrace. Both venues have live music & tend to keep going later than many of the other clubs.

☆ **Ona, a ne neka druga** [162 B1] Grobljanska 9, Zemun; ☎ 3076 613; ⏰ 21.00–04.00 Tue–Sun. In the Gardoš area of Zemun, close to the Millennium Tower, the name translates as 'She, not some other', which gives a clue that this bistro-club is dedicated almost exclusively to women. Men are tolerated – just about – with a female accomplice. The waiters are all male & a certain amount of high-spirited & good-natured girlish (or womanly) (mis)behaviour is permitted. Definitely a place for women to enjoy themselves in a fun, non-threatening atmosphere. Live music some nights.

☆ **Plastic** [103 F3] Takovska 34; m 064 6403 956; ⏰ 23.00–05.00 Fri/Sat. Formerly known as Mondo, this remains one of Belgrade's most prestigious clubs & you may need to queue to get in. It attracts a fairly youthful crowd, the atmosphere is hot & sweaty, & the music played is electronica in its various forms – house, techno, drum 'n' bass, etc. There are guest appearances by well-known DJs most w/ends. The club is also home to the Paži Škola DJ bar. The Takovska premises are winter only: in summer, the action moves to a *splav* close to the 25 Maj sports centre.

☆ **Tilt** [102 C2] Bulevar Vojvode Bojovica 30; m 063 377 763; ⏰ 22.00–04.00. Located in the parking area of Beton hala, this is currently one of the city's most popular nightclub venues.

☆ **Tramvaj** [103 G5] Ruzveltova 2; m 065 8726 825; w tramvaj.rs; ⏰ 09.00–01.00. Tramvaj can be found just down from Vukov Spomenik, towards Novo Groblje on Rustelova. It has an English pub-like atmosphere with good, cheap draught beer. Live musicians perform here most nights of the week.

☆ **Underground** [114 A4] Pariska 1a, opposite the Swedish Embassy; m 063 333 344; ⏰ 22.00–05.00. Romantically located in the 18th-century catacombs beneath Kalemegdan Park, this has long been one of the city's top clubs, with an enormous dance floor, famous DJs at w/ends, hiphop music & strobe lighting. For the faint-hearted, there are also quieter sitting areas away from the dance action.

FLOATING RESTAURANTS AND CLUBS (*SPLAVOVI*) These can mostly be found clustered along the Danube shore near the Hotel Jugoslavija and along the Sava north of Brankov most in New Belgrade. More can be found at the northern end of Ada Ciganlija, close to the 25 Maj sports centre in Dorćol and also along the west bank of the Sava River near Blok 70 in New Belgrade.

☆ **Acapulco** [102 A1] Kej oslobođenja bb; m 063 220 111; w splavakapulko.rs; ⏰ 11.00–04.00. With Mexican associations that are rather tenuous, this raunchy raft close to Hotel Jugoslavija is a prime location for live Serbian pop & rock music. A night here may well be an interesting spectacle, watching Belgrade's new money strut its stuff, but it is mostly the preserve of the well-heeled, young & beautiful.

☆ **Amfora** [102 A1] Kej oslobođenja bb; ☎2699 789; ⏰ 10.00–01.00. This is possibly the smartest & most exclusive of all the *splavovi* along here. A smart dress code is enforced.

☆ **Bibis** [102 A2] Kej oslobođenja bb; ☎3192 150; ⏰ 10.00–02.00. Bibis is one of the most popular of the *splav* café-nightclubs along the riverfront just south of the Hotel Jugoslavija. This one has photos of famous sportsmen on the walls & is patronised by good-looking athletic types. This

3

is one of the few *splavovi* that are open during the winter months. Similar upmarket places close by are: Amsterdam [102 A2] & Monza [102 A2].
☆ **Freestyler** [102 C4] Brodarski bb; m 062 8002 020; w splavfree.rs. At the Sava Quay, this popular *splav* has themed nights & a mix of musical styles.
☆ **Hua Hua** [102 B2] Ušće (near Yachting Club Kej); m 062 262 212; w huahuasplav.com; ⏰ 22.00–04.00. Ethno, ex-Yugoslav & turbo-folk music mostly.

GAY BELGRADE Belgrade's gay scene is low key to say the least. Considerable discretion is in order as open displays of affection between those of the same sex are likely to provoke hostility in some quarters.

See w gej.rs, w belgrade-gay.com and w gay-serbia.com for more information.

Clubs
☆ **Apartman** [114 A7] Karađorđeva 43/3; m 064 1876 235. Private gay parties on Fri/Sat.
☆ **Musk** [115 F6] Makedonska 28; m 065 6564 060
☆ **Pleasure** [103 E4] Kneza Miloša 9 (off courtyard next to Turkish Embassy); ⏰ 23.00–late Fri/Sat

Gay-friendly cafés, bars and restaurants
☆ **Bar 24** [103 H6] Kajmakčalanska 22; m 060 7070 777; ⏰ 18.00–late
☆ **Downtown** [114 D5] Čika Ljubina 7; ⏰ 09.00–midnight
☆ **Egal** [114 C6] Obilićev venac 3a; m 062 440 169
☆ **Smiley** [115 E7] Terazije 5; ⏰ 13.00–01.00
☆ **Zaplet** [103 H6] Kajmakčalanska 2; ☎ 2404 142; ⏰ 11.00–23.00 Tue–Sun

CULTURE AND FESTIVALS

Belgrade is a city soaked in culture and, apart from the numerous museums and galleries that can be visited at any time of year, there are plenty of special annual cultural events, especially outside the winter months, that embrace every aspect of the arts. All of the arts are well represented, with theatre, cinema, visual arts and music all being celebrated in annual events. There are also a number of events that cater especially to children and young adults. See pages 110–11 for a list of annual events.

MUSIC Belgrade has a dynamic and ever-changing music scene with something for everyone from classical string quartets to trance. Many pubs, clubs, café-bars, restaurants, and even sometimes bookshops, put on live music in the evenings. To witness live Serbian traditional music, you can be pretty much guaranteed hearing something in the 'national' restaurants along Skadarska, as some have their own resident musicians on hand to serenade customers. For pop music or jazz, try some of the more upmarket pubs and cafés; they often advertise what is coming up with fly posters. The website of the Tourist Organisation of Belgrade (**w** *tob.rs*) has a listing of some of the more major musical events during any particular month. A more comprehensive listing appears in the monthly (Serbian-language only) magazine *Yellow Cab* (**w** *yc.rs*).

Classical For classical music, one of the main venues is the **Beogradska Filharmonija** [114 C4] at Studentski trg 11 (**✆** *3282 977*; **w** *bgf.co.rs*). It is also worth trying to find out what is coming to **Guarnerius** [115 G5], a beautifully restored recital hall located at Džordža Vašingtona 12 (**✆** *3345 237*; **w** *guarnerius.rs*) and at the former national theatre, **Madlenianum** [162 B2], now a private opera house, in Zemun.

Occasional concerts are also staged by the various cultural institutes, particularly the **French Cultural Institute** on Knez Mihailova [114 D5] and the **Spanish Cervantes Institute** nearby [114 D5]. The **Fresco Gallery** [114 C3] has a small concert hall that occasionally puts on performances by classical musicians and vocal groups, as does the **Ethnographic Museum** [114 C4].

BEMUS, the Belgrade Music Festival, is held annually in October, with many international artistes and orchestras performing at a range of venues throughout the city. Information on the performance schedule can be found at the website **w** bemus.rs.

Rock and pop For rock music there are frequent live performances by solo artists and groups at the Youth Cultural Centre **Dom Omladine** [115 F6] on Makedonska 22 (**✆** *3220 127*; **e** *dobinfo@domomladine.org*; **w** *domomladine.org*). These tend to span the wide range of genres from hiphop to jazz, with rock guitar bands being perhaps the best represented. Dom Omladine also has a booking office that can inform on coming events in the city. Other venues include the **SKC (Student Cultural Centre)** [103 E5] at Kralja Milana 48 (**✆** *3602 009*; **w** *skc.org.rs*), **KST (Klub studenata tehnike)** [103 F4] at Bulevar kralja Aleksandra 73 (**✆** *3218 391*; **w** *kst.org. rs*), **Tramvaj** [103 G5] (**m** *065 8726 825*), **Hala sportova** [102 A3] in New Belgrade, and the **'Pinki' sports centre** [162 B2] in Zemun (**✆** *193 971*). The **Gun Club** [102 D5] (**✆** *2443 007*; **☉** *20.00–03.00 daily*) at Miloša Pocerca 10 is another young, studenty place for live rock music, with local and international bands playing nightly. **Mikser House** [114 A7] at Karađorđeva 46 (**✆** *2626 068*; **w** *mikser.rs*) holds various musical events throughout the year at its base in Savamala. Bigger, internationally famous names tend to play at the **Sava Centar** [102 B4] (**✆** *2206 000*; **w** *www.savacentar.net*) at Milentija Popovića 9 in New Belgrade.

Folk and Roma music This is often much the same thing really, as Roma musicians are pragmatic and tend to play whatever is requested of them, be it regional Serbian folk tunes or popular film themes. This occasionally upsets folk purists of the ultra-traditionalist variety. Roma combos usually come in two forms: string bands with violins, guitars and accordions – the sort that entertain diners in Skadarlija – and brass bands that play at weddings and outdoor celebrations. In Belgrade, there are often brass musicians hanging around looking for work at the patio of St Mark's Church or at Kalenić Market, which lies close to a nearby registry office. These bands have the endearing habit of sometimes rehearsing on the street close to tall buildings, like those near the railway station, that provide natural amplification for what is already pretty loud music – a magical sound cutting through the rumble and clatter of rush-hour traffic.

Apart from occasional residencies at restaurants and at some *splavovi* Roma musicians have little in the way of regular or advertised gigs.

Jazz and Latin Both jazz and Latin music are popular in Belgrade and there are several regular venues where sessions take place. For jazz fans visiting the city at the right time of year there is also the **Summertime Jazz Festival** in late June and early July at the Sava Centar [102 B4] (w *www.savacentar.net*) and the **Belgrade Jazz Festival** (w *bjf.rs*) in the last week of October based at Dom Omladine [115 F6] (w *domomladine.org*).

♪ **Bašta Jazz Bar & Restaurant** [114 A7] Male stepenice 1; m 062 8711 475
♪ **Big Dill Jazz Club** [103 E5] Resavska 32; ↘3231 302
♪ **Jazz Club Rif** [103 F6] Mačvanska bb; m 064 0022 606
♪ **Ptica Jazz Club** [103 F4] Dalmatinska 98; m 064 6109 984

THEATRE There are plenty of Serbian-language productions but very few in English. It may be worthwhile contacting the following to see if any English-language productions are coming up.

🎭 **Atelje 212** [115 H7] Svetogorska 21; ↘3247 342; w atelje212.rs. This attractive theatre, opened in 1956, specialises in modern theatre & new works.
🎭 **Belgrade Drama Theatre** (Beogradsko dramsko pozorište) [103 G6] Mileševska 64a; ↘2837 000; w bdp.rs
🎭 **BITEF Theatre** [115 H5] Skver Mire Trailović; ↘3243 108; w bitef.rs. This utilises the unfinished Evangelist church at Bajloni Market, which was adapted for theatrical use in 1988–89. It is the home stage of the BITEF (Belgrade International Theatre Festival) that is held in the city each Sep.
🎭 **Madlenianum** [162 B2] Opera House Glavna 32, Zemun; ↘3162 533; w operatheatremadlenianum.com. This is for opera mostly but it also puts on some theatrical productions.
🎭 **National Theatre** (Narodno pozorište) [115 E6] Francuska 3; ↘3281 333; w narodnopozoriste.

co.rs. The National Theatre is the largest & oldest theatre in the city, opposite the National Museum on Trg Republike. In addition to drama the National Theatre also stages performances of ballet & opera.
🎭 **Theatre T** (Teatar T) [103 F4] Bulevar kralja Aleksandra 77a; ↘422 012. This newly redecorated theatre tends to put on Broadway-style musicals like *New York, New York*.
🎭 **Yugoslav Drama Theatre** (Jugoslovensko dramsko pozorište) [102 E5] Kralja Milana 50; ↘2644 447; w jdp.co.rs. Next to the SKC (Student Cultural Centre), this theatre, established in 1947, was damaged in a fire in 1997 but was reopened in 2003. Together with the National Theatre it is one of the most prestigious theatres in the city.
🎭 **Zvezdara Theatre** (Zvezdara teatar) [103 H6] Milana Rakića 38; ↘2414 527, 2417 155; w zvezdarateatar.rs. Like Atelje 212, this is well known for its regular staging of contemporary, modern & foreign works.

CULTURAL CENTRES All the following put on regular exhibitions featuring the visual arts as well as staging occasional musical and theatrical events. The foreign national centres also usually have a selection of foreign-language libraries and newspapers:

American Corner [115 F6] Makedonska 22; ☎3227 694; w americancorners.rs

Belgrade Culture Centre [114 D6] Knez Mihailova 6; ☎2621 469; w kcb.org.rs; ⏰ 09.00–20.00 daily

Belgrade Youth Centre (Dom Omladine) [115 F6] Makedonska 22; ☎3220 127; w domomladine.org

British Council [115 E7] Terazije 8/II; ☎3023 800; w britishcouncil.rs

Centre for Cultural Decontamination [103 E5] Birčaninova 21; ☎2681 422; w czkd.org

Cervantes Institute (Spain) [114 D5] Čika Ljubina 19; ☎3034 182/3; w belgrado.cervantes.es

French Cultural Centre [114 D5] Zmaj Jovina 11; ☎3023 600; w ccf.org.rs

Goethe Institue (Germany) [114 C4] Knez Mihailova 50; ☎3031 810; w goethe.de/belgrad

Italian Institute [102 D5] Kneza Miloša 56; ☎3629 137; w www.iicbelgrado.esteri.it

Russian Centre for Science & Culture [103 E4] Kraljice Natalije (Narodnog fronta) 33; ☎2642 178; w ruskidom.rs

Student Cultural Centre (SKC) [103 E5] Kralja Milana 48; ☎3602 009; w skc.co.rs

CINEMA Belgrade's cinemas show all English-language films with their original dialogue and Serbian subtitles. Those listed below show the same range of Hollywood movies that you might expect at home. The **Muzej Kinoteke** at Kosovska 11 next to the Union Hotel [115 F7] (☎ *3248 250*) shows classic films. They print a monthly programme of what is coming up, and have the same information available on their website (w *kinoteka.org.rs*).

Each year in February and March, **FEST**, the Belgrade International Film Festival, takes place at a variety of venues throughout the city: Sava Centar, Belgrade Cultural Centre, Dom Omladine and the Yugoslav Archive. About 70 films are shown over a period of ten days. Details of the programme may be found at w fest.rs.

🎬 **Akademija 28** [103 E5] Nemanjina 28; ☎3616 020

🎬 **Dom Omladine** [115 F6] Makedonska 22; ☎3248 202

🎬 **Dom Sindikata** [115 F7] Dečanska 14; ☎3234 849

🎬 **Kinoteka** [103 F7] Kosovska 11; ☎ 3248 250

🎬 **Kosmaj** [115 E7] Terazije 13; ☎3227 279

🎬 **Kozara** [103 E4] Terazije 25; ☎3235 648

🎬 **Odeon** [103 E4] Narodnog fronta 45; ☎2643 355

🎬 **RodaIntermezzo Cineplex** [102 A7] Požeška 83a; ☎2545 260

🎬 **Sava Centar** [102 B4] Milentija Popovića 9; ☎3114 322

🎬 **Cineplexx** [102 A5] Jurija Gagarina 16; ☎2203 400

🎬 **Tuckwood Cineplex** [102 D5] Kneza Miloša 7; ☎3236 517

Outdoor screenings During the summer months (May–October), the following have screenings outdoors:

🎬 **Kafe Ada** [102 A6] Ada Ciganlija 2; ☎544 601

🎬 **Tašmajdan** [103 F4] Ilije Garašanina 26; ☎3231 533, 432 616

🎬 **Zvezda** [103 E4] Terazije 40; ☎687 320

CASINOS You can try your luck and get a taste of the Belgrade gambling (under) world at the following:

☆ **Fair Play** [115 E7] At the Hotel Kasina, Terazije 25; ☎3233 613

☆ **Grand Casino** [102 A1] Bulevar Nikole Tesle 3; ☎2202 800

☆ **London** [103 E4] Kralja Milana 28; ☎2688 530

☆ **Slavija** [103 E5] Hotel Slavija, Svetog Save 2; ☎2441 120

SPORTS

Football The most popular spectator sport is, of course, football, although basketball and tennis are not that far behind. This is taken very seriously, with fans swearing loyalty to one or other of the main teams at an early age. It can be difficult obtaining tickets for a high-profile international game or a local derby.

The main teams, and their corresponding home grounds, are listed below. Other Belgrade teams, such as FK 'Obilić', have known glory in the past but have since fallen on hard times.

FK 'Crvena Zvezda' [103 E7] Ljutice Bogdana 1a; ✆3672 060, 3672 070; w redstarbelgrade.info. The Red Star stadium, renamed the Rajko Mitić stadium in 2014 after the club's greatest footballer hero, is the largest in the country, seating over 55,000. Red Star's hard-line supporters call themselves Delije (roughly translated as 'heroes') – a name seen sprayed on walls across the city – & they are not to be messed with. In the early years of the 21st century a lowered standard of play, coupled with the predictable violence that attends derby matches, resulted in a severe drop in attendance figures. The derby played on 11 May 2005 in the semi-final of the Serbia & Montenegro Cup had a crowd of only 8,000 attending, an all-time low. Things have picked up somewhat since then.

FK Partizan [103 E7] Humska 1; ✆648 222; w partizan.co.rs. Originally recruited from the ranks of the Yugoslav army, this team's supporters are called Grobari, 'graverobbers', a name which seems wholly appropriate whenever a fixture takes place between Partizan & Red Star. Matches between these fierce rivals – referred to as the 'eternal derby' – are lively affairs & often feature fireworks used in ways not recommended by the manufacturer. Disappointment in a poor result is sometimes expressed by setting fire to the seats in the stands. Generally speaking, non-derby matches tend to have a little less of a Battle of Kosovo atmosphere about them.

FK Radnički Novi Beograd Tošin bunar, New Belgrade. Radnički are a lower-league side based in New Belgrade with a small, but fierce fan base – a bit like a Balkan version of Millwall FC.

Basketball Basketball is also immensely popular and the two main teams echo the names of Belgrade's football clubs: Crvena Zvezda ('Red Star') and Partizan. Their home courts are based at Belgrade Fortress. The 2005 European Basketball Championships were held in Serbia, in Belgrade, Novi Sad, Vršac and Podgorica (Montenegro). This engendered a lot of interest for a sport in which Serbians tend to excel although the national team did not do particularly well on this occasion.

Swimming In summer you can do what the locals do and swim from the beaches on the shoreline of Ada Ciganlija in the middle of the River Sava. There is also a discreet nudist beach here. Another beach is at the Lido opposite Zemun on Veliko Ratno Ostrvo (Great War Island) in the middle of the confluence of the Sava and Danube rivers. This can be reached by walking across the seasonal pontoon bridge that is set up in July and August. All sites off map, unless otherwise noted.

Swimming pools

11 April Novi Beograd, Autoput 2; ✆672 939, 671 547

25 May [102 D1] Tadeuša Košćuška 63; ✆2622 578

Košutnjak Kneza Višeslava 72; ✆3555 461

Tašmajdan Ilije Garašanina 26; ✆6556 500

Running The Belgrade 'Stark' Marathon takes place every year in the second half of April, attracting up to 1,500 participants, including 70 international runners from 35 countries. There is also a 5km 'Race of Joy', in which up to

20,000 participants take part. A Children's Marathon starts at Belgrade Zoo a week before the main event.

Cycling The annual 'Tour de Serbie', established in 1939, generally starts in Belgrade and takes place over a week in June. For information, see **w** tds.co.rs.

Sports centres For more participatory sports action, Belgrade has a number of well-equipped sports centres. All sites off map, unless otherwise noted.

'25 Maj' sports centre [102 D1] Tadeuša Košćuška 63; ☎ 2622 578
City Centre for Physical Fitness [103 E5] Deligradski 27; ☎ 658 747
SC [103 H7] Šumice Ustanička 125; m 063 279 306

Sports Centre Voždovac Crnotravska 4; ☎ 2660 826. South of the centre in Voždovac suburb.
Sports Recreational Centre Banjica Crnotravska 4; ☎ 2668 700
Sports Recreational Centre Tašmajdan [103 F4] Ilije Garašanina 26–28; ☎ 3247 512

SHOPPING

Although increasing in popularity in recent years, Belgrade is not as yet on any sort of widely recognised tourist trail and so traditional souvenir tat, all too common elsewhere in eastern Europe, is fairly minimal and only available in a small number of places, mostly tourist information centres and at the stalls along Knez Mihailova and the entrance to Kalemegdan Park.. There are plenty of genuine handicrafts that are worth buying: embroidery, wickerwork, knitted garments and crochet work, in addition to copperware products and Serbian crystal. Leather products are also generally of high quality, and the city is full of shoe shops selling high-quality footwear, although the prices are by no means cheap. As well as shoes, there are also leather suitcases, handbags and jackets worthy of consideration.

Shops in Belgrade are normally open 08.00–20.00 Monday–Friday, 08.00–15.00 on Saturdays, closed on Sundays. There is often a long lunch break from noon until mid afternoon. Grocery stores keep longer hours: usually 06.30–20.00 in the week, 06.30–18.00 on Saturdays and 07.00–11.00 on Sundays. Many supermarkets stay open longer than this, until late in the evening. In keeping with Belgrade's tendency to go out and stay out late, most of the smart shops along Knez Mihailova, as well as the bookshops like Plato, stay open until late in the evening, until midnight in some cases.

At the top end of Knez Mihailova by the **City Library** [114 C4] is a line of **craft stalls** that sell handmade novelty and pottery items. Additionally, there are usually women selling embroidery and crochet work near the main entrance to Kalemegdan Park; they sometimes also sell their goods from small stalls along the middle section of Knez Mihailova.

A reasonable range of **postcards** is available throughout the city, both at pavement stalls and in bookshops, but the ones dating from 1999 showing bomb-damaged Belgrade with typically Serbian, sardonic humour ('The children's playground, designed by NATO' captioning a shot of boys frolicking in twisted wreckage; and, 'Sorry, we didn't know it was invisible – Greetings from Serbia' on a card showing a downed 'undetectable' F-117A spy plane) are becoming increasingly hard to find.

HANDICRAFTS, GIFTS AND SOUVENIRS
Beogradski Izlog (Belgrade Window) [114 D6] Knez Mihailova 6/Trg Republike 5; ☎ 2631 721;
⊕ 09.00–21.00 Mon–Sat, 10.00–15.00 Sun. Has a wide range of specialised calendars, notebooks,

3

posters, postcards, T-shirts, glassware & tea mugs, all with a Belgrade theme.

Beosuvenir [114 D7] Zeleni venac, Jug Bogdanova 2; ☎ 2631 423; ⏰ 08.00–20.00 Mon–Fri, 09.00–17.00 Sat, 10.00–15.00 Sun. Ceramics, rugs, national costumes.

Ethnographic Museum [114 C4] Studentski trg 13; ☎ 3281 888; ⏰ 10.00–17.00 Tue–Sat,

09.00–14.00 Sun, closed Mon. The museum has a selection of handicrafts on sale in its gift shop.

Galerija Singidunum [114 C5] Knez Mihailova 40; ☎ 2185 323

Makadam [114 A6] Kosančićev venac 20; ☎ 2630 272; ⏰ 08.00–20.00 Tue–Sun. Arts & crafts, wines, jewellery.

COMMUNIST MEMORABILIA The **Museum of Yugoslav History** gift shop at the entrance to the **House of Flowers** memorial centre [102 D7] has a wide range of Tito- or Yugoslavia-related items for sale: posters, postcards, books, T-shirts, mugs, pencils and even mouse mats.

For those whose sense of irony is truly deep, there are usually stalls along Knez Mihailova or in Kalemegdan Park that sell nationalist items like *četnik* flags and Radovan Karadžić T-shirts and calendars. It is probably best to keep a straight face if you decide to make an ironic purchase of any of these.

ART Many of the **art galleries** have copies of their work for sale, together with Serbian-language catalogues of the works on display. The Ethnographic Museum at Studentski trg 13 [114 C4] (☎ *3281 888*) also has a good gift shop. For naive art, a wide range of paintings is available at **Naive art – atelier Davidović** [102 A3] (*Bulevar Mihaila Pupina 161/17, II floor, New Belgrade;* ☎ *2121 536*).

Art sales galleries

AS Gallery [115 F5] Skadarska 27; ☎ 3239 242

Beograd [114 A6] Kosančićev venac 19; ☎ 3033 923

Dada [115 E7] Čumićeva 54; ☎ 3242 091

Fabris [102 B4] Milentija Popovića 23; ☎ 3112 866

Gallery 1250 [115 E7] Čumićevo sokače 56; m 064 2588 421

Radionica Duše [102 B4] Milentija Popovića 9; ☎ 2206 114

Remont [114 C6] Maršala Birjuzova 7; ☎ 3223 406

Sebastijan Art [114 B4] Rajićeva 12; ☎ 185 653

Singidunum [114 C5] Knez Mihailova 40; ☎ 2185 323

FASHION AND ACCESSORIES Knez Mihailova has almost the same range of modern clothes shops that you might expect of any major Italian city. Prices are not cheap but you get what you pay for.

For smart, designer boutiques and a privileged, chi-chi atmosphere, there is the **New Millennium Centre** shopping mall [114 D6] (⏰ *10.00–21.00*) at Obilićev venac 16, just off Knez Mihailova, while City Passage, Obilićev venac 20, which leads through to the Millennium Centre, has much of the same sort of thing. In New Belgrade, there is a similar range of exclusive boutiques in the cavernous **Sava Centar** building [102 B4] at Milentija Popovića 9. There is also a shopping centre at **Piramida** at Jurija Gagarina, Blok 44.

The **Choomich Design District** [115 E7] (*Čumićevo sokače;* ⏰ *noon–20.00 Mon–Fri, noon–18.00 Sat*), housed in a once-abandoned two-storey shopping centre close to Terazije and Trg Republike, is home to more than 30 local fashion designers, some young, some more established.

Original Serbian fashion design

Dragana Ognjenović [114 B5] Kneza Sime Markovića 10; ☎ 3628 838; w draganaognjenovic.

com. Home-grown Belgrade design with the emphasis on black.

Identity [115 E6] Makedonska 30; ☎3284 044; w jspfashion.com. Quirky fashion design for women.

Kjara [114 D4] Višnićeva 7; ☎3285 908; w kjara.rs. A wide range of original clothing, shoes, jewellery & accessories.

Milan St Marković Jove Ilića 129; ☎2462 893, 474 417; w milanmarkovic.com. Some way south of the centre in Voždovac suburb.

P...S...Fashion [114 D6] Knez Mihailova 23; ☎ 3287 085; w ps.rs

Uppa Druppa [114 F4] Takovska 25; ☎3347 375. A boutique with an original range of quaint designer clothes, hats, shoes & bags as well as some distinctive jewellery.

Verica Rakočević [114 C3] Jevremova 12; ☎2189 394; w vericarakocevic.com. Expensive *haute couture* design by a well-regarded Belgrade fashionista.

FOOD AND DRINK

Bombonicija [114 D4] Gavrila Principa 14; ☎2623 171. This quaint, old-fashioned sweet shop makes all its own confectionery products, including a wide range of Turkish delight.

Hanan Sweets [115 G7] Svetogorska 2; ☎3345 304. A wide range of take-away *baklava* sold by the kilo & gift-wrapped.

Julieta [114 C5] Đure Jakšića 11; ☎2637 690. Cuban cigars, fine chocolate, wines & whisky.

Vinoteka [115 F6] Makedonska 24; ☎3224 047. This has a good selection of wines from various Serbian vine-growing regions.

Vinoteka Beograd [103 E7] Bulevar oslobođenja 117; m 063 8406 395. A huge range of national & international wines.

Vinoteka Royal [114 A7] Karađorđeva 3; ☎3033 025. Another place with a wide selection of wines.

MUSIC The best selection of CDs in the Old Town is probably at the Dallas Music Shop upstairs at the **Vulkan** bookstore [115 E7] (*Sremska 2;* ☎*2639 060;* ⊕ *09.00–22.00 Mon–Sat, 11.00–22.00 Sun*), which has a good range of folk, jazz, world and pop releases, as well as music DVDs. Vulkan has several other branches around the city; check its website (w *knjizare-vulkan.rs*) for locations. Serbian CDs generally cost 700–1,000din, while those of foreign artists, 1,000–1,600din. The trade in bootleg CDs is not what it was but there are still street and market stalls that sell copies of popular titles for 300–400din, although they tend to concentrate more on DVDs and computer games these days.

For vinyl, the **Gun Club** at Miloša Pocerca 10 [102 D5], south of the railway station, has a weekly record market on Sundays. The best place to go for fans of rare Yugoslav vinyl is **Yugovinyl** [103 H5] (*Toplička 35;* ☎*3863 439;* ⊕ *noon–20.00 Mon–Fri*) in the east of the city, just off Dimitrija Tucovića south of Novo Groblje – an Aladdin's Cave of rare vinyl of all sorts of genres including jazz and Yugo-rock. **Leila** record shop and gallery at Kralja Petra I 41 (page 129) also has a good selection.

BOOKS AND MAGAZINES Most of Belgrade's better bookshops are to be found in the Old Town in the vicinity of Knez Mihailova. **Vulkan** [115 E7] (*Sremska 2;* ☎*2639 060;* w *knjizare-vulkan.rs;* ⊕ *09.00–22.00 Mon–Sat, 11.00–22.00 Sun*) has a good range of English-language books and magazines. There are several other branches around the city – check its website for locations. A good selection of foreign-language books can also be found at **IPS-Akademija** [114 C5] at Knez Mihailova 35 (☎ *2636 514;* ⊕ *09.00–23.00*), located in a beautiful neo-Baroque building. **Plato** [114 C4] at Knez Mihailova 48 (☎ *2625 021*) is another good place for English- and other foreign-language books. **Apropo** [114 C5] (*Cara Lazara 10;* ☎*2625 839;* ⊕ *10.00–20.00 Mon–Fri, 10.00–16.00 Sat, closed Sun*), just off the main Knez Mihailova drag, is both a bookshop and a cosy café. In Vračar, south of the city centre, the **Magellan Bookshop** [103 F5] (*Makenzijeva 51/Kode Kapetana 2;* ☎*2450 365;* w *knjizaramagelan.com*) has a good selection of secondhand books in English.

MARKETS Much of Belgrade's commerce is carried out in far less refined surroundings than the places mentioned above – either at the **street stalls** that line some of the main roads or at outdoor markets. Although they have tightened up recently, copyright laws in Serbia are lax, to say the least, and so 'genuine' Versace clothing, Cartier shoes, computer software and recent-release CDs and DVDs are sometimes available at knockdown prices. The clothes packaging may look suspect, and the cover art on the CDs may be slightly blurry, but the chances are that if you cannot tell the difference then it is unlikely that anyone else will be able to do so either. Whether or not such facsimile items infringe copyright outside Serbia is a moot point of course.

Belgrade's largest open-air market in the city centre is at **Kalenić pijaca** [103 F5] at the bottom end of Njegoševa, within sight of the enormous dome of St Sava's Church. It is a dense warren of activity that starts early and is open every day but at its busiest on Friday and Saturday mornings. Every imaginable type of food produce is sold here: vast piles of seasonal fruit, heaving mounds of greens and onions, sheets of pastry dough, plastic bags of handmade pasta, strings of peppers, rounds of cheese, hams, wooden tubs of *kajmak*, and enough garlic to dispatch any vampire straight back to Transylvania. With most of the stalls run by unhurried, cheerful women in headscarves, Kalenić is the spirit of the Serbian countryside transposed to the city. As well as food produce, and an adjoining area devoted solely to flowers, the market also has a section where chain-smoking Roma men sell a range of quite bizarre antiques – perhaps 'bric-a-brac' is a better term for the items on display here. Search amongst the broken 1940s wireless sets, World War II Partisan medals and broken watches for your own bargain. Haggling is quite acceptable.

Closer to Stari Grad, just below McDonald's and the city bus stops on Brankova, is **pijaca 'Zeleni venac'** [114 D7], a market area selling fruit and vegetables, household goods and clothing.

At the bottom of Skadarlija is **Bajlonova pijaca** [115 G5], named after the brewery nearby, that has a number of stalls selling fruit, vegetables and dairy produce as well as clothes and bric-a-brac.

In New Belgrade there is a large open-air market at **Buvlja pijaca** [102 A5] on Proleterske solidarnoste, near the railway bridge at Blok 43. The market extends outside as those individuals who cannot afford to rent a stall sell their goods from pitches on the pavement beneath the railway bridge. It is a colourful and noisy place, with the odd beggar and wandering Roma accordionist. Seeing the limited goods that some of these have to sell is a reminder that this is a rather poor part of the city.

Just down the road from Buvlja pijaca at Blok 70 on Bulevar Jurija Gagarina is the so-called **Chinese Market**, which as the name implies is central to New Belgrade's sizeable Chinese community. It is also one of the cheapest places to buy imported goods in the whole city.

OTHER PRACTICALITIES

COMMUNICATIONS
Post Belgrade's **main post office** is located on Tavoska 2, near Sveti Marko Church [103 E4] (✆ *3210 069*), while the more conveniently located **central post office** [114 D5] is at Zmaj Jovina 17. Other branches are at: Slobodana Penezića Krcuna 2 [102 D4], Šumadijski trg 2a, and Glavna 8 in Zemun [162 B2] (⊕ *08.00–20.00 w/days, 08.00–15.00 Sat, with some branches also opening on Sun*).

The cost of sending a standard letter within Serbia is 23din. For anywhere in Europe it costs 70din for up to 20g and then the tariff increases to 170din up to 100g. A postcard costs 40din. Post from Serbia to the United Kingdom takes around a week. All of the major express courier companies like DHL and FedEx have offices in Belgrade. All offices are off map, unless otherwise noted.

The basic ZIP code for Belgrade is 11000.

Express mail couriers
✉ **DHL** Jurija Gagarina 36; ☎ 3105 500

✉ **FedEx** Express Autoput 22; ☎ 3149 075

✉ **TNT** [103 G2] Venizelosova 29; ☎ 3332 555

✉ **UPS** Nikola Tesla Airport; ☎ 2286 422

Telephones Phone calls can be made from any post office, where you are directed to a booth and pay for a call when you have finished. The code for dialling abroad is 00; you then dial the country code then the city and the recipient's number. To phone Belgrade from abroad, you must first dial the international access code (which is usually 00), then 381 for Serbia; then you dial the city code 11 and the number. The telephone centre in the central post office [102 D5] (☎ *3234 484*) is open 07.00–midnight Monday–Friday and 07.00–22.00 at weekends; at the central post office, calls can be made from 07.00 to 22.00 daily. A simpler solution may be to buy a Halo card from a kiosk or post office and use it at one of the red Halo street phones; 600din gets you about 10 minutes to the UK.

Be aware that over the past few years some **local Belgrade phone numbers** have changed. In particular, most, but not all, six-figure numbers beginning with a '6' have had a '2' added to make a seven-figure number. This is an ongoing process. This guide has strived to be as up to date as possible but if a phone number does not work and it begins with a '6' then it is worth trying to redial by adding a '2' in front of it.

Mobile phones All mobile-phone numbers in Serbia begin with 06: 062 and 063 for Telenor (formerly Mobtel); 064 and 065 for MTS Telekom Srbija; 060 and 061 for VIP Mobile.

060, 061 VIP Mobile [114 C4] Knez Mihailova 21; m 060 1234; w vipmobile.rs

062, 063 Telenor [115 F7] Kosovska 49; m 063 9000; w telenor.co.rs

064, 065 MTS [103 E4] Trg Nikole Pašića 7; m 064 789; w mts.telekom.rs

Internet Internet cafés are much less common than they were a few years ago due to an increase in home computer ownership and the widespread availablity of Wi-Fi, which is found in almost every café, restaurant and hotel in the city, as well as other places like the lobby of the **Municipality of New Belgrade** (*Bulevar Mihaila Pupina 167*) and the park at Studentski trg.

EMBASSIES A full list (downloadable pdf file) of foreign embassies and consulates in Belgrade can be found at w mfa.gov.rs/diplomatic_list.pdf.

🅔 **Australia** [102 B4] Vladimira Popovića 38–40; ☎ 3303 400

🅔 **Canada** [103 E4] Kneza Miloša 75; ☎ 3063 000 (consular section: ☎ 3063 039)

🅔 **France** [114 B4] Pariska 11; ☎ 3023 500 (consular section: ☎ 3023 561)

🅔 **Germany** [102 D7] Neznanog Junaka 1a; ☎ 3064 300

🅔 **Netherlands** [115 E5] Simina 29; ☎ 2023 900

🅔 **United Kingdom** [103 E5] Resavska 46; ☎ 3060 900 (consular section: ☎ 3061 072); e (general): belgrade.man@fco.gov.uk, (consular): belgrade.consular@fco.gov.uk

🅔 **United States of America** [102 D7] Bulevar Kneza Aleksandra Karađorđevića 92; ☎ 7064 000

EMERGENCY SERVICES

Police ☏92

Fire Department ☏93

Ambulance ☏94

Motoring assistance in Belgrade ☏987

MEDICAL SERVICES There are **24-hour dentists** on duty at Obilićev venac 30 [114 D6] (☏ *635 236*) and Kneginje Zore (Ivana Milutinovića) 15 [103 F5] (☏ *4441 413*).

State-run clinics

✚ **Clinical Centre of Serbia – Emergency Centre** [103 E5] Pasterova 2; ☏3617 777, 3618 444

✚ **KBC Zemun** [162 B2] Vukova 9; ☏3772 666

✚ **KBC Zvezdara** [103 H5] Dimitrija Tucovića 161; ☏3810 969

Private clinics

✚ **Bel Medic** Koste Jovanovića 87; ☏3091 000; ⏰ 24hrs, with ambulance for emergencies. South of the city centre in Voždovac suburb.

✚ **Dr Ristić policlinic** Narodnih heroja 38, Novi Beograd; ☏2693 287

✚ **Petković Clinic** [102 B7] Koste Glavinica 5d; ☏2662 777

✚ **Vizim Clinic** [103 F3] Knez Miletina 36; ☏3390 000

Dentists

✚ **Beldent** [114 B7] Brankova 23; ☏2634 455

✚ **Dr Cvijetinović** [114 D2] Strahinjića bana 20; ☏2185 802

✚ **Savadent** [103 G2] Đure Daničića 15; ☏3349 164

✚ **Zepter Dental Clinic** [102 C4] Kralja Petra I 32; ☏3283 880, 3283 881, 3283 882

Pharmacies (24hr)

✚ **Prvi maj** [103 E5] Kralja Milana 9; ☏3241 349

✚ **Sveti Sava** [102 D5] Nemanjina 2; ☏6643 170

✚ **Zemun** [162 B2] Glavna 34; ☏2618 582

MONEY AND BANKING

Credit cards This is the simplest way to get hold of local currency, using one of the city's numerous ATMs. The most widely accepted credit and debit cards are Visa, closely followed by MasterCard and Cirrus, and cash can be withdrawn from ATMs bearing these symbols. Maestro and Visa Electron debit cards may also be used where the symbol is displayed. American Express and Diners Club are not so well accepted, although they may be used in payment for goods in some shops, top hotels and car-rental agencies.

On the whole, you do not need to look far for an ATM in the city centre and Old Town – they are everywhere. For travellers arriving by plane, there is an ATM at the arrivals hall (downstairs) of Belgrade's Nikola Tesla Airport, which will accept Visa, Visa Electron, Visa Plus, MasterCard, Maestro and Cirrus cards.

Travellers' cheques As travellers' cheques are now more or less a thing of the past, cashing them can present more difficulty: American Express, Thomas Cook and Visa travellers' cheques can still be exchanged at some banks, while Eurocheques can usually be cashed at branches of ProCredit banka. Generally speaking, branches of **Komercijalna banka** or **Raiffeisenbank** are the best bet but beware of high commission charges. For both cash and travellers' cheques the preferred foreign currency is the euro, closely followed by the US dollar.

Cash Foreign currencies can be easily exchanged at most banks, post offices or exchange offices.

Banks are generally open from 08.00 to 19.00 on weekdays and from 08.00 to 15.00 on Saturdays. Some banks and post offices are also open on Sundays.

The Société Générale banka, which has a branch at Kralja Petra I 21 [114 B4] (☏*3011 607*), will also allow foreigners to open a bank account in Belgrade, as well as facilitating Western Union fast cash transfers (✆ *3115 525;* e *transfer.novca@socgen. com*). Western Union have a strong representation in Serbia and are probably the best way to have money sent from abroad. They have their own toll-free number with English-speaking operatives. Check for Belgrade locations at w westernunion. com.

SUGGESTED ITINERARIES

ONE DAY If you are in the city for just a single day then most of your time should be spent in and around Stari Grad, the Old Town. You might wish to spend the morning visiting St Sava's Church just south of the city centre at Vračar before heading north to Trg Republike to have lunch at one of the restaurants nearby. After lunch, a leisurely stroll along Knez Mihailova will give you opportunity to window-shop and to experience the bustling but easy-going atmosphere of modern-day Belgrade. You should ensure that you see the Orthodox Cathedral and perhaps have a drink at the '?' café across the street to get a flavour of the atmosphere of old Belgrade. Ideally, you should then try to visit Kalemegdan Park an hour or two before sunset. This is where native Belgraders go to relax and to take the air and it is a thoroughly enjoyable experience to go and join in with them.

For atmosphere, dinner should be in one of the restaurants along Skadarska, a sloping cobbled street a 5-minute walk east of Trg Republike. Here, you can eat Serbian national food served by waiters in national dress to the accompaniment of Roma musicians. If you still have any energy left after all of this, and are not too stuffed from your meal, you could then investigate Belgrade's club scene. A couple of clubs lie nearby in the area near the top end of Knez Mihailova and Kalemegdan Park. A more relaxing alternative would be to take a late evening stroll along Knez Mihailova (the *korso* can last until the early hours) before having a nightcap at one of the street cafés here, or perhaps at one of the trendier café-bars along nearby Obilićev venac.

TWO OR THREE DAYS With two or more days you should endeavour to do all of the above; extra time will allow you to spread it all out a little more. On the second day, you might wish to visit New Belgrade in the afternoon – at least the Danube shore there – and take an evening stroll along the Danube walkway before having dinner in one of the fish restaurants along the New Belgrade or Zemun shore. Another possibility is to visit Zemun during the daytime. If you go nowhere else in Serbia then this, at least, will give you a better idea of what a smaller, more traditional Serbian town is like. A second day should give you the opportunity to visit one or two of the museums in the city: you should endeavour to visit both the Ethnographic Museum and Military Museum, or for something more quirky, perhaps the Nikola Tesla Museum. It probably makes more sense to enjoy one thoroughly rather than try to rush through several. For a slightly different night-time scene on a second or third day you might wish to investigate the smart cafés along Strahinjića bana, Belgrade's so-called 'Silicone Valley'.

THREE DAYS OR MORE A lengthier stay will allow you to get out to more far-flung parts of the city, to visit the 'House of Flowers' at Topčider Park and perhaps look in on some of the more specialist, but equally interesting museums that the city has to offer – the house of Vuk Karadžić or the Fresco Gallery. By now you might feel in need of a break and in mind to take a day trip somewhere. Smederevo, with its magnificent medieval riverside castle, is within easy reach, as is Pančevo; even Novi Sad, Serbia's second city, can be reached in 2 hours by bus or train, although if time allows it is best to stay the night to fully appreciate the different atmosphere that the city has to offer.

WHAT TO SEE AND DO

PLACES TO VISIT
Stari Grad – the Old City Many of Belgrade's most appealing landmarks lie within this comparatively small area. The Old City may be defined as being the part of the city that lies southwest of Dunavska, with its western boundary circumscribed by Karađorđeva and Kalemegdan Park, and its southern limit set by Brankova. Stari Grad's southeastern boundary is vaguer, but undoubtedly it extends as least as far as Skadarska, a leafy, cobbled street of restaurants serving up national cuisine. This haystack-shaped concentration of Belgrade's older buildings is bisected by Vase Čarapića, an important artery that connects Trg Republike, the spiritual heart of the city, with Kalemegdan Park by way of Studentski trg. The pedestrian thoroughfare of Knez Mihailova (sometimes called Kneza Mihaila) runs parallel to this.

Trg Republike (Republic Square) is as good a place as any to begin. This large, elongated square is flanked by the imposing Neoclassical edifice of Narodni Musej – the **National Museum** [115 E6] – at its north side, with the **National Theatre** [115 E6] (originally built in 1869, bomb-damaged during World War I and rebuilt with a new façade in 1922) just across Vase Čarapića to the east. The National Museum has been closed since 2003 because of structural instability. A complete rebuild is planned at some stage in the future. Dominating the part of the square that stretches up to link with Knez Mihailova is **Dom štampe (The House of the Press)** [115 E6], a glass and concrete example of 1950s socialist architecture and a window cleaner's nightmare. The square has been renamed recently as Trg Slobode – Freedom Square – but most simply refer to it as 'Trg'. A set of fountains divide the square at this side, stretching down to reach the **equestrian statue of Prince Mihailo Obrenović** [115 E6], who reigned from 1839 to 1868 and was widely hailed as a great liberator of Serbia from the Turks. The prince points steadily south, towards the lands that were still under Ottoman rule during his reign and which were yet to be liberated in the name of the motherland. The base of the statue, which was unveiled in 1882, has relief work that depicts episodes from the struggle against Turkish domination. This famous landmark is at the heart of the city and the statue has become an important meeting place for young Belgraders who say, '*Kod konja*' to each other ('Meet you at the horse'), which suggests that his steed has earned greater notoriety than the prince himself.

Bohemian Skadarlija Not far from Trg Republike, leading off north from 29 Novembra (now sometimes referred to by its new name: 'Bulevar despot Stefana'), just beyond the National Theatre and opposite the post office there, is the tiny bohemian enclave of **Skadarlija** [115 F/G5]. This corner of the city was first settled by Roma in the 1830s who occupied the abandoned trenches in front of Belgrade's defensive walls. Their flimsy Gypsy huts were replaced by more solid buildings in the middle of the century as the area became home to craftsmen and lower-rank bureaucrats. The street received its current name in 1872 in honour of the Albanian city of Shkoder and, by the turn of the 20th century, Skadarska Street had become a focus for the city's bohemian life and a haunt of Belgrade's artists, actors, writers and musicians. The writer Đura Jakšić lived here and his former home is still used as a poetry venue for occasional 'Skadarlija nights'. Belgraders like to compare Skadarlija with Montmartre in Paris but this is probably pushing things a bit. Effectively, the area consists of just one principal street, Skadarska, together with a couple of lanes that lead off it. Skadarlija does its level best to conjure up the atmosphere of bygone times in the city, albeit in a slightly self-conscious fashion. The street itself is picturesque enough – narrow, cobbled and leafy with plane trees – but its main attraction, particularly in summer, is the concentration of 'national' restaurants that are squeezed in along here. Running all the way down the street is a chain of old-time restaurants, all of which compete with each other to be the oldest, the most authentic, have the oddest name – My Hat, the Three Hats, the Two Deer, There Are Days, etc – and host the best musicians.

The appeal is there for both locals and visitors. Large groups of friends and extended families gather here to drink, eat and celebrate; tourists come to gawp at the spectacle of Serbs enjoying themselves and to absorb the bohemian atmosphere. The food is Serbian with frills: plentiful grease, grilled meat and *kajmak*. The formula is similar whichever restaurant you decide to patronise: slick waiters circulate with endless plates of meat as Gypsy bands surround diners at their tables and play for tips. For the price of a few euros the musicians will perform requests.

Skadarlija can be a great night out, but it can also be a disappointment to those expecting to be seamlessly plunged back in time to witness some sort of bohemian Arcadia. The whole experience should not be taken too seriously: how much fun you have is really a matter of attitude. Skadarlija is certainly the 'real' Serbia, but it is also the closest that Belgrade comes to having any sort of tourist trap (see also, page 126). There is a market, **Bajlonova pijaca** [115 G5], and a line of florists running along Džordža Vašingtona at the bottom end of the street. The mock-Ottoman kiosk here was a gift from the Bosnian city of Sarajevo to Belgrade in 1989 and a reflection of friendlier times before the hostilities of the 1990s.

Around Studentski trg Returning to Trg Republike, and then continuing up Vase Čarapića, past the post office and the Plato café, you soon reach the quiet, green rectangle of **Studentski trg** [114 D4]. This was originally a Turkish graveyard, which was later cleared to make way for a marketplace. When the Serbs took over the administration of the city the market area was transformed into a public park. The building facing the square at Studentski trg 1 is the former residence of Captain Miša Anastesijević, an important 19th-century city merchant and business associate of Prince Miloš. The building, with a light-coloured facia and red ornamentation, was built in 1863, and is a combination of Gothic, Roman and Renaissance styles. Today it is the seat of the rector's office of Belgrade University. The **Ethnographic Museum** [114 C4] stands on the square's northern side. Also on Studentski trg, at the corner of Braće Jugović and Višnjićeva, is the *türbe* **of Sheik Mustapha** [114 D4], a Muslim holy man. This is one of the few Turkish monuments that still survive in Belgrade. It was built in 1784 as a mausoleum, and originally stood in the courtyard of a dervish monastery that has now completely vanished. Clearly, the Sheik is still venerated in some quarters: when I last visited the *türbe*, a group of Roma women were involved in kissing the locked doorway, posting dried flowers through the window, tying scraps of cloth to the metal grille and collecting plants from the grass outside.

Up to Kalemegdan **Kalemegdan Park** [114 A2] is nearby: a leafy, green refuge from the city, busy with strolling couples at any time of year, and situated on a bluff overlooking the confluence of the Sava and Danube rivers. The main path leading through it towards the fortress is lined with gift stalls and the stands of peanut vendors,

3

while other walkways meander off into the shade of birch and chestnut trees. Busts of various national heroes stand on plinths at some of the intersections. Covering a total of 30ha, this is the biggest park in the city: a vast complex of fortifications and gardens that, as well as serving as a home for the Belgrade Fortress and Military Museum, also contains an Arts Pavilion, the Belgrade Zoo and the fine Balkan-style *konak* of the Cultural Monuments Protection Institute. From the park's higher reaches, marvellous views may be had of the Sava and Danube rivers below, the high-rise buildings of New Belgrade on the opposite bank, and the wooded countryside of the pancake-flat Pannonian Plain that lies north of the city limits, and which draws the eye to a hazy vanishing point far upstream. The view is best in the morning – or better still, in the early evening, when the *bloks* of Novi Beograd are silhouetted with the setting sun and the river gives off a silvery glow. Despite famous Viennese waltzes that claim a contrary colouration, the Danube's waters are resolutely brown most of the time (those of the Sava River are said to be black!). In the opposite direction, low hills stretch away to the south, towards central Serbia. It is at this time of day that Belgraders are most likely to linger here, strolling, talking, playing chess and sometimes singing and dancing in impromptu groups. It is also a favourite spot for courting couples, and quite rightly so: it is without doubt the city's most romantic spot.

The park was created in 1867 by Prince Mihailo Obrenović on the occasion of Belgrade Fortress being handed back to the Serbs. The project was put in the hands of Emilijan Josivović, Belgrade's first urban planner. Originally, it only extended as far as the stone stairway leading up to the lower terrace but after 1931 the park was extended to include the upper city. The horse chestnut trees that were planted at this time are a splendid sight when in flower in late spring.

Walking along the western pathway above the Sava River you soon come to the **Messenger of Victory (Pobednik)** monument [102 C2], a landmark that was inaugurated in 1928 to commemorate the tenth anniversary of the breach of the Salonica front. This defiant and proud statue by Ivan Meštrović was originally intended to stand in the city centre but had to be relocated here due to prudish complaints about its full-frontal nudity and quite obvious masculine attributes. Now it stands looking west over the Sava River, facing unashamedly towards New Belgrade and to Austria and Hungary beyond. Despite the story relating to its forced relocation the figure looks very much at home here, proudly surveying the confluence of the two rivers. As well as its more obvious manly charms, Meštrović's warrior figure has two symbols of Serbian nationhood incorporated into its design: in his left hand, the warrior holds a falcon to symbolise Slavic freedom, and in the right, a sword representing the defence of peace. Belgrade has been required to take up this sword of peace many times, usually at great cost to its citizens, but at no time was the city's freedom more threatened than during the Nazi bombings and subsequent occupation of World War II. As a reminder of this, four graves of more recent heroes lie nearby, to the right of the main path just before entering the King Gate from below. Among these are those of Tito's right-hand man in the Partisan struggle, Ive Lole Ribar, and the Marxist, Moše Pijade, one of the theoreticians that helped to give Tito an ideological framework for his reconstruction of post-war Yugoslavia.

Meštrović has another work located in the gardens nearby: his **Monument of Gratitude to France** [114 A3], which was erected in 1930 and depicts a figure bathing. It is dedicated to the French who perished in Yugoslavia whilst fighting in the Great War. Symbolically, the statue is meant to represent the soldiers as bathing in the waters of courage. It is an altogether different monument from the Messenger of Victory, and being of a softer, more feminine nature, has never aroused the same degree of controversy. Close to this monument, behind the bouncy castle and kids' electric trucks and beneath the shade of trees is a fountain that depicts a figure wrestling heroically with a snake, a 1906 work of sculptor Simeon Roksandić that is entitled *The Struggle*. The walks and pathways in this part of the park contain several more busts and statues; they are mostly dedicated to famous Belgrade poets and writers.

Also contained within the park, to the north of the main entrance, is the **Art Pavilion 'Cvijeta Zuzorić'** [114 B2]. **Belgrade Zoo** [114 C1] (*Mali Kalemegdan 8;* \ *2624 526;* **w** *beozoovrt.rs;* ⊕ *from sunrise to sunset daily; admission 300/400din adult/child*) lies beyond this, spread across the park's northern slope. When Nazi Stuka dive-bombers attacked the fortress in 1941 they hit the zoo too, damaging many of the cages and allowing some of its more dangerous inmates to wander freely through the capital's ruined streets. Rebecca West, who visited before the German bombs fell, describes it as being 'a charming zoo of the Whipsnade sort'.

Kalemegdan Park gets its name from a combination of two Turkish words, *kale*, which means field, and *megdan*, meaning battle. The name refers to the plateau itself rather than the fortifications that were built upon it that are simply known as the **Belgrade Fortress** [114 A2]. Less martially, the Turks also referred to the site as '*Fitchir-bayir*' ('hill for meditating'); clearly, the park still fulfils much the same function for many of Belgrade's citizens today. Being such an obviously strategic site, high above the surrounding plain, with clear views in all directions overlooking the confluence of two great rivers, it seems no wonder that it was occupied and defended at the first opportunity. The first military defences here were built by the Celts, later to be expanded by the Romans during their tenancy of the site. Later, in the medieval period, the fortress was rebuilt, and ramparts constructed around the Lower Town, by the Serbian leader Despot Stefan Lazarević who managed to cling on to power here despite rapid Turkish expansion to the south. When the Turks finally arrived, the fortress fell into neglect and it was not until the arrival of the Austrians at the beginning of the 18th century that the fortress was reconstructed in its present form. A good idea of the development of the fortress can be had by studying the models on display at the **Belgrade Fortress Museum** [114 A2] next door to the clock tower. This also clearly indicates how the small manmade harbour on the Danube below was created and defended, as well as how it subsequently vanished from sight.

There are remnants of the earlier structures still in existence, like some of the medieval fortifications, but much has been re-used as building materials, or as a foundation for subsequent rebuilding. Some deep wells remain that are of Roman origin: the 60m-deep so-called **Roman well** [114 A3] (⊕ *09.00–21.00 daily; admission 100din, free on the last w/end of the month*) by the King Gate below the Victory monument was rebuilt by the Austrians in 1731 to ensure a safe water supply to the fortress. A double spiral staircase leads 35m down 208 steps to the water level. It was here at the site of the Roman well that Stefan Lazarević used to hold court in the 15th century and, of the surviving medieval fortifications, the most impressive date from the period of his rule. Most notable is the **Despot's Gate (Despotova kapija)** [114 A1] at the northeast corner of the complex, which is named after Stefan Lazarević himself, the best-preserved of the fortifications from that period. This gate formed the main entrance to the upper town in medieval times; above the gate stands the Dizdar Tower that is now used as an astronomical observatory.

Beyond this lies the **Zindan** or **Prison Gate** [114 A1], constructed in the middle of the 15th century a few years before the Despot's Gate to provide a heavily fortified entrance to the fortress. The Zindan Gate consists of two low round towers that could be defended with cannons, with a bridge crossing the ditch to the entrance between them. A dungeon was installed in the cellars underneath, hence the name. Across the drawbridge in front of the Zindan Gate is the late 17th-century Leopold Gate, which was built to honour the Austrian emperor of the same name; the initials L.P. (Leopoldus Primus) have been carved into it as evidence of this. A short distance to the north is **Jakšić Tower** [114 A1], a late 15th-century tower that was removed by the Austrians in the early 18th century and reconstructed in 1938; this looks down over two churches: the Rose Church of Our Lady (Crkva Ružica) and the smaller, later church of St Petka. The **Rose Church of Our Lady** [114 A1] is said to stand on the same spot as an older church that was built during the reign of Stefan Lazarević, but which was razed by the Turks during their 1521 invasion. The current building was originally built as an arsenal during the 18th century but later converted into an army chapel called the Ružica or Rose Church between 1867 and 1889. It was restored in 1925. The icons represent several contemporary prominent figures from this time: King Petar, Prince Aleksandar, Tsar Nicholas II and politician Nikola Pašić. Immediately above this church at Kalemegdan is **Church of St Petka (Sv Paraskeva)** [114 A1], built on the site of a sacred spring of the same name. The spring was considered to have miraculous powers for barren women and Belgrade's women still come here in large numbers on 27 October, the *slava* of the church's patron. The current church was built in 1937 to the design of Momir Korunović.

Elsewhere within the fortress complex, features of interest of a later construction include Sahat-kula, the **Clock Tower Gate** [114 A2] (⊕ *09.00–21.00 daily*), built in the second half of the 18th century above the south entrance to the Upper Town and used by the Turks as a lookout, and **Karađorđe's Gate** [114 A3], reached by taking the path to the right of Meštrović's monument to France, which was constructed in the mid 18th century and so-named because the eponymous leader of the First Serbian Uprising passed through it to enter the city in 1806. The **Outer Stambol Gate** [114 B3] directly opposite dates from the same period. The paths from both gates converge in front of the **Gallery of the Museum of Natural History** [114 A3] built in 1835 by the Turks as a guardhouse and which, rather surprisingly, is of Classical design. In front of this the Inner Stambol Gate, constructed in the late 18th century with fine stone blocks, leads into the fortress.

Standing near the centre of the Upper Town is one of Belgrade's three surviving Turkish religious monuments, the **Tomb** (or in Turkish, *türbe*) **of Damad-Ali Paša** [114 A2], which dates from 1783 and was built to commemorate a vizier who was killed at Petrovaradin in 1716. The focal point of the Upper Town, the **Military Museum** [114 A3], is situated in a building that used to house the Military Geographical Institute and, dating from 1923–24, is not as old as it might appear to be on first glance. The museum is easy to find; just look for the neat ranks of World War I and II tanks and anti-aircraft guns that fill the ditches surrounding it.

All of the above are to be found in the Upper Town sector of Kalemegdan but the Lower Town, the riverbank zone of the fortress, has a few sights of its own, although far more has been destroyed here. The Baroque **Charles VI Gate (Kapila Karla VI)** [102 C1] was built in 1736 as a ceremonial entrance to the city and bears a coat of arms that shows a boar's head being pierced by an arrow. A late 18th-century cannon foundry stands next to the gate, later to become an army kitchen. Nearby stand a **hammam**, built around 1870 for the Serbian army, which these days serves as a planetarium for an astronomical society, and a building from around 1820 that was originally the kitchen for the Turkish garrison. In addition to that of Charles VI, three more gates lead into the Lower Town: the **Vidin Gate** [102 C1], built by the Turks in the mid 18th century, and two earlier 15th-century **Eastern gates** that lead into the Lower Town from the Vidin Gate. The latter were damaged by Allied bombing in 1944. The most prominent feature in the whole Lower Town area is the 15th-century **Nebojša Tower** [102 C1], which stands near the river on Bulevar Vojvode Bojovića, and was originally constructed around 1460 to protect the harbour with cannons. There was great resistance here during the 1521 siege of the city by the Turks: only after setting fire to the tower was the Lower Town successfully taken. Later, during Ottoman rule, it became a dungeon and torture chamber.

BELGRADE WATERFRONT – TRANSFORMING SAVAMALA INTO SERBIA'S DUBAI

At the heart of Savamala, next to the Hotel Bristol, stands the Geozavod building that once housed the Institute of Geophysics. A striking Art Nouveau structure that had long been neglected and allowed to deteriorate over the past century, the Geozavod has been restored in recent years for use as a marketing centre for the new *Belgrade Waterfront* scheme, a large model of which can be seen in the elegant hall of the first floor.

The scheme was unveiled by Prime Minister Aleksandar Vučić in June 2014: a €3.5 billion project to develop Belgrade's waterfront in the characterful and bohemian, if somewhat run-down, Savamala district of the city. The project, funded by Middle East money, plans to redevelop this neglected part of Belgrade by building state-of-the-art hotels, offices and condominiums where crumbling housing and warehouses currently stand next to the confluence of the Sava and Danube rivers. The centrepiece of this development is to be a sky-piercing glass skyscraper, the tallest in southeast Europe. The developer is the Abu Dhabi-based Eagle Hills, chaired by Mohamed Alabbar, who was previously involved with building the world's largest shopping mall and tallest building in Dubai.

Hardly surprisingly, such a grandiose scheme has divided opinion. Many critics are dubious whether such a scheme is suitable for an economically struggling city such as Belgrade, and are sceptical about the prosperity the developer claims that it will bring to the city. Soon after the announcement of the development a dedicated opposition movement under the banner of '*Ne da(vi)mo Beograd*' ('We won't let Belgrade d(r)own') – its mascot, a giant yellow duck – took to the streets to protest, and in Savamala in particular, fresh graffiti started to appear on the district's soot-blackened walls.

The potential benefits are, of course, fairly obvious in a city in which unemployment runs at around 25% – a promise of anything up to 20,000 jobs – but critics of the scheme point out numerous irregularities in the way *Belgrade Waterfront* has been implemented thus far, suggesting that the original agreement is contrary to Serbian law, that local people have not been consulted, and that adequate affordable housing has not been provided. More serious still is the claim that people who lived in the area had been summarily evicted in April 2016 with just one day's notice before their houses were demolished, an action that led to more angry protest in the days that followed.

It remains to be seen how successful an ambitious top-down gentrification project such as this will be in terms of improving the prosperity and general quality of life of most of Belgrade's citizens. There are also serious doubts whether the full allocation of promised funds will be forthcoming from the Arab sponsors. At the time of writing, *Belgrade Waterfront* remains a matter of 'watch this space' – or rather, watch *that* space.

For information on the planned development, see the website w belgradewaterfront.com.

Following Bulevar Vojvode Bojovića beneath the rise of Kalemegdan Park will soon bring you to the **Savamala** waterfront (see box, page 151), a formerly industrial area that, at the time of writing, was scheduled for large-scale development. **Beton hala** [102 C2] here, a long parade of concrete former warehouses at Belgrade Port next to the river, has in recent years become a popular night-time entertainment zone with a few clubs and plenty of voguish cafés and restaurants like Cantina de Frida, Comunale and Toro.

Around Upper Knez Mihailova Returning to the Upper Town and leaving Kalemegdan Park by its southern entrance to traverse the pedestrian crossing on Pariska, you will find yourself at the very top of pedestrianised **Knez Mihailova**. Heading south, you pass the terminus for tram numbers 19, 21, 22 and 29 on your left, fronted by a line of stalls selling all manner of souvenir porcelain; the next street running across is Kralja Petra I. Turning down this street to the left, and passing a few restaurants on the way, you reach the Royal, which is, rather surprisingly, Belgrade's oldest hotel. Just beyond here, at Gospodar Jevremova 11, is the city's only surviving mosque (at one time there were 30 in the city). The **Bajrakli Mosque** [114 D3], which dates from the Turkish re-conquest of the city in 1690, and was built as a memorial to Sultan Suleyman II, has clearly seen better days. Its name means 'the flag mosque', a reference to the method in which the call to prayers was signalled in the past. The mosque lost its original minaret during the second period of Austrian rule in the city when it was converted into a Jesuit church for a while. When the Turks left the city for good it was abandoned but it was eventually reopened in 1893 to serve those Muslims that remained in the city. Somehow, this solitary remnant of the Muslim faith gives the impression of deliberately hiding itself away in a city that these days is predominantly Orthodox. (The spirit of Orthodoxy is actually very close, just around the corner at the **Fresco Gallery** [114 C3] on Cara Uroša, and the gallery itself was built on the site of a former synagogue destroyed during World War II, so clearly Christians, Muslims and Jews used to live cheek by jowl around here.) The mosque has good reason to hide itself perhaps; it was badly damaged by fire during the riots that were the backlash of anti-Serb riots in Kosovo in March 2004. It has since been restored and continues to be used by the city's small Muslim community.

Dorćol ('four roads') The mosque marks the edge of the city neighbourhood known as **Dorćol**, its name coming from the Turkish *dört yol*, meaning 'four roads'. The four roads in this case originally referred to the crossroads where Cara Dušana crosses Kralja Petra I but now the name is used to describe the whole of the quarter that stretches northwards from Skadarlija to Kalemegdan, and eastwards from Studentski trg to the Danube riverbank. Formerly, Dorćol was host to a cosmopolitan community of Turks, Austrians, Greeks, Jews, Vlachs and Serbs. The 19th-century Jewish community occupied the area delineated by the streets of Tadeuša Košćuška, Visokog Stevana, Braće Baruh and Dunavska (one of Belgrade's first synagogues was built here, at the corner of Solunska and Jevrejska), while the neighbouring Turkish quarter of Zerek lay in the streets that surrounded the intersection of Kralja Petra I and Cara Dušana – the *dört yol* crossroads itself. The first church to be established in this multi-cultural enclave was that of **St Alexander Nevsky (Svetog Aleksandar Nevski)** [115 G4] at Cara Dušana 63. The proposal for a church in the Dorćol area first came from Russian volunteer troops stationed in Belgrade at the end of the 19th century. It was arranged that a mobile military chapel consecrated to the Russian saint be brought to Belgrade, and half a century later, in

1928–29, a church dedicated to the same saint was constructed at this location. The church is in the style of the Morava School and it has a white marble iconostasis that contrasts nicely with its smoke-blackened interior. The iconostasis was originally intended for the Karađorđević mausoleum at Oplenac but was bequeathed to the church by King Aleksandar. The northern choir has a monument to the soldiers killed in the conflicts of 1876–78, 1912–13 and 1914–18. In the southern choir is a monument to Tsar Nicholas II of Russia and King Aleksandar I.

Along Kralja Petra I Street Nowadays, Dorćol is a largely working-class residential area with a far more homogeneous population. Dorćol has its share of high-density housing and can seem a little down at heel in places, particularly in its northern reaches approaching the river. This is not to say that it seems threatening in any way: the area has a genuine neighbourhood feel to it and it seems that everyone who lives here is at least on nodding terms with everyone else. At its northern edge on the Danube, near the '25 May' Sports Centre, there is a popular promenade that follows the river east towards the Danube quay and west to Kalemegdan Lower Town; a route which is busy in summer evenings with cyclists, courting couples, dog walkers and locals enjoying the fresh river air.

More of the area's Jewish history can be discovered at the Jewish History Museum back on Kralja Petra I Street. **Kralja Petra I** has a number of other interesting sights. Heading uphill back towards Knez Mihailova you come to a pair of fine Art Nouveau buildings on the right-hand side just before you reach the junction with the pedestrian street. The building at number 41 with the green-tiled façade dates from 1907 and was the house of a city merchant called Stamenković. Next door at number 39 is another fine secessionist-style building that has a motif of a female face flanked by two doves above its upper balcony. This was built in the same year as its neighbour for Aron Levi, a wealthy Belgrade Jew. In great contrast, facing them on the opposite side, is the 1997 Zepter building, designed by the architects Branislav Mitrović and Vasilije Milutinović, a postmodern steel-and-glass edifice that looks as if it has been slickly shoe-horned into the limited available space. It is worth going round the back of this interesting building to take a look at the semicircular rear entrance that faces on to the narrow alleyway off Uzun Mirkova. Crossing Knez Mihailova, the street plunges downhill once more, and the **National Bank of Serbia (Narodna banka Srbije)** [114 B4] is on your left at number 12. This Renaissance-inspired building was built in 1890 and it is this same branch that still serves as the

A ZAHA HADID DEVELOPMENT FOR KALEMEGDAN?

A large plot of land between Kalemegdan Fortress and the Dorćol riverfront is currently awaiting development. Originally owned by Beko, a company that went bankrupt, the land has been bought by Lamda Development, a Greek company that is part of a holding company with EFG Bank and EKI Petrol. The Greek company approached the studio of Zaha Hadid to come up with a project for the land and the Iraqi-British architect came up with a stunning plan for the development: a sweeping modernist design that connects with the surrounding landscape and incorporates essential public spaces and public transition between the fortress and the riverfront. It is highly unlikely that such an ambitious, expensive plan will ever be realised but, for those interested, the design can be seen online at **w** zaha-hadid.com/architecture/beko-masterplan.

National Bank's headquarters today. It is claimed that the bank was built upon the site of Roman *thermae* that stood here during the 1st or 2nd century AD. Further down, on the opposite side at number 7 is the Kralja Petra I Elementary School, another neo-Renaissance building constructed in 1905–06, and designed by Serbia's first woman architect, Jelisaveta Nacić. Continuing down from here you arrive at the **Orthodox cathedral (Saborna crkva Sv Arhangela Mihaila)** [114 B5]. The Holy Archangel Michael Church, better known as the 'Gathering church', was constructed between 1837 and 1840 on the orders of Prince Miloš Obrenović, who is buried here in the crypt together with his two sons, Mihailo and Milan. The church, a mixture of Classical and Baroque styles, was designed by the Pančevo architect Kvarfeld, and occupies the site of an earlier church that dates back to 1728. The interior contains a finely carved iconostasis by Dimitrije Petrović and icons by Dimitrije Avramović. During World War II, the relics of Prince Lazar were brought here for safe keeping, away from the hands of the Ustaša who had already stolen the prince's rings from his corpse in its resting place at a monastery in the Fruška Gora. This conferred considerable importance on the cathedral as a pilgrimage centre, until 1987 when Lazar's remains were sent on a nationwide tour prior to being deposited in their final resting place at Ravanica Monastery. Prince Lazar was not the only revered Serbian to be interred here: Vuk Stefanović Karadžić, the scholar responsible for phoneticising Serbian and producing a definitive dictionary of the language is also buried in the church's graveyard, together with Dositej Obradović, another great Serbian educator and writer. There is a museum dedicated to the legacy left by these two scholars quite nearby on Gospodar Jevremova. Next door to the cathedral is the **Museum of the Serbian Orthodox Church** [114 A5], and opposite is the **'?' café** [114 B5]. This café – a traditional Serbian *kafana* – was built in the 1820s by a man called Naum Ičko, who later sold it to Prince Miloš Obrenović. The prince made a present of it to his personal healer, Hećim Tomi, who decided to open it as a *kafana*. The property changed hands several times, as did its name, being known at first as 'Tomi's kafana', then 'Shepherd's Inn', and then 'By the Cathedral'. There were objections by the ecclesiastical authorities to this last name and so a temporary sign showing a question mark was put up, which ended up becoming its name. Setting its individual history to one side, the '?' is a rare Belgrade example of a wooden-framed, Turkish–Balkan building, as well as being a fine location for a drink or a meal (see also, pages 125–6). To get an idea of a rather grander style of living during the early 19th century in Belgrade you could take a look at nearby **Princess Ljubica's Konak** [114 B5] around the corner on Kneza Sime Markovića, a building that looks particularly impressive when lit up at night.

Back to Knez Mihailova

Returning to the pedestrian street of **Knez Mihailova**, there are a number of fine buildings that are worth a look whilst walking south towards Terazije. The urban terrain that was later covered by the street dates back to the original Roman settlement of Singidunum, later developed during the Turkish period to become an area of houses, drinking fountains and mosques. The street itself was laid out in 1867 by Emilijan Josimović, the same city planner responsible for Kalemegdan Park, and it was immediately occupied by the great and the good of Belgrade society. In 1870, the street was given the name it still bears today. At number 56 is the **Library of the City of Belgrade** [114 C4], which was formerly the Srpska Kruna Hotel, built in 1869 in a Romantic style. Virtually opposite at numbers 53–55 is a slightly later, Renaissance-style building that originally served as the private home of the influential lawyer, Marko Stojanović. In 1937, it was turned into a gallery space for the **Academy of Fine Art**. Continuing further down the street, you pass several grand buildings, all dating from the 1870s, constructed in a transitional style that lies somewhere between Renaissance and Romantic. At number 49, you pass the former headquarters of OPTOR, the coalition of opposition groups so instrumental in bringing about Milošević's downfall. This used to be the setting-off point for demonstrations, by way of the nearby Plato café at Studentski trg. Further down, at number 33 is the neo-Renaissance building of the **Nikola Spasić Foundation**. At the junction of Knez Mihailova and Đure Jakšića stands the **Soldiers' Fountain (Delijska česma)** [114 C5], close to the site of an earlier Turkish fountain destroyed by the Austrians. At the next junction, where Zmaj Jovina crosses the street, the Progress Palace dominates the surrounding buildings. Built in 1994 by the architect Miodrag Mirković, the design is a postmodernist combination of styles from different epochs, with a rounded corner façade of reflective glass. Continuing south, you pass the French Cultural Centre. Opposite sits the Press building, Dom štampe, with fountains leading the way down to Trg Republike. Just a little further on and you reach **'Albania' tower** [115 E7], at the corner of Knez Mihailova and Kolarčeva. This building, dating back to just before World War II, was Belgrade's first skyscraper. Somehow, it managed to avoid the attentions of the German bombers in 1941. This is the end of the pedestrianised zone and where Knez Mihailova ends, so do the southern limits of Stari Grad, the Old City.

South of Terazije – the modern city
The sights of modern Belgrade are fewer and farther between than those of Stari Grad, but they are interesting nevertheless, especially when considering the city's more recent history. A short walk along Terazije from its junction with Knez Mihailova soon brings you to the imposing and attractive façade of the **Hotel Moscow** [103 E4]. This building, built in Art Nouveau style in 1906 for the 'Russia' insurance company, is one of Belgrade's more notable landmarks, but the view across to the neon signs of Terazije and its dull row of traffic-grimed buildings is overall less pleasing. There are some fine buildings nevertheless: at Terazije 34 is the Krsmanović House built originally in 1885 as a merchant's house but used between 1918 and 1922 as the court of Aleksandar I Karađorđević and it was from here, in December 1918, that the Kingdom of Serbs, Croats and Slovenes, later to become the Kingdom of Yugoslavia, was proclaimed.

Sitting opposite the Hotel Moscow is the equally large but rather less grandiose Hotel Balkan. Walking down Prizrenska from here will soon bring you to **Zeleni venac** [114 D7], an important terminus for the city's bus network and the prized location of another McDonald's branch. From the terrace above the bus park you can see the chequerboard-patterned roofs of Zeleni venac, condemned by some hard-line nationalists for echoing the Croatian national emblem in its design. In the street behind, hidden away at Maršala Birjuzova 19, is the city's only currently active synagogue, built in 1924–25 on a piece of land donated by the Belgrade Municipality. The gate leading into it appears to be locked nearly all of the time. Steps lead up from this rather woebegone street to Obilićev venac and a whole parade of trendy cafés.

South of the Hotel Moscow, Terazije morphs into traffic-crazed **Kralja Milana** (formerly called Marshal Tito, in the days when the idea of a united Yugoslavia was still a source of pride). It is along here that, more than anywhere else in the city, resonances of the former republic make themselves known: the crowded trams clattering along the street, the faded neon Cyrillic lettering, some lacklustre shops and dusty department stores – all seem to hark back to the recent past, the 1970s perhaps. The stylish cafés and designer boutiques of Knez Mihailova already seem another world away; as if the recently introduced free-market economy, so fêted in the streets just north of here, could not spread beyond some unseen economic fault line that ran east to west somewhere in the vicinity of the Hotel Moscow. This is purely illusory of course, but for a brief moment, walking down Kralja Milana, it can almost seem as if Balkan-style socialism is still alive and well.

Terazije has one or two sights of its own: on the left-hand side at number 39 is the **Smederevo Bank** building [103 E4], built in the secessionist style in 1912 as an office and residence for a prominent Belgrade merchant. On the right opposite are two impressive buildings. The first, at number 34, is the **Krsmanović House**, built in 1885 in a neo-Baroque style as a family dwelling for a city merchant. The house served as a temporary royal palace between 1918 and 1922 and it was here that the Kingdom of Serbs, Croats and Slovenes (to become Yugoslavia in 1929) was declared in December 1918. Another secessionist building, the **Photography Studio of Milan Jovanović** [103 E4], is at number 40, with a relief showing two cupid figures with a camera above the entrance. These days the entrance to the studio leads into the Zvezda cinema. Opposite at Terazije 41 is the building of the **Ministry of Justice** [103 E4], constructed in 1883, with a mural by Ibrahim Ljubović of a hot-air balloon on the gable above it. Just beyond this on the right-hand side is the **Ministry of Education** [103 E4], which was originally built in 1870–71 but had its façade altered considerably in 1912 to the secessionist style. The ornamentation above the door shows two female heads and the Serbian coat of arms, along with interweaved motifs that reflect the influence of the Morava School.

A little further on, just off the street on the edge of Pionirski Park to the left, stands the **City Hall** [103 E4], built in 1882 as the royal palace of the Obrenović dynasty in an Italian Renaissance style. The building now houses the mayor's offices and is the premises of the Belgrade City Assembly; it was also used by Tito for a while in the early days of the post-war Yugoslav republic. Sadly, the stained-glass windows that represent scenes of Partisan struggle during World War II are not on view to the general public. Next door to City Hall, across some gardens and a newly restored fountain, stands the **New Palace** [103 E4], which was built between 1913 and 1918 for Petar I Karađorđević. This was restored after being badly damaged during World War I and reoccupied in 1922 when it became the official residence of the Serbian royal family until 1934 when King Aleksandar was assassinated. Today the building serves as the seat for the Serbian State Assembly. It is interesting to note how the residencies of the two rival dynasties have now been usurped to serve the somewhat gentler rivalries of city and state. A little further down on Andrićev venac, the **Ivo Andrić Museum** [103 E4] makes use of the former residence of the writer and Nobel Prize winner. There is also a monument to him at the street corner.

Kneza Miloša leads downhill off Kralja Milana to the right. It was this part of the city that took the brunt of some of the most damaging of the 1999 NATO attacks, with cruise missiles homing in on the government buildings of the Federal and Republican Ministries of Internal Affairs. The building of the Republican Ministry of Justice on nearby Nemanjina Street was also hit shortly after, and the twin towers of the Yugoslav Ministry of Defence, which stood on the corner of Kneza Miloša and Nemanjina, were bombed twice, on 29 April and 7 May of that same year. The US Embassy complex at Kneza Miloša 50 was abandoned just before these raids took place, to be lightly vandalised in the weeks that followed. The crumpled remnants of the buildings remain in place, quite deliberately it might seem: a defiant symbol of what was perceived as an unjust NATO campaign and Serbia's demonisation by the wider world. The contorted concrete and exposed girders are, undeniably, a chilling testament to precision bombing; indeed, they look as if they have suffered from freakishly localised earthquakes. The large obelisk-like edifice in the background to the carnage is the **'Belgrade Girl' building (Beograd anka)** [103 E4], which towers above the junction of Kneza Miloša and Kralja Milana.

Heading back towards the centre along Kralja Milana and then turning right along Dragoslava Jovanovića next to the park to reach Bulevar Aleksandra (formerly Bulevar Revolucije), **Trg Nikole Pašića** [103 E3–4] lies directly on the left. This is the youngest of the city's squares, built in 1953 along with its central fountain, and originally known as Marx and Engels Square. The Nikola Pašića monument at the square's centre is a recent (1998) addition. The Classical-style **State Union Parliament Building** [103 E4], formerly the Federal Parliament, pre-dates the square, building having started in 1906, with completion in 1936. In front of the main entrance stand two groups of prancing black horses. It was in front of here that many of the opposition rallies against the Milošević regime took place in October 2000.

A little further down, at the edge of Tašmajdan Park stands **St Mark's Church (Crkva svetog Marka)** [103 E4]. This Serbian–Byzantine-style church in yellow and red was built between 1931 and 1936, and occupies the site of an older church from 1835. St Mark's has been constructed as a larger-scale copy of the Gračanica Monastery in troubled Kosovo, one of the most hallowed religious monuments of the Serbian psyche. The hall interior is quite bare, and dominated by four massive pillars supporting the roof, but the church contains a rich collection of icons from the 18th and 19th centuries, as well as the sarcophagus that contains the remains of the Serbian emperor Dusan who died in 1355, which were moved here from the Saint Archangel's Monastery in Prizren. The church also contains the tomb of Patriarch German Ćorić. Next door to St Mark's, and dwarfed by its bulk, is a tiny, jewel-like Russian church that was built by Russian exiles fleeing the October Revolution of 1917.

On Aberdareva, directly behind the church, stands the RTS Serbian state television headquarters. The technician's wing of this building was hit by a NATO missile on the night of 22–23 April 1999, killing 16 RTS workers and wounding 18 others. What makes this even worse is that it would appear that management were fully aware that the building was going to be targeted but had decreed that any employee leaving the building during working hours, even in the event of an air raid, would be threatened with martial court. A monument to the victims stands overlooking the site in Tašmajdan Park and asks the simple question, *Zašto?* – 'Why?' **Tašmajdan Park** [103 E/F4] is a pleasant, leafy space that is popular with Belgraders, especially families with young children. Tašmajdan is named after the former quarry that was located at the site of the park. Much of the stone for Belgrade's older buildings came from here. As a consequence the ground underneath the present-day park is riddled with galleries and tunnels. During the First National Uprising in 1806, some of the rebels had their camp here. A funereal tradition continued following the Roman construction of catacombs here and there used to be a cemetery here, but the graves were transferred to Novi Groblje in the 19th century.

Another green space nearby, to the north of Tašmajdan Park, and sandwiched between Takovska and 29 Novembra is the **Jevremovac Botanical Garden** [103 F3] (*Takovska 43;* ✆ *768 857, 767 988;* ⊕ *1 May–1 Nov 09.00–19.00 Mon–Fri, 11.00–18.00 w/ends; admission 100din; free guided tours are given on Sat at noon starting from the main gate*). The garden is actually a unit of the University of Belgrade's Biology faculty, and was formerly an estate owned by Prince Milan Obrenović. It was donated to the university in 1889 on the condition that it was named after the prince's grandfather, Jeverem, from whom he had inherited the estate. There is only one entrance, at the corner on Takovska. The gardens cover 5ha and have about 250 species of tree and shrub, both native and exotic. Some of these are labelled with their names in Serbian, English and Latin together with a distribution map. There is also a hothouse, constructed in 1892, and the offices of the Institute of Botany. The hothouse, which was once one of the very best in eastern Europe but now looks a little careworn,

3

is jam-packed with exotics but only the central section was open during my visit. Signs from the hothouse indicate the direction of the Japanese Garden (Japanski Vrt), which has all the ingredients you might expect: a pool, a shallow stream, sensitively placed rocks, a wooden footbridge, stone pagodas and a pavilion.

Returning to Tašmajdan Park then heading southeast along Bulevar kralja Aleksandra you pass by Belgrade University's Faculty of Technical Sciences, with its large seated statue of Nikola Tesla, just before reaching **Ćirilo and Metodije Park** [103 F5]. This small park is probably better known for the monument it contains – the **Vuk Memorial statue (Vukov spomenik)** [103 F5]. The statue by Đorđe Jovanović, which stands at the park's western edge, was unveiled in 1937 to celebrate the 150th anniversary of Vuk Karadžić, the famous Serbian linguist and ethnographer. The statue depicts the great educator seated with book in hand, sporting a moustache so large that soup would have been out of the question. The park is also the location of Belgrade's only **underground station**, a state-of-the-art white elephant that is well worth a look (see box, page 106).

Returning back along Bulevar kralja Aleksandra towards the Old City, and then turning left down Beogradska, you pass close to the **Nikola Tesla Museum** [103 F5] as you cross Krunska. Beogradska continues down to **Slavija Square** [103 E5], which might already have been your first experience of Belgrade if you arrived in the city by way of the airport transfer bus. The uninspiring monolith of the Slavija Hotel dominates the scene, and buses, taxis and trams speed dizzily around the roundabout before being catapulted centrifugally in one of seven possible directions, principally along the main arteries of Kralja Milana, Nemanjina or Bulevar JNA. There is really little reason to linger here. A better bet is to walk back a block north, to Njegoševa – a smarter, quieter street strewn with designer cafés and trendy bars along its entire length. By turning right and following this street you will soon arrive at Kalenić Market, Belgrade's most interesting outdoor locale for the sale of fresh produce.

The **Temple of St Sava (Hram svetog Save)** [103 E6] is also within easy grasp from Slavija Square – just a short walk south to the Vračar neighbourhood – and the church's enormous dome can be seen from all over the city, gleaming through Belgrade's haze in all directions like a beacon. Size apart, the church is undeniably a highly impressive structure: a neo-Byzantine colossus with echoes of St Sophia in Istanbul. The site at Vračar was chosen because it was the same place where the Ottoman ruler, Sinan Pasha, had the holy relics of St Sava burned in 1594, having seized them from Mileševa Monastery in Raška in southwest Serbia. This humiliation left a very bitter taste and it was decided, on the 400th anniversary of the event in 1894, that a huge memorial church would be erected on the spot where the sacrilegious act had taken place. Building it was anything but straightforward: the time taken over St Sava's construction must compare to that of cathedral-building in medieval times. Even today, the church's interior is still not quite complete, although with the relative peace that reigns in Serbia these days there is at least an end in sight (see box, page 164).

The much smaller church to the north of St Sava's is the Old Chapel of St Sava that was relocated here in 1935. Its interior contains rich frescoes, the work of Dragan Marunić. A large landscaped area fronts both churches to the west leading down to Bulevar JNA. On the south side of this stands the National Library of Serbia, constructed in 1970 to replace the earlier one that was burned to the ground in the Nazi bombing raids of 6 April 1941. On the west side, on a small mound facing Bulevar JNA, is a **monument to Karađorđe** [103 E6], erected in 1979 on the 175th anniversary of the First National Uprising.

Dedinje and Topčider Park This area, south of the city centre, has smart residential enclaves, several large parks and sports clubs, as well as a few museums and galleries. Topčider Park is a vast green space, close to the residential enclaves of Dedinje and Senjak, and was the first of the city's parks to be created. It sprang up around the residence of Prince Miloš Obrenović with the wide-scale planting of plane trees in the 1830s. The name derives from Turkish, meaning 'Valley of Cannons', as it was here that the Turks set up makeshift foundries to produce the cannons used for the 1521 attack on the city. Later, the area was used for vineyards and the summer residences of the wealthy but in 1831, after having had a *konak* built for his wife and children in town, Prince Miloš gave instructions for the setting up of a park and settlement here. He ordered the construction of a church, a *kafana* and an army barracks, in addition to a mansion for himself that was to be designed by the same architect, Hađi-Nikola Živković, who had been responsible for his wife's residence near to the cathedral (page 154). The building, now housing the permanent collection of the **Historical Museum of Serbia**, is in Serbian–Balkan style, with some elements of central European influence. The prince stayed here only occasionally during his first reign, which ended in 1839, but this became his permanent home throughout his short, second reign that began in 1859. He died here on 14 September 1860.

There are a number of monuments that lie close to Prince Miloš's residence: an **obelisk** erected in 1859 to celebrate Prince Miloš's re-establishment of the Obrenović dynasty; the **Monument to Archibald Reiss**, a Swiss who accompanied the Serbs through Albania in 1915; and the **Monument to the Woman Harvester**, dating from 1852 and one of the oldest surviving monuments in the city.

South of Prince Miloš's mansion, Dedinje stretches away to the east of Rackovički put, while to the west lies wooded Košutnjak Hill with its maze of walking paths. To the north, hemming Dedinje in, with yet more greenery is **Hajd Park** [102 C7] (pronounced in the same way as London's famous green space). Close to Hajd Park is the **Museum of Yugoslav History** [102 D7], sometimes referred to as the Museum of 25 May, which is just one of a complex of three buildings. While the main building hosts temporary exhibitions and events, its older sister museum up the hill houses a collection of gifts donated to Tito from heads of state around the world. Just a little further up the hill is Tito's mausoleum, the **House of Flowers** [102 D7] (*Kuća Cveća;* ⊕ *09.00–15.00 Tue–Sun*); the cloying name is perhaps something of a euphemism to avoid drawing too much unwanted attention to the deceased founding father of federal Yugoslavia (see *Museum of Yugoslav History and Josip Broz Tito Memorial Complex,* pages 169–72).

Much of Dedinje is quite self-consciously exclusive, with luxurious mansions glimpsed behind thick, protective hedges and expensive German cars swishing the tarmac; a natural abode for foreign ambassadors, film stars, politicians and Belgrade's new money. With the anonymity desired by some of its residents, it is perhaps not surprising that the neighbourhood, while pleasant enough, is rather lacking in real character. But Dedinje also has the common touch, and plays host to the home grounds of two of Belgrade's most well-known football teams – **FK Crvena Zvezda** (Red Star) Belgrade and **FK Partizan** [103 E7] (page 138). The aggressive and tribalistic graffiti that decorates the exterior walls of both of these grounds injects a tougher and grittier element into what is primarily an upper middle-class neighbourhood. This is perfect if you are both wealthy and a football fan. A short distance to the southwest, hidden away atop **Dedinje Hill**, is **the Royal Compound**, which consists of two palaces, a church and other buildings in a parkland setting of 135ha. Group visits to the Royal Compound may be made from 1 April to 31 October on Saturdays and Sundays. The

3

maximum group size is 50 and prior registration is mandatory. Tickets may be booked at the Tourist Organisation of Belgrade office at Makedonska. No food and drink, bulky luggage or smoking is allowed within the compound; shorts should not be worn.

The **White Court (Beli Dvor)** was built as a summer residence for King Aleksandar I between 1934 and 1937. The king was assassinated the year construction began and it became the home of the prince regent, Paul, instead. The house, by architect Aleksandar Đorđević, is in Palladian style, similar in design to the English country house Ditchley Park. The interior, in the styles of Louis XV and Louis XVI, was by the French firm Jansen who were also responsible for the White House in Washington. After World War II Beli Dvor became the official residence of President Tito although he tended to use it mainly for official functions as did Slobodan Milošević during his presidency later on. The house has since been returned to the Serbian royal family and has become the residence of Crown Prince Alexander II since his return to Serbia in 2002.

The **Old Court (Stari Dvor)**, sometimes referred to as the Royal Palace, was built between 1924 and 1929 for King Aleksandar I. It was designed in the Serbian–Byzantine style by the architects Zivojin Nikolić and Nikolai Krassnoff, both members of the Royal Academy. The entrance hall is decorated with copies of medieval frescoes from Dečani and Sopoćani monasteries while the drawing rooms, the Blue and Gold salons, with carved wooden ceilings and brass chandeliers, are in Baroque and Renaissance styles respectively. Along with Beli Dvor, the Old Court is also home to a valuable collection of paintings mostly of the Renaissance School. The basement, which has a wine cellar, a billiards room and a projection room, is decorated in the style of the Kremlin's Terem Palace in Moscow with motifs of the Russian firebird legend and scenes from Serbian national epics.

The **Palace Church of St Andrew the First-called**, which lies to the south of the Old Court and was built at the same time, is based upon the model for King Milutin's church at Studenica. It is also influenced by the Church of St Andrew on the Treska River in Macedonia. The frescoes inside are copies of those found in Serbian medieval monasteries and were painted by a team of Russian painters under the supervision of the exile Nikolai Krassnoff.

Northwest of Dedinje, on a site alongside the Sava River, is the development that makes up the Belgrade Fair complex. South of here, **Košutnjak Hill (Doe Hill)** is a 330ha expanse of mixed forest and open areas that is criss-crossed by numerous walking trails. It owes its name to the deer that once roamed here, as it was a royal hunting reserve until 1903 when it was opened to the public. Despite the fact that this park witnessed the murder of Prince Mihailo Obrenović in 1868, Košutnjak has become a favoured picnic spot for many of Belgrade's citizens. Horse-drawn carriages are available for hire for trips around the park, and it is worth seeking out the enormous 200-year-old plane tree that has branches so massive it requires braces to keep them up. The park area contains two specialised facilities: Pionirski grad ('Pioneer's town') with its sports and recreational centre, and Filmski grad ('Film town') with studios and buildings to service the film industry. The Košutnjak Sports and Recreational Centre lies further down the hillside with football pitches, tennis, volleyball and basketball courts, athletics tracks and several swimming pools. There is also a ski practice slope open all year. Lying at the foot of the hill is a spring called **Hajdučka česma** that is reputed to have been favoured as a resting spot for members of the Obrenović dynasty when they went on their hunting forays; the name roughly translates as 'Brigand's Fountain'. This lies close to the spot where Prince Mihailo was killed.

New Belgrade This part of the city, west of the Sava River, is a post-war appendage that serves as the location for Belgrade's five-star hotels, the Hyatt Regency and the Continental. It is a mixture of vast, low-cost housing projects or *bloks*, and tall office buildings, with a few sports centres, embassies, shopping centres and business complexes like the Sava Centar, to complete the mix. First glimpses are unprepossessing: if the image of this concrete jungle were transposed to northern Europe, say to London or Paris, it would represent the sort of crime-blighted no-go areas that are best avoided. However, here across the water, mean architecture does not necessarily signify mean streets; it may be unattractive but Novi Beograd is by no means dangerous. The simple truth is that for the casual visitor there is little in the way of traditional sightseeing among the concrete canyons of the new town.

Most of the interest lies along the riverbank, with numerous boats and rafts moored along both the Sava and Danube shores offering entertainment in the form of cafés, restaurants and nightclubs. Most of the riverside life is within the vicinity of **Brankov most** [102 C3], the most northerly of the four road bridges linking New Belgrade with the Old Town. **Park prijateljtsva (People's Park)** [102 B2] extends north from this bridge, between the river and Bulevar Nikole Tesle, the main road that continues west to Zemun. The park contains the purpose-built building of the Museum of Contemporary Art, which was closed to the public in 2007 for reconstruction and extension. The first phase of reconstruction was partially completed in 2010 but the building remains closed awaiting a complete interior remake at the time of writing (for listing details, see pages 168–9). The **Sava Centar** at Milentija Popovića 9 [102 B4] (↟ *2206 000;* w *www.savacentar.net*) is a large entertainment and business complex next to the Continental Hotel Beograd. Covering a site of 10ha, in addition to a 4,000-seat theatre and 15 conference halls, there are also business offices, exhibition halls, cinemas, restaurants and a shopping mall with smart boutiques. The Sava Centar also hosts concerts by famous national and international artists. For cheaper prices than chi-chi Sava there are two other options in New Belgrade. There is the **Buvlja pijaca** open-air market near the railway bridge at Blok 43 along nearby Proleterske solidarnosti, and the so-called **Chinese Market** that lies west along Bulevar Jurija Gagarina at Blok 70 and, which as its name implies, is central to New Belgrade's Chinese community.

Continuing west towards Zemun you reach the **Church of St Vasilje of Ostrog** at Partizanske avijacije 21A, which is interesting on two counts: its age and its design. This is the newest Orthodox church in Belgrade, begun in 1996 and completed in 2001, and constructed by donations made by devotees of St Vasilje of Ostrog, a reputed miracle worker. It is of an unusual rounded design, with large round windows and a detached bell tower.

Zemun Continuing west along Bulevar Nikole Tesle from New Belgrade, the unprepossessing hulk of the Hotel Jugoslavija [162 D4] soon appears on your right. It is round about here that another sprawl of *splavovi* starts to appear along the waterfront, stretching from here all the way to the centre of Zemun.

Zemun is now a Belgrade municipality but it used to be a separate town. The town is, in fact, much older than Belgrade. With such a favourable position on the banks of the Danube, some sort of settlement existed here even in Neolithic times. Later, in the 3rd century BC, the area was settled by a Celtic tribe, the Scordisci, who named the town Taurunum. The current name probably came about with the arrival of the Slavs, with the name derived from the Slavic term for the dugouts – *zemnica* – that housed the original inhabitants. With the arrival of the Austrians in 1717 the town came under Habsburg control and it was developed as an important fortification along

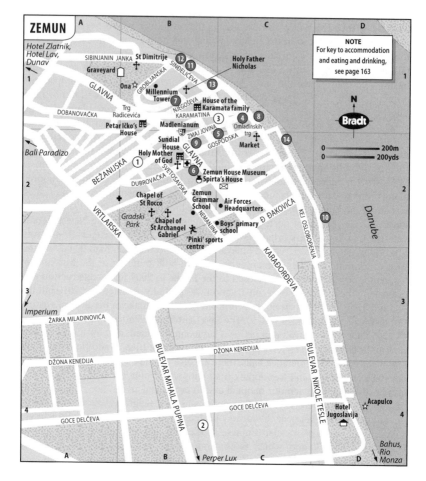

NOTE
For key to accommodation
and eating and drinking,
see page 163

Hotel Zlatnik,
Hotel Lav,
Dunav

SIBINJANIN JANKA   St Dimitrije   12   SINĐELIĆEVA   11

Graveyard

Holy Father
Nicholas

GLAVNA   Ona   GROBLJANSKA   13

Millennium
Tower   7   NJEGOŠEVA   House of the
Karamata family

DOBANOVAČKA   Trg
Radicevića   KARAMATINA   3

Petar Ičko's
House   Madlenianum   ZMAJ JOVINA   4   8   Omladinskih
trg   14

Sundial
House   9   GOSPODSKA   5   Market

Bali Paradizo   Holy Mother
of God   1   GLAVNA

BEŽANIJSKA   SVETOSAVSKA   6   Zemun House Museum,
Spirta's House

DUBROVAČKA   Zemun
Grammar   Air Forces
Headquarters

VRTLARSKA   Chapel of
St Rocco   School

Gradski
Park   Chapel of
St Archangel
Gabriel   Boys' primary
school   NEMANJINA   Đ ĐAKOVIĆA   10   KEJ OSLOBOĐENJA

'Pinki' sports
centre   KARAĐORĐEVA   Danube

3   Imperium
ŽARKA MILADINOVIĆA

DŽONA KENEDIJA   DŽONA KENEDIJA   BULEVAR MIHAILA PUPINA

GOCE DELČEVA   BULEVAR NIKOLE TESLE   Acapulco

GOCE DELČEVA   2   Hotel
Jugoslavija   4

A   B   Perper Lux   C   D   Bahus,
Rio
Monza

0   200m
0   200yds

N

Bradt

the border with the Ottoman Empire. The town's importance as a trade centre on the border of two conflicting empires helped to boost its standing as a cultural centre, with handicrafts and industry becoming central to the town's economy. By the start of the 20th century, Zemun had become one of the most economically developed regions of Serbia. Nowadays, Zemun has something of a reputation of a mafia centre – the stamping ground of the so-called 'Zemun Clan' – and many of the building projects that are currently taking place there are said to be financed with monies gained from various nefarious deeds. Such gangsterism is not at all apparent on the ground; indeed, if anything, Zemun has rather a staid, sleepy provincial feel to it. For accommodation and restaurant listings, see pages 120–2, 128–9 and 131–2.

What to see and do The Zemun Fortress, mentioned in documents from the 9th and 10th centuries, is the oldest building in the town but most of the remains that stand today only date back to the 15th century. A far better-preserved, later structure, still standing in the centre of the fortress area is the **Millennium Tower (Milenijumska kula)** [162 B1], which was built by the Hungarians in 1896 to celebrate the 1,000th anniversary of their state. The tower, which was partially restored in 1962, is often referred to as **Sibinjanin Janko's Tower (Kula Sibinjanin Janka)** and sometimes also

Gardoš Tower. The Millennium Tower has a prominent vantage point at the top of Gardoš Hill, which makes it a landmark from even as far away as Belgrade Fortress in the Old Town. To reach it, turn right at Trg Radičevića at the end of Glavna, Zemun's main street, go down Njegoševa then turn left at the church up Sinđelićeva and left again at Grobljanska. The tower, which is something of a hotchpotch of styles, sits in a field overlooking the Danube. There is a café next door, a convenient place for a rest and a drink after climbing the tower. Just across the road is the distinctively yellow, neo-Byzantine **Church of St Dimitrije** [162 B1] that has an iconostasis by Pavle Simić. The large and lovingly tended graveyard by the church is an interesting and peaceful place to wander in for a while. Next door is a restaurant with an outdoor terrace, an excellent place for a meal or a drink. From both the tower and the restaurant there is a magnificent view over Zemun's rooftops and the Danube to Belgrade beyond.

Compared with Belgrade, Zemun abounds with fine old houses, mostly in the vicinity of Glavna Street. At Dubrovačka 2 is the **Sundial House** [162 B2], built at the beginning of the 19th century in a mixed Classical and Baroque style. The famous Serbian writer Jovan Subotić spent his last years at this house. Nearby at **Petar Ičko's House** [162 B1] on the corner of Bežanijska and Svetosavska is a merchant's house dating from 1793 that reflects a style transitional between Classicism and Baroque. Along Karamatina on the way to the tower is the **House of the Karamata family** [162 B1], built in 1764 for a wealthy merchant and bought in 1772 by Dimitrije Karamata whose descendants still live in it. The house has a well-preserved 18th- and 19th-century interior. On Glavna itself there is **Spirta's House** at number 9 [162 B2], a residence built for a Vlach family in the mid 19th century in a neo-Gothic style. It now houses the **Zemun House Museum** (page 175). At number 6 is a single-storey, late 18th-century dwelling in a Classical style, the birthplace of Dimitrije Davidović, secretary to Prince Miloš Obrenović, diplomat, statesman and founder of Serbian journalism.

Further south along Glavna is the **Air Forces Headquarters** [162 C2], an interesting modernist building designed by Dragiša Brašovan that dates from 1935. There are Art Deco touches to the building's design that relate to its function, such as round windows that bring to mind the business end of a jet engine; the architect's concept was that the building resemble a fighter jet although, as a whole, the building tends to look like a ship more than anything else. Another aerial theme can be seen on the façade that faces on to Glavna where there is a large figure of Icarus, the work of sculptor Zlata Markov. The building was bombed in the 1999 NATO campaign and has only been partially repaired since; a plaque outside lists the names of the victims.

Continuing along V Bunja to Nemanjina at the other side of the square, backing on to Trg JNA at number 25 is the **Boys' Primary School** [162 C2] that dates from

Belgrade Београд   WHAT TO SEE AND DO

3

1913 and displays a mixture of Neoclassical and secessionist styles. Turning right along Nemanjina you pass the Pinki Sports Centre to come to the **Zemun Grammar School** [162 B2] on the left, a neo-Renaissance building from 1879. This is at the north end of **Gradski Park** [162 B2], Zemun's largest green space. The park was built on the former site of the quarantine area of Kontumac, the largest of several quarantine complexes that used to sit on the border of the Austrian and Turkish domains and functioned in the 18th and early 19th centuries. All that remains of the complex today are two chapels: the **Quarantine Chapel of St Rocco** [162 B2], built in 1836 as a Roman Catholic chapel, and the **Quarantine Chapel of St Archangel Gabriel** [162 B2], a Baroque-style Orthodox chapel of 1786. Of the two, the former appears to be sadly neglected while the latter now serves as a women's monastery.

Zemun has two other churches of note: at Njegoševa 43 at the base of Gardoš Hill beneath the Millennium Tower stands the **Church of the Holy Father Nicholas** [162 B1], which is the oldest Orthodox church in the Belgrade area. It was constructed in Baroque style between 1725 and 1731 on the same site as an earlier church of the pre-Turkish period. Many icons in the church are the work of the 19th-century Zemun artist Živko Petrović, while the fine iconostasis was painted by Dimitrije Bacević.

The bell tower was reconstructed in 1870. On the other side of Glavna at Rajačićeva 4 is the Baroque-style **Church of the Holy Mother of God** [162 B2], the biggest church in Zemun, which was built between 1775 and 1783. Like the previous church it also contains many icons and paintings by local artist Živko Petrović. The iconostasis is the work of Aksentije Markovića and Arsenije Teodorović.

If you are not in the mood for seeking out specific churches or old houses, a good route to follow is to turn right off Glavna near the Central Hotel, and walk down Gospodska, a pedestrian street with shops and fine old houses that leads down to the Danube. At the bottom of the street is an **open-air market** [162 C2], pijaca Zemun, in front of the church. A very pleasant riverside walk can be made from here in either direction. As in New Belgrade, Zemun has a concentration of riverside clubs and cafés along the Danube waterfront here that are quiet or closed by day, busy by night. Many of the restaurants along Kej oslobođenja – Šaran, Skala, Sent Andreja, Aleksandar, Stara Kapitanija – make the perfect venue for a leisurely meal on a balmy summer evening.

To reach Zemun from central Belgrade take a number 84 bus. You could combine a day trip with a visit to the Museum of Contemporary Art in New Belgrade, or even base yourself here (pages 120–3).

MUSEUMS Belgrade has many top-quality museums. Rather than trying to see too many in too little time you should pick and choose to follow your own particular interests. That being said, there are some that have great appeal even though their subject matter may not seem immediately enticing. For example, the Military Museum at Kalemegdan tells a fascinating story of Serbia's history, even for those not normally interested in military matters, while the Nikola Tesla Museum provides an affectionate testimony to an eccentric genius and is not solely of interest to scientists. The Museum of Yugoslav History, and especially the 'House of Flowers', cannot fail to impress any visitor who has a memory of the international influence that Tito's Yugoslavia once had. Unfortunately, at the time of writing the Museum of Contemporary Art and the National Museum remain closed awaiting radical reconstruction. Most, but not all, museums are closed on Mondays, and most have a nominal admission fee.

Andrić Memorial Museum [103 E4] (*Spomen muzej Ive Andrića; Andrićev venac 8;* ℡ *3238 397;* w *ivoandric.org.rs;* ⏱ *10.00–18.00 Tue/Wed & Fri/Sat, 10.00–14.00*

> ## TWIN TOWERS – BELGRADE STYLE
>
> New Belgrade's most obvious landmark is perhaps the 'Genex' building at Blok 33, a massive edifice of two connected towers that can be seen from all over the city. The 35-storey building, otherwise known as Belgrade's Western Gate (Zapadna kapija Beograda), has mixed residential and commercial use spread throughout two separate towers joined together by a high corridor. A revolving restaurant caps the shorter of the two towers. The building was designed in the brutalist style in 1980 by the architect Mihailo Mitrović and today it is the second-highest building in Belgrade after the Ušće Tower, recently rebuilt after suffering extensive damage during the 1999 NATO campaign. Many city residents would have you believe that a motorway passes between the towers but this is apocryphal: the main dual carriageway to Nikola Tesla Airport and Novi Sad passes just to the side of it.

Sun, closed Mon; admission 200din) Located at the home of the Yugoslav diplomat, writer and Nobel Prize winner (1892–1975), four rooms of his former home have been converted into a museum to show the life and work of the writer.

Banjica Concentration Camp Museum [103 E7] (*Muzej Banjičog logora; Pavla Jurišića Šturma 33;* \ *2630 825;* w *mgb.org.rs;* ⊕ *10.00–17.00 Wed–Fri; admission 200din*) This is located just south of the FC Red Star Belgrade stadium, on the same site as the World War II concentration camp that was set up here in June 1941 and saw the deaths of thousands of Slavs, Jews and Roma.

Belgrade Fortress Museum [114 A2] (*Beogradska Tvrđava; Upper Town, Kalemegdan;* \ *2620 685;* w *beogradskatvrdjava.rs;* ⊕ *09.00–21.00 daily; free entry*) Not to be confused with the more martial collection of the Military Museum, this small museum has a permanent display of models showing the development of the complex, plans and texts relating to the evolution of the fortress, and some of the tools used by the builders.

Ethnographic Museum [114 C4] (*Etnografski muzej; Studentski trg 13;* \ *3281 888;* w *etnografskimuzej.rs;* ⊕ *10.00–17.00 Tue–Sat, 09.00–14.00 Sun, closed Mon; admission 150din, Sun free*) This well-maintained museum has a fascinating range of ethnographic artefacts from all over Serbia, Kosovo and Vojvodina with the emphasis on regional dress and village economy. The ground floor is given over mostly to costumes, the first floor to textiles, and the second floor to agriculture and traditional economy. Of particular interest are the bridal costumes formerly worn by the women in parts of Serbia like Šumadija, with their elaborate caps incorporating coins, dried flowers and peacock feathers. There is a detailed exhibit on *čilim* manufacture that shows all aspects of the weaving and dyeing of the cloth, as well as demonstrating the important role the monasteries had in promulgating these skills. Old photographs show the unusual sight of village men spinning, and it is interesting to note how the distaff is of great spiritual importance to Serbs, associated as it is with many folk beliefs and customs. Elsewhere on the second floor, scattered amongst the displays, are strange Bosnian Bogomil gravestones with ghoulish, cartoon-like faces. The museum has a shop selling a range of books, craftwork and postcards, and a special exhibition area. Occasionally, musical and other cultural events are put on in the museum's large lecture hall.

Fresco Gallery [114 C3] (*Galerija fresaka; Cara Uroša 20;* \ *2621 491;* w *narodnimuzej.rs;* ⊕ *10.00–17.00 Tue–Wed & Fri, noon–20.00 Thu, noon–20.00 Sat, 10.00–14.00 Sun, closed Mon; admission 200din, also valid for Vuk & Dositej museum, Sun free*) This is actually a branch of the National Museum that is filled with quality replicas of some of Serbia's most important religious art. It is a good idea to familiarise yourself with the contents of this gallery first if you plan on venturing into the Serbian backcountry to see the real thing. Although the spiritual atmosphere of a city museum cannot compare to that of a half-hidden monastery in a remote valley, at least the copies on show here can be viewed with greater ease than many of the originals, being far more conveniently positioned and better lit. Concerts of classical music, particularly religious choral works, are sometimes staged in the main hall.

Gallery of the Museum of Natural History [114 A3] (*Galerija prirodnjački musej; Mali Kalemegdan 5;* \ *3284 317;* ⊕ *winter 10.00–17.00 Tue–Sun, closed*

Mon, summer 10.00–21.00 daily; admission 100din) Located in a former Turkish guardhouse at the fortress, on the way to the Upper Town, the museum presents its exhibits thematically and, as well as interesting displays of Serbian fauna, there is also a large collection of mineral samples and fossils on show. The headquarters of the museum is at Njegoševa 51 (❦ *3442 147;* w *nhmbeo.rs;* ⊕ *winter 10.00–18.00 Tue–Sun, closed Mon, summer 10.00–21.00 daily*), where the material on display is organised into four sections: mineralogy, palaeontology, zoology and botany.

Jewish History Museum [114 C3] (*Jevrejski istorijski muzej; Kralja Petra I 71a;* ❦ *2622 634;* w *jimbeograd.org;* ⊕ *10.00–14.00 Mon–Fri, closed w/ends & holidays; admission free*) As much a research centre as anything else, this museum has a fascinating display that charts the history of the Jewish community in the former Yugoslavia from first arrivals until the present day. Much of the focus is on the persecution and privations suffered by the Jewish community during World War II, and their participation in the National Liberation War. One particularly chilling panel indicates how the Jewish population was virtually wiped out during the Holocaust.

The museum is more or less opposite the Hotel Royal. Enter the doorway and take the stairs to the first floor where you will see the entrance and can ring the bell.

Jovan Cvijić Museum [115 H6] (*Muzej Jovana Cvijića; Jelene Ćetković 5;* ❦ *3223 126;* ⊕ *10.00–18.00 Tue/Wed & Fri/Sat, noon–20.00 Thu, 10.00–14.00 Sun, closed Mon*) A museum set up in the former home of the internationally renowned geographer, scientist and academic, Jovan Cvijić (1865–1927).

Manak's House [114 B7] (*Manakova kuća; Gavrila Principa 5;* ❦ *633 335;* w *etnografskimuzej.rs;* ⊕ *10.00–17.00 Tue–Sat, 09.00–13.00 Sun, closed Mon; admission free*) A detached part of the Ethnographic Museum, this houses a collection of objects, costumes and jewellery relating to the peoples of southern Serbia that was accumulated by the painter Hristofor Crinilović (1886–1963).

Military Museum [114 A3] (*Vojni musej, Belgrade Fortress;* ❦ *3343 441;* w *muzej. mod.gov.rs;* ⊕ *10.00–17.00 Tue–Sun, closed Mon; admission 200din*) Here you'll find a huge collection of military hardware and associated paraphernalia from all periods of Serbian history, including an enormous range of weaponry, paintings, engravings, uniforms and flags, as well as items of specific interest like a Turkish suit of armour that dates back to the 1389 Serbian defeat at the Battle of Kosovo. Virtually all of the labelling is in Cyrillic but the significance of much of what is on display is self-evident enough. The collection is as much a history of Serbia itself as it is a mere display of military effects: a turbulent and violent history that can be charted as a relentless succession of invasions and conflicts. Perhaps the most moving of all of the rooms is the very last one, which deals with Serbia's most recent conflicts and inspires the visitor to reflect on the cyclical nature of human conflict in the Balkans.

Museum of African Art [102 C7] (*Muzej Afričke umetnosti; Andre Nikolića 14;* ❦ *2651 654;* w *museumofafricanart.org;* ⊕ *10.00–18.00 daily; admission 150din*) This museum, located in the suburb of Senjak, features the private collection of Yugoslav diplomats, Veda and Dr Zdravko Pečar. Most of the permanent exhibits are from West Africa, with particular emphasis on masks and magical objects. The museum can be reached by taking bus number 44 from Kneza Miloša and getting off at the first stop after the Topčider roundabout.

Museum of Automobiles [115 G7] (*Muzej automobile; Majke Jevrosime 30;* ℘ *3034 625;* ⊕ *09.30–19.00 Mon–Fri; admission 100din*) This houses the collection of Bratislav Petković and includes about 50 historically important automobiles together with motor accessories and archives relating to the development of motor sport. Although full of sleek and beautiful (and very valuable) vintage and classic cars, pride of place has to go to a faithful copy of Del Boy and Rodney's *Only Fools and Horses* Robin Reliant three-wheeler complete with faux leopard-skin upholstery. The building, designed by Russian architect Valeriy Stashevsky, was constructed as the first public garage in the city centre. Theatrical performances also take place in the museum on occasion.

Museum of the City of Belgrade [114 C6] (*Muzej grada Beograda; Zmaj Jovina 1;* ℘ *2630 462;* w *mgb.org.rs*) This is the headquarters of a collection of over 130,000 artefacts. It is divided into three departments: art, archaeology and history. There is no permanent exhibition due to lack of space and exhibitions are staged elsewhere. Enquiries may be made about the whereabouts of exhibitions during normal office hours.

Museum of Contemporary Art [102 C3] (*Muzej savremene umenosti; Ušće 10, Blok 15, New Belgrade;* ℘ *3115 713;* e *msub@msub.org.rs;* w *msub.org.rs*) This purpose-built gallery is in New Belgrade in parkland by the banks of the Danube. The museum, established in 1958, houses a large collection of Yugoslav painting and sculpture of the 20th century. Unfortunately the museum has been closed since 2007 awaiting extensive renovation, some of which was completed in 2010. When it will finally reopen is uncertain. For the time being, there is the **Salon Gallery of the Museum of Contemporary Art** [114 B4] in the Old Town at Pariska 14 (page 175), which stages the work of foreign artists in addition to putting on exhibitions of acknowledged Serbian artists. Additional galleries under the auspices of the

---

PASSING THE BATON FOR COMRADE TITO

The tradition began on the eve of Tito's 53rd birthday when the first mass relay of Yugoslav youth was organised. The runners were to carry batons containing written birthday messages, which they would relay to their leader in Belgrade.

The first relay baton set off from Kumrovec in Croatia, Tito's birthplace, but in following years the journey started from different places throughout Yugoslavia, marking anniversaries of events from the history of Yugoslav nations and celebrating its various ethnic groups. The batons were carried over a period of months along predefined routes. They were carried underwater by divers, to mountain tops by climbers, by parachutists jumping from aeroplanes; lightweight miniature ones were even transported by carrier pigeons. The public was informed daily about the progress of the batons by radio and television reports.

More than 20,000 relay batons were made during the first 12 years of the tradition. They were made by artisans and were usually of wood or metal, with decorative features such as a five-pointed star or a torch on the top. The culmination of the relay was always on 25 May, Tito's official birthday, when the baton would be handed over to Tito at the Yugoslav People's Army stadium (now the home ground of FK Partizan).

Museum of Contemporary Art are the **Gallery-Legacy of Milica Zorić and Rodoljub Čolaković**, south of the centre in Dedinje (*Rodoljub Čolaković 2;* ⊕ *noon–20.00 Wed–Mon; admission free*), and the **Gallery of Petar Dobrović** [114 C4] (*Kralja Petra I 36/IV;* ⊕ *10.00–17.00 Fri–Sun; admission free*).

Museum of FC Red Star Belgrade [102 D7] (*Musej FK Crvena Zvezda; at the FC Red Star Belgrade stadium at Ljutice Bogdana 1A;* ☏ *3224 412;* w *redstarbelgrade. com;* ⊕ *10.00–14.00 Mon–Sat, closed Sun; admission free*) This is where you can see Red Star Belgrade's impressive collection of trophies including the UEFA Champions cup of 1991. As well as an impressive display of silverware, there are photographs and newspaper cuttings relating to the club's illustrious history. The museum entrance is located to the right of the main doors, just beyond the souvenir shop. Go through the glass door and climb the stairs; the museum is located next to the directors' boardroom on the first floor at the end.

Museum of Science and Technology [115 G3] (*Muzej nayke i tehnike; Skenderbegova 51;* ☏ *3037 850, 3037 950;* w *muzejnt.rs;* ⊕ *10.00–20.00 Tue–Sun, closed Mon; admission 200din*) This museum has 20 collections showing Serbia's scientific and technological heritage. Occasionally exhibitions are staged at the gallery of the Serbian Academy of Arts and Sciences at Knez Mihailova 35.

Museum of the Serbian Orthodox Church [114 A5] (*Musej Srpske pravoslavne crkve; Kralja Petra I 5;* ☏ *3025 136;* w *spc.rs;* ⊕ *08.00–16.00 Mon–Fri, 09.00–noon Sat, 11.00–13.00 Sun; admission free*) A collection, housed in the Serbian Patriarchate next to the Orthodox cathedral, which illustrates the development of the Serbian Orthodox Church, with manuscripts, icons, religious objects and artefacts such as the robes of King Milutin.

Museum of Vuk and Dositej [114 D3] (*Muzej Vuka i Dositeja; Gospodar Jevremova 21;* ☏ *2625 161;* ⊕ *10.00–17.00 Tue/Wed & Sat, noon–20.00 Thu, 10.00–14.00 Sun, closed Mon; 200din, also valid for Fresco Gallery*) The Vuk and Dositej Museum is dedicated to the work of two great scholars and national heroes. Vuk Stefanović Karadžić (1787–1864) was a self-taught linguist who devised the first Serbian dictionary and single-handedly reformed the Serbian language. Dositej Obradović (1742–1811) was a great writer, philosopher and educator. The museum is housed in the Turkish residence in which Obradović founded the first Serb high school in 1808; Vuk Karadžić was one of the first pupils here. The part of the museum dedicated to Dositej Obradović is on the ground floor, while the first floor deals with the life and work of Vuk Karadžić. Exhibits include a copy of the plaque that commemorates Obradović's 1784 residency in London at St Clement's Court, EC4, and a copy of John Bowring's English translation of Vuk Karadžić's poetry from 1827. The bust of Vuk Karadžić on display, like the monument at Vračar, confirms that he sported a quite splendid moustache in his later years. Virtually all of the captions are in Cyrillic but there may be a guidebook in Serbian and English available. To enter, go through the gate to the back of the building and ring the bell.

Museum of Yugoslav History – Josip Broz Tito Memorial Complex [102 D7] (*Muzej istorije jugoslavije; Botićeva 6;* ☏ *3671 485;* w *mij.rs;* ⊕ *winter 10.00–18.00, summer 10.00–20.00, closed Mon; admission 400din, free on 4 May & 25 May & every 1st Thu of month, free tours at 11.00 & noon on w/ends*) This quite extraordinary memorial complex in Dedinje can be reached by taking a number 41

3

Nikola Tesla was born during a lightning storm at the stroke of midnight on 10 July 1856. His midwife is reported to have exclaimed, 'He'll be a child of the storm', to which his mother replied, 'No, of light'. His parents were both Serb, although he was born in present-day Croatia, where he spent his early life. Tesla was educated in Karlovac, in Croatia, before going on to study electrical engineering in Graz, Austria.

In 1881, he moved to Budapest to work as chief electrician for the American Telephone Company. During his time with the company, Tesla invented a device known as the telephone repeater, a precursor to the modern wireless telephone, although he did not patent his invention until many years later.

In 1882, he moved to Paris to work as an engineer for the Continental Edison Company, where he began to develop devices that utilised rotating magnetic fields: the prototype of the induction motor. Two years later, he moved to the United States to work for the Edison Company in New York. He arrived in the country with four cents in his pocket (he had been robbed aboard ship), a book of poetry and a letter of recommendation. While working for his new employer, Edison offered Tesla US$50,000 if he could improve upon his design for direct-current dynamos. Tesla worked for nearly a year on this and made considerable improvements, but when he approached his boss for the money he was told, 'Tesla, you don't understand American humour.' This blow caused Tesla to resign, and to form his own company, Tesla Electric Light and Manufacturing, but this came to nought as his investors pulled out over his plan for an alternating current motor. Subsequent unemployment drove the scientist to work as a labourer for a while, in order to finance his next project.

In April 1887, Tesla began investigating what would later be called X-rays, experimenting with high voltages and vacuum tubes. He became a US citizen in 1889, and two years later established his own laboratory in Houston Street, New York, where he lit up vacuum tubes as evidence for the potential of wireless power transmission. He went on to demonstrate the first neon light tubes at the prestigious World Columbian Exposition of 1893 and, more importantly, illuminated the Exposition with electricity that used his alternating current, removing any doubt about its usefulness. During this period, direct current was still the standard, and Edison, who was unwilling to lose patent royalties on direct current to a former employee, misused Tesla's ideas to construct the first electric chair for the state of New York in order to promote the idea that alternating currents were deadly.

Soon, Tesla was in partnership with George Westinghouse to commercialise a system of transmitting power over long distances. Together they won a contract (over Edison and General Electric) to harness the potential of Niagara Falls and generate hydro-electricity. Eventually, Edison's General Electric Company reluctantly adopted Tesla's AC system.

Tesla went on to invent numerous gadgets and devices, many of which were way ahead of their time. Some, such as radio remote-control systems and electric igniters for petrol engines, are widely used today, while others, such as the 'electric laxative', demonstrated an eccentricity that was unlikely to win converts.

In 1899, Tesla moved his research to Colorado Springs where he devoted himself to experiments with high voltage and electrical transmission over distances. Here, he constructed electrical devices of Dr Frankenstein proportions, most notably his Magnifying Transmitter, a 52ft-diameter electrical coil that was capable of generating millions of volts and sending lightning arcs 130ft long. Witnesses claimed that they saw a blue glow like St Elmo's fire emanating from the environs of the laboratory, while sparks emitted from the ground as they walked. On one occasion, a backfeeding power surge blacked out the whole of Colorado Springs.

During his time at Colorado, Tesla recorded cosmic waves emitted by interstellar clouds and red giant stars, which prompted him to announce that he was receiving extraterrestrial radio signals. But the scientific community did not share his enthusiasm and rejected Tesla's data; research into cosmic signals – radio astronomy, as it is known today – did not yet exist. Undaunted, Tesla would spend the latter part of his life trying to send signals to Mars.

In the early years of the 20th century, Tesla fell down on his luck. In 1904, the US Patents Office awarded the patent for radio to Marconi, even though this innovation was clearly based on Tesla's earlier demonstrations, and in May 1905, some of Tesla's patents expired, halting his royalty payments. In 1907, in financial crisis, he freed Westinghouse from payment on his induction motor patent for a nominal sum. Lack of funds meant that his biggest project so far, the Wardenclyffe Tower facility on Long Island, begun in 1900, had to be abandoned.

By 1916, he was living in poverty; and it was around this time that Tesla started to exhibit symptoms of obsessive–compulsive disorder: he became obsessed with the number three – very Serbian – and felt compelled to walk around a block three times whenever he needed to enter a building. His genius was still undiminished though, and in 1917, he set out the principles of modern military radar in the *Electrical Experimenter* journal. He even developed the concept of something he called the 'death ray', an idea he tried to get Neville Chamberlain, the British prime minister of the time, interested in. But Tesla was a gentle, altruistic soul who hated war, and even his proposed death ray, or teleforce, was primarily a defensive weapon, a particle beam that would supposedly protect a nation from invasion by air or sea.

By the time of his death in 1943, Tesla had more than 700 patents to his name. But that did not stop him dying half-forgotten and in debt. Despite his scientific genius, he was a naïve businessman who was frequently used and abandoned by contemporaries whose names are far better known than his today.

For many years Tesla remained a fairly obscure figure in the annals of scientific achievement, despite cameo appearances on Serbian banknotes and US postage stamps, and having an asteroid and a moon crater named after him (ironically one on the dark side). In 2006, the 150th anniversary of his birth, Tesla finally started to receive wider recognition. The year was proclaimed 'Nikola Tesla Year' by Serbia, Croatia and UNESCO, Belgrade's international airport was renamed 'Nikola Tesla Airport', and a statue of the inventor was unveiled on the Canadian side of Niagara Falls. In the same year, the Hollywood movie *The Prestige*, a film concerning two rival New York magicians at the turn of the century, featured a subplot that involved Nikola Tesla as a supporting character, a role which was played by David Bowie no less.

For a full biography read *The Man Who Invented the Twentieth Century: Nikola Tesla, Forgotten Genius of Electricity* by Robert Lomas (Headline, 2000).

trolleybus from Studentski trg or a number 40 running down Kneza Miloša. Get off at the second stop after turning into Bulevar Mira. The museums are reached by following the path uphill from the road past the bandstand and the pond. There are three main buildings in the complex, all part of the Museum of Yugoslav History. The large building seen from the road is what used to be known as the Museum of the 25th of May, taking its name from the former Yugoslav leader's birthday. This used to house a large collection of Tito memorabilia but these days serves as an administrative centre and as an exhibition space. There is no permanent exhibition here but upstairs is a large gallery space for art exhibitions.

To visit Tito's mausoleum at the 'House of Flowers' (Kuća cveća), head to the gatehouse that doubles as a souvenir shop to the left of the main building and follow the footpath past lawns and trees to the building that contains his tomb. These days the House of Flowers receives just a fraction of the visitors it once had. There is a quiet renaissance though, and Slovenes in particular are starting to make the pilgrimage once more; indeed, a large group of Slovene Hell's Angels have been paying an annual visit for the past few years. Many others from the countries that used to constitute Yugoslavia now come to pay their respects too, particularly on 25 May.

The mausoleum has an opening roof that covers a centre court landscaped with cheese plants. Tito's grave lies centre stage under a large marble slab that bears the simple inscription: 'Josip Broz Tito 1892–1980'. A corridor around the tomb leads to several rooms. The Chinese room is filled with ornate lacquer-work furniture and a carpet showing hunters on horseback, with angels around the edge (Tito was a keen hunter although the angel motif does not sit so well with his communist proclivities). The state room next door has a heavy wooden desk and bookcase, and a dark broody portrait of a weary Tito sat at his desk, beleaguered by the weight of state. Another room to the left is filled with the ceremonial batons (*štafeta mladosti*) that, each year on the occasion of his birthday, were relayed 9,000km around the federation by Yugoslav youth before being presented to the president in JNA stadium. The tradition survived him but the very last baton made its final journey in 1987 (see box, pages 24–5).

Walking back down the path to the entrance with the House of Flowers to your rear there is a building to the right, known as the Old Museum, which houses a large collection of gifts made to Tito during the course of his presidency. This is quite an extraordinary collection and probably just a small fraction of the gifts he received during the long years of his rule. There are numerous folk costumes from the states of the former Yugoslavia and beyond (Tito apparently enjoyed dressing up) as well as musical instruments, swords, pistols and other assorted weaponry. There are a few curiosities too, like a varnished turtle shell and a one-string violin that appears to have been carved out of a single piece of limestone. The gifts came from all over the world although it is apparent that political fellow travellers – China, some African states and the revolutionary movement in Bolivia – were often those most lavish with their donations. The most touching exhibits though are the personal gifts made by ordinary Yugoslav women: cushions, scarves, waistcoats and even woolly socks, embroidered with '*Drugu Titi*' and red star motifs. The small shop at the gatehouse is the place to purchase all manner of Tito souvenirs – mugs, posters, books, T-shirts and so on.

National Museum [115 E6] (*Narodni muzej; Trg Republike 1a;* ☎ 3306 048; w *narodnimuzej.rs; currently closed*) Founded in 1844, the National Museum possesses a priceless collection of artefacts from all periods of Serbian history – prehistoric (including findings from Lepenski Vir), Roman, Graeco-Illyrian, medieval and Ottoman – as well as an impressively wide range of classical and modern art, both Serbian and foreign, including a few paintings by Rubens and Tintoretto, a number of 19th-century French masters – Renoir, Manet – some works by Picasso, and English artists like Sickert and Nash. The museum's greatest treasure is *Miroslav's Gospel*, which, dating from around 1190, is the earliest example of a Cyrillic manuscript in existence.

The National Museum is without doubt one of the best collections in Europe, having over 200,000 exhibits in total, but the tragedy for the visitor is that most of the collection cannot be viewed for an indefinite period until reconstruction of the building is complete (not for the first time: J A Cuddon in his 1968 *Companion Guide to Jugoslavia* remarks that during his research the museum was closed for a whole 18 months while roof repairs were carried out).

Nikola Tesla Museum [103 F5] (*Muzej Nikole Tesle; Krunska 51 (on the corner with Prote Mateja);* \ *2433 886;* e *info@tesla-museum.org;* w *tesla-museum.org;* ⏲ *10.00–18.00 Tue–Sun, closed Mon; admission 500din including English-language guided tour*) Nikola Tesla was a great Serb physicist and inventor who almost, but not quite, became an international household name. Many say that if it were not for occasional stubbornness and a poor sense of financial management, Tesla might have ended up as famous as Edison or Einstein.

Despite a lack of international recognition, he remains a Serbian national hero, and it is his face that currently decorates the 100din note. You may note that Tesla bears an uncanny resemblance to the young Frank Zappa, another famous eccentric.

The museum has captions in English, and a guidebook is available in Serbian and English. Regular tours in English are given by the enthusiastic and knowledgeable staff. Some of the rooms relate to Tesla's scientific work, and have a number of hands-on displays and dynamic working models that are fun for children and adults alike. There is also a wonderful poster that shows Tesla nonchalantly reading a book while surrounded by enormous arcs of electrical discharge. You somehow wonder if he had PR representation trying to cultivate the image of 'mad scientist'. Two more rooms are dedicated to the personal life of the physicist. The urn containing his ashes is housed here too, as well as his death mask. (See box, pages 170–1.)

Pedagogy Museum [114 C3] (*Pedagogski muzej; Uzun Mirkova 14 (close to Kalemegdan Park);* \ *2625 621;* w *pedagoskimuzej.org.rs;* ⏲ *10.00–17.00 Tue–Sat, 10.00–15.00 Sun, closed Mon; admission 150din*) This small museum was established in 1896 by the Association of Teachers in Serbia with a view to preserving the various school books, teaching aids and other artefacts used in elementary education over the centuries. The museum documents the Serbian history of education from the 9th century until the beginning of the 20th. There is also a reconstruction of a typical 19th-century classroom as part of its permanent exhibition. Although there are no captions or illustrative material in languages other than Serbian, it is easy enough to make sense of most of what is on view.

Prince Miloš's Mansion [114 D7] (*Konak kneza Miloša, Rakovički put 2 (Topčider);* \ *2660 422;* w *imus.org.rs;* ⏲ *summer 10.00–20.00, winter 11.00–16.00 Tue–Sun, closed Mon; 200din*) In the Topčider suburb, south of the centre, this houses the exhibition of the Historical Museum of Serbia. The permanent display is entitled 'Serbian Revolution 1804' and is dedicated to the 1804 uprising. The display includes documents, arms, flags and personal possessions of Prince Miloš and Karađorđe that relate to the insurrection against Turkish rule. In front of the museum grows one of the oldest and most beautiful plane trees in Europe.

Princess Ljubica's Konak [114 B5] (*Konak Kneginje Ljubice; Sime Markovića 8;* \ *2638 264;* w *mgb.org.rs;* ⊕ *10.00–17.00 Tue/Wed & Fri/Sat, noon–20.00 Thu, 10.00–14.00 Sun, closed Mon; admission 200din*) This *konak* is an early 19th-century mansion demonstrating the architecture, furniture and interior design of that period. This luxurious dwelling was an inspiration of Prince Miloš Obrenović, who had the mansion designed by architect Nikola Živković. The prince's wife and two sons moved into this Turkish-style residence in 1831, just after its completion, and lived here for the next ten years. After restoration in 1970, it was turned into a museum. The *konak* gives a good insight into the luxurious living conditions that royalty and the upper classes of the period enjoyed. There are several beautifully reconstructed rooms, all in the so-called Serbian–Turkish style that blends Ottoman spaciousness with a more formal, Western rigidity. The rooms are filled with exquisitely carved furniture collected from a number of Belgrade houses. Some are very Turkish in style, with exquisite *čilim* carpets, carved wooden *mashrabiyya* screens and low seating around a central area, while others reflect a central European influence that would have been considered very modern for the time. There is also a Turkish-style *hammam* with a raised marble slab and a ceiling punctuated with cut-out stars but this was closed for technical reasons at the time of visiting. Downstairs in the cellar is a large exhibition space that is given over to temporary exhibitions.

PTT Museum [103 E3] (*PTT muzej; Majke Jevrosime 13;* \ *3064 171;* w *www. pttmuzej.rs;* ⊕ *10.00–15.00 Mon–Fri, 11.00–19.00 1st Sat of month, otherwise closed w/ends; admission free*) This museum, which chronicles the history of the Serbian post office, might be of interest to philatelists and holidaying postmen.

Railway Museum [102 D4] (*Železnički musej; close to the station at Nemanjina 6;* \ *3610 334, ext 5079;* w *zeleznicesrbije.com;* ⊕ *09.00–15.00 Mon–Fri, Sat/Sun scheduled group visits only; admission free*) This has a permanent exhibition that traces the history of Serbian railways since 1849.

Theatre Museum [114 D3] (*Muzej pozorište umetnosti Srbije; Gospodar Jevremova 19;* \ *2626 630;* ⊕ *09.00–15.00 Mon–Sat, closed Sun; admission free*) This is tucked away on the same street as the Museum of Vuk and Dositej and presents the historical development of the theatrical arts in Serbia.

Yugoslav Aeronautic Museum [102 A4] (*Muzej Vazduhoplovstva; Belgrade Nikola Tesla Airport;* \ *2670 992;* w *muzejvazduhoplovstva.org.rs;* ⊕ *summer 09.00–18.30, winter 08.00–16.00; admission 600din*) Housed in a modernist purpose-built structure that looks like an enormous glass tyre, this collection of nearly 50 exhibits includes World War II aircraft like the Spitfire, Hurricane and Messerschmidt, together with Russian MiG fighters, helicopters and gliders. There are also parts of the downed American stealth fighter that Serbians are so fond of displaying. Outside the museum lie the battered remains of numerous other decommissioned planes that did not make it into the collection.

Yugoslav Cinematic Museum [115 F7] (*Jugoslovenska kinoteka; Kosovska 11;* \ *3248 250;* w *kinoteka.org.rs;* ⊕ *15.00–23.00 daily; admission free*) This is located on the same street as the Hotel Union and is home to the Yugoslav film archive. Visits can only be organised during film screenings.

Zemun House Museum [162 B2] (*Zavičajni musej Zemuna; Glavna 9, Zemun;* \
3165 234; ⊕ *for visits by appointment; this museum was undergoing reconstruction at the time of writing*) The material on display here illustrates the development of Zemun, once a completely separate town from Belgrade, from prehistory through to the present day.

Zepter Museum [114 C5] (*Muzej Zepter; Knez Mihailova 42;* \ *3283 339;* w *zeptermuseum.rs;* ⊕ *10.00–20.00 Tue/Wed, Fri & Sun, noon–22.00 Thu & Sat, closed Mon; admission 200din, Sun free*). This private art museum, located in a beautiful Neoclassical building that was once a bank, was opened to the public in 2010. It houses over 350 Serbian artworks from the last 60 years and also has themed special exhibitions and events.

GALLERIES

🏛**Art Pavilion** 'Cvijeta Zuzorić' [114 B2] Mali Kalemegdan 1; \2621 585; ⊕ 10.00–20.00 Mon–Sat, 10.00–14.00 Sun. The exhibition space of the Association of Fine Artists of Serbia (ULUS), this gallery is a showcase for the work of its members & for renowned foreign artists. Special exhibitions are staged twice annually in spring & autumn.

🏛**Đura Jakšić House** [115 F5] Skadarska 34; \3230 302; ⊕ 08.00–15.00 & 19.00–23.00 daily

🏛**Gallery 'O3one'** [102 C3] Uzun Mirkova 10/ II; \3287 107; w eng.o3one.rs; ⊕ noon–19.00 Mon–Sat, closed Sun

🏛**Gallery of Fine Arts Faculty** [114 C5] Knez Mihailova 53; \630 635; ⊕ 10.00–20.00 Mon–Fri, 10.00–14.00 Sat/Sun

🏛**Gallery of Students' Culture Centre** [102 E5] Kralja Milana 48; \3602 036; w skc.org.rs; ⊕ 10.00–17.00 Mon–Fri, 10.00–14.00 Sat, closed Sun

🏛**Gallery of the SULUJ** [115 E7] Terazije 26/II; \2685 780; w galerijasuluj.wordpress.com; ⊕ 11.00–18.00 Mon–Fri, 11.00–14.00 Sat/ Sun. The SULUJ (the Union of Yugoslav Artistic Associations) gallery puts on a wide range of exhibitions of work of Serbian & foreign artists.

🏛**Gallery of the ULUS** [114 C5] Knez Mihailova 37; \2623 128; ⊕ 10.00–20.00 Mon–Fri, 09.00–16.00 Sat, closed Sun. This, the other gallery of the Association of Fine Artists of Serbia, has put on a themed autumn exhibition since 1928.

🏛**Ilija M Kolarac Foundation** [114 C4] Studentski trg 5; \2635 073; w kolarac.rs; ⊕ 10.00–20.00 Tue–Sun, closed Mon

🏛**Salon of the Museum of Contemporary Arts** [114 B4] Salon Muzeja savremene umetnosti, Pariska 14; \2630 940; w msub.org. rs; ⊕ noon–20.00 Wed–Mon, closed Tue. This gallery, part of the (currently closed) Museum of Contemporary Art, stages a variety of temporary modern art exhibitions in an elegant building close to Kalemegdan Park.

🏛**SANU Gallery of the Serbian Academy of Arts and Sciences** [114 C5] Knez Mihailova 35; \2027 244; w sanu.ac.rs; ⊕ 10.00–21.00 Tue/ Wed & Fri/Sat, 11.00–16.00 Thu, closed Mon

🏛**Youth Hall Gallery** (Dom Omladine) [115 F6] Makedonska 22; \3225 453; ⊕ 10.00–22.00 Mon–Sat, closed Sun

PARKS AND ESCAPES As has already been mentioned, Belgrade has a generous amount of green space at the disposal of its citizens. In addition to those places already mentioned – Kalemegdan, Tašmajdan, Topčider – the following are important places for rest and relaxation within the city boundaries.

Ada Ciganlija [102 A6–7] This long, flat island near the mouth of the Sava River, between the suburb of Čukarica and New Belgrade, is the preferred leisure spot of many Belgraders, especially in summer when tens or even hundreds of thousands migrate to its beaches at weekends. Like Zemun, its name is supposed to have a Celtic origin, coming from a combination of *singa* ('island') and *lia*, a word for submerged ground. Much of the island is covered in deciduous forest but there are extensive beaches that face on to the artificial 4km-long lake that

*Dragan Simić, bird blogger and guide (e birdingserbia@gmail.com, ✎ @albicilla66,
f BirdingBalkansAndBeyond)*

The **confluence of the Sava and the Danube rivers**, together with the river branches, ponds, willow and poplar forests of the Danube floodzone, along the northern bank, some dozen kilometres up and downstream, is surprisingly rich in birdlife. The local bird list is some 210 species long, about 100 of them breeding in the area. Another important breeding area is the neighbouring fish farm 'Mika Alas' in the suburb of Krnjača (reachable by buses numbers 95 and 96; leave the bus at Sebeški Canal stop). The most significant breeding birds of the area include black stork (easily observed during migration), ferruginous duck (especially numerous at the fish farm) and black kite. Night and squacco herons are easily seen, while purple herons require a bit of effort. The reedbeds of Mika Alas offer penduline tits. The area hosts about six pairs of white-tailed eagles, easily seen at the very confluence (one pair breeds at the Veliko Ratno Island Reserve, in the inner-city zone – by the time this edition is published their nest-cam should have gone live on the internet). A 700 pair-strong mixed heronry is located downriver, closer to Pančevo town. Waterbirds become more numerous on migration and during winter (especially during cold spells, when more than 20,000 birds of 35 species gather at the Danube, many of them east of Veliko Ratno Island, including scaup, velvet scoter, smew and black-throated diver). At the same time, by the downstream end of Ada Ciganlija Island in the Sava River, up to 7,000 pygmy cormorants, one-tenth of their European population, roosts in willow groves – the biggest known winter roost anywhere!

Perhaps the easiest place to observe waterbirds in the cold months is at the **Ušće Park** (Park prijateljstva) at the New Belgrade banka [102 B2], overlooking Veliko Ratno Island, and in front of it, merely 80m away, Malo Ratno islet. Here you can easily observe roosting pygmy cormorants, as well as teal, kingfisher, white-tailed eagle, and with a bit of luck, black-necked grebe, wigeon, gadwall, pintail, ferruginous duck, and uncommon species such as red-crested pochard, long-tailed duck and Caspian tern; from late February onward – garganey; from the end of March – night heron, and little egret at the beginning of April.

The very best wetland birding around Belgrade can be found some 40km north along the Zrenjanin road, at the villages of **Baranda and Sakule** (and, until recent degradation of a local fish farm, in neighbouring Čenta as well). Both (or all three) villages have their fish farms teeming with birdlife. Breeding birds include

was created by damming both ends of the island in 1967. These beaches have water for bathing that is cleaner and warmer than the Sava River itself and are very popular with bathers in summer. In addition to swimming, the lake provides an ideal environment for a whole range of watersports including rowing, sailing and water polo, and national and international championships are frequently held here; there is also a discreet nude-bathing beach 1km upstream of the main beach area. In addition to the beaches there are other distractions in the form of open-air cafés and floating restaurants, as well as shops, picnic areas, bicycle hire, pony rides, minigolf courses, and even bungee jumping. There is a marina in the Čukarica channel for boats, yachts and small ships. In summer, outdoor musical events are sometimes staged here.

ferruginous duck, greylag goose, numerous white stork (one-fifth of the national population can be found in the villages along the River Tamiš), numerous bittern, a mixed colony of cormorants, herons and even spoonbill and glossy ibis in addition to the largest colony of whiskered tern in the country. The first record of breeding cattle egret in Serbia after the 1800s was here in 2008. Among the passerines, bluethroat is easily found. The rarest breeding birds of the area are black stork and white-tailed eagle. The bird list of this part of the Tamiš River is about 215 species, 110 of them breeding species. Also, this area is an important migration stopover for large flocks of wildfowl, cormorants, herons, spoonbills, waders, gulls and terns. Recent rarities include Dalmatian and white pelicans, whooper swan and collared pranticole.

Some 18km to the south and reachable by buses numbers 401, 403, 405, 407 and 408, **Mount Avala** is a low, gentle sloping, wooded mountain (at lower altitude with hornbeam and maple, and oak on southern slopes; at higher altitude, beech, with northern slopes planted conifers). One can follow a marked walking path, about 5km long and with 300m of altitudinal difference, crossing the mountain from west to east, ending in the village of Beli Potok (take bus number 402 to return to the city). The bird community is typical of such habitats, with raptors such as buzzard, goshawk and hobby, woodcock (very hard to see), tawny owl (there is even one recent surprise record of an eagle owl), woodpigeon, six species of woodpeckers – great, middle and little spotted, green, grey-headed (rare) and black (about four pairs); robin, song thrush, blackbird, blackcap, chiffchaff, goldcrest, wren, five species of tits – great, blue, coal, marsh and long-tailed – nuthatch, short-toed treecreeper, raven, chaffinch, hawfinch, etc; in winter these are joined by mistle thrush, firecrest and bullfinch.

Another place to look for woodpeckers would be the oak forest of **Košutnjak** where Syrian woodpecker is common, while grey-headed and black woodpeckers were recorded recently but remain uncommon.

Among the most colourful birds of Belgrade are bee-eaters, breeding at the very ends of the city: in the Zemun loess bluff in the north, behind the church on Vojvođanska, and further along the same loess bluff in the west; in the east, in an abandoned clay pit on the northwest slope of Lešće Hill. Bee-eaters return from Africa by the beginning of May; in the second half of July they are already forming flocks and by mid-August they migrate south. Please always remember to keep a respectful distance near breeding sites.

See also box, pages 8–10.

As you come from the city to the north, Ada Ciganlija announces itself with the sight of a large jet of water spurting from the lake, Lake Geneva-style, and a curious set of concrete monuments that locals call 'Stonehenge' for very obvious reasons. On a summer's weekend at least, you will also be greeted by the sight of an awful lot of exposed flesh. The main entrance to the island is by way of the causeway, the road across the northern end of the lake. Bike hire is available on the other side of the causeway – an ideal way of getting around, especially if you would like to circuit the lake.

Ada Ciganlija can be reached from Stari Grad or the city centre by taking one of the A1 buses that run from Zeleni venac. The bus calls in every 20 minutes or so in summer and drops off and picks up near the barrier by the entrance to the island. Other buses stop fairly near to the entrance – 92, 55 and 56. If you are driving be aware that there is quite restricted parking available on the island and cars must pay to go beyond the barrier. Many locals avoid this by driving down the narrow road that runs parallel to the south side of the lake and finding a place to park here. There are also boats to the north shore of Ada Ciganlija from the quay in New Belgrade at Bloks 44 and 70 that charge about 100din return (bicycles can be taken on the boats).

The north shore of the island can be reached by ferry from New Belgrade. Crossing the island past the sports centre you will soon come to the north shore. The shore here is very different from that around the lake itself: instead of an open beach, the trees at the water's edge give more the impression of a mangrove swamp. There are hundreds of rafts along the shore here, half-hidden by the trees, often reached by rickety wooden walkways. A few of them serve as cafés or restaurants but most are privately owned, the pride and joy of Belgraders who come here to potter about at weekends. It is an atmospheric place and surprisingly peaceful once out of sight and earshot of the hordes that crowd around the lake beach.

Just to the left of the volleyball courts and a couple of raft cafés are the piers for ferries across to Blok 70 in New Belgrade. There are two or three boats that ply this route, which leave regularly in summer between 08.00 and 21.00 and charge a nominal fee. The journey takes about 5 minutes or so and provides a good view of the smaller island, **Ada Medjica**, and the picturesque line of brightly coloured rafts stretching westwards along Ada Ciganlija's northern shore. Once you reach the Sava's north shore turn left then follow the wide path that soon appears to the right – this will lead you through the tower blocks of Blok 70 and bring you out at the Chinese Market on Jurija Gagarina, an interesting place in its own right and a great place for bargains. A number 11 tram from here will take you back over the Sava past the bus station to Kalemegdan Park and Dorćol.

Novo Groblje (New Cemetery) [103 H4] The New Cemetery is actually the oldest existing cemetery in Belgrade. It was founded in 1886 and, shortly after the cemetery at Tašmajdan closed, remains of the great and the good were moved here. The cemetery is large, with several different sections and over 1,500 sculptural monuments. Just before the entrance, on Ruzeltova to the south, is the French Military Cemetery, with neat straight rows of white crosses representing the French soldiers killed during World War I. At the cemetery's far northern edge, next to the Italian military graveyard, is the British equivalent, in this case dating from World War II.

The New Cemetery is a fascinating place to wander at will, examining monuments and enjoying the dense shade of the lime trees and respite from the heavy traffic outside. Many of the graves, in typical Orthodox fashion, have little fenced compounds around them and a bench for visitors. There are several grand memorial monuments scattered throughout the cemetery. At the far north is the memorial that stands above the cemetery of the victims of the 1941 and 1944 bombings. South of this, just off the main driveway, stands the Serb ossuary from World War I that contains the remains of around 4,000 Serb soldiers; nearby is the memorial of the Russian soldiers and officers who lost their lives during World War I, which has a splendid sword-wielding winged angel towering above it. The mundane is equally moving: most Orthodox graves have an engraving of the face of the deceased, or a life-size statue. Some of them allow fashion to give clues to the time of their demise, like the statue of a young woman wearing a miniskirt, who was cut off in her prime in the early 1970s.

On the other side of Ruzeltova is the **Jewish Cemetery**. At the bottom of it is a slightly forlorn 1952 monument to the Jewish victims of fascist terror, the work of architect Bogdan Bogdanović, with rusting hands and Star of David. Unlike the cemetery over the road, usually quietly busy with mourners attending the graves of their loved ones, this is more likely to be deserted, although it is still in use. Next door to the Jewish Cemetery is the **Memorial Cemetery of the 1944 Liberators of Belgrade** that holds the graves of over 2,000 Partisan and Red Army soldiers. This was opened in 1954 on the tenth anniversary of the liberation of Belgrade.

Veliko Ratno Ostrvo (Great War Island) [102 B1] This flat, heavily wooded island was formed by deposition at the confluence of the Danube and Sava rivers. It got its current name during the Austrian occupation of Belgrade in 1717 and, because of its strategic position between both Zemun and Belgrade, it was a constant source of friction between the Turks and the Austrians. They divided the island between them in 1741 but during the next conflict in the latter part of the 18th century the Turks took it over once more and used it as a base from which to bombard their enemy in Zemun. Karađorđe's rebels reconquered it during the First National Uprising in 1804 but abandoned it soon after.

These days it serves as a refuge for wildlife, especially birds, and a place of relaxation for Belgrade's masses. The northern tip of the island has the Lido Beach, which can be reached by ferry and sometimes in summer by a pontoon bridge from Zemun.

OTHER PLACES OF INTEREST
Belgrade Fair complex [102 B6] (*Beogradski Sajam; Bulevar Vojvode Mišića 14;* \ *2655 555;* e *info@sajam.rsu;* w *sajam.rs*) The Belgrade Fair is a trade and convention centre that puts on a variety of trade shows throughout the year as well as the occasional concert. The complex consists of about 20 separate buildings covering an area of around 40ha next to the Sava River just to the north of Ada Ciganlija. Regular events and shows are staged here throughout the year: February, March and October see a number of fashion events, April is car-show month and May the time of a technology fair. In October the Belgrade Book Fair takes over (and rooms in Belgrade's cheaper hotels become hard to find). A furniture fair follows this in November and the year ends with the, by now traditional, New Year's Fair. In spring 2005, the country's first Erotic Fair was staged here, which raised quite a few eyebrows in the city.

NEARBY CITY ESCAPES

RAKOVICA MONASTERY This monastery, located 12km south of the centre in wooded hills on the edge of the city, was founded in the late 14th century by Radul I the Black who married Prince Lazar's daughter. It was destroyed by the Turks in the 16th century but restored in 1861–62 under the patronage of the Obrenović dynasty. The mid 16th-century church is in the style of the Morava School and has a collection of icons from the 18th and 19th centuries and an iconostasis that dates from 1862, a donation of Prince Mihailo. The monastery is the resting place of two influential figures from the First Serbian Uprising: Vasa Čarapić, who died in the siege of Belgrade in 1806, and Naum Ičko who signed a deal with the Turks in that same year.

The monastery can be reached from the city centre by taking a number 37 bus from the stop on Francuska (or on Kneza Miloša near the junction with Birčaninova) and travelling all the way to the terminus. The monastery lies just beyond to the south.

VINČA (ВИНЧА) Vinča, 14km from the centre of Belgrade on the Smederevo road, is home to the remains of a Neolithic settlement that covered 10ha on the banks of the Danube River. Excavations in 1908 discovered evidence of several turf houses and the remnants of a considerably developed material culture. Artefacts found include stone and bone implements and weapons, earthenware vessels, anthropomorphic and zoomorphic figurines, and jewellery made of semi-precious stones. The collection is shared between the National Museum, the Belgrade City Museum and the Vinča collection at the Faculty of Philosophy at the University of Belgrade. Evidence suggests that at its peak around 3800bc the Vinča culture extended further than any other Neolithic territory in Europe at the time, before being surpassed by Bronze Age cultures. The archaeological site (*Belo Brdo 17, Vinča;* ✆ *806 5340;* e *office@mgb.org.rs;* ⊕ *10.00–16.00 Tue, Wed, Fri, noon–18.00 Thu, 10.00–18.00 Sat/ Sun, closed Mon*) is open to visitors between 1 April and 31 October.

MOUNT AVALA Some 18km south of Belgrade, Mount Avala is a popular summer day trip for many of Belgrade's citizens. There are a few hotels and restaurants at the mountain for those who wish to stay over.

The 511m peak stands out dramatically from the flat, agricultural terrain of the Danube and Sava valleys, and Avala serves as a natural plinth for the **Unknown Soldier Monument** that has pride of place on top of it. This striking work by the sculptor Ivan Meštrović was constructed in 1938 as a tribute to Serbian soldiers killed in World War I. Nearby is a monument dedicated to Soviet war veterans who died in an air crash in 1964 while on their way to Belgrade to celebrate the 20th anniversary of the liberation of the capital. In the village of Jajinci is a **Memorial Garden** that pays tribute to the 80,000 Yugoslavs executed by the Nazis during World War II. The mountain itself is covered in a mixture of coniferous and deciduous forest, and has been under state protection since 1859. The town of Žmov dominated the mountain top in the medieval period, controlling the access roads to Belgrade. In the 15th century, the town was seized by the Turks who built a fortress on the summit. The most recent reminders of war are the severely damaged buildings and rubble that remain from when the 195m tower of the RTS state television network was targeted in the 1999 NATO bombing raids. The **Avala tower** has since been rebuilt and the new 205m-high tower (w *avalskitoranj.rs*), the tallest manmade structure in Serbia, was officially opened in April 2010, the 11th anniversary of the NATO air raid. It has an observation deck (⊕ *summer 09.00– 20.00, winter 09.00–17.00; admission 150din*), from which most of Belgrade and its surrounding area can be seen.

If you do not have your own transport take a bus bound for Mladenovac from the main bus station. This will drop you off at the junction by the main road from where you can walk up to the summit. It is a stiff climb but you may be able to find a taxi here that could take you up, allowing you to return on foot. A better plan in summer is to catch the seasonal open-top Lasta bus that leaves on weekends from Trg Nikole Pašića at 09.00, noon and 15.00, returning to Belgrade at 11.00, 14.00 and 18.00. At weekends, from the end of May until the end of August, bus number 400 runs to and from Avala from Voždovac (the last stop on trams 9, 10 and 14, or trolleybus lines 40 and 41) every 40 minutes. Other excursions that could easily be done as a day trip would be to visit **Pančevo**, **Smederevo** or **Novi Sad** (see pages 278–81, 181–7 and 230–53 respectively).

4

Along the Danube

Serbia's share of the Danube's 3,000km odyssey from source to sea is a mere 588km. Nevertheless, the stretch of the river that passes through Serbia is one of its most dramatic sections, transforming in a few short miles from a wide, muddy channel to the narrow defile that squeezes through the Iron Gates, where the spectacle of towering limestone cliffs on either side takes the focus away from the river for once.

The Đerdap Dam, the river's swansong within Serbia's boundaries, might seem prosaic, even unsightly, but it cannot be denied that the project remains nothing less than an engineering miracle and that Serbia – and Romania – would be all the poorer without it.

After leaving Serbian soil the Danube continues eastwards, circumscribing the border between Romania and Bulgaria, but even within Serbia the river is an immense physical barrier that forms a natural border between Serbia proper and the autonomous province of Vojvodina. In broader historical terms, the river has always provided the boundary between the influence of Austria, Hungary and central Europe to the north and west and that of the Near East, Byzantium and the Ottoman Empire to the south and east.

SMEDEREVO (СМЕДЕРЕВО)   *Telephone code 026*

Leaving Belgrade, the first town of significance reached by heading east along the Danube is Smederevo, a port and industrial town of about 70,000 inhabitants, a sizeable proportion of which are internally displaced people from Kosovo. The town is mostly of interest to visitors because of its outstanding **fortress**. The fortress is remarkable for the sheer scale of its defences and for its state of preservation,

TRAVEL ALONG THE RIVER DANUBE

Unless you are taking part in a river cruise, travelling east along the Danube from Belgrade may not turn out to be as immediately romantic as you might have imagined. There is no public river transport to link the key towns or sites along the river these days, and so the journey must be done by road. A self-driven hire car is the simplest option but if you do not have your own transport all of the main sites can still be visited using a combination of public buses and a little ingenuity.

An increasingly popular option is to travel along the river by bicycle. The Serbian portion of the **Danube Cycling Route**, the *Donauradweg* (w *danube-cycle-path.com*), is now fully signed between the Hungarian and Bulgarian borders (see box, page 183).

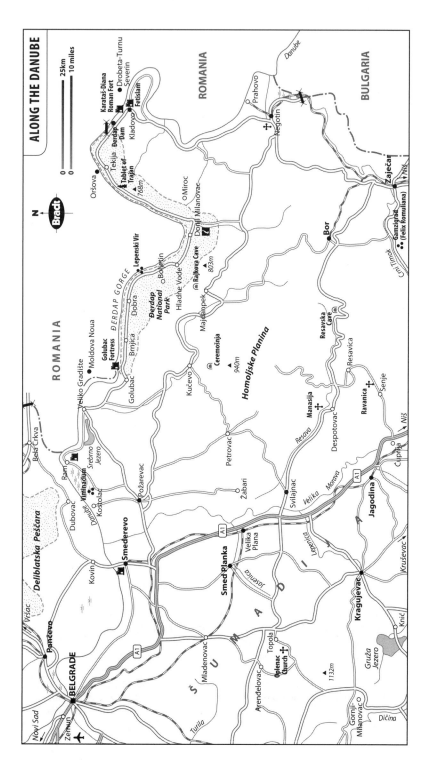

ALONG THE DANUBE

0 ——— 25km
0 ——— 10 miles

N

Bradt

CYCLING THE DANUBE

Cycling experts from Hungary, Croatia, Serbia, Romania and Bulgaria, with support from the German Technical Cooperation (GTZ) GmbH, have been working on developing a cycle route along the Danube River from Budapest to the Black Sea since 2003, a route that forms just part of EuroVelo Route 6 (w *eurovelo.com/en/eurovelos/eurovelo-6*) that connects the Atlantic Ocean with the Black Sea. Together, they have produced a detailed cycling map and a website in English and German (w *danube.travel*) that contains plentiful information on routes, accommodation options and facilities, cultural attractions, suggested campsites and surface conditions along the way. The set of maps *Donauradweg – from Budapest to the Black Sea* (in German only) have been produced by Kartographie Huber and can be ordered online at w amazon.de or w kartographie.de. The Serbian section of this route, now complete, is undoubtedly the most significant move for cycle tourism ever made in Serbia and each year an increasing number of cyclists from all over Europe and beyond are coming to make use of it.

The Serbian section is in seven stages that begin at Bački Breg on the Hungarian border and end at Bregovo, just beyond Negotin, on the frontier with Bulgaria. Detailed maps of each stage can be downloaded from the w danube.travel website, as can full details of the sights and facilities of the route along the way. The total length of the route through Serbia is about 665km and this takes in cities along the river like Novi Sad and Belgrade in addition to smaller places like Sombor and Negotin that lie a little way from the water. A ferry is used to cross the river from north to south between Banataska Palanka and Ram east of Belgrade. There are also plenty of suggestions for detours away from the river and consequently the amount of time taken for the passage through Serbia is very much up to the individual. It could be done in a few days by athletic types in a hurry – or over a leisurely fortnight by those wishing to fully explore the Danube hinterland.

For those who want a supported cycle tour along the river, ACE Adventure (w *ace-adventurecentre.com*) offers a seven-night, eight-day tour along sections of the route between Belgrade and Kladovo for €770. This is available between June and October, and takes in Smedervo, Skorenovac (the most southerly Hungarian community in Europe), Golubac and Lepenski Vir, is fully van-supported, and enables clients to cycle as little or as much as they wish. A self-guided option is available from €560.

which is impressive considering that, like many similar sites in cash-short Serbia, Smederevo Fortress has languished in cheerful neglect for centuries.

Paradoxically, this neglect is actually part of the fortress's charm, as is its informal use for leisure purposes by Smederevo's citizens. In warmer weather, funfairs are frequently set up within its grounds, groups of boys fish in the moat, and young couples take advantage of the fortress's many hidden nooks and crannies for their afternoon trysts – all encouraging signs that local people are prepared to make the most of this ready-built theme park on their doorstep. Concerts sometimes take place within the walls of the fortress in summer. The fortress is open 08.00–20.00 daily. One-hour guided tours can be arranged through the tourist office for 1,000din (page 186).

4

HISTORY Smederevo began life as a Roman settlement on the route from Singidunum to Viminacium. In 1427, it became the new Serbian capital, when the Hungarians took over Belgrade again following the death of Stefan Lazarević. The castle is triangular in shape, with five gates, 25 large towers, double ramparts and a moat. At one end of the complex is a smaller stronghold that consists of a palace and a citadel, which has its own moat and four bastions. On one of the bastions is the date of the building, 6938, the number of years reckoned by the Orthodox Church to have elapsed since the world was first created, which corresponds to the date 1430 in the Roman calendar. Considering that the castle was erected very quickly, within a year from 1429–30, its dimensions are hugely impressive: the walls of the keep at the north of the inner fortress are about 5m thick, and the total distance around the perimeter is about 1.5km.

The castle's construction was by order of Đurađ Branković, son of Vuk, who was despot at the time. The notion was to provide an impenetrable barrier to the Turkish advance that was taking place during this period. One legend states that the impoverished peasants who built the castle were obliged to provide thousands of eggs to mix with the mortar in order to firmly secure the stones, while another asserts that it was Branković's tyrannical Greek wife, Jerina (known by her subjects

THE DANUBE RIVER

After the Volga, the Danube is the second-longest river in Europe and the only major one to flow from west to east. It flows for a total of 2,850km from a source in the Black Forest Mountains in Germany to the delta on the Black Sea coast of Romania, passing through Germany, Austria, Slovakia, Hungary, Croatia, Serbia, Bulgaria and Romania along the way, and draining a basin of more than 817,000km². The river is navigable by ocean-going vessels as far as Braila, Romania, and by river craft up to Ulm in Germany. In addition, about 60 of its 300 tributaries are also navigable, principally the Morava, Drava, Tisza, Sava and Prut, three of which flow through Serbia. Four national capitals lie along the river's route: Vienna, Bratislava, Budapest and Belgrade.

The river has always served as a crucial route between western Europe and the Black Sea. In the 3rd century AD, it formed the northern boundary of the Roman Empire, and the fortresses that they built along its banks served as the main line of defence against invasion by Goths, Huns and Slavs from the north and east. Some of the Roman settlements subsequently grew to become important cities like Vienna (formerly the Roman settlement of Vindobona), Budapest (Aquincum) and Belgrade (Singidunum). One millennium later, instead of constituting a defensive line, the river actually facilitated invasion, most notably that of the Ottoman Empire's advance into central Europe.

By the 18th century, the Danube had become an important commercial link between the nations of central and eastern Europe; by the 19th century, the river linked the industrial world of the West (especially Germany) with the agricultural areas of the Balkan Peninsula, enabling a two-way flow of consumer goods and raw materials. Both the Treaty of Paris of 1856 and the Treaty of Versailles of 1919 promoted free navigation along the entire length of the river and established a European commission responsible for supervising the river as an international waterway. A Danubian Convention was signed after World War II, which allowed just the countries along the Danube itself to participate in the supervision of the river.

as 'Damned Jerina' and said to bathe only in milk), who gave the order for the castle's construction. Either way, it is undeniable that a great deal of forced labour had to be recruited to build such an extensive and imposing structure in such a short time.

The Turks eventually arrived to subdue the fortress but it took them more than 20 years to do so. Smederevo Fortress was finally surrendered in 1459 to Sultan Mehmet I, which marked the final victory of the Ottoman Turks over Serbian territory. Immediately, the Turks made the castle the headquarters of their *pašalik* in the region and it remained in Turkish occupation, with the exception of a brief period of Austrian control, until 1805 when Karađorđe formally received its keys following his initial successes with the First National Uprising. Having survived the medieval period more or less intact, the fortress suffered considerable damage in far more recent times when a German ammunition depot blew up part of it in 1941 claiming more than 5,000 lives, and then later in 1944 when it was bombed by Allied forces.

Also in Smederevo is an early 15th-century monastic church, the **Dormition of the Virgin Mary**, that dates from around the same time as the fortress and may be the burial site of Đurađ Branković. The church is built in a mixture of Byzantine and Morava styles, in brick and stone with three apses and a central dome, and contains some 17th-century frescoes that illustrate the life of Christ and the Psalms.

The Danube provides a source for water supplies, irrigation and fishing but its most important role is that of allowing the movement of freight and the provision of hydro-electricity. Several countries have built dams and power plants along the length of the river, the most prominent being the Iron Gates project developed by co-operation between the former Yugoslavia and Romania that is located at the end of the narrow defile of the river that forms the border between Serbia and Romania.

In recent decades the Danube's ecosystem has been sorely damaged by the increase in traffic and pollution, and much of its waters have become unfit for irrigation or drinking water as a result of this. Species such as white-tailed eagle, black stork, Dalmatian pelican and sturgeon that used to characterise the river have now become endangered. Raw sewage from the cities, agricultural run-off, industrial waste and the spillage of ship oil have all played their part in the deterioration of what was once an undeniably romantic river.

On 31 January 2000, 100,000m³ of waste water contaminated with cyanide and heavy metals spilled over from a mine at Baia Mare, Romania, into the River Lupus. This deadly cargo soon passed downstream through tributaries to reach the River Somes, the Tisza and finally the Danube itself, killing hundreds of tonnes of fish and necessitating the shutting off of water pumps in Belgrade. This was not the only disaster in recent times. A year before, the NATO bombing of Yugoslavia clogged the river by destroying bridges, slowing the river's flow and altering its ecosystem; even more serious was the release of chemical spills into the river from factories bombed during the hostilities. Currently, the United Nations Environment Programme (UNEP), the European Union and the World Wide Fund for Nature (WWF) are all active in attempting to clear the river and restore it to its original state. Following the Romanian cyanide incident, the WWF has recommended a five-step recovery plan that involves: a clean-up of the contamination near the mine at Baia Mare; a monitoring programme along the whole length of the river; an improvement in water quality; the conservation of areas unaffected by the spill that can contribute to the recolonisation of the river; and a river basin management plan.

4

The town's other main church, the **Church of St George**, is located in the central Republic Square and is the third-largest church in Serbia dating from 1854. This imposing white church, designed by the Czech architect, Jan Nevola, is built in the Romantic style and blends Serbian medieval heritage with Baroque influences. The interior and the iconostasis were painted by the Russian artist, Andrea Vasilevich Bicenko. The **Smederevo Museum** at Omladinska 4 (*Muzej u Smederevu*; ℡ *222 138*; w *mus.org.rs*; ⏰ *10.00–17.00 Mon–Fri, 10.00–15.00 Sat/Sun, closed Mon; admission 100din*) is also worth a look. The town is also home to a large, 300-year-old **mulberry tree** under which the keys of the town were handed over to Karađorđe by the Turkish commander during the First Serbian Uprising in 1805. The tree is under state protection.

The Smederevo region is well known for its **winemaking** tradition. Two nearby cellars that may be visited are Mali Podrum Radovanović in the village of Krnjevo (*Dositejeva 10*; ℡ *821 085*; w *podrumradovanovic.rs*), which produces Chardonnay, Cabernet Sauvignon and Riesling, and the Gitarić Cellar in Dobri Do (℡ *742 174*) that produces Smederevka white wines.

GETTING THERE AND AWAY To reach Smederevo from Belgrade there are at least a dozen or so **buses** a day from the Lasta bus station, most of which continue on to Bela Crkva. Some of these go via the motorway and are a little more expensive, although not necessarily quicker. Most take the more scenic route via Grocka, along a high ridge above the River Danube. The fare is around 500din. The bus station (℡ *222 245*) in Smederevo is close to the castle, as is the railway station (℡ *221 222*), although there are no trains to Belgrade, just services to Požarevac and Lapovo on the Belgrade–Niš line. There is also a frequent bus service to Vršac, via the towns of Kovin and Bela Crkva north of the Danube.

TOURIST INFORMATION There is a very helpful tourist information centre at Kralja Petra I 18 (℡ *615 666*; e *turizam.info@smederevo.org*; w *smederevowelcome.com*; ⏰ *08.00–20.00 Mon–Fri, 09.00–19.00 Sat*).

WHERE TO STAY AND EAT Smederevo's state-run Hotel Smederevo in the town centre closed for business several years ago. The town's close proximity to Belgrade makes it highly suitable for a day trip but should you wish to stay there, try the following options. For food, there are a handful of restaurants, cafés and bakeries situated around the main square.

Apartments Mir (6 rooms) Ante Protiča 21; ℡288 820; m 063 7550 840. Modern en-suite rooms in the town centre, all with bathroom, satellite TV & AC, & shared ground-floor kitchen. **€€**

Dunavski Plićak Guest House (3 rooms) Manastirska Rampa, 9km east of Kovin; m 062 582 105; e cdromiceva@gmail.com; w guesthousedp. zohosites.com. Some distance from Smederevo, & on the other side of the river, this simple but cosy cycle-friendly guesthouse makes an excellent stopover for cyclists following the Eurovelo 6 Danube route. **€€**

Hotel Car (43 rooms) Đure Daničića 66; ℡642 042; e office@cartourism.net;

w cartourism.net. Crisp & modern hotel & restaurant a little way south of the town centre. **€€**

Konak (2 rooms) Ljubička 3; ℡612 7635; m 064 2493 207; e prenocistekonak@yahoo.com. Private lodging in a townhouse just south of the centre. **€€**

Restaurant & Lodging Hamburg (12 rooms) Šalinačka bb; ℡4150 555; m 065 5484 484; e office@hamburgrestoran.rs; w hamburghotels.rs. Fairly close to the centre on the main road to Kovin, 1km from the bridge, this restaurant has sgl, dbl & trpl rooms with bath, AC & Wi-Fi. **€€**

✕ Vila Jugovo-S Beogradski put bb;
☎647 271; **m** 060 4520 270; **w** vilajugovo.rs.
On the main Belgrade road by the river, this has
national cuisine, live music & terrace seating.
€€€–€€

✕ Zamak Kralja Petra I 19; ☎613 406; **m** 063
283 981; ⊕ 09.00–midnight Tue–Sun, closed
Mon. In Smederevo's pedestrian zone, this smartish
place has international dishes that include pasta,
pizza, steaks & salads. Live music. €€

OTHER PRACTICALITIES
$ Bank Alpha banka: 11 Kralja Petra 1; ☎222 045   ✉**Post office** Karađorđeva 10; ☎222 568

FROM SMEDEREVO TO VELIKO GRADIŠTE

From Smederevo as far as Ram, where there is a campsite and a ruined 16th-century
castle, the river continues to divide Vojvodina from the rest of Serbia. The Danube
is wide up to this point, with low islands surfacing here and there mid stream.
Unfortunately there is no road following the river on this stretch and so the only way
to trace the route between these two points is by boat. The road from Belgrade goes via
Požarevac, the home town of Slobodan and Mira Milošević, to rejoin the Danube at
Veliko Gradište, a minor resort. From here the landscape on the opposite bank belongs
to that of a different country altogether – Romania. The main road veers away from the
Danube once more to join the river again just before the sleepy settlement of Golubac.

VIMINACIUM (ВИМИНАЦИЈУМ) The **Roman city** of Viminacium used to stand close
to what is now the small town of Kostolac, close to the Danube north of Požarevac.
Viminacium was the capital of the Roman province of Moesia Superior and was rebuilt
by Justinian I after being destroyed by marauding Huns in 440. In the late 6th century, the
city was destroyed once and for all by Avar raiders. The site (**m** *062 232 209;* **e** *vimkost@
gmail.com;* **w** *viminacium.org.rs;* ⊕ *May–Sep 09.00–19.00, Nov–Feb 09.00–16.00, Mar
& Oct 09.00–17.00, Apr 09.00–18.00; entrance 500din*) may be visited throughout the
year on any day apart from 1 January. A guided tour in Serbian or English is included in
the entrance price. There is no direct public transport to the site, although buses from
Požarevac run to the thermo-electric station at Kostolac, which is just 1km from the
site. A taxi from Požarevac is a more reliable option if you do not have your own vehicle.
The site has remains of aqueducts, mausoleums, *thermae* and a basilica. A large quantity
of Roman coins and jewellery and ceramics have been found on the site but the most
significant find in recent years has been the mammoth skeleton that was unearthed on
the site in June 2009, which although originally thought to be around 1.5 million years
old, now appears to be much older at around five million years.

RAM (PAM) **Ram Castle** stands on a low hill above the river beyond the village
of Kostolac, 20km west of Veliko Gradište. This strategic fortress with four towers
and a central donjon (keep) was constructed during the time of Sultan Bayezid
II. Conveniently, there's a rare **ferry** across the river here to Stara Palanka on the
Vojvodina shore. It leaves at roughly 40-minute intervals during daylight in the
summer months, with just four departures a day in October, November and March
at 06.00, 10.00, 11.30 and 15.00 and three a day in December, January and February
at 07.00, 10.00 and 13.30. There is a handful of restaurants at the ferry dock on the
Vojvodina side, one of which, **Dunav** (☎ *013 851 094;* €€), has rooms. There is also
the **Restoran Lederata u Ramu** (☎ *672 152;* €€), specialising in fish dishes.

SREBRNO JEZERO (СРЕБРНО ЈЕЗЕРО) Between Ram and Veliko Gradište, Srebrno
Jezero (Silver Lake) is a 14km-long curving oxbow **lake** created by damming

a branch of the Danube at Zatonje village in 1971. The lake is a popular fishing and bathing resort in summer. There are several options for staying here if you are making your way along the Danube in a leisurely manner and not rushing towards the major sights (see below). Increasingly popular, the resort can sometimes be very busy in summer. Further hotel building, along with the construction of golf courses, shopping malls and marinas, is planned for the future.

VELIKO GRADIŠTE (ВЕЛИКО ГРАДИШТЕ) *Telephone code 012*

Veliko Gradište itself is a pleasant-enough riverside town, with some attractive late 19th-century buildings and a peaceful riverside park. The town was home to a Roman *castrum* (defensive site or fort) at the time of the emperor Hadrian and later became important for the trade of cattle during the medieval period. The park is right next to a ferry dock that has a passenger ferry across to the Romanian town of Moldova Noua each day at 09.00; the return ferry is at 15.00 (14.00 Serbian time).

Tourist information
Vojvode Putnika 2; ☎ 012 663 179; w tovg.org

Where to stay and eat

Vila In (8 rooms) Jezerska 23; ☎ 7663 400; m 063 1629 664; w vila-in.com. A small, attractive, lakeside holiday complex at Srebrno Jezero. All rooms come with kitchen & balcony. €€

Vila Lago (15 rooms) Beli Bagrem; ☎ 662 759; m 063 7718 400; w vilalago.net. €€

Vila Tamaris (4 rooms) Jezerska 27; ☎ 663 104; m 063 326 573; w vilatamaris.com. Private rooms with AC, cable TV & minibar. €

✗ **Srpska Kuća** Beli Bagrem; ☎ 661 161. A national restaurant with rooms available at Srebrno Jezero. €

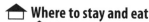

GOLUBAC (ГОЛУБАЦ) *Telephone code 012 (also Kučevo)*

Golubac town – a village really – is quite unremarkable but takes its name from the very impressive fortress that lies just a few kilometres east. Sitting mid stream in the river here, facing the town, is the large, flat island of Moldova, which belongs to Romania. Golubac makes a good stopover – there is a hotel and adequate facilities – although it can hardly be said that it is a dynamic sort of place: it is the sort of town where the locals think nothing of going shopping on their tractors.

Golubac Fortress lies 5km east of the town, about a 50-minute walk along the main road from the hotel. It is possible to walk the first part along a riverside walkway, but the path soon peters out and the main road soon becomes the only option.

The castle is clearly visible from the town itself but as soon as you start walking it disappears around a headland and only reappears once you are almost upon it. Walking along the road you have to be aware of the steady stream of cars and articulated lorries heading for Romania that rush past at unnerving speed, although, in May, with nightingales singing in the lush vegetation above the road, and croaking frogs flopping into the water below, you can easily be lulled into believing that this part of Serbia is still a rural idyll. The impression is shattered as soon as the next rumbling truck speeds past.

The walk is well worth the effort: Golubac is the perfect fairy-tale castle, wonderfully set off by its location in the rugged landscape at the head of the Đerdap Gorge. There are nine ruined towers in all, each between 20m and 25m high. The castle's crumbling ramparts climb high up the hillside above the main road, which passes through two of the lower gateways. The extensive walls are impressively thick, with an average width of 2.8m. With a towering profile that complements the rugged geology surrounding it, Golubac is undoubtedly one of the most beautiful castles along the river's length. If the aspect seen from the road is impressive enough, then the view from the river is even more splendid, especially in the golden light of an early summer's evening.

The fortress built by Hungarians, who called it Galambocz, on the same site as the Roman Castrum Columbarum, probably sometime in the second half of the 13th century, although this is uncertain as the first written record that relates to it is from 1335. Golubac was captured by the Turks in 1391 and changed ownership several times before being finally reclaimed by the Serbs in 1867. On the Romanian side of the river lie the remains of another castle, Laslovar, although this is in a far more ruinous state.

The fortress marks the beginning of the narrowing of the Danube at the Iron Gates and the western limit of the Đerdap National Park; there is a noticeboard to this effect immediately before it. There is a disused limestone quarry just before the sign and directly opposite is a roadside truckers' restaurant, which looks as if it only opens sporadically. As is the case for most ruined castles in Serbia, there is absolutely nothing in the way of interpretive material and no limits imposed on where you can wander. Although clambering among its ramparts is a tempting proposition, there are absolutely no safety barriers. The rock is quite slippery, and it is an awfully long way to fall down, so be cautious and be very careful where you put your feet. For an excellent view over the fortress, follow the stony track that leads up to the top of a cliff and a quarry from the west side of the fortress.

GETTING THERE AND AWAY The small **bus station** provides connections along the Danube in both directions as far as Belgrade or Kladovo, as well as occasional (usually once a day) buses that go inland to places like Kučevo or Krivača. There are nine buses a day that run the 150-odd kilometres between Golubac and Belgrade, and seven heading east towards Kladovo.

WHERE TO STAY AND EAT Accommodation at Golubac is simple enough as there is a single two-star hotel. There may also be private rooms to rent on the main road just east of Golubac Fortress, and further east in the villages of Brnjica and Dobra. Besides the *kafana* listed below, other options for **food and drink** include **Café Fenix** in the village and the café at the bus station. There are a few **supermarkets** for provisions; the best-stocked one is next to the Golubački Grad Hotel. There is also a post office opposite the hotel and a branch of the Vojvodina banka.

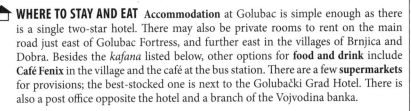

Golubački Grad Hotel (50 rooms) Golubački trg 4; ☏ 678 207; e hotelgolubacki@mts. rs; w hotelgolubacki.co.rs. This stands by the river to the east of the bus station & looks like a sort of rustic conference centre. The hotel's reception staff are welcoming & the food at the hotel's restaurant (€€) is quite reasonable, which is just as well as there are few other enticing options around. €€

Vila Dunavski Raj (8 rooms) Beogradsko sokace Vinci bb; ☏ 679 616; m 062 8987 366; e viladunavskiraj@gmail.com; w viladunavskiraj. rs. A family-run hotel with plentiful sports facilities located 7km north of Golubac in Vinci. €€–€
Kafana Zlatna Ribica Cara Dušana 28; ☏ 232 598; w kafanazlatnaribica.com. A national restaurant by the petrol station near the river that also has 10 rooms to let (€€). Discounts for longer stays. €€–€

THE HOMOLJSKE REGION (ХОМОЉСКЕ ПЛАНИНЕ)

Running parallel south of the river between Golubac and Donji Milanovac are the hills of the Homoljske range, which extend to the southeast almost as far as the industrial town of Bor. This is one of the most overlooked regions of Serbia,

THE *RUSALIJKE* OF DUBOKA

One of the most well known of the Vlach settlements in the Homoljske region of Serbia is Duboka, where in the past, local women used to go into painful trances during the Whit Sunday festivities. The trances were considered to be a form of spirit possession in which prophecy and soothsaying took place. The ritual that surrounds the trances probably derives from syncretism between Slavic pagan practices and older Balkan beliefs and it was believed that, during a trance, the women became possessed by nymph-like beings. The trance was accompanied by sacred music played on bagpipes and violins: a repetitive melody that could only be played at this time of year. The women involved in this practice were known as *rusalijke* but, as Anne Kindersley reflects in her travelogue, *The Mountains of Serbia*, they were dying out even in the late 1960s. Whether or not the practice of falling into trance still occurs is highly debatable: Kindersley expresses disappointment in not having witnessed the spectacle, although she relates that the neighbouring village of Ševice was said to have a *rusalijka* of greater reliability.

and home to a number of Vlach villages that still retain some of their traditional customs and crafts. Despite their relative proximity to Belgrade, the Homoljske hills are one of the least-known parts of the country, and although it is difficult to explore without your own transport, a leisurely exploration of this region would undoubtedly pay dividends. The obvious centres to use as a base are the small towns of **Kučevo** and **Majdanpek**, both of which have hotels and a reasonable range of facilities. The excellent **tourist information centre** at Donji Milanovac can also provide information about the region and make bookings for private accommodation in the Majdanpek municipality in villages such as Rudna Glava and Crnajka.

KUČEVO (КУЧЕВО) AND MAJDANPEK (МАЈДАНПЕК) Every year at the end of May, the regional centre of Kučevo hosts a series of events as part of the 'Homolje Motifs' celebrations, in which local skills such as gold-panning in the Pek River, Vlach cooking, spindle making, sheep milking and wool spinning are demonstrated, along with a variety of sporting competitions for local shepherds to participate in. These events are staged together with performances of folk music and dance from the Vlach community. Also, at the beginning of July, the FESTEF film festival takes place in the town.

Specific information on events can be had from the Veliko Dugošević Cultural Centre and the Kučevo Municipal Tourist Organisation (*Svetog Save 114;* ☏ *850 666;* e *tokucevo@gmail.com;* w *tokucevo.org*).

Getting there and away Daily **buses** run from Belgrade to Kučevo and on to Majdanpek. There is a daily bus from Kučevo to Golubac on the Danube. Eight buses a day link Majdanpek with Donji Milanovac. A single daily **train** leaves Belgrade in the late afternoon, stopping in Kučevo on its way to Bor.

Tourist information The office can be found in Majdanpek at Trg Svetog Save bb (☏ *030 584 204;* e *rajkova.pecina@toom.rs;* w *toom.rs*) and in Kučevo at Svetog Save 114 (☏ *850 666;* e *tokucevo@gmail.com;* w *tokucevo.org*).

Where to stay and eat

🏠 **Golden Inn** *** (49 rooms, 8 apts) Svetog Save 10; ✆ 030 581 338; e goldeninnhotel@gmail. com; w goldeninnhotels.rs. Formerly the Hotel Kasina, this 3-star is the sole Majdanpek hotel choice. €€

🏠 **Hotel Rudnik** ** (51 rooms) Svetog Save 96; ✆ 852 266; e marketing@hotelrudnik.com; w hotelrudnik.com. Based in Kučevo, this 2-star hotel also has a restaurant. €€

🏠 **Pasko** (2 rooms) Mali sokak 4/16; m 062 501 552. On the 4th floor of an apartment block, private rooms in the centre of Majdanpek. €

✗ **Homoljski Motivi** Trg Veljka Dudoševića, Kučevo; ✆ 852 154; w restoranhomoljskimotivi. com. Large, long-established restaurant with traditional Serbian food & atmosphere. €

CAVES OF THE HOMOLJSKE REGION One of Serbia's most beautiful caves, **Ceremošnja**, first discovered in 1952, is situated close to Kučevo, 15km from the town at the foot of the Homoljske hills. This was the second cave in Serbia to open as a show cave for the public. Of Ceremošnja's 775m depth, some 431m are accessible to visitors. An underground river, the Strugarski Potok (Little River), runs through the cave. This leads to the largest underground chamber of the complex, called the Arena, with a 20m-high domed ceiling that is lined with calcite and adorned by numerous stalactites and stalagmites. From the Arena visitors pass through another chamber, called Dveri, to resurface 100m from the cave entrance after passing underground waterfalls and more highly decorated underground chambers. As is often the case with tourist cave complexes, many of the speleological features have been accorded human attributes. Visiting hours are 09.00–18.00 daily from 1 April to 31 October, or by prior appointment in the winter months. More information can be obtained from the Kučevo Tourist Office (see opposite).

Just 2km from Majdanpek, at the spring of Mali Pek, is **Rajkova Cave** (✆ 030 584 204; e rajkova.pecina@toom.rs; ⊕ 1 Apr–31 Oct 09.00–18.00 daily, by prior arrangement in winter), a river cave that has the Rajkova River running through it. The cave's total length is 2,304m, 1,410m of which can be followed on a tourist path. The system consists of two separate caverns, both of which have two levels. As usual, inventive biomorphic descriptions are applied to its rock features: Egyptian goddess, sleeping bear, etc.

ĐERDAP NATIONAL PARK (НАЦИОНАЛНИ ПАРК ЂЕРДАП)

The Đerdap National Park (*Kralja Petra 1 br 14a, 19220 Donji Milanovac;* ✆ 030 215 066; e office@npdjerdap.org; w npdjerdap.org) is generally better known as the 'Iron Gates National Park', a reference to the old Roman name, Porta Ferea, which was used to describe the narrowing of the limestone cliffs above the River Danube. The national park's western boundary begins at the fortress at Golubac and stretches as far east as the dam near Sip – a total of about 64,000ha.

Topographically speaking, the park's most noteworthy feature is the Đerdap Gorge itself, which stretches for well over 100km in a boomerang shape from Golubac to Tekija, forming the longest composite valley in Europe. Rather than a single entity, the gorge is actually a compound river valley made up of four separate gorges – Gornja Klisura, Gospođin vir, Veliki and Mali kazan and Sipska Klisura – each of which is separated from its neighbour by ravines. This spectacular section of the Danube abounds in superlatives: at **Gospođin vir** (*vir* means whirlpool) the waters are up to 82m deep, one of the greatest recorded depths in the world for a river channel (and now even deeper with the dam); at the canyon of Kazan, the cliffs rise up to 600m above the river, which has narrowed at this point to a mere 150m wide. The highest point within the park's boundaries is the 768m-high Mt Miroč.

Of the 1,100-plus plant species found in the park, the most significant in scientific terms are those Tertiary relict species such as Turkish hazel (*Corylus columa*), walnut (*Juglans regia*) and yew (*Taxus baccata*): all survivors from before the glacial period. The yew was considered to be a holy tree by Serbs in times past, stemming from its ability to regenerate itself from a stump after felling, and a sprig of yew kept in a wallet was said to prevent money from leaving it. In addition to these ancient relict species, trees like oaks, maples, elms, limes and hornbeams are all present in great numbers and, of herbaceous plants, there is one species endemic to the Đerdap Gorge: the Đerdap tulip (*Tulipa hungarica*).

Of the larger mammals found within the park, jackal (*Canis aureus*), lynx (*Lynx lynx*) and brown bear (*Ursus arctos*) are probably the most notable – and also the most elusive. With luck and determination, chamois (*Rupicarpa rupicarpa*) may be seen scrambling around on the higher rock pinnacles. Of the birds found here, raptors such as golden eagle are well represented, while other rarities like black stork also have a refuge here. During winter and on passage migration, the flooded waters of the lower Danube play host to large populations of wildfowl such as smew, pochard and goldeneye.

LEPENSKI VIR (ЛЕПЕНСКИ ВИР)

LEPENSKI VIR (ЛЕПЕНСКИ ВИР) From Golubac, the river narrows markedly as it is squeezed between the limestone cliffs of the Iron Gates. The next village, Brnjica, has the Toma restaurant but little else to warrant a halt. The road continues past the minor settlement of Dobra, where a large medicinal herb processing plant, financed by Belgian investment, became operational in October 2008, using the premises of an abandoned textile factory. Donji Milanovac is the next settlement reached, a small port and another good option for an overnight stay. Donji Milanovac possesses no specific sights of its own but does have some nice river views, an excellent tourist information centre and a good range of accommodation options. For many, the main reason for stopping here is to see the site of Lepenski Vir, which sits in a recess of the riverbank just off the main road 14km northwest of the port.

The early settlement of Lepenski Vir was first uncovered in 1965 during one of the exploratory digs that preceded the building of the Đerdap Dam. The site was excavated in the following year, and in 1967 the distinctive stone sculptures that were to make the site famous were discovered. The stone sculptures, which are mostly stylised, life-size heads, are quite remarkable and appear to show human faces with the lips of fish. The carvings date back as far as about 5350BC and are the oldest Mesolithic sculptures in all of Europe.

Although nothing is certain, the heads probably represent depictions of the primitive gods that the people of Lepenski Vir worshipped. It may also have been that Lepenski Vir served as some sort of religious centre, as fish and deer bones have been found in such numbers that they suggest they may have been used for sacrificial purposes. Whatever the true role of the settlement, Lepenski Vir was undoubtedly a well-chosen site: up on a raised shelf just above the Danube's waters, with plentiful fish in the river and game in the forest, although there is nothing to suggest that agricultural practice took place in any form. Altogether, some 85 huts have been discovered here: a large settlement for Mesolithic times.

In 1970, the Lepenski Vir finds were moved to higher ground 35m above the original site to avoid the flooding that took place when the Đerdap Dam was opened. By 1985, a total of 15 superimposed Mesolithic settlements had been discovered at the site, all dating from between 7000BC and 4600BC. A protective, all-weather roof was installed over the site in 2010.

The **Lepenski Vir Visitors Centre** at Boljetin village near Donji Milanovac (☏ 030 501 501; m 062 216 559; e *office@lepenski-vir.org*; w *lepenski-vir.org*; ⊕ May–Aug

09.00–20.00 daily, shorter hours rest of year, closed Feb; admission 400/200din adult/ child) is under the tutelage of the National Museum in Belgrade (w en.narodnimuzej. rs). The museum contains some of the tools and utensils that were uncovered during the excavations, as well as the stone heads themselves. Next to the museum is a small open-air exhibit of traditional architecture of the region with typical high-capped chimneys and arched verandas. These few houses were saved and rebuilt here after their original location, Poreč Island in the Danube, was submerged when the Iron Gates Dam became operational.

DONJI MILANOVAC (ДОЊИ МИЛАНОВАЦ) *Telephone code 030*

Although it is quite feasible to visit Lepenski Vir from Golubac, or from further along the Danube at Tekija, the closest place to stay to visit the site is at nearby Donji Milanovac, a new town that was completely rebuilt after its namesake disappeared under the lake following the construction of the dam. As well as serving as a base for visiting the museum and as a centre for pleasant walks in the locality, the town is a good choice for an overnight stay having plenty of options for accommodation and dining. The headquarters of the Đerdap National Park is in the building opposite the bus station, as is the very helpful and organised tourist information centre.

Donji Milanovac has something of an unusual history: a town that has been moved so many times that the settlement itself, rather than the people that live here, could be said to have a nomadic nature. Originally, there was a settlement close to the modern-day town that moved wholesale to Poreč Island in the middle of the Danube in order to avoid the attentions of the Turks. Following the Second Serbian Uprising, the settlement reverted back to the less flood-prone mainland in 1832 and its name was changed to Milanovac in honour of Prince Milan Obrenović, the eldest son of Miloš Obrenović. The prefix Donji (Lower) was added to distinguish it from Gornji (Upper) Milanovac that was established around the same time. With the building of the Đerdap Dam in 1970 and the subsequent raising of the Danube's water level, it became necessary to move the town once again, this time 3km upstream on a higher ridge. Apart from two historical buildings and the church that were moved here along with the town's population, everything else you see today is less than 40 years old. Despite this modernity, Donji Milanovac is an attractive enough place, with lovely views, a pleasant river promenade and a distinctly laid-back air.

GETTING THERE AND AWAY The **bus station** offers a reasonably frequent service in either direction to Belgrade or Kladovo, as well as eight buses a day inland to Majdanpek and five to Boljetin. If you do not have your own transport it is also possible to use these buses to reach Lepenski Vir from Donji Milanovac: you can catch a Belgrade-bound bus and get dropped at the turn-off for the museum and then later flag down a bus heading to Kladovo for the return journey. Be sure to check the times thoroughly first though at the bus station. A better bet is probably to go there by taxi – many taxi drivers in Donji Milanovac will offer a deal of driving to Lepenski Vir and back and waiting an hour for €12–15 – enquire at the tourist information centre or Hotel Lepenski Vir. There is no left-luggage facility at the bus station.

TOURIST INFORMATION The tourist information centre is just across from the bus station in a new purpose-built building at Kralja Petra I bb (✆ 591 400; m 065 5656 555; e tic@toom.rs; w toom.rs; ◷ 09.00–21.00). The very helpful, English-speaking staff here can organise private rooms in the town and in Majdanpek municipality in addition to providing information on local attractions. There is also an internet café and art gallery and a wireless connection is available for those carrying their own laptop.

🏠 WHERE TO STAY

There are also many **private rooms** (€) for rent in the town that can be easily booked through the tourist information centre (page 193). Some of these are located high up in the village and offer excellent views of the Danube below; others are more conveniently situated closer to the centre. For longer stays, family apartments are also available.

🏠 **Hotel Lepenski Vir** (265 rooms, 10 suites) 📞 590 211, 590 212, 590 215; e lepenskivir@ open.telekom.rs; w hotellepenskivir.co.rs/index. asp?lang=en. Described by one correspondent as 'a cross between Hotel Moskva and Fawlty Towers', this large, slightly faded 3-star hotel stands on the hill just above the town & many of its rooms offer excellent views over the Danube. Facilities include a large restaurant, conference facilities, swimming pool, tennis courts, disco. €€€–€€

🏠 **Prenociste Vidikovac** (3 rooms) Radnička Ulica bez broja; 📞030 590 374, 591 315; m 063 416 386; e clientservices@hoteldonjimilanovac. com; w hoteldonjimilanovac.com. This B&B, with just 6 beds in 1-, 2- and 3-bed rooms, has panoramic views. Located at the top of the hill beyond Hotel Lepenski Vir. €

🍴 WHERE TO EAT AND DRINK

As well as the facilities at the hotel, there are several restaurants and cafés in the town. There are also a few basic cafés and grilled meat places on the strip next to the bus station.

🍴 **Poreč** Kralja Petra I bb; 📞86 805. Next door to the tourist information centre, this restaurant has 2 terraces: 1 facing the street, the other behind facing the Danube. €€

✳ 🍴 **Zlatna Ribica** Kapetana Miše 38; 📞596 304; m 064 4061 585. The recommendation of almost everyone in town, & with good reason, this

restaurant, a little way back from the river towards the church, serves up excellent fish & grilled meat dishes at very reasonable prices. There is an outside dining area in the summer. €€

☕ **Teuta Coffee Bar** Kralja Petra I; 📞590 026. A laid-back coffee bar with views over the Danube River.

WHAT TO SEE AND DO

Donji Milanovac stretches steeply uphill for a surprising distance from the Danube shore. Any climb on foot up and away from the town should repay the effort with excellent views. If you can manage to find your way up to the white concrete cube structure that sits on top of a hill opposite another hill with radio masts across the inlet of the Poreč River, then you will be rewarded with a panoramic view of the whole region. The best way to achieve this is to walk uphill past the church and then just keep turning along any street that seems steeper than the one you are already on. Eventually you should reach the outskirts of the town and some open meadows with marvellous expansive views.

The Kazan defile

From Donji Milanovac, the Danube steers north to enter the defile of Kazan, the Turkish word for **cauldron**. These once-rapid waters are now calmed by the presence of the dam downstream, and the water remains sluggish as the river narrows and cliffs loom high on both sides. After about 15km the river reaches its narrowest point before opening up again a few kilometres further on. If you are travelling on the river itself then you should keep a lookout for the **Tablet of Trajan** that is set into the cliff face above the water. This has been moved from its original location lower down to allow for the raised waters created by the dam.

The tablet was originally erected by the Roman emperor Trajan in AD102 to commemorate the completion of a road along the defile that had been begun in AD28 and which had previously been abandoned as being impossible. The tablet also acknowledges Trajan's successful campaign against the Dacians. Although the road, which was cut into the bare rock, was undoubtedly an engineering miracle, no-one could accuse Trajan of false modesty. The sign reads: 'The Emperor Caesar, son of the divine Nerva, Nerva Trajan Augustus Germanicus, great pontiff, tribune for the fourth time, father of the country and consul for the fourth time, has conquered the mountain and the river and opened this road.'

Before the construction of the dam, the deep, turbulent waters of the Kazan defile were host to enormous sturgeon of up to 900kg, whose caviar promoted a lucrative industry in Kladovo further downstream. With their migration route to the Black Sea blocked off forever by the dam's construction, these monster fish (actually two separate species: white sturgeon and stellate sturgeon) are now merely a memory.

Travelling by car or bus, the road climbs up high above the gorge before dropping down to the river again just before Tekija. The views here are magnificent, with dark, craggy rocks and the Danube's waters looming far below; the silhouettes of birds of prey soaring high overhead. Over on the Romanian side of the river, you may notice the head of a mysterious warrior figure that has been fashioned in the cliff face by the deft use of explosives. Somehow the ingenuity of this enterprise is eclipsed by its own tastelessness: nature at its most elemental, such as here, needs no such embellishment.

TEKIJA (ТЕКИЈА) *Telephone code 019*

The attractive sprawling village of Tekija is another suitable place to stop for the night. Tekija is even quieter than Golubac, but it is a pleasant enough place that offers some delightful walks in the vicinity, especially west along the river. Food and accommodation are available at the Motel Tekija, which is just up the hill, following the steps that lead up to the church, 100m or so before the bus pull-in area.

GETTING THERE AND AWAY Occasional **buses** and **minibuses** run the final 27km on towards Kladovo. Belgrade-bound buses can be flagged down at the bus pull-in.

WHERE TO STAY AND EAT The **Restoran Đerdapsko Jezero** (*Avrama Petronijevića 14*; ☎ *805 116*; €) has five rooms and is a quiet, inexpensive place to stay, with a restaurant terrace that looks out over the river. The food speciality here is fish along with the usual grilled meat and salads (€).

Other dining possibilities in Tekija include the **Restoran Panorama** (*Hajduk Veljkova 40*; ☎ *804 024*; €€) just before the town to the west by the bridge, and the **Kafana Alas**, which is on the road at the start of the village.

WHAT TO SEE AND DO
The Đerdap Dam Just before reaching Kladovo, near the village of Sip, the enormous hydro-electric complex of the Đerdap Dam stretches across the river. The dam was built between 1962 and 1974 as a joint Yugoslav–Romanian venture, with contributions from other Danubian countries and the Soviet Union, at a total cost of around US$500 million. The dam's vital statistics cannot fail to impress, being 448m wide at the bottom and 1,278m at the top and rising 30m above the waters of the Danube, a river which in turn stands 35m higher than it did previously. Đerdap's annual hydro-electric capacity is a staggering 10.5 billion

kilowatts. A cheap and dependable supply of energy was only part of its bounty, however: with the aid of two locks, 310m long and 34m high, the calmed waters of the resultant lake meant that ships of up to 5,000 tonnes could navigate between Belgrade and the Black Sea for the first time. The road running across the wall of the dam leads to an official border post, and forms a useful link with the nearby port of Drobeta-Turnu Severin in Romania. Although the construction of the dam undoubtedly caused ecological harm in some quarters – most famously in blocking the migration route of the river's giant sturgeon – it also created new habitat for other species: the newly formed lakes helped provide a vast wildfowl wintering ground that had not existed before.

Karataš-Diana Roman Fort A little beyond the dam, at the village of Karataš, lie the ruins of a Roman fortress locally referred to as 'Diana'. This fort was originally built during the reign of Trajan but it was destroyed several times over by the successive raids of Huns, Goths and Avars before being rebuilt and enlarged by Emperor Justinian in the 6th century. Another tablet commemorating Trajan's exploits, similar to the one at the Kazan defile, has been discovered here. There is not that much to see now of what once must have been a vitally important frontier post: just extensive foundations and low, round towers built with alternating layers of stone and flat Roman bricks. Although it is not particularly rewarding in archaeological terms, the site affords good views in both directions and is probably the closest point at which you can direct your camera towards the Đerdap Dam without arousing unwanted interest from the police.

KLADOVO (КЛАДОВО) *Telephone code 019*

The riverside town of Kladovo lies 10km beyond the dam. Along with Negotin, this small town is the most important urban centre in this far-flung corner of the country, but that isn't enough to prevent Kladovo having the slightly stagnant air of a town that has seen better days. The town used to be famous for its caviar factory but, after the construction of the dam, and the subsequent calming of the waters, the famous giant sturgeon of the Iron Gates were no longer to be found and the bottom fell out of the industry. Kladovo gives the impression of being overwhelmed by what is clearly the much larger settlement of Drobeta-Turnu Severin just across the Danube. The town lies in the shadow of the extensive industrial units, cranes, gantries and docks of its Romanian neighbour and seems a little intimidated by the brash enterprise taking place there. From the Kladovo shore, you can sometimes even hear the sound of work sirens announcing the beginning and end of shifts in the Romanian port. Many Kladovo citizens have never seen their neighbour up close though. Overall, Kladovo is a pleasant enough place, if somewhat nondescript, and there are one or two things to see if you are passing through or staying here overnight.

GETTING THERE AND AWAY The **bus station** has seven buses a day along the Danube that travel to and from Belgrade; otherwise, the majority of services are to destinations in eastern Serbia: Niš via Zaječar, Bor, Leskovac and Negotin. A few daily buses cross the border to reach Drobeta-Turnu Severin in Romania. It is not possible to walk across the dam into Romania; you have to travel by car or bus.

TOURIST INFORMATION Information can be found at Dunvaska 16a (☏ *801 690;* w *kladovo.org.rs*).

WHERE TO STAY

Hotel Aquastar Danube (45 rooms, 9 suites) Dunavski jej 1; 810 810; e info@ hotelkladovo.rs; w hotelkladovo.rs. Kladovo's first 4-star hotel, opened in 2008, with 2 restaurants serving traditional & international food, & 2 bars, 1 with a terrace next to the promenade. Conference rooms, swimming pool & wireless internet. Bus & boat tours arranged. €€€

Hotel Djerdap (143 rooms) Dunavska 5; 801 010; e agencija@djerdapturist.co.rs; w hoteldjerdap.com. This 3-star high-rise hotel next to the Danube has large, comfortable rooms with cable TV, some of which afford a view over the river, the distant Đerdap Dam & the docks of Drobeta-Turnu Severin across the river in Romania. The hotel has a conference hall, hair salon, aperitif bar & 2 restaurants. €€

WHERE TO EAT AND DRINK

The Hotel Djerdap has a cavernous restaurant typical of most large, three-star hotels. The Hotel Aquastar Danube also has two good, if rather expensive, restaurants. Elsewhere, there are a few booths opposite the museum that offer snacks and fast food. Along the Danube promenade is **Natura** (807 600; €€–€), which has fish as its speciality. However, the best bet for a leisurely meal or a pleasant drink is probably along Kralja Aleksandra (formerly Maršala Tita), close to the museum, pedestrianised May–September, where there is a choice of several cafés, a couple of patisseries, two national restaurants and yet more pizzerias.

Tekijanka Plus Kralja Aleksandra 5; 800 400. National dishes, pizzas & salads. €€–€

Zero Kralja Aleksandra 28; 803 636. Pizzas & pasta. €€–€

Elite Pizzeria Kralja Aleksandra 11; 808 580; 07.00–midnight. Excellent savoury pancakes as well as pizzas here. €

OTHER PRACTICALITIES

$ Bank Komercijalna banka: 22 Septembra 19; 800 585

Health-care centre Dunavska 1–3; 801 455
Post office 22 Septembra 1; 801 237

WHAT TO SEE AND DO In the town itself there is a small **Orthodox church**, dedicated to St George. This has a fairly crude copy of the Miloševa White Angel painted on to one of the walls, in which the androgynous features of the original have been rendered entirely feminine by a less-skilled hand. Close by is the **Đerdap Museum of Archaeology** (Arheološki Muzej Đerđapa) (open 10.00–17.00 daily, closed Mon; admission 100din) that has Bronze Age pottery, Roman jewellery and amphora vessels for storing wine, and copies of the Lepenski Vir heads to look at. Captions are in Serbian and English.

Opposite the museum is a short strip of fast-food kiosks and just beyond here, at the town's western limit, is a small lake and sports field. Just to the east of here, running south from 22 Septembra, the town's high street, is Kralja Aleksandra, a street full of open-air cafés, which is pedestrian-only during the summer months. The bus station is to be found further east on Stefanije Mihailović that runs parallel to the high street, away from the water.

Perhaps it is the close proximity of Romania but for some reason Kladovo seems to have more than its fair share of *menjačnica* exchange offices: along 22 Septembra, the town's main thoroughfare, almost every other doorway seems to be one.

The town has an extensive promenade along the riverfront that makes for an interesting, if not especially scenic, evening stroll. Further along this, to the east of the Hotel Djerdap there is a small beach where the town's young people bathe in the summer, although given the proximity of the docks at Drobeta-Turnu Severin

THE KLADOVO TRANSPORT

Kladovo achieved notoriety during World War II as being the stumbling block for what came to be known as the Kladovo Transport. In November 1939, following the dire signals given by the Anschluss and Kristallnacht, a group of about 1,200 central European Jews set off from Bratislava by boat in an attempt to reach Palestine via the Danube and the Black Sea. At the Hungarian–Yugoslav border they were transferred mid stream from the riverboat *Uranus* to three Yugoslav vessels. The refugee fleet was stopped at the Yugoslav–Romanian border near Kladovo and directed to remain in Serbia.

Aware of their plight, the Federation of Jewish Communities in Yugoslavia undertook relief efforts on behalf of the stranded refugees. They rented an additional barge to alleviate the cramped living conditions on the three boats and, in July of 1940, they opened a school in Kladovo just before the whole group was ordered to transfer to a refugee camp in Šabac in western Serbia.

Sixteen months later, in the spring of 1941, the transport was issued with 207 legal immigration certificates for Palestine, but these were restricted solely to youths between the ages of 15 and 17. The group left on 15 March 1941, travelling by train through Greece, Turkey, Syria and Lebanon to reach their goal. When the Germans arrived in Yugoslavia in mid-April all outside support of the transport was cut off and the thousand refugees that remained became dependent on the neighbouring Croatian Jewish community in Ruma for food and other supplies.

Soon after, both men and women from the transport were conscripted for forced labour. In July, they were relocated once more, this time to the city's fortress that had been turned into a concentration camp known as the Sava. Later that same summer, as reprisals against Partisan forces who had temporarily taken control of part of the city, the entire population of Šabac, including the Jews of the transport, was rounded up by German troops. The prisoners, who were intended to help build a concentration camp in Jarak, Croatia, were forced to run a 23km death race to the site, after first having been kept for two nights without food or water. Those who could not keep up were shot without mercy. Four days later, after the Germans decided to abandon the site, the prisoners that were still alive were marched back to Šabac.

On 11 October 1941, the surviving Jewish males at the Sava camp were transferred to Zasavica, where they were killed along with 160 Roma. Four months later, the Jewish women and children from the transport were taken to the concentration camp in Sajmište, where they were all killed in gas vans over the next few months. Only one member of the group imprisoned in Sava concentration camp lived to survive the war.

and the river's less than perfect environmental record, the best advice might be to stay on dry land.

The Roman settlement of **Diana** is just a few kilometres to the west, within sight of the Đerdap Dam at Sip, and **Fetislam**, a ruined Turkish fort, stands on the outskirts of town in the same direction. The fort's inner walls were constructed on the base of a Roman *castrum* in the 18th century and the three outer gateways all have plaques in Ottoman Turkish that commemorate the renovation of 1739. The Turks remained here until 1867. These days the fort itself is rather overgrown with long grass.

Negotin lies just away from the Danube very close to the borders of both Romania and Bulgaria. It is a somewhat larger town than Kladovo and seems a little livelier, in summer at least, although it is still wholly provincial in character. Unlike Kladovo, the town's economic base has little to do with the Danube. The river, which is only 10km away at this point, already seems distant and of little consequence, although a fair proportion of the town's population work at the struggling chemical factory at the village of Prahovo, which is on the Danube.

Unemployment is higher than average in the surrounding region and many of the local population, particularly Vlachs, have left to work abroad in Austria or Germany, returning only for brief summer visits. Wine production is an important part of the local economy, with many vineyards in the surrounding area, some of which can be visited. The town stands on the Danube Cycle Route and makes a convenient stopover for cyclists to and from Bulgaria. Negotin is also on the Iron Curtain Cycle Route #13.

GETTING THERE AND AWAY Negotin is just 1 hour away from Kladovo by a regular service from the modern **bus station** (542 999). Other buses run to Belgrade, Zaječar, Niš, Bor, Leskovac, Donji Milanovac and nearby villages.

The only trains that run from Negotin's **railway station** (542 069) are to Zaječar four times a day, in addition to a local service to Prahovo on the Danube. Inconvenient train times make the bus a better option.

TOURIST INFORMATION
Kraljevića Marka 6; 547 555; e toonegotin@ gmail.com; w toon.org.rs

WHERE TO STAY Negotin has seen several new small hotels open for business in recent years. It is also possible to find **private rooms** staying with local families in the nearby villages of Rajac, Rogljevo, Tomnič, Popovica, Šarkamen, Čubra, Sikole and Bukovo. The tourist information centre can provide details and help with booking.

Hotel Beograd (16 rooms, 2 apts) Trg Stevan Mokranjac 2; 547 000, 545 588; e info@ hotelbeograd.rs; w hotelbeograd.rs. Housed in a 125-year-old building in centre of town next to the pedestrian zone. All rooms come with unique furniture & AC. Wi-Fi in the lobby bar. €€

Hotel Vila Delux (12 rooms, 3 apts) Naselje Gradiste bb; 548 885; e viladelux@gmail.com; w vila-delux.eu. A small, modern 4-star hotel, close to the centre of town, with restaurant, satellite TV & Wi-Fi. €€

Pension Vila Kristina (7 rooms, 1 suite) Dositeja Novakovića bb; 545 885; e info@ vilakristina.rs; w vilakristina.rs. Centrally located modern rooms in a quiet location, with bar, conference room & car parking. €€

Pension Vila Tea (14 rooms) Stanka Paunovića 13; 570 180; e tea1@nadlanu.com. Central modern pension with satellite TV, internet connection, restaurant, car parking & free laundry service. €€

Hotel Ineks Krajina (65 rooms, 10 apts) Trg Đorđa Stanojevića 1; 542 853; e inexhotel@ live.com; w hotelinexnegotin.com. Renovated in 2013, this former state-run hotel overlooks the town's main square close to the central park. Rooms have en-suite bathrooms & satellite TV. Restaurant & business facilities. €€–€

Guesthouse Stanisavljević (3 rooms) Stojanka Radosavljević 10; m 063 8266 685. A homely place to stay in the centre of town. Diligently run by tennis coach Bojan & his wife Vesna, this welcoming cyclist-friendly guesthouse has cosy rooms & a terrace & shady garden for relaxing in hot weather. The ever-helpful Bojan can help organise trips to Vratna Canyon & the surrounding countryside & visits to the stone wine cellars in Rajac. €

4

🏠 **Hostel 019** (18 rooms) JNA 1a; **m** 065 9119 019; **w** hostel019.weebly.com. A conveniently located hostel on the top floor of the new shopping mall building in the centre of town. €

🏠 **Hostel Olimpik** (20 beds) Vere Radosavljević 6; ☎ 549 270; **m** 063 8110 298; **e** olimpikng@gmail.com. Small central hostel located opposite the Krajina Museum. €

✘ **WHERE TO EAT AND DRINK** For snacks, there are stalls opposite the church, next to the equestrian statue, while the **Inex Café**, opposite on the corner of the street that leads down to the museum, has good prices and a pleasant, outdoor location. There are other cafés, pizzerias and bakeries along the street between the equestrian statue and the Hotel Ineks Krajina, as well as along the street that leads to the Krajina Museum.

✘ **Hajduk Veljkov Raj** Rade Nedeljković 2; ☎ 545 600; ⊕ Mon–Sat. National restaurant with dining hall & outside terrace. €€–€

✘ **Kafana '202+'** Trg Đorđa Stanojevića 14; ☎ 545 600; **m** 063 777 164; ⊕ 08.00–23.00 Mon–Sat, 13.00–23.00 Sun. Grill restaurant with a good choice of wines & large servings of *rostilj*. €€–€

✘ **Konak** Hajduk Veljkova 1; **m** 064 1348 730; ⊕ 07.00–midnight. A courtyard & underground cellar-restaurant close to the church that offers a good selection of traditional Serbian meat dishes. Live music some nights. €€–€

WHAT TO SEE AND DO The centre of town, a 10-minute walk from the bus station, is dominated by a large yellow Baroque church built in 1876 and an equestrian statue overlooking a shady park with a large World War I monument. Beyond here, a handful of outdoor cafés line two busy shopping streets that lead away from the statue and church. In the opposite direction, there is a newish shopping mall just around the corner from a 1970s square.

If you are staying overnight here there is little specific to see other than the **Krajina Museum** (*Muzej Krajine; Vere Radosavljević 1;* ☎ *545 072;* **w** *muzejkrajine.*

GHOSTS FROM THE DEPTHS

In the summer of 2003, one of the worst droughts for many years pushed water levels of the Danube River to record lows. In eastern Serbia, the river fell to a level not seen since records began in 1888, revealing the rusting wrecks of German gunboats dating from World War II. One such ship at Prahovo, close to the Romanian and Serbian borders, had been abandoned in the water since 1944, having first been dynamited by its retreating German crew. Despite the attempts at wilful destruction by its original owners, the newly revealed boat still retained its rotating gun turret and metal holders for shells. Now, 60 years after being abandoned, it stood in just a metre of water. Not wishing to look a gift horse in the mouth, a few resourceful locals took advantage of the ship's surprise reappearance and helped themselves to still-usable electrical cable from the wreck.

The ship was just one of 130 vessels that had been scuppered by the Germans as they retreated from the advancing Soviet Black Sea Fleet in 1944. Using dynamite, the Germans sank their ships in rows across the river in a last-ditch attempt to slow down the Soviet fleet. Many of the ships were subsequently removed from the water when the Đerdap Dam was built but others, including a hospital ship, had remained almost forgotten until the drought exposed them anew.

org.rs; ⊕ *08.00–18.00 Tue–Fri, 10.00–14.00 Sat, Sun & holidays).* This has plenty of Roman artefacts in its garden and a permanent display inside that shows the development of the region. The grave of **Hajduk Veljko Petrović**, a protagonist of the First National Uprising, lies near here, buried in the grounds of a small church that dates to 1803. Hajduk Veljko is very much a local hero and it is his equestrian statue that dominates the square in the town centre.

A couple of monasteries lie in close proximity to the town. Just 3km away is **Bukovo Monastery** that has some 17th-century frescoes that survived a 19th-century renovation. Five kilometres to the north is **Koroglaš Monastery** at the edge of Miloševo village. The church here is the supposed burial site of King Marko Kraljević who was said to have been mortally injured while fighting the Turks alongside Despot Stefan Lazarević at the Battle of Rovine across the Danube. Further afield, **Vratna Monastery**, about 40km from Negotin, was founded in the 14th century, attacked in the early 19th century and then rebuilt in 1817. Today, it serves as an active nunnery. Close to the monastery are some impressive **stone arches** above the Vratna river canyon – Veliki Prerast, Mali Prerast and Suvi Prerast – created by natural erosion. A path leads up steeply through woodland to the first two (Veliki and Mali) arches from the right-hand side of the monastery entrance. Suvi ('Dry') Prerast lies further away but can be seen from Mali Prerast.

The area around Negotin is an important wine-producing region with some excellent and distinctive reds, even though these are not as well known as the products of other Serbian viniculture regions like Fruška Gora or Vršac. There are many **wine cellars** in the immediate vicinity of the town. The photogenic village of **Rajac** has a total of 270 stone cellars, while equally attractive **Rogljevo** has a complex of about 150, mostly dating from the 19th century. **Štubik**, about 25km northwest of Negotin, has about 30 cellars in total, although once there were over 300. The village of Smedovac on the road between Rogljevo and Rajac also has some cellars. Many of the village wine cellars may be visited for tours and tastings. At Rajac, the Vukašinović winery (m *063 250 080*) produces Gamay blended with Vranac, Sauvignon Blanc and Chardonnay. The Bogdanović Cellar (☏ *442 867, 531 724*), also in Rajac, is another possibility. Vino Grade (☏ *541 120*) at Rogljevo produces Burgundy, Gamay, Cabernet Sauvignon, Riesling and Chardonnay, while the Ivanović Cellar (☏ *532 728*) in the same village produces Bahus red wine, a blend of Gamay, Burgundy, Začinak and Semillon.

Like the Homoljske range further west, Negotin lies at the centre of a region populated by a number of Vlach villages, some of which, like **Slatina**, have their own celebrations at certain times of year. A large number of the Vlachs have emigrated to Austria or Germany for work in recent years but they often return to their home villages in summer for the holidays. Nearby at Prahovo and Radujevac, the Danube finally leaves Serbian territory. It was at Prahovo in the hot, drought-ridden summer of 2003 that the river's waters dropped so low as to reveal the prows of long-forgotten German gunboats that had been rusting mid stream for the past 60 years (see box, opposite). Since that summer the river has continued to behave erratically, with the complete opposite – widespread flooding – taking place in the spring and summer of 2005 and again in April 2006 when its waters reached the highest level for a century.

Heading from Negotin towards the Bulgarian border at Bregovo, a secondary road leaves the main road towards the village of Srbovo, a village of large houses with iron fences. The road continues through the village as a pot-holed track towards the river and, after passing a dyke and eventually turning southwards, leads to an iron, communist-period **watchtower** that offers a view of three countries and the River Danube. There is a bus service from Negotin as far as Srbovo.

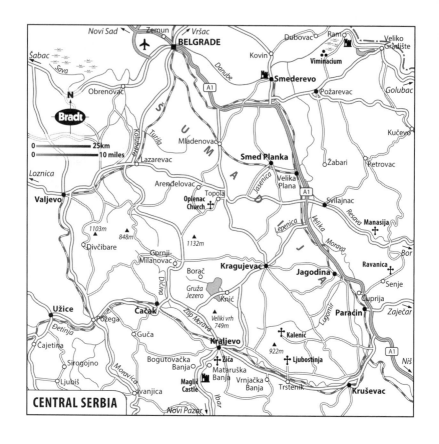

CENTRAL SERBIA

UPDATES WEBSITE

You can post your comments and recommendations, and read the latest feedback and updates from other readers online at **w** bradtupdates.com/ serbia.

202

5

Central Serbia

Immediately south of Belgrade and the Danube and Sava rivers lies the region of central Serbia usually referred to as **Šumadija**, the 'wooded land'. And wooded it is in places, with dense stands of lush deciduous woodland containing species like oak, hornbeam and small-leaved lime. More generally though, this is a region of rolling farmland with small farmsteads, tidy villages, healthy-looking pigs feasting on corn husks and seemingly endless orchards of pear and plum trees. In contrast to the old-world ways of the countryside, the towns and cities of the region are, by and large, industrial.

The region is the heart of old Serbia and probably has the most homogeneously Serb population in the whole country, lacking the central European component of Hungarians, Slovaks and Croats that is found north of the Danube in Vojvodina, and the Muslim population that predominates further south in the Sandžak and Kosovo.

The region was settled in the main during the 15th and 16th centuries by Serbs who had been driven north by their defeat at the Battle of Kosovo. When the Turks slowly started moving north to consolidate their victory, some of the recent settlers feared the consequences of Ottoman rule and moved once again to Hungary or Bosnia.

Later migrations at the end of the 17th century saw the region almost completely deserted once more. The Šumadija was finally resettled in the latter years of the 18th century when some of the less prosperous and land-hungry Serbs from Vojvodina moved south of the Danube to clear patches of woodland in order to create smallholdings.

Central Serbia was at the heart of the First and Second national uprisings against Turkish rule, in 1804 and 1815 respectively. It also saw the formation of guerrilla bands during World War II and led the struggle against Nazi occupation, which brought great suffering to the region. Today, the combination of a tradition of fierce independence, coupled with a population that is almost entirely Serb, has meant that central Serbia has become the natural homeland of Serbian nationalism: Tomislav Nikolić, founder of the Serbian Progressive Party and President of Serbia since May 2012, is a native of Kragujevac.

For the visitor, the main sights in this region are the monasteries, which are almost inevitably set deep in half-hidden valleys in the most sumptuous of rural surroundings. Some of these can easily be reached by public transport; others require more effort. The countryside itself is a delight, and the slow rhythm of life in the villages and small towns of the Šumadija offers a glimpse of a bygone age that has now passed much of Europe by. This is worth experiencing first hand if you get the opportunity.

The larger towns and cities of the region have perhaps less to offer, although they are mostly unavoidable as either overnight bases or transport centres. While it is certainly true that all of the urban centres of central Serbia hold great historical interest, it is undeniable that in some cases their history has been so violent and devastating that there is sometimes little to see in specific sights on the ground. Nevertheless, these are the towns and cities where modern Serbia was forged. What some of them might lack in monuments, they make up for with atmosphere, culture and a deep sense of history. Kragujevac is a case in point.

KRAGUJEVAC (КРАГУЈЕВАЦ) *Telephone code 034*

I always feel myself close to the inhabitants of Kragujevac because I remember the heroism of a whole people.

Jean-Paul Sartre

The city of Kragujevac, capital of the Šumadija region, has the fourth-largest urban population in Serbia with about 180,000 citizens. In contrast to the bucolic delights of the lush Šumadija countryside, Kragujevac is a modern industrial city with little to tempt the casual visitor, although its proximity to both Ljubostinja and Kalenić monasteries makes it a suitable destination for an overnight stay. Although there are few sights in the city itself, those fascinated by Serbia's more recent history will find interest at the **Šumarice Memorial Park** [205 A1] and museum at the city's outskirts, which commemorate the dreadful events that took place here during World War II.

HISTORY The settlement of Kragujevac probably originates from the first half of the 15th century, in the time just before Serbia came under Turkish rule. The subsequent Turkish occupation was not continuous. Twice the town was wrested from the Turks to fall under Austrian rule, first in the 17th century, then in the 18th century between 1718 and 1739. Following the First National Uprising in 1804, Kragujevac was liberated from Turkish rule until 1813, when the town was briefly reoccupied until the Second National Uprising in 1815, after which the Turks left the town for good. Shortly after this, in 1818, Prince Miloš Obrenović made Kragujevac the capital of the new Serbian state and it retained this status until 1841 when it was abandoned by the Constitutionists in favour of Belgrade. The new capital developed quickly: the city's first printing house and theatre were established here in 1833, closely followed by a newspaper in 1834, a military academy in 1937 and a high school in 1838. In addition, the first Serbian constitution was proclaimed here in 1835, along with the first notions of an independent electoral democracy.

By the beginning of the 20th century, Kragujevac had become an important centre for socialism. Socialists had first taken control of local government in 1876 and the first socialist representative of the Serbian Parliament, Dr Mihailo Ilič, was elected here in 1903.

During World War I, Kragujevac was the seat of the Serbian Supreme Headquarters. In 1918, near the close of the war, a military riot took place in the barracks here, with an uprising of soldiers – mostly Slovak – rioting against Austro-Hungarian rule. The uprising was quickly crushed and 44 of the soldiers involved, all Slovak, were shot on Stanovljansko field close to the town.

After a relatively peaceful inter-war period Kragujevac was occupied by Nazi troops on 11 April 1941. As a response to this, the local Communist Party made a decision in July of that year to form a Partisan detachment and start an uprising against German rule. The limited success of the Partisans soon caused Hitler to worry about the danger of Serbian insurrection so he ordered that brutal measures be taken to stop the revolt in its tracks. As a consequence, savage reprisals were meted out by the Nazis on a scale that can only be considered genocidal. In the

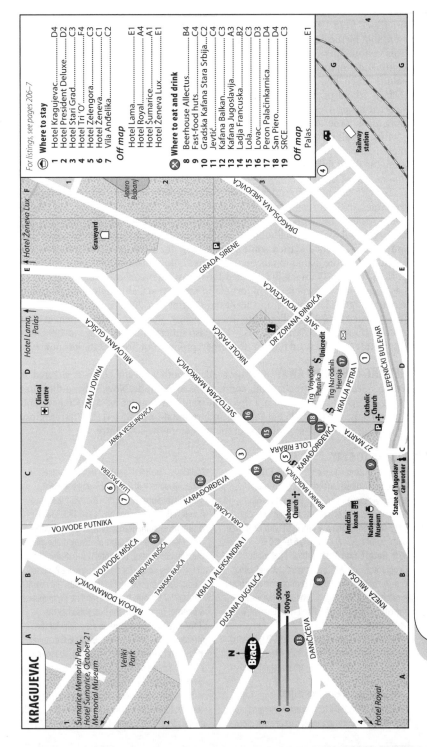

KRAGUJEVAC

brief spell from 19 to 21 October 1941, more than 7,000 male citizens of the town were shot by the Nazis in retaliation to the killing of German troops in an ambush. This vast number was determined by General Franz Böhme, the German military commander in Serbia, who ordered that 100 adult males be shot for every German soldier killed, and 50 for each one wounded. Three hundred of those killed were, in fact, school pupils, and another 40, their teachers. Although they supposedly selected males over 15 years of age, the Nazis also murdered boys much younger than this in order to make the numbers up.

This appalling crime against humanity is commemorated in stone at the memorial park but somehow the gesture hardly seems necessary: in Kragujevac it seems as if the folk memory of the event has somehow permeated the very bricks and mortar of the place.

The city continued to suffer in more recent years when the Zastava car factory, the largest in the former Yugoslavia, was bombed by NATO on 9 April and 11 April 1999. Around 160 workers were injured in the raids, and the destruction of the factory meant that the livelihoods of 38,000 people were taken away overnight. The industrial decay had started some years earlier: the Kragujevac car industry was already in decline thanks to sanctions and economic hardships during the Milošević period; the NATO attack precipitated its almost total collapse. Thankfully, there has been a minor turnaround in fortune in recent years, although unemployment remains high. Fiat bought up the Zastava factory in 2008 and pledged a total investment of €700 million into the company that would be renamed Fiat Automobiles Serbia. Zastava Arms, which also suffered bomb damage in 1999, was restructured in 2005 and remains the largest producer of firearms in the country.

GETTING THERE AND AWAY Kragujevac, being both large and centrally situated, is well connected, with frequent bus connections to Belgrade, Novi Sad and the other main centres of central Serbia. Infrequent train connections exist to Kraljevo and Lapovo only. The **bus** [205 F4] (✆9802) and **train stations** [205 F4] (✆9803) are close to each other, on the opposite side of the river from the city centre.

 WHERE TO STAY

⌂ **Hotel Ženeva Lux** ★★★★ [205 E1] (6 rooms, 7 suites) Slobode bb; ✆356 100; e office@zenevalux.com; w zenevalux.com. A smart modern hotel on the northern edge of town with both rooms & suites, all with TV, jacuzzi bath, minibar, Wi-Fi & AC. €€€€–€€€

⌂ **Hotel Lama** ★★★★ [205 E1] (21 rooms) Beogradeska 75; ✆372 817; e info@hotel-lama. com; w hotel-lama.com. A comfortable new hotel located in a quiet neighbourhood to the north of the city. All rooms with cable TV, minibar, AC & Wi-Fi. €€€

⌂ **Hotel President Deluxe** [205 D2] (9 apts) Janka Veselinovića 52; ✆405 935, 491 365; e president@ptt.rs. A small, smart establishment in the city centre. €€€

⌂ **Hotel Royal** ★★★ [205 A4] (7 rooms, 1 apt) Gružanska 17; ✆300 410; e hotel.royal@gmail.com. 2km from the centre in a quiet part of town called

Mala Vaga, the Hotel Royal is a modern business hotel. All rooms with cable TV & minibar. €€€

⌂ **Hotel Šumarice** ★★★ [205 A1] (98 rooms, 6 suites) Desankin venac bb; ✆336 180, 336 181; e sumarice@sumaricedoo.com; w sumaricedoo. com. Managed by the same company that owns the Hotel Zelengora, this hotel is situated well out of the centre on the far side of Šumarice Park, so it is probably most useful to those with their own transport. All rooms have AC, satellite TV, minibar & internet connection. The hotel also has the 'Tito Suite' that was furnished especially for the president's stay here in 1978. €€€ (€€ in annex)

⌂ **Hotel Zelengora** ★★★ [205 C3] (23 rooms, 2 suites) Branka Radičevića 22; ✆336 254; e zelengora@sumaricedoo.com; w hotelzelengora.com. This hotel, in a stylish old building located in a pedestrian zone by the church on Karađorđevića, is one of the best in town. All rooms have AC, TV, minibar & internet connection. Restaurant, garden & aperitif bar. €€€

🏠 **Vila Anđjelika** *** [205 C2] (14 rooms) Luja Pastera 13; ☎365 461; e info@adjelika.rs; w andjelika.rs. A stylish new hotel with 7 standard suites & 7 luxury apartments, all with Wi-Fi, cable TV & minibar. €€€

🏠 **Hotel Stari Grad** *** [205 C3] (25 rooms) Karađorđeva 10; ☎330 591; e info@hotelstarigrad. rs. The Stari Grad is a small, stylish private hotel in the city centre that is mostly geared towards businessmen. €€€–€€

🏠 **Hotel Kragujevac** ** [205 D4] (112 rooms) Kralja Petra I 21; ☎335 811, 335 812; e recepcijac@hotelkragujevac.com; w hotelkragujevac.com. This central hotel is a fairly typical, high-rise state-run concern. Reasonable rooms vary in price slightly, depending on which floor you are on. Some rooms are categorised as 'lux'. Good central location & a reasonable restaurant. €€

🏠 **Hotel Tri 'O'** ** [205 F4] (23 rooms) Vojislava Kalanovića 3; ☎353 764; e hotel. kragujevac@tri-o.rs. Located next to a car wash but quiet & highly convenient for the bus & train stations, this good-value hotel has modern studio rooms with TV, free Wi-Fi & AC. Buffet b/fast. €€

🏠 **Hotel Ženeva** *** [205 C1] (11 rooms, 2 suites) Luja Pastera 19; ☎330 605; e hotelzeneva@gmail.com; w hotelzeneva.com. An ultra-modern, stylish hotel located just outside the city centre. All rooms with cable TV, minibar & Wi-Fi. €€

🍴 **WHERE TO EAT AND DRINK** Just before the bridge on 27 Marta near the market is a small enclave of **fast-food huts** serving *čevapčići* and *pljeskavica* [205 C4]. Going in the opposite direction, the **San Piero** [205 D4] (*27 Marta;* ☎ *367 077;* €€€–€€) is an international restaurant serving steaks and seafood located on the second floor of the shopping centre opposite Trg Vojvode Putnika. Continuing across 27 Marta from Kralja Petra I, the **Kafana Balkan** [205 C3] (*Kralja Aleksandra 94;* ☎ *334 304;* €) is just beyond the corner of Karađorđevića and Radičevića, and serves traditional Serbian food. For drinks and snacks, there are outdoor **café-bars** all the way along the pedestrian street of Kralja Petra I, along Kralja Aleksandra, the extension of Karađorđevića that leads to Šumarice Park, and also along Lole Ribara, another pedestrian street that runs north off Karađorđevića that also has a couple of pizzerias. **Lola** [205 C3] at the top of the pedestrian area, at the corner of Miloja Pavlovića and Svetozara Markovića, is a café very popular with the city's young set. For pancakes, **Peron Palačinkarnica** [205 D4] (m *064 6774 311;* €) has a terrace extending in front of a marooned railcar near the Hotel Kragujevac at Kralja Petra 1 bb. **Bakeries** can be found just about everywhere in the city. A conveniently situated sit-down place is **Jevtić** at 27 Marta 17 [205 C4]. The best patisserie in the city is probably **SRCE** [205 C3] (*Kneza Miloša 3;* ☎ *304 320;* w *srce-sweets.co.rs*), which has a stylish elegant interior, a huge range of sweets and cakes and, for what it's worth, a non-smoking section. The list below gives some further suggestions for places to dine in the city.

🍴 **Beerhouse Allectus** [205 B4] Daničićeva 21; ☎501 228. Not just beer but also good food in a relaxed bohemian atmosphere. €€–€

🍴 **Lovac** [205 D3] Svetozara Markovića 17; ☎336 501. Local food. Restaurant has a small interior but there is a nice garden for dining in summer. €€–€

🍴 **Palas** [205 E1] Darinke Radović 5; ☎371 319. Traditional Serbian restaurant in the north of the city, with grilled meat, fish, traditional Šumadija dishes & live music Wed–Sun. €€–€

🍴 **Gradska Kafana Stara Srbija** [205 C2] Karađorđeva 7; ☎333 262. Traditional restaurant serving large portions at very reasonable prices. €

✳ 🍴 **Kafana Jugoslavija** [205 A3] Daničićeva 52; m 066 365 200. 'Yugostalgia'-themed *kafana* in which Tito memorabilia & maps of the former Yugoslavia republic create a tangible atmosphere of the good old days. Decent tasty meals include BBQ dishes & a good range of beers. Live music on occasion. €

🍴 **Ladja Francuska** [205 B2] Vojvode Mišića 1; ☎334 414. Good Serbian cooking, low prices & live music. €

5

OTHER PRACTICALITIES

$ Bank Unicredit banka [205 D4] Srete Mladenovića 2; ✆337 770

✚ Clinical centre [205 D1] Zmaj Jovina 30; ✆505 050

✉ Post office [205 D4] Karađorđeva 6; ✆366 190

ℹ Tourist information centre [205 D3] Zorana Đinđića 114; ✆335 302, 301 306; e info@gtokg. org.rs; w gtokg.org.rs

WHAT TO SEE AND DO The large Šumarice Memorial Park [205 A1] (w *spomenpark. rs*) on the city's western edge is both outdoor space and memorial. The park stands on higher ground that is a good 2–3km from the city centre, on the edge of rolling countryside with grassy meadows and haystacks.

Spread in a wide circuit around the park are various monuments that commemorate the tragic events of October 1941. These include the *Monument of Pain and Pride* (1951) and the *Monument to Resistance and Freedom* (1961) by A Grzetić, the *Monument to the Executed School-Pupils and Teachers* (1963) by M Živković, the *One Hundred for One Monument* (1980) by Nandor Glid and the *Monument against Evil* (1991) by M Romo among others. To visit all of the monuments following the circular path that connects them takes between 1½ hours and 2 hours in total.

At the entrance to Šumarice Park stands the **October 21 Memorial Museum** [205 A1] (*Memorijalni muzej 21.oktobar;* ✆ *335 607;* ⊕ *summer 08.00–18.00, winter 08.00–15.00 daily; nominal admission fee; a guide service is available*), sometimes referred to as the Genocide Museum, a curious building composed of 33 towers of different heights that create the impression of a basalt rock formation or a chemical salt crystal. In the entrance hall is a piece of symbolic sculpture made from soldiers' helmets hung on a spray of rifles bayoneted into a base. The museum contains photographs and texts documenting the lives of some of the 7,000 shot by the Nazis on the tragic day in question.

In the city centre itself, there is the **National Museum** [205 C4] (*Narodni muzej Kragujevac; Vuka Karadžića 1;* ✆ *333 302;* ⊕ *10.00–15.00 Tue–Fri, 10.00–14.00 Sat/ Sun*), with a small archaeological, historical and ethnographical collection in the *konak* that was the former **Palace of Prince Miloš** at Svetozara Markovića 2. This and the **Amidžin Konak** [205 C4] that dates from 1820 and stands next door is virtually all that is left of the old town – that which was not destroyed in two world wars was cleared for development in the immediate post-war years to make room for the car production plant that grew out of the Crvena Zastava (Red Flag) military factory. These days Kragujevac's industrial heyday is represented in mere stone: in front of the Zastava offices, across the concrete bridge at the end of Marta 27, is an interesting and rather heroic **statue of a Yugoslav car worker** [205 C4], a poignant sight now that the industry is no longer the conquering hero that it once was. A more fitting legacy, perhaps, are the tens of thousands of beaten-up but lovingly maintained Yugos and Zastavas that continue to kick up dust on the roads throughout the region, all of which, at some stage, would have passed through these same factory gates.

THE KNIĆ (КНИЧ) AREA *Telephone code 034*

Lying roughly halfway between Kragujevac and Kraljevo is the small country town of Knić. Although there is nothing specific to see in the town, it is central to a particularly lovely part of the Šumadija that is ideal for walking or cycling. There are also a few sights of interest close by, so Knić could serve as a suitable base for exploration.

Close to the town is the 9km² **Gruža Lake**, a popular location for watersports and fishing while, just to the south, is the 749m peak of **Veliki vrh**, the highest point in the area.

Thirteen kilometres northwest of Knić, on a back road that meanders towards Čačak, is the small village of **Borać**, which has some ruins of an old medieval town, towering above the village on a craggy bluff, that dates back to the time of Stefan Lazarević. The most remarkable thing here is the 14th-century, so-called '**hidden church**' that has three of its sides sheltered by a cliff face and its fourth concealed by a lush stand of 100-year-old lime trees. The church dates from 1350 and, true to its name, does not reveal itself until you are right at its door. The house by the gate has the key if you want to go inside. There is also an interesting old graveyard nearby. Another attractive village in the region, just 4km from Knić, is **Grabovac**.

More information on local attractions can be had from the **tourist office** in Knić (\ 510 115, 590 491; e toknic@ptt.rs) in the centre of the town, which can also assist with accommodation in the area. Staying with a family in the area would enable you to get a closer look at the rural way of life here.

For more formal accommodation in the area there is the **Hotel Eurogaj** (\ 591 128, 591 111; e eurogaj@feman.co.rs; w eurogaj.rs; €€), a large motel with 29 rooms and 12 apartments (€€€) just beyond the lake at Knić. The restaurant serves local Šumadija dishes. The **Restoran Putnik** on the main Čačak to Kragujevac road next to Lake Gruža also has rooms available (\ 871 519; €€). Nearby is the large and stylish **Klub Restoran Arsenijević** that serves Šumadija food in a traditional setting (\ 871 836; €€).

KRALJEVO (КРАЉЕВО) *Telephone code 036*

Like Kragujevac, Kraljevo is another industrial town that has largely been rebuilt since World War II, although its roots belong to the 19th century when it was the seat of the Obrenović dynasty. Originally known as Rudo Polje, Karanovac and then Rankovićevo, the town took on its present-day name (meaning 'king's town') in 1882. During the immediate post-World War II period, when such reminders of a monarchist past were unpopular, it briefly changed its name back to Rankovićevo once more but reverted back to Kraljevo from 1955 onwards. The city was badly damaged in World War II and suffered almost as much as Kragujevac in terms of the brutal Nazi reprisals that were visited upon the civilian population of the town. More recently, during the 1999 bombing campaign, several targets in and around Kraljevo were hit by NATO bombs, destroying some railway lines and a bridge. The town's population has grown considerably since the 1990s to accommodate a relatively large influx of refugees from Kosovo and Bosnia. Little is left of the town's 19th-century heritage and what you see today is largely the result of socialist town planning. The town was hit by a 5.6 magnitude earthquake in November 2010, which damaged many buildings, cut off water and power supply and killed two people. Kraljevo is a convenient stopover for **Žiča Monastery**, which lies just outside the town, and could also be used as a base for visiting **Studenica**, **Kalenić** and **Ljubostinja**.

GETTING THERE AND AWAY Kraljevo is an important transport hub and one of Serbia's better-connected towns. The **local and long-distance bus stations** [210 E1] stand side by side at the top of Oktobarskih Žrtava just north of the centre. There are many daily buses that run to Belgrade, seven of which originate in Kraljevo. Six buses a day run west to Zlatibor, and many more go east to Kragujevac and Kruševac. There is a frequent bus service south to Raška and Novi Pazar, and even far-flung destinations like Subotica and Vranje can be reached directly from the town. There are also three buses a day to Studenica Monastery: one early in the

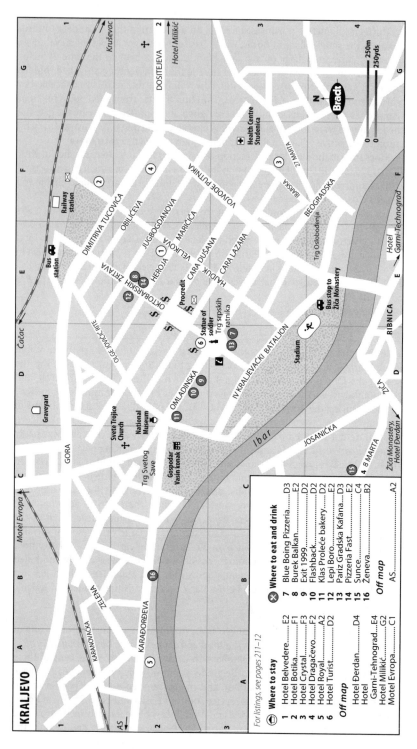

KRALJEVO

For listings, see pages 211–12

① Where to stay
1 Hotel Belvedere......E2
2 Hotel Botika..........F1
3 Hotel Crystal.........F3
4 Hotel Dragačevo......F2
5 Hotel Royal...........A2
6 Hotel Turist..........D2
Off map
   Hotel Đerdan........D4
   Hotel
   Garni-Tehnograd...E4
   Hotel Milikić........G2
   Motel Evropa.......C1

✖ Where to eat and drink
7   Blue Boing Pizzeria......D3
8   Burek Balkan............E2
9   Exit 1999...............D2
10 Flashback...............D2
11 Klas Prolece bakery.....D2
12 Lepi Boro...............E2
13 Pariz Gradska Kafana....D3
14 Pizzeria Fast...........E2
15 Sunce...................C4
16 Ženeva..................B2
Off map
    AS.......................A2

Health Centre
Studenica

Bus stop to
Žiča Monastery

Statue of
soldier
Trg srpskih
ratnika

Procredit

Railway
station

Bus
station

Graveyard

Sveté Trojice
Church

National
Museum

Gospodar
Vasin konak

Trg Svetog
Save

Trg Oslobođenja

Stadium

Motel Evropa

Kruševac

Hotel Milikić

DOSITEJEVA

DIMITRIVA TUCOVIĆA

OBILIĆEVA

JUGBOGDANOVA

HEROJA

VELIKOVA

MARIČIĆA

VOJVODE PUTNIKA

CARA DUŠANA

CARA LAZARA

HAJDUK

OKTOBARSKIH ŽRTAVA

OLGE JOVIČIĆE

GORA

OMLADINSKA

IV KRALJEVAČKI BATALJON

JOSANIČKA

Ibar

RIBNICA

BEOGRADSKA

IBARSKA

17 MARTA

4. 8 MARTA

Žiča Monastery,
Hotel Đerdan

Hotel
Garni-Technograd

KARAĐORĐEVA

ZELENA

KARANOVAČKA

AS

Čačak

250m
250yds

N

Bradt

210

morning, one mid morning and one early afternoon. Two of these buses go on to Novi Pazar, and you change at Ušće where a connection will be waiting; the early afternoon bus appears to be direct. It is best to check these details with the tourist information centre or at the bus station (✆ 313 444).

Train connections [210 F1] are much more limited, with five trains a day to Čačak, two to Kragujevac, two to Kruševac and two to Kosovska Mitrovica in Kosovo via Ušće. Be aware that some of these leave at inconvenient times like the early hours of the morning. For train enquiries, ✆ 313 555.

TOURIST INFORMATION [210 D3] (*Trg srpskih ratnika 25;* ✆ *316 000, 311 192;* e *jutok@tron.rs;* w *jutok.org.rs*) Situated on the southwest side of the square, this tourist information office is run by helpful staff who speak English and do their best to accommodate the needs of foreign visitors.

🏠 **WHERE TO STAY** All of the following lie either within town or within reasonable distance outside it.

🏠 **Hotel Crystal** [210 F3] (26 rooms) Ibarska 44; ✆ 329 140, 329 150; e office@hotelcrystal.rs; w hotelcrystal.rs. A plush & stylish hotel, offering good value & facilities for the price. All rooms come with internet access, minibar, cable TV & AC. Pleasant bar & small restaurant with buffet b/fast. €€€

🏠 **Hotel Garni-Tehnograd** **** [210 E4] (21 suites) Kovanlučka 1; ✆ 373 300; e office@hoteltehnograd.com; w hoteltehnograd.com. South of the river in a quiet part of town, this has suites of various sizes, all with AC, internet connection, kitchen & high-tech AV devices. €€€

🏠 **Hotel Milikić** [210 G2] (7 rooms) Disteleva bb; ✆ 382 001, 382 002; e office@hotelmilikic.com; w hotelmilikic.com. On the Kragujevac road, 3km from the town centre, all rooms have internet connection, cable TV & AC. €€€

🏠 **Hotel Royal** ** [210 A2] (9 rooms) Karađorđeva 107; ✆ 354 004, 353 999; w hotelroyalkv.com. This smart modern hotel has been in operation since 2003 & still looks pristine. Rooms have TV & minibar, with AC in the summer months. It has its own good restaurant & will accept Visa credit cards. €€€

🏠 **Hotel Turist** **** [210 D2] (67 rooms, 5 apts) Trg srpskih ratnika 1; ✆ 322 366; e hotel@hotel-turist.net; w hotel-turist.net. Originally a state-run hotel, closed down in 2006, this large establishment on the central square has since been completely refurbished. Aimed primarily at the business traveller, it has plain, spacious rooms, congress centre, wellness centre & sauna. Top-floor restaurant has fine views & good food. €€€

🏠 **Hotel Belvedere** [210 E2] (6 apts) Heroja Maričića 67; ✆ 313 333; e info@belvedere.rs; w www.belvedere.rs. A small hotel with apartments with cable TV, internet access & minibar. €€

🏠 **Hotel Botika** [210 F1] (29 rooms) Naselje Moše Pijada 1A; ✆ 366 800, 366 801; e hotelbotika@gmail.com; w hotelbotika.rs. Very close to the railway & bus stations, this sparkling new hotel has a restaurant, internet access & AC in the rooms, & use of a wellness centre that includes sauna, jacuzzi & gym. €€

🏠 **Hotel Đerdan** [210 D4] (9 rooms) ✆ 5816 250, 5817 417; e djerdan@gmail.com; w djerdan.co.rs. Just outside Kraljevo on the road to Žiča, about 1km short of the monastery. €€

🏠 **Hotel Dragačevo** [210 F2] Obilićeva 49; ✆ 235 056, 231 613; m 064 4557 955; e hoteldragacevo@gmail.com; w hoteldragacevo.rs. A tidy new hotel with its own restaurant near the railway station. €€

🏠 **Motel Evropa** [210 C1] (8 rooms, 2 suites) 7 Sekretara skoja, Jarčujak; ✆ 351 945. A neat place attached to a restaurant & offering B&B accommodation in a village 4km out of town on the Čačak road. €€

🍴 **WHERE TO EAT AND DRINK** The list below offers some restaurant suggestions. For a drink, there is a whole string of café-bars along Omdalinska like **Flashback** [210 D2] and **Exit 1999** [210 D2] that have outdoor terraces and stay open late.

There are also a couple of decent bakeries along here, such as **Klas Proleće bakery** [210 D2]. Oktobarskih Žrtava has a few pizzerias and fast-food places like **Pizzeria Fast** [210 E2] and **Burek Balkan** [210 E2].

✕ **AS** [210 A2] Karađorđeva 219; ☎ 352 032. This restaurant has a terrace by the river, good service & national cuisine. €€

✕ **Sunce** [210 C4] 8 Marta bb; ☎ 361 810, 361 555; w restoransunce.rs. A smart, upmarket restaurant with an international menu that offers fish dishes. €€

✕ **Ženeva** [210 B2] Karađorđeva 51/4; ☎ 316 111, 316 112, 316 113. On the left bank of the River Ibar, with an outdoor terrace, this has both Serbian & international dishes. €€

✕ **Blue Boing Pizzeria** [210 D3] Trg srpskih ratnika 22; ☎ 320 990. This is close to the tourist office. €

✕ **Lepi Boro** [210 E2] Oktobarskih Žrtava 15; ☎ 328 328. A pleasant, friendly national restaurant with good food. Not everything on the menu might be available, however. There is also a very basic *ćevapčići* place next door. €

♀ **Pariz Gradska Kafana** [210 D3] Trg srpskih ratnika 43; ☎ 359 660. This *pivinica* (beer hall) on the main square has a genuine *kafana* atmosphere. As well it might – it has been functioning for over 100 years. The only modern touches are the flatscreen TV & the comedy 'No Smoking' signs on the wall. This has the standard range of Serbian dishes & good draught beer. €

OTHER PRACTICALITIES

$ **Bank** Procredit [210 E2] Cara Lazara 44; ☎ 317 290
✚ **Health Centre** Studenica [210 F3] Jugbogdanova bb; ☎ 301 988

✉ **Post office** [210 E2] Cara Lazara 37; ☎ 303 013

WHAT TO SEE AND DO Apart from nearby Žiča Monastery, there is little to see in the town itself although Kraljevo serves as a pleasant enough base for the region. Kraljevo is best enjoyed by a leisurely stroll up and down the pedestrian-only street of Omdalinska and having a drink in one of the numerous outdoor cafés there.

The central square, **Trg srpskih ratnika (Square of the Serbian Warrior)** [210 D3], is actually a circle, around which most of the town's activity rotates. In the centre stands a large, sombre **statue** of the eponymous warrior with a gun and a banner, around which in summer small children in battery-powered cars endlessly circulate while their parents sit on benches and chat.

Heading west along Omdalinska you soon come to a leafy park and the small square of Trg Svetog Save. The elegant, Neoclassical **National Museum** [210 D2] (*Narodni muzej; Trg Svetog Save 2;* ☎ *337 960, 315 350;* ⏱ *09.00– 20.00 Tue– Fri, 09.00– 13.00 Sat/Sun, closed Mon*) stands opposite this. The park houses the **Gospodar Vasin Konak** [210 C2], a 19th-century residence from the time of the Obrenović dynasty.

Žiča Monastery [210 D4]

This is situated just outside Kraljevo, across the Ibar River in one of the town's southern suburbs. It is about a 45-minute walk from the centre, or you could take a taxi or a local bus heading towards the village of Mataruška Banja; as you approach the monastery, you will see its three cupolas and red walls emerging through its screen of trees. Buses leave about every half an hour or so from Kraljevo's local bus station, just east of the long-distance station, from where there are sometimes also inexpensive share taxis. Be sure to catch a bus that says 'Prekov Žiče' as some Mataruška Banja buses go by a different route. You can also pick a bus up at the bus stop on the north side of the river before the bridge [210 E4].

Žiča is distinctive from all other Serbian monasteries in being painted a rusty red colour, an echo of the monasteries at Mt Athos in Greece. With a single aisle, a semicircular apse and a narthex on the western side, it is a prime example of the **Raška School** and, at one time at least, was one of the grandest representatives of this style in all of Serbia. Nowadays, following an extensive repair programme that aimed to correct the damage of previous centuries, the monastery's natural ambience has been adversely affected by so much well-meant restoration: it is still grand but somehow it lacks atmosphere. Sadly, most of the original frescoes have been destroyed, either by plundering Bulgarians in 1290, or by later Turks infuriated at the portrayal of the human image. All that remains of the earlier frescoes are fragments around the main cupola and the *Crucifixion* in the south transept. *The Dormition of the Virgin* on the west wall is later, probably 14th century.

Despite its artistic losses, Žiča's historic pedigree is faultless and the monastery holds a special place in the affections of many Serbians. It was here that Serbia's patron saint, **St Sava**, founded the first patriarchate on his return from his long sojourn at Mt Athos. A golden thread is said to have led him to the site, and it is this legend that gives the monastery its name (*žiča* means cord or thread).

The construction of the main church began about 1206 and it was finished around 1217. Shortly after, Žiča became the seat of the newly independent episcopacy in 1219 and the monastery became the place of coronation for Serbian kings, the first of which was Stefan, Sava's brother, subsequently referred to as Stefan Prvovenčani (the First Crowned), who reigned until 1223.

Following the damage done by marauding Bulgarians at the end of the 13th century, the monastery was reconstructed under the auspices of archbishops Jevstatije, Nikodin and Danilo II, only to be plundered several times more in later centuries under Turkish rule. The first major reconstruction was in 1562, and again in the 18th century. After the First National Uprising in the early 19th century, Karađorđe constructed some new residential buildings before the monastery came under attack once more. What remains today is the result of extensive restoration work done in the period between 1925 and 1935, in addition to that carried out in more recent years.

EAST OF KRALJEVO

Halfway to Kruševac on the E-761 east of Kraljevo is the small industrial town of Trstenik. Just to the north of here lies the **Ljubostinja Convent**. As the monastery is only a 5km walk from the town, it makes an easy day trip from either Kraljevo or Kruševac. The frequent **buses** that link these two towns all stop at Trstenik. There is also the occasional **train**. Trstenik's bus station is at the southeast corner of the town. To reach Ljubostinja, walk north from the bus station past the church then turn left along the next street until reaching a junction. Turn right to cross a steel bridge across the Morava River and then follow the road to the edge of the village where there will be a sign pointing to the right towards the monastery. Soon after, there is another sign pointing left. Follow this minor road for about 3km, climbing gently to reach the monastery. There is a roadside café just past the monastery on the left.

LJUBOSTINJA CONVENT (МАНАСТИР ЉУБОСТИЊА) Ljubostinja is an easy hour's walk from Trstenik in a typical Šumadija setting of gentle, green, forested hills. The monastery buildings include a magnificent black-and-white timbered *konak*, a large number of convent buildings and a church within a walled paddock. It is still very much a working monastery and the nuns here keep busy making wine and honey when not involved with more spiritual concerns (or recording an album of Orthodox chants as they did in 2002). Photography within the monastery grounds is not permitted.

Externally, the church is a fine example of the Morava School, with intricately sculpted windows and doors. Inside, the frescoes are something of a disappointment with only fragments surviving, the best being those in the narthex. The west wall of the north side of the door has portraits of Prince Lazar and Princess Milica, with their sons, Stefan and Vuk, on the other side.

The church was founded by Lazar's widow, Princess Milica, and was built between 1402 and 1404 following her husband's death at the Battle of Kosovo in 1389. An inscription in the step below the door that leads from the narthex to the naos identifies the builder, one Rade Borojević. There is a secret door in the northeast corner of the narthex that leads to a narrow staircase, once used as a hideaway and place to store treasure.

Princess Milica spent her last years here in the monastery, becoming a sister along with many other noblewomen widowed by the Battle of Kosovo. Her tomb lies in the naos.

KALENIĆ CONVENT (МАНАСТИР КАЛЕНИЧ)

KALENIĆ CONVENT (МАНАСТИР КАЛЕНИЧ) The convent of Kalenić stands 20km or so north of Ljubostinja on a hillside of the Gledićke range deep in the Šumadija countryside, 12km west of the village of Oparić next to the small settlement of Kalenićki Prnjavor. Unfortunately, Kalenić is probably the most inaccessible monastery in the whole of Serbia and almost impossible to reach by public transport – a great pity because this monastery, completed around 1415 by Bogdan, a Serbian noble, is a masterpiece of the Morava School and probably represents the culmination of its art. The monastery was abandoned and semi-ruined by the 17th century but was restored by Prince Miloš Obrenović in 1823 and even more meticulously between 1928 and 1930.

The exterior of the church is outstanding, and resembles that of Prince Lazar's Church in Kruševac, decorated with stripes and chequerboard patterns, and adorned with a wide array of motifs that include lions, birds, centaurs and gryphons. Intricate rosettes and minutely carved geometric designs surround all of the windows and portals. Inside, it is no less striking and the overall effect is one of grace and balance. The frescoes are mostly well preserved, having been restored during the 1950s. It should be noted how the proportions of the compositions combine with the building's dimensions; in particular, the way that the scenes in the frescoes are graded with height, becoming larger as they reach up to the cupola.

The most noteworthy of the narrative frescoes is without a doubt the *Marriage Feast at Cana* in the southern apse, which depicts Christ and the Virgin in the setting of a medieval Serbian wedding. The fresco is remarkable for its period detail: the Virgin appears to be speaking to Christ about the wine, while two old men in the background are happily sampling it; the groom is about to prick the finger of his bride in the part of the ancient Serbian ritual that symbolises the mixing of blood – a custom that survived until not so long ago. Other frescoes include a portrait of the monastery's patron Bogdan with his wife Milica and his brother Peter on the north wall of the narthex.

To reach Kalenić with your own car, do not try to continue north after visiting Ljubostinja as the direct road to Prevešt is in very bad condition. It is best to seek local advice. Without private transport, getting here is going to present a problem. Buses run from Kragujevac, Kruševac and Jagodina/Svetozarevo to Oparić, a village south of Belušić, but the monastery is still 12km west of here so hitchhiking might be an option. If there is a group of you, hiring a taxi from Trstenik to do a round trip to Ljubostinja and Kalenić and back is probably the easiest solution.

Vrnjačka Banja, just to the west of Trstenik, is a spa resort that is held in high esteem by middle-class Serbs who are devotees of spa-tourism. A resort of this kind is probably of limited appeal to most foreign visitors but it does at least offer a wide range of facilities and comfortable places to stay for anyone touring the area. The resort is in the wooded foothills that lie beneath the 1,147m Goč Mountain.

The beneficial qualities of the waters of Vrnjačka Banja have a long history that dates back to Roman times. Development of the current resort started back in 1868 and it remains one of the most popular spas in the country. There are three mineral springs at the spa – two cold and one warm: the warm spring has an average temperature of 36.5°C and is used mainly for bathing, and the cold, between 14°C and 25.7°C, for drinking. The spa is recommended for the treatment of diabetes, diseases of the gastro-intestinal tract, pancreas, kidney and urinary tract, as well as for cardiovascular conditions.

GETTING THERE AND AWAY Frequent **buses** run here from both Kraljevo and Kruševac. There are plenty of direct buses from Belgrade and other large Serbian cities too.

TOURIST INFORMATION Visit the tourist and sports centre (*Vrnjačka 6/2;* \ *611 106, 611 107;* e *office@vrnjackabanja.co.rs;* w *vrnjackabanja.co.rs*).

WHERE TO STAY There are over 10,000 beds in the resort so you have plenty to choose from. It is very much a buyer's market and so you should be able to find something suitable in your price range. Just a small sample of the hotels and pensions found in the resort are listed below.

Hotel Vila Aleksandar ** (19 rooms, 4 suites) Heroja Čajke 7; \617 999; e aleksandarvila@todor.rs; w aleksandar. todorhoteli.rs. In a renovated villa in the heart of Vrnjačka Banja, this is one of the most elegant places to stay in town. All rooms have minibar & cable TV; most have balconies. €€€

Hotel Merkur *** (252 rooms) Bulevar srpskih ratnika 18; \5155 141; e info@vrnjcispa. rs; w www.vrnjcispa.rs. Large centrally situated hotel with fitness centre, pool & sauna. €€

Hotel Železničar * (60 rooms) Gavrila Principa 3; \612 368. €€

Hotel Zvezda *** (124 rooms) Vrnjačka 12; \611 770; e prodaja@htpfontana.com; w htpfontana.com. €€

Pansion Vuk *** (18 rooms) Olge Jovičić 10; \612 131, 618 370; e vukaca@gmail.com; w pansionvuk.com. €€

Vila Kraljica (5 rooms) Nemanjina 22; \616 565; e kraljicavb@open.telekom.rs; w kraljica. co.rs. Rooms above a national food restaurant. €€

Vila Lenka 2 **** (8 apts) Beogradska 12A; \4522 350; m 063 201 590; e office@vilalenka2. com; w vilalenka2.com. Comfortable modern apartments with dbl- or trpl-bed rooms. Cheaper for stays over 3 days. €€

WHERE TO EAT AND DRINK Most of the town's hotels are geared up to providing full or half board, so to take at least your evening meal at your hotel certainly represents better value. Otherwise, there are numerous cafés, fast-food and pizzeria places scattered around town.

Kraljica Nemanjina 22; \611 565; m 065 777 3540; w kraljica.co.rs. National cuisine, seafood & pizzas, with an outdoor terrace in the town centre. €€

Kruna Slatinski venac 3; \613 513; w restorankruna.rs. Old-fashioned, traditional restaurant serving up national cuisine. €€

✗ Savka Gavrila Pricipa 6; ☎617 434. Smart restaurant/cocktail bar with Italian food located in a stylish villa. €€

✗ Vuk Olge Jovičić 10; ☎612 131. A decent pizza place that also has lodgings. €€

✗ Etno Kuća Kraljevačka 19A; m 062 1568 395. Local Serbian cooking amid rustic fittings. €

KRUŠEVAC (КРУШЕВАЦ) *Telephone code 037*

This medium-sized town on the Zapadna Morava River, a western tributary of the Morava, is noteworthy for its fort and its well-preserved 14th-century church of the Morava School. Although aerial photo shots on postcards make the town look like a cheerless 1970s high-rise jungle, on the ground things seem quite different and Kruševac is an easy-going, relaxed sort of place that makes a good base for an overnight stop. As well as its convenient position for visiting the monasteries of Kalenić and Ljubostinja, the town also has a handful of sights of its own worth visiting.

HISTORY The town was founded in the 1370s and had become Prince Lazar's capital by the time of the Battle of Kosovo in 1389. It was from the fortress at Kruševac that the Serbian army under Lazar's command set off for its fateful encounter in June of that year.

Despite the Serbian defeat at the hands of the Turks it was a further 60 or so years before the Turks finally wrested the city from Serbian control, by which time the majority of the population had fled north to safety. Kruševac remained in Turkish hands for the next 400 years until it was finally liberated by Serbs in 1833.

Kruševac's citizens have long been referred to as *čarapani* (sock-wearers) thanks to one event during the First National Uprising in which a company of Serbian rebels, led by Mladen Milanović, managed to steal into the town at night completely unnoticed by the Turkish troops. This feat was achieved by the rebels removing their boots and entering the town silently in their socks, hence the name.

GETTING THERE AND AWAY Kruševac lies at the southeastern corner of central Serbia. It is well connected to Belgrade and the **bus station** [217 C1] (☎ 421 555, 21 706) has a frequent service that is more or less hourly, as well as to other destinations in southern and central Serbia. Numerous daily buses also run to the nearby resort of Vrnjačka Banja, many via Trstenik (for Ljubostinja Convent). Less regular services link the town with destinations east of the Morava River like Ćuprija, Jagodina and Niš.

An infrequent and slow train service runs west from the **railway station** [217 C1] (☎ 28 888) to Kraljevo and north to Jagodina from where there are connections to Belgrade and Niš.

TOURIST INFORMATION [217 B/C2] (*Majke Jugovića 3;* ☎ *445 180;* e *turizamkrusevac@mts.rs;* w *turizamkrusevac.com;* ⏱ *08.00–20.00 Mon–Fri, 09.00–15.00 Sat*) Close to the Kosovo monument, a little way along Majke Jugovića, this office has information and English-language literature about local attractions, a small selection of souvenirs and very helpful staff.

⌂ WHERE TO STAY

⌂ **Hotel Biser** [217 A2] (12 rooms, 3 apts) Kosovska 18; ☎421 606, 421 610; e info@ hotelbiser.rs; w hotelbiser.rs. Close to the sights of the centre, with stylish modern rooms complete with AC, internet access, cable TV & minibar. €€

✳ ⌂ **Hotel City** [217 B3] (9 rooms, 2 apts) Veselina Nikolića 18; ☎3502 100, 202 634; e jetcitydoo@gmail.com; w cityhotel.rs.

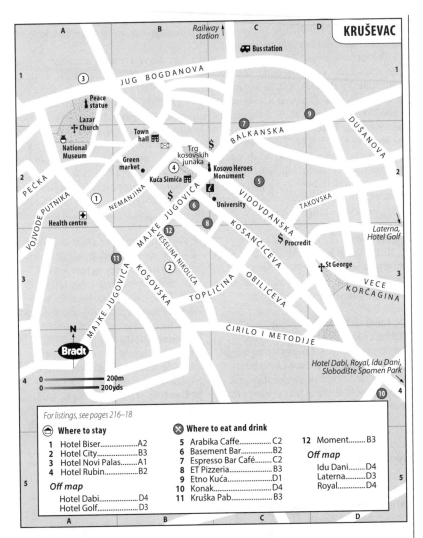

KRUŠEVAC

For listings, see pages 216–18

A good-value small hotel in a quiet street just off pedestrianised Majke Jugovića. Spick & span spacious rooms & helpful staff. **€€**

🛏 **Hotel Dabi** *** [217 D4] (42 rooms, 5 apts) Dostojevskog; ☎ 491 061; e hoteldabi@gmail. com. 10mins from the centre, this hotel has clean simple rooms & a large restaurant serving national cuisine. **€€**

🛏 **Hotel Golf** ** [217 D3] (12 rooms) Gavrila Principa 74; ☎ 460 563, 3462 820; e info@ hotelgolf.co.rs; w hotelgolf.co.rs. 2km from the town centre. All rooms with AC, minibar, cable TV & internet connection. **€€**

🛏 **Hotel Novi Palas***** [217 A1] (18 rooms) Gazimestanski trg (formerly Trg mira) 7; ☎ 442 378; e mak037palas@gmail.com. With both standard & lux category rooms, all of which have AC, cable TV & Wi-Fi. This modern, good-value hotel, formerly the 'Niš Fam', also has a casino. **€€**

🛏 **Hotel Rubin***** [217 B2] (61 rooms, 4 apts) Nemanjina 2; ☎ 425 535. This large, slightly run-down state-run hotel faces out on to the town's central square. The hotel has its own restaurant & bar; currency exchange & free Wi-Fi are offered in the foyer & private parking is available. Prices depend on which floor you choose: the 1st floor is more expensive. **€€**

✗ WHERE TO EAT AND DRINK Many restaurants don't give opening times but noon to 23.00 or midnight is a safe assumption.

The area around Trg kosovskih junaka has several cafés, pizzerias and a *poslastičarnica* with outdoor seating. Tucked away in a side street behind Vidovdanska at Čolak Antina 5 is **Arabika Caffe** [217 C2] (✆ *440 430*; w *arabika.rs*), a large café-*poslastičarnica* with a non-smoking section upstairs. As well as a huge choice of sweets and cakes, it also serves light meals like pasta dishes. Several cafés and bars like **Basement Bar** [217 B2], and fast-food take-aways and pizzerias such as **Moment** [217 B3] (m *064 2244 377*; €) can also be found along Majke Jugovića, a narrow pedestrianised street that runs south from the Kosovo monument in the central square. At the top of Balkanska, **Espresso Bar Café** [217 C2] is a lively bar that seems much more like a pub than a coffee bar in atmosphere. Just beyond the bottom end of Majke Jugovića, the **Kruška Pab** [217 B3] (*Kosovska 42*; m *065 8763 213*) has a wide range of beers and live music some nights.

✗ ET Pizzeria [217 B3] Kajmakčalanska bb; ✆ 442 895. More than just a pizza place, this is a bit more upmarket than most with a decent range of Italian dishes. Small cosy interior with varnished floors & larger covered terrace area. No sign of aliens. €€

✗ Konak [217 D4] Nikole Tesle (formerly Radomira Jakovljevića) 5; ✆ 443 410; e info@konak.rs; w konak.rs. A restaurant serving national cuisine located not in a traditional *konak* but in a modern building with an interesting interior. A wide-ranging menu that includes excellent grilled meats. They also have rooms to rent. €€

✗ Royal [217 D4] Milosava Kostića; ✆ 460 870, 460 820. A large restaurant with an outdoor terrace area & cosy interior that serves both Serbian & international dishes. Live music most nights. €€

✗ Idu Dani [217 D4] Kneza Miloša 66; ✆ 462 255. A traditional restaurant with outside seating close to the river at the east end of town. €€–€

✗ Laterna [217 D3] Dragomira Gajića 86; ✆ 3538 107; w laterna.rs; ⊕ noon–midnight. Italian & Serbian food in a cosy room with open fireplace. €€–€

✗ Etno Kuća [217 D1] Balkanska 35; ✆ 422 244. A lively & popular local restaurant with trestle tables, the usual range of grilled food & salads, & draught Jelen beer. €

OTHER PRACTICALITIES

$ Bank Procredit [217 C3] Mirka Tomića 99; ✆ 418 480

⊞ Health centre [217 A2] Kosovska 16; ✆ 414 000, 421 826; w zckrusevac.org.rs

✉ Post office [217 B2] Nemanjina 2; ✆ 413 713

WHAT TO SEE AND DO Kruševac's most important sight is undoubtedly the 14th-century **Lazar Church (Crkva Lazarica)** [217 A2] that stands in the grounds of the ruined fort. To find the fort and church, walk west from the Hotel Rubin past the post office and the elegant Neoclassical **town hall** [217 B2], then turn left and head south briefly before taking the road that leads off to the right. This will soon bring you to the **archaeological park**.

The church, built about 1380 and restored by Prince Miloš Obrenović in the 19th century, is a typical example of the **Morava School**, with an Orthodox cross plan, a central cupola, mixed brick and stone masonry, and elaborate, decorative carvings around the doors and windows. Although all of the original frescoes have been lost, destroyed by Turkish iconoclasts, externally the church is in remarkably good condition for its age. In fact, its appearance seems almost new, the decorative red brickwork still bright and in pristine condition and the stone carvings hardly worn.

It must be said that the church may be too fussy for some tastes: with numerous arches and mouldings, rose windows, carved dragons and over-the-top tracery. Somehow, the overall effect is all a bit too much – an overstatement.

The church stands central in the park that once held **Lazar's Fortress (Kruševački grad)**. Apart from some defensive walls, there is little that remains of the fort today but a noticeboard points you in the right direction if you want to work out where Prince Lazar's Palace, the stables, blacksmiths and kilns used to stand. At the north end of the park, close to Jug Bogdanova is an interesting **peace statue** [217 A1], showing a pair of arms that rise from the ground to gently clasp the world in its hands.

Prince Lazar's Palace is now reduced to its foundations but the **National Museum** [217 A2] (*Narodni muzej;* ⊕ *08.00–18.00 Tue–Sat, 09.00–14.00 Sun & holidays, closed Mon; small admission fee*) that stands in the park, and which dates from 1863, is well worth investigating. Downstairs are several rooms devoted to reconstructed frescoes, fragments of stoneware, illustrated manuscripts, medieval pottery and glassware, together with stone arrowheads and axes from the Neolithic period. On one wall is a medieval map showing the extent of Greater Serbia between 1371 and 1459, but pride of place must go to the glass cabinet that contains a cloak that was supposedly worn by Prince Lazar himself. The cloak – grey with yellow brocade and stylised animal motifs that seem to lie somewhere between a dog and a lion – has something of a Chinese appearance about it. Somehow, its authenticity seems doubtful. It looks more of a dressing gown than a cloak, but perhaps it was just the thing for relaxing in after a hard day on the battlefield.

Upstairs, the museum has a display of interesting modern paintings all related to the Battle of Kosovo theme, many of which were created especially for the 600th anniversary of the battle in 1989. The history of the Kruševac region is represented by numerous letters and newspaper cuttings from the 19th century. There is also an ethnographical exhibit of beds, looms, clothes and tools used in homes in the region and, interestingly, a large stuffed wolf skewered on a stake. The wolf has a length of wool and a garland of chilli peppers and corn tassels hung around its neck; a bell hung from its tail. This appears to have some sort of talismanic value as old black-and-white photographs show villagers dressing up a dead wolf in the same manner in a winter ceremony. Unfortunately, all of the captioning is in Cyrillic Serbian.

Perhaps the most interesting object on display is the wooden mock-up made from sculptor Ivan Meštrović's 1912 plan for his proposed monument, Vidovanskog Hrama, which was intended to be built at Kosovo Polje, the site of the fateful battle. The scale of the project was truly monumental, which might go part of the way to explain why it was never even started. The design incorporates the sort of militaristic, superhuman aesthetic that Mussolini so admired. The ground plan is that of an enormous Orthodox cross, with an outer and an inner temple area divided by colonnaded walkways. At the entrances that lie at each point of the cross, ranks of lions and horses guard the steps that lead up to them. In the centre of the design is a tower composed of warrior figures stacked on each other's shoulders. Given the spectre of conflict that continues to haunt troubled Kosovo, it is probably just as well that it was never built. The museum has a small shop at the entrance.

The **town centre** itself has one or two things of note. Standing in the centre of Trg kosovskih junaka, the main square, is the **Monument to Kosovo Heroes** [217 B/C2], a winged angel that is the work of sculptor Đorđe Janković, commemorating the Battle of Kosovo and dating from 1904. Just off the square on the east side, around the corner from Majke Jugovića café-bar street is a very elegant stucco building that is the main building of the **university** [217 C2]. At the top end of Majke Jugovića, close to the main square, is **Kuća Simića** [217 B2] (☉ *08.00–16.00 Mon–Fri, 08.00– 15.00 Sat*), a museum house in Turkish–Balkan style that dates from 1833. A small park at the end of Vidovdanska, east of Trg kosovskih junaka contains a church dedicated to **St George** [217 D3], built in 1904 in the Serbian–Byzantine style with alternating red and yellow layers of stone. This was built on the remains of an earlier church dating from 1838. Beyond this is a small shopping centre.

Kruševac is also home to an excellent **green market** [217 B2], one of the best in Serbia and at its most animated on Saturday mornings. The market site is found along the street that runs south from Hotel Rubin. There is a permanent covered area where clothes, furniture, tools and household appliances are sold, as well as a densely packed outdoor spread of stalls selling all manner of fruit, vegetables, mushrooms, fish and meat, along with locally produced dairy products like white cheese and *kajmak*. Animal lovers may baulk at some of the sights here: the bulk of chickens that change hands are still alive and clucking, and on the street outside, larks and captured songbirds are sold in tiny cages. With its colourful population of Roma vegetable vendors, and burly village women in headscarves selling eggs from buckets, there is a strong hint of the Middle Eastern bazaar here.

A little way out of town to the south is the **Slobodište Memorial Park (Spomen-park Slobodište)** [217 D4], an area of undulating wooded parkland that, like its counterpart in Kragujevac, contains a collection of monuments dedicated to those who were killed by Nazi forces during World War II. The park is close to the former location of a prison camp where mass shootings of partisans and citizens took place between 1941 and 1943, especially in the summer of 1943 when over 1,000 people were executed, mostly by Albanian and Bulgarian troops. The memorial complex was designed by Bogdan Bogdanović, an architect, politician, one-time Belgrade mayor and critic of Slobodan Milošević, who died in 2010. The trail begins at a stone arch (*Gate of the Sun*) that is flanked by two mounds like Neolithic barrows. The most evocative monuments in the complex are the set of wing-like sculptures that zigzag up a slope towards woodland at the top of the site. To reach the sculpture park from the city centre, head along the right fork at St George's church at the eastern end of Vidovdanska to go along Dositijeva and Hajduk Veljkova to eventually reach a roundabout by a large sports centre and a plane on a plinth. Bear right here to follow the footpath next to the main highway and after about a kilometre, take one of the footpaths to the right that lead through trees into the park. The site is about a 40-minute walk from the city centre.

TOPOLA (ТОПОЛА) *Telephone code 034*

Regular buses run to and from Belgrade and take around 1½ hours. Some through buses *en route* to Kragujevac and Kraljevo also stop here. The **bus station** is just north of the centre.

TOURIST INFORMATION The tourist information office is on Kraljice Marije 4 (☎ *6814 172;* e *info@topolaoplenac.org.rs;* w *topolaoplenac.org.rs;* ☉ *10.00–18.00 daily*); there is also a small information booth opposite the museum.

🏠 **WHERE TO STAY AND EAT** Topola is an easy day trip from Belgrade. If you wish to stay in the vicinity, there are various options. There are also private rooms available in some of the surrounding villages – enquire at the tourist information office.

The nearby spa town of **Aranđelovac**, the home of Knjez Miloš mineral water, has further options for staying in the vicinity, such as the Hotel Izvor below. The Vajat restaurant at Kneza Miloša 173 (m *064 1573 689*; €€) on the main street near the park is recommended for its fish soup.

🏠 **Hotel Izvor** ***** (89 rooms) Mišarska bb, Aranđelovac; ✆700 400; e office@a-hotel-izvor.com; w a-hotel-izvor.com. A large, luxurious hotel that is part of a spa & wellness resort complex. Prices include HB & unlimited use of aqua park & wellness centre. €€€€€

🏠 **Hotel Oplenac** ** (40 rooms) Oplenačka bb; ✆811 430; e recepcija@hoteloplenac.com; w hoteloplenac.com. This 2-star, situated just below Topola's church, has its own restaurant. €€

🏠 **RC Baikal** (14 rooms) Mije Todorovića bb; ✆813 878; e rezervacije@rcbaikal.com;

w rcbaikal.com. Combined restaurant & accommodation complex 2.5km outside Topola on the Aranđelovac road. All rooms with minibar, TV & internet access. €€–€

✖ **Vožd** Jovana Skerlića; ✆6811 365; w restoranvozd.com. A traditional Serbian restaurant in the centre of Topola with a summer garden. €€–€

✖ **Breza** Krajiških Brigada 25; ✆812 463. Downhill from Topola centre, this has good Serbian food. €

WHAT TO SEE AND DO The prime reason for visiting the small town of Topola, 65km south of Belgrade, is to visit the **Karađorđe Mausoleum** on the hill of **Oplenac** just outside the town. An all-inclusive ticket for the church, museum and King Petar's house should be bought before you start.

Topola served as Karađorđe's campaign headquarters during the First National Uprising and the leader's bones are still here in the church that was built for him – a curious, Byzantine-style structure dedicated to St George. Because of Karađorđe's revered status as a national hero of the First National Uprising, the mausoleum at Oplenac is venerated throughout Serbia and considered an important national shrine. Whether or not it holds the same appeal for foreign visitors is largely dependent on their taste for white marble and wall-to-wall mosaics.

The glistening white **Mausoleum Church of St George (Crkva Sv Đorđa)** is on top of the hill at the south side of the town, set among pines and well-tended gardens. The church was founded by King Petar I and consecrated in 1912. It was damaged during World War I and partly rebuilt in the 1920s; the mosaics that cover the interior were created during this period.

Most of the walls and ceiling of the church are covered with mosaics copied from frescoes in Serbian monasteries. Altogether there is said to be a total of 725 compositions taken from as many as 60 medieval churches and monasteries. There were reputedly over four million pieces used here, of 15,000 different shades. The mosaics are well executed and the colours are vivid.

Scenes from St George's life decorate the narthex while, in the south apse, is the **Gallery of Serbian Medieval Rulers**, in which each ruler is depicted beneath episodes from the life of Christ. St Simeon and scenes from the life of St Sava decorate the pillars that support the dome above the naos, and the altar bears frescoes that depict the *Apostles*, the *Last Supper* and the *Road to Golgotha*. Resting on a floor of polished, coloured marble, Karađorđe's remains inhabit a grand coffin in the southern choir, while the northern end holds a similar white marble sarcophagus that contains those of King Petar I, the church's benefactor. Downstairs in the crypt, the entrance of which is guarded by the figures of archangels Michael and Gabriel, more mosaics glint down on a series of onyx tombs, many of which remain unoccupied. Altogether, there are 19 other members of the Karađorđević dynasty interred here, spanning a total of five generations, but the mausoleum was constructed for a dynasty that did not survive for as long as expected and, although the tombs of King Aleksandar, murdered in Marseilles in 1934, and his mother are found here, there are many more vacant niches that will never be filled.

King Petar's House stands opposite the church (⊙ *3481 1280;* ⊕ *09.00–17.00 Tue–Sun*). This was the refectory where the king lived while he was overseeing the construction of the church. The other main sight is the nearby **Karađorđev Konak Museum** (⊕ *09.00–17.00 Tue–Sat*) that stands on the site of what used to be Karađorđević Castle at Kraljice Marije 2. The Balkan-style *konak* where Karađorđe lived, and which now houses the museum, is now the only extant part of the town's former fortifications. The museum contains artefacts of his life: his gun, a letter written to Napoleon and a painting that depicts his beheading in 1817, upon the order of Prince Miloš Obrenović.

VALJEVO (ВАЉЕВО)   *Telephone code 014*

This town of around 60,000 inhabitants, 100km south of Belgrade, has a few specific sights and is a pleasant, relaxing place to visit. The town stands on the Kolubara River, a tributary of the Sava, surrounded by low mountain ranges with the 1,103m peak of Divčibare about 30km to the southeast. The linguist and compiler of the modern Serbian language, Vuk Karadžić, was a native of the town and there is a moustachioed monument to him in front of the old railway station. Supposedly, Valjevo is the place where the most grammatically perfect Serbian is spoken, although this is unrelated to the Vuk Karadžić connection.

HISTORY Valjevo was a significant trading post for the Serbs during the early 15th century and became increasingly important after capture and subsequent enlargement by the Turks in 1458. The town was badly damaged during the Austro-Turkish wars of the 18th century but played a significant role in both the First and Second national uprisings in which the decapitation of two local dukes, Aleksa Nenadović and Ilije Birčanin, in 1804 became a powerful catalyst for the uprising against Turks in the region.

Once liberated from Turkish rule, the town started to expand once more, necessitating a move of its centre from the south side to the less-restricted north side of the Kolubara River. By the end of the 19th century, the town was one of the most prosperous in all Serbia.

Like many provincial Serbian towns, Valjevo was targeted during the 1999 NATO air campaign. The town's 'Krušik' industrial plant was struck along with some residential apartment blocks north of the centre. The town hospital was also damaged in the raids.

GETTING THERE AND AWAY Valjevo's **bus terminal** [223 D4] (⊙ *221 482*) is a relatively modern place east of the centre that has television screens showing timetables for arrivals and departures. There are good connections with Belgrade and two buses a day leave for Novi Sad via Šabac, on a direct route that avoids Belgrade. There are also a reasonable number of services southwest towards Zlatibor and Tara, and even a couple that cross the border to Banja Luka in Bosnia. The town lies on the Bar–Belgrade railway and so there are a couple of relatively fast **train** connections [223 D4] (⊙ *221 697*) each day north to Lazarevac and Belgrade and south to Užice.

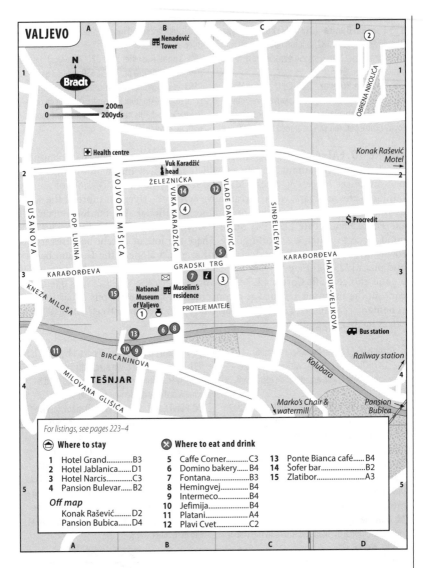

VALJEVO

N

Bradt

0 ———————— 200m
0 ———————— 200yds

☩ Health centre

Nenadović Tower

Vuk Karadžić head

ŽELEZNIČKA

GRADSKI TRG

National Museum of Valjevo

Muselim's residence

PROTEJE MATEJE

Konak Rašević Motel

$ Procredit

🚌 Bus station

Railway station

Marko's Chair & watermill

Pansion Bubica

VOJVODE MISIĆA

POP LUKINA

DUŠANOVA

VUKA KARADŽIĆA

VLADE DANILOVIĆA

SINĐELIĆEVA

KARAĐORĐEVA

HAJDUK-VELJKOVA

KARAĐORĐEVA

KNEZA MILOŠA

BIRČANINOVA

TEŠNJAR

MILOVANA GLIŠIĆA

Kolubara

OBRENA NIKOLIĆA

For listings, see pages 223–4

🏠 **Where to stay**

1   Hotel Grand...............B3
2   Hotel Jablanica........D1
3   Hotel Narcis...............C3
4   Pansion Bulevar......B2

Off map
    Konak Rašević.........D2
    Pansion Bubica.......D4

✖ **Where to eat and drink**

5   Caffe Corner............C3
6   Domino bakery.......B4
7   Fontana.....................B3
8   Hemingvej................B4
9   Intermeco................B4
10 Jefimija.....................B4
11 Platani......................A4
12 Plavi Cvet.................C2

13 Ponte Bianca café......B4
14 Šofer bar.......................B2
15 Zlatibor.........................A3

TOURIST INFORMATION [223 B3] Information can be found at Proteje Mateje 1/1
(✆ *221 138;* e *tovaljevo@mts.rs*).

🏠 WHERE TO STAY

🏠 **Hotel Grand** **** [223 B3] (35 rooms,
5 suites) Trg Živojina Mišića 1; ✆ 227 133, 232 112;
e hotelgrandvaljevo@narcisdivcibare.com;
w narcisdivcibare.com. The smartest hotel in town,
with its own national restaurant & conference
facilities. €€€

🏠 **Hotel Narcis** *** [223 C3] (78 rooms,
4 apts) Vlade Danilovića 1; ✆ 221 140;

e hoteldivcibare@narcisdivcibare.com;
w narcisdivcibare.com. Fully renovated in 2009, all
rooms come with TV, modern bathroom & minibar.
€€€–€€

🏠 **Hotel Jablanica** ** [223 D1] (51 rooms)
Obrena Nikolića 18; ✆ 222 367, 227 415. Tucked
away in the northern part of town close to the
hospital. €€

🏠 **Pansion Bubica** [223 D4] (11 rooms) Mirka Obradovića 1; 📞229 182; e info@bubica.co.rs; w bubica.co.rs. Clean & stylish pension close to the Kolubara River. €€

🏠 **Pansion Bulevar** [223 B2] (12 rooms) Vuka Karadžića 36; 📞220 185; e pansionvaljevo@gmail. com; w bulevarvaljevo.com. This pleasant, small town-centre pension was upgraded in late 2009.

Small, old-fashioned rooms with AC, satellite TV & internet connection. €€

🏠 **Konak Rašević** [223 D2] (10 rooms) Radomir Đurđevića bb; 📞231 659; m 063 842 9503; e info@konakrasevic.com; w konakrasevic. com. About 4km from the centre of town on the Belgrade road, this motel has clean simple rooms with AC & cable TV. €

✖ **WHERE TO EAT AND DRINK** The area around the riverbank has plenty of café-bars and restaurants, many of which have live music in summer. The pedestrianised street of Kneza Miloša [223 A3] has a procession of trendy outdoor cafés and bars, while Birčaninova across the river has more of the same as well as restaurants that tend to be more traditional. The outdoor terrace of the **Ponte Bianca café** [223 B4] on Trg Vojvode Mišića by the footbridge is a good place to watch the world go by. There are lots of decent bakeries in the town, three on the upper part of Vuka Karadžića alone – the **Domino** bakery and pizza [223 B4] (*Trg Vojvode Mišića 10;* 📞 *347 755*) opposite the museum is a good choice. **Caffe Corner** [223 C3] (*Karađorđeva 93;* 📞 *238 238*) is open very early in the morning and makes a convenient stop for early bus departures, as is **Fontana** [223 B3] (📞 *220 443*), a café-bakery on the same street. The list below offers further suggestions.

🍷 **Šofer bar** [223 B2] Vuka Karadžića 56; 📞221 476. Relaxed café-bar with comfortable armchairs. There is also an adjoining restaurant. €€

✖ **Hemingvej** [223 B4] Čika Ljubina 12; 📞242 627. On the corner by the bridge, this is a stylish bar that serves pizzas & decent pasta & chicken dishes. €€–€

✖ **Intermeco** [223 B4] Birčaninova 36; 📞230 461. By the bridge in the Tešnar district, this traditional Serbian restaurant has an outdoor riverside terrace. €€–€

✖ **Jefimija** [223 B4] Brčaninova 40; 📞214 765. A traditional Serbian restaurant in the Tešnar district. €€–€

✖ **Platani** [223 A4] Birčaninova 149; 📞3522 991. On the edge of town across the river, this homely traditional restaurant has good food & wine & a shady garden for summer dining. €€–€

✖ **Plavi Cvet** [223 C2] Vlade Danilovića 31; 📞221 816. Small cosy restaurant with tasty Serbian food at good prices. €€–€

✖ **Zlatibor** [223 A3] Trg Vojvode Mišića 13; 📞221 524. A friendly, old-fashioned restaurant with attentive waiters, an English menu, & fish as well as grilled meat dishes. Try a *valjevska snicla* – pork *escalope* covered with cheese, an omelette, bacon bits & *kajmak*. You can order cheese by the kilo here too! €€–€

OTHER PRACTICALITIES
$ **Bank** Procredit [223 D2] Doktora Pantića 118; 📞244 723

✚ **Health centre** [223 A2] Vladike Nikolaja 5; 📞227 112

✉ **Post office** [223 B3] Vuka Karadžića 5; 📞294 013

WHAT TO SEE AND DO The historic **Tešnjar quarter** [223 A/B4], a centre for 19th-century trade, on the south bank of the Kolubara River, has a pleasant old-fashioned charm; its cobblestone streets now house many of Valjevo's cafés, restaurants and workshops. This well-preserved street is something of a living museum and is considered sufficiently authentic to have been used as the setting for a number of Serbian period films over the past few years. Kneza Miloša, a pedestrian zone on the opposite bank that is lined with cafés, is another enjoyable place for a stroll.

The town's oldest building is **Muselim's residence** [223 B3], a rare 18th-century Turkish building (⏰ *10.00–17.30 Tue–Sat*), whose cellar served as a prison for dukes Aleksa Nenadović and Ilije Birčanin as they awaited execution in 1804. It now houses a permanent display of costumes, weaponry and documents that relate to the national uprisings of the early 19th century. This same building used to house the collection of the town museum but this moved in 1969 to new premises at Trg Vojvode Mišića 3, close to the Hotel Grand. The **National Museum of Valjevo** [223 B3] (*Narodni muzej Valjevo; Živojina Mišića 3;* ☎ *221 041, 224 641;* e *info@museum. org.rs;* w *museum.org.rs;* ⏰ *10.00–18.00 Tue–Thu, 10.00–21.00 Fri, 10.00–18.00 Sat, closed Sun/Mon*) is now located in an elegant 19th-century building that was formerly the old grammar school.

The **Nenadović Tower (Kula Nenadovića)** [223 B1] stands on Kličevac Hill just north of the town centre. It was built in 1813 by Jakov Nenadović and his son Jevrem as a storehouse for munitions, and utilised stone from another nearby ruined tower. The three-storey tower fell into Turkish hands shortly after construction and was used by them as a dungeon. To reach the tower, walk north along Vojvode Mišića across a bridge over a little stream and past a junction with Bolera Pizza on the right and an army camp on the left. Take the next road to the right after a bus stop. Close to here, immediately east of Vojvode Mišića, at the junction of Železniča and Vuka Karadžića, is an alarmingly large **sculptured head** [223 B2] of the town's most famous son, Vuk Karadžić, complete with voluminous moustache.

RAVNA GORA

Ravna Gora (Flat Hill) is the name given to the upland plateau west of the 864m peak of Mt Suvobor that lies between the towns of Gornji Milanovac and Valjevo. In recent years Ravna Gora has become a place of annual pilgrimage for Serbian royalists who travel here each May to pay tribute to the memory of Dragoljub Mihailović, the World War II Chetnik leader. The date is significant because it was on 13 May 1941 that Colonel Mihailović gathered his royalist forces to declare their uprising against the German occupation of Yugoslavia and instigate what became known as the Ravna Gora Movement. As things panned out, the Chetniks were to become embroiled in a far more complex battle that counted Josip Broz Tito's rival Partisans among their enemies alongside the Nazis and the Ustaša. After the end of the war, following a victory by Partisan forces that had received both Allied and Soviet support, Mihailović was executed by Tito's new communist government after a trial that found him guilty of treason.

In recent years, the Chetnik movement has been rehabilitated to some extent and the royalist ideal has proved popular with nationalists polarised by what they see as the failure of communism. A monument to Mihailović – or 'Uncle Draža' as he is known by his followers – was erected in the 1990s, together with a church dedicated to St George that was completed in 1998. For the past few years, gatherings of tens of thousands of nationalist sympathisers have been taking place here each May, most notably on the Saturday that follows 13 May. As might be expected, such gatherings are accompanied by rousing nationalist songs, fluttering Chetnik flags and the plentiful consumption of grilled meats and *rakija*.

The south of the town also has a couple of interesting sights. **Marko's Chair (Markova stolica)** [223 C4] is a view spot over the town and the Kolubara River that is reached by taking the track that leads up off Birčaninova once it has turned south from the main Tešnar zone. There is also an attractive **watermill** [223 C4] on the River Gradac, a tributary of the Kolubara River, best reached by following Knez Mihailova southeast from Birčaninova and turning right just after the railway.

6

Vojvodina

The name Vojvodina translates as 'Duchy' or 'Dukedom', a reference to the long years in which this vast tract of land north of the Danube belonged to the Austrian Empire. The region had been inhabited since Palaeolithic times before the Romans first visited the area in the 1st century BC. By the beginning of the 2nd century AD, under the command of the emperor Trajan, most of the Banat was under Roman rule. The Romans built the town of Sirmium as their capital, choosing a site by the Danube where present-day Sremska Mitrovica is located. No fewer than four emperors were born here – Aurelianus, Probus, Gratianus and Constantius II – before the town was conquered by Hungarians in AD441, thus ending Roman rule in the region. It was subsequently destroyed by the Avars in 582.

A migration into the region began in the second half of the 4th century and continued until the end of the 9th century. The settlers were of diverse origins: Byzantines, Huns, Avars and Slavs. Magyars started to arrive in number during the 9th century and Hungarians ruled Vojvodina until the 16th century. Serbs started to settle the region from the 14th century onwards, with the result that Vojvodina's population was a relatively balanced Serbian–Hungarian mix by the early 16th century.

In 1526, following the Battle of Mohács, on the River Danube in present-day Hungary, the Ottomans took control of Vojvodina. This precipitated a massive depopulation of the region and it remained this way until the late 17th century when the Habsburg Empire successfully laid claim to the region.

Following their new territorial gains, the Austrians were intent on setting up a defensive zone between themselves and the Turks. They encouraged new migrants to settle in the region, which by now had become quite sparsely populated. Many came to take advantage of the offer, attracted by the promise of fertile farmland. Among the first to arrive were more Serbs from the south, ever fearful of a Turkish resurgence in their homeland. Within a relatively short period of time, something in the order of 40,000 Serb families took up residence here in the latter part of the 17th century. Land was not the sole attraction: the Austrians were pragmatists and allowed Serbs to freely practise their Orthodox religion, which encouraged others to follow in their steps. Soon after this migration a new Serbian Orthodox Patriarchate was established at **Sremski Karlovci** near present-day **Novi Sad**, the same town in which the Treaty of Karlowitz had been signed in 1699 to legitimise the Habsburgs' claim on the region.

Other migrants followed in the wake of the Serbs, especially those in search of land or freedom from persecution – or both. What ensued created an ethnic and cultural mix unsurpassed anywhere in Europe at the time. The Serbs were soon joined by **Hungarians**, **Croats**, **Romanians**, **Slovaks**, **Germans**, **Roma** and many others, even by migrants from much further away, like **Greeks** and **Macedonians**

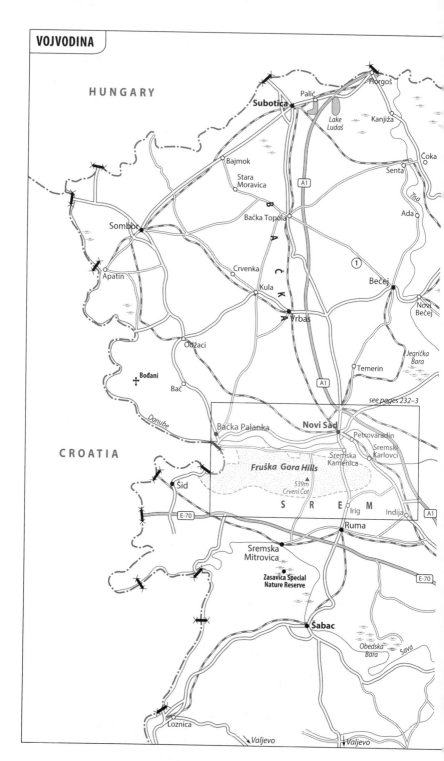

HUNGARY

Subotica
Palić
Lake Ludaš
Horgoš
Kanjiža

Čoka

Bajmok
Stara Moravica
A1
Senta
Tisa
Ada

Bačka Topola

B
A
Č
K
A

Crvenka
Kula
Vrbas

1

Bečej
Novi Bečej

Sombor

Apatin

Odžaci

Jegrička Bara

Temerin
A1

Bođani
Bač

Danube

Bačka Palanka
Novi Sad
see pages 232–3
Petrovaradin
Sremski Karlovci

CROATIA

Fruška Gora Hills
Sremska Kamenica

539m
Crveni Čot

Šid
E-70

S   R   E   M
Irig
Indija
A1

Ruma

Sremska Mitrovica

Zasavica Special Nature Reserve

E-70

Šabac
Obedska Bara
Sava

Loznica
Valjevo
Valjevo

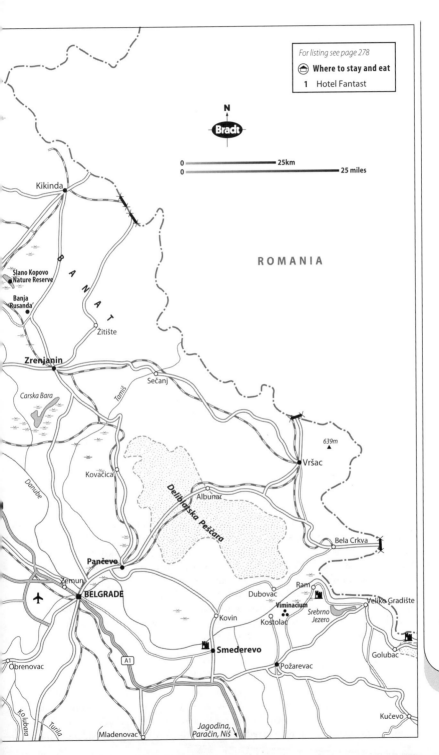

For listing see page 278

⊖ **Where to stay and eat**
1   Hotel Fantast

N

Bradt

0 ▬▬▬▬▬▬▬ 25km
0 ▬▬▬▬▬▬▬▬▬▬ 25 miles

Kikinda

R O M A N I A

B
A
N
A
T

Slano Kopovo
Nature Reserve

Banja
'Rusanda'

Žitište

Zrenjanin

Sečanj

Tamiš

Carska Bara

639m ▲

Vršac

Kovačica

Deliblatska Peščara

Albunar

Donube

Bela Crkva

Pančevo

Zemun

Ram

Dubovac

Veliko Gradište

BELGRADE

Viminacium

Srebrno
Jezero

Kovin

Kostolac

Golubac

Obrenovac

A1

Smederevo

Požarevac

Kolubara

Turila

Mladenovac

Jagodina,
Paraćin, Niš

Kučevo

Vojvodina

6

from the south, and **Ruthenians** from the Ukraine. This human tapestry has left its mark on the land and the same cultural diversity still exists in Vojvodina today as the descendants of the original settlers continue to speak their native languages and observe the cultures of their forefathers within the boundaries of modern Serbia.

With the abolishment of the military frontier between 1867 and 1881, Bačka (Hungarian: Bacska) and the Banat came under Hungarian rule, while Srem was claimed by the crown of Croatia-Slavonia. The end of World War I, and the dismantling of the Austro-Hungarian Empire that followed, allowed the three Vojvodina provinces to form a union with what was then known as the Kingdom of Serbia on 25 November 1918. Shortly after, on 1 December of the same year, Vojvodina officially became part of the newly formed Kingdom of Serbs, Croats and Slovenes, which went on to become known as Yugoslavia from 1929 onwards. After a brief occupation by Axis powers during World War II the province was restored to Yugoslavia once more and became part of Marshal Tito's new communist state. Later, in 1974, Vojvodina was given full autonomous status within the Yugoslav federation, a freedom that was subsequently rescinded by Slobodan Milošević in 1990.

It is to the credit of Yugoslavia's post-war leaders that the province's cultural diversity has been preserved and even encouraged. Following World War II, Vojvodina's children were taught in schools that allowed their native tongue to be used as well as Serbo-Croat. Such tolerance in the face of the rampant nationalism at work in other parts of the country goes some of the way to explain why Vojvodina's citizens are not always completely happy with the political machinations that take place in central government in Belgrade. The loss of the province's autonomy in 1990 did little to win hearts and minds in favour of the Milošević government, or to proselytise for the Serbian nationalist cause. However, Milošević's inglorious fall from power in 2000 allowed a new era of reform to flourish and, in 2002, the province's autonomy was partially restored by the Omnibus Law that affirmed the provincial administration's jurisdiction over matters such as health, education and social care. A new statute was adopted by the Vojvodina Provincial Assembly in 2008, and after minor amendments was approved by the Serbian Parliament the following year. The statute was officially proclaimed in December 2009 and came into force on 1 January 2010.

Vojvodina is composed of three discrete geographical divisions: **Srem**, **Bačka** and **Banat**. In a region in which the land for the most part is endlessly flat, it is the province's rivers that create the geographical divisions. Srem is the region that lies south of the Danube and north of the Sava, and which extends west into northeast Croatia. It contains the only noteworthy hills in the province – the **Fruška Gora** range. North of here, the province is divided laterally by the Tisa River; the western portion is known as Bačka and the eastern part, which, in geographical terms at least, extends into southeast Romania, is the Banat.

This chapter will first deal with the Vojvodina capital, **Novi Sad,** and its immediate surroundings to the south that belong to **Srem** – Sremski Karlovci, Fruška Gora, Sremska Mitrovica – before dealing with the rest of **Bačka** – Sombor, Subotica – and then the area east of the Tisa River, the **Banat**.

NOVI SAD (НОВИ САД) *Telephone code 021*

Capital of Vojvodina and, with a population of more than a quarter of a million, Serbia's second-largest city, Novi Sad is a relatively prosperous, commercial, industrial and university town on the north shore of the Danube in the Bačka region of the province. Long referred to as the 'Serbian Athens', Novi Sad has always been a centre of culture and learning and the atmosphere of its small but elegant city centre seems somehow a little more refined than that of the capital. Instead of looking south and east as Belgrade has historically done, Novi Sad's cultural ties are firmly to the north and west.

With a diverse and mixed population of Serbs, Hungarians, Croats and Slovaks, together with a sizeable but rather downcast Roma population, the city's cultural resonances bring to mind Budapest and Vienna rather than Belgrade or Sarajevo. As one writer has already noted, Novi Sad can be said to be the most easterly city in western Europe, and the most westerly city in eastern Europe. Famous sons – or rather, daughters – of the city include Mileva Einstein, née Marić, wife of Albert (the great man himself lived here for a few years before World War I), and Monica Seleš, former world number one tennis star (page 57).

The city's most striking feature, the **Petrovaradin Fortress** [233 G5], is not in Novi Sad itself but across the Danube in the separate town of Petrovaradin (which belongs to Srem rather than Bačka). Three bridges link the two sides of the river and, although all of these were destroyed during the hostilities of 1999, they have all since been replaced. The city centre has a number of noteworthy buildings, mostly in the Baroque style, together with some excellent museums and art galleries. It is also a very lively city, with a large student population and a dynamic café-bar scene.

It is quite feasible to visit the city as a day trip from Belgrade if time is short but a longer stay here will pay dividends. Not only are there various sights in the city to enjoy, Novi Sad also serves as an excellent base for trips to other parts of Vojvodina, as well as excursions into the **Fruška Gora** hills that lie just to the south.

HISTORY Originally known as **Petrovaradinski sanac** (Petrovaradin's trench), the city was renamed Novi Sad, 'New Plan', following a 1748 royal decree that awarded the settlement free city status. The term 'Serbian Athens' came into play during the 19th century when Novi Sad became famous as a centre of culture and learning. The city's theatre, the oldest in Serbia, was established during this period.

The original settlement had developed in tandem with the growth of the fortress at Petrovaradin across the river. This had started life as a Roman fort, with further fortifications being added in the medieval period. It was here in 1716 that the Turkish army were soundly defeated by the forces of Prince Eugene of Savoy. Most of what remains of the fortress today dates from around this time.

A large part of Novi Sad was destroyed in 1848 during a garrison revolt by Hungarian soldiers, who bombarded the city from their vantage point for a number of months. They were finally tricked into surrendering but only after they had succeeded in flattening almost two-thirds of the town. Consequently, much of what remains today dates from the latter part of the 19th century and after.

During World War II, Novi Sad was once again occupied by Hungarian troops, this time by those of the Axis persuasion, while across the Danube in Petrovaradin, Croatian Ustaša troops had control.

With the NATO attacks against Slobodan Milošević's rogue-state Yugoslavia in the spring of 1999, Novi Sad came once more under bombardment and went on to suffer greater casualties than the capital did in terms of human life, environmental pollution and destroyed infrastructure. The attacks came as a surreal spectacle for the city's bemused population. It was hard to understand just why they were being targeted: few of them were fans of their leader's nationalist policies and besides, Kosovo, the epicentre of the hostilities, was at the other end of the country.

NATO missiles first struck the city on 24 March 1999. In the days that followed, further attacks hit two of the bridges that connected Novi Sad with Petrovaradin and

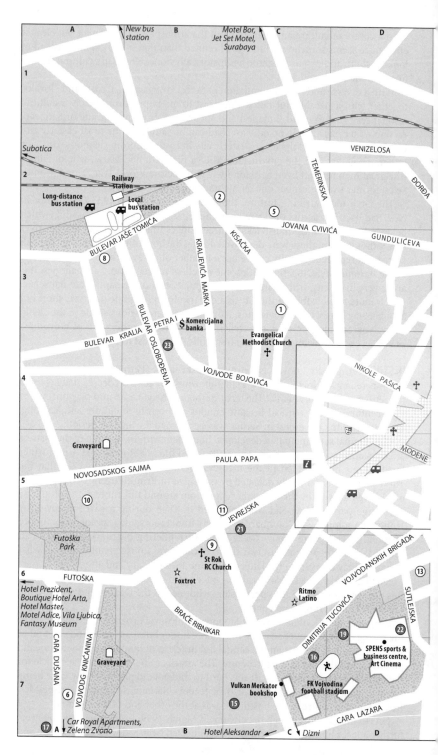

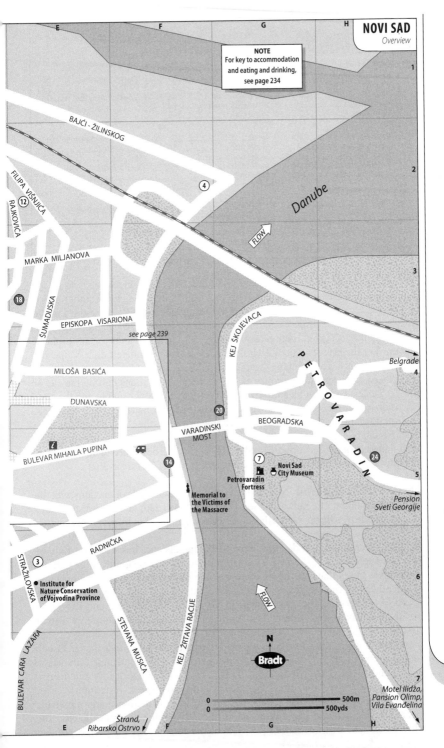

NOTE
For key to accommodation
and eating and drinking,
see page 234

E   F   G   H

1

BAJĆI - ŽILINSKOG

FILIPA VIŠNJIĆA

RAJKOVIĆA

12

4

2

Danube

FLOW

MARKA MILJANOVA

ŠUMADIJSKA

18

3

KEJ SKOJEVACA

EPISKOPA VISARIONA

see page 239

MILOŠA BASIĆA

P E T R O V A R A D I N

Belgrade

4

DUNAVSKA

20

BEOGRADSKA

VARADINSKI
MOST

24

i

BULEVAR MIHAILA PUPINA

14

7

Novi Sad
City Museum

Petrovaradin
Fortress

5

Pension
Sveti Georgije

Memorial to
the Victims of
the Massacre

RADNIČKA

3

STRAŽILOVSKA

Institute for
Nature Conservation
of Vojvodina Province

6

FLOW

BULEVAR CARA LAZARA

STEVANA MUSIĆA

KEJ ŽRTAVA RACIJE

N

Bradt

0   500m
0   500yds

Motel Ilidža,
Pansion Olimp,
Vila Evanđelina

E   F   G   H

Štrand,
Ribarsko Ostrvo

🛏 **Where to stay**

1	Bela Lađa.....................C3	6	Hotel Ile de France...........A7	11	Planeta Inn.......................B5
2	Bonaca Apartments.....B2	7	Hotel Leopold I................G5	12	Podbara............................E2
3	City...................................E6	8	Hotel Novi Sad..................A3	13	Voyager Apartments.....D6
4	Hotel Aurora..................F2	9	Hotel Panorama Garni.....B6		
5	Hotel Garni Rimski.......C2	10	Hotel Park..........................A5		

Off map

Boutique Hotel Arta........A6	Jet Set...................................C1	Pension Sveti Georgije.....H5
Car Royal Apartments.....A7	Motel Adice.........................A6	Vila Evanđelina.................H7
Hotel Aleksandar.............C7	Motel Bor............................C1	Vila Ljubica.......................... A6
Hotel Master...................... A6	Motel Ilidža........................ H7	Zeleno Zvono.....................A7
Hotel Prezident.................A6	Pansion Olimp..................H7	

✖ **Where to eat and drink**

14	Atelje.................................F5	19	Ognjište.........................D6	*Off map*
	Bela Lađa.................(see 1)	20	Parobrod.........................G4	Dizni.....................................C7
15	Borsalino..........................C7	21	Pekara Klas....................C5	Surabaya.............................C1
16	Chicken Tikka...................C7	22	Plava Frajla....................D6	
17	Dvor...................................A7	23	Savoca Pizzeria.............B4	
18	Kafanica Đorđa.................E3	24	Trag.................................H5	

Sremska Kamenica south of the river. On 5 April, Novi Sad's oil refinery was hit for the first time, releasing a large cloud of toxic smoke over the city. Another attack on the refinery came two days later as NATO attempted to destroy the third of the city's bridges. The oil refinery continued to be targeted and, on the night of 16 April, explosions that occurred there released dangerous chemicals into the atmosphere. The third of the bridges – the Žeželj Bridge – was finally rendered useless after the attacks of 26 April. The bombing campaign continued until 9 June, by which time the oil refinery had been attacked once again, electrical installations outside the city at Rimski Šančevi had been hit cutting off the electricity and water supply, and the city's television transmitter, sited in the Fruška Gora to the south, had been badly damaged.

The Liberty Bridge that leads to Sremska Kamenica across the Danube River has since been rebuilt. It is expected that the new Žeželj Bridge that will replace the temporary road–railway bridge used for trains and heavy vehicles will be opened to traffic in 2017. The city is set to become one of three European Capitals of Culture in 2021.

GETTING THERE AND AWAY Novi Sad has excellent bus and rail connections with the rest of the country. The railway station [232 A2] (📞 *443 200*) and long-distance bus station sit side by side on the north side of the town about 1km from the city centre.

By bus Over 30 buses a day link Novi Sad's **long-distance bus station** at Bulevar Jaše Tomića 6 [232 A2] (📞 *444 021, 444 022, 444 023*) with Belgrade; some of these are express buses that use the motorway, while others are slower and stop more frequently along the way. Fares are between 500din and 800din, depending on the speed of the service. The larger towns in Vojvodina like Subotica and Zrenjanin are also well connected, with at least ten departures a day, but even more distant destinations like Niš or Novi Pazar have at least one direct daily service. The city has a number of international services too, with fairly regular buses to Vukovar, Osijek and Zagreb (Croatia), Sarajevo and Banja Luka (Bosnia), Budapest (Hungary), Ohrid and Skopje (Macedonia) and Budva, Tivat and Podgorica (Montenegro). The bus station has the usual facilities you would expect: restaurants, cafés, snack kiosks, *garderoba*, pay toilets, but no tourist information. Large timetable boards, inside and out, give full details of the services to and from the city. The city has another **new bus station** [232 A1] at the corner of Sentandrejski put and

Novosadskog partizanskog odreda a little further out near 'Novosadska Mlekara' (Novi Sad's dairy plant), but this was not being widely used at the time of writing.

Buses to closer destinations in the immediate Novi Sad area like Sremski Karlovci, Sremska Kamenica, Begeč and Veternik leave from the terminus beside the long-distance bus station, in front of the train station. Some of these services, like buses to Sremski Karlovci, may also be picked up in the city itself.

By train All of the trains that link Belgrade with Budapest and the north stop at Novi Sad's **railway station** [232 A2] (✆ 443 200) and so there are relatively good rail connections too. Originating in Belgrade, two trains a day serve Budapest and Vienna, one in the morning and one late at night. Of the domestic services, 11 trains leave daily for Subotica, three run to Sombor, two to Zrenjanin and there is an overnight service to Bar on the Montenegrin coast. The trains that run to Belgrade are generally a little slower than the bus but they are also slightly cheaper. The exceptions are the international services that stop here *en route* to the capital. If travelling to Belgrade by train avoid catching those bound for 'Beograd Centar' only, as this station is inconveniently situated for getting to the Old City by public transport (it is intended that it will eventually replace Belgrade's current main station near the bus station).

By air Novi Sad does not have its own commercial airport, but it is only 1 hour's drive from Belgrade's Nikola Tesla Airport. Arriving from abroad, it is possible to pre-book a transfer between Budapest or Belgrade Airport and Novi Sad with local taxi firms like **Genelux** (✆ 4722 492) or **Heligon** (m 064 2320 816); these charge for the whole vehicle so the cost will be dependent on the total number of passengers – if all seats are taken it will be around €10 per person. Transfers can also be booked online at w belgradeairporttransfer.com. The Air Serbia office is at Bulevar Mihajla Pupina 18 [239 F3] (✆ 457 585, 457 588; e novisadto@airserbia.com; w airserbia.com).

GETTING AROUND
City bus Most of what you will want to see in Novi Sad is close enough to visit on foot but a couple of the city bus services are useful, in particular those that link the city centre with the long-distance bus and railway stations. To reach the city centre from the bus or train station, take a number 4 bus from the line of bus stops in front of the train station. This heads towards the centre along Bulevar oslobođenja, the main road into the centre, turns left along Jevrejska and then right along Uspenska and on to Bulevar Mihajla Pupina where you can alight for the central pedestrian zone. To reach the long-distance bus or train station from the centre, simply reverse the process and catch a number 4 heading in the opposite direction. To reach Petrovaradin Fortress from the centre take bus number 3. The fare for a single journey in the city is 55din and you pay the driver.

Taxi The minimum fare is around 100din. To take a taxi from the train or bus station to a central hotel should cost about 200–300din. The following are reliable taxi firms that can be called by phone.

🚗 **City plus** ✆4724 333, 450 450
🚗 **Delta** ✆553 333
🚗 **Dobro Jutro** ✆322 222
🚗 **Elit** ✆500 555

🚗 **Lux** ✆6300 000
🚗 **Maxi Novosađani** ✆451 111
🚗 **Naš** ✆6300 300
🚗 **Pan** ✆455 555

Car hire

🚗 **Europcar** [232 A3] Hotel Novi Sad, Bulevar Jase Tomića 1; ☎443 188; w europcar.com

🚗 **Inex** [233 E6] Stražilovska 3; ☎526 666

🚗 **Sixt** [232 A5] Hotel Park, Novosadskog sajma 35; ☎549 520; w sixt.co.uk

TOURIST INFORMATION [239 A4] (*Jevrejska 10;* ☎ *6617 343, 421 811;* e *tons@turizamns.rs;* w *novisad.travel/en;* ⊕ *09.00–17.00 Mon–Fri, 10.00–15.00 Sat, closed Sun*) This excellent information centre in the city centre has helpful and dedicated English-speaking staff that can provide visitors with city maps, museum information and details of current events, as well as advising on accommodation and transport. They have numerous brochures available detailing the city's museums and galleries, as well as booklets on aspects of Novi Sad's diverse ethnic make-up and history.

There is another office at Bulevar Mihajla Pupina 9 [239 E3] that keeps shorter working hours (☎ *421 811, 421 812;* ⊕ *08.00–16.00 Mon–Fri, closed w/ends*).

For further information on Novi Sad and Vojvodina, see w visitvojvodina.com, w vojvodinaonline.com or w visitnovisad.rs.

LOCAL TOUR OPERATORS Below are listed some of the main operators in the city:

Autoturist [239 C2] Mite Ružića 2; ☎523 863, 451 156; e autoturist.ns@gmail.com; w autoturist-ns. com. This operator runs trips to the Fruška Gora monasteries & the wine cellars at Irig. They also do excursions to Sremski Karlovci, Kovilj & the castle & agricultural museum at Kulpin.

Bon Voyage [239 B3] Kralja Aleksandra 14; ☎6621 244, 6611 944; e office@bonvoyage.rs; w bonvoyage.rs. This is an operator that runs a number of city tours, wine excursions & trips to Fruška Gora monasteries.

Donna Vista Travel [239 D2] Dunavska 6; ☎426 126, 425 705; m 063 539 013; e donatour@open. telekom.rs. Organises traditional dinners at rural *salaš* & monastery tours.

Elnostours [232 D6] Maksima Gorkog 10; ☎528 244; also Trg Slobode 2; ☎524 778; e elnostours@ elnostours.rs; w elnostours.rs. Wine-tasting, monastery tours, Novi Sad sightseeing & Fruška Gora hiking are all offered by this operator.

GoTravel [232 B3] Bulevar oslobođenja 20; ☎3284 604; e info@gotravel.rs; w gotravel. rs. Provide a guide service for Novi Sad & surroundings, & Fruška Gora monasteries. Also vineyard tours.

Magelan Corporation [239 C1] Nikole Pašića 7; ☎420 680, 4721 741; e office@magelan.rs; w magelan.rs. Magelan provide a wide range of services: walking tours of Novi Sad & Petrovaradin

Fortress (min 4 persons); full- & half-day boat trips on the Danube (min 6–8); mountain-bike tours of Fruška Gora that last 2–8hrs (min 6); full-day visits to the Fruška Gora monasteries; full-day birdwatching/photo safari tours of Fruška Gora with a guide (6–10 persons); & Sremski Karlovci wine & honey excursions. They can also organise longer trips that take in more of Vojvodina & Serbia (page 64).

Market Tours Bulevar Cara Lazara 55; ☎468 409, 6367 712; e markettours.ns@gmail.com; w markettours.co.rs. Market Tours organise Danube boat tours between Apr & Oct (min 5 persons). They can also arrange fishing w/ends (or weeks) on the Danube, as well as Fruška Gora monastery tours & Sremski Karlovci vineyard visits. They are able to provide fishing permits & rent out boats for those with an interest in fishing.

PanaComp Bulevar Cara Lazara 96; ☎466 075, 466 076, 466 077; e info@panacomp.net, office@ panacomp.net; w panacomp.net. PanaComp is an incoming tourist agency offering a wide variety of tour packages that take in Novi Sad, Fruška Gora & beyond.

Stalis Tours [232 C5] Pap Pavle 27; ☎421 257; m 063 506 823; e stalisns@eunet.rs; w stalis. co.rs. Stalis offer day tours of Srem, Novi Sad historical sightseeing tours & visits to Salaš 137.

 WHERE TO STAY As you might expect for a city of this size, there is a good variety of places to stay. There is now a good choice of upmarket hotels in the city as well as plenty

of reasonable mid-range choices. In addition to hotels, several hostels have opened for business in recent years to fill some of the gap in the budget market, and those listed below are just some of the more long-standing ones. Websites like w hostelworld.com, w hostels.com and w hostelbookers.com offer a wider selection that can be booked online. Apartments and motels are also available, though some are outside the town centre and thus best suited to those travelling by car.

In general, accommodation prices tend to be a little higher in July when the EXIT festival is on, especially in the hostels and smaller boutique hotels (for details of the festival, see pages 245–7).

Sremska Kamenica is a satellite town, 5km away in Srem across the Danube and has a few more options for those who do not wish or need to be in the city centre. See page 241 for listings.

Luxury

🏠 **Hotel Leopold I** ***** [233 G5] (45 rooms, 13 suites) Petrovaradinska tvrđava bb; ☎ 4887 878; e office@leopoldns.com; w leopoldns.com. An elegant & luxurious 5-star located at the Petrovaradin Fortress across the river with some of the best views in the city. Rooms (€€€€€) on the 1st floor are in late Renaissance style, while those on the 2nd come with modern décor (€€€€) & are less expensive. Suites are named after famous historical figures. Italian, Thai & national restaurants & aperitif bar. €€€€€–€€€€

🏠 **Hotel Park** ***** [232 A5] (182 rooms, 57 apts, 6 residences) Novosadskog sajma 35; ☎ 4888 888; e info@hotelparkns.com; w hotelparkns.com. This large hotel is situated well away from the city centre, close to Futog Park & the site of the Novi Sad Fair & Sajmiste Sports Centre. The hotel was taken into private ownership in 2004 to be completely refurbished & reopened as the city's first 5-star hotel in 2006. It offers the whole range of facilities & services you might expect of a top-notch hotel: car rental, limousine service, sauna, swimming pool, a large conference hall, à la carte restaurant, aperitif bar & fitness centre. It even provides boxes & a kitchen for dogs. €€€€€–€€€€

Upmarket

🏠 **Hotel Aleksandar** **** [232 C7] (20 rooms, 7 suites) Bulevar Cara Lazara 79; ☎ 4804 400; e recepcija@aleksandar-hotel.com; w hotel-aleksandar.rs. A modern business hotel with facilities that include aperitif bar, restaurant, exchange office, plasma TV lounge & conference hall. All rooms have AC, cable TV, internet connection & minibar. €€€€–€€€

🏠 **Hotel Centar** **** [239 B3] (40 rooms, 2 suites) Uspenska 1; ☎ 4776 333; e recepcija@ hotel-centar.rs; w hotel-centar.rs. A brand-new, futuristic-looking hotel in the heart of the city centre opposite the National Theatre. Large stylish rooms, non-smoking available & special room designed for disabled visitors. €€€€–€€€

🏠 **Hotel Prezident** ***** [232 A6] (39 rooms, 5 apts) Futoška 109; ☎ 4877 444; e reservations@prezidenthotel.com; w prezidenthotel.com. Convenient for Novi Sad Fair site but less so city centre, aimed squarely at a business clientele, this has a wellness centre & indoor swimming pool. Standard rooms have Wi-Fi, minibar & flatscreen TVs. Suites have jacuzzi & terrace. Lower rate at w/ends. €€€€–€€€ (presidential suite €€€€€)

Mid-range

🏠 **Boutique Hotel Arta** *** [232 A6] (10 rooms, 2 suites) Heroja Pinkija 12; ☎ 6804 500; e office@boutiquehotelarta.rs; w boutiquehotelarta.rs. A small, stylish boutique hotel with modern décor, located in the south of the city. Bar, garden & Wi-Fi. €€€

🏠 **Hotel Ile de France** **** [232 A7] (14 suites) Cara Dušana 41; ☎ 6362 382; m 063 1939 784; e office@iledefrance.co.rs; w iledefrance. co.rs. This relatively new hotel in an elegant Baroque building close to Futoški Park offers suites with a luxurious French ambience. Each suite has balcony, dining room, TV & internet connection. A buffet b/fast is provided. Secure car parking. €€€

🏠 **Hotel Master** **** [232 A6] (47 rooms, 7 suites) Brace Popović bb; ☎ 4878 700; e office@a-hotel-master.com; w a-hotel-master.com. Another well-appointed business hotel near Novi Sad Fair.

⊖ **Where to stay**

1	Downtown...........................C2	5	Hotel Putnik.................D3	9	Lazin...............................B2
2	Fontana...............................B1	6	Hotel Veliki...................C1	10	Sova...............................C3
3	Hotel Centar......................B3	7	Hotel Vojvodina.............C3	11	TAL Centar....................C2
4	Hotel Mediteraneo...........D2	8	Hotel Zenit....................D2	12	Teresa...........................A2

✕ **Where to eat and drink**

13	Alla Lanterna......................E1	21	Gondola..........................E3	30	'Only Fools and
14	Arhiv...................................D2	22	Irish Pub 'Red Cow'......D2		Horses' Pub.................C2
15	Čerčil..................................B1	23	La Forza..........................C2	31	Pasha.............................E2
16	Cezar...................................C3	24	Lazino Tele..................... B2	32	Pivnica Gusan..............C2
17	Dva Anđela.........................C2	25	Lipa.................................C2	33	Sečuan......................... D2
18	EmChi..................................A2	26	London Pub....................B2	34	Šeherezada
19	Evropa poslastičarnica.....D2	27	Marina............................B4		poslastičarnica...........C2
20	Fish & Zeleniš....................B1	28	Martha's Pub..................C2	35	Trčika.............................B4
	Fontana.........................(see 2)	29	Modena...........................C3		

All rooms with AC, minibar & internet acces. Room suitable for disabled persons. €€€

🏠 **Hotel Mediteraneo** ** [239 D2] (11 rooms) Ilije Ognjanovića 10; ☎ 427 135; e mediteraneo@sbb.rs; w hotelmediteraneo.rs. A modern, central hotel in the pedestrian zone close to the Hotel Putnik. The nicely furnished rooms are en suite & have AC, cable TV, internet access & phone. €€€

🏠 **Hotel Novi Sad** *** [232 A3] (112 rooms) Bulevar Jaše Tomića bb; ☎ 442 511; e info@ hotelnovisad.rs; w hotelnovisad.co.rs. This large, traditional hotel is very convenient for the bus & train stations but at some distance from the city centre. It has a 250-seat restaurant, conference hall, cocktail bar, sauna, discotheque & bar. €€€

🏠 **Hotel Panorama Garni** ** [232 B6] (10 rooms, 2 suites) Futoška 1a; ☎ 4801 800; e panorama@neobee.net; w hotelpanorama. co.rs. Small, central hotel with rooms that have AC, minibar, TV & internet connection. On the upper floor of a large building at a major crossroads, the entrance can be a little difficult to find first time. Take the lift to reception on the 4th floor. Excellent views from rooms over the city. €€€

🏠 **Hotel Zenit** ** [239 D2] (19 rooms) Zmaj Jovina 8; ☎ 6621 444, 6622 035, 6621 444, 6621 327; e info@hotelzenit.co.rs; w hotelzenit.co.rs. This cosy, well-run hotel, established in 1997, is right in the heart of the city centre just off Trg Slobode. Although its front entrance is through a pedestrian arcade, it has its own private parking area at the rear, reached by going along Ilije Ognjanovića by the Putnik Hotel. With just 19

rooms, it tends to fill quite fast. The rooms are modern, airy & quiet although the inner-facing rooms that lack outside windows are not such a good deal. Free coffee & Wi-Fi are available around the clock. €€€

🏠 **Hotel Aurora** *** [233 F2] (42 rooms) Beogradska kej 49B; ☎ 4871 400; e office@ hotelaurora.rs; w hotelaurora.rs. A mid-range choice in the north of the city with spacious, good-value AC rooms with minibar, internet access & satellite TV. Free parking & river view from some rooms. €€€–€€

🏠 **Hotel Putnik** *** [239 D3] (77 rooms, 6 apts) Ilije Ognjanovića 24; ☎ 6615 555; e info@ hotelputnik.rs; w hotelputnik.rs. Fully renovated in 2010, this good-value old favourite has a very handy central location just off Trg Slobode. Bar, restaurant, exchange office & congress centre. All rooms with AC, internet access, TV & minibar. €€€–€€

🏠 **Pension Sveti Georgije** **** [233 H5] (18 rooms, 2 apts) Okrugićeva 1; ☎ 432 332; e info@svetigeorgije.co.rs; w svetigeorgije. co.rs. In Petrovaradin, this pension doubles as an old people's retirement home so is probably not suitable for those who want to party. Each room has minibar, TV & AC. Long-term lease can be arranged. €€€–€€

🏠 **Planeta Inn** **** [232 B5] Jevreska 36/ Gajeve 1; ☎ 421 021; m 063 1421 021; e planetainnhotel@gmail.com; w planetainn. com. Above the 'Planeta 021' shopping centre, so 'handy for the shops' is rather an understatement. Good-value, comfortable rooms with AC, satellite TV, minibar & Wi-Fi. €€€–€€

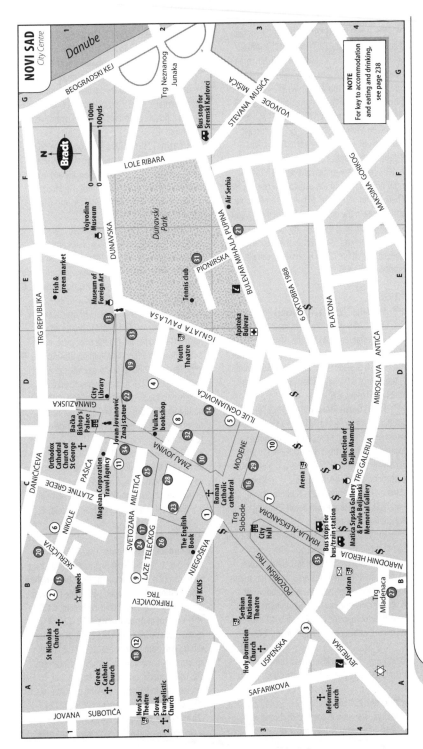

NOVI SAD
City Centre

Danube

BEOGRADSKI KEJ

Trg Neznanog
Junaka

Bus stop for
Sremski Karlovci

STEVANA MUSIĆA

VOJVODE MIŠIĆA

MAKSIMA GORKOG

NOTE
For key to accommodation
and eating and drinking,
see page 238

LOLE RIBARA

Vojvodina
Museum

Dunavski
Park

Air Serbia

BULEVAR MIHAJLA PUPINA

21

6 OKTOBRA 1988

PLATONA

ANTIĆA

MIROSLAVA

0   100m
0   100yds

N

Bradt

Fish &
green market

Museum of
Foreign Art

13

33

Tennis club

PIONIRSKA

31

Apoteka
Bulevar

TRG REPUBLIKA

DUNAVSKA

IGNJATA PAVLASA

Youth
Theatre

19

4

14

ILIJE OGNJANOVIĆA

5

10

32

8

30

MODENE

20

16

7

Roman
Catholic cathedral

City
Library

22

GIMNAZIJSKA

Jovan Jovanović
Zmaj statue

Bačka
Bishop's
Palace

Orthodox
Cathedral
Church of
St George

34

11

Magelan Corporation
Travel Agency

PAŠIĆA

ZLATNE GREDE

DANIČIĆEVA

NIKOLE

ŠKERLUĆEVA

2   15

Wheels

6

25

MILETIĆA

SVETOZARA

24   17

LAZE TELEČKOG

26

9

The English
Book

28

23

1

Trg
Slobode

KNS

NJEGOSEVA

POZORIŠNI TRG

TRIKOVIĆEV
TRG

Serbian National
Theatre

Holy Dormition
Church

USPENSKA

St Nicholas
Church

Greek
Catholic
Church

18   12

Novi Sad
Theatre

Slovak
Evangelistic
Church

JOVANA   SUBOTIĆA

SAFARIKOVA

Reformist
church

JEVRESKA

Collection of
Rajko Mamuzić

TRG GALERIJA

Matica Srpska Gallery
& Pavle Beljanski
Memorial Gallery

Arena

Bus stops for
bus/train station

City
Hall

KRALJA ALEKSANDRA

NARODNIH HEROJA

Jadran

Trg
Mladenaca

27

3

ZMAJ JOVINA

VULKAN bookshop

  239

Vojvodina   NOVI SAD (НОВИ САД)

6

✻ 🏠 **Hotel Veliki** *** [239 C1] (58 rooms, 2 apts) Nikole Pašića 24; ☎ 4723 840; e info@veliki.rs. w veliki.rs. A newish establishment in the heart of the city close to many sights & restaurants. Spacious modern rooms with Wi-Fi, AC & cable TV. Discount offered in hotel restaurant. €€€–€€

🏠 **Hotel Vojvodina** *** [239 C3] (58 rooms, 2 apts) Trg Slobode 2; ☎ 6622 122; e office@hotelvojvodina.rs; w hotelvojvodina.rs. This establishment, built in 1854, is the city's oldest hotel & has a very convenient central location right next to the Catholic cathedral & the City Hall. There is a fountain, a small bar & a comfortable sitting area in the upstairs lobby. Rooms are quite spacious & those at the back, not facing the square, tend to be quieter. The cavernous restaurant downstairs, where b/fast is served, is usually empty. €€€–€€

Budget

🏠 **Fontana** [239 B1] (12 rooms) Nikole Pašića 27; ☎ 6621 779; w restoranfontana.com. The Fontana restaurant, close to the city centre, has a few rooms to rent. The rooms are simply furnished but clean & pleasant with bathroom, AC & minibar, & the service is friendly. B/fast is served in the courtyard below. €€

🏠 **Hotel Garni Rimski** ** [232 C2] (15 rooms) Jovana Cvijića 26; ☎ 443 231, 444 765; e rimski@sezampro.rs; w hotelrimski.com. This hotel is located in a quiet street fairly close to the bus & railway stations. All rooms are complete with bathroom, central heating, cable TV, telephone & minibar. Free internet access & photocopying. The hotel has a restaurant with a non-smoking section & a conference room. €€

🏠 **Bela Lađa** [232 C3] (14 rooms) Kisačka 21 & Zlatna grede 15; ☎ 422 552, 500 190; e resbelaladja@yahoo.com; w belaladja.com. This is a friendly family restaurant that has rooms to rent – some are above the restaurant itself & some in an annex nearby. All rooms at annex have bathroom, cable TV & AC; all but 1 above restaurant at Kisačka share bathroom. €€–€

Hostels Below is just a small sample of the many hostels that Novi Sad has to offer.

🏠 **City** [233 E6] Radnička 21; ☎ 6447 208; e nscityhostel@gmail.com; w cityhostel.rs. 4-, 6-, 8- & 10-bed dorms & 1 dbl room. €

🏠 **Downtown** [239 C2] Njegoševa 2/II; ☎ 524 818; m 060 3060 090, 061 6032 9642; e downtownnovisad@gmail.com, info@hostelnovisad; w hostelnovisad.com. With superb central location next to the Catholic cathedral. Free internet, cable TV, no lockout. 4-, 6- & 8-bed dorms & private dbl rooms available with shared bathroom. €

🏠 **Lazin** [239 B2] Laze Telečkog 10; m 063 443 703; e lazinhostel@hotmail.com; w lazinhostel.net. Located in pedestrian zone on 2 levels, each with shared kitchen & living room. 1 sgl room, 2 twins & 4-, 6- & 8-bed dorms. Free internet & cable TV. €

🏠 **Podbara** [233 E2] Đorđa Rajkovića 28; ☎ 551 991; e hostel.podbara@gmail.com; w hostel-novisad.com. Well-recommended peaceful & friendly hostel, a little way north of the city centre, with clean rooms & helpful landlady. €

🏠 **Sova** [239 C3] Ilije Ognjanovića 26; ☎ 6615 230, 527 556; e contact@hostelsova.com; w hostelsova.com. This popular, highly rated hostel, close to Modene in the city centre, has helpful hosts & a friendly & homely atmosphere. €

🏠 **Teresa** [239 A2] Svetozara Miletića 43; m 062 1837 272; e hostelteresa@gmail.com; w hostelteresa.rs/en. With dorm, dbls with shared bathroom (€€) & 6- & 8-bed apartments, this new central hostel has AC, Wi-Fi & a large common terrace area. €

🏠 **Zeleno Zvono** [232 A7] Ilariona Ruvarća 26; ☎ 6402 949; m 060 0702 963; e galfi@mts.rs; w prepnocistens.com. A hostel in the Telep district of the city south of Futoški put. Range of rooms – sgl, dbl & trpl – with AC & TV. Free internet. €

Apartments

🏠 **Bonaca Apartments** [232 B2] (22 apts) Kisačka 62a; ☎ 446 600; e bonaca@nadlanu.com. New sgl, dbl & trpl apartments close to the railway & bus stations. All equipped with cable TV, minibar, AC, internet access, kitchen & bathroom. €€€

🏠 **Car Royal Apartments** **** [232 A7] (13 rooms) Cara Dušana 71; ☎ 6362 200; e car.ap@sbb.rs. 3km from the city centre, the Car (Tsar) apartments have modern, simply furnished sgl, dbl, trpl & quad rooms all with AC, minibar, Wi-Fi & satellite TV. Underground parking available. €€€

🏠 **Voyager Apartments** **** [232 D6] (20 apts) Stražilovska 16; ☎ 453 711; e voyageragencijja@sbb.rs; w voyagerns.co.rs.

Well-equipped city apartments that can be rented for short or long stays. Buffet b/fast provided. €€€

🏠 **TAL Centar *** ** [239 C2] (6 rooms) Zmaj Jovina 23; 📞 6613 813; m 061 2080 262; e talcentar@neobee.net; w talcentar.rs. Down a passageway on the corner of Zmaj Jovina & Dunavska. These Lončar tourist agency rooms are good value & ideally placed in the city next to the pedestrian zone. All rooms come with kitchen, bath, AC, cable TV & Wi-Fi. €€

🏠 **Vila Ljubica** [232 A6] (5 apts) Mikole Kočiša 6; 📞 422 595. 5 2-person apartments. €€

Motels

🏠 **Jet Set** [232 C1] (13 rooms) Temerinski put 41; 📞 414 511; m 063 540 536; w jetset-ns.co.rs. This has a conference hall & a national restaurant with seating for 150. €€

🏠 **Motel Adice** [232 A6] (15 rooms) Branka Ćopića 62; 📞 543 000, 543 111. 3km from the city centre in the Adice district, all rooms come with TV, power shower & internet connection. A free carwash is included in the price. €€

🏠 **Motel Bor** [232 C1] (12 rooms) Temerinski put 57a; 📞 6412 424, 6411 013; e office@vilabor. rs; w vilabor.rs. At the edge of Novi Sad, 1km from the E-75 *autoput*. The motel has its own restaurant. €

Kamenica

🏠 **Motel Ilidža** [233 H7] (17 rooms) Ledinački put 1; 📞 461 158. This is a small motel that has a restaurant & private parking for guests. €€

🏠 **Pansion Olimp** [233 H7] (5 rooms) Miloša Obilića 8; 📞 463 295; e olimp@ptt.rs. €€

🏠 **Vila Evanđelina** [233 H7] (16 rooms) Branislava Bukurova 2; 📞 464 111, 464 222; e vila. evandjelina@tehnounion.rs; w vilaevandjelina. com. Rooms with TV, AC & minibar. Grill restaurant, bar & secure parking. €€–€

✗ **WHERE TO EAT AND DRINK** Novi Sad is well provided with restaurants of every type. The squares and pedestrian areas around Trg Slobode, Modene and Zmaj Jovina are full of bars, cafés and pizzerias with plentiful outdoor seating in the warmer months of the year. Zmaj Jovina has several courtyards leading off it to the east that have more hidden-away cafés and restaurants, and Laza Telečkog, a narrow pedestrianised street that leads off to the west, is lined with a dense concentration of lively bars. Of the traditional restaurants, several places have *alaska čorba* on the menu, a local, paprika-rich fish soup. Paprika is used widely in Vojvodina cookery, part of the Hungarian legacy. The Vojvodina wines on offer at many of these restaurants are well worth sampling too, particularly those from the vineyards of Sremski Karlovci in Fruška Gora and those from Vršac in the east of the province.

Bakeries abound too, especially around the crossroads where Jevrejska and Bulevar oslobođenja meet, where you'll find **Pekara Klas** [232 C5] among several others. **Cafés** range from the traditional to the ultra hip, from quaint to quirky. There is even an **'Only Fools and Horses' Pub** [239 C2] at Zmaj Jovina 2, with the waiting staff decked out in T-shirts bearing a Robin Reliant three-wheeler logo – a far cry from Peckham.

Restaurants
City centre

✗**Arhiv** [239 D2] Ilije Ognjanovića 16; 📞 4722 176; ⏰ 08.00–midnight Mon–Sat. A smart, central restaurant located in a cosy basement that serves above-average, imaginative Vojvodina dishes like chicken stuffed with pears & almonds in a red wine sauce. €€€

✗**Čerčil** [239 B1] Nikole Pašića 25; 📞 525 132; w cercil.rs; ⏰ 08.00–22.00 Mon–Sat. Čerčil (Churchill) is a large, popular restaurant spread over several rooms that has good steaks, homebaked bread & an extensive wine list. €€€

✗**Pasha** [239 E2] Pionirska 1; 📞 6616 189; w pasharestoran.com; ⏰ noon–midnight daily. A modern international restaurant right by the park, this has Italian favourites like pasta & pizza as well as a good choice of fish & salads. Good wine list. €€€–€€

✗**Surabaya** [232 C1] Primorska 26; 📞 6413 400; w surabaya.rs; ⏰ 09.00–23.00 Mon–Sat. This is a rare (unique?) thing in Serbia – an

Indonesian restaurant. Surabaya is located next to the Apollo business & shopping centre, in the north of the city. It also serves Chinese food. €€€–€€

✳ ✕ **Alla Lanterna** [239 E1] Dunavska 27; ✆6622 022; w allalanterna.rs; ⏰ 08.00–midnight daily. This is a popular pasta & pizza place at the end of the pedestrian stretch of Dunavska. It has a vaulted ceiling with wrought-iron chandeliers. All of the walls are elaborately decorated with tiles & patterns made with pebbles that have been cemented in place. The English menu has a few vegetarian items on it, as well as a wide selection of pizzas. The pasta dishes like *spaghetti carbonara* & *arrabiatta* are also very good & reasonably priced. In winter, the tables fill quickly & you may have to wait, especially on w/end nights; in summer, the situation is generally easier as more tables are placed outside on the street. €€

✕ **Dva Anđela** [239 C2] Laze Telečkog 14; m 063 1134 567; ⏰ 09.00–23.00 Mon–Thu, 09.00–01.00 Fri/Sat, 11.00–23.00 Sun. Pizza, pasta dishes & good salads right in the heart of the pedestrian zone. Despite the ultra-modern décor, there is a wood oven for pizzas. €€

✕ **EmChi** [239 A2] Svetozara Miletića 43; m 061 2055 293; w emchi.rs; ⏰ 10.00–22.00 daily. This is a rarity: a vegetarian restaurant. EmChi, with its clean pine décor, offers an imaginative range of vegetarian dishes that includes sandwiches, soups, salads & tasty, Middle East-influenced vegetable dishes. €€

✕ **Fish & Zeleniš** [239 B1] Skerlićeva 2; ✆452 002; w fishizelenis.com; ⏰ 11.00–23.00 Mon–Fri, 11.00–midnight Sat, 13.00–22.00 Sun. This innovative & understandably popular restaurant in the city centre serves up imaginative 'fish & vegetable' (ie: the name of the restaurant) dishes with a Greek or Mediterranean twist, also risottos, salads & pastas. Décor & staff are charming & the place has a cosy, relaxed atmosphere. €€

✕ **Fontana** [239 B1] Nikole Pašića 27; ✆6621 779; w restoranfontana.com; ⏰ 07.00–midnight daily. Fontana is a fairly upmarket Serbian restaurant, located just off Zmaj Jovina, that has several wood-panelled rooms inside, & a pleasant courtyard with secluded seating around a fountain outside. Excellent grilled meat dishes & huge portions. There is live folk music here some nights. €€

✕ **La Forza** [239 C2] Katolička porta 6; ✆4720 500; w laforza.rs; ⏰ 08.00–23.00 Mon–Sat, 15.00–23.00 Sun. La Forza is a central pizzeria that also offers a wide variety of pasta dishes & pancakes. €€

✕ **Gondola** [239 E3] Bulevar Mihajla Pupina 18; ✆456 563; w gondola-restoran.rs; ⏰ 08.00–midnight daily. Another pizzeria run by the same company as Alla Lanterna. This one is outside the pedestrian zone close to the tourist information office. €€

✕ **Lipa** [239 C2] 7 Svetozara Miletićeva; ✆6615 259; ⏰ 07.00–23.00 Mon–Fri, 07.00–01.00 Sat/Sun. Located on a street that runs off Zmaj Jovina, this old-fashioned national restaurant has a wide selection of typical Vojvodina dishes & usually a very good-value fixed 'menu of the day' on offer. Outdoor seating on a terrace as well as down in the wine cellar. Live music at w/ends. €€

✕ **Marina** [239 B4] Trg Mladenaca 4; ✆424 353; ⏰ 08.00–23.00 daily. This is a café-bar-restaurant by the Registry Office arch at Trg Mladenaca, which serves fairly standard Serbian & Italian fare. The pizzas are both large & tasty. There is a separate dining area with a pleasant atmosphere but this is spoiled to some extent by the loud music that emanates from the bar area. €€

✕ **Modena** [239 C3] Trg Slobode 4; m 064 8038 800; w modena-caffe.rs; ⏰ 08.00–23.00 Mon–Fri, 08.00–01.00 Sat/Sun. This is a popular central café-pizzeria with modern interior décor & an outside terrace. B/fast dishes are served until 13.00. €€

✳ ✕ **Pivnica Gusan** [239 C2] Zmaj Jovina 4; ✆425 570; w pivnicagusan.rs; ⏰ 09.00–midnight daily. In a courtyard off Zmaj Jovina this is as much a place for beer as it is for food – hence the '*pivnica*' tag. There is a convivial outdoor seating area & live music on some nights. €€

✕ **Sečuan** [239 D2] Dunavska 16; ✆529 693; ⏰ 09.00–23.00 Mon–Fri, 09.00–01.00 Sat/Sun. This 3-star Chinese restaurant close to the bottom of the pedestrian part of Dunavska has become something of a Novi Sad institution over the years. It is said to be the oldest Chinese restaurant in Serbia. As well as decent Sichuan cuisine & *dim sum*, it also serves Serbian dishes. €€

Around the centre

✕ **Atelje** [233 F5] Kej Žrtava Racije 2; ✆457 929. On the Danube riverbank opposite the fortress, this is one of the city's swankiest restaurants with a wide-ranging international menu & an impressive wine list. €€€

✗ **Dvor** [232 A7] Cara Dušana 58; ☎468 970; ⏰ 09.00–midnight daily. Smart, traditional restaurant with national cuisine. €€€

✗**Bela Lađa** [232 C3] Kisačka 21; ☎6616 594; w belaladja.com; ⏰ 08.00–midnight daily. A traditional restaurant that offers local dishes, especially game, & a wide selection of Vojvodina wines at very reasonable prices. The walls are stacked high with shelves of wine bottles from all over the world & there is traditional music to accompany your meal most nights. On the house on the other side of the street is a plaque indicating that Einstein lived here for 2 years between 1903 and 1905: his wife was from Novi Sad. €€

✗ **Borsalino** [232 C7] Vojvođanska 24; ☎468 088; w borsalino.rs; ⏰ 08.00–midnight daily. A small, above-average pizzeria that is off the usual tourist beat. €€

✗ **Chicken Tikka** [232 C7] Dimitrija Tucovića 3; ☎453 052; w chicken-tikka.co.rs; ⏰ 08.00–midnight Mon–Sat, 10.00–midnight Sun. If you hanker after the UK's favourite dish you might come here & be disappointed. The emphasis is actually on chicken dishes rather than Indian food but other types of typical Serbian meat are also available. The restaurant is located outside Novi Sad's main football ground: Stadium 'FK Vojvodina'. €€

✗ **Kafanica Đorđa** [233 E3] Jovanovića 2; ☎6611 783; w restoran-kafanica.rs; ⏰ noon–midnight Mon–Sat. A popular backstreet restaurant that serves delicious Vojvodina dishes chosen from a changing blackboard menu. €€

✗ **Ognjište** [232 D6] Dimitrija Tucovića 3; ☎450 594; ⏰ 09.00–01.00. Ognjište is a cosy, traditional restaurant that is decorated in a style something like a *hajduk*'s hideout, with dusty antiques, quaint wooden furniture, old lamps & all manner of curiosities hanging from the walls. This friendly restaurant, tucked away behind the football stadium, serves both Mediterranean-style & typical Serbian dishes at very reasonable prices. €€

✗ **Parobrod** [233 G4] Kej Skojevaca bb, Petrovaradin; m 063 598 998; ⏰ 09.00–midnight daily. A *splav* or floating restaurant across the river in Petrovaradin close to the bridge. Lots of river fish dishes including *alaska čorba* (fish chowder). A *tamburica* band play at w/ends. €€

✗ **Plava Frajla** [232 D6] Sutjeska 2; ☎6613 675; w plavafrajla.com; ⏰ 09.00–midnight Mon–Fri, 09.00–01.00 Sat/Sun. This reasonably priced restaurant in the SPENS Sports & Business Centre specialises in Vojvodina cuisine. Popular with locals for the quality of its food, this has some rather odd decorative features, such as chairs suspended from the ceiling. Live music at w/ends. €€

✗ **Savoca Pizzeria** [232 B4] Bulevar oslobođenja 41; ☎521 111; w picerijasavoca. com; ⏰ 08.00– midnight, 08.00–01.00 Sat/Sun. Decent pizza place close to the bus & train stations. Also pasta & risotto. €€

✗ **Trag** [233 H5] Preradovićeva 2, Petrovaradin; ☎431 989; ⏰ 10.00– 23.00 daily. This traditional Serbian restaurant specialising in fish & game dishes is located across the Danube in Petrovaradin. €€

✗ **Dizni** [232 C7] Bulevar oslobođenja 92; ☎6616 810; w diznipalacinke.com; ⏰ 09.00– 23.00 Mon–Fri, 09.00–midnight Sat/Sun. A very popular pancake place that has a wide range of sweet & savoury choices. €

Bars, cafés, snacks and take-aways

✗ **Cezar** [239 C3] Modene 2; ☎6623 538. A central pizzeria that has seating inside & out, & which sells pizza by the slice, either to eat on the premises or to take away. It also sells several varieties of *burek* & *pita*, like mushroom & potato – all excellent – as well as sandwiches & draught beer. €€

☕ **Evropa poslastičarnica** [239 D2] Dunavska 6. This café-patisserie is an excellent place to stop for coffee, ice cream & cakes.

🍺 **Irish Pub 'Red Cow'** [239 D2] Zmaj Jovina 28; ☎427 136; ⏰ 09.00–01.00 Mon–Fri, 09.00–02.00 Sat/Sun. If you've visited any eastern European Irish pubs before, you'll know what to expect. A youthful hangout with downstairs bar & upstairs attic.

🍺 **Lazino Tele** [239 B2] Laze Telečkog 16; ☎6612 265. Pub that has live music some nights & DJs at w/ends. Good choice of drinks.

🍺 **London Pub** [239 B2] Laze Telečkog 15; ☎421 881. Good selection of draught beers, a lively atmosphere &, naturally, a Union flag.

🍺 **Martha's Pub** [239 C2] Laze Telečkog 3; ☎611 038. Another lively but relaxed place in this hedonistic enclave. With an upstairs bar, downstairs patio & a sign that confusingly asserts 'God save the pumpkins'. *Medovača* – honey-flavoured *rakija* – is one of the choice drinks here.

📺 **Šeherezada poslastičarnica** [239 C2] Zmaj Jovina 19; ✆ 6623 280. Wonderful selection of delicious cakes & ice creams. Outdoor tables on Zmaj Jovina near the Bishop's Palace.

📺 **Trčika** [239 B4] Kralja Aleksandra 14; m 064 1124 588. Also called 'Tramvaj', this is an old tram carriage that serves as a café with more tables & chairs spilling out on to the street at the edge of the pedestrian zone.

NIGHTLIFE AND ENTERTAINMENT Novi Sad seems to be a very young city and at weekends the bars and cafés along Laze Telečkog and Zmaj Jovina are buzzing until the early hours with a glamorous under-30 crowd. Some of the places listed above have DJs and dancing and effectively cross over into club territory. As for **nightclubs** proper, the scene is not as big as it is in Belgrade but it is lively nevertheless. Check with the tourist office for what is currently hot (page 236). Below are a few suggestions.

Clubs

☆ **Foxtrot** [232 B6] Futoška 23; ✆ 6622 904; ⏰ 08.00–01.00. A daytime café that turns into a live music venue at w/ends.

☆ **Ritmo Latino** [232 C6] Sremska 9; ✆ 528 095. No prizes for guessing the predominant type of music here. There's also R&B & hiphop, DJs & occasional live bands.

☆ **Trema** [239 B3] SNP, Pozorišni trg 1; ✆ 451 232; ⏰ 10.00–02.00. A bar-club upstairs in the National Theatre building.

☆ **Wheels** [239 B1] Natošićeva 4; ✆ 522 557; ⏰ 19.00–01.00. This unpretentious jazz club attracts a wide range of live performers.

Cinemas

🎞 **Arena** [239 C3] Bulevar Mihajla Pupina 3; ✆ 447 690; w arenacineplex.com

🎞 **Art Cinema Vojvodina** [232 D7] SPENS Sport & business centre, Sutljeska 2; ✆ 4882 222

🎞 **Jadran** [239 B4] Poštanska 5; ✆ 528 838

🎞 **KCNS (Novi Sad Cultural Centre)** [239 B2] Katolička porta 5; ✆ 528 972; w kcns.org.rs

Theatres

🎭 **Brod Teatar (Boat theatre)** Beogradki kej; m 063 865 5083; e brod@neobee.net; w brodteatar.rs. Theatrical performances using a boat for a stage.

🎭 **Novi Sad Theatre – Ujvideki Szinhaz** [239 A2] Jovana Subotića 3–5; ✆ 525 552; e szinhaz@eunet.rs; w www.uvszinhaz.com. Hungarian-language theatre company.

🎭 **Serbian National Theatre** [239 B3] Pozorišni trg 1; ✆ 520 091, 6621 411; e biletarnica@snp.org.rs; w snp.org.rs

🎭 **Theatre – Pozorište Mladih (Youth Theatre)** [239 D2] Ignjata Pavlasa 4–8; ✆ 525 884, 520 543; e office@pozoristemladih.co.rs; w pozoristemladih.co.rs

FESTIVALS AND EVENTS Novi Sad is host to numerous cultural events throughout the year. Details about current events in the city can be obtained from one of the Novi Sad Tourist Organisation information centres or from their website (w *novisad.travel*). The list below details just some of the events that take place annually in the city.

February–March Late March sees the **Novi Sad International Half Marathon** (w *marathon.org.rs*) take place along the banks of the Danube River.

April The **Novi Sad Musical Festival** (w *muzickaomladina.org*) is a series of performances by Serbian and international artists at various venues throughout the city at the end of April. The music is mostly classical but there are also some jazz and folk performances.

May–June The **Sterijino Pozorje** theatre festival is held at the end of May and the beginning of June (*information from Sterijino Pozorje, Zmaj Jovina 22;* ✆ *451 273;* e *office@ pozorje.org.rs;* w *pozorje.org.rs*).

EXIT MUSIC FESTIVAL

The event that has attracted the most attention in recent years is the EXIT Music Festival (w *exitfest.org*) staged at Petrovaradin Fortress in early July, which now attracts anything up to 200,000 festival-goers annually. Even back in 2006, an estimated 150,000 attended overall (the biggest draw was Billy Idol, who had 45,000 at his performance). It has grown even more in the years since and EXIT is currently said to be the largest music festival in southeast Europe. As well as increasing in size, EXIT has also gained considerable prestige over the past few years, winning a 'Best European Festival' award in 2007. Since then, EXIT has been nominated every year for this award and also received four nominations for 'Best Major Festival'. EXIT's Dance Arena was also voted one of three best destinations for electronic dance music by American *Vibe* magazine in 2013.

During the EXIT festival, the fortress area is given over entirely for musical performances and around 20 stages of varying sizes are erected to take advantage of the spectacular setting and impressive acoustics. Despite an emphasis on electronics and rock, some of the smaller stages concentrate on music that is not so obviously 'urban'; these have included a Fusion stage, a World Music stage, a Metal Hammer stage, a Latino stage, a Reggae One Love stage and a Roots and Flowers stage in the past, although they change from year to year. Daily performances start around 19.00 and finish very late.

For accommodation, two festival campsites on the opposite bank of the Danube provide camping places for 12,000 and put on a few low-profile musical events of their own – so do not expect an undisturbed night's sleep. The alternative is to stay at a hostel or hotel in the city, but it is wise to book very well in advance. Hardly surprisingly, beds in the city tend to cost more during EXIT.

Prices are a real bargain for what you get: an all-inclusive four-day ticket costs around €120 and a camping pass, €40. At this price it might be just about possible to buy a do-it-yourself package of cheap return flight from England to Belgrade, bus or train Belgrade to Novi Sad, entrance ticket and camping permit for not much more than the entrance price to one of the UK's summer music festivals! Early-bird tickets sold in the winter before the festival are usually available at discounted prices; eTickets may be bought online at w www.exitfest.org. For help with organising transport and accommodation in Serbia, EXITTRIP.org (e *info@exittrip.org*) are an official EXIT tourism partner and provide an online booking service. In the UK, ExitConnectUK.com, the UK visitors EXIT festival information site (*suite 217, 99 Warwick St, Leamington Spa, Warks CV32 4RB;* \ *01926 827557;* m *07505 960674;* e *info@EXITconnectUK.com*) can provide practical information and help organise accommodation and airport transfers.

Over the past few years EXIT has attracted (mostly British) international names like Emeli Sande, Napalm Death, The Prodigy, Bastille, George Clinton and David Guetta as well as home-grown stars from Serbia and the Balkan region.

Further information about the festival and line-up may be found on the EXIT website w exitfest.org.

The **Tour de Serbia International Cycling Race** (w *tds.co.rs*) takes place in mid- to late June and usually takes in Novi Sad at some stage.

June–July The Novi Sad Cultural Centre (*Katolička porta 5;* \ *528 972;* e *info@kcns.org.rs;* w *kcns.org.rs*) organises the **Digital Arts Festival** and the

STATE OF EXIT – A BRIEF HISTORY

The festival first began in 2000, a very critical year in Serbia's history, as the brainchild of two university students Dušan Kovačević and Bojan Bošković. The plan was twofold: to provide entertainment for Serbia's youth and to raise political awareness and engender anti-Milošević protest. The first festival stretched through the summer of 2000 and took place at various stages around the campus of the University of Novi Sad and the Danube's left bank. Serbian bands like the Orthodox Celts, Eyesburn and Darkwood Dub put in appearances several times over the summer months and the event finally came to an end on 24 September, just two weeks before Milošević's fall from power.

In 2001, the festival moved across the Danube to its present site at the Petrovaradin Fortress. The ethos behind that year's festival was a twofold celebration: of being finally rid of Milošević and also of Serbia's opening up to the wider world after years of isolation. EXIT – Noise Summer Fest, as it became known, received generous funding from the new authorities in Belgrade, who wanted to be seen to visibly support the event and who actually attended in considerable numbers, hungry for the photo opportunities it offered. This time, instead of lasting all summer, the event was over a more manageable nine days. It was an enormous success.

EXIT 2002 brought in more DJ acts and foreign artists like the Asian Dub Foundation, Transglobal Underground and Roni Size. Despite success on the ground, the event, again over nine days, ended up making a loss of €300,000. This led to claims of financial mismanagement along with public criticism that the event was too long and had too few big international stars. In response to this, EXIT 2003 was shortened to four days and was more aggressively advertised by its 'State of EXIT' marketing campaign. There was a noticeable shift towards the commercial with each of seven stages having a separate commercial sponsor. The change in philosophy seemed to work and, that year, international acts such as Tricky, Misty in Roots, the Stereo MCs, Chumbawumba and Soul II Soul all performed to ecstatic crowds.

EXIT 2004 had a troubled start. Three weeks before the event one of the organisers was arrested for embezzlement but no charges were ever pressed. To some it looked as if the event was coming under some sort of political persecution.

International Festival of Alternative and New Theatre (INFANT) in late June and early July. The **International Film Festival** also takes place at the Arena Cineplex [239 C3] (w *eng.cinemacity.org*) in late June. Come in July for the popular **EXIT Music Festival** (page 245), which is by far the largest outdoor festival in the region, attracting tens of thousands of visitors from all over Europe.

August The **Days of Brazil Samba Carnival** takes place in the city centre during this month.

September The **Street Artist Festival** (w *ulicnisviraci.com*) takes place at various venues throughout the city in early September.

October The **Novi Sad Marathon** (w *marathon.org.rs*) is held during October. **Tesla Fest** is an annual international festival that celebrates technological innovation and creativity.

Despite the setbacks, EXIT went ahead and, once again, it was a great success with Iggy Pop stealing the show.

It was around the time of EXIT 2004 that the foreign media started to take an interest. In 2005, the festival was covered by BBC Radio 1 for the first time and awareness of the festival reached a much wider, international audience. This was not all that surprising as MTV had already recorded the festival the previous year. There were concerns this year that the newly elected mayor of Novi Sad, Maja Gojković, the Serbian Radical Party candidate, might become obstructive because of the event's left-leaning, internationalist reputation. No such thing happened, however, and the city continued to support the festival. This tacit endorsement by the Radicals and the abandonment of a minute's silence for the Muslim victims of Srebrenica (it was the tenth anniversary of the event) was seen by some on the left as a selling out by the organisers. Whatever the political machinations, the music was as impressive as ever, with international names like the White Stripes and Fat Boy Slim headlining the bill. However, the weather was less impressive, with torrential rain putting a damper on proceedings. Perhaps it was the inclement weather that attracted so many foreigners for the first time. With over 150,000 present, 15,000 were from outside Serbia and a good proportion of these were British. These, no doubt, felt right at home if they had any experience of the UK's Glastonbury Festival where rain and mud are virtually de rigueur.

EXIT 2006, with Franz Ferdinand (an apposite band name for this region), Morrissey, Billy Idol and the Pet Shop Boys all headlining, had 22 stages in all, featuring a wide variety of musical styles that ranged from hiphop to reggae. For the first time even unknown bands had a chance for their place in the spotlight on the Future Shock stage, which gave everybody an opportunity to perform. Perhaps partly because there was no Glastonbury Festival in the UK that year, there were more foreign visitors than ever, with an estimated 5,000 UK visitors. The following year saw 190,000 visitors come to the festival, 51% of whom were foreigners according to B92. This was the same year that EXIT won the UK Festival Award for the Best European Festival. By 2012, EXIT attracted up to 200,000 attendees over the whole four-day period, a figure that has been maintained in the years since.

November The **Novi Sad Jazz Festival** is also organised by the Novi Sad Cultural Centre (**w** *kcns.org.rs*) with international artists, ensembles, workshops and exhibitions.

SHOPPING
Souvenirs

City Sales Gallery [239 C2] Zmaj Jovina 22 – Ilije Ognjanovića 4; ✆421 651; **e** marta@citygallery.co.rs

Ethno Food [239 E1] Dunavska 27; ✆ 451 885; **m** 066 1054 548; **w** ethno-food.com

Etno Art Travel [232 D7] Bulevar Cara Lazara 29; ✆360 587, 365 341, 466 940

Novi Sad Kibicfenster [233 E6] Stražilovska 21; ✆522 663, 522 944; **m** 063 8814 734

NS Škrinja [239 E1] Dunavska 17; **m** 063 412 169

Souvenirs Prestige [239 C2] Zmaj Jovina 2; ✆571 131

Bookshops Not surprisingly for a cultured city with a large student population, there are good bookshops to be found scattered around the centre. The ones listed below stock a reasonable amount of English-language material.

6

MB Libro [232 D7] Sutjeska 2; 622 134; ⊕ 08.00–20.00 Mon–Fri, 09.00–14.00 Sat. Inside SPENS Sport & Business Centre.
Solaris [232 D7] Sutjeska 2; 6624 387. Inside SPENS Sport & Business Centre.
The English Book [239 B2] Njegoševa 14; 528 777; e bookshop.novisad@englishbook. rs; w englishbook.rs; ⊕ 08.00–20.00 Mon–Fri,

09.00–16.00 Sat. As its name suggests, the only bookshop in the city stocking exclusively English-language books.
Vulkan [239 C2] Zmaj Jovina 24; 426 843; ⊕ 09.00–22.00. The best bet overall for English-language books in the city.
Vulkan Merkator [232 B5] Bulevar oslobođenja 102; 6368 498; ⊕ 09.00–22.00

OTHER PRACTICALITIES

Banks There is no shortage of banks and places to change money in Novi Sad. Those listed below all have ATMs for cash withdrawal.

$ **Delta banka** [239 C4] Bulevar Mihajla Pupina 4
$ **Komercijalna banka** [232 B3] Bulevar Kralja Petra I 11
$ **Novosadska banka** [239 C4] Bulevar Mihajla Pupina 3

$ **Raiffeisen banka** [232 B5] Bulevar oslobođenja 56a
$ **Vojvođanska banka** [239 C3] Trg Slobode 5–7

Health There is a very elegant, traditional-style **pharmacy** close to the centre at Apoteka Bulevar [239 D3] (*Bulevar Mihaila Pupina 7;* 420 374).

Internet Dunavski Park is a Wi-Fi hot spot for those travelling with their own laptop. Many city-centre pubs and cafés also provide free Wi-Fi access.

Post and telephone services The main **post office** and **telephone centre** [239 B4] is on the corner of Bulevar Mihajla Pupina and Narodnih Heroja. The telephone centre is open 24 hours a day; there are also Halo pay phones outside.

WHAT TO SEE AND DO Most of the city's sights are within a small area of the centre. The hub is spacious **Trg Slobode** [239 C3], with the neo-Gothic brick-clad Roman Catholic cathedral on one side of the square and the City Hall facing it on the other. In the centre of the square stands a statue of **Svetozar Miletić** (1826–1901), one of the most prominent Serbian politicians of the 19th century – a 1939 creation of the seemingly ubiquitous Ivan Meštrović. The statue was hidden during the Hungarian occupation of World War II but put back in place in 1944. The figure, in a strident, almost ranting, pose faces towards the cathedral, his back turned on the elegant **City Hall** (Gradska kuća) [239 C3]: the neo-Renaissance, two-storey building that is a copy of the town hall in Graz, Austria. The **Roman Catholic cathedral (Katedrala – Rimokatolička zupna crkva imena marijina)** [239 C2] opposite was built between 1893 and 1895, at the same time as the City Hall, on the site of a former 18th-century church. The building, with three naves and a 76m-high tower, is not a cathedral at all – the seat of Bačka's bishopric is actually further north in Subotica – but rather, a parish church dedicated to Mary. Over the years it has been its impressive size, rather than its ecclesiastical status, that has caused it to be known as the 'cathedral'. The interior is richly carved, with four altars and 20 windows designed by Czech and Hungarian stained-glass craftsmen. The roof has a steep pitch and is strikingly patterned with multi-coloured Zsolnai tiles.

The pedestrian area of the square continues along café-lined Zmaj Jovina to the Bačka Bishop's Palace at its eastern end and the Orthodox cathedral just beyond this. The **Bačka Bishop's Palace (Vladicanski dvor)** [239 D1] is the residential palace

top	Southeast Serbia offers numerous opportunities for hiking in an unspoiled mountainous landscape (TON) page 339
above left	Cycling is a popular sport in Serbia, and the area around Mount Avala is ideal for mountain biking (BJ/ANTOS) page 183
above right	White-water rafting on the Ibar River (DB/ANTOS) page 315
below	Kopaonik is Serbia's top ski resort with a total of 44km runs reaching up to 2,017m (DB/ANTOS) page 319

above left   Krušedol Monastery in the Fruška Gora Hills (P/S) page 261

above right   Church at Drvengrad – this small ethno-village was constructed as a film set by the director Emir Kusturica (LM) pages 311–12

left   The Church of St Peter just outside Novi Pazar is the oldest in the country, dating from the 8th or 9th century (P/S) pages 326–7

below   Subotica's elegant synagogue was one of the first of many Art-Nouveau buildings to be constructed in the city (STO) page 274

<table>
</table>

top	Stroll by colourful houses on the picturesque bank of the River Timok in Knjaževac (LM) pages 365–7
above left	A carved head in the rock on the Romanian side of the Kazan defile, where the Danube reaches its narrowest point in the Đerdap National Park (m/S) pages 194–5
above right	The Šumarice Memorial Park in Kragujevac has many monuments that commemorate the tragic events of October 1941 (BM/S) page 208
below	The Lepenski Vir visitor centre by the River Danube near Donji Milanovac sits on slightly higher ground than the original Mesolithic settlement (DB/ANTOS) pages 192–3

above   The Dragačevo Trumpet Festival is held
          in the small village of Guča every August
          (sd/A) page 302

left   A musician playing bagpipes, one of many
          traditional Serbian instruments – folk
          music is an important part of Serbian
          national culture (SS) page 51

below   Folk dancers in Sremski Karlovci
          (DB/ANTOS) pages 253–7

above   The open-air museum at Sirogojno was built with the idea of recreating a typical 19th-century Zlatibor homestead (TW/S) pages 308–9

middle top   Serbian food is both hearty and healthy, featuring plenty of locally grown organic produce (DB/ANTOB) pages 82–6

middle bottom   Street traders selling their wares outside the entrance to the Turkish fortress in Niš (LM) page 358

bottom left & right   Taste local wine in one of the wine-tasting regions near Vršac or Sremski Karlovci, or sample *rajika* made from ripe plums (A/S and DB/ANTOS) pages 86–7

above The twisting Uvac canyon in western Serbia is one of the few places in the country where griffon vultures can be found (AT/S) pages 330–1

left The 'House on the Drina' is a small wooden fishing lodge that perches on a rock in the middle of the River Drina at Bajina Bašta (AL/S) page 315

below Haystacks are a common sight throughout rural Serbia (DB/ANTOS)

above The 'Šargan Eight' Railway winds through the precipitous mountain scenery of Mokra Gora (DB/ANTOS) page 310

right Autumn colours in the region near Užice (J/D) pages 293–300

below The atmospheric landscape of Đavolja Varoš is located in a remote region near the border with Kosovo (DB/ANTOS) pages 378–9

top   One of the largest winter gatherings of migrating common cranes in Europe — up to 20,000 birds — can be seen at Slano Kopovo near Novi Bečej in Vojvodina (LM) page 278

above left   Bee-eaters (*Merops apiaster*) are among the most colourful birds who breed outside Belgrade (FS/S)

above right   Distinctive ear tufts characterise the pensive eagle owl (*Bubo bubo*), found in Đerdap and Ovcar-Kablar gorges (KB/S) page 7

below   A hikers' and birdwatchers' paradise, Tara National Park is also home to the endemic Serbian spruce (*Picea omorikca pancic*) (BJ/ANTOS) page 7

of the Serbian Orthodox bishop in Novi Sad. It was constructed in 1901 on the site of a former palace that dated from 1741. The building style is curiously eclectic: a mix of secessionist and Serbian Romanticism, with pseudo-Moorish plasterwork decoration on red brick. In front of the palace stands a statue of **Jovan Jovanović 'Zmaj'** (1833–1904) [239 D1], the city's famous doctor and poet.

The **Orthodox Cathedral Church of St George (Saborna crkva svetog Georgija)** [239 C1] lies just behind the palace. The present church was erected on the same site as an older one from 1734, which was burnt out, like so much else, by the Hungarian shelling of the city in 1848 and 1849. The restoration took place between 1860 and 1880, with a second phase of work from 1902 to 1905, when the bell tower was erected. Inside, there is a total of 33 icons on the iconostasis and two larger icons by the local painter Paja Jovanović who also designed the stained-glass windows.

Leading off from here is the pedestrian street of **Dunavska**, one of the city's most attractive thoroughfares with many 18th- and 19th-century buildings. The **City Library** (1895) [239 D1] is on the corner with Gimnazijska and further down, close to the junction with Ignatja Pavlasa, is the **Museum of Foreign Art (Galerija – Zbirka Strane Umetnosti)** [239 E1] at number 29. Beyond here, the street runs along the edge of a pleasant park with a small lake – Dunavska Park – a leafy escape from the city bustle. The park's fountain has a sculpture *The Nymph* as its centrepiece, the 1912 work of Đorđe Jovanvić, a prominent Serbian sculptor of the period.

Continuing along Dunavska past the park, you soon arrive at the busy traffic artery of Beogradski kej and the wide River Danube just beyond it, with a superb view of Petrovaradin Fortress looming high above the opposite bank of the river. The three bridges that formerly crossed the river were all destroyed during the 1999 NATO bombing raids but have since been replaced. **Varadin Bridge (Varadinski most)** [233 F5], which leads directly across to Petrovaradin, has a plaque that reads: '*Varadinski most – original one destroyed April 1st 1999 by NATO, killing citizen of Novi Sad Oleg. M. Najov, aged 29.*' Nearby, is a small statue of a man playing a tamburica that looks uncannily like Alfred Hitchcock. It is not the film-maker, however, but a memorial to a local musician: '*Janko Balaž 1925–1988.*' Walking south from Varadin Bridge along Beogradski kej next to the Danube River you soon reach a war memorial opposite the junction with Maksima Gorkog. The **Memorial to the Victims of the Massacre** [233 F5], which commemorates the January 1942 massacre in which 800 Jews (and 700 Serbs) were murdered in the city by Hungarian units, is a touching work that depicts a family group of man, woman, child and baby. Beneath it is a Hebrew inscription, a reminder of Novi Sad's once sizeable Jewish population. Stretching across the river to the left is a line of concrete supports, all that remains of **Franz Joseph Bridge (Franz Josef most)**, the city's third bridge destroyed by NATO bombs in 1999. Now the supports have no other purpose than providing high-rise accommodation for gulls and cormorants. From the memorial, a walking, running and cycling track leads all the way south to Štrand and Ribarsko Ostrvo (Fish Island). **Štrand** [233 F7] (🕐 *08.00–midnight Mon–Fri, 08.00–02.00 Sat/Sun; small admission fee, free after 22.00*), a large river beach on the Danube bank near Freedom Bridge in the city suburb of Liman, is enormously popular in summer. In fine weather, thousands come here to bathe, have leisurely picnics, enjoy the sun or relax in the shade of the large park that backs the beach. Beyond here lies **Ribarsko Ostrvo (Fisherman's Island)** [233 F7], which is home to fish restaurants, cafés, nightclubs, sailing clubs and a tourist resort.

Returning to the Orthodox cathedral, and walking northwest along Pašićeva, you come to the entrance of the grounds of the church of St Nicholas located in a quiet, shady corner between Pašićeva and Đure Jakšića streets. The small **St Nicholas Church (Nikolejevska crkva)** [239 B1] is the oldest Orthodox church in Novi Sad, mentioned in official records from 1739 as the endowment of the Bogadanović family, wealthy merchants in the city at that time. The church served as both a Serbian and a Greek Orthodox place of worship for many years. It was damaged in the 1849 bombardment of the city, and again in 1862, after which it was renovated at the expense of benefactors Jovan and Marija Trandafil. The church, unusually, has a small gold-plated onion dome in the style of a Russian Orthodox church. This was probably a symbolic response to the generous donations it received from the Russian Church after being damaged in the 1862 uprising. Mileva and Albert Einstein's sons were christened here in 1913.

There are many more churches dotted around Novi Sad, which is to be expected given the multi-ethnic make-up of the city. Scattered around the city centre are the places of worship of a broad range of denominations: as well as Orthodox and Roman Catholic there are Greek-Catholic, Reformist, Pentecostal, Adventist, Slovak-Evangelistic, Baptist and Methodist. There is also a synagogue – before World War II Novi Sad had a sizeable Jewish population.

The **synagogue** [239 A4] is on Jevrejska (Jew Street) at number 9, with other important buildings previously owned by the Jewish community flanking it on both sides. The whole complex, all constructed using the same light-yellowish brick, was built in 1909, designed by the architect Lipot Baumhorn (1860–1932). The synagogue – a three-nave basilica, smaller but similar in design to that in Szeged, Hungary – was the fifth to be built on exactly the same spot. It has stained-glass windows throughout and a large rose window facing the street, along with golden letters in Hebrew that spell out the invitation: 'This is the house of worship for all nations.' The building came through World War II relatively unscathed, serving at the end of the war as a collective centre for Jews deported to the concentration camps. Services were revived in 1945 but ten years later nearly all of Novi Sad's surviving Jewish community migrated to Israel, leaving the building largely redundant as a place of worship. In 1991, the synagogue was handed over to the city for a period of 25 years. It is now a regular concert venue for both classical music and jazz. The building next door at number 7, formerly a Jewish school, currently serves as a ballet school.

Walking back along Jevrejska from the synagogue, the city's main post office dominates the corner with Bulevar Mihaila Pupina. Immediately behind this is the small wedge-shaped square of **Trg Mladenaca (Newlyweds Square)** [239 B4] by the registry office, with a curious Baroque-looking arch in the centre, purpose-built for wedding-photo opportunities. Crossing the road back towards Trg Slobode you cannot fail to notice the vast concrete structure of the **Serbian National Theatre** at Pozorišni trg (Theatre Square) [239 B3]. The building is large – very large (ground area: 20,000m²) – and seems rather out of scale with its surroundings, having more the appearance of a university campus building or a conference centre rather than a theatre. There are three stages inside, the largest of which seats 700.

Museums and galleries

The city has a number of excellent galleries and museums, which, in most cases, are efficiently organised and well run. The tourist office can advise on specific interests but a brief overview is detailed below. Note that winter opening hours (from November to March) may be more restrictive than those given below so it is best to check before visiting.

Fantasy Museum [232 A6] (*Muzej igračaka fantasy; Olge Petrov 36/27;* **m** *060 6555 3365, 063 1553 365;* **e** *muzej_fantasy@hotmail.fr;* **w** *muzejfantasy.com;*

admission 170din) This fascinating toy and wax museum has a collection of over 5,000 dolls, toy soldiers, doll's houses, puppets and children's toys mostly from the early 20th century. Opening hours are subject to change, so it is best to phone first.

Collection of Rajko Mamuzić [239 C4] (*Galerija Rajka Maumuzića; Vase Stajića 1;* \ *520 223, 520 467;* e *glurm@mts.rs;* w *galerijamamuzic.org.rs;* ⊕ *09.00–17.00 Tue–Sun*) This collection represents the work of post-World War II Serbian/Yugoslav painters. It was presented to the city of Novi Sad as a gift in 1972.

Gallery of Matica Srpska [239 C4] (*Galerija Matice Srpske; Trg Galerija 1;* \ *4899 000;* e *info@galerijamaticesrpske.rs;* w *galerijamaticesrpske.rs;* ⊕ *10.00–18.00 Tue–Thu & Sat, noon–20.00 Fri; admission 100din*) This collection was founded by Matica Srpska in Budapest in 1826 and opened to the public in 1847. In 1864, the gallery was transferred to Novi Sad and it was placed in its current building in 1958. The gallery, one of the best collections of paintings in the country, represents Serbian artists working in Vojvodina from the 17th to the 20th century.

The collection is spread throughout 19 rooms, and laid out in chronological order. The ground floor is given over to copies of frescoes taken from various Fruška Gora monasteries. The works on the first floor are mostly 18th century, and are largely of a religious nature and by unknown artists. In the rooms representing the 19th century, the works of Pavle Simić (1818–76) and Đura Jaksić (1832–78) feature heavily but there are also some fine, very human portraits by Pavel Burković (1772–1830) and by Nikola Alexsić (1811–73), whose women all seem to wear a provocative expression that lies somewhere between conspiratorial and sexually precocious. Displayed among the works from the early 20th century are the rather sinister self-portraits of Stefan Meksić (1876–1923). In one of these, a worried-looking man is portrayed smoking a cigar and drinking wine while a violin-playing skeleton leers at him from over his shoulder: clearly the work of an artist preoccupied with his own mortality. Other artists from this period, like Šerban, have work that displays a riot of Impressionistic colour – like Van Gogh on acid – while experimental artists like Sava Šumanović (1896–1942), who was killed by Croatian Ustaša during World War II, have works like *Sailor with Pipe* (1920–21) and *Two Nudes* (1930) that display both Structuralist and Cubist influences.

Institute for Nature Conservation of Vojvodina Province [233 E6] (*Pokrajinski zavod za zaštitu prirode; Radnička 20a;* \ *4896 301;* e *info@pzzp.rs;* w *pzzp.rs;* ⊕ *08.00–19.00*) The Institute has a collection of over 60,000 items from various fields of study: geology, palaeontology, botany, ornithology, etc. Among an extensive display of animal skeletons, stuffed birds, dioramas and fossils, the most impressive item is the skull and tusks of a woolly mammoth from the Pleistocene period.

Museum of Novi Sad – Foreign Art Collection [239 E1] (*Dunavska 29;* \ *551 239;* e *muzejgradanovogsada@gmail.com;* ⊕ *09.00–17.00 Tue–Sun; admission 100din*) The work on show here is the legacy of Dr Branko Ilić and includes artworks from the Renaissance right up to the 20th century. Most of the collection comes from the central European region.

Museum of Vojvodina [239 E1] (*Muzej Vovojdine; Dunavska 35–37;* \ *420 566;* w *muzejvojvodine.org.rs;* ⊕ *09.00–19.00 Tue–Fri, 10.00–18.00 Sat/Sun; admission 150din*) This large, rambling, but excellent museum is housed in two buildings next door to each other opposite Dunavska Park. The museum at number 35 deals with the archaeology, earlier history and ethnology of the province, from Palaeolithic origins right up to the *belle époque* period of the late 19th century. At number 37 next door, the focus is on more recent history – from the first half of the 20th century up until the end of World War II. There is much to see here, especially in the sections on archaeology and early history, but the museum's greatest treasure is undoubtedly that of a beautifully preserved Roman helmet fashioned from pure gold.

Novi Sad City Museum [233 G5] (*Muzej grada Novog Sada; Petrovaradin Tvrđava 4;* \ *6433 145, 6433 613;* e *muzelgrada.ns@gmail.com;* w *museumns.rs;* ⊕ *09.00–17.00 Tue–Sun; admission 200din*) The standard display on show here concerns the cultural history of the city, with a selection of fine and applied art from the mid 18th to the mid 20th century that includes paintings, religious icons, musical instruments and furniture. There are also curiosities like the remains of an enormous wooden boat, probably of Celtic origin, that was dredged from the bottom of the Danube (a similar one can be found in the museum at Sremska Mitrovica). With some advance notice, the museum staff can organise tours of the fortress's underground galleries. Tours take place between 10.00 and 17.00 and cost 500din for a guided tour in English.

Pavle Beljanski Memorial Gallery [239 C4] (*Spomen-Zbirka Pavla Beljanskog; Trg Galerija 2;* \ *4729 966;* e *kontazt@pavle-beljanski.museum;* w *www.pavle-beljanski.museum;* ⊕ *10.00–18.00 Wed–Sun, 13.00–21.00 Thu; admission 100din, Thu free*) This gallery, first opened to the public in 1961 in a purpose-built building designed by architect Ivo Kurtuvić, is composed entirely of the work of Serbian artists from the late 19th and the first half of the 20th century. The collection of paintings, sculpture and tapestries was bequeathed to the city by Pavle Beljanski, a prominent Novi Sad lawyer and diplomat. The memorial hall, opened in 1966, as a gift of his family, is a reconstruction of Beljanski's living and working space, with paintings, books, furniture and personal objects.

Petrovaradin Fortress [233 G5] This impressive fortress has often been referred to as the 'Gibraltar of the Danube'. Petrovaradin started life as a Roman fortress and various additions were made through the medieval period. That which exists today, however, dates almost entirely from the early 18th century, when the fortress was comprehensively enlarged and fortified by the Austrians after their successful defeat of the Turkish army in 1692. The notion was to build on this success and construct an invincible barrier that would prevent further Turkish expansion into central Europe. The French military architect Sebastian Vauban was enrolled and the massive project was begun.

Although the Turks returned for a final battle in 1717, the fortress was already a white elephant by the time the fortifications were complete. By now, any serious threat of attack had almost completely vanished; not only had the Turks become far less of a threat as the 18th century progressed but the nature of warfare had changed so much that the fortress was rendered redundant. The enormous expenditure that had been made in terms of cash, materials and manpower was, in hindsight, a profligate waste of resources.

It was not a complete waste of time, however; the fortress's extensive **underground galleries** have been put to good use as dungeons from time to time, playing host to some very distinguished prisoners. Karađorđe was imprisoned at Petrovaradin during the First National Uprising at the start of the 19th century and Marshal Tito himself spent a brief time in custody here when he was a young NCO in the Austrian army, getting himself into trouble as a firebrand socialist. Other guests to the fortress, coming as distinguished foreign visitors rather than prisoners, have included the Ethiopian emperor, Haile Selassie, and the young Prince Charles.

The construction of the tunnels was a massive task that took an enormous toll in terms of human life. The convicts forced to labour on its construction called it the 'Castle of Death' with good reason, as many thousands perished during the excavation of the underground galleries. It took a total of 88 years to build; work began in 1692 and was not completed until 1780.

There are 18km of galleries in all, at four different levels beneath the fortress. The original idea was that, if the fortress were attacked, then up to 30,000 men could hide underground and cover the surrounding area by firing their muskets through the 18,000 loopholes that had been installed. Very few people knew the layout of the tunnels in their entirety. Officers would be familiar with just their own small section of the tunnel complex and numerous devices were installed to fool or trap the enemy if they were smart enough to find their way into part of the tunnel system.

Today, only 1km of the tunnel complex is open but even this is still highly impressive. As well as a tourist attraction, the tunnels have found modern usage as an ideal location for horror films – if you take a tour you may notice remnants of fake cobwebs here and there.

Above ground, there are other things to see. Many of the original buildings have been converted for alternative usage: the **City Museum** [233 G5] (see opposite) is housed in buildings that originally served as a barracks and an arsenal; the Historical Archive of Novi Sad is housed in another block of barracks, and the long terrace of barracks that look out over the Danube has been converted into the Hotel Leopold I and a variety of art studios. Between the Hotel Leopold I and the Historical Archive is a small street of craft shops. The seating area immediately below the clock tower – **Ludwig's Bastion** – and the terrace of the adjoining restaurant both offer excellent views over the Danube River and Novi Sad beyond. You may notice that the hands on the **clock tower** are the wrong way round, with the minute hand replacing the hour hand and vice versa. The reason for this is that it is said to make them easier to see at a distance. The clock is said to run fast in summer and slow in winter, the result of a worn mechanism. Notwithstanding this, for many years, a clock tax was imposed by the Austrians, which was applicable to any household able to view the clock tower from their home. Under Habsburg rule, the privilege of knowing the correct time did not come free.

Petrovaradin Fortress is a relatively short walk over the bridge from central Novi Sad or you can reach it by catching bus number 3 to Petrovaradin. A taxi should cost around 250din.

SREMSKI KARLOVCI (СРЕМСКИ КАРЛОВЦИ) *Telephone code 021*

This small historic town, 11km southeast of Novi Sad on the banks of the Danube, is one of the most attractive in all Serbia. The tree-shaded central square, Trg Branka Radičevića, named after the Romantic poet Branko Radičević, a native of the town, has a 1770 **marble fountain** [254 C3] with four lion figures as its centrepiece. Historically, Sremski Karlovci's most important building is the so-called **Peace Chapel (Kapela Mira)** [254 C6], which stands on a hill at the south end of the town. This curious, circular building commemorates the signing of the Treaty of Karlowitz on 26 January 1699 that brought peace between the Turks and

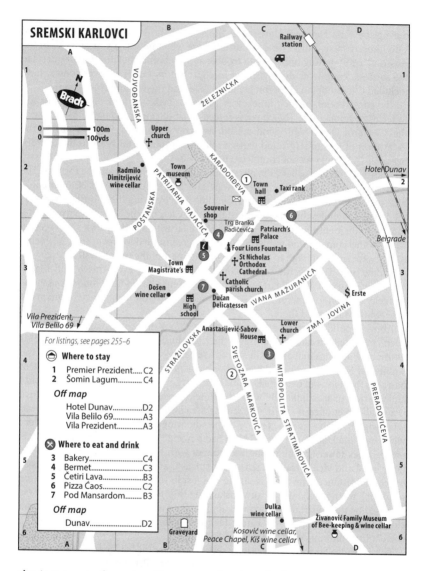

SREMSKI KARLOVCI

For listings, see pages 255–6

Where to stay
1 Premier Prezident..... C2
2 Šomin Lagum............. C4

Off map
Hotel Dunav................D2
Vila Belilo 69................A3
Vila Prezident.............A3

Where to eat and drink
3 Bakery....................C4
4 Bermet....................C3
5 Četiri Lava...............B3
6 Pizza Ćaos..............C2
7 Pod Mansardom.........B3

Off map
Dunav..........................D2

---

the Austrians in the region. The current chapel was built in 1817 and mimics the shape of a Turkish military tent with four entrances to enable all of the participating parties to enter the room at the same time, thus putting them on equal terms. The chapel's windows are said to be patterned on the Union Jack flag – a nod of recognition to Britain, which was a co-signatory of the treaty that was eventually signed after 72 days' careful negotiation. The Peace Chapel has recently been fully restored with UNESCO funding.

GETTING THERE AND AWAY To reach Sremski Karlovci by **bus** from Novi Sad, take bus number 61 or 62 from Bulevar Mihaila Pupina before Varadin ridge. Buses leave every 20 minutes or so between 06.00 and 21.00. You can get off at the stop next to the railway station [254 C1] and walk along Karađorđeva to the central square or, if you prefer, stay on it as it continues through the town. Catching buses back into Novi Sad it is probably easier to wait at the stop by the station [254 C1].

By **rail**, there is the seasonal **Romantika** tourist train service from Belgrade in summer. This runs on weekends, leaving Belgrade in the morning for the 1½-hour trip to Sremski Karlovci. The same train departs Sremski Karlovci in the late afternoon to arrive back in Belgrade in the early evening. Tickets range in price according to class and whether the train is diesel- or steam-powered. Tickets, which include free parking at Belgrade station, free bicycle transportation, a walking map and free sightseeing tour, can be purchased at Belgrade and Novi Sad stations or at travel agencies like Magelan. Check with Serbian Railways (w *serbianrailways.com*) for the current timetable.

TOURIST INFORMATION [254 B3] (*Patrijarha Rajačića 1;* ✆ *882 127;* e *info@ karlovci.org.rs;* w *karlovci.org.rs*) The tourist office on the main square is very helpful and well resourced, with plenty of information about the history of the town as well as more general detail about the Fruška Gora area. It can also help arrange local accommodation, organise wine tours and sell you a detailed map of the town.

🏠 **WHERE TO STAY AND EAT** Dining and accommodation options are listed below, but there are also *sobe* to rent at Ivana Mažuranića 5 (✆ *882 849;* €) and quite a few more options for staying in **private rooms** in and around the town. Enquire at the tourist office for further suggestions.

As well as the eating options listed, there is also a good **bakery** [254 C4] that sells *burek*, *pite* and pizza slices on Mitropolita Stratimirovića opposite the Lower church, and a few **fast-food stalls** around the corner by the post office on Trg Branka Radičevića. **Pizza Ćaos** [254 C2], located near the taxi stand, is another option.

🏠 **Premier Prezident** ***** [254 C2] (15 rooms, 3 suites) Karađorđeva 2; ✆ 884 111; e reservations@premierprezidenthotel.com; w premierprezidenthotel.com. In the centre of town, this luxurious small hotel in mock Baroque style has comfortable kitschy rooms, welcoming staff & excellent b/fasts. Spa, gym, swimming pool & parking. Probably more 4-star than 5-star overall. €€€€

🏠 **Hotel Dunav** *** [254 D2] (47 beds, 5 suites) Dunavska 5; ✆ 884 008; e hotel@ hoteldunav.co.rs; w hoteldunav.co.rs. Situated on the bank of the River Danube at the edge of town & aimed at both tourists & business visitors. All rooms come with TV, minibar & AC. A swimming pool & a dock for tourist ships are planned for the future. €€€

🏠 **Vila Prezident** **** [254 A3] (6 rooms, 2 apts, 1 suite) Belilo 71; ✆ 883 325; m 062 506 451; e vilaprezident@gmail.com; w vilaprezident. com. 1km from the town centre, all en-suite rooms with AC, TV, internet. Smoking & non-smoking. Restaurant with live music & own wine cellar. €€€–€€

🏠 **Šomin Lagum** [254 C4] (3 rooms) Svetozara Markovića 8; ✆ 883 855; m 062 1643 865; e info@ sominlagum.com; w sominlagum.com. 3 dbl rooms in a 200-year-old family house. €€

🏠 **Vila Belilo 69** [254 A3] (23 rooms) ✆ 884 101; m 062 1958 844; e vilabelilo@gmail. com. 2km from town centre on the Stražilovo road. Rooms have cable TV, minibar & internet connection. €€

✗ **Bermet** [254 C3] Trg Branka Radičevića 5; ✆ 884 544; w bermetvilla.com; ⏰ 07.00–23.00 Mon–Thu, 07.00–01.00 Fri/Sat, 08.00–23.00 Sun. Using premises that once belonged to the now-defunct Hotel Boem, this has a perfect location right on the square, with a sunny outdoor terrace & a decent choice of drinks & national dishes. €€

✗ **Četiri Lava** (Four Lions) [254 B3] Trg Branka Radičevića 3; m 060 7658 106; ⏰ 09.00–22.00 daily. A traditional tavern named after the famous fountain, with a good range of Vojvodina dishes to select from & live music most evenings. €€

✗ **Dunav** [254 D2] Dunavska 5; ✆ 881 666; w restorandunav.rs; ⏰ 08.00–23.00 daily.

There are several cellars in town where you can sample local wines. The tourist office can help organise visits.

Došen [254 B3] Karlovačkih đaka 10; 301 785, 881 974; e vinarijadosen@hotmail.com. In the centre of town, this winery produces Bermet, Chardonnay & Merlot.

Dulka [254 C6] Poštanska 8 i Karlovačkog Mira 18; 571 711, 881 797; e dulka@eunet. rs; w dulka-vinarija.com. Currently run by the 4th & 5th generations of the Dragoljović family of winemakers, the main wines here are Riesling & Župljanka. They also produce brandies such as Komovica & Lozovača.

Kiš [254 C6] Karlovačkog Mira 46; 882 880, 882 564; e info@vinarijakis.com; w vinarijakis. com. Following a family winemaking tradition that is nearly 2 centuries old, this is a good place to sample the local Riesling, as well as white & red Bermet.

Kosović [254 C6] Karlovačkog Mira 42; 882 842; e info@vinarijakosovic.com; w vinarijakosovic.com. A small vineyard producing high-quality wines: Riesling, Vranac, red & white Bermet.

Radmilo Dimitrijević [254 B2] Patrijarha Rajačića 5; 881 911

Živanović [254 D6] Mitropolita Stratimirovića 86; 881 071; e muzejpcelarstva@gmail.com; w muzejzivanovic.com. This is the same family concern that runs the bee-keeping museum.

This international restaurant specialising in fish dishes is part of the Dunav hotel complex. €€

✗ **Pod Mansardom** [254 B3] Mitropolita Stratimirovića 2; 884 140; m 063 8660 545;

🕑 Tue–Sun. An old-fashioned, traditional restaurant located near the high school. Friendly service & good fish & roast meat dishes. Also wine & souvenir shop. €€

OTHER PRACTICALITIES

$ **Bank** Erste banka [254 D3] Zmaj Jovina 18; 881 351

✉ **Post office** [254 C2] Trg Branka Radičevića 1; 881 735

WHAT TO SEE AND DO Surrounding Trg Branka Radičevića is an array of buildings from the 18th and early 19th century: a Neoclassical **town hall** [254 C2] built between 1806 and 1811, a Baroque Orthodox **cathedral** [254 C3] constructed between 1758 and 1762, with a 19th-century façade, and a considerable number of 18th-century houses. The cathedral, dedicated to St Nicholas, has a splendid carved iconostasis by Teodor Kračun and Jakov Orfelin, with icons by other renowned 18th-century Serbian artists. Several of the wall paintings are by Paja Jovanović, a prominent Serbian painter of the period. Next to the cathedral stands the **Patriarch's Palace** [254 C3] that was built in 1894 to replace its older premises. The palace formerly had an impressive library and treasury but these were badly looted by Ustaša troops during World War II. Today the building serves as both the residence of the Bishop of Srem and the summer abode of the patriarch.

Another building of note is the **high school** [254 B3], which as an institution in the town dates from 1791. The current building, built in 1891, is a striking combination of traditional Serbian and secessionist styles. The former neo-Byzantine Patriarchate at Patrijarha Rajačića 16 nearby is now home to the **town museum (Gradski musej)** [254 B2] (✆ 881 637; 🕑 09.00–17.00 daily), which provides an archaeological, historical and ethnographical account of the town and surrounding area, in addition to having a gallery of work by local artists from the 18th century to the present.

The **Upper church (Gornja crkva)** [254 B2] in the northern part of the town was originally founded at the end of the 15th century as a nunnery, a property of the monastery at Hilandar in Greece. It was rebuilt in 1737. The **Lower church (Donja crkva)** [254 C4] south of the main square dates from the first quarter of the 18th century and has a very old and beautiful plane tree in its churchyard. Across the road from here is the **house** [254 C4] that used to belong to one of the town's wealthiest merchants, Dimitrije Anastasijević-Sabov, who was instrumental in financing the opening of the original high school in 1791. The house, dating from 1790, has many interesting Rococo features that include wrought-iron bars at the windows and stone ornamentation. On the same street at Mitropolita Stratimirovića 86b is the **Živanović Family Museum of Bee-keeping** [254 D6] (*Muzej pčelarstva podorice Živanović;* \ *881 071;* e *muzejpcelarstva@gmail.com;* w *muzejzivanovic.com;* ⊕ *10.00–19.00 Mon–Fri*) that gives an interesting historical background to what is an important part of the rural economy in these parts. As well as photographs and newspaper cuttings that document seven generations of Živanović bee-keeping, there is some interesting archaic bee-keeping equipment and a replica of a church-shaped beehive that used to be kept in the garden. The proprietor Žarko also has a 300-year-old wine cellar, where you can sample and buy his wines, which include an award-winning, herb-infused Bermet dessert wine that featured on the wine list of the *Titanic*. Žarko's son speaks good English.

FRUŠKA GORA NATIONAL PARK (НАЦИОНАЛНИ ПАРК ФРУШКА ГОРА)

By any standards these are not especially high – or spectacular – but this modest range of hills, 80km long and clearly visible to the south from Novi Sad, provides welcome relief from what is otherwise the occasionally monotonous, flat terrain of Vojvodina.

The highest point of Fruška Gora (Holly Mountain) at **Crveni Čot** is a mere 539m above sea level, but what makes this range a delight is its lush, forested slopes filled with wildlife, a plethora of hiking trails, and the monasteries tucked away half-hidden in the folds of the hills, mostly on the southern side of the range. On the same warmer slopes, woodland gives way to agriculture at the lower reaches, and sunflowers, orchards and grapevines take advantage of the sunshine and adequate rainfall. Some of Serbia's better wines hail from the vineyards of this area. Above 300m, the hills are almost entirely covered by forest: this is the densest concentration of small-leaved lime (linden) in Europe.

The whole area has been a national park since 1960, and covers an area of 22,460ha. Animal life includes deer, lynx, marten and wild boar, although you would be very lucky to see any of these on a casual visit. The birdlife is prodigious and the hills and valleys are said to have over 700 species of medicinal herb (page 7).

The national park headquarters (\ *463 666;* w *npfruskagora.co.rs*) is at Sremska Kamenica but there is an information centre at Iriški venac, where there is also a gift shop and museum.

GETTING THERE AND AROUND With your own transport, you can meander around the Fruška Gora to your heart's content. Without a car, it is much easier to take one of the tours provided by one of the agencies in Novi Sad or Belgrade (see pages 236 and 109 for tour operator listings). If you just want to walk or mountain-bike in the hills – both worthwhile pursuits – there are numerous hiking and biking trails that stretch across the range. The widely available *Geokarta 1:60,000 Fruška Gora* tourist map gives a good overview of these.

Public transport into the Fruška Gora is sparse and rather inadequate. Although pleasant forays into the hills can be made from Sremski Karlovci, visiting the monasteries themselves entails an awful lot of walking and backtracking. However, it is just about possible. A suggested itinerary is outlined below.

A day's walk in the Fruška Gora using public transport

From Novi Sad's long-distance bus station, take a bus heading for Šabac or Sremska Mitrovica and ask to be let off at Iriški venac. There are several buses leaving in the morning, fewer in the afternoon. Get off at the crossroads at the top of the hill, by the Venac restaurant, then follow the woodland track that leads east through the picnic area behind the restaurant. Following the red and white triangles marked on the trees will lead you to the Hotel Venac, a rather forlorn-looking building that is currently closed. Attached to one of the trees in front of the hotel is a small sign in Cyrillic that points to a downhill track and says something to the effect of: 'Manastir Novo Hopovo – 1 hour'. The narrow track leads down through dense woodland, fragrant with lime blossom and alive with the sound of birds and insects in summer.

After about 45 minutes you will come to an open area where there is another track leading sharply off to the left. Ignore this for the time being – you will return this way later. Just ahead is a motorable dirt track that bends sharply around a fishing pond. Take the right-hand fork of this, which will lead you across meadows to **Novo Hopovo Monastery**, another 10 minutes' walk away.

After visiting the monastery, return to the fork by the pond. From here, take the track back in the direction you originally came from and fork right through a meadow. Very soon, you should see a metal sign nailed to a tree that points up to the right and indicates 'Staro Hopovo 2.2km' away. This track climbs up steeply through woodland at first, then starts to level off as it passes an isolated house with a vineyard. Soon it meets a wider track at a junction by another house and garden. Turn left. This track leads past meadows, fields and orchards, with open views of the valley below. If you are here at the right time of year you can help yourself to delicious plums from the trees that skirt the track.

Staro Hopovo Monastery is soon reached, situated in a sloping meadow beneath pine woodland – a lovely, peaceful spot. A few dedicated monks are hard at work restoring it but the church still remains in quite a ruinous state. From Staro Hopovo, you can continue along the track a little more until you reach a small shrine by a stream and a wooden footbridge. There is a water pipe inside the shrine and the water from it seems to be fine to drink: a good place to top up canteens.

The track continues north then east along a route known as the Fruška Gora Transversal. It eventually leads to **Grgeteg Monastery** by a meandering route that climbs back up to the ridge of the hill. This is still a long way distant, however – a good 10km further on. Unless you have limitless time and energy, it is better to return the way you came, as far as the house at the T-junction by the track from Novo Hopovo. Instead of turning right to retrace your previous steps, continue straight in a southerly direction. The track leads slowly down, passing fields of sunflowers, vines and maize. Eventually it will lead you to the small town of **Irig**. The bus station is at the bottom end of the town, next to a road sign that points towards Krušedol Monastery 7km away. From here you can get a bus to take you back to Novi Sad – they run throughout the afternoon until early evening. There is also a direct bus to Belgrade at 16.15. According to the bus station timetable, a local bus runs to Krušedol at 13.15 – another possibility if you have made an early start – but unfortunately there is no bus back to Irig after this one, so you would have to return on foot.

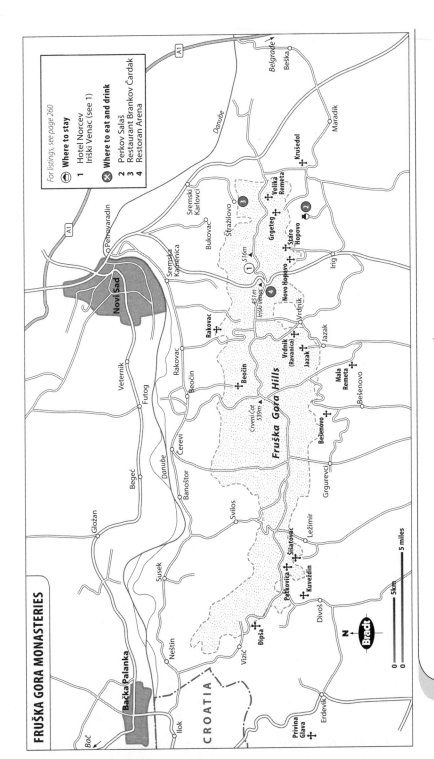

FRUŠKA GORA MONASTERIES

For listings, see page 260

Where to stay
1 Hotel Norcev
   Iriški Venac (see 1)

Where to eat and drink
2 Perkov Salaš
3 Restaurant Brankov Čardak
4 Restoran Arena

CROATIA

Novi Sad

Fruška Gora Hills

Belgrade

Danube

A1

Bačka Palanka

WHERE TO STAY AND EAT *Map, page 259*

The best gateway to the park is by way of the historic town of Sremski Karlovci, which is worth a visit in its own right.

If you want to stay in the area, rather than travel the short distance from Novi Sad, there are a few possibilities. The best idea is probably to stay in Sremski Karlovci, which lies just outside the national park, but if you would like to be a little closer there is the **Restaurant Brankov Čardak** (✆ 883 530) at **Stražilovo**, 4km from Sremski Karlovci, inside the national park in the Fruška Gora foothills. The restaurant has six two-bed bungalows to rent that are equipped with bathroom, television, refrigerator and heating during the winter. The restaurant serves grilled meat, fish and game dishes.

Another option would be to stay at **Iriški Venac** (*telephone code 022;* €€–€), a cluster of buildings around a crossroads in the eastern end of the range 500m above sea level, or Hotel Norcev (details below).

Hotel Norcev * (39 rooms, 5 apts) Put Partizanski odreda bb; ✆ 4800 222; e office@norcev.rs; w norcev.rs. A newish hotel set in woodland that has plenty of sports facilities like swimming pool, gym & sauna. €€€–€€

✗ Perkov Salaš m 064 1156 465; e perkovsalas@yahoo.com; w salasi.info; ⏲ 11.00–20.00. Situated to the east of Irig, towards Grgeteg Monastery. This *salaš* (country ranch) serves both as a rustic restaurant & a country-life museum with lots of ox-carts, ploughs & looms around the place. €€

✗ Restoran Arena ✆ 461 524; w oppidulumarena.rs. Located in trees right by the crossroads. This restaurant serves game & meals containing organic woodland produce like snails, herbs & mushrooms. €€

WHAT TO SEE AND DO

Monasteries of Fruška Gora In the period between the 16th and 18th centuries, a total of 35 monasteries were built in these hills. Today, just 17 remain, tucked away along the length of the range. Some, like Bešenovo, Kuveždin and Šišatovac, are just ruins these days. Others, like Divša, Rakovac, Grgeteg, Jazak, Staro Hopovo and Velika Remeta, which have suffered similar heavy damage, have been completely or partially restored, although nothing can realistically be done to faithfully restore the frescoes that formerly graced Krušedol, Vrdnik, Mala Remeta, Petkovica and Privina Glava monasteries.

The monasteries were founded during the period of wars and migrations caused by Turkish occupation further south. They became vital communities that ensured that Serbian identity and Orthodox religion would survive through difficult times. They also became places of pilgrimage, filled with sacred art and the relics of Serbian saints that attracted both pilgrims and patrons alike.

It would take a real enthusiast to visit all of the monasteries, and it is probably best to concentrate on just two or three in order to avoid 'monastery fatigue', a temporary psychological state that is even more common in central Serbia than it is here. The monasteries of Fruška Gora are not as old as those further south that belong to the Raška and Morava schools, nor are their frescoes as well preserved or impressive. If you are short of time and have to make a decision between the two, it would be better to see just those in central and southern Serbia. Nevertheless, a day or two spent visiting monasteries in Fruška Gora is a delightful way to see the best of the Vojvodina countryside. If you decide to visit just two or three, then Novo Hopovo, Krušedol and Vrdnik are the ones probably most worthy of your time.

Some of the more outstanding monasteries of Fruška Gora are detailed below.

Krušedol This lies 8km east of the small town of Irig, and was founded in the early 16th century by Đurađ Branković, who ruled Serbia for about ten years before becoming an archbishop. It has been destroyed and reconstructed on several occasions since. Most of its frescoes are from the mid 18th century although a few 16th-century remnants remain. The church, which also contains the remains of many members of the Branković family, as well as King Milan Obrenović (died 1901), was used as a prison by the Ustaša during World War II – many Partisans were tortured and murdered here. This is probably the most visited monastery in the Fruška Gora range.

Grgeteg Further to the west, Grgeteg was founded between 1465 and 1485 by Despot Vuk Grgurević. The monastery was deserted before the great migration but was renovated by Bishop Isaija Đaković in 1708. It has been restored again in recent years. Grgeteg has an icon of Mother Trojerućica that is a copy of the famous icon from Hilandar Monastery at Mt Athos, Greece.

Novo Hopovo Built in 1576, the monastery is located 7km from Irig, next to the main road that leads to Novi Sad. The church shows a Byzantine influence in its design, rather like those of the Morava School, and has an elegant 12-sided dome that is encircled by colonettes. Inside, there is the famous fresco of *The Massacre of the Children at Vitlejem* by the painter Teodor Kracun. The monastery was badly damaged during World War II, its iconostasis torn down and religious treasures stolen.

Velika Remeta Close to Sremski Karlovci in the eastern part of Fruška Gora, Velika Remeta was built, entirely of bricks, during the 16th century. There is some

THE 'WILD MAN' OF FRUŠKA GORA?

In the winter of 1996, two friends from Novi Sad, Sreta Spasović and Dejan Radulov, went walking in the hills of Fruška Gora. After stopping at the house of Dejan's mother-in-law in Sremski Karlovci, they headed first to Zmajevac, where they rested, and then on towards Brankovac. For a change they decided not to follow the marked path but instead find their way through the woodland. Deep into the woods they heard a loud cracking of branches and, thinking that it might be a roe deer, headed towards the source of the noise. They came to a small clearing but, instead of the expected deer, they claim they saw something much more remarkable: a man-like creature completely covered in brown hair, almost 3m tall. They describe the hunch-backed creature as having hands that were disproportionately large, as being broad-shouldered with an immense head that resembled an orang-utan's, only bigger. On seeing the two hikers, who at this stage were both paralysed with fear, the creature screamed and darted into the woods at incredible speed. Sreta suggested that they try and follow the 'wild man' but Dejan was not keen. They followed its tracks in a northeastern direction until they suddenly disappeared without trace: it was as if it had disappeared underground, or taken off and flown. Returning to the area the next day, they could find no trace of the creature or its tracks.

Make what you will of this report – perhaps the moral of the tale is that it is better to stick to the footpaths!

evidence to suggest that the monastery already existed in 1509. The bell tower, built 1733–35, is one of the tallest in the region at nearly 40m high. Most of its frescoes were destroyed during the last war.

Mala Remeta Founded by Dragutin Nemanjić, it lies 2km west of Jazak. Monks from Žiča Monastery came here to live at the end of the 17th century. The original church was destroyed by the Turks and the present one dates from 1759.

Vrdnik (Ravanica) The monastery lies close to Vrdnik, a former mining settlement. The date of its founding is unknown but it is mentioned in documents from 1589. Monks from the monastery of Ravanica in eastern Serbia arrived here in 1697, bringing with them the relics of Prince Lazar. Lazar remained here until World War II when he was temporarily moved (with German assistance) to Belgrade to prevent his remains falling into disrespectful Ustaša hands (page 345). The current church dates from 1811.

Jazak The monastery lies 2km north of the village of the same name. It probably dates from the first half of the 16th century. The relics of King Uroš Nejaki were kept here from 1705 to 1942.

SREMSKA MITROVICA (СРЕМСКА МИТРОВИЦА) *Telephone code 022*

This town on the Sava River to the south of Novi Sad in western Srem, just off the main Zagreb–Belgrade highway, has a long history of settlement that goes back 7,000 years. The earliest colonists here were Illyrians, later followed by Celtic settlers, but the greatest undertaking was undoubtedly made by the Romans who built **Sirmium** on the same site as the modern town, close to the banks of the Sava River.

Sirmium was an extensive settlement that was far more than a mere garrison, having all of the usual trademarks of Roman sophistication: baths, mosaic floors, public sewage systems, a hippodrome and palaces. Sirmium, under the rule of Emperor Galerius, became one of the four capitals of the Roman Empire after the Diocletian partition in the late 3rd century AD. It went on to become an important Christian centre before being conquered and destroyed by Avars in 582. After this, the town fell into obscurity for a long period and was ruled in turn by Byzantines, Hungarians and Serbs under Despot Đurađ Branković. In 1521, Ottoman Turks conquered the town and ruled for the next two centuries until Habsburg rule took over in the 18th century. During World War II Sremska Mitrovica became part of the NDH (Independent State of Croatia) and life was especially tough for the town's Serbian majority, who suffered greatly at the hands of the Ustaša. When the war ended the town was incorporated into the province of Vojvodina in 1945.

Much of what the Romans left still lies under the streets of the modern town, awaiting the will and the finance necessary to excavate (the town has the world's only unexcavated horse-racing arena). However, there are a couple of places in town where the foundations have been cleared enough to appreciate the scale and sophistication of Sirmium without needing to have a trained archaeologist's eye. The town's museums also have plenty of interest, with some fine pieces of Roman sculpture.

GETTING THERE AND AWAY There are around 20 buses a day from Novi Sad and ten or so from Belgrade. Four daily buses also run from nearby Ruma. Being close to both the Croatian and Bosnian borders there are also international connections: five buses run from Banja Luka in the Republka Srpska entity of Bosnia and Herzegovina, and two more from Brčko.

Sremska Mitrovica is on the main Ljubljana–Zagreb–Belgrade train line and so all through trains stop here at the town's rather grim railway station.

The **train** (✆ 712 422) and **bus stations** (✆ 714 147) stand side by side, a 20-minute walk from the town centre. A war memorial in the form of an obelisk with the communist red star stands in the road between the two stations – a rare sight in modern Serbia.

TOURIST INFORMATION
i Svetog Dimitrija 10; ✆ 618 275; e turistorgsm@ yahoo.com; w tosmomi.rs

WHERE TO STAY AND EAT
Sremska Mitrovica is an easy day trip from either Novi Sad or Belgrade but there are several options if you want to stay over. In addition to what the hotel restaurants have to offer, there is also a reasonable choice of dining options.

Apartments Passage (10 apts) Kralja Petra I 84; ✆ 623 845; e passageapartmani@gmail.com; w apartmanipassage.com. Apartment accomodation with modern facilities near the town centre. €€

B&B Atrium (5 rooms) Kralja Petra I 5/11; ✆ 612 613. A clean & good-value B&B with modern facilities & an excellent location in the town centre. €€

Hotel Sirmium ** (55 rooms) Vuka Karadžića 8; ✆ 226 333. This Yugoslav-era hotel, in the centre of town, is close to everything that you might wish to see. The foundations of a Roman palace are just outside the entrance & the Museum Srem is immediately opposite, facing the park. €€

Hotel Srem ** (17 rooms) Fruškogorska bb; ✆ 638 216; e hotelsremkpz@gmail.com. A little more basic but cheaper than the Sirmium. €

Vila Bela Ruža (8 rooms) Stevana Sremca 89a; ✆ 640 400, 640 644; e belaruza@neobee.net. On the banks of the Sava River, this restaurant has 8 rooms for guests, all having AC & satellite TV. €

Restaurant Probus Promenada; ✆ 623 860. Down by the banks of the Sava River, Probus has a wide choice of Serbian, Hungarian & Italian dishes & live music at w/ends. €€

Riblja Čarda Rubin No1 ✆ 610 925. Down at the old pontoon bridge, this place is, as its name implies, a fish restaurant. €€

Restaurant Balkan 11 Dositejeva; ✆ 622 0100. National dishes on the menu here. €

Caffe Aureus Masarikova bb; ✆ 510 550. In the park by the museum & in a nice shady spot for a drink in warm weather.

WHAT TO SEE AND DO
Although there are no specific buildings to point out, Sremska Mitrovica has an interesting mix of building styles and to wander down through its streets to the river is a pleasant experience. Among the weather-worn 18th- and 19th-century façades are a surprising number of old-fashioned shops that seem to have changed little since Tito's time.

Remains of the extensive **Roman town** of Sirmium are clearly visible in the few places around the town where excavation has already taken place. The best is found near the river along the main road running south from the Hotel Sirmium, at a fork in the road a few hundred metres past the Orthodox Church of St Demetrius. In the triangle of land formed by the junction – Trg Žitni (Grain Square), a small plaza surrounded by 19th-century shops and dwellings – are the excavated remains of what would have been one of the **trade quarters** of the Roman town.

There is also evidence of a high street that would have been one of the main traffic routes connecting the River Sava with the town's forum. Fragments of the pedestrian zone are quite clear, especially the public sewer with its arched brick roof that still remains in places. In the south part of the site some remains of the city wall can be seen.

Vojvodina   SREMSKA MITROVICA (СРЕМСКА МИТРОВИЦА)

6

Continuing down the road from here you soon arrive at the river. There is a large new pedestrian suspension bridge arching across to the south bank of the Sava, and a river promenade to follow in either direction should you so wish. The road to the right of the Roman site leads to the small white 16th-century **Church of St Stephen**, which has a few cafés clustered around it. This modest church, typical of those built during the Turkish period, has an 18th-century iconostasis painted by Teodor Kračun and now serves as a **museum of church art**.

The other major Roman excavation in the town is just behind the Hotel Sirmium at the corner of Dr Adžije and Branka Rajičevića. This probably represents some of the remains of an **emperor's palace** and most likely belonged to one of Constantine's sons. It is likely that more of the palace will be revealed in the future, when the excavations over the road outside the Srem Museum are completed. So far, a beautiful marble head of Diana has been discovered here, giving further evidence that the palace was the property of a powerful and influential figure. The Diana head should be on display in the museum at some stage in the future. Further evidence that a palace existed here is supported by findings around the town that reveal traces of a large hippodrome. If this were the palace of someone as important as an emperor's son then it would have been positioned right next to the hippodrome; so far, all of the evidence seems to point towards this.

The **Museum of Srem (Musej Srema)** is divided into two sites. Opposite the Hotel Sirmium at Trg Svetog Stefana 15 (\ 623 245), in the large building facing the park, is the part of the museum that displays the ethnographic and art collection. The other site is an 18th-century nobleman's house, virtually opposite the church at Vuka Karadžića 3 (\ 621 150; e sm.muzejsm@neobee.net; ⊕ 09.00–15.00 Tue–Fri, 09.00–13.00 Sat, both museums are closed Sun/Mon). This branch deals with the palaeontology and archaeology of the region and serves as the home of CAID, the Centre for Archaeological Excavation and Documentation on Sirmium. Downstairs in the courtyard is an impressive array of Roman finds from Sirmium: statues, columns and intricately carved coffins. Most impressive of all is the blackened skeleton of an enormous wooden canoe-like boat that was dredged from the mud of the Sava River some years ago, and is similar to the one in the collection at Petrovaradin Fortress in Novi Sad. Upstairs, there is a reconstruction of a Celtic house and a Roman tent, various pottery finds and some mammoth and giant elk bones. All of the labels are in Serbian although there is a limited amount of interpretive material in English downstairs.

The **Orthodox Church of St Demetrius** opposite the museum is also worth a quick look. The church was constructed in 1794 on the site of an old marketplace. It has a finely detailed iconostasis and stained-glass windows that feature Lazar, Stefan Nemanja and other members of the Nemanjić dynasty.

Obedska Bara Bird Sanctuary

Obedska Bara Bird Sanctuary This, one of the three Ramsar Convention wetland sites in Vojvodina, consists of an area of marsh and floodplain on the north bank of the Sava River 65km west of Belgrade, close to the town of Šabac. The reserve lies inside an old oxbow lake with open water areas, extensive reed-beds and wet meadows.

Over 200 bird species have been recorded here. Black stork breed here and white-tailed eagle and lesser-spotted eagle have both been seen. Typical birds present here include great white egret, spoonbill and little bittern. There is also a heronry of 250-plus birds.

The sanctuary is reached from the main Belgrade–Zagreb E-70 motorway by taking the Pećinci village exit and continuing south to the village of Obrež at the oxbow lake. Accommodation is available at the **Obedska Bara Hotel** (*15 rooms*; ☎ *022 488 622;* €€–€) in Obrež village.

Zasavica Special Nature Reserve
The Zasavica reserve is situated in a small enclave of Srem that lies immediately south of the Sava River close to Sremska Mitrovica. It consists of around 2,000ha of protected wetland that is made up of meadows, canals, creeks and the Zasavica River itself. The area was first put under protection in 1997 on the recommendation of the Institute for the Protection of Nature in Serbia.

Zasavica has over 200 plant species including water lilies (*Nymhaea alba* and *Nuphar luteum*) and some rare relict species that are included in Serbia's *Red Data Book*. The reserve is also host to around 120 bird species, 80 of which breed, as well as a number of rare reptiles and amphibians, and elusive aquatic mammals like otters. Fishing is permitted in specific locations of the reserve, and carp, pike and golden carp are all present in its waters.

Information and guides are provided by the managing authority, Pokret gorana, based at Svetog Save 19, Sremska Mitrovica (☎ *614 300;* e *zasavica@zasavica.org.rs;* w *zasavica.org.rs*).

The Sremska Mitrovica tourist agency **Anitours** (*Trg Vojvođanskih brigada 4;* ☎ *613 466*) can also help provide tourist information as well as organising accommodation and tours.

SOMBOR (СОМБОР) *Telephone code 025*

The medium-sized town of Sombor lies in the northwest part of Bačka close to both the Croatian and Hungarian borders. Sombor is a pleasant, leafy sort of place with an attractive central square and a leisurely pace of life. Although Serbs form the majority, the town also has a sizeable Hungarian, Croatian and Bunjevci (Catholic Serb) population and most signs and notices in the town are written in two languages. The town, which along with Subotica and Vršac must count as one of the most attractive in Vojvodina, is especially appealing in autumn when the leaves turn yellow and cover the streets in drifts.

The town, first recorded as Sent Mihalj (St Michael) in 1340, fell to the Turks in 1541 and became an administrative centre for the Ottoman Empire that was populated mainly by Serbs. It was plundered by Tartars during the 1593–1606 war with Austria and many of the Serbs living here fled north to safety to be later replaced by Bunjevci, themselves refugees from Dalmatia. Sombor was liberated from Turkish rule in 1687 when it came under Habsburg jurisdiction and in 1749 it gained 'free royal city' status. Sombor is often referred to as Ravangrad (Flat Town) by many of its citizens, a name coined by its best-known writer Veljko Petrović, but its other appellation, 'Green City', seems equally appropriate, as the town boasts more trees and greenery than any other settlement of its size in the country. Both names suit Sombor perfectly: it is, indeed, both green and flat.

Leaving the bus station, a sign points you along a tree-lined road towards the centre. Walking for 10 minutes in this direction, you arrive at a quiet leafy park and the lofty twin-towered **Carmelite church of Svetog Stafana** to the right. Adjacent to the church is the splendid mustard-yellow *Županija* or **Prefecture** building. The central Trg Svetog Trojstva (Holy Trinity Square) with its large, orange-painted town hall is just one block further on, along Pariska. The square is surrounded by attractive buildings on all sides: the **town hall** in Neoclassical style is dated 1842, the date of its reconstruction. Opposite the town hall at Trg Svetog Trojstva 2 is the **Milan Konjović gallery** (☎ *412 563;* w *konjovic.rs;* ⏰ *08.00–19.00 Tue–Fri,*

09.00–13.00 Sat/Sun; admission 100din), devoted to the work of Milan Konjović (1898–1993), a well-known artist who originated from Sombor but spent a lot of time abroad. Adjacent to the town hall is an outdoor market area that is overlooked by a wall-mounted sundial with an inscription in Hungarian painted beneath it. The words translate, somewhat menacingly, as *'One of these is your last'*, referring of course to the hours delineated by the sundial's shadow. Alongside the gallery, a pedestrian street in yellow brick leads down to Trg Republike and the near-defunct Hotel InterNacion. The **City Museum** (*Trg Republike 4;* \ *422 728;* w *gms. rs;* ⊕ *09.00–18.00 Mon–Fri, 09.00–13.00 Sat/Sun; admission 100din)*, a handsome Habsburg building, stands on the north side of Trg Republike. Heading east from Trg Svetog Trojstva along pedestrianised Laze Kostića soon brings you to Kralja Petra I, a wide pedestrian thoroughfare that leads up from the park that surrounds the Carmelite church and the Prefecture building. This is lined on both sides by numerous splendid 19th-century and *fin-de-siècle* buildings, some a little dilapidated, others newly renovated. One of the most notable buildings along here is the **Serbian Reading Room (Srpska Čitaonica)**, established in 1845. On the pavement nearby stands a life-size bronze statue of a photographer with a tripod.

A little way north of Trg Svetog Trojstva is the **Catholic Church of the Holy Trinity (Crkva Presvetog Trojstva)**, built in a Baroque style in 1763 for the town's Bunjevi community on the site of old Turkish buildings. More notable, perhaps, is the **Orthodox Church of St George (Crkva Svetog Đorđa)** at the northern end of Kralja Petra I, which is in mixed Baroque, Rococo and Classical styles and dates from 1761. The church has a very ornate iconostasis of 1866 that has two rows of columns decorated with gilded vines and flowers, and a mural by Pavle Simić that depicts *The Ascension of Christ*. Nearby, stands the **Orthodox Church of St John (Crkva Svetog Jovana)** that was purportedly built on a site previously occupied by a mosque. The elaborate iconostasis here dates from 1809 and is the work of Pavle Đurković. The oldest building in town is of Turkish origin, a large *konak* that was formerly the summer residence of the Belgrade *paša* and became the town's first post office in 1789.

One thing that you may notice in Sombor, and also in Subotica, is the large number of bicycles in the town. It seems that everyone rides them here, both young and old. It makes sense topographically speaking – northern Bačka is as flat as *palačinke* and the residential areas of low-rise Vojvodina towns like Sombor are usually quite spread out. It is, in part, the bicycles that help to reinforce the impression of unhurried calm in the town. Watching the cyclists making slow, shaky progress across the cobbled square, with bulging bags of tomatoes and onions slung from the handlebars, can have a slightly soporific effect, rather like watching a tank of tropical fish.

GETTING THERE AND AWAY To reach Sombor by **bus**, you can take one of the several daily buses that come from Belgrade via Novi Sad. There are also a couple more that originate in Novi Sad. There are ten buses a day that leave for Subotica, as well as a morning service to Zagreb in Croatia and Baja in Hungary.

There is a limited **railway** service with a few trains daily to and from Novi Sad, Subotica and Vrbas but nothing direct from Belgrade. The train station is a 20-minute walk north of the town centre.

TOURIST INFORMATION

i Trg Cara Lazara 1; \ 434 350; e info@ visitsombor.org; w visitsombor.org; ⊕ 07.30–15.00 Mon–Fri

i Kralja Petra I 18; \ 420 041; ⊕ 09.00–14.00 Mon–Sat. Another tourist office with a gift shop.

WHERE TO STAY AND EAT There are plenty of other places to eat in the town centre like **Gradska kafana** (*Trg Svetog Đorđa;* ☎ *412 373;* €) and cafés like **Star** (*Trg Svetog Trojstva 3;* ☎ *418 066;* €) and **Centar** (*Kralja Petra I 22;* ☎ *434 555;* €), which are good for a drink or a snack. Pizzerias are plentiful: **Mamma Mia** (*VI licke divizije 1;* ☎ *442 202;* €) and **Piccolina** (*Avrama Mrazovića 2;* ☎ *412 820;* w *piccolina.co.rs;* €) are both reasonable options. For more formal dining and a choice of traditional Vojvodina fish dishes there is **Vila Tamara** on the Apatin road, which also has a few rooms to rent (see below).

🏠 **Garni Hotel Andrić ★★★** (15 rooms) Trg Koste Trifkovića 3; ☎ 422 422; e recepcija@hotelandric.co.rs; w hotelandric.co.rs. A well-appointed central B&B-style hotel. Rooms with AC, minibar, cable TV & internet connection. €€€

🏠 **Vila Kronić ★★★** (23 rooms) Čonopljanski put 30; ☎ 429 900; m 063 1174 748; e gradskakafana.so@gmail.com; w vilakronic.com. Just outside the town to the northeast, a modern motel with its own restaurant. €€

🏠 **Vila Tamara ★★★** (3 rooms, 2 suites) Apatinski put; ☎ 434 110; e office@vila-tamara.com; w vila-tamara.com. A restaurant with rooms on the Apatin road, 3km from Sombor. €€

✗ **Café Des Arts** Kralja Petra I 18; ☎ 422 432. On pedestrianised Kralja Petra I, this has a courtyard & a quaint interior that seems half café-bar, half museum-gallery. Intimate bohemian atmosphere; occasional music events. €€

✗ **Gentlemens** Venac Petra Bojovića 2; ☎ 302 016; w restorangentlemens.com; ⏲ Tue–Sun. Large, elegantly furnished restaurant serving huge portions of Serbian grill favourites. €€

✗ **Stari Slon** Venac Radomira Putnika 21; ☎ 412 979; ⏲ 08.00–midnight. Traditional *kafana*-style restaurant on the main road just north of the Holy Trinity church. €€

✳✗ **Emma's Fusion** Venac Petra Bojovića 13; ☎ 301 302; w emmasfusion.com. Bright, simply furnished café-restaurant serving a limited but inspired menu of dishes from around the world including several vegetarian choices. There's even an English b/fast for those in need of such things. Good for drinks too. €€–€

✗ **Pollini** Trg Svetog Trojstva 18–19; m 063 8888 041. Next door to the entrance to the town hall, this has a quirky interior that cannot have changed much since Yugoslav times. Good place for coffee, beer or light meals & pizzas. €

BAČ (БАЧ) *Telephone code 021*

The small town of Bač, in south Bačka to the south of Sombor, gives its name to the region. It is one of the oldest towns in Vojvodina and Neolithic remains and evidence of a Roman settlement have been found in the area. In the 10th century, the area became part of the Kingdom of Hungary and in 1085 a new bishopric was founded here. The town eventually fell to the Turks in 1529 who took control of the fortress for almost the next two centuries. Today it is of interest for the evocative ruins of its medieval fortress and its Franciscan monastery.

GETTING THERE AND AWAY Direct **buses** run to Bač from Novi Sad and Belgrade; local services from Bačka Palanka and Odžaci.

🏠 **WHERE TO STAY AND EAT** Both of the accommodation options listed below have their own restaurants. The town centre also has the **Košava** (*Maršala Tita 60;* ☎ *771 070;* €), serving Serbian and international food. There are a number of fish restaurants in the vicinity of the town where *riblja čorba* (fish soup) is the speciality: **Kod Bujaka** (*JNA 14;* ☎ *771 232;* €€) in Bač itself, **Ranč** (*Bereva 25;* ☎ *776 358;* €€) in Bođani, and **Čarda kod Nećka** (*Dunavski kej;* ☎ *779 208;* €€) and **Kod Mikavice** (*Dunavski kej;* €€), down on the banks of the Danube at Bačko Novo Selo.

Hotel Central Lux (14 rooms) Maršala Tita 1; \772 200. As its name implies, this is central & comfortable although not necessarily 'lux'. All rooms come with TV & AC. Restaurant. €€

Pension Jakić (4 rooms) Dose Đerđa 30; \770 707. A pension that doubles as a restaurant; close to the centre. €

WHAT TO SEE AND DO

Bač Fortress Constructed between 1338 and 1342, just to the west of the present-day town, the fortress was held by various different factions during the chaos that followed the collapse of the Hungarian state in 1526 before being taken into the possession of the Turks in 1529. After liberation from Turkish rule, the fortress was partially destroyed as a measure to prevent it being used by Hungarian rebels. Despite this, it remains the best-preserved medieval fortress in the province. The brick-built fortress has a pentagonal plan with a defensive tower at each corner. Inside the walls is a taller central tower of the donjon, which had important defensive and observational roles. The remains of a Gothic chapel are still visible on the north side of the complex.

Franciscan monastery The monastery dates to 1169, and belonged to an order of Templars until it was taken over by Franciscans in 1301. Under both the Templars and the Franciscans, the monastery served as a hospital, one of the first in this part of Europe. The Turks converted it into a mosque during their occupancy and after their expulsion the monastery was almost completely rebuilt in 1743. The Romanesque apse and the large Gothic bell tower built upon 12th-century foundations are probably the most interesting features, along with the remnants of 15th-century frescoes that survive.

Orthodox Monastery of Bođani Located 15km west of Bač, the monastery was founded following a miracle that is said to have restored the eyesight of a merchant called Bogdan in 1478. The church was erected on the site of the spring where the miracle occurred and the monastery was named after its founder. The original buildings were destroyed by the Turks during their occupation, then rebuilt before being destroyed once again following the Rákóczy Uprising that took place in 1703. The present-day church was built in the Baroque style in 1772, and painted in 1739 by the famous fresco painter Hristofor Žefarović, who incorporated contemporary 18th-century detail into his work. In 1991, the monastery changed from a male order to a female one when it was taken over by an order of nuns. Today it is male once more and home to monks from Kovilj Monastery. A chapel with a spring and a small museum dedicated to the work of Hristofor Žefarović can be found in the western wing of the residence.

SUBOTICA (СУБОТИЦА) (Hungarian: Szabadka) *Telephone code 024*

If you travel from Hungary, and particularly from Szeged, with its colourful secessionist buildings, Subotica does not come as too much of a surprise; if anything it seems more of a continuation of that which has gone before. The border does not seem to count for much here and you do not suddenly plunge into a Serbia that is culturally at odds with anything you have seen further north. There is good reason for this: like the rest of Vojvodina, Subotica has spent far longer under Hungarian control than it has as part of Serbia but, unlike most of the other large towns in the province, it has always had a majority Hungarian population as well. It remains very much a Hungarian town, even today. To complicate matters further, that which is not Hungarian in the town is almost as likely to be Croatian as it is Serbian, although this ethnic variation is nowhere near as obvious.

Subotica, the second most populous centre in Vojvodina after Novi Sad, and the administrative centre of the North Bačka district, is Serbia's most Hungarian town by a long chalk. Signs on the street are dual-language, and many local newspapers, radio stations and television channels use the Hungarian language rather than Serbian.

The Magyar influence even extends to the food, with paprika and *gulaš* featuring heavily on many menus.

For the visitor, the novelty of all this depends on which direction they are heading. Travelling from the south, it can come as a pleasurable jolt that Serbia suddenly seems a long way distant; that Turkish influences are nowhere to be seen, and that the hegemony of the Orthodox Church has suddenly faded away. Coming from the north, it may just seem like more of the same. Either way, the gaudy elegance of middle European secessionist architecture is a dominant feature of the townscape. Love it or hate it, it is the architecture of the town that is Subotica's greatest draw.

HISTORY The town was first documented in the late 14th century as a free trading post protected by the Hungarian crown. After the Battle of Mohács in 1526, Subotica became the capital of Jovan Nenad, the self-proclaimed emperor of the short-lived Serbian Empire that existed in Bačka and parts of Banat and Srem from 1526–27. Turks ruled the city between 1542 and 1686 and during this period, as elsewhere in Vojvodina, they encouraged Orthodox Serbs from the south to settle in the area. The city became part of the Habsburg Empire military border zone following the Turkish defeat at Senta in 1697. This precipitated a further colonisation of South Slavs, this time Bunjevci (Catholic Serbs) from Dalmatia. Subotica grew during this period and progressed from being a mere garrison to becoming a sizeable market town. A civil charter was granted in 1743 and many of the Serb population left after this in protest at the loss of the privileges that they had previously been granted as servants of the Habsburg Empire. Many of these migrated to New Serbia in the Ukraine, where they were granted land by the Russian authorities. Some gave their new settlements the same names as their previous homes – Subotica, Senta, Sombor, etc.

In 1779, Maria Theresa of Austria proclaimed Subotica as a Free Royal Town and the town changed its name for a while to Maria Theresiopolis. The population quadrupled during the 19th century and an increasing number of Hungarians and Jews settled in the town. Subotica's so-called 'golden age' began around 1867. In 1869, a railway was built, which allowed it to develop even more rapidly, and in 1896, an electrical power plant was constructed. It was during this period that Subotica developed its treasury of *fin-de-siècle* architecture. The majority of the town's most notable buildings date from around the turn of the 20th century when the taste for architecture in the bold, central European secessionist style was at its peak. The resort of Palić, on the shores of the nearby lake, was developed around the same time, closely followed by the inauguration of a tram service to ferry citizens to and from the new resort.

Following World War I, when the city ceased to belong to Austria-Hungary and became part of the Kingdom of Serbs, Croats and Slovenes, Subotica's prosperity started to wane as it was reduced to the role of border town at the far north of the newly founded country that was later to become Yugoslavia. Nevertheless, with a population of over 100,000, it found itself the third-largest city in the kingdom after Belgrade and Zagreb.

During World War II Subotica was occupied by Hungarian troops. Around 4,000 Jews were deported from the city to face almost certain death in concentration

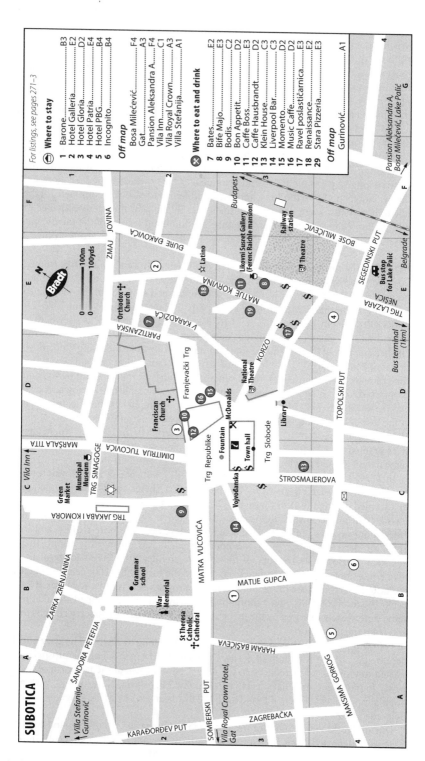

SUBOTICA

For listings, see pages 271–3

Where to stay

1	Barone	B3
2	Hotel Galleria	E2
3	Hotel Gloria	D2
4	Hotel Patria	E4
5	Hotel PBG	B4
6	Incognito	B4

Off map

	Bosa Milećević	F4
	Gat	A3
	Pansion Aleksandra A	F4
	Vila Inn	C1
	Vila Royal Crown	A3
	Villa Stefanija	A1

Where to eat and drink

7	Bates	E2
8	Bife Majo	E3
9	Bodis	C2
10	Bon Appetit	D2
11	Caffe Boss	E3
12	Caffe Hausbrandt	D2
13	Klein House	C3
14	Liverpool Bar	C3
15	Momento	D2
16	Music Caffe	D2
17	Ravel poslastičarnica	E3
18	Renaissance	E2
29	Stara Pizzeria	E3

Off map

	Gurinović	A1

270

camps, while many others – Serbs, Hungarians, Croats, Bunjevci and Jews – joined the Partisan resistance movement to fight the Axis forces. Since the 1990s the city's Serb population has been swollen by refugees from Croatia, Bosnia and Kosovo, while some Croats and Hungarians chose to leave during the Milošević period. Despite this, Hungarians still form the majority in the city and, according to a 2013 government survey, make up 33% of the population (Serbs constitute 30%; Bunjevci, 9%; Croats, 9%).

GETTING THERE AND AWAY Subotica lies on the Belgrade–Novi Sad–Budapest railway line and so has good connections both north and south. Two express trains run direct to Budapest daily from Subotica's **railway station** [270 F3] (*Bose Milićević bb;* \ *555 606*); they originate in Belgrade and arrive in Subotica around 3 hours later, one in the middle of the night and the other at midday. Two more trains go to Szeged in Hungary, one in the morning and the other in the early afternoon. From Szeged, there are connecting services to Budapest by train or bus (the express trains from Belgrade do not travel via Szeged). Three further train services link Subotica with the capital and Novi Sad, but these do not continue over the Hungarian border. Daily train services from Subotica serve other destinations in Vojvodina: five to Sombor, two to Kanjiža, four to Senta and two to Kikinda.

The railway station is conveniently situated in the town centre near to the Likovni Susret gallery.

The **bus station** [270 E4] (\ *555 556*) is located a little further out of town, about 1km along the main Novi Sad–Belgrade road. It can be reached by taking a number 1 bus from the town centre. There are more than 20 buses a day to Belgrade, 20 to Novi Sad, five to Senta, five to Niš and three to Kikinda as well as plenty of local services to places like Bajmok. A daily bus leaves every evening for Sarajevo in Bosnia and Herzegovina.

GETTING AROUND All of Subotica's main sights are within the fairly compact town centre. Two local bus services are useful: the number 1 bus that runs along the Belgrade road to and from the bus station, and the number 6 service that can be caught at the corner of Maksima Gorkog and Trg Lazara Nešića, which goes to Lake Palić.

TOURIST INFORMATION [270 C3] (*Trg Slobode 1;* \ *670 350;* e *office@visitsubotica. rs;* w *visitsubotica.rs;* ⏱ *08.00–16.00 Mon–Fri, 09.00–13.00 Sat, closed Sun*) Located at the town hall, the office has English-speaking staff and can provide maps of the town and information on sights of interest in both Subotica and Lake Palić. They also have several English-language publications for sale on the region.

WHERE TO STAY
Hotels

⌂ **Hotel Galleria** **** [270 E2] (80 rooms, 10 suites) Matije Korvina 17; \ 647 111; e hotel@ galleria-center.com; w galleria-center.com. A business hotel & conference centre with a range of comfortable rooms & suites including 2 for guests with disabilities. Spacious rooms, with AC, minibar, TV, safe & internet connection. Also has the Panorama restaurant with good views over the city. €€€ (apts €€€€)

⌂ **Hotel Gloria** **** [270 D2] (28 rooms, 4 suites) Dimitrija Tucovića 2; \ 672 010; e info@ hotelgloriasubotica.com; w hotelgloriasubotica. com. A centrally located tourist hotel. Stylish modern rooms come with AC, cable TV, internet access & minibar; most have a balcony. Good-value sgl rooms (€€). €€€

⌂ **Hotel Patria** **** [270 E4] (141 rooms, 7 apts) Đure Đakovića bb; \ 554 500; e info@ hotelpatria.rs; w hotelpatria.rs. Renovated in

2008, all rooms in this conveniently central hotel now have AC & cable TV. Facilities include a bar & café, a 250-seat restaurant, wellness centre & a congress hall. There is an exchange office & a travel agency in the lobby. €€€

🏠 **Hotel PBG ★★** [270 B4] (27 rooms, 2 apts) Harambašićeva 21; 554 175, 556 542; e info@ pbghotel.co.rs; w pbghotel.co.rs. The PBG is a small, tidy privately run hotel, built in 2001, in the south part of the town, just 5mins from the centre. It has a restaurant, a conference room & reserved parking. All rooms are equipped with TV, Wi-Fi & minibar. €€€–€€

🏠 **Vila Royal Crown ★★★★** [270 A3] (9 rooms, 2 apts) Somborski put 75; 533 666. Just outside Subotica on the Sombor road. All rooms with Wi-Fi, AC, cable TV & minibar. €€€–€€ (apts €€€)

🏠 **Gat** [270 A3] (13 rooms) Gundulićeva 42; 557 345; e gatsubotica@gmail.com; w gat. subotica.info. A large restaurant south of the centre with simply furnished, good-value sgl, dbl & trpl rooms with bath, AC & Wi-Fi. €€

🏠 **Pansion Aleksandra A ★★★** [270 F4] (28 rooms) Segedinski put 86; 686 840; e aleksandra@yunord.net. On the outskirts of Subotica on the road to Lake Palić. All rooms with satellite TV & bath. Conference hall, coffee bar & pizza restaurant. €€

🏠 **Vila Inn** [270 C1] (9 rooms) Aleja Maršala Tita; 544 122; e villain.subotica@gmail.com; w vilainn.rs. Clean, good-value accommodation in a central location close to the pedestrian zone. €€

🏠 **Villa Stefanija** [270 A1] (8 rooms) Bajski put 12; 580 804; e villastefanija@yahoo.com. On the Kelbija road, a 15min walk from the city centre, with sparsely furnished sgl, dbl & trpl rooms all with AC, private bath & internet access. Min stay 2 days. Free parking. €€–€

Hostels

🏠 **Barone** [270 B3] (16 rooms) Matije Gupca 2; 562 601; e hostel.barone@gmail.com; w barone.hostel-evropa.com. AC rooms of various sizes, from 1- to 6-bed (€ pp), with bath, TV. Shared coffee lounge. €€–€

🏠 **Bosa Milećević** [270 F4] (15 rooms) Studenska Centar, Segedinski put 11; 650 501; e smestaj@scsu.org.rs; w scsu.org.rs. Cheap student accommodation in clean twin rooms with shared bathroom & toilet. €

🏠 **Incognito** [270 B4] (13 rooms) Huga Badalića 3; 559 254; e info@hostel-subotica.com; w hostel-subotica.com. Close to the city centre, all rooms with TV & Wi-Fi. Both dorms & private rooms come with shared bathrooms. Restaurant. €

✖ **WHERE TO EAT AND DRINK** Subotica has a few restaurants in the centre that specialise in local dishes, as well as several pizzerias and numerous outdoor café-bars. **Matije Korvina** [270 E3], formerly Engelsova, just off the pedestrianised Korzo, is a narrow pedestrian street of elegant frontages that is almost entirely given over to cafés, bars and restaurants, a very popular place to hang out on warm summer evenings. In addition to Caffe Boss (see opposite), good places along here to eat, or to just have a drink, are **Stara Pizzeria** [270 E3] (551 835; €€€–€€) at number 5, and the above-average pizzeria **Renaissance** [270 E2] (555 001; w renaissance.co.rs; ⏰ 09.00–midnight; €€€–€€) at number 13.

The area around Trg Republike and the town hall also has a number of café-bars like **Momento** [270 D2] and **Bon Appetit** [270 D2] (555 889; w bon-appetit. rs; ⏰ 11.00–20.00), some with outside tables. **Music Caffe** [270 D2] (525 342) has sumptuous cakes and a non-smoking area downstairs. As well as serving as a café, **Bodis** [270 C2] (Rudića 1; 559 258; €€) is one of the oldest pastry shops in the city. Another elegant caffe-poslastičarnica is **Caffe Hausbrandt** [270 D2] (410 000), on the corner facing Trg Republike. **Ravel poslastičarnica** [270 E3] (554 670) at Branislava Nušića 2, just off Korzo, is another delightful coffee and cake shop.

A central bar worth checking out is **Klein House Social Bar and Art Gallery** [270 C3] (m 063 7093 636; ⏰ 09.00–23.00 Mon–Thu, 09.00–midnight Fri/Sat) at Štrosmajerova. This is effectively an art gallery that multi-tasks as a wine bar, performance space and Hungarian cultural centre. A good selection of wine by the glass is available at a very reasonable price. A good place for a beer is **Bife Majo**

[270 E3] (✆ *556 982*; ⊕ *09.00–midnight*) next door to the Likovni Susret gallery, an inexpensive, old-fashioned place where the walls are covered in photos and posters of sports teams. The Wi-Fi connection here is surprisingly good. For die-hard Liverpool FC fans and homesick scousers there is the **Liverpool Bar** [270 C3] (*Petra Drapšina 10*; ✆ *556 777*; ⊕ *07.30–midnight*), which has a good selection of draught beers and the constant reminder that 'You'll never walk alone'. This has live music some nights.

Elsewhere for musical entertainment, some of the places along Matije Korvina like **Latino** [270 E2] (✆ *523 410*) and the Renaissance pizzeria have live music some nights, especially in summer, as does Bodis (see opposite) at weekends. Ask at the tourist office about other venues in the town.

✳✗ **Caffe Boss** [270 E3] Matije Korvina 7–8; ✆551 111; **w** bosscaffe.com; ⊕ 07.00–midnight Mon–Fri, 07.00–01.00 Sat, 09.00–midnight Sun. As well as a large indoor dining area, this large café-restaurant has a terrace that stretches along both sides of the street & serves as a popular pizzeria, café & bar with a good range of pizzas, salads & pasta dishes. €€€–€€
✗ **Bates** [270 E2] Vuka Karadžića 17; ✆556 008; **w** batessubotica.com; ⊕ 10.00–22.00 Mon–Thu

& Sat, 10.00–midnight Fri, 11.00–16.00 Sun. A family restaurant serving traditional dishes & local specialities in cosy surroundings. Live tamburica group on Fri evenings. €€
✗ **Gurinović** [270 A1] Bajski put; ✆554 934; ⊕ noon–22.00. A well-regarded national restaurant, located a little way out of the centre, with plenty of local dishes on the menu. Dine in a tastefully decorated dining room or attractive garden. €€

OTHER PRACTICALITIES
💲**Bank** Vojvođanska banka [270 C3] Trg Slobode; ✆555 200

📖 **Library** City Library [270 D3] Cara Dušana 2; ✆553 115

WHAT TO SEE AND DO The Art Nouveau **town hall** [270 C3], built in 1908–10, is easily the town's most impressive building even if it is not to everybody's taste. With fancy gables and towers, patterned brickwork and gaudy colours, it is an architectural mishmash of styles that could be said to verge on the tasteless. The rhythm of its design might be described as heavily syncopated – frenetic even – but what it lacks in harmony it makes up for with sheer cheerfulness. As well as the town's administrative offices, the building houses several banks, restaurants, gift shops and the municipal museum. There is even a branch of McDonald's, a singular location for a fast-food chain that prides itself on the uniformity of its product.

It is possible to take a tour up to the town hall's 45m **clock tower**. Departures are at 12.00 from Tuesday to Friday. You are supposed to have a minimum group of five persons but they seem to be quite flexible about this. There is a small admission charge to the watchtower. It is a steep climb but from the top you are rewarded with a marvellous view over the town and surrounding countryside. Telescopes are provided for a closer look at the world below.

Another good thing about taking a clock-tower tour is that you get to take a peek inside the everyday working part of the town hall where Subotica's citizens go about their business, filling in forms, queuing outside offices and so on. This would seem perfectly normal were it not for the elaborate interior decoration found throughout: it seems as if every surface has been stencilled with a variety of naive floral patterns in pastel shades, rather like the designs on a Slovakian chest of drawers. For the bureaucrats of Subotica town hall it must be like working inside an architectural chocolate box.

Facing the town hall is the **National Theatre** [270 D3] (Narodno Pozorište in Serbian, Népszínház in Hungarian) (✆ *554 700*; **w** *suteatar.org*), which originally dates from 1854, making it the oldest theatre in the country. Because of serious structural damage two-thirds of the original Neoclassical building was demolished in 2007 to allow a reconstruction to be erected on the site. The rest of this central zone is contemporary with the town hall and several other examples of the Art Nouveau/secessionist style can be seen along the pedestrian street of Korzo, such as the building that now houses the Continental Bank building, which has heart shapes around the windows and painted shutters on the upper floor.

Behind the town hall, in the park that merges into Trg Republike, is a large **fountain** [270 C3] in an electric shade of cobalt blue, which is especially striking when illuminated at night. Not for the first time in the town, it seems as if the hand of the Catalan maverick, Gaudí, has been at work here but the fountain is a fairly modern addition to the urban landscape and was designed in 1985 by the architect Svetislav Vičena. The brilliant blue ceramic tiles come from the Zsolnai porcelain factory in Pécs, Hungary.

There are more secessionist buildings nearby at the northern end of Dimitrija Tucovića but the most important remaining edifice in this style is the imposing synagogue that stands alone close to the town's market area. The **synagogue** (1902) [270 C1], on the south side of Trg Oktobarske revolucije, was one of the first Art Nouveau buildings to be constructed in Subotica, designed by Dezsó Jakab and Marcell Komor who were responsible for several other buildings in the town including the town hall. The architects have recently been honoured in the renaming of the square, which is now known as Trg Jakab i Komora. The temple has a large green hexagonal dome, with curved gables and large rose windows that are crowned by smaller ones with Star of David brickwork. Now that virtually all of Subotica's Jewish community have gone – either killed during World War II or as migrants to Israel – the building is rarely used and it is starting to look run-down.

The town's **Municipal Museum (Gradski musej)** [270 C1] (*Trg Sinagoge 3;* ☎ *555 128;* w *gradskimuzej.subotica.rs;* ◴ *10.00–18.00 Tue–Sat; admission 100din*), which used to be housed in the town hall, has moved in recent years to a new building on the same street as the synagogue. As well as a large pottery section it has a large ethnographic and archaeological collection from the Subotica region, with plenty of local costumes and musical instruments as well as oddments like bee-keeping equipment and an enormous 1831 wine press. All captions are in three languages: Hungarian, Cyrillic Serbian and Croatian.

Almost opposite the synagogue is the town's **marketplace** [270 C1], which in autumn is full of local produce like peppers and mushrooms. You can buy garlic by the kilo here, live trout in buckets, enormous plastic bags of pre-shredded cabbage and paprika in industrial quantities (Horgoš, the epicentre of Serbian paprika production, is just a few kilometres up the road).

The twin-towered **Catholic Cathedral of St Theresa of Avila (Katedrala Svete Terezije Avilske)** [270 A2] is nearby. The cathedral was built in two separate stages at the end of the 18th century and was the tallest building in the town before the construction of the town hall. In the churchyard is an interesting **statue of the Holy Trinity** that shows God the Father and Jesus atop a pillar with a radiant sunburst above. Beneath them is the Virgin Mary surrounded by a group of four angels. This 1815 monument formerly stood in front of the town hall.

Directly opposite the cathedral stands a Social Realist memorial by Toma Roksandič, erected in the 1950s and dedicated to 'the victims of Fascism'. On one side is a panel of naked men locked in combat; on the other, simply the dates 1941–1945.

On the other side of town near the railway station is perhaps the best example of Art Nouveau architecture in the entire country, the 1904 **Ferenc Raichle mansion**, which is home to the **Artistic Encounters Modern Art Gallery** (**Moderna galerija Likovni Susret**) [270 E3] (♦ 553 725, 552 651, 533 850; e *liksus@open.telekom.rs*; ✆ 08.00–18.00 Mon–Fri, 09.00–noon Sat; admission 200din). Once again, it seems like it came straight from the sketch pad of Gaudí but it is, in fact, the work of the eponymous Ferenc Raichle, who was also responsible for the **city library** [270 D3] and the **grammar school** [270 B2]. Originally designed as a dwelling house, it has now found new life as a gallery of contemporary art.

Lake Palić
Palić started life as a spa in the mid 19th century. By the turn of the 20th century it had become a popular health resort and vacation spot for the wealthier citizens of the region. During this period a number of flamboyant Art Nouveau public buildings were erected, most notably the 1912 **water tower** and the Grand Terrace on the lake, and the wooden **women's lido** of the same year that extends out into the lake.

Palić has a picturesque location and makes for a pleasant outing from Subotica. It may strike some visitors as a bit of a theme park but, in fairness, this is exactly what it was designed to be.

If you decide to spend some time here there are a variety of things to do at the lake. There are beaches for swimming, tennis courts, bikes for hire and a zoo. Both boating and fishing are permitted on the lake. Alternatively, there are plenty of waterside cafés to watch the world go by from. The **zoo** (*Krfska 4;* ♦ *753 075;* w *zoopalic.co.rs;* ✆ *09.00–15.00*) is also considered to be one of the best in Serbia.

Getting there and away A number 6 **bus** from Subotica will bring you here, as will one of the local **trains** that run twice a day between Subotica, Horgoš and Szeged in Hungary. The main bus stop for the lake is by the water tower, which you really cannot miss as it resembles a giant ice-cream cone by the roadside; from here, walk along a shady avenue of trees to reach the lake. Emerging from the arch at the end of the avenue you arrive at an attractive fountain just before the lake promenade. Walking left leads to the Hotel Prezident, while turning right will take you past an Art Nouveau house that looks as if it has been transported from Disney World and on to the four-star fish restaurant, Riblja Čarda. There is lots of artsy statuary to look at along the way.

Tourist information
🛈 Park heroja 13; ♦ 753 111; e info@palic.rs; w palic.rs; ✆ 08.00–16.00 Mon–Fri, noon–19.00 Sat/Sun

🏠 **Where to stay and eat** There is no shortage of places to stay or eat at the resort; below are just a few suggestions. There are also many **private rooms** (*sobe*) available; look for signs around the town. The tourist information centre (see above for contact details) can help with bookings. Many of these are listed on their website.

For **drinks and snacks**, Palić has quite a number of cafés positioned close to the water itself. Two of the best four-star **restaurants** in Palić are run by the Elitte Palić company that also owns the Park and Jezero hotels: **Restoran Riblja Čarda** (♦ *755 040;* w *elittepalic.rs;* €€), which specialises in fish dishes, and **Restoran Mala Gostiona** (♦ *753 447;* w *elittepalic.rs;* €€).

More places can be found on the main road to Horgoš: **Jadran** (*Horgoški put 35;* ♦ *755 104;* €€), which has both international and domestic cuisine, and **Admiral** (*Horgoški put 66;* ♦ *754 427;* €€). There are more basic places close to the water tower and bus stop to Subotica, like **Caffe-pizzeria Don Corleone** (*Horgoški put 65;* ♦ *753 324;* €€) and **Picerija Pub** (*Horgoški bb;* ♦ *753 103;* €).

Vojvodina   SUBOTICA (СУБОТИЦА)

6

🏠 Hotel Park i Jezero **** (Park: 26 rooms, 4 suites; Jezero: 28 rooms) Park heroja 15; 📞753 245; e office@elittepalic.rs; w elittepalic.rs. The Park & Jezero are 2 hotels that stand next to each other in woodland close to the beach. Both are protected 19th-century Art Nouveau buildings that share the same management & reception area. Spa & fitness centre, sauna, bicycle & horse rental available. The Park is a little more expensive than the Jezero. €€€

🏠 Hotel Prezident **** (40 rooms, 4 suites) Olge Penavin 2; 📞622 662; e info@hotelprezident. com; w hotelprezident.com. This smart hotel, 50m from the water & next to a park, is probably the best choice at Lake Palić. It has its own bar & restaurant, a guarded car park, conference room, terrace & garden, as well as a Turkish bath & a jacuzzi. All rooms come equipped with TV, minibar & phone. €€€

Lake Ludaš This nature reserve is close to Lake Palić, just a few kilometres further east along the Horgoš–Szeged road. It has been listed as a wetland of international importance since 1977 and, because of its importance for waterfowl, is one of three protected Ramsar sites in Serbia. In 1994, Ludaš was given the status of a special nature reserve. Fittingly, the lake and nature reserve's name derives from the Hungarian word for goose, which is *ludas*.

There have been 214 bird species recorded at the lake and over 40 are regular nesters. Typical species include squacco heron (*Ardeola ralloides*), bearded tit (*Panurus biarmicus*), marsh harrier (*Circus aeruginous*), bittern (*Botaurus stellaris*), white stork (*Ciconia ciconia*), black-necked grebe (*Podiceps nigricollis*), purple heron (*Ardea purpurea*) and little bittern (*Ixybrychus minutus*). Ludaš also serves as an important feeding station for passage migrants. In addition to being a haven for waterbirds the lake is home to other scarce creatures like pond terrapin (*Emys orbicularis*), a decreasing and endangered species in Serbia.

The reserve is managed by the **Palić-Ludaš** public enterprise in collaboration with the Belgrade-based Institute for Protection of Nature in Serbia and the Ministry of the Environment.

Bačka Topola and around The small town of Bačka Topola (*telephone code 024*) lies 34km south of Subotica, halfway to Srbobran. The town, which developed in the 18th century, has an ethnically mixed population with Hungarians being in the majority with around 60% of the population. Less than 5km north of the town is the village of **Zobnatica**, famous for its extensive stud farm where English thoroughbred horses have been bred for over 200 years. An annual **horse festival** (*Zobnatičke konjičke igre*) takes place at the racetrack here on the second weekend in September and horseriding is available all year at the visitor complex where there is also a museum of horsebreeding and a zoo.

On the road between Bačka Topola and Bajmok, **Stara Moravica** (Hungarian: Bácskossuthfalva) is a large attractive village that is almost entirely Hungarian. There is a nearby lake for fishing, canoeing and birdwatching. Although it is mostly not on a commercial scale, winemaking is an important village tradition here, with many local families having a small vineyard and a wine cellar.

Getting there and away Regular buses running between Subotica and Bačka Topola stop at Zobnatica village. Stara Moravica has far fewer services although it is easy to reach by taxi from Bajmok or Bačka Topola.

Tourist information
🄸 Maršala Tita 30, Bačka Topola; 📞715 310; e tourg@stcable.co.rs

Where to stay and eat

Stara Moravica village farmhouse
Mikloša Zrinjskog (Boračka) 28, Stara Moravica; m 063 567 795; w stara-moravica.com. A cosy self-catering village farmhouse with an orchard owned by a Dublin couple that sleeps up to 6. Fully equipped kitchen, wood stove, bikes & canoe. Home-cooked meals can be provided by arrangement. €€ (1–4 persons), €€€ (5+ persons)

Hotel Jadran*** (20 rooms, 3 apts)
Subotički put, Zobnatica; 715 641, 715 842; e hotel-jadran@open.telekom.rs; w zobnatica.rs. Next to Zobnatica Lake just north of Bačka Topola. All rooms with TV & minibar. €€

BEČEJ (БЕЧЕЈ) *Telephone code 021*

Bečej is a quiet country town of around 25,000 that sits on the eastern border of Bačka by the Tisa River northeast of Novi Sad. Novi Bečej lies just to the east, across the Tisa in Banat. The town grew up around a 13th-century Hungarian castle that stood on an island in the middle of the Tisa River. The castle was taken into Turkish ownership in 1551 and remained so for the next century and a half. It was destroyed after the Treaty of Karlowitz in 1699 and in 1701 a Serb military camp was established in the settlement under the present-day name. From the middle of the 18th century onwards, Hungarians started to settle here, replacing Serbs who began to leave once the military post had been abandoned. This shifting demographic balance created ethnic tensions in the town and violent clashes took place between the two rival groups in 1848, damaging many of the town's buildings.

Most of the town's buildings date from the period after this clash. The **town hall** in the central square Trg oslobođenja dates from 1884, while the three-towered Neoclassical **Orthodox church** opposite was built between 1851 and 1858 to replace an earlier structure that was destroyed by fire during the 1848 clash. Similarly the town's original **Catholic church**, built in 1830, was restored in 1870 following extensive damage in 1848.

GETTING THERE AND AWAY To reach Bečej by **bus** there are reasonably regular services to and from Novi Sad and Zrenjanin. Less frequent services connect the town with Subotica, Kikinda, Bačka Topola and Senta. **Novi Bečej**, on the other side of the River Tisa, has better bus connections to Kikinda as well as **train** services to Kikinda, Zrenjanin and Belgrade.

WHERE TO STAY If you have your own transport, **Fantast Castle** is one of the better places to stay located on the Bačka Topola road (page 278).

Hotel Tiski Cvet Trg oslobođenja 1;
771 140; e info@tiskicvet.com; w tiskicvet.com. Situated close to the river in Novi Bečej & a convenient base for exploring the Slano Kopovo Nature Reserve that lies a few kilometres northeast of the town. €€€–€€

Hotel Bela Lađa (20 rooms) Zelena bb;
6915 608, 6915 908. A newish 3-star close to the town centre. €€

Villa Via Bečej (18 rooms) Svetozara
Markovića 45; 6919 833; e villavia.becej@gmail.com; w becej-hotel.com. Close to the town centre, this new hotel is popular with sports teams using the nearby sports centre. It features non-smoking rooms with cable TV, bath & internet access & has a restaurant on site. €€

WHAT TO SEE AND DO The hotel and tourist complex **Fantast Castle**, to the south of Subotica in the eastern part of Bačka, is a popular overnight stop for organised tours of the region. 'Fantast' is located on the Bačka Topola–Bečej road, 14km west

Close to Novi Bečej, a little way to the east just off the road to Bašaid, is **Slano Kopovo**, a seasonal natron lake and salt marsh amidst a vast flat plain of meadows and marginal agricultural land used for herding that is also probably the best place in Serbia to observe the migration of **common cranes** in the winter months. To see the cranes flying low in formation against a winter sunset is a thrilling spectacle, not just in visual terms, but also for the remarkable noise that thousands of these birds collectively make.

With up to 20,000 common cranes stopping here on migration, along with as many as 14,000 white-fronted geese and a vast number of ducks like mallard, teal and wigeon, this is the southernmost important resting place for the bird in central Europe. Many of the cranes, *en route* to winter quarters in North Africa, arrive via Hungary to the north and navigate their way here by following the course of the Tisa River south (Slano Kopovo is the remains of an ancient meander of the river's former course).

Perhaps surprisingly, the management of the nature reserve is a collaborative effort between conservationists and sympathetic hunters who have declared the area off-limits for shooting – a model of co-operation between interested parties that has enabled a unique wildlife site such as this to thrive.

---

of Bečej. The complex includes the castle (now a hotel), a horse stud, a chapel and a parkland area. The 'castle', which is really more of a folly than anything else, was built at the beginning of the 20th century by Bogdan Dunđerski, a local landowner and the richest man in Vojvodina at the time. The building, which is in a mixture of Neoclassical, Baroque and Romance styles, has four towers, the largest of which resembles the donjon of a medieval castle, hence the name. Tours of the castle are available on request, horseriding lessons may be had at the stud and there are tennis courts for the use of guests.

As well as the facilities listed above, the three-star **Hotel Fantast** [map, page 228] (*Bačko-topolski put bb, 21200 Bečej;* ☏ *6913 531;* **€€€–€€**) has 18 rooms, two suites, a 90-seat restaurant, café and conference room.

PANČEVO (ПАНЧЕВО) *Telephone code 013*

Pančevo, administrative centre of the **South Banat**, is an industrial town of around 100,000 that lies close to Belgrade on the River Tamiš, a tributary of the Danube. Despite its troubled recent history, Pančevo has a quiet, relaxed town centre with a number of churches and attractive 19th-century buildings, which makes a good half-day trip from the capital. Interesting walks may be had down by the Tamiš River and there are some pleasant places to eat and drink down at the waterfront.

Maggie O'Kane, writing about the bombing of Pančevo in *The Guardian* newspaper in April 1999, said that it was 'the kind of town that will probably never make it into a guide book'. So here goes.

HISTORY Although the town existed as an important centre of Serbian culture during the Turkish occupation, Pančevo expanded during the early 18th century when it received migrations of Serbs from Romania and German colonists from the Upper Rhine region.

During Habsburg rule the town was made up of two separate municipalities: one Serb and one German. In 1794, these were united into one. Germans remained a major ethnic group in the town up until World War II, constituting 36% of the city population according to the 1910 census. In comparison, the same census revealed that 42% were Serbs and 16% Hungarians. Nowadays, Serbs make up at least 80% of the population.

Pančevo came under the Belgrade city administration between 1929 and 1944 but reverted back to Vojvodina in the years that followed the Axis occupation to become the administrative centre of the South Banat district. The modern town has grown up around its post-World War II petrochemical industry.

Of all the damage wreaked in the 1999 NATO bombing campaign, Pančevo was undoubtedly the worst affected. On the night of 18 April 1999, NATO attacked the town's HIP chemical complex that produced petrochemicals and fertilisers. Fires and explosions at the factories caused huge quantities of toxic chlorine compounds to be released into the air and river, and large tracts of land were polluted with oil derivatives, mercury, ammonia and acids. A large area of farmland around the town was affected and withered, blackened crops lay dead in the fields, poisoned by noxious air and water. Many inhabitants of the area fell ill as a consequence, some of whom subsequently died. The Pančevo area had long been considered a cancer black spot, the cause attributed to inadequate environmental control of its petrochemical industry. Following the bombing and the release of vinyl chlorine monomer into the air at levels a staggering 10,600 times above the recognised safe limit, the situation became considerably worse. The effects of this widespread ecological catastrophe are still being felt in the area and the Pančevo district remains one of the most ecologically damaged regions in all Serbia.

GETTING THERE AND AWAY Pančevo can be easily reached from Belgrade by taking one of the trains that run more or less hourly from Karađorđev Park station near St Sava's Church. As well as Belgrade services, Pančevo Glavna station has four trains a day to Vršac and two to Zrenjanin and Kikinda. Fairly regular buses run to Belgrade, Vršac and Zrenjanin, although some of the Belgrade buses only go as far as the Dunav bus station in the north of the city by Dunavska most. Pančevo Glavna **railway station** (✆ 341 111) and the **bus station** (✆ 510 455) are some distance from each other in the town. The railway station is a 20-minute walk south of the city centre, while the bus station is more central, to the east of the river. Another quick and easy way to reach Pančevo from Belgrade is to take one of the **minibuses** that run regularly from Bulevar Despota Stevana (29 Novembra) close to Pančevački Bridge. These will drop passengers off in the town centre *en route* to the bus station and Chinese Market.

 WHERE TO STAY AND EAT The large state-run Hotel Tamiš is currently closed and up for sale. Below are a few accommodation and dining options. There are a couple of boat restaurants down by the river here, such as **Kakadu** (*Kej Radoja Dakića;* ✆ *342 166;* €).

🏠 **Guesthouse Perla** (5 apts) Vuka Karadžića 5; ✆ 344 546; w perla.co.rs. Close to the town centre & bus station, all apartments with AC, Wi-Fi & TV. Swimming pool & sauna. Lower rates for longer stays. €€€–€€

🏠 **Family Garden** (12 rooms) Stevana Supljikča bb; ✆ 378 240. Small hotel with restaurant in a quiet area near the train station. All rooms en suite with heating, Wi-Fi, TV; some have a balcony overlooking the park. €€

🏠 **Konak Miloša** (8 rooms) Trebinjca 5; ✆ 333 102; e konakpancevo@gmail.com. A quiet, good-value place near the town centre. Clean, tidy rooms with bath, TV, AC & internet access. €€–€

✖ Poco Loco Braće Jovanića 15; ✆ 355 222, 355 333; w pocoloco.co.rs. In the city centre, this smart restaurant also doubles as a club. €€

✖ Vetrenjača Trg mučenika bb; ✆ 351 222. Down by the river, this restaurant in the form of a windmill has all the usual Serbian grilled meat favourites as well as freshwater fish dishes & delicious pancakes. There's an outside terrace by the water for dining in good weather. €€

✖ Citadela Restaurant Dimitrija Tucovića 63; ✆ 354 487. On the main street that leads from the railway station to the centre; has a summer garden. €€–€

✖ Kafić Voz m 064 2904 913; ⏱ 09.00–01.00. Down by the Tamiš River, an old railway locomotive & several carriages serve both as a café-bar & unofficial railway museum. The bar counter is in a converted 3rd-class carriage, with wooden seats &

old black-&-white photos & railway memorabilia on the walls. The outdoor terrace is covered with a wrought-iron supported roof, part of an old platform shelter. The other carriages belong to the Serbian Trainspotters Club, while the locomotive is the property of the Belgrade Railway. The trains that used to arrive at the railway station that once stood here provided the large quantities of grain required by the nearby Weifert brewery, once an important feature of the town. This was formerly the oldest brewery in Serbia but it has since been bought up by Heineken & subsequently closed. Georg Weifert (Đorđe Vajfert), who founded the brewery with his father Ignatz, & later became Governor of the National Bank of Serbia in 1890, is portrayed on the current Serbian 1,000 dinar note. €€–€

WHAT TO SEE AND DO Other than a pleasant stroll along the river, the biggest draw for most Serbian visitors to the town is the large open-air market, known locally as the **Chinese Market**, that stands next to Pančevo Glavna railway station. This has a lot of cheap smuggled goods from Romania on sale and is considered to be a great place for bargains.

The city centre is focused around the square of Trg Kralja Petra I, which has the 1833 Neoclassical Town Magistrates' building at number 7 that now serves as the **town museum (Gradski musej)** (✆ 342 666). The museum has an interesting ethnographic and historical collection and a permanent exhibition of paintings that include *Migration of the Serbs* by Paja Jovanović, a famous and rather iconic image that shows the Serb migration into Habsburg territories in 1690.

Pančevo has a handful of interesting churches. The mid 18th-century **Catholic Church of St Carl Boromeo (Crkva Katolička Sv Karla Boromeski)** began life as a Franciscan monastery; a chapel was built on the south side in 1853 and its slim, square bell tower was added in 1858 during renovation. The neo-Baroque **Mother of God Assumption Church (Crkva sa dva tornji)**, dating from 1810, stands on Dimitrija Tucovića, its two towers rising above the surrounding rooftops to create a local landmark. The church's benefactor was Karađorđe who is said to have provided the wood for firing the church's bricks. The church developed slowly: the interior was not finished until 1836, the towers completed in 1855 and the side doors added to the western wall in 1861. The frescoes in the interior were not completed until 1928. Nearby is the **Church of the Transfiguration (Crkva Preobraženja)**, in a contrasting neo-Byzantine style, with a central dome and independent bell tower.

The south part of the town used to be the German municipality and continued to be the part of town where ethnic Germans lived long after the Serb and German boroughs combined to form a single entity. Evidence of this can be seen in the 1905 neo-Gothic **Evangelistic church** that stands on Svetislava Kasapinović.

Vojlovica Monastery lies just outside the town to the south on the road to Starčevo, next to the oil refinery in the predominantly Slovak village of the same name that has since become a Pančevo suburb. The monastery was founded in the 15th century. Legend attributes its founding to Prince Lazar's son, Despot Stefan Lazarević, but its true origin is uncertain. The monastery has been badly damaged many times, first by the Turks during their occupation and later by Austro-Hungarian troops during World War I. The monastery was last restored in the 1980s but these days it seems a strange juxtaposition of the sacred and profane, with the buildings set amidst the pipes and paraphernalia of the industrial zone that surrounds them.

KOVAČICA (КОВАЧИЦА) *Telephone code 013*

This small but sprawling town lies directly north of Pančevo in the middle of a flat agricultural landscape of sunflower fields and far horizons. Kovačica is well known for two things: its majority **Slovak population** and its tradition of **naive painting**.

The town is quite spread out with long, tree-lined avenues radiating off a central park with a church; not really that different from many others in Vojvodina, except that the church, dating to 1829, is Slovak Evangelist rather than Serbian Orthodox. Generally, the Slovak influence is not that pronounced but it can be seen in the houses, some of which have small plaques that record the householder's name on the gable, along with the date of construction. There are more blonde-haired children than usual too, as you might expect, and a few older women riding around on bicycles who still wear the traditional Slovak embroidered apron over their black voluminous skirts.

Slovaks first came to the area 200 years ago as soldiers of the Austrian army on the front line against the Ottomans. In return for their services to the Habsburgs they were given land to farm. The tradition of naive painting started in 1939 when two locals, Martin Paluška and Ján Sokol, began to paint. The tradition developed in the 1950s when Paluška, Sokol and a few others formed a painting club and more Slovaks from Kovačica, Padina and the surrounding area took up paintbrushes to try and represent the rural environment they lived in. The first exhibition took place in 1952 on the occasion of the 150th anniversary of the Slovaks' arrival in Kovačica; three years later the first gallery of naive art was opened. Kovačica's fame as a centre of excellence for naive art has blossomed over the years since and local painters Zuzana Halupova and Martin Jonaš in particular have built up an international reputation. Famous overseas visitors to the village galleries have included former French president Francois Mitterrand, the actresses Sophia Loren and Ursula Andress, footballer Pelé, cellist Mstislav Rostropovich and even, it is claimed, the Rolling Stones.

GETTING THERE AND AROUND Buses run from Belgrade's **BAC bus station** to Kovačica several times a day. The journey takes just over an hour and costs around 150din. More frequent services run to Pančevo and Zrenjanin. The infrequent **trains** that run to Zrenjanin from Belgrade also stop in Kovačica. To reach the art galleries and workshops from the bus stop on the main road, turn right past the park and church and walk for 5 minutes; they are on the right-hand side of the road beyond a few shops and cafés.

TOURIST INFORMATION
i Maršala Tita 50; 660 460; e office@took.org. rs; w took.org.rs

🏠 **WHERE TO STAY AND EAT** Kovačica is an easy day trip from Belgrade but if you want to stay there is just one hotel, **Hotel Olymp-Insit**, although at the time of writing this was closed for restoration. Fortunately, there is also **private accommodation** (*all €*) available in the town with various local hosts. All can provide meals and all can be reserved through the Tourist Organisation of Kovačica (660 460; e took.booking@ gmail.com).

Other places to eat include **Cervene Vino** (*Maršala Tita 76;* m *063 8685 923;* €€), which has Slovak food and folk music; **Srdiečko** (*Maršala Tita 27;* ☎ *661 344;* €€), another restaurant that serves Slovak national cuisine, and **U Susedov** (*Masarikova 66;* ☎ *660 778;* €€), which offers Serbian national food. There are several cafés scattered around the town centre like **Caffe Sport** and **Fagan**.

🏠 **Ana Boboš** JNA 75; ☎ 661 196; m 061 1139 822; e annabobos@yahoo.com.au

🏠 **Ana Šipicki** Janka Bulika 79; ☎ 662 019; m 063 1206 357

🏠 **Marijana Farkaš** Nikole Tesle 97; ☎ 662 148; m 063 8890 506

🏠 **Zuzana Venjarski** Martina Kukučina 5; ☎ 661 525; m 062 8504 309; e viktor.venjo@gmail.com

WHAT TO SEE AND DO A large and varied collection of the work of the Kovačica artists can be seen at the **Gallery of Naive Art** (*Galerija naivne utmetnosti; Masarikova 65;* ☎ *661 157;* w *naivnaumetnost.com;* ⊕ *08.00–16.00 Mon–Fri, 10.00–16.00 Sat/Sun*), the state-run gallery in the town. Naive art is not to everybody's taste but there is a striking amount of variety in the work on display and many of the painters here have instantly recognisable styles. The themes, of course, are all rural, but even these cover a wide range of subject matter.

Next door to the state gallery is the private **Gallery Babka** (☎ *661 631;* e *office@babka-center.com;* w *babka.rs*), with a more limited range. They have reproductions and small cameos for sale as well as full-size paintings. In the same group of buildings are the workshops of several practising artists. One that is well worth visiting and which welcomes visitors is that belonging to **Zuzana Holúbeková** (*Masarikova 65;* ☎ *660 521, 661 929;* m *062 438 353*), whose work has quite a marked erotic quality about it. The **Martin Jonaš Memorial House (Spomen kuća Martina Jonaša)** (*Čaplovičova 25;* ☎ *661 157*), which has 150 paintings along with the painter's collection of books, furniture and Slovak costumes, can also be visited with prior notice.

KIKINDA (КИКИНДА) *Telephone code 0230*

Kikinda, the administrative centre of the **North Banat**, close to the Romanian border is a pleasant enough place to spend a night or two although, in truth, it is probably not worth making a special detour for unless you have a penchant for mammoths or owls. If you do have an interest in either or both of these, then Kikinda is quite unparalleled as a destination.

Archaeological evidence points towards the Kikinda region being settled back in the Bronze and Iron ages. At the site of Gradište at nearby Iđoš artefacts from the Neolithic age have also been discovered. The most exciting find, however, was back in 1996 when the most complete skeleton of a **steppe mammoth** ever found was discovered in a local brickworks. The skeleton now resides in the municipal museum. Today the town's industry revolves around the manufacture of tiles – it is home to the country's largest tile factory – and signs around the town proudly proclaim: 'Kikinda – Tile capital.' In recent years, the town's central square has also become well known as the winter roosting place for an astonishingly large number of long-eared owls (see box, opposite).

GETTING THERE AND AWAY The town is somewhat out on a limb, deep in the Banat, and its best connections with the rest of Serbia are through Zrenjanin to the south. A dozen or so buses go each day to Belgrade from Kikinda's **bus station** (☎ *23 770*) and a similar number leave for Novi Sad and Zrenjanin. Three daily buses run to Subotica and three to Bečej.

KIKINDA – A SERBIAN PARLIAMENT... OF OWLS

There are no two ways about it: during the cold winter months, the small town of Kikinda, hard against the Romanian border in northeast Serbia is, for a period at least, the owl capital of the world. It is not the only place in the region favoured in this way – northern Vojvodina holds hundreds of roosting sites for long-eared owls – but in sheer number and ease of viewing, Kikinda is undoubtedly the most impressive.

The owls arrive around late October, using the trees of the town's central square as a daytime roost before heading off into the surrounding countryside each evening to hunt rodents. Owl numbers increase as the winter progresses and at their peak there may be up to 750 perched in the trees around the Church of St Nikola that is the centrepiece of Trg srpskih dobrovoljaca. Individual trees may hold anything up to 25 or 30 owls perched together. The birds are generally tolerant of being viewed as long as visitors do not create too much disturbance. The same tolerance is also true of Kikinda's citizens, who are proud of their town being so favoured by the owls and take great pleasure in showing outsiders the best trees to view.

Why they roost in such large numbers, and why they choose an urban setting such as this is down to several factors. Northern Vojvodina, thanks to traditional farming practices, is rich in rodents – voles mostly – that is the long-eared owl's main source of food. In winter towns are generally a few degrees warmer than the surrounding countryside and so Kikinda, in the heart of vole country, with its tolerant people and leafy central square, ticks all the right boxes. Numbers invariably fluctuate in response to the quantity of rodents available: the winter of 2009–10 came with a maximum count of 734 birds; in 2016–17, the number of owls was reduced to a still very impressive 160 or so. Whatever one's interest in birds in general, Kikinda's winter long-eared owl roost is a spectacular and unforgettable sight to behold.

For those who wish to travel here in the company of expert birders, The Urban Birder (w *theurbanbirder.com/tours*) usually offers tours to this destination in early winter.

Kikinda also has a **railway station** (✆ *23 114*) on the edge of the town, which has a limited service to Subotica and Zrenjanin. The single-carriage train that used to run across the Romanian border to Jimbolia twice a day is sadly no longer in service.

TOURIST INFORMATION In the town hall at Trg srpskih dobrovoljaca 12 (✆ *26 300*; e *turizam@kikinda.org.rs*; w *kikinda.org.rs*).

WHERE TO STAY AND EAT Kikinda has a wealth of café-bars but few proper restaurants. The main square, Trg srpskih dobrovoljaca, has some café-bars facing on to it, and the streets that lead on to the square have more cafés, as well as a number of ice-cream parlours and bakeries. There are a couple of **pizzerias** along the south side of the square, to the west of the town hall. Further on, across the next junction, is a large **bakery** with an outdoor seating area. Another decent place for cakes and coffee is **Caffe-Picerija Macchiato** (*Trg srpskih dobrovoljaca 19*; ✆ *29 779*) on the main drag between Hotel Narvik and the main square.

Vojvodina   KIKINDA (КИКИНДА)

6

At the time of writing, Kikinda's main hotel, Hotel Narvik, was closed for business but there are a number of places offering pension accommodation in the town.

🏠 **Belavila** (12 rooms) Svetosavska 178; ☎434 354; w belavila.rs. This national restaurant also has bright modern rooms to rent. €€–€

🏠 **Hostel Paparazzo** (7 rooms) Zorana Đinđića 5l; m 060 1435 435; e sova0230@gmail.com. Clean sparse rooms above the Café Sova. €

🏠 **Pension Bukva** (5 rooms) Pere Segedinca 36; m 2105 200. €

☀✗ **Twenty** Trg srpskih dobrovoljaca 28; ☎435 158; w twenty.rs; ⏲ 08.00–midnight. A smart &

very popular restaurant with chandeliers & sparkly mirrors that serves a wide variety of well-prepared pizzas, salads & pasta dishes. Open kitchen with a huge pizza oven but sadly no no-smoking area. Also offers comfortable accommodation (2 rooms, 1 apt; €€) in pristine, modern rooms. €€

✗ **Conti Pizzeria** Svetosavska, blok GA 3; ☎34 443. Has a reasonable selection of pizzas & pancakes. €

FESTIVALS AND EVENTS Around the second Saturday of September, **Mamutfest** (w *kika-mamut.com*) takes place at the town museum to coincide with the date of the mammoth's discovery. **Pumpkin Days** (*Dani ludaje*), held in mid-October, is a local three-day festival in which locals get to show off their home-grown pumpkins and gourds. Not only are there competitions for the biggest and heaviest fruits but lectures on pumpkin cultivation also take place, as well as cooking competitions that involve – naturally – the use of pumpkins. To date, the largest pumpkin has weighed in at 247kg, and the longest gourd measured over 2m.

The **International Jazz & Blues Festival** is a music festival held in November that features performers from the Balkan region and beyond.

OTHER PRACTICALITIES There are plenty of banks in the town centre that have Visa-friendly ATMs. These include the **Vojvođanska banka** and the **Central banka** on the main square, and the **Delta banka** on the road south of the main square, parallel to and west of the road that has the Hotel Narvik. The **post office** lies at the end of the shady café street that runs south from the square between the two churches.

WHAT TO SEE AND DO All of Kikinda's sights are in the central square of **Trg srpskih dobrovoljaca**. The most arresting is the pastel-pink, 1894 **town hall**, which is built in Neoclassical style with ornate stucco work. Along the square to the west is the **Orthodox Church of St Nicholas** (Srpska pravoslavna crkva Svetog Nikole), built in 1773 on the site of an older church. Across the square from the church in the Neoclassical **Kurija** court building is the **town museum** (*Narodni muzej Kikinda; Trg srpskih dobrovoljaca;* ☎ 21 239; w *muzejkikinda.com;* ⏲ *10.00–20.00 Tue–Sat; admission 150din*) that has the famous steppe mammoth skeleton excavated on the premises of the town's brick factory among its exhibits. The remains of the mammoth are on display behind glass upstairs but even more impressive is the reconstructed whole skeleton that stands as the centrepiece to the courtyard by the museum entrance. The museum also has an ethnological and archaeological collection that is quite impressive for a town of this size. The gift shop sells all manner of mammoth- and long-eared-owl-themed gifts, as does the gift shop attached to the informal tourist information place just across the square. Kikinda also has one of two surviving **Suvača** (horse-powered dry mill) in Europe, that used to be utilised for grinding flour and paprika. The building, dating from 1899 and operational until 1945, is now occasionally used for theatre performances and concerts.

This, the largest town in the **Banat region** and the third largest in Vojvodina, was known as Bečkerek during the medieval period. In 1936, the city changed its name to Petrovgrad in honour of King Petar Karađorđević, and in 1946 it became Zrenjanin, the name given in memory of Žarko Zrenjanin, a local communist and war hero who died at the hands of the Nazis in 1942. Zrenjanin is too close to Novi Sad to really warrant an overnight stay as, despite its considerable size, it has little in the way of attractions when compared with the Vojvodina capital. That said, there are a few things to see here if you wish to break your journey for a few hours.

GETTING THERE AND AWAY The **bus station** (☏ 541 00) is on the edge of the town, a 20-minute walk or short bus ride from the town centre. Local buses run past the bus station and along Bulevar Beogradski towards the centre; you get off at the turn-off to the town centre where there is a large mural of horses on a gable end. This road, 29 Novembra, leads directly to Trg Slobode and the town centre.

A limited railway service links Zrenjanin's **train station** (☏ 530 388) with Belgrade and Pančevo to the south and Kikinda to the north.

TOURIST INFORMATION At Koče Kolarova 68 (☏ 523 160; w *visitzrenjanin.com*). There is also a tourist information centre at Subotićeva 1 (☏ 581 890).

WHERE TO STAY AND EAT There are a few options for accommodation in Zrenjanin and no shortage of places to eat, especially restaurants serving national food. Below are a few suggestions for both.

Hotel Vojvodina **** (76 rooms, 15 suites) Trg Slobode 3–5; ☏ 561 233; e recepcija@hotel-vojvodina.rs; w hotel-vojvodina.rs. Recently privatised & renovated, this has 2 restaurants, café-bar, summer garden terrace, billiards club & car park. All rooms have minibar, TV, internet connection & AC. Separate floors for smokers & non-smokers. €€€

Guest House Luxotel **** (6 rooms, 2 apts) Laze Lazarovića 6; ☏ 563 457; e luxotel@beotel.rs; w luxotel.co.rs. A modern guesthouse with cable TV, minibar & AC in each room. Indoor swimming pool & sauna. €€€–€€

Vila Filadelfija (6 rooms) Ive Lole Ribara 7; ☏ 528 840; e info@filadelfija.com; w filadelfija.com. Pleasant simple rooms in a 19th-century town house close to the centre with cable TV, AC & internet access. Use of kitchen. €€

Boemi Ninić Pančevačka 38a; ☏ 542 345. A small 'ethno' restaurant with outdoor seating & local food. Live music at w/ends. €€

Burence Strosmajer 55; ☏ 569 344. Traditional restaurant specialising in beef & turkey grilled dishes. Live folk music on Thu. €€

Kamel Karađorđević trg 100; ☏ 530 270. Traditional restaurant located in the park next to the football stadium. €€

Tri Soma Karađorđević trg; m 064 4262 162. Another restaurant in the park with live music & seafood. €€

Monaco Nemanjina 18; ☏ 562 270. Italian pizzeria & coffee bar. €

WHAT TO SEE AND DO The central square of **Trg Slobode** is attractive, with ornate lamp posts and a large neo-Baroque **town hall**. The building, painted in two pastel shades of avocado green, originally dates from 1816 but did not receive its present-day façade until its reconstruction in 1887. It underwent extensive restoration in 2004. Behind the town hall is Gradski bašta, the town park, which is a pleasant green space with fountains, statues and a pavilion. Next to the town hall is the town's Romanesque-style **Catholic church** built in 1864–68 by Stevan Đorđević. Leading off Trg Slobode is **Kralja Aleksandra I**, a pedestrian thoroughfare that has several restaurants and cafés. This comes to an end at Trg Republike, where a pedestrian bridge leads over the Bečej River. The bridge was built in 1971 to replace an earlier and narrower iron bridge by the Eiffel Company. Another, older (1904) footbridge, **Mali most** (small bridge), can be reached from Trg Slobode by way of Subotica Street.

Banja 'Rusanda'

Rusanda spa lies just north of Zrenjanin at Melenci on the road to Novi Bečej, on the east side of Rusanda Lake. The spa offers a variety of therapies alongside facilities for sports training. (*For further information:* \ *315 0409;* e *office@banjarusanda.rs;* w *banjarusanda.rs.*)

Carska Bara

The Stari-Begej-Carska Bara complex is situated to the southeast of Zrenjanin, close to the village of Ečka, and an appealing destination for anyone interested in wildlife. This 1,767ha reserve, designated as one of just three Ramsar Convention sites in Serbia, is actually a complex of various wetland ecosystems that include lakes, swamps, meadows and forest. With 250 recorded species (140 breeding, the rest migrants) and the largest marsh harrier population in Serbia, the reserve is of special importance to wetland birds. All eight European species of heron are said to nest here. The reserve also provides a valuable habitat for marsh flora, scarce mammals like European otter and a variety of fish species like carp, pike and perch.

Currently, Carska Bara is mostly used for scientific research, school visits and recreational pursuits like sports fishing, which is permitted in certain areas of the complex. Interest in birdwatching is still at a fairly low level in Serbia but it is on the increase. A visit to the reserve is a feature of the birdwatching and photographic safari packages run by Magelan Corporation (page 236). They also run one-day trips from Belgrade.

If you would like to visit independently, accommodation can be found in the village of Ečka at the following:

🏠 *Where to stay*

🏠 **Hotel Kaštel Ečka **** (38 rooms, 7 suites) Novosadska 7, Ečka; \ 554 800; e office@ kastelecka.com; w kastelecka.com. This hotel, effectively a 'hunting manor', used to belong to the Lazar family, who were merchants of Armenian origin & who built the village's Catholic church where Franz Ferdinand married Sofia. €€€

🏠 **Hotel Sibila ***** (24 rooms) Ribnjak Ečka fish farm, Lukino selo, Ečka; \ 884 646; e hotelsibila@ribnjakecka.com; w hotelsibila. com. The hotel can organise birding boat tours of the reserve, as well as photo safaris, horseriding & excursions in horse-drawn carriages. Meals can be provided. €€

VRŠAC (ВРШАЦ) *Telephone code 013*

The medium-sized town of Vršac lies out on a limb in the southeast Banat and is not a place you would pass through unless you were heading for Timişoara in Romania. This is a pity as it has a fair amount to offer and is worth considering as an excursion in its own right. Although there are adequate places to stay, it is possible to visit the town as a lengthy day trip from Belgrade.

Two things make Vršac stand out from other towns of the Banat. Firstly, the town's surroundings come as a welcome break from the interminably flat relief that characterises the rest of the region. Vršac stands on the edge of a hilly border region known as the **Vršačke planine** that rises above the Pannonian Plain in a way that seems quite dramatic after having made the mental adjustment to big skies and long horizons. The southern slopes of the Vršac hills are home to vineyards that produce a quite distinctive red wine.

The town's other distinguishing feature is its abundance of architecture from the Habsburg period, with an interesting mix of 18th-century Classical buildings alongside others that betray a more wayward neo-Gothic influence.

Vršac has its own aerodrome that is not used for commercial flights but by the flying school that has its base here. The track at the aerodrome has also played host to the Serbia and Montenegro Motorcycle Grand Prix. With the construction of the state-of-the-art Millennium Sports Centre to the east of the town centre, Vršac was chosen as a provincial venue for the European Basketball Championships hosted by Serbia in 2005.

GETTING THERE AND AWAY More or less hourly buses run every day between Belgrade and Vršac, as well as others to Novi Sad and Niš via Bela Crkva and Smederevo. There are more limited services to Vatin and Markovac, villages that lie close to the Romanian border. Six daily buses run to nearby Bela Crkva, and there is a single early morning service to Kikinda. The **bus station** (◊ *822 866*) is a flat, 20-minute walk northwest from the town centre along Miloša Obilića.

Train services are less frequent. There are five trains a day between Vršac and Belgrade Dunav station via Pančevo Glavna, which take about 1 hour 40 minutes. Two trains leave each day for Timişoara in Romania, one in the morning and one early evening. The journey takes about 2 hours, although Romanian local time is 1 hour ahead of Serbia. The **railway station** (◊ *832 422*) is a 20-minute walk southwest of the town centre.

TOURIST INFORMATION There are two branches: one at the side of the town hall building, the other nearby on Dvorska (◊ *832 999, 831 055*; e *toovrsac013@gmail.com*; w *to.vrsac.com*).

🏠 **WHERE TO STAY** *Map, page 288*

🏠 **Hotel Villa Breg** ***** (44 rooms, 4 apts) Goranska bb; ◊ 831 000; e reception@villa-breg.com; w www.villabreg.com. Villa Breg is a newish, well-appointed luxury hotel that sits on a hill overlooking the town. Top-notch facilities include a restaurant with a terrace & panoramic view, bar, business centre, conference hall & swimming pool. €€€€

🏠 **Motel Vetrenjača** ** (31 rooms) Beogradski put bb; ◊ 801 156; e vetrenjacadoobenst@gmail.com; w www.vetrenjaca.co.rs. Built in the shape of a windmill, this motel has rooms with AC, satellite TV & minibar. Restaurant, café & congress hall. €€€

🏠 **Hotel Srbija** *** (78 rooms, 8 suites) Svetosavski trg 12; ◊ 815 545; e office@hotelsrbija.rs; w hotelsrbija.rs. This 6-storey hotel just east of the main central square should always have space. Room prices depend on the size of bed & which floor it is on – the luxury rooms with AC, minibar & satellite TV cost more. Facilities include restaurant, banquet hall, conference hall, bowling alley & discotheque. €€€–€€

🏠 **Stari Mlin** (13 rooms) Đure Daničića 11; ◊ 283 0155; e starimlin@oktobar.rs. Cosy, clean & good-value rooms above a large restaurant set back from the road near the market. €€

✕ **WHERE TO EAT AND DRINK** *Map, page 288*

For eating, the **Hotel Srbija** has its own bunker-like dining room (€€) and the **Hotel Villa Breg** has an attractive but expensive restaurant (€€€). Otherwise, there are several more decent choices for food in town. For **fast food**, there are plenty of take-aways along Vuka Karadžića between the twin-spired Catholic cathedral and Gradski Park. For snacks there are plenty of *poslastičarnica* scattered around the town centre like **Calzone** and **Gelato**.

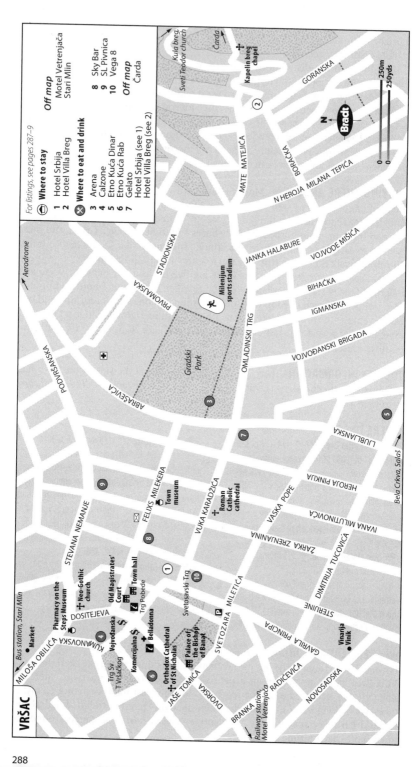

VRŠAC

For listings, see pages 287–9

Where to stay
1 Hotel Srbija
2 Hotel Villa Breg

Off map
Motel Vetrenjača
Stari Mlin

Where to eat and drink
3 Arena
4 Calzone
5 Etno Kuća Dinar
6 Etno Kuća Rab
7 Gelato
Hotel Srbija (see 1)
Hotel Villa Breg (see 2)

8 Sky Bar
9 SL Pivnica
10 Vega 8

Off map
Čarda

Kula breg
Čarda

Kapelin breg chapel

Sveti Teodor church

GORANSKA

N HEROJA MILANA TEPIĆA

BORAČKA

MATE MATEJIĆA

JANKA HALABURE

VOJVODE MIŠIĆA

BIHAĆKA

IGMANSKA

VOJVOĐANSKI BRIGADA

Milenijum sports stadium

OMLADINSKI TRG

LJUBLJANSKA

HEROJA PINKIJA

VASKA POPE

IVANA MILUTINOVIĆA

ŽARKA ZRENJANINA

DIMITRIJA TUCOVIĆA

GAVRILA PRINCIPA

STERIJINE

SVETOZARA MILETIĆA

Vinarija Vinik

NOVOSADSKA

Bela Crkva, Salaš

RADIĆEVIĆA

BRANKA

DVORSKA

JAŠE TOMIĆA

Palace of the Bishop of Banat

Orthodox Cathedral of of St Nicholas

Svetosavski Trg

Roman Catholic cathedral

Town museum

FELIKSA MILEKERA

VUKA KARADŽIĆA

Trg Pobede

Town hall

Old Magistrates' Court

Neo-Gothic church

STEVANA NEMANJE

Pharmacy on the Steps Museum

DOSITEJEVA

KUMANOVSKA

Vojvodanska

Komercijalna

Belladonna

Trg Sv T. Vršačkog

MILOŠA OBILIĆA

Bus station, Stari Mlin
Market

Aerodrome

STADIONSKA

PRVOMAJSKA

PODVRŠANSKA

ABRAŠEVIĆA

Gradski Park

Railway station; Motel Vetrenjača

Bradt

N

250m
250yds

0
0

For **drinks**, the central square of Trg Svetog Teodora Vršačkog is lined with cafés on both sides and has plenty of outdoor seating in summer. There are also a number of **café-bars** like **Sky Bar** in the area around Hotel Srbija.

✕ Etno Kuća Dinar Dimitrija Tucovića 82; `830 024; w etnokucadinar.rs. A national restaurant with a quaint rustic interior & an outdoor terrace. Good variety of traditional Vojvodina dishes. €€

✕ Etno Kuća Rab Trg Svetog Teodora Vršačkog 15; `837 338; w rab.rs. Effectively this is a wine cellar that has live music at w/ends but functions more as a straightforward restaurant during the week & at lunch times. €€

✕ SL Pivnica Žarka Zrenjanina 4; `838 037. Restaurant in the vaulted rooms of the local SL brewery, established in 1742. Probably a better choice for beer than food. €€

✕ Arena Gradski Park; m 060 8435 053. Tucked away in the park. €€–€

✳✕ Vega 8 Svetosavski trg 11; `830 080. A large cellar restaurant with excellent food, low prices & friendly service. Good choice of local wines too. €€–€

✕ Čarda Kula bb; `837 109. On the road leading up to the church of Sveti Teodor, this is a relaxed rustic place with grilled meat & Hungarian dishes. €

SHOPPING Vršac is well known for its distinctive red wine. A good selection can be found at the shop tucked away behind the Hotel Srbija. Cellars to visit include **Vinarija Vinik** (*Novosadska 1;* `*834 169*) and **Kuća Vina Rab** (*Trg Svetog Teodora Vršačkog 11;* `*837 338; w rab.rs*). The town's most well-known wines are Vržole Noir and Vržole Blanc.

OTHER PRACTICALITIES

$ Banks & ATMS Komercijalna banka: Trg Sv T Vršačkog. Located by the drinking fountain; Vojvođanska banka: located in the attractive round building at the bottom of the square.

✛ Hospital Abraševićeva bb; `839 538
✚ Pharmacy Belladonna pharmacy: Dvorska 13a; `823 107
✉ Post office Žarka Zrenjanina 15; `309 072

WHAT TO SEE AND DO Vršac is a town whose Habsburg heritage is only too apparent. While there are a few specific sights well worth seeking out, much of the charm of the town lies in its domestic architecture as, unusual for Serbia, there are whole streets that have changed little in 200 years. One such street is **Jaše Tomića**, which runs east–west across Dvorska, the high street at the bottom end of Trg Svetog Teodora Vršačkog. There is an impressive row of period houses in the Vojvodina style running along here, in particular numbers 30/30a next to Dom Omladine, and the bright yellow residence a little further along that is dated 1608. Dvorska is also the location for the **Palace of the Bishop of Banat (Vladičanski dvor)**, a large yellow Baroque building with a shiny green-glazed tiled roof that dates originally from 1759 but which was later rebuilt. Inside the palace, the **Chapel of Holy Archangels Michael and Gabriel (Kapelom svetih arhangela Mihaila i Gavrila)** has some fine icons by Nikola Nesković. On the other side of the street is the **Orthodox Cathedral of St Nicholas (Saborna crkva Svetog Nikole)**, built 1783–85, with paintings by Paja Jovanović and an iconostasis that was originally painted by Pavle Đurković but which has since had most of its panels clumsily restored.

Nearby, just to the north of Trg Pobede and on the corner of Kumanovska and Stefan Nemanje, is the **Pharmacy on the Steps Museum (Apoteka na stepenikama musej)**, with the entrance on steps above the street as the name implies. This was the town's first pharmacy, opened in 1784 and operational until 1965 when it became a museum. There are two exhibitions on display here: one concerning medicine and another dedicated to the work of the artist Paja Jovanović, whose brother worked here. Unfortunately, to visit this museum you have to time your visit carefully as, according to the notice on the door, it is only open 10.00–13.00 and 15.00–19.00 on Sundays, but check at the tourist office to see if the opening hours have since been extended. Just around the corner, where Dositejeva meets Stefan Nemanje, is a rather curious Romanian **neo-Gothic church** with red and yellow brickwork, a cupola and a tower inlaid with the ceramic images of saints.

Facing Trg Pobede, the imposing chocolate-coloured **town hall**, built in 1757, is a mixture of Classical and Gothic styles. Continuing east along Vuka Karadžića you come to the twin spires of the neo-Gothic **Roman Catholic cathedral (Rimokatololički hram)** that was constructed between 1860 and 1863 and later rebuilt. The **town museum** (*Gradski muzej Vršac; Žarka Žrenjanina 20;* \ *838 053;* w *www.muzejvrsac.org.rs;* ⊕ *08.00–15.00 & 17.00–19.00 Thu, 10.00–13.00 & 17.00– 19.00 Sun; admission 100din*), which is close by, more or less parallel to, the Roman Catholic cathedral on Anđe Ranković, has an interesting ethnographic exhibit and an art collection that has a special selection dedicated to the painter Paja Jovanović who was born here. Also worth seeking out in town is the **Old Magistrates' Court (Stari Sudije za prekršaje)**, another neo-Gothic building built in 1860.

Kula breg

Clearly visible from anywhere in town is Kula breg, a **15th-century defensive tower** that surveys the plains from its 400m vantage point on a round volcanic hill immediately above Vršac. Although close scrutiny does not reveal very much more about the site, it is as good a destination as any for a walk outside the town.

The best approach on foot is to head east from the Hotel Srbija along Vuka Karadžića past the Catholic cathedral and continue up the wide, gently sloping road that passes through Gradski Park. Fairly soon, you will pass the gleaming new Millennium Sports Complex on your left. Just beyond here you come to a four-way junction. Take the narrow road that is the second from the right – the least likely-looking candidate. This leads up to a series of steep steps that pass through a smart new housing development and eventually reaches a small white chapel, **Kapelin breg**, which although clearly visible from the town below, seems to disappear into the trees as you get increasingly close. Kapelin Breg, also known as the Chapel of the Holy Cross, is the oldest church in Vršac, constructed between 1720 and 1728. In 1739, it became dedicated to St Rok, the protector from plague (there was an outbreak of plague in the town during that same year). Just above here is the main road and, on the other side of it, a meadow with a noticeboard, picnic tables and small amphitheatre. The larger **Church of St Teodor (Crkva Svetog Teodor Vršačkog)**, also visible from the town, is just off the road to the left down a track. There is a car park area to the left of the road and a rustic café-restaurant with a garden next to it.

To reach the **tower** (*admission 100din*) from here you have two options. The first is to follow the main road for a couple of kilometres. The road bends anticlockwise around the hillside and eventually you will see a sign and a drinks hut from where there is a steep path that leads uphill to the tower and the radio mast. The other option is to follow the track that leads into the woods from the car park restaurant. When you come to a parting of the ways take the right fork. This brings you to a wide track that more or less follows the contour line of the hill in a clockwise direction. There are a few rocky outcrops from which to admire the view before the path ventures into thick woodland that is very fragrant with lime blossom in summer. The track eventually circles the hill and brings you out on the main road at the drinks hut where the path leads up to the tower. Realistically, there is probably not much difference in the actual distance for either approach but it is certainly more pleasant walking through woodland on a hot day than it is to follow tarmac.

There is not much to see once you arrive at the tower, apart from the view of the Pannonian Plain, the town and the **aerodrome**. There are some rough foundations at the base of the *kula* but little else other than the tower itself. The view is excellent, and the tower has quite a foreboding presence about it, which adds to the atmosphere. The walk from the town should take an hour and a half or so, depending on how often you stop for breath.

If you are driving to Kula breg, the road to take is the one towards Bela Crkva and then turn left off this up the hill along the road that is signposted: *Turistički put Breg.*

BELA CRKVA (БЕЛА ЦРКВА) *Telephone code 013*

The pretty town of Bela Crkva (White Church), 35km south of Vršac, is tucked away in a pocket of Serbia that is surrounded on three sides by Romania. It is a fairly pristine place, without much industry and set in fairly flat but pleasant countryside. The River Nera, which more or less defines the frontier, is close by, as are several small lakes and the Danube–Tisa–Danube Canal. So much water has inevitably meant that the town has been dubbed the 'Venice of Vojvodina' but this is overstating the case somewhat.

Like Vršac, Bela Crkva has a number of Baroque façades in its centre, but the town is most renowned for its **Flower Carnival** that takes place each summer.

The town has an interesting history. After centuries of invasion and occupation of the area by groups as diverse as Avars, Slavs, Hungarians, Turks and Bulgarians, Bela Crkva was established in 1717 by Count Claudius Florimund of Marcia. The town became heavily colonised by German settlers in the 18th century, who developed different trades and industries, in particular viniculture. The first grapes were harvested in 1733 and by 1816 wine traders from as far away as Vienna were visiting the town to buy its produce. Serbs, Romanians and others later joined the earlier migrants but the town remained predominantly German until 1945.

After World War I and the subsequent break-up of the Austro-Hungarian Empire, Bela Crkva found itself right on the border of the new entity of the Kingdom of Serbs, Croatians and Slovenes. Consequently, much of its economic power was lost as roads were cut and markets were denied. Following the next war, and the bitterness that ensued after years of Nazi occupation, virtually all of the Germans left the town for good.

Today, the town promotes its fresh air, fishing and bathing. There is a **beach** in town that has swimming facilities such as showers and changing cabins, and undeveloped beaches can be found at some of the nearby lakes. There is also a **town museum**, dating from 1877, that has paintings by 19th-century local artists and a small archaeological collection.

As well as the 100-year-old Flower Carnival that takes place in late June there is also a catfish-catching competition held each summer.

WHERE TO STAY AND EAT There are two campsites, **Auto Camp BC Jezera** (✆ 853 486) and **Srbija** (✆ 853 708), as well as the following:

Vila Oaza (11 rooms) Zelegorska 3; m 064 2930 686; w vilaoaza.com. At the entrance to town, this has rooms with AC, Wi-Fi & cable TV. Sauna. €€–€

Pension Laguna (24 roooms, 15 apts) Jezerska 1; ✆ 851 270. €

Vila Jezero (29 rooms) Jezerska bb; ✆ 851 771. Close to the water, with its own restaurant. €

DELIBLATO SANDS (DELIBLATSKA PEŠČARA) (ДЕЛИБЛАТСКА ПЕШЧАРА)

This unique area of remnant sand dunes left over from the drying up of the Pannonian Sea forms a northwest to southeast arc between Bela Crkva and Belgrade. Much of the area has been afforested as a means of preventing land erosion and the unique habitat provided by this has created a suitable environment for a variety of species of animal and plant. Nearly 2,000ha of its roughly 30,000ha are protected as reserve.

On the remaining land, hunting is popular, with the majority of hunters coming from Italy, Germany and France. The most famous predator here, however, is the wolf. Wolves used to be considered vermin here and numerous attempts were made to eradicate them throughout the 19th century. By 1912, the wolf population was almost completely wiped out but the Deliblato wolves managed to increase their numbers slightly through the 20th century, despite continued persecution.

The whole area is excellent for birdwatching, and is home to rare species like imperial eagle (*Aquila heliaca*), corncrake (*Crex crex*) and saker falcon (*Falco cherrug*). The Novi Sad-based travel agency Magelan Corporation offer one-day birdwatching tours of Deliblatska Peščara that start from Belgrade. If you are driving your own vehicle, you should head for the villages of Dolovo, Mramorak, Deliblato and Šušara that lie between Pančevo and Bela Crkva. A little further south near Dobovac, close to the Danube shore, you may see great-spotted eagles, hoopoes and bee-eaters in summer and large conglomerations of ducks in winter. The area south of Gaj, which if you have your own vehicle can be explored by taking a rough sandy track south of the main road, with luck may yield saker falcons and ground squirrels.

7

West and
Southwest Serbia

The gently rolling countryside of central Serbia becomes increasingly dramatic as you venture west or south from Kraljevo. From Čačak west, the main road follows the course of the Ovčar River, a tributary of the Morava, a region of small monasteries hidden away in the valleys of forested hills. Beyond here lies Užice, an interesting industrial town with an important place in modern Yugoslav history. Further west, close to the Bosnian border, is the Zlatibor region, an upland farming area with Kraljeve Vode (Partizanska Vode), a resort popular with Serbian holidaymakers, at its centre. Although west Serbia is not a distinct region in any political sense, it does have a character all of its own, which seems to echo the dark green mountains of Bosnia that lie beyond.

Heading south from Kraljevo along the River Ibar, the predominantly Muslim region of Raška (alternatively referred to as 'Sandžak', a derivation of the Turkish word *sanjak*) is soon reached: a poor, but starkly beautiful, region that historically has served as a buffer zone between Orthodox Serbia and Muslim Bosnia.

The highlights in this southwestern part of the country are undoubtedly the monasteries of Studenica, Sopoćani and Mileševa, all tucked away in gorgeous lush valleys; Novi Pazar with its Turkish bazaar atmosphere and ancient churches that lie just outside the town; the majestically bleak highlands of the Pešter plateau that rises to the west of Novi Pazar; and the small villages of the Zlatibor region – Mokra Gora with its fascinating switchback railway and Sirogojno with its open-air folk museum. Winter-sports enthusiasts will also find plenty to amuse themselves with in the ski resort of Kopaonik.

UŽICE (УЖИЦЕ) *Telephone code 031*

HISTORY Although nothing is immediately apparent from its appearance, this city, formerly known as Titovo Užice, holds a unique place in modern Serbian and Yugoslav history. It was here, in the autumn of 1941, that the Užice Republic was declared: a free Partisan state that lasted a mere 67 days until the town was surrendered to the Germans after a heroic defence. For the brief time that the republic lasted, Užice became the headquarters of the war effort and the strategic centre from which Tito planned his Partisan operations.

Although it was a short-lived liberation, a provisional government was set up in the town, and presses put to work to print propaganda and newspapers. The eventual evacuation and defeat, when it came, was quite dreadful, with horrifying losses as the German army took back the town with its 10,000-strong strike force. This was to be one of the Partisans' worst defeats. With such overwhelming odds, it was inevitable that Užice would sooner or later fall back into Nazi control; nevertheless, the town was defended almost to the last man. As a result of this, Tito

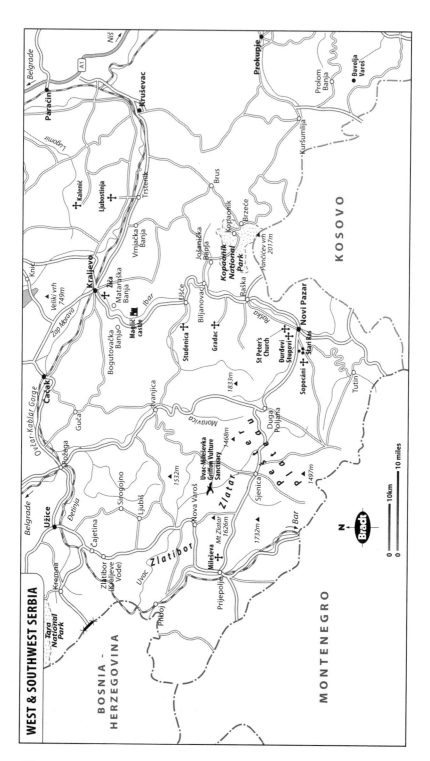

WEST & SOUTHWEST SERBIA

felt obliged to tender his resignation as Partisan leader; it was, of course, rejected outright. Following the appalling losses at Užice, the Partisans made a desperate withdrawal across the Zlatibor Planina, a march made in the depth of winter in which they suffered further casualties.

The city was renamed Titovo Užice in 1946 in honour of the Partisan leader and kept the name until 1992, when the prefix was consigned to history. The large statue of Josip Broz Tito that had formerly stood in the central square had already been removed the previous year.

Today, the city is a reasonably attractive sort of place, set deep in the valley of the Đetinja River, a tributary of the Zapadna Morava, at an altitude of 411m, surrounded by lush, dark green hills. With blocks of public housing climbing up the hillsides, Užice has a prosperous, if somewhat utilitarian, air about it. The city has grown quite rapidly since World War II and today has a population approaching 60,000 that are mainly employed in the chemical industry and copper and aluminium processing. The city centre is testament to the occasional successes of modern urban planning and, although it is quite compact, it has a light and airy feel, despite the plentiful presence of concrete high-rises, the most notable of which is the concrete skyrocket of the Hotel Zlatibor. Užice's concentration of high-rises has led the city to be sometimes referred to as 'Serbia's Hong Kong', which is perhaps wishful thinking. The city's most famous son, for the time being at least, is former Manchester United defender Nemanja Vidić.

Coming from the west, Užice's most notable landmark is clearly visible before the modern town opens up to view in the valley below: high on a bluff above the river, the ruins of a medieval fortress look down over the town, with steep stone walls and terraces like an Inca ruin. This fortress gives evidence to a strategic importance that has existed since Roman times.

The city may have Celtic origins but the first mention of the town comes from a document in the archives of Dubrovnik from 1329, when a trade colony was developed here. It was conquered by the Turks in the middle of the 15th century, and by the 17th century had become an important craft and cultural centre. Užice became a military base at the time of the wars between Austria and Turkey in the late 17th and early 18th centuries and played a crucial role in the First National Uprising. In 1805, the town was liberated from the Turks by Serbian insurrectionists, only to fall under Ottoman rule once again in 1813. In 1862, the Turks finally left after another siege and a great fire that virtually destroyed the town. The city was finally connected to Belgrade by railway in 1912. With the exception of the fortress and some churches, most of what can be seen today is post-World War I. The German bombardment of 1941 was not quite the last word in the military action that Užice would witness: in the hostilities of 1999, the city post office was hit by a NATO bomb, killing and injuring a number of civilians and putting 18,000 phone lines out of use. The reasoning behind this seemingly pointless attack remains unclear.

GETTING THERE AND AWAY Užice's **bus** (❧ 521 765) and **train** (❧ 513 165) stations stand side by side on the south side of the river, just 5 minutes' walk from the city centre. The bus station has facilities including left luggage, cafés and shops, with a currency exchange upstairs. There are plenty of buses to Belgrade that go via Čačak and Gornji Milanovac, a journey that takes about 3 hours. Four buses a day run to Novi Sad, two of which are direct via Valjevo, two via Belgrade. There are 20 buses a day that run a shuttle service to nearby Čačak, while several buses also run to points further east like Kraljevo, Kruševac, Kragujevac and Niš, as well as to local destinations in western Serbia. Buses to Zlatibor leave about every half-hour.

This short-lived republic was the first territory in Nazi-occupied Europe to be liberated, although its freedom was transitory and lasted no longer than a few months. This military mini-state was set up in autumn 1941 by Tito's Partisan resistance movement. Its territory, which was no more than 200km², was circumscribed by the Drina River to the west, by the Uvac River to the south and by the Zapadna Morava River to the east. Its northern boundary was loosely defined by the Skrapež River and an imaginary line drawn between Valjevo and Bajina Bašta. The population of the republic was probably around 300,000 and, although it turned out to be short-lived, a government made up of people's councils called *odbors* was formed in the republic's capital, Užice. Here, a newspaper (*Borba – The Struggle*) was printed, while the town's factories continued to operate under their new command. The Germans reoccupied the territory in November 1941 following attacks on the city by Chetniks. Most of the Partisan soldiers made their escape west or south to find more secure territory to fight from, while the local populace were forced to suffer bitter reprisals from the re-invading Germans. *Užička republika*, a Yugoslav film of 1974 directed by Žika Mitrović, used the short-lived republic as the historical backdrop for a stirring tale of anti-fascist struggle and intertwined love stories.

The city lies on the Bar–Belgrade train line and so there are plenty of services in either direction, stopping at Priboj and Prijepolje (for Mileševa Monastery) going south, and Valjevo and Lazarevac, heading north to Belgrade.

There is a small airport nearby but currently this does not handle commercial flights.

TOURIST INFORMATION AND LOCAL TOUR OPERATORS For information about travel, hotels and excursions in the region, the **tourist information centre** at Dimitrija Tucovića 52 (✆ *500 555;* w *turizamuzica.org.rs*) can offer assistance. For booking services, local travel agencies like **Riva Turs** (*Petra Ćelovića 20;* ✆ *511 660*) should be able to help. For booking or confirming flights, there is an Air Serbia office at Dimitrija Tucovića 64 (✆ *513 870*).

⌂ WHERE TO STAY *Map, opposite*
For a city of 60,000, there are few accommodation choices in Užice. Fortunately, the Hotel Zlatibor rarely fills.

⌂ **Hotel Zlatiborska Noć** (31 rooms, 6 apts) Bela Zemlija bb; ✆ 572 910; e rezlatiborskanoc@ open.telekom.rs; w zlatiborskanoc.rs. Large hotel complex geared towards business visitors, inconveniently situated 6km outside Užice on the road to Zlatibor. Fitness centre, 2 restaurants, private pools, poolside bars & business centre. €€€

⌂ **Hotel Zlatibor** *** (142 rooms, 6 apts) Dimitrija Tucovića 149; ✆ 516 188; e office@ hotel-zlatibor.com; w hotel-zlatibor.com. You cannot fail to notice this 3-star skyscraper in the centre of town, dominating the square south of Trg Partizana. There is a circular bar in the vast reception area & a large adjoining restaurant that resembles a glazed car park. The rooms are clean, the staff are friendly, & the views over the town from the upper floors are good. Some rooms have been refurbished in recent years, & there is also an exchange office, bar, hairdresser & business centre. €€

⌂ **Eco Hostel Republik** (4 rooms) Zelje Durica 34; m 064 3226 316; e reception@republik.rs;

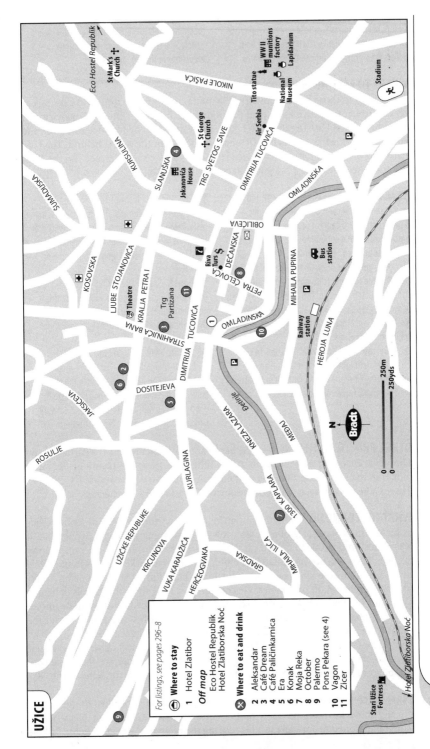

UŽICE

For listings, see pages 296–8

Where to stay
1 Hotel Zlatibor

Off map
   Eco Hostel Republik
   Hotel Zlatiborska Noć

Where to eat and drink
2 Aleksandar
3 Café Dream
4 Café Paličinkarnica
5 Era
6 Konak
7 Moja Reka
8 October
9 Palermo
   Pons Pekara (see 4)
10 Vagon
11 Zicer

Eco Hostel Republik

St Mark's Church

NIKOLE PAŠIĆA

St George Church

TRG SVETOG SAVE

Jokanović House

SLANUŠKA

KURSULINA

ŠUMADIJSKA

KOSOVSKA

LJUBE STOJANOVIĆA

Theatre

KRALJA PETRA I

Trg Partizana

STRAHINJIĆA BANA

DIMITRIJA TUCOVIĆA

DOSITEJEVA

JAKŠIĆEVA

ROSULJE

UŽIČKE REPUBLIKE

KRCUNOVA

VUKA KARADŽIĆA

HERCEGOVAKA

GRADSKA

MIHAILA ILIĆA

1300 KAPLARA

KNEZA LAZARA

Detinje

KURLAGINA

Riva Turs

DEČANSKA

PETRA ČELOVIĆA

OBILIĆEVA

OMLADINSKA

MIHAILA PUPINA

Bus station

Railway station

HEROJA LUNA

MEĐAJ

DIMITRIJA TUCOVIĆA

Air Serbia

Tito statue

National Museum

WWII munitions factory

Lapidarium

Stadium

OMLADINSKA

Stari Užice Fortress

Hotel Zlatiborska Noć

Bradt

N

250m
250yds

7

w republik.rs. Dorms & private rooms in a slightly wacky 'eco' hostel that has furniture made from pallets & ex-army equipment. Geared towards providing a sociable hostel experience for young people, the staff can help organise various excursions in the region. €€–€

✗ WHERE TO EAT AND DRINK *Map, page 297*

In addition to those listed below, Trg Partizana has a line of coffee and cake places on its eastern side, such as **Zicer** at the bottom end next to Dimitrija Tucovića. On the other side is **Café Dream** (✆ *602 302*). More cafés can be found across from the Hotel Zlatibor, while others like **October** are located in the streets behind. The **Café Palačinkarnica** next to the Jokanovića House has a nice shady terrace and the **Pons Pekara** bakery beneath it is a good place to have breakfast.

✗**Aleksandar** Kralja Petra I 16; ✆518 110; w aleksandargold.com; ⊕ 11.00–midnight daily. A national restaurant serving all of the usual Serbian dishes that sometimes has live music. €€

✳✗**Moja Reka** 1300 Kaplara 24A; ✆555 075; ⊕ 10.00–midnight daily. On the shore of the River Đetinja close to a nightclub, this is a relaxing spot in early evening. Plenty of fish dishes on the menu, as well as soups, pancakes, salads & specialities like 'Turkey à la Moja Reka'. Good wine list. Outdoor tables in summer. €€

✗**Palermo** Vuka Karadžića 19; ✆555 143; ⊕ 15.00–midnight daily. Intimate Italian restaurant west of the centre, with pizza & pasta as well as various fish & meat dishes. €€

✗**Era** Dimitrija Tucovića 142; ✆518 645; ⊕ 10.00–23.00 Mon–Sat. This is a cosy traditional restaurant where you can try out the *kajmak* that the city is reputedly famous for. The *teleći čorba* (veal soup) here comes highly recommended. €€–€

✗**Konak** Kralja Petra I 6; ✆510 207; ⊕ 11.00–midnight daily. Next door to Aleksandar, this is another national restaurant with rustic fittings & the standard Serbian menu choices. Garden for summer dining. €€–€

✗**Vagon** Mihaila Pupino bb; ✆517 000; ⊕ 08.00–midnight Mon–Sat, 14.00–midnight Sun. Resembling a train wagon near the river bank, this has mostly Italian food like pasta & good pizzas as well as Serbian dishes & savoury pancakes. Outdoor dining area. €€–€

OTHER PRACTICALITIES Most of the **banks** are clustered around Trg Partizana and Dimitrija Tucovića; most have an ATM, otherwise there are plenty of exchange offices in the same area. Find the **post office** at Obilićeva 6 (Dečanska) (✆ *590 874*). There's a **health centre** at Miloša Obrenovića 17 (✆ *561 255;* w zcue.rs).

WHAT TO SEE AND DO The author Brian W Aldiss, writing in 1966, describes Užice as having the appearance of a frontier town so swarming with wild people that 'it was almost impossible to drive a car down the main street' and where 'every sturdy Serbian dame was accompanied by a child, a lamb, or a porker'. Aldiss found Užice to be a place where 'men sat alone, clutching sharp knives and devouring hunks of meat and bread off bare tables'. He concludes, stating that, 'the morals of Titovo Užice are reputed to be low; one has only to see the place to believe the rumour' before confessing that he did not have enough time at his disposal to spend the night there. Alas, things have changed somewhat since then: these days, Serbian dames are far more slender and Užice's men use more genteel cutlery to eat their pizza as they sit quietly with their girlfriends. However, despite the humdrum trappings of modern provincial life, there are a few things worth seeing in the city.

Stari Užice Fortress This medieval fortress perches on a rock just to the west of the city above the river, probably on the same site as an earlier Roman *castrum*. It is first mentioned historically in 1373, during the reign of the brutish noble, Nikole

Altomanović, but little is known of the detail of its subsequent demise. Despite a complete lack of interpretive material, it is well worth a visit for the view at least – east across the modern city, and west over the green valley of the Đetinja River and on to the hills of the Zlatibor range. Although the fortress remains undiscovered and unexploited by the Serbian tourist industry it has not been overlooked by local youths, and the presence of extensive graffiti – both crude *četnik* ciphers and less politically motivated scrawl – has had an undesirable effect on what might otherwise be a numinous atmosphere.

To reach the fortress, either walk west along Kurlagina, then take a left on to Gradska, which will take you uphill to reach it. Alternatively, walk along the river west from the centre – it does not matter which side you choose, as there are plenty of footbridges. You will soon reach a small hydro-electric plant and a waterfall. Steps lead up to the right to reach the iron bridge that crosses the river here, actually a decommissioned railway crossing. It is possible to follow the old railway line, west along the valley through tunnels and over more bridges; this has some potential for a rewarding mountain-bike route, although as it stands, the bridge crossings would be extremely hazardous on two wheels until some sort of protective barrier was put in place. Hiking is a possibility too: with a number of paths leading off temptingly in several directions, there is undoubtedly great walking potential to be explored in the hills around the city.

Returning to the iron bridge, steps lead up a narrow path through woodland. This soon reaches a road higher up where you turn right past some houses, then sharp left at the next junction along Gradska, which leads straight up to the fortress. The fortress, which clings to the steep summit, has unprotected precipitous drops on all sides, so care is required.

Partisan Square (Trg Partizana) If this guide had been written two decades earlier I would be advising you to visit the giant statue of an austere, greatcoat-wearing Tito in this, the city's central square. Unfortunately, in 1991 the statue was removed to leave a large, empty space where it formerly stood. Although it is easy to understand why Užice, and Serbia in general, wants to shed painful memories of the recent past, it seems a pity that there is nothing whatsoever to remind us of the heroic struggle that took place here in 1941 – another case of praiseworthy and valiant babies being thrown out with communist bath water. Now Trg Partizana appears to be too large for a city of such modest size, and lacks any real focal point. In summer, its eastern flank is lined by outdoor cafés, which take up some of the space, but still the square seems a little forlorn, as if haunted by the ghost of the ousted statue.

Museums and churches
National Museum (*Narodni muzej Užice; Dimitrija Tucovića 18;* \ *521 360;* e *nmuzejuzice@ptt.rs;* w *nmuzice.org.rs;* ⊕ *summer 08.00–17.00, winter 08.00–15.00, closed Mon; admission 200din*) The museum, formerly known as the Museum of the 1941 Insurrection, occupies the same building that was the headquarters of Tito's Popular Army of Liberation in the autumn of 1941. The same building also once served as the Bank of Yugoslavia. It contains a number of exhibits from the war effort during this period, together with displays from later, communist times. A small tank is parked outside the entrance. Opening times are given above but these do not appear to be strictly adhered to. Entrance tickets can be bought inside the building on the right and these also include entrance to the long underground sheds in the cliff face behind the museum. These served as a **munitions factory** during

World War II. One has been preserved as such, with plenty of ammunition-making machinery in place, along with black-and-white photographs and interpretive material. The other has been recently converted into a **lapidarium** for a collection of Roman stones and statues found in the region. The **statue of Tito** in a greatcoat, which was removed from its original home in Trg Partizan in 1991, can be found here. Hidden away from public gaze behind the museum buildings, it is almost invisible from the street despite its impressive size.

Jokanovića House (*Slanuška 10a;* \ *513 035;* ☉ *summer 08.00–17.00 daily, winter 08.00– 15.00 daily; admission 100din*) This typical 19th-century house, also known as the 'Pećara', is preserved as a cultural monument with a permanent ethnographic exhibition.

Nearby is the grey-washed **Church of St George** (1844) that occupies the same cobbled square that is a popular hangout of the city's student population. Užice's other noteworthy church is the whitewashed **St Mark's Church** (1829), which has a rustic wooden bell tower that was added in 1890. The church holds icons and engravings from the 17th to the 19th centuries.

ČAČAK (ЧАЧАК) *Telephone code 032*

Halfway between Kraljevo and Užice, the large industrial town of Čačak on the Zapadna Morava River has little to offer the casual visitor other than a gateway to Guča, an ordinary provincial town for 51 weeks of the year but a quite extraordinary place during the annual Dragačevo Trumpet Festival that takes place there each summer.

Čačak played a prominent role in the anti-Milošević protests of October 2000 when the outspoken mayor of the town, Velimir 'Velja' Ilić, organised an enormous convoy of over 10,000 protesters from Čačak to Belgrade, personally leading them through numerous police road blocks on the morning of 5 October. The Čačak convoy was as much carnival as it was protest group and included 50 buses and 1,000 cars in its ranks to transport the protesters. Ilić also took the precaution of taking a bulldozer with him, to assist in negotiating the blockades. On arrival in Belgrade, the machine was used to smash a way into the entrance of the Serbian RTS television building. Later, after spearheading the storming of the parliament building, Mayor Ilić's supporters were heard singing: 'We are the Čačak boys, bulldozers are our toys.'

The image stuck in people's minds and as a result of Čačak's central role in the countrywide protest the mayor soon became better known by his new nickname, 'Bulldozer' Ilić.

Despite the laudable anti-Milošević pedigree, Čačak was quite badly damaged by the 1999 NATO bombing campaign, in particular the 'Sloboda' factory which, though producing only vacuum cleaners, was identified as a military target.

GETTING THERE AND AWAY Twenty buses a day connect Čačak's **bus station** (\ *221 461, 222 211*) with Belgrade; many more go to Kraljevo, Užice, Gornji Milanovac and Kragujevac.

A limited **train** service (\ *222 518*) runs east to Kraljevo and Kruševac, and west towards Užice.

TOURIST INFORMATION The office at Gradsko šetalište bb (\ *342 360, 343 721;* e *toc@ptt.rs;* w *turizamcacak.org.rs*) may be able to provide further suggestions on places to see in Čačak.

WHERE TO STAY There are a few hotels, a couple of motels and an adequate selection of restaurants in town if you want to stay but it is probably advisable to press on to either Užice or Kraljevo.

🏠 **Hotel Beograd ** ** (31 rooms, 4 apts) Gradsko šetalište 20; 📞 224 594; e office@hotel-beograd.rs; w hotel-beograd.rs. A central hotel, built in 1900, that has some nice Art Nouveau touches. Restaurant, café, meeting hall. €€

🏠 **Hotel Prezident ** *** (52 rooms, 6 suites) Bulevar oslobođenja bb; 📞 371 404, 371 417. This modern business hotel lies just 1km from the centre. All rooms have satellite TV, phone & en-suite bathroom. Swimming pool, sauna & fitness centre. €€

🏠 **Motel Čačak** (21 rooms) Bulevar oslobidilaca; 📞 361 030. €€

🍴 **WHERE TO EAT AND DRINK** There are plenty of cafés and a decent number of traditional restaurants scattered around town. Some suggestions are listed below:

🍴 **Moravski Alasi** Kneza Miloša 66/1; 📞 345 509. Elegant restaurant specialising in fish dishes. €€€–€€

🍴 **Car Lazar** Dr Dragiše Mišovića 46; 📞 222 392; w moravacacak.com. Čačak's oldest *kafana*, serving national food in a traditional setting. €€

🍴 **Lovac** Gradski Bedem 2; 📞 333 646. Comfortable & stylish restaurant with national food. Also has 5 rooms. €€

🍴 **Romansa** Lomina 38; 📞 221 799. National restaurant with live music every night. €€

🍴 **Brvnara** Kneza Vase Popovića 15; 📞 349 132. Rustic wooden setting & national food. €

🍴 **Proleće** Župana Stracimera bb; 📞 341 852. A modern pizzeria in the city centre. €

🍺 **City Pub** Gospodar Jovanova 22. A *pivnica* (beer hall) that really does look quite like a pub.

WHAT TO SEE AND DO Today, the town is a fairly dull, modern place of about 100,000 with little to see other than the **Church of Christ's Assumption** in the town centre that used to be part of the Gradac Monastery that the town developed around. The church, built in the late 12th century, served as a mosque during the Turkish occupation. Most of the original decoration has gone but there are still patches that can be seen. It has an iconostasis that dates from 1846.

The **National Museum** (*Narodni musej Čačak; Cara Dušana 1;* 📞 *222 169;* e *camuzej@sbb.rs;* w *cacakmuzej.org.rs/files/Vodic_Engleski.pdf;* ⏰ *09.00–17.00 Tue-Fri, 09.00–13.00 Sat/Sun; admission free*) is located in an early 19th-century *konak* known as **Konak Jovan Obrenović** that has the coat of arms of the Obrenović dynasty painted on to its front wall. The museum's permanent display includes an exhibition of the town's history since the medieval period and some Roman and Illyrian artefacts.

GUČA (ГУЧА) *Telephone code 032*

Guča is a small market town 18km southwest of Čačak that lies at the foot of the Krstac hills. In recent years this anonymous little town has become famous for the annual **Dragačevo Trumpet Festival** that takes place in August (see box, page 302). Since the first festival was organised in 1961 the event has grown beyond anyone's imagination. Attendance is now said to be over 500,000 over the whole five days of the festival, and up to 200,000 on Saturday, the most crowded day. This may be a slight exaggeration but it is certainly big – very big – and any hope of finding somewhere to stay during the festival should be abandoned unless prior arrangements have been made.

THE DRAGAČEVO TRUMPET FESTIVAL

Officially called *Dragačevski sabor trubača* but better known simply as 'Guča', this extraordinary annual event, as much sociological spectacle as it is music festival, is now half a century old. Over the past ten years it has grown to become an enormous national spectacle, which is now televised. In this time 'Guča' has become internationally famous as a sort of Serbian bacchanal, a riotous village fair on steroids, but it has far more modest origins.

Trumpets were first introduced into Serbian life by Prince Miloš Obrenović, who ordered the formation of the first military band in 1831. It was probably the presence of a large amount of decommissioned military brassware that led to the trumpet (along with other brass-band instruments like flugelhorn, tuba and baritone) being adopted as the musical instrument of choice for all sorts of social occasions: births, baptisms, weddings, *slava* days and church festivals. Many musicians in south and central Serbia, Roma especially, took to playing the trumpet as a result; they had their advantages over more traditional instruments, being harder-wearing, easier to keep in tune and, most important, they were much louder.

The first Dragačevo Assembly of Trumpet Players was held in 1961 (Dragačevo is simply the district to which the town of Guča belongs) in the yard of the Church of St Michael and St Gabriel in the town. It remained a small, almost clandestine, celebration for a number of years, a reflection of the political atmosphere at the time, which did not always approve of celebrations that did not directly involve the state.

Over the past ten years the Guča festivities have grown enormously, and are now attended by trumpet players, brass bands, folk song and dance groups from around the world. Some old hands say that the festival has become over-commercialised (there is much sponsorship these days by Serbian beer companies) and over-attended by those more interested in the riotous party atmosphere than the music itself. Certainly, the immodest consumption of food and drink seems to have become as important as the music itself in recent years. In 2002, it was estimated that over 300,000 attended during the three days of the festival. In 2004, when 500,000 were said to have attended, the festival was extended by another day to become a four-day event. In 2007, it was extended once more, this time to five days and on this occasion even national rock star Goran Bregović turned up to perform with his Weddings and Funerals Band. 2010 marked the festival's 50th anniversary, a massive spectacle barely recognisable from the modest event that had set the ball rolling back in 1961. By 2012, the festival had extended to a week-long event, opening on Monday morning and not finishing until the following Sunday. Estimates of total visitor numbers are now considered to be in excess of 600,000 annually.

Past stars of the festival include Milan Mladenović, Ekrem Sajdić, Elvis Ajdinović, Fejat Sejdic and Zoran Sejdic. The greatest star of all, and multiple winner of the *Zlatna Truba* 'Golden Trumpet' award, is the Roma trumpet player, Boban Marković from Vladičin Han in southern Serbia (an area rich in brass bands and exemplary musicians), who was so good they had to ban him to give the rest of the competition a chance. Now his son Marko is proving equally talented. As no less than trumpet maestro Miles Davis himself remarked when he visited the festival, 'I didn't know you could play trumpet that way.'

More about the festival can be found at w guca.rs.

If you want to visit the festival, it is highly advisable to organise transport in advance and essential to pre-book accommodation. One option is to book through the website at **w** guca.rs, which offers transportation Belgrade–Guča–Belgrade for €40 return, and four nights' accommodation, including breakfast, in a private home in the town from €135 per person. Transportation and three nights' accommodation are slightly discounted at €150 per person when they are booked together. Groups of ten or more may be eligible for a special price (*contact is Dejan Ćirić;* **m** *063 8979 092;* **e** *info@guca.rs*). The Dutch tour operator **Time to Travel** (*w guca-festival.com/ about-us-time-to-travel/about-us*) also runs packages to the festival that are aimed at low-budget travellers.

Several other tour operators run all-inclusive Guča festival packages (see page 64 for options). All packages should be booked well in advance as places are limited. The other, braver, option is just to arrive with a tent, find a pitch somewhere and just hope for the best; as anyone who has attended will tell you, sleeping is a fairly low priority at the festival.

The website has a message board for past and prospective Guča visitors and some excellent videos and photo galleries that really bring home the noise and mayhem of the event. Be warned! Guča is not an event for the faint-hearted. But if your idea of fun is five sleepless days of drunken, noisy pandemonium fuelled by a diet of beer and greasy meat (Guča visitors consumed 800,000 litres of beer in 2009!) then this might be just your thing. It helps if you like trumpets … and beer … and meat.

WHERE TO STAY As already stated, a bed will be impossible to find during the trumpet festival unless it has been pre-booked. This can be done either through the website **w** guca.rs or by using an online agency such as **w** booking-hotels.biz or **w** accommodationguca.com. The rest of the year, accommodation can be found at the following:

Hotel Zlatna Truba *** (31 rooms, 3 suites) Trg Slobode; ☎854 459. €€

'Vajat' Apartments (4 rooms, 6 apts) ☎861 146, 861 093; **e** vajati@eunet.rs; **w** vajati. com. Just southwest of Guča in the village of Gornji Kravarica. €€

WHAT TO SEE AND DO Although it is a pleasant enough place, it is very unlikely that you would visit Guča for any other purpose than attending the trumpet festival. Across the street from the Hotel Zlatne Truba is **Dom Kultur (Culture House)** where live concerts are put on during the festival. Turning right at Dom Kultur there is the famous **Statue of the Trumpet Player** that celebrates the festival at the next corner. Turning left here brings you to the square where most of the tent restaurants are and where most of the off-stage live music takes place during the event. The brass competition itself is held in a football field at the edge of town.

Other musical events in the Čačak region

Guča may have the lion's share (page 301), but it does not have a complete monopoly on musical events in the area. In late July, a flute-playing festival takes place in the village of Prislonica, just to the north of Čačak. The **'Oj Moravo' Flute-player Assembly** is an annual gathering in which folk music is performed on the *frula*, an indigenous Serbian form of the flute. Like Guča, this is essentially a competitive event, and the best *frula*-player is chosen from competing entrants. As well as music, there are other traditional activities such as folk dancing and poetry readings. Contact the Čačak Tourist Office for more information (page 300).

AROUND ČAČAK

MONASTERIES OF THE OVČAR-KABLAR GORGE Leaving Čačak in a westerly direction along the E-761 towards Požega and Užice, the road runs alongside the picturesque Ovčar-Kablar Gorge. The area is something of a playground for the nearby industrial centres and the Morava River is lined with fishing lodges along much of the way. A few places along the main road also offer *sobe* to passing travellers. Hidden away high above the river in dense woodland, is a succession of **17th-century monastery churches**. The monasteries are for the most part small and remote, dating from a time when monks were compelled to hide themselves away from the Turks as much as possible. The ten that lie along the gorge are deemed in some quarters, somewhat fancifully, to constitute a Serbian equivalent of Mt Athos. They nearly all require a detour and, although interesting enough and in lovely surroundings, they are probably not worth devoting too much time to if you are planning to visit, or have already seen, the cream of Serbian monasteries like Studenica, Sopoćani or Manasija.

Probably the most accessible is **Vavedenje Monastery**, close to the main road just 8km from Čačak, which dates from 1452 and has a painted doorway from the early 19th century. The **Church of the Annunciation at Blagoveštenje Monastery** lies above the village of **Ovčar Banja**. The church was built in 1602 and, as well as a fine iconostasis, houses several important manuscripts in its library, the most notable being a Holy Gospel from 1552. The frescoes were painted in 1632, the work of a local artist. **The Holy Trinity Monastery (Manastir Svete Trojice)** on the opposite bank originates from 1694, although there are vestiges of 13th-century design in its construction. The church contains two icons dated 1635: *Christ with the Apostles* and the *Mother of God with the Prophets*. The **Sretenje Monastery** is close by – at least, as the crow flies – situated on the southwest slope of Mt Ovčar at a height of 800m above sea level. The monastery is home to an 18th-century Russian icon: *Mother of God with the Child*. The monastic library was burned down during World War II but a handful of 16th-century documents and Bibles were saved. **St Nicholas's Monastery (Manastir Nikolje)**, the oldest of all of these monasteries, dating probably from the middle of the 15th century, on the river's north bank has been destroyed several times in its turbulent history but still retains some interesting frescoes.

The rest of the monasteries are of more recent date but have all been built on the site of older monastic foundations. Close to the peak of Mt Kablar is a small church, dedicated to St Sava, built close to a mineral spring that is said by locals to cure eye problems.

ZLATIBOR (ЗЛАТИБОР) *Telephone code 031*

Zlatibor is the name given to a mountain range and a region rather than a particular place, although the tourist centre of **Kraljeve Vode** (previously Partizanska Vode) at the heart of the region is often referred to simply as 'Zlatibor'. Roughly speaking, Zlatibor corresponds to the area west of Užice that extends as far as the Bosnia and Herzegovinan border, and to the south almost to Nova Varoš. It is a region of high mountains, pine forest and alpine meadows, with little in the way of large settlements other than the market town of Čajetina that serves as a sort of lower town to the resort. For an upland region it is surprisingly well connected: the E-761 leads east from Užice through the sprawling community of Kremna to the Bosnia and Herzegovinan border and Višegrad just beyond – an important route that links

Belgrade with Sarajevo – while the main Bar–Belgrade railway passes through, linking the south of the region, Priboj, with the north, Užice, after a brief excursion into the territory of Republika Srpska in Bosnia and Herzegovina.

Being only 4 hours from Belgrade by road, Zlatibor is a firm favourite with domestic tourists: many come to Kraljeve Vode in winter to ski, or in summer to walk and escape the big-city heat. The spectacular 'Šargan Eight' railway line that runs from **Mokra Gora** is also immensely popular, as is the Village Museum complex at **Sirogojno**.

For the foreign visitor, perhaps the best way to enjoy the region is to explore the possibilities for **village tourism** and base yourself in one of the villages such as **Kremna** and **Gostilje**, which offer accommodation and board with local families – a great way to experience rural life and to enjoy delicious home-produced fare that is far superior to anything you could buy in a restaurant.

GEOGRAPHY OF THE ZLATIBOR REGION Zlatibor gets its name from a combination of *zlato*, meaning gold, and *bor*, pine. The whole area is a vast rolling plateau that is geographically defined by the territory between the rivers Sušica and Uvac, the eastern slopes of Mt Tara and the western slopes of Murtenica. The average altitude of the Zlatibor region is around 1,000m above sea level. As its name suggests, the region is characterised by large expanses of coniferous forest composed of pine, fir and spruce, together with upland meadows and pasture. The highest mountain in the region is Tornik at 1,496m. In the northern, limestone, part of the region the only river is the Sušica, whose name means 'dry', a reference to its periodic disappearance during the summer months. Accompanying the limestone are the expected geological features like caves and springs: Zlatibor abounds in speleological phenomena and a total of 98 caves and 44 pits have been identified in the region. The greatest of these is 1,691m-long **Stopića Cave (Stopića pećina)** that lies off the Sirogojno–Užice road, 30km from Užice. The cave boasts a 30m-wide, 18m-high entrance and the deepest rimstone pool in Serbia. In contrast to the limestone, the main rock type, away from the northern and eastern fringes of the plateau, is green serpentine and this forms the largest serpentine massif in Serbia.

Zlatibor enjoys a sunny, sub-alpine climate but, with about 100 snowy days a year, there is also an abundant supply of snow for skiing between November and March. The region is equally popular in the summer months, especially in July and August, and Serbians come here in large numbers to walk, relax and breathe the cool mountain air.

ZLATIBOR (KRALJEVE VODE) The tradition of tourism at Zlatibor began early in the 19th century when Prince Miloš Obrenović chose to spend his summers on the mountain. Following the arrival of King Aleksandar Obrenović in 1893, the small settlement of Kulaševac soon became known by its new name of Kraljeve Vode (King's Water). In response to the honour, the king built the fountain that still stands in the town centre on which is engraved: '*Kralj Aleksandar I, 20 avgusta 1893.*'

At the beginning of the 20th century, the town had just a few private summer houses owned by wealthy Užice residents but, after 1927, when the first bus line was opened from Užice, the construction of new houses, restaurants and hotels soon began in earnest. After World War II the name changed again to Partizanska Vode (Partisan's Water) to reflect Yugoslavia's new political direction. Although the town has since reverted to its original name, some maps and signs continue to use this name today.

Zlatibor-Kraljeve Vode is pleasant enough but, unless you are a sociologist interested in studying the Serbs at play, there are probably better choices in the region. It is very much a purpose-built resort and consequently it lacks any real character. The pine forest that reaches almost as far to the town is attractive but the extent of ongoing building development is such that you need to walk a long way from the town centre in order to get a sense of undisturbed nature. On the plus side, Zlatibor does make a good alternative to Užice as a base for exploring the region, as excursions to places like Mokra Gora and Sirogojno are relatively easy to arrange here in season. The town is also a suitable base if you have your own transport, as the well-developed infrastructure here guarantees that you will be well catered for in terms of accommodation and food.

GETTING THERE AND AWAY Buses run frequently to and from Belgrade, Užice and more local destinations, and there are even some direct services to destinations as far away as Subotica and Niš. There is a Zlatibor stop on the Bar–Belgrade railway but this is some way out of town. The **bus station** (✆ 841 244) is located next door to the Tržni shopping centre.

TOURIST INFORMATION AND LOCAL TOUR OPERATORS The Zlatibor Tourist Organisation can organise excursions to a variety of places in the region like Sirogojno, Mokra Gora or Drvengrad. Other tour operators, working from kiosks beside the bus station, include **Zlatiborturs** (✆ 845 957) and **Zlateks** (✆ 841 244; w zlateks.rs).

⁊ Zlatibor Tourist Organisation Miladina Pećinara 2, Zlatibor; ✆841 646, 848 015, 845 103; e info@zlatibor.org.rs; w zlatibor.org.rs, w zlatibor.org; ⊕ 08.00–20.00 daily

WHERE TO STAY There is a huge range of accommodation to choose from, with hotels of all classes, as well as simpler pensions and apartment complexes that are generally more amenable to longer stays. Most hotels offer half or full board as standard.

There are also plenty of **private rooms** available; look for 'sobe' signs around the town. The Zlatibor Tourist Organisation also has comfortable accommodation in a purpose-built block next door to the tourist information centre (see below).

Away from the resort in the neighbouring town of **Čajetina** to the north, there is the two-star **Motel Inex** (*Zlatiborska 18*; ✆ 841 021; €€–€), while in the village of **Ljubiš** in the southeast there is the three-star **Pansion Ljubiš** (✆ 801 091, 801 151; e simex-lju@ptt.rs; €€).

⌂ Hotel Mona Zlatibor **** (90 rooms) Miladina Pećinara 26; ✆841 021; e hotel@ monazlatibor.com; w monazlatibor.com. With standard rooms & spacious studio apartments, this also has 2 restaurants & a bar-café. €€€

⌂ Special Institute Zlatibor-Čigota ✆841 141, 597 236; e office@cigota.rs; w cigota.rs. It is not compulsory to participate in their weight-loss programme if you wish to stay here. Swimming pool & sauna. €€€

⌂ Hotel Olimp **** (33 rooms, 7 suites) Miladina Pećinara 1; ✆842 555; e hotelolimp@ mts.rs; w hotelolimp.com. With restaurant, fitness club & jacuzzi. €€€–€€

⌂ Hotel Palisad *** (328 rooms) Jexero 66; ✆841 151, 841 161; e prodaja@palisad.rs; w palisad.rs. This large complex at the centre of the resort is owned by an ex-basketball star. This has the 'Zlatni Bor' restaurant serving national dishes, sometimes with traditional music. €€€–€€

⌂ Hotel Zelenkada **** (50 rooms) Gajeva 1; ✆846 345, 846 382; e pttugost@gmail.com. Rooms with balconies in what looks like a huge ski lodge. €€€–€€

⌂ Dunav Resort **** (24 rooms, 7 suites) Rujanska bb; ✆841 126, 841 181; e info@ dunavturist.rs; w dunavturist.rs. Right next to Tržni shopping centre, with fitness centre, conference hall, aperitif bar, billiards parlour & restaurant with a summer terrace. €€

🏠 **Zlatibor T O Konačište** (8 rooms) Miladina Pećinara 2; 🖀845 103; e info@zlatibor.org.rs; w zlatibor.org.rs. Comfortable, modern rooms in a block next door to the tourist information centre just north of the lake. All rooms with TV, bath & Wi-Fi. B/fast provided at restaurant next door; HB is also possible. Discount given for stays over 3 days. €€

✖ WHERE TO EAT AND DRINK
There are numerous places in the town centre for food and drink. As many of the hotels provide full board to their guests, most places in the centre just offer drinks and snacks. However, in addition to a few proper restaurants, there are pizzerias and other places serving cakes, pancakes and ice creams dotted around town, and a handful of 24-hour fast-food *roštilj* places too. Most of the cafés have summer outdoor seating that allows patrons to soak up the ultraviolet while they sip their cappuccinos. The local speciality is *Zlatiborska pršut*, a dark, intensely flavoured mountain ham, and several restaurants feature this on the menu. A few central establishments are listed below.

☕ **Feniks** Tržni centar; 🖀848 017. Delicious fancy cakes & excellent coffee at this posh conservatory-like café-*poslastičarnica*. €€€–€€

✖ **Beli Dvor** Tržni centar; 🖀841 340. A traditional Serbian restaurant in the heart of town. €€

✖ **Grand Zlatibor** Tržni centar 66; 🖀848 123; w grandzlatibor.rs. A 3-in-1 affair, with an Irish pub at street level & a nightclub below. The rather smart restaurant is upstairs. €€

✖ **Jezero** Kraljevi Konaci bb; 🖀841 100. On the shore of Zlatibor's small lake, this has standard Serbian fare & an outdoor terrace that overlooks the water. €€

✖ **Zlatni Bor** Naselje Jezero; 🖀845 077. Overlooking the square by the lake, this national restaurant has all the Serbian favourites at reasonable prices. €€–€€

☕ **Pizzeria Fama i Café Mondo** Tržni centar; 🖀845 217. Near the entrance to the Tržni shopping centre, this comfortable, well-lit café-pizzeria has a good range of pizzas, pancakes & sandwiches. €

WHAT TO SEE AND DO The centre of the town is very compact, with a dense concentration of souvenir shops, cafés and restaurants close to the bus park. Close by, next to the King's Fountain, is a small artificial lake surrounded by pines that is used for bathing and sunbathing in summer and for skating in winter. For a swim in wilder surroundings, there is an artificial beach called **Kod komša** 7km away, where the natural course of a stream has been interrupted and enclosed with stones. Do not expect the water to be warm. Meanwhile, in the town itself, an Olympic-size, open-air swimming pool is under construction. The **Čigota Institute** also has a heated indoor swimming pool that is open year-round to its guests.

Zlatibor developed as a **ski centre** in the period between the wars. There are three ski lifts in operation and a choice of slopes that vary in level of difficulty. There is also a track for cross-country skiing. The beginners' slopes are at **Obudovica**, just to the west of the town centre, with those at the **Tornik Sports Centre** at nearby Ribnica more suitable for experienced skiers. More information on skiing at Zlatibor can be had from w skijanje.rs. The town also has numerous walking paths in the vicinity and that, together with skiing in the winter, is one of its greatest draws, but health tourism is important here too and many Serbs come for treatment.

The clear, pure air of Zlatibor has given it a reputation for healing a variety of heart and respiratory complaints as well as for disorders of the thyroid; indeed, there is a clinic dedicated solely to thyroid problems at the crisply titled **Special Institute for the Prevention and Treatment of Thyroid Gland Disorders and the Rehabilitation**

West and Southwest Serbia   ZLATIBOR (ЗЛАТИБОР)

7

of **Patients**. Another therapy that the town specialises in is weight loss following a course of treatment called the Čigota programme.

The town is also a popular choice for basketball and football teams preparing for tournaments, and for summer sports camps in tennis and swimming.

There are a number of **festivals** held in the town: at the end of July, Zlatibor hosts a trumpet festival; at the end of August, an international film festival, known as MEFEST, is held; and at the end of February, the town plays host to a hunters' gathering called the 'Wolf Chase' in which oxen are roasted, lectures on hunting are given and moving targets ranging from clay pigeons to real wolves are shot at by trigger-happy macho types – needless to say, it is probably not to everyone's taste.

VILLAGES IN THE ZLATIBOR REGION

SIROGOJNO (СИРОГОЈНО) *Telephone code 031*

The **Open-Air Museum 'Old Village'** (*Muzej na otvorenom 'Staro Selo';* ✆ *3802 291;* e *staroselo@ptt.rs;* w *sirogojno.org.rs;* ⊕ *Apr–Oct 09.00–19.00, Nov–Mar 09.00–16.00 daily; admission 150din*) was set up here in 1979 by the Yugoslav Republic Institute for the Protection of Cultural Monuments with the idea of recreating a typical 19th-century Zlatibor homestead. The buildings were collected from all over the region, dismantled and then reconstructed here on this hillside site. There are examples of all the components you would expect in a 19th-century homestead: a house, a cottage – specially built for married members of the family and just used for sleeping – a guesthouse, dairy, granary, forge and animal compounds. The buildings are complete with furniture and fittings, and display artefacts typical of the economy and period; they are also used to stage demonstrations of traditional village skills from time to time.

The museum is set out in the same way as a typical homestead, positioned on a sunny slope with the highest point reserved for the living quarters, with stables, pigsties, sheep pens and vegetable plots a little lower down. All of the buildings are covered with a steeply pitched shingle roof, a safeguard against the considerable winter snow that this region receives.

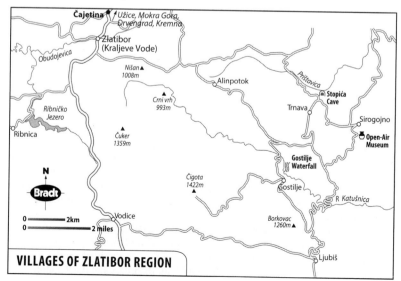

VILLAGES OF ZLATIBOR REGION

If you want to stay over, there are some traditional wood cabins that each have between two and five beds. Each cabin comes equipped with a small kitchen, a fireplace and television (✆ *call to book 3802 291*). There's a traditional inn on site too that has typical Serbian staples on offer like *kajmak*, *pršut*, cheese and black bread.

Even without the interest of the museum, Sirogojno is an attractive place, high on a hillside with lovely views across the valley. The small, pristine white **Church of St Peter and St Paul** stands close to the museum site, dating from 1764. At the museum entrance are various craft stalls selling high-quality hand-knitted woollens, wooden craft items and mountain dairy produce like cheese and *kajmak*. The handmade jumpers, designed by Dobrila Vasiljević-Smiljanić, and knitted by Zlatibor women for the past 30 years, are world famous; they are not cheap but they still offer exceptional value for money when bought at the source here. The wool used, apparently, is imported from Iceland rather than from local sheep. The museum itself has an excellent gift shop that sells a wide range of textiles, basketry, dried herbs, home-produced jams and cheeses, as well as a staggering (quite literally, if you drink too much) range of herb-flavoured fruit *rakija*.

Sirogojno can be reached by fairly regular **buses** from Užice.

Around Sirogojno Quite close to Sirogojno, near the village of Roždanstvo on the Užice–Sirogojno road, is the **Stopića Cave (Stopića pećina)**. The cave, which is 1,650m long, has an entrance 35m wide and 18m high.

GOSTILJE (ГОСТИЉЕ) *Telephone code 031*
This village, a centre for village tourism, just south of Sirogojno, has idyllic surroundings and is perfect for walking. Gostilje is a sleepy, peaceful place, with expansive views of the valley and the limestone outcrops that stand proud of the forest west of here. There is also a waterfall close to the village that can be easily reached by a short walk. Heading down from the car park by the bridge, you pass a watermill and a flat meadow that doubles as a football pitch. A path leads down to the waterfall just beyond a very basic, but beautifully situated, campsite. Apart from the stunning scenery, the village's only other diversion is a fish farm full of thrashing trout.

 Where to stay The village of **Ljubiš**, another 7km south, has accommodation at the **Pansion Ljubiš** (✆ *801 091, 801 151;* e *simex-lju@ptt.rs;* **€€**).

MOKRA GORA (МОКРА ГОРА) *Telephone code 031*
The small village of Mokra Gora (Wet Mountain), close to the Bosnia and Herzegovinan border, is where you embark on the spectacular **Šargan Eight Railway (Šarganska osmica)**. The railway is so-called because of extreme curvature of the tracks and the shape they make when seen from below. The track changes direction to such an extent that it is difficult to work out which direction you are travelling in after you have been on board for a while (see box, page 310).

Approaching Mokra Gora from Užice, you may notice the outline of a traditional-looking village set high on a small plateau above the village. This is the village of Drvengrad (Timber Town) that was constructed by film director Emir Kusturica as a set for his 2004 film release, *Život Je Čudo* (Life is a Miracle).

Mokra Gora is a small, pleasant village but the real reason for visiting is to take a ride on its unique railway. The Šargan Eight Railway, with its charming wooden carriages and sensational views, is a wonderful excursion and certainly not just one for rail buffs. The train leaves Mokra Gora station for Šargan-Vitasi twice a

THE 'ŠARGAN EIGHT' RAILWAY

In a former life, the short stretch of convoluted track that is now called the 'Šargan Eight' used to just be one small section of the narrow-gauge line that connected Belgrade with the Bosnian capital, Sarajevo. The train was a lifeline for many communities that had previously been poorly connected and, until its closure in 1974, the Ćira train used to link the isolated villages in this part of western Serbia with the outside world.

The difficult, mountainous terrain of western Serbia ensured that it was a spectacular journey through steep cuttings and rocky gorges. Some sections were more problematic than others, however; in particular, the short section between Mokra Gora and Šargan-Vitasi. Although the horizontal distance between these two stations was a mere 3.5km, the height difference between them was a daunting 300m. Clearly, no ordinary train could cope with an incline this steep. The engineers came up with an ingenious solution to the problem and designed a loop in the shape of a number eight to connect the two stations. The loop – soon to be known as the Šargan Eight – was about 13.5km long and included 22 tunnels and ten bridges and viaducts along its length.

After 50 years of successful service, the Ćira line was declared to be unprofitable and the decision was made to close it down; the last train ran on 28 February 1974. Around 25 years passed by until fresh ideas of reopening the railway started to emerge, this time as a tourist route. During 1997 and 1998, villagers from around Mokra Gora organised voluntary work brigades to make the course of the railway passable once more. The route was finally cleared during the months of the NATO bombing in 1999, with the additional help of the Serbian army. Narrow 760mm-gauge track was laid along an 8km length of the line, a committee was formed to take charge of the railway's revitalisation, and professional assistance of the Želnid Railway Museum was sought. The emphasis was on authenticity: stations at Mokra Gora, Jatare and Šargan were reconstructed exactly as they had been in 1925 when the line was first opened.

Two museum trains – *Škoda* and *Elza* – were overhauled and put into service, and authentic wooden passenger coaches were repaired and refurbished. Since its inauguration as a tourist line, the Šargan Eight has become a rare success story in troubled times. It has even captured the interest of film-maker, Emir Kusturica, who used the railway as the setting for his 2004 movie *Život je čudo* (*Life is a Miracle*) and built a film-set village on a hill above Mokra Gora.

Now the line continues to Višegrad in the Republika Srpska, although trains only run once a week at present. See opposite for more details.

day between 1st April and 31 October at 11.45 and 13.30, taking about 40 minutes to cover the short distance downhill (in winter, trains run to a different timetable and may only run as far as Jatare and back; check w serbianrailways.com for more information). It returns to Mokra Gora after a 15-minute break and takes an hour for the uphill return journey. A return ticket costs 600din for an adult, 300din for a child. The 13.30 departure is the one generally reserved for group excursions, so there is a slim chance that this one may be full if you have not pre-booked. A limited number of tickets are sold for standing-only passengers – if this is the case, try and get a place on the small platform at the rear of the train.

It is possible to hire the whole train for a bespoke trip, which costs between 60,000din and 120,000din, depending on the time of day or night and whether or not you wish to charter a steam engine.

For further information on times, see **w** serbianrailways.com. Advance tickets can be reserved at the **Šarganska osmica booking office** (\ *510 288, 510 688;* **e** *buking.sargan8@srbrail.rs*) or bought at **Mokra Gora** (\ *800 003*), **Belgrade** (\ *011 3602 899*), **Novi Sad** (\ *021 420 700*) or **Niš** (\ *018 291 328*) railway station ticket offices.

Getting there and away Mokra Gora village is connected to Kremna and Užice by public **bus**, although it is harder to get something going back east in the late afternoon as most transport will be coming across the border from the Republika Srpska. All-inclusive **railway** trips may be booked through some Zlatibor travel agencies like Zlatiborturs or through the Zlatibor Tourist Organisation (**w** *zlatibor.org.rs*).

⌂ **Where to stay and eat** Mokra Gora railway station has its own **hotel** (\ *800 505;* **€€**) and **restaurant** right on the platform, although this is often fully booked up with groups. There are also numerous '*sobe*' signs around the village advertising private lodgings.

DRVENGRAD ('TIMBER TOWN'; ДРВЕНГРАД, ALSO KNOWN AS KÜSTENDORF)
Telephone code 031
(\ *800 686000;* **m** (*reservations*) *064 8830 213;* **e** *info@mecavnik.info;* **w** *mecavnik. info;* ⊕ *09.00–21.00 for visitors throughout the year; admission 250/140din adult/ child*) This is the small **ethno-village** above Mokra Gora on Mećavnik Hill that was constructed as a film set by film director Emir Kusturica. In addition to creating the site as a set for filming *Life is a Miracle*, Kusturica wanted the village to serve as a tribute to Serbian cultural traditions and become a settlement where artists could work:

> I lost my city during the war. This is why I wished to build my own village. It bears a German name: Küstendorf. I will organise there seminars for people who want to learn how to make cinema, concerts, ceramics, painting. It is a place where I will live and where some people will be able to visit from time to time. There will of course be other inhabitants who will work there. I dream of an open place with cultural diversity which sets up against globalisation.

The buildings, which include a tiny church dedicated to St Sava, are all of wood and built in typical 19th-century Zlatibor style with steeply pitched roofs. The village is certainly beautiful, with stunning views across to Bosnia, but, unlike Sirogojno, it is hardly typically 19th-century in function, having a swimming pool, a cinema in the basement of the main house ('Underground') that shows Kusturica's films, a library devoted to the works of Ivo Andrić (a native of Višegrad, not so far away across the border in Bosnia) and the 'Macola' art gallery. There is also a restaurant that serves national food. In keeping with Kustarica's interests in film and culture, the village's streets have been given the names of film-makers or famous international figures from the fields of sport, arts and science: Diego Maradona, Che Guevara, Bergman, Fellini, Novak Đoković and so on.

The village, which is often referred to as 'Mećavnik', the name of the hill that it stands on, was inaugurated on 25 September 2004 with the premier screening of Kusturica's film *Life is a Miracle*. Kusturica has subsequently received the

Philippe Rotthier European Architecture Award from the Brussels Foundation for Architecture for his project.

The first **Küstendorf Film and Music Festival** (w *kustendorf-filmandmusicfestival. org*) was held in the village in January 2008 with the aim of screening the work of film students from Serbia and abroad. In 2009, the main guest of the festival was the American film director Jim Jarmusch who held a workshop. A retrospective of Jarmusch's films was screened and there were also musical performances by Kustarica's own No Smoking Orchestra. The festival continues to take place in January each year.

Getting there and away Drvengrad village can be reached **on foot** by walking uphill from Mokra Gora railway station. At the level crossing gates west of the platform, go straight across and look for the path that climbs uphill and bears to the right past farm buildings – there should be a 'Mećavnik' sign or two along the way although the route is fairly obvious. To reach Drvengrad village by **car**, go back towards Užice a short way, then take the road that joins from the left after the railway crossing.

For those who would like to stay in the village, there is the four-star **Hotel Mećavnik** (✆ *3152 000;* m *(reservations) 064 8830 213;* e *info@mecavnik.info;* w *mecavnik.info;* €€), although there is little chance of finding a room at the time of the film festival or around New Year.

KREMNA (КРЕМНА) *Telephone code 031*
Kremna is a rather spread-out village that lies on the main E-761 road to Bosnia and Herzegovina, just to the south of the Tara National Park. As well as being at the heart of a beautiful area for walking, Kremna could provide a good base for visits to Mokra Gora and the Tara National Park. The town is best known for the 'Kremna prophecies', in which two illiterate shepherds during the late 19th century had Nostradamus-like visions of the future of their country (see box opposite).

Buses run to the village from Užice, usually *en route* to Republika Srpska across the border.

Where to stay There is a motel in town with 12 rooms, **Motel Šargan** (✆ *808 455;* €), and rural homestay accommodation (€) with village households can be booked through w *visitserbia.org*.

TARA NATIONAL PARK (НАЦИОНАЛНИ ПАРК ТАРА)
Telephone code (Bajina Bašta & park villages) 031

The Tara National Park lies just to the north of Kremna, in the panhandle circumscribed by the bend of the River Drina that extends northwest into Bosnia and Herzegovina. Tara, which includes both the Tara and Zvezda mountain ranges, was declared a national park in 1981. The park covers an area of about 22,000ha that lie between 250m and 1,500m above sea level.

The park is almost entirely composed of high mountains and deep gorges, three-quarters of which are covered by forest, together with the caves and springs typical of a karst landscape. Tara is home to a rare endemic tree species, the Pančić (or Serbian) spruce (*Picea omorikca pancic*), that is now confined to just a small area of the park and under state protection. Several species of rare and threatened birds and mammals like golden eagle and brown bear are present within the park's boundaries.

THE KREMNA PROPHECIES

During the late 19th century, in the village of Kremna in the Zlatibor region of western Serbia, a local shepherd, Mitar Tarabić, found himself subjected to disturbing visions of the future. Tarabić was an illiterate, uneducated man and so narrated these revelations to his godfather, an Orthodox priest called Zaharije Zaharić who, although sceptical, wrote down the shepherd's prophecies in his notebook. When Mitar died in 1899, this ability to predict the future passed over to his nephew, Miloš.

Many of the predictions possessed a quite uncanny accuracy. One prophecy was that the Serbian king and queen would be assassinated and replaced on the throne by a Karađorđević. In 1903, this came to realisation when Aleksandar and Draga Obrenović were assassinated by their own guards to be replaced by Petar Karađorđević who became King Petar I. Other prophecies were more wide-ranging. They predicted that the Serbs would renounce their name (Yugoslavia?) and that a man who was not a Serb, who had blue eyes and a star on his forehead, would rule for a long time. This same man (surely Tito?) was also predicted to live to a ripe old age and die as a result of a leg injury.

Further Tito prophecy is related here by the priest:

> Mitar told me that the man with blue eyes and the star upon his forehead, would break the long-lasting love with our Christian Orthodox brothers, the Russians. He would not be grateful to them for the fact that he was sitting on our throne because they had put him there in the first place. A great hatred would erupt between us and the Russians. Blood would be spilled among our people. These wounds would be quickly healed and we would again be friends with the Russians, but never sincerely, only formally, pretending for the sake of others not to understand how we cheat and lie to each other.

Both Mitar and Miloš predicted that there would be a total of three world wars and that their priest scribe would die the same year that the first war ended. Ever accommodating, Zaharije Zaharić died as predicted in 1918. The events of the Yugoslav wars of the 1990s were also apparently anticipated, with the Tarabićs predicting that Serbia's neighbours would unite against them. A further revelation was that a man who came from a village that bore his name would unite the Serbian people, who would then rise and 'chase out the godless'.

Perhaps it was no coincidence then, that Petar Tarabić, a direct descendant of the prophetic duo, was on hand to greet President Vojislav Koštunica (whose family came from the village of Koštunici) when he visited Kremna in late August 2000, just a couple of months before Slobodan Milošević was ousted from power.

The prophets fail to mention who would win the third of the world wars in which 'evil ones will ravage the whole Earth and men will start to die in great numbers' but at least conclude that after this the world would become a happy place where people would live such long lives that they would 'forget when they were born'.

A local expert on the Kremna prophets is Dragan Pjević, who has opened a small museum in the village.

West and Southwest Serbia   TARA NATIONAL PARK (НАЦИОНАЛНИ ПАРК ТАРА)

7

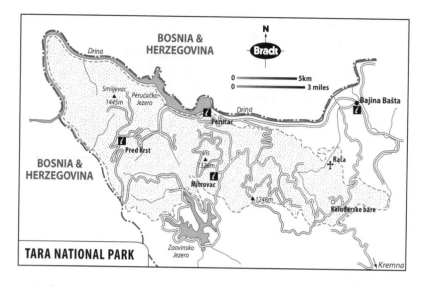

BOSNIA &
HERZEGOVINA

Drina

Smiljevac
▲1445m   Perućačko
Jezero

Drina

Perućac

Pred Krst

BOSNIA &
HERZEGOVINA

Vis
▲326m

Mitrovac

Rača

1248m

Kaluđerske bare

Bajina Bašta

Zaovinsko
Jezero

Kremna

TARA NATIONAL PARK

0 ——————— 5km
0 ——————— 3 miles

Bradt

Facilities can be found within the park at Kaluđerske bare, where there is a hotel complex, at Perućac and at Mitrovac, which has a children's recreational centre and some catering facilities.

GETTING THERE AND AWAY Three roads lead into the park: one from Bajina Bašta directly by way of the Bajina Bašta–Kaluđerske bare road; a second from Bajina Bašta along the Perućac–Mitrovac road, and another from Kremna on the road that leads to Kaluđerske bare. The road that continues through to Bosnia and Herzegovina at Kamenica does not constitute an official border crossing point. There is limited public transport within the park. Bajina Bašta is well connected to Užice by bus and has a few services each day to Perućac as well as to Valjevo.

TOURIST INFORMATION The **Bajina Bašta Tourist Information Centre** is at Milana Obrenovića 34/II (📞 865 370, 865 900; e turizam@taradrina.com; w taradrina.com). Information about the park can be had from the Tara National Park headquarters at Bajina Bašta (*Milenka Topalovića 3, 31250 Bajina Bašta;* 📞 863 644; e office@nptarag. rs; w nptara.rs), just outside the park boundary. There is also an information centre at Mitrovac (📞 859 732) and a visitor centre at Perućac Lake.

 WHERE TO STAY AND EAT The websites w tara-planina.com and w tara-apartmani. com also have details of many private apartments to rent in the Tara National Park.

Kaluđerske bare and Perućac

🏠 **Beli Bor **** (125 rooms) Kaluđerske bare; 📞 593 852, 593 598; e recepcija.belibor@mod. gov.rs; w hotelitara.mod.gov.rs. At Radmilovac, a few km from Omorika. National restaurant, sports facilities, conference room & nightclub. €€

🏠 **Omorika ***** (156 rooms, 8 suites, 2 apts) Kaluđerske bare; 📞 593 901; e recepcija.omorika@ mod.gov.rs; w hotelitara.mod.gov.rs. Each room with bath, satellite TV & phone. €€

🏠 **Vila Drina** (13 rooms, 2 suites) Nikole Tesle bb, Perućac; 📞 862 451; w taragreen.rs. All rooms with satellite TV, minibar & internet access. €€

🏠 **Javor *** (28 rooms) Kaluđerske bare; 📞 593 901, 593 550. Next door to Omorika. Has a national restaurant with live music. €

Bajina Bašta

🌟 🏠 **Hotel Turist **** (3 rooms, 11 apts) Svetosavska 95, Bajina Bašta; 📞 866 570; e info@

hotelturist.rs; w hotelturist.rs. With helpful staff &
spacious, well-appointed rooms, this modern hotel
makes an excellent base for exploring the Tara
region. Restaurant, Wi-Fi, cable TV, AC. €€€–€€

🏠 **Hotel Drina** *** (79 rooms, 6 suites)
Vojvode Mišića 5, Bajina Bašta; 📞862 452;
w taragreen.rs. In the centre of town, with its own
restaurant that offers FB. €€

WHAT TO SEE AND DO The Drina Gorge that separates Serbia from Bosnia and
Herzegovina is also an integral part of the park and can be toured by boat. Various
water-based activities such as white-water rafting are offered along the river here.
Check w raftingtara.com for further information. As well as hiking, the park is also
one of the best places in the country for mountain biking (page 78).

Bajina Bašta is a pleasant border town that has some interesting domestic
buildings and serves as a good base for visiting the park with your own transport.
The town also has some sights of its own worth seeing. Most famous of these is
undoubtedly the **House on the Drina (Kućica na Drini)**, a wooden fishing hut that
perches improbably on a rock in the middle of the River Drina. Much photographed,
the building is featured on numerous book covers and postcards and posters about
the Tara region. To reach it from the town centre, head east along Svetosavska past
the bus station and then turn left along the main Belgrade road. Continue for a
kilometre or so through an industrial area to a point where the road meets the river.
Here there are a couple of restaurants and a parking area along with an information
board and a view of the House on the Drina. For a better view, follow one of the
paths that lead down towards the river. Hilltop Bosnian mosques can be seen
on the other side of the Drina River, which serves as an international boundary
here. The Drina house was originally built in the late 1960s by local youths who
transported the wood by boat and canoe. Six kilometres to the south of Bajina Bašta
is **Rača Monastery** that was founded in the late 13th century by King Dragutin. It
was restored in the 16th century to become an important centre for the copying of
liturgical texts but was destroyed by Turks in the late 17th century. The monastery
was reconstructed in 1795 by Hadži Melentius Stefanović, a protagonist of the First
National Uprising. The current church dates from 1826. *Miroslav's Gospel*, now in
the National Museum of Belgrade, was stored here during the years of World War
II. For a brief taste of the national park, there are several marked trails that lead into
the surrounding forest from the monastery. A good one to try is the one that leads
up to the spring at Lađevac, a beautiful walk through dense beech woodland with
shady picnic spots along the way. The trail can be very muddy in places after wet
weather. A taxi to Rača Monastery costs around 400din each way.

SOUTH ALONG THE IBAR VALLEY

The road leading south from Kraljevo follows the Ibar River towards Raška, Novi
Pazar and the territory of the Sandžak. It is a beautiful drive, with densely forested
green hills on either side of the narrow valley. The river, fast flowing even at Kraljevo,
becomes increasingly turbulent as it progresses upstream, shadowed by the main
road. Steep, wooded slopes rise on both sides but, here and there, tiny, garden-sized
plots of agriculture appear where there is just enough flat land to cultivate a few crops.

Two spa resorts lie just off this road: **Mataruška Banja** to the east, about 12km
from Kraljevo, with accommodation available at the three-star **Hotel Termal** (*Žička
28*; 📞 036 5411 366; €€), and **Bogutovačka Banja** 10km further on, a couple of
kilometres west of the village of Bogutovac on the main road. Both have the usual
spa facilities as well as hotels. Further information on these may be had from the
helpful Kraljevo tourist office.

After about 20km or so, the medieval castle of **Maglič** appears to the left, high on a bluff above a bend in the river. Maglič Castle was constructed in the 13th century to give control over the Ibar Valley. It was restored and strengthened during the reign of King Milutin by Danilo II, a 14th-century archbishop who wished to protect himself from marauding factions. You might assume, given the castle's forbidding and impregnable appearance, that he was entirely successful in his venture, but the castle eventually fell into Turkish hands in 1438. Like many of Serbia's abandoned castles, Maglič probably looks more impressive from a distance – and especially from below, where it maintains a sense of scale and dominance over the surrounding landscape. Buses will stop here, should you wish to get off and explore; there is a footbridge a little further on beyond the bus stop, which you can use to cross the river before clambering up to the ruins.

The road continues a further 25km south to the small town of **Ušće** at the confluence of the Ibar and Studenica rivers, where there is the turn-off to Studenica Monastery. The road to take is the one immediately before the town, just north of the river. The road to Studenica climbs up steeply through pine forest, snaking its way through a series of tight bends. The monastery is reached about 12km from the junction, although it will probably seem further than this by the time you get there.

STUDENICA MONASTERY (МАНАСТИР СТУДЕНИЦА)
Deliberately remote, the Monastery of Studenica sits in splendidly mountainous surroundings, high above the river that bears the same name, and even higher above the Raška Valley, a dozen kilometres to the east. Originally established by Stefan Nemanja at the end of the 12th century, this is undoubtedly one of the country's greatest monasteries and one of the holiest places in the Serbian national psyche.

The monastery consists of three churches within an oval walled complex (originally there were nine). The largest of these, and central to the complex, is that of the **Church of Our Lady (Bogorodičina crkva)**, completed in 1196. This church, the prototype of the Raška School, takes its influence from both Romanesque and Byzantine sources. The exterior is of polished marble, unique in Serbian medieval architecture, with elaborately sculptured leaves, figures and mythological beasts in the Romanesque style decorating the windows and doorways.

Inside, the effect of smooth marble is marred by a clumsily executed exonarthex, added by Radoslav, one of the later rulers of the Nemanjić dynasty, who added this maladroit extension around 1230. Entrance to the interior is made through the exonarthex. Inside, the iconostasis, with its unusually cheerful-looking representations of Jesus, Mary and God, dates from the 16th century. The marble tomb of Stefan Nemanja is situated in a chapel to the right of the exonarthex beneath a fresco that shows him holding a model of the church and being presented to Christ and the Virgin. It was at Studenica that Stefan Nemanja abdicated before his retirement to Mt Athos in Greece. His body was returned here after his death. His feast day is 24 May and there is an annual pilgrimage to celebrate the event. Stefan's son, Stefan Prvovenčani, is entombed here too, and his body lies in the exonarthex in an elaborate 19th-century walnut casket inlaid with designs in mother-of-pearl and ivory.

Most of the original frescoes, completed in 1209, and probably the work of a single artist, were repainted in 1569. They are divided into an upper part that has a gilded background, a middle part with a yellow background and a lower part, with a blue background. The work reflects a development in the Serbian tradition in which there is an increased emphasis on the human form, its physical strength and its definition of character. Exceptions to the 16th-century repainting are part of the

Annunciation and the *Crucifixion*, which adorns the west wall and shows the figure of Christ flanked by St John and the Virgin. The colours used here – blues, maroon and gold – are particularly deep and rich.

Next door, and tiny in comparison, is the **King's Church (Kraljeva Crkva)**, built by King Milutin in 1314. The frescoes here are very well preserved and represent some of the greatest religious art in the country, painted in the period when Serbian fresco art was at its peak. The north wall has the fresco of the *Birth of the Virgin*, which shows how Serbian artists had gone beyond mere symbolism by this date to become increasingly interested in portraying realism and technique. To the left of the Virgin child, a woman holds a tray of surgical instruments while the figure of Destiny fans the newborn; in the foreground, a woman is portrayed testing the temperature of the water with the back of her hand.

The third remaining church is the early 13th-century **Church of St Nicholas (Sveti Nikola)**, which has a few surviving frescoes of interest and a 17th-century iconostasis.

It should not be forgotten that Studenica is no mere museum but a thriving, working community that, while welcoming visitors, is not in the least dependent on them for its existence. For the monks here, the monastery is both a religious retreat and a workplace where spiritual contemplation is mixed with more mundane tasks like chopping wood and growing vegetables. Visitors are steady and frequent but rarely overwhelm the tranquillity of the place. Rather than just visit as a day trip, it is also possible to stay for longer and absorb the peaceful atmosphere here. There is an **Upper Hermitage** built into the rock face further up from the monastery and this could provide the target for an enjoyable walk. Ask how to reach it at the monastery.

Getting there and away The best way to reach Studenica if you do not have your own car is by bus from Ušće. These are relatively infrequent but there should be around five in total throughout the day. In most cases the same bus will return to Ušće from the monastery after a short break there. Avoid missing the return bus as it is a 12km walk back to Ušće; at least it is downhill.

Getting to Ušće from either Kraljevo or Novi Pazar should present no problems, as passing buses can be flagged down on the main road. There are also buses to Kraljevo that originate from the town.

Where to stay and eat For accommodation, the monastery's own **Studenica Guest House** (m *064 6467 492*; €), next door to the monastery, has simple but acceptable rooms. For food, as well as the hotel restaurant, there is a fairly basic restaurant near the entrance to the complex by the road.

Ušće has several basic places to eat but nowhere to stay in the town itself.

KOPAONIK (КОПАОНИК) REGION *Telephone code 036 (& Raška)*

South of Ušće, the road enters the historic territory of the Sandžak. Ten kilometres after leaving Ušće, at the village of **Biljanovac**, a road leads off to the left bound for the high pasture and ski runs of **Kopaonik**. This is Serbia's prime ski-resort area and, for some winter holidaymakers, all they get to know of the country. This is a pity because, although the region has undeniable natural beauty, the resort itself has the ambience you might expect from a popular winter sports destination. It is perfectly possible to visit in summer of course, thus avoiding both the ski-season crowds and the often unpleasant mugginess of the lower altitudes, but even then it may be difficult to ignore exactly where you are: a slightly brash, purpose-built ski resort.

GETTING THERE AND AWAY Driving your own **car**, the best way to come is to turn off the Kraljevo–Novi Pazar road at Biljanovac and head towards the small town of **Jošanička Banja**, with its Turkish *hammam* and constant source of warm spring water, 10km along this route. Just beyond the town is a road to the right that leads to the **Monastery of Gradac**, founded in the late 13th century by Jelena, the wife of King Uroš I, and mother of kings Dragutin and Milutin. The church is in a style that combines Gothic and Byzantine elements, and has some resonance with Studenica in that it would appear that its craftsmen had some familiarity with the religious architecture of western Europe. The frescoes within – a *Crucifixion* on the west wall, a *Dormition of the Virgin* on the north wall, and scenes from the life of the Virgin in the narthex – are all badly damaged.

From Jošanička Banja the road winds up through spectacular mountain scenery to the resort at Kopoanik, and then on to **Brzeće**, an alternative base in the region, some distance beyond.

By public **bus** – not an easy option unless you find direct transport to and from Belgrade – you must travel beyond the junction at Bilanovac and on to Raška to find a connecting service.

KOPAONIK NATIONAL PARK (НАЦИОНАЛНИ ПАРК КОПАОНИК)

Geography Kopaonik was declared a national park in 1981. It is not a single peak but a flattish plateau-like massif called Suvo Rudište with several peaks rising above the 1,700m of the plateau. The national park is spread over 12,000ha, the boundaries of which are defined by natural phenomena: the valleys of the Ibar to the west, Jošanica to the north, the Rasina and Gornija Toplica to the east, while its southern slopes blend into the northern reaches of Kosovo above Leposavić. The highest of the peaks is **Pančićev vrh** at 2,017m.

The area's main features were formed by massive earth movements some 70 million years ago, the deep clefts formed creating a path for the flow of andesite-basalt that was responsible for the rich mineral deposits in the area. The mineral wealth associated with this rock form – iron, copper, lead and silver – is found in abundance throughout the massif. Consequently, the area became an important mining centre and this was the mainstay of the local economy before tourism was developed in the area. The name Kopaonik is derived from this practice (*kopati* means 'to dig').

Because of an altitude that is in excess of 1,600m, the Kopaonik area has a sub-alpine climate, tempered to some extent by its southerly latitude and its plateau shape. The relative flatness of the massif means that cloud tends not to sit on the mountain for long and so, without this cloud cover, Kopaonik is exposed to the sun for extended periods in winter, making it warmer than might be expected. Nevertheless, snow cover remains for an average of 159 days a year from November through to May, providing a long and relatively stable ski season. On average, Kopaonik enjoys 200 sunny days a year, with most rainfall coming in summer in July and August.

Natural history The flora of Kopaonik is particularly rich, with numerous species of tree, fern, moss and herbaceous plant. The foothills have forests of oak, Turkey oak, hornbeam and common pear, which give way to beech forest higher up as far as 1,500m. Above the belt of beech forest is a zone of spruce forest, now much depleted after heavy deforestation in the past. At the highest elevations, above 1,800m, mountain juniper (*Junipeus nana*) finds a foothold due to the species' tolerance of extreme cold. Now pasture has replaced the high alpine forest in many places. Mountain cattle-rearing was formerly important here, with the animals spending the warmer months grazing on the high meadows. Now this activity is starting to die out and many of the meadows are being cultivated.

The evergreen zone holds a number of rare bird species that include red crossbill as well as a species of grasshopper that is more usually found in Siberia. Larger animals like wolves, hares and foxes survive here despite reduced numbers, but bear, lynx, deer and wildcat have all disappeared in recent years.

KOPAONIK RESORT The **Kopaonik Ski Centre** provides a total of 44km of ski paths. There are 22 chair lifts and drags. The resort is at an altitude of 1,770m and the highest station reaches 2,017m. There are four nursery slopes. Of the main slopes, 12 are designated 'easy' runs; five, medium; while two are considered difficult. The longest ski run is 3.5km long and the maximum vertical rise is 521m. As well as the vertical ski runs, there are also around 20km of cross-country tracks.

🏠 **Where to stay** If you come on an organised tour here your accommodation will, of course, already be provided. If you decide to visit independently then you can expect a wide selection from which to choose. Below is just a small sample of the hotels and apartment complexes available at the resort and a couple of options at **Brzeće** nearby (*telephone code 037*). Prices tend to be higher in the winter skiing season, especially in the period around New Year and Orthodox Christmas.

🏠 **Grand Hotel & Spa** **** (171 rooms) ✆5471 977; e info@mkresort.com; w mkresort.com. This is probably the most luxurious hotel in Kopaonik, part of a spa complex that has an indoor swimming pool, jacuzzi, sauna, indoor tennis court & fitness centre. €€€€

🏠 **Apartments Konaci Deluxe** **** (407 apts) ✆5471 977; e info@mkresort.com; w mkresort.com. This massive 3-winged complex, which belongs to the same MK Mountain Resort company as the Grand Hotel & Spa, stands as a centrepiece to the resort. Apartments with small kitchen & bathroom. €€€

🏠 **Hotel Junior** *** (111 rooms) Brzeće; ✆833 355; e info@junior-kopaonik.com; w juniorhotel.rs. €€€

🏠 **Apartment Complex JAT** **** (130 apts) ✆5471 043, 5471 044, 5471 045; e jatkop@ptt.rs; w jatapartmani.com. Apartments with kitchen & satellite TV. The 'Romantika' restaurant in the complex serves national dishes. €€

🏠 **Jugobanka** ** (80 rooms) ✆5471 062, 5471 040. Located close to 5 ski lifts. €€

🏠 **Olga Dedijer***** (65 rooms) ✆5471 033. A typical alpine resort hotel, with restaurant, nightclub, gym & shop. €€

🏠 **Putnik** *** (95 rooms) ✆5471 130; e putnik-kop@putnik.com; w putnik-kop.com. Situated just 200m from the 'Sunny Valley' ski lift, with 2 restaurants, a shop & a large sun terrace. €€

🏠 **Tourist Apartments Kopaonik** *** (61 apts) Brzeće; ✆823 099, 823 130; w kopapartmani.co.rs. €€

🍴 **Where to eat and drink** The resort is well served by restaurants and bars, mostly attached to hotels and apartment complexes. The following are just a few more options:

🍴 **Naša Kuća** ✆5471 193. Popular with a trendy young crowd & serving international food. €€€

🍴 **Zvrk** ✆5471 977. Part of the Grand Hotel complex, this restaurant on 2 levels with an open fire is one of the best in the resort. €€€

🍴 **Bakina Kuhinja** m 062 474 630. 'Grandmother's Kitchen', ie: traditional Serbian cooking. €€

🍴 **Buongiorno Casa Pizza** m 062 1721 523. Pizzeria. €€

🍴 **Kopanički Vajat** ✆5471 782. National restaurant. €€

Sandžak, the Turkish term used to describe its administrative provinces and this predominantly Muslim corner of southwest Serbia (and northeast Montenegro), is sometimes used as an alternative to Raška, the term that most Orthodox Serbs prefer. The region, which remained a buffer zone between Serbia and Montenegro until late in the 19th century, was the last part of Serbia to be liberated from Turkish rule, remaining as part of the Ottoman Empire until 1912 and the First Balkan War when it was overrun by Serbian and Montenegrin troops. At the end of World War I, Raška was included in the newly created Kingdom of Serbs, Croats and Slovenes.

Following the establishment of Serbian and Montenegrin regional governments in the region, many of Raška's Muslims migrated to Turkey with the encouragement of both the newly established kingdom and Turkey itself. This migration continued even into the years that followed World War II, with deals continuing to be struck between communist Yugoslavia and the Turkish government. The reasons for this unexpected co-operation were twofold: from the Yugoslav position, there were doubts about the loyalty of its Muslim citizens and it was happy to let them go; from Turkey's point of view, it was an ideal opportunity to help populate vast uninhabited areas of Anatolia. It is estimated that over a million inhabitants of modern-day Turkey are actually of Raška origin – more than the current population of both the Serbian and Montenegrin Raška today.

Muslims have continued to leave since the last agreement between Yugoslavia and Turkey was signed in 1954, mostly to western Europe or Bosnia and Herzegovina, and mainly driven by economic hardship. The current trend for an exodus of the Serbian Orthodox population is actually something of an anomaly, a phenomenon that has occurred largely in the wake of the Kosovo crisis.

In topographical terms, Raška, which straddles both sides of the Serbian–Montenegrin border, is largely a remote region of forest, mountains and few decent roads. It is the rearing of livestock that is the main economy here, rather than the fruit-growing and arable farming that is the mainstay further north, although as might be expected in a mainly Muslim province, pigs are conspicuous by their absence.

Raška is noticeably poorer than the rest of western and central Serbia and, according to many of its inhabitants, largely neglected by central government. The figures bear this out: the GDP of predominantly Muslim Novi Pazar is 53% of the Serbian average, and in Sjenica, which is 85% Muslim, it is even lower at 41%; in nearby towns that have a Serbian Orthodox majority, the GDP is higher; 87% in the case of Raška town. The poverty, the politics and the ethnic imbalance mean that some parallels can be drawn with the situation in Kosovo, except that here the large Muslim population is not of Albanian origin but ethnic Slavs who converted to Islam in the distant past. Thankfully, the ethnic violence that has torn Kosovo apart in recent years has had no equivalent here, although the situation can often be tense around election time.

RAŠKA *Telephone code 036*

Continuing along the main road south of Ušće, the first town of any size is Raška, 18km beyond the Kopaonik turn-off. **Raška** is a spread-out, sizeable place, about 20km north of Novi Pazar, with a reasonable amount of industry stretching along the roadside. There is not that much to see in the town other than an interesting street market on Wednesdays when essential rural goods like wooden barrels and horse harnesses are sold. Other than this, it is not a particularly attractive place. However, if it is late in the day and you are travelling on to Kopaonik, you should be prepared to spend the night here as buses to the resort are infrequent. There are a few places advertising rooms (*sobe*) around the town as well as the central, two-star **Hotel Prestige** (*Predraga Vilimonovića 2;* ☎ *736 688;* e *office@hotelprestige.co.rs;* w *prestigeraska.com;* €€) and the **Motel Karavan** (*Predraga Vilimonovića 81;* ☎ *733 409;* e *karavan@beotel.net;* €), 600m from the centre on the Novi Pazar road. Further south, along the main road close to Novi Pazar, is the three-star **Hotel Oxa** (☎ *020 371 381;* e *oxa@gmail.com;* w *hoteloxa.com;* €€).

All **buses** heading south tend to stop in Raška; it is here that a main road branches off with the railway to follow the River Ibar into Kosovo by way of the troubled town of Kosovska Mitrovica.

Beyond Raška, the road follows the river that takes its name from the town until, after a further 20km, the region's capital, Novi Pazar, is reached.

NOVI PAZAR (НОВИ ПАЗАР) *Telephone code 020*

Sitting among low hills where the River Raška has its confluence with the Ljudska, is the large town of Novi Pazar (New Bazaar), capital of the region. Almost immediately upon arrival you notice how different it seems from similar-sized towns to the north like Kraljevo or Čačak. Other than in Kosovo, Novi Pazar is the town with the most pronounced Islamic atmosphere in the country: instead of church domes, it is minarets that stab the skyline, and rather than the relaxed and carefree mixing of the sexes that takes place throughout most of Serbia, men and women seem to live more separate existences here. Almost everywhere you look there are coffee houses full of huddled groups of men drinking small glasses of *čaj* or *Turska kafa*, talking and playing backgammon in a haze of cigarette fog. Even without the existence of mosques and old Ottoman buildings, such characteristics give evidence that this is still very much a Turkish town and, despite the worst excesses of 1970s Yugoslav town planning, modernisation has failed to destroy the distinctly Muslim character of Novi Pazar. Having said all of this, it is important to note that the town also possesses three extremely important historic Orthodox buildings in its immediate vicinity: tangible reminders of Raška's pre-Islamic period – the Church of St Peter, St George's Pillars and Sopoćani Monastery.

Although Novi Pazar has some of the appearance and atmosphere of Kosovo, its Muslim population is composed, not of Albanians, but of Serbs who converted to Islam centuries ago. These proselytised Serbians are now commonly referred to by the rest of the population as Bosniaks, Muslims, or even 'Turks', which in this context might be considered a pejorative term. Whether it is a product of religion, culture or development – or all three – the atmosphere here is markedly different from the rest of the country. The steady Orthodox migration away from the Novi Pazar region that has taken place over the past ten years, talked up by fears of cultural domination and Kosovo-type repression, has contributed to the Muslim character of the town in many ways. It is not just the visible backdrop of mosques, tea houses and narrow bazaar streets that define this character, but also in the way people carry out their daily life: in Novi Pazar, the evening *korso* is dominated by groups of strolling young men, few restaurants openly sell alcohol, and many women cover themselves up in the Islamic manner.

There seems to be a slightly conspiratorial air about the place, as if trouble is expected on the horizon. Given the sad realities of nearby Kosovo, this is, perhaps, reasonable enough, but, up to now at least, the town and province have managed to avoid the spiteful conflict that has blighted their neighbour.

In some ways this is one of the most interesting towns in the country, which makes it all the more mysterious why there is so little information about the place.

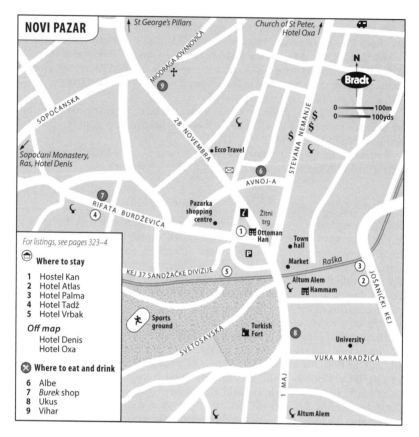

NOVI PAZAR

↑ St George's Pillars

Church of St Peter,
Hotel Oxa ↑

MIODRAGA JOVANOVIĆA

SOPOĆANSKA

28 NOVEMBRA

Sopoćani Monastery,
Ras, Hotel Denis

● Ecco Travel

AVNOJ-A

STEVANA NEMANJE

N

Bradt

0   100m
0   100yds

⑦ RIFATA BURDŽEVIĆA ④

Pazarka
shopping
centre

Žitni
trg

① 🏛 Ottoman
Han

Town
hall

For listings, see pages 323–4

🛏 **Where to stay**

1   Hostel Kan
2   Hotel Atlas
3   Hotel Palma
4   Hotel Tadž
5   Hotel Vrbak

Off map
   Hotel Denis
   Hotel Oxa

✖ **Where to eat and drink**

6   Albe
7   *Burek* shop
8   Ukus
9   Vihar

KEJ 37 SANDŽAČKE DIVIZIJE ⑤

Market

Raška ③

Altum Alem ②

🏛 Hammam

JOŠANIČKI KEJ

Sports
ground

SVETOSAVSKA

Turkish
Fort

⑧

University

VUKA KARADŽIĆA

1 MAJ

Altum Alem

The reason for all this is most probably political. There is a palpable nervousness about what might happen in Novi Pazar in the future. Having had its religious institutions secularised, and its town centre ripped apart by Yugoslav town planners in the 1960s and 70s, much of Novi Pazar seems keen to return to its Turkish roots in the post-Milošević period. Certainly, the Islamic character of the town is becoming increasingly more pronounced as the cultural balance has changed in favour of the Muslim community. Until a couple of decades ago, Novi Pazar was a town with a fairly even Orthodox–Muslim mix. Nowadays, its population is something like 90% Muslim, an imbalance caused partly by the higher birth rate of the Muslims and partly by the recent migration of many Orthodox Serbs away from the region. A small influx of ethnic Serb refugees from Kosovo has helped to redress this balance to some extent, however. Naturally, this demographic shift continues to alarm those Orthodox Serbs that remain – by 2011, comprising just 16% of the municipal population and much lower in the city itself. Fears of Kosovo-style divisions and a general resentment and distrust of central government in Belgrade have done little to allay such fears.

It is undeniable that the Raška region, and Novi Pazar in particular, has suffered long years of neglect, with a distinct lack of investment in its industry, services and infrastructure. Unemployment is much higher here than elsewhere in the country, the roads are even worse than usual, and the statistics show that public health in the region is well below the national average. It is no wonder then that a certain degree of resentment is in the air.

This is not to paint too bleak a picture: Novi Pazar is not a place of widespread extremist sentiment – it is nothing like Saudi Arabia, or Pakistan, or even Egypt – but its Islamic character, which was suppressed and diluted as part of the former Yugoslavia, continues to strengthen with time. In recent years, there has been a noticeable increase in fundamentalist Wahhabi sympathisers – a group of them broke up a folk music concert in 2006 claiming that the music was 'satanic' – but these hold beliefs that are at odds with the vast majority of the town's moderate Muslims who have no sympathy with their extremist views and aggressive tactics.

True to its Ottoman roots, the town today feels more like Turkey than anywhere else in Serbia; indeed, it is probably closer to old Turkish traditions than a lot of Turkish Mediterranean towns that have embraced mass tourism in recent years. Until recently, the town was probably most famous for its textile industry, particularly for the manufacture of denim jeans, which it churned out in great quantity and in a variety of guises and fashion labels, genuine and otherwise. Cheap imports, mostly from China, have put an end to this and the town's unemployment figures have soared. Inevitably perhaps, a minority in the town have turned to easier ways of making money and drug smuggling has become a fact of life in recent years. Despite a local GDP that is supposedly about half the national average, the number of expensive German cars cruising up and down Stevana Nemanje each night is a sight to behold – a visible reminder of the ill-gotten gains of some of the town's 'traders'.

GETTING THERE AND AWAY Novi Pazar is well connected by **bus** to most parts of Serbia. Several buses run each day to Belgrade, a journey of just over 5 hours. There is also one bus to Podgorica (in Montenegro) and one to Skopje in Macedonia, two to Novi Sad, four to Niš, five to Kragujevac, seven to Kraljevo, ten to Sjenica, nine to Raška and a couple to Baćica on the Pešter plateau. Fairly frequent services also run to Sarajevo and Istanbul, and there is a daily service to Priština in Kosovo.

Novi Pazar has no rail service, nor airport, but **bus information** can be found at ☏318 354.

TOURIST INFORMATION In theory, this can be found at 28 Novembra 27 (☏ 338 030; e info.tonp@live.com; w tonp.rs), although they seem reluctant to open their office.

A tourist agency that may be able to help with local travel arrangements and organise tours is **Ecco Travel** (28 Novembra 54; ☏ 314 859, 311 575; e eccodoo@gmail.com; w ecco.rs). They speak both English and German.

🏠 **WHERE TO STAY** Map, page 322

🏠 **Hotel Atlas** ** (32 rooms, 4 apts) Jošanički kej bb; ☏601 101; e info@hotelatlas.rs; w hotelatlas.rs. A modern hotel with spacious rooms next to the river behind the market. €€€–€€

🏠 **Hotel Tadž** **** (25 rooms) Rifata Burdževića 79; ☏311 904, 316 838; e info@hoteltazdnd.com; w hoteltazdnd.com. By far the best hotel in town, this gleaming new private hotel is just a few years old & offers modern comforts in plain, well-appointed rooms that come with AC, satellite TV & minibar. It is situated near the river

just a few mins' walk west of the centre. The hotel has its own private parking area; you drive right through the building to reach it – quite literally. €€€–€€

🏠 **Hotel Denis** **** (7 rooms) Nedžad Ramović; ☏360 120; e hotel-denis@neobee.net. 5km from Novi Pazar on the road to Tutin. €€

🏠 **Hostel Kan** *** (13 rooms) Rifata Burdževića 10; ☏315 300; m 065 3315 300. This is not really a hostel but a small private hotel, located right in the town with modern en-suite rooms with minibar & cable TV. The rooms are clean but rather cramped & with thin walls, & somewhat overpriced for what they offer. €€

🏠 **Hotel Oxa *** (35 rooms) Postenje bb; ☏ 371 381; e oxa@gmail.com; w hoteloxa. com. Just out of town on the Raška road, this is a comfortable business hotel with modern, well-appointed rooms. €€

🏠 **Hotel Vrbak *** (30 rooms) 37 Sandžačke divizije; ☏ 314 844, 314 548; e office@hotelvrbak; w hotelvrbak.com. This very odd, state-run hotel in the town centre is hard to miss. The hotel's design is a weird hybrid of neo-Oriental & 1970s space station. Rooms on 3 levels surround the central atrium that houses the reception desk.

There are some nice design touches here & there: lozenge-shaped windows, fancy wrought-iron work & stained-glass windows. In different surroundings, the Vrbak might appear impressive but here, in the centre of an old Turkish town, it looks rather out of place. Nevertheless, I am sure the architects must have won a prize for their work – for originality at least. This was virtually empty of guests when I last visited but still operational. Take the spiral staircase to reach the 1st-floor lobby & reception. €€

🏠 **Hotel Palma *** Jošanički kej bb; ☏ 335 400, 335 401. No-nonsense place to stay, with spacious rooms. €

✘ WHERE TO EAT AND DRINK *Map, page 322*

For dining, all of the hotels have their own restaurants but none of them are really anything special. Although there are one or two pizzerias dotted about, the best bet really is to eat in the bazaar area where there are numerous *čevapčići* places that offer good food at very affordable prices. The **Ukus** on 1 Maj (€), the road leading up through the bazaar to the Altum Alem mosque, is particularly good, with a choice of salads and sweets as well as *čevapčići* and other grilled meats. Another good option is the Turkish kebab place on Stevana Nemanje, next door to the National Bank of Greece. Elsewhere, there are *mlečni* restaurants all around town, and especially near the centre along 28 Novembra and Stevana Nemanje streets. *Mlečni* refers to milk, rather like milk bars, an indication that these places do not serve alcohol. A good *mlečni* place just off Stevana Nemanje that also does good coffee and pizzas is **Albe** (m 063 604 858). If you want a beer or something stronger then you could try one of the trendy café-bars with darkened windows and booming music up near the bus station. The **Vihar** (€) near the church on Miodraga Jovanovića also serves alcohol. For Turkish coffee or *ćaj*, there are numerous options in the bazaar, especially near the old *hammam*, along 28 Novembra, or up near the bus station. However, these places do tend to be male preserves and female visitors will probably feel uncomfortable if not unwelcome; better to use one of the more upmarket café-bars that are also quite plentiful. For cakes, snacks, and especially for *burek*, there are numerous possibilities all around town. There is an excellent **Turkish *burek* shop** opposite the Hotel Tadž and a couple more along Stevana Nemanje.

OTHER PRACTICALITIES For money, the **Eksimbanka** and **National Bank of Greece** have branches on Stevana Nemanje, the road that leads to the centre from the bus station. Both of these have ATMs, as does the **Raiffesien banka** that is found in the walkway of the large concrete block on the right-hand side of Stevana Nemanje as you head into town. There is a **post office** on 28 Novembra. For everyday items, there is the **Pazarka shopping centre**, a large supermarket close to the central square of Žitni trg.

WHAT TO SEE AND DO Part of the pleasure of being in Novi Pazar is to simply absorb its vaguely exotic atmosphere. The evocative sound of the *muezzin* – the call for prayer five times a day – that emanates from the mosques is a reminder that Turkey and the Middle East are not so very far away. The smells are redolent of the East too, with the ever-present, sweet-and-sour aroma of roasting coffee beans and grilling *čevapčići* managing to overpower the stench of exhaust fumes even in the heart of the town centre. Unfortunately, if you arrive by public transport the first smell that will greet you at the bus station will probably be emanating from the neglected toilet facilities there, so make a swift exit, turn left at the traffic lights and a 10-minute walk will bring you to the town centre.

The central square of Žitni trg is little more than a large car park but it lies close to most of the town's major sights and all of the important modern and bazaar streets radiate from this central hub. With one or two exceptions, everything worth seeing in Novi Pazar is no more than a 10-minute walk from here.

The old **Turkish quarter** lies east over the bridge from here beyond the **Turkish Fort (Tvrđava)** that looks down over the central square, the grubby river and the dubious architecture of the Hotel Vrbak. The fortress, which dates from the 15th century, was formerly the seat of the Turkish *sanjak* in the region, and is home to a pleasant park these days. It was originally built to a triangular plan probably on the order of Iša-Bey Išaković, the town's founder. New buildings and reinforcements were added later, between the end of the 17th century and the middle of the 19th. Some of the original ramparts remain, together with an octagonal watchtower, but otherwise there is little to see. Nevertheless, its benches offer cool shade on a hot summer's day, and there is a good view from the terrace of the park's outdoor café.

Heading south over the bridge from the square, a narrow cobbled road, 1 Maj, leads through the old bazaar area to the early 16th-century mosque of **Altum Alem**, the most important Turkish building in the town. Access to the mosque can be gained through the courtyard at number 79, which houses several Ottoman-period graves and the entrance to an Islamic school. Altum Alem, built by the master builder Abdul Gani, is of a square plan, with a dome and a spacious porch covered with cupolas that are not typical for the region. There is a wooden gallery and a colourful *mihrab* within.

The road that leads to the mosque is lined with small restaurants that specialise in *čevapčići*; coffee houses, butchers' shops and small bakeries selling *burek*; closer to the bridge is a small enclave of shops that specialise in gold jewellery. Close to the bridge is a ruined **hammam** – Turkish bath – that probably dates from the 1460s and which was endowed to the town by its founder Iša-Bey Išaković. It is a symmetrical structure with facilities for simultaneous bathing by men and women.

The only thing that spoils the enjoyment of wandering these bazaar streets is the constant stream of exhaust-belching traffic that keeps you on your toes. The Serbian tradition of parking on any available piece of pavement is taken to its extreme here, constantly forcing pedestrians out into the narrow street into the path of taxis and minibuses.

Back across the bridge to the north there is an outdoor market area along the river, opposite the bazaar area. Most of the items on sale are household utensils and cheap clothing, especially the cut-price jeans for which the town used to be famous. On the square itself, you will probably see men with suitcases selling duty-free cigarettes, together with makeshift stalls selling Islamic texts, Korans and stylised scenes of the *Kaaba* in Mecca.

On the north side of Žitni trg is an old **Ottoman Han** (inn) dating from the 17th century, part of which currently serves as a restaurant and a guesthouse. This comprises a group of four buildings facing on to a common courtyard. In the past, the upper floor would have been reserved for the accommodation of passing traders (it still is), while other parts would have housed the cattle and animal stock that the visitors brought with them. In contrast to this, on the opposite side of the square, is the **Hotel Vrbak**, one of the most unusual hotels in the country. It is hardly beautiful but the

Hotel Vrbak cannot fail to impress, and gives weight to the theory that however much communist-period architects were under instruction to produce cheap, utilitarian housing for the proletariat, they were given completely free rein when it came to the design of hotels; that is, as long as they stuck to a vaguely futuristic concept. The Vrbak is a prime example of this: a wacky architectural conceit that was taken seriously by a planning committee and immortalised in concrete – a curious combination of retro-Ottoman and modernism. The building consists of two hexagons joined together on two sides, with an extension reaching south across the lacklustre river channel that passes unglamorously through the town. Inside, the cavernous atrium has a vaguely oriental feel to it. The rooms themselves are decorated with wooden friezes and are equipped with hexagonal mirrors, leather pouffes and Turkish-style lamps. The Balkan commentator, Misha Glenny, who passed through this way in the early 1990s, describes the building as drab, depressing and shoddy, and remarks that it is 'a prince among such hotels'. It is almost exquisitely ugly, and fits in perfectly with the brutal modernisation that the rest of the town centre underwent in the 1970s. Still, it is not without interest: for aficionados of the old Eastern-bloc aesthetic, the Hotel Vrbak is a real gem. There is more curious 1970s architecture to be seen nearby at Bulevar AVNOJ-a, where an enormous and rather eccentric apartment block stands with a covered shopping street beneath.

AROUND NOVI PAZAR

Novi Pazar's other sights of interest lie just outside the town and belong to the Orthodox rather than the Islamic or communist traditions. Studenica Monastery is also well within range for a day trip from the town.

CHURCH OF ST PETER (CRKVA PETROVA) This wonderfully atmospheric church lies at the base of a grassy hill, about 3km south of the town centre. To reach it, walk along Stevana Nemanje past the bus station, keep going as far as a six-way roundabout and take the turning that more or less leads straight on (the church is signposted). Keep going through the outskirts of town and you will eventually see the church up on a bluff to the left. You may notice, walking this way out of town, that this northern part of Novi Pazar is still predominantly Serbian Orthodox. The telltale signs are all there: Cyrillic rather than Latin signs on shops and houses; Orthodox death notices pinned to doors; crates of Jelen beer bottles stacked outside cafés.

The small Church of St Peter is the oldest in the country, dating from the 8th or 9th century – the only pre-Nemanjić church in existence anywhere in Serbia – and was the seat of the Orthodox See of Raška for a period of almost 900 years. It was here that Stefan Nemanja held the council that outlawed the Bogomil heresy in Serbia.

The church is circular in plan with a central cupola and three radial apses. It is built in a style that shows the influence of an earlier Byzantine tradition, and which probably arrived in Serbia via the Adriatic. It is highly likely that the church was constructed on a site that was sacred to earlier settlers in the region as, in 1958, the 5th-century grave of an Illyrian prince was discovered beneath the floor here, along with a number of accompanying burial items like jewellery, masks and ceramics in the Greek tradition that are now in the keeping of the National Museum in Belgrade.

The interior is dark, and consists of a single, circular nave surrounded by the tombs of a number of Serbian princes. In the apse to the right, steps lead down to a sunken font where St Sava is purported to have been baptised. Such frescoes that survive are severely chipped and in poor condition but their use of unusual colours – red and black – lends considerably to the mysterious atmosphere that this small church possesses. Outside the church is an evocative cemetery of heavily weathered old gravestones stained yellow and gold with lichens.

If the church is locked, the woman in the house next door has a key, although there may also be a priest in attendance who will show you around. A donation to the church collection box is appreciated.

ST GEORGE'S PILLARS (ĐURĐEVI STUPOVI) A few kilometres to the west of Novi Pazar, the monastic Church of St George (Đurđevi Stupovi) occupies a wistful, windswept site, high on a hill above the town. This 12th-century church was originally created by Stefan Nemanja and contains some weather-beaten frescoes, most notably one of St George on a galloping steed. Some of the other frescoes have long been removed to the National Museum in Belgrade for protection and the site has recently been restored with a large expanse of plate glass to keep out the elements, which, although providing protection, does little for its general aesthetic appeal. The monastery was badly damaged during the Ottoman period and it is a wonder that any of its frescoes have survived considering that they were exposed to the elements for centuries. In recent years, the site has been undergoing restoration to become a functioning monastery once more. Since 1979 it has been listed as a UNESCO World Heritage Site along with the complex at Stari Ras and Sopoćani Monastery.

Đurđevi Stupovi is visible high on a hill from St Peter's Church and, in theory at least, it is possible to reach it by walking up the grassy track that leads west up the hill from St Peter's Church. After a while the track becomes indistinct but as long as you keep heading in the same direction – roughly WNW – you should eventually manage to reach the monastery. A more straightforward way to reach the monastery is to take the road (Kolubarska) that leads north from Miodraga Jovanovića in the town, just beyond the petrol station next to the Sveti Nikole Church. It is a long uphill slog and so a taxi is probably a better idea – a return trip should cost in the order of €10. Ideally this could be part of a combined trip that also takes in Sopoćani Monastery.

SOPOĆANI MONASTERY (МАНАСТИР СОПОЋАНИ) This is undoubtedly the most important site in the region. The monastery lies about 16km west of the town, along a wild and lonely road that penetrates deep into the Raška heartland. The best way to reach it if you do not have your own transport is to take a taxi from Novi Pazar's central square. The cost should be about €15–20 there and back, including an hour's stop at the monastery. If you just wish to be deposited there it should be something more like €12–14. There are no buses.

The road, which is quite pot-holed in places, heads west from Novi Pazar along a beautiful valley filled with pine forest. About halfway to the monastery, you reach the ruins of **Stari Ras**, which now just consist of a lot of foundations and low walls. It is probably not really worth stopping here, as there is not much to see on the ground, but you could negotiate a brief stopover with your taxi driver should you wish to do so.

Ras was the ancient capital of the Nemanjić kings, and dates from the 9th century. It became the capital of the early Serbian kingdom of **Raška**, a name that is still used to describe this southwest region of the country. The city was severely damaged in the 12th century in clashes between the Serbs and the Byzantines but remained the capital until 1314. As Novi Pazar developed as the new regional centre, Ras dwindled in importance. Nowadays, it would take a trained archaeological eye to make much sense of the little that remains. If you want to stay there is accommodation nearby at the **Motel Ras** (\ *020 361 578*), which is also home to the recommended Pazarište restaurant.

Sopoćani Monastery lies beyond, higher up and close to the source of the Raška River that gushes from a spring in the rock. Founded in the middle of the 13th century by King Uroš I, the Monastery of Sopoćani is one of the finest examples of the Raška School. It was severely damaged in 1689 and completely abandoned at the end of the 17th century, allowing it to fall to ruin. Considering that the monastery stood as a roofless ruin for the best part of two centuries, it is quite remarkable that so many fine frescoes have survived. Many have managed to evade the worst effects of the elements during Sopoćani's long period of neglect and the renovated monastery is home to some of the greatest religious art in Europe and, many would agree, the highest achievement of all Serbian art. An English-language booklet is on sale at the monastery, as well as candles, icons and postcards of the frescoes. It may be a good idea to buy a few of these as photography of the church's interior is not permitted.

The centrepiece of the complex is the **Church of the Holy Trinity** (Crvka Svete Trojice), built in an adapted Romanesque style with narthex, naos, semicircular apse and cupola. In the 14th century, Emperor Dušan added an exonarthex, which collapsed some years afterwards leaving just the belfry standing. Surrounding the church, monastery buildings of the same period – a refectory, kitchens, monks' cells and a water fountain – all now lie in ruins.

The frescoes in the narthex date from 1270 and depict subjects new to Serbian iconography at the time, like *The Last Judgement* and the *Legend of St Joseph*. As well as praising God, the frescoes here celebrate and elevate the grandeur of the Nemanjić dynasty: Queen Anne, the mother of Uroš, is depicted almost as reverentially as a Virgin figure would be, and on the east wall, the council of Stefan Nemanja is portrayed as an equal alongside the seven ecumenical councils. Details from the life of Stefan Nemanja portray him as a monk at Mt Athos, and the subsequent movement of his body to the Monastery of Studenica.

The greatest works, however, are in the naos. The *Dormition of the Virgin* on the west wall shows Christ holding a baby in swaddling clothes, with the Apostles standing alongside in a carefully composed group. The figures portrayed are very human, demonstrating great dignity and calm; the colours used are bright but subtle – green, maroon and gold – and the overall effect created is one of emotional but serene resignation. The north wall has the *Birth of Christ*, the *Descent into Limbo* and the *Transfiguration*; the west, the *Crucifixion*, *Presentation at the Temple* and *Christ among the Learned Men*. All of these were executed a little earlier than the narthex paintings, the creation of master painters from Constantinople at work around 1265. They show a brilliance and visionary quality that can only be compared to some of the creations of the Italian Renaissance that followed. Impending Turkish rule would see to it that Serbian art would not be able to develop beyond this early inspirational blossoming.

There is accommodation next door to the monastery at the **Hotel Sopoćani** (✆ *020 313 663;* €), should you wish to spend more time here. Apart from the obvious benefit of having more time to study the frescoes, it would be a wonderfully restful experience to spend the night, or even a few days, here. Sopoćani, like all Serbian monasteries, is located in extraordinarily beautiful surroundings and the potential for quiet walks in the surrounding hills must be endless.

WEST OF NOVI PAZAR Heading south, Novi Pazar is pretty much the end of the road
before Montenegro or Kosovo is reached. There are daily buses to Priština in Kosovo from Novi Pazar and if you want to visit Montenegro there are also plenty of buses that run to Rožaje, from where you can pick up connections to points beyond.

Heading west towards Nova Varoš and Prijepolje, the road climbs up high from the Raška Valley to skirt the edge of the **Pešter plateau**, a very isolated sheep-and-cattle-raising area that borders Montenegro. With your own transport, this would be a fascinating region to explore with plenty of time at your disposal and a full fuel tank. It is one of the remotest parts of the country, without many towns to speak of, and consists mostly of open moorland and endless swathes of gently undulating pasture. The plateau is also quite high in altitude and suffers from extremely cold weather in wintertime. Not for nothing is Pešter sometimes termed 'the Serbian Siberia'.

Without a car, the best you can do is to take the bus through Sjenica to Nova Varoš and Prijepolje. There is a daily through bus from Novi Pazar that leaves in the morning, contrary to what it says on the bus station departures board.

Leaving Novi Pazar, there is a steep climb up to the hilltop village of Duga Poljana, which has some shops and a restaurant but no hotel. From here you travel across a high, bare plateau. There are a few fields here and there but mostly it is cattle country that brings to mind the more upland parts of Northumberland or the North York Moors. It is a lonely but spectacular landscape, with a rambling farmstead standing in isolation by the road every few kilometres. The clear, upland air, the gently undulating terrain and the lack of trees makes it possible to see for miles in any direction. Just before the town of **Sjenica** is reached, a sign by the roadside proclaims the altitude to be 1,509m above sea level.

SJENICA (CJEHИЦA) *Telephone code 020*

Sjenica lies in a natural bowl, high on the plateau, surrounded by pine forest and bleak pasture. Even in summer, it is easy to understand why it is considered to be the coldest town in Serbia. With the exception of Tutin that lies further south, close to the Montenegrin border, this has the highest Muslim population of all the towns in the Raška region. Life is tough here, eking out an existence in a hostile landscape, but the locals seem to do well enough given their circumstances. There is little specific to see here but the town stands in the middle of magnificent landscape and so there is the temptation of using Sjenica as a base for walks in the surrounding countryside.

The town itself seems surprisingly large because of its rather rambling nature: space is not at a premium up here on the plateau. Nor is there any clear-cut demarcation made between where the town stops and the countryside begins – cows are led around on ropes to graze on any available plot of wasteland. There are a few nods made to Sjenica's urban status: a leafy, central square with a large new mosque; a national-style restaurant next door to the tiny bus station; and a few basic pizzerias nearby.

The town's only hotel, the two-star Hotel Borovi, is set in pine woodland, a couple of kilometres back towards Novi Pazar.

GETTING THERE AND AWAY There are infrequent **buses** that leave Sjenica for Prijepolje, Novi Pazar, Belgrade and Kragujevac daily, but it is best to seek confirmation of the departure times first if you intend on catching any of these. Quite amazingly, there is also a direct bus to Istanbul, which stops in Sjenica on its way from Sarajevo.

After Sjenica the road climbs through pine forest and pasture to reach Nova Varoš after a further 37km. There is another road shown on maps that links Sjenica directly with Prijepolje but it is in poor condition and virtually all vehicles heading for that town make a detour through Nova Varoš.

7

TOURIST INFORMATION Information can be found at Trg Svetozara Markovića (📞 744 843; e info@turizamsjenica.com; w turizamsjenica.com).

🏠 WHERE TO STAY AND EAT

🏠 **Hotel Lane** *** (9 rooms) 📞 744 223; e hotel-lane@hotmail.com; w hotel-lane.rs. Much newer & a little more luxurious than the Borovi (below), the hotel is located on Njegoševa in the town centre, which has modern facilities & its own moderately priced restaurant. €€

🏠 **Hotel Borovi** ** (40 rooms) Milanovana Jovanovića bb; 📞 741 242; e hotelborovi@gmail. com; w hotelborovi.com. Set in pine woodland just off the main road, this place is a couple of kilometres east, back towards Novi Pazar. The hotel restaurant (€) is friendly & inexpensive but be aware that much of what appears on the menu may not be available. Better to let the waiter tell you what the cook is able to prepare to avoid disappointment. €€–€

NOVA VAROŠ (НОВА ВАРОШ) *Telephone code 033*

Nova Varoš is a medium-sized alpine town sprawling up and along both sides of the valley. There is a noticeably larger Serbian Orthodox population here than further east and, unusual for this part of Serbia, the domes of Orthodox churches are as visible in the town as are minarets. After travelling through the Pešter plateau, Nova Varoš may strike you as quite urbane and sophisticated but unless you have a particular reason for being here it is probably best to push on south to Prijepolje and Mileševa Monastery. Should you need it, there is B&B accommodation at **Apartments Bona Fides** (📞 63 222; €) above a pizza restaurant at Oslobodilaca bb.

ZLATAR MOUNTAIN Mt Zlatar (highest point, 1,627m) lies close to the town of Nova Varoš. There is a resort here, surrounded by spruce and birch forest and meadows that are carpeted with wild flowers in late spring. Lying at some considerable altitude, the climate is halfway between Mediterranean and alpine but generally it is sunny. The resort offers skiing in winter along with summer recreations such as tennis and swimming. Fishing and sailing may be done at nearby lakes, while the whole area is perfect for energetic walking in summer.

Tourist information (*Karađorđeva 36, 31320 Nova Varoš*; 📞 62 621; e tozlatar@verat.net; w zlatar.org.rs). The tourist organisation 'Zlatar' offers information about the Nova Varoš–Zlatar area.

🏠 Where to stay

🏠 **Hotel Panorama** ** (138 rooms) Babića Brdo bb; 📞 61 784; e hotelpanoramazlatar@gmail. com; w hotelpanoramazlatar.com. €€

UVAC AND MILEŠEVKA GRIFFON VULTURE SANCTUARY For birdwatchers, the Griffon Vulture Sanctuary at the Uvac-Mileševka Dam is close at hand. The sanctuary consists of several limestone gorges surrounded by forest and pasture, which supplies the birds with their food, mostly dead calves. The griffon vulture, one of Serbia's largest birds weighing between 6kg and 11kg and with a wingspan of up to 2.8m, has an important role in the food chain as it exists solely on carrion. Uvac, Mileševka and nearby Trešnjica canyons are the only places where the birds can be found in Serbia. Nesting socially in groups on cliffs, the birds start mating at the age of five and remain monogamous, living for up to 40 years.

Thanks to careful management, numbers have increased in recent years from just seven individuals in 1990 to several hundred. In 1999, there was considerable concern for the fate of the vultures when a NATO plane crashed into the Mileševka canyon close to the nest sites – griffon vultures are prone to abandon their nests when disturbed – but they seem to have survived this annoyance. At last count there were over 300 birds and 67 nesting pairs. More than 50 tonnes of food is provided to the griffon vulture feeding station annually.

A road leads down to the dam wall from Nova Varoš by way of the village of Komarani. You will need to arrive early in the morning if you want to see them sitting on their nests and their roost ledges, as the birds take to the thermals after about 09.00. The vultures range over an incredibly large territory searching for the carrion that they feed on and you may be lucky enough to see one along the Sjenica–Nova Varoš road as I once did.

PRIJEPOLJE (ПРИЈЕПОЉЕ) *Telephone code 033*

Prijepolje lies 27km southwest of Nova Varoš on the main train line that links Bar on the Montenegrin coast with Belgrade. The town itself is scenically situated but has little to see other than an **Orthodox church** built in the Raška style, similar to Mileševa, but dating from the late 19th century. There are also three mosques and a handful of old houses in the Serbian–Balkan style. Above all, Prijepolje serves as a convenient base from which to visit the Mileševa Monastery.

GETTING THERE AND AWAY The **railway station** (\ *712 094*) stands next to the small **bus station** (\ *714 085*) at the southern end of town. Five trains a day run north to Belgrade via Užice and Valjevo, and the same number south to Montenegro via Bijelo Polje and Podgorica. Buses are less numerous and serve mostly local destinations. The railway station has one restaurant upstairs and another outside by the car park but it's a bit of a gloomy place for a lengthy wait. Unfortunately, there is no left-luggage facility whatsoever, which is a nuisance if you are just passing through the town to take a look at Mileševa Monastery. The best thing to do, if you wish to visit Mileševa, is to take a taxi from the railway station and have it wait for you while you look around the monastery. This way, you can take your bag with you. The return trip to the monastery, including a reasonable wait, should cost no more than €8.

TOURIST INFORMATION
i Trg Bratstva i jedistva 1; \ 710 140;
e toprijepolje@gmail.com; w turizamprijepolje.org.rs

WHERE TO STAY AND EAT Because the town is well connected by train, and to a lesser extent by bus, it is not necessary to spend the night here. However, two options exist. There is also **Hotel Park** (\ *712 033*; €) on the road to Mileševa Monastery.

Dining possibilities include **Gradska kafana** (*Valterova 48*; \ *712 882*; €), a fairly traditional *kafana*, and **Pingvin** (*Trg Dimitrija Tucovića*; \ *782 292*; €). There are also a few places close to the railway station.

Hotel Mileševa *** (104 rooms) Novovaroška bb; \ 711 078. With restaurant, coffee bar & swimming pool. €€

Motel Grbo (12 rooms) Bjelopolski put; \ 710 504; m 063 652 774. At the exit of town on the road to Bijelo Polje. €€–€

MILEŠEVA MONASTERY (МАНАСТИР МИЛЕШЕВА) The monastery lies 6km up a valley to the east of Prijepolje, on the southern slopes of Mt Zlatar. As soon as you arrive at the monastery you cannot fail but notice the large Serbian Orthodox flags

7

flying on poles outside the entrance – as much a political gesture as anything else in this predominantly Muslim part of the country. Further along the valley, the dramatic-looking ruins of a medieval castle are visible on a crag in the distance. This is Mileševac Castle, which was, most probably, the stronghold of a long-deceased Bosnian king, although local legend tells of it being built at the whim of a rich woman who did not know what to do with her wealth.

Other than the church, there is not much to see of the monastery buildings themselves; quite clearly, Mileševa is poor and in decline. However, a few monks hang on and will be pleased to show you round, although you will be lucky to find anyone who speaks English, or anything written in English at the monastery shop.

Mileševa was founded by the grandson of Stefan Nemanja, Vladislav, in about 1234. It was originally planned as his mausoleum but the monastery was to gain greater fame when it became the final resting place of Vladislav's uncle, St Sava. Soon after his death, a cult developed around St Sava's relics, one which was observed by both Orthodox Christians and Muslims alike. This alarmed the Turkish authorities to the extent that they had the saint's remains taken to Vračar in present-day Belgrade, where they were burned. A legend tells that his body rose from the flames and hovered in the sky above. The spot chosen for the burning has subsequently become the site for the construction of Belgrade's enormous St Sava's Church.

The main body of the church consists of one single space, since the wall that separated narthex and nave collapsed many centuries ago. Since the collapse, the church is usually described by what may be termed its 'blue' and 'gold' parts, the predominant colours used in the frescoes. The frescoes were executed around the same time as the church was built and were the work of three men, Dimitrije, Đorđe and Teodor, who were most probably native Serbs. On the north side of the narthex are representations of the Nemanjić kings: Stefan Nemanja, the founder of the dynasty; Stefan Prvovenčani and his brother, St Sava; Vladislav, the church-founder, and his brother Radoslav. Facing this on the south wall is a fresco that depicts the Virgin leading Vladislav, who is carrying a model of Mileševa, towards Christ. Above this is the most familiar of all the frescoes here: the *Angel of the Resurrection* – better known simply as the *White Angel* – a cool, rather androgynous, figure that casts his eyes serenely down on the observer in a slightly superior, almost haughty manner. This iconic image oozes mystical power and has, in recent years, been adopted by the United Nations as an emblem, having earlier been projected across the Atlantic as part of a pioneering UK–USA satellite link-up. The image has been much copied but, like the smile on the *Mona Lisa*, the enigmatic quality of the original has been hard to replicate. Just above the *White Angel*, and hard to see in the gloom, is a serene representation of the *Virgin of the Annunciation* scene next to a *Deposition* that shows Christ being lovingly tended to by Mary Magdalene and the Virgin.

ONWARD TRAVEL TO KOSOVO

Kosovo declared full independence from Serbia on 17 February 2008. The new republic is not currently recognised by the Serbian government or by the majority of countries in the world at present. Among EU countries, the independent state is as yet unrecognised by Spain, Greece, Romania, Slovakia and Cyprus. The issue of Kosovo is a highly emotional one for many Serbs but, whatever the rights or wrongs of the politics of the current situation, it cannot be denied that historically Kosovo has been a hugely important cradle of Serbian culture – certainly in the past if not in the present. The most obvious reminders of Serbian culture in Kosovo are its Orthodox churches and monasteries, some sadly desecrated and damaged beyond repair, others still glorious. This brief overview gives a potted history and describes some of Kosovo's more remarkable religious buildings. To find out more about Kosovo, see *Kosovo: The Bradt Guide*; page 392.

A BRIEF HISTORY OF KOSOVO In early medieval times, the region now known as Kosovo was inhabited mostly by Serbs but after Prince Lazar's defeat at the Battle of Kosovo Polje in 1389, close to present-day Priština, much of the Serb population moved north to escape from Turkish subjugation. This created a vacuum and the territory abandoned by the fleeing Serbs was taken up by land-hungry Muslim settlers of both Turkish and Albanian origin. Neighbouring Albania became an independent state after the Second Balkan War in 1913 and the neglected backwater of Kosovo came under Serbian control once more as the Serbian-dominated Kingdom of Slavs, Croats and Slovenes emerged.

During World War II, many Kosovars and Albanians fought against the Partisans in the hope that the Nazi invasion of Yugoslavia would help bring about a post-war pan-Albanian state, although, no doubt, an equal number fought on the Partisan side too. Tito's 1945 victory kept Kosovo as part of Serbia within the new Yugoslav socialist federal state. Meanwhile, neighbouring Albania became an isolationist and deeply suspicious Stalinist state under Enver Hoxha. Because of a deep mistrust of any nationalist agendas that might threaten the new socialist state, the Albanian language and even Albanian customs were declared illegal in Kosovo.

The 'Albanian question' became more of an issue as the 20th century progressed. At the beginning of the century, Albanians made up only one-third of the province's population but by the 1960s it had become two-thirds. This dramatic change of Kosovo's ethnic make-up was brought about by two factors: the much higher birth rate of the Albanians, with families of six children being considered pretty average, coupled with the gradual departure of ethnic Serbs from the province. Even before the 1999 crisis and the mass exodus that followed, Serbs were leaving Kosovo in droves. It is estimated that about 60,000 Serbs left Kosovo during the 1970s, a time of reasonable stability. At the time of writing, the percentage of ethnic Albanians that make up Kosovo's current population is uncertain, but it must be in the order of 85–90%.

Serious rioting in the province in 1968 forced Tito to change his policy and make some reforms, of which the recognition of Albanian and Turkish as official languages was probably the most vital. He gave Kosovo a greater degree of autonomy and increased financial support to what was, without doubt, the most neglected corner of socialist Yugoslavia. This was probably too little, too late, though. Unemployment remained extremely high compared with prosperous states like Slovenia and Croatia, and a lot of the money coming into the province went on ill-conceived schemes like building Priština's skyscrapers, which had little bearing on the lives of Kosovo's poor.

Despite the reforms it was still the case that, by and large, the Serbs that lived here were better off in terms of jobs and positions of power, while the Albanians had to contend with unprofitable farming, mining and manual labour, or seek employment abroad. Many did, and left in droves to work as migrant labourers in the West. It is not because of a successful education system that so many middle-aged Kosovars are able to speak German today.

In 1981, student protests soon turned to widespread riots that gave voice to long-held resentments. Very soon, nine were dead and hundreds were injured as demonstrators confronted the Yugoslav authorities. The Yugoslav army were sent in, resulting in hundreds of protesters being arrested and given long prison sentences on charges of sedition.

In 1988, it was the Kosovo Serbs' turn to protest. They felt that now it was they who were being discriminated against by a newly empowered Albanian majority. With a long-repressed majority finally finding their feet (the Albanians) and the former elite sensing that they had become the new victims (the Serbs), the necessary conditions were in place for all-out conflict. As had happened elsewhere in the unforgiving political climate of the Balkans, a violent cycle of revenge and counter-revenge was slowly starting to gather momentum. The Kosovo situation had been tense for years but the state-sanctioned repression of the Yugoslav federation had usually kept a lid on it. When the former Yugoslavia started to break up in the early 1990s many eyes focused on Kosovo and predicted, not unreasonably, that this would be the next flashpoint.

It is a matter of opinion as to how great the effect of Slobodan Milošević was on the war in Kosovo. Milošević came to power in 1987 and gained popular support with his promise that he would put an end to the violence against the Serbs in the province. In 1990, rather than give in to Albanian calls for greater autonomy, he abolished the autonomous status of the province, which caused further resentment among the Kosovar Albanians. Shortly after, the regional parliament in Priština declared full independence from Serbia for Kosovo, a futile gesture perhaps, but one which led to further repression of Kosovo's Albanians by Milošević's forces.

By the mid 1990s, the Kosovo Liberation Army (KLA) started to emerge as a force dedicated to fighting for an independent Kosovo (and a Greater Albania). In the eyes of many Kosovar Albanians the KLA were 'freedom fighters' but they were viewed as straightforward terrorists by the Serbian government. In January 1998, the KLA began a series of attacks on Kosovan Serbs in the province. Milošević responded by sending in troops to quash the unrest.

By the summer of 1998, the violence had escalated to a full-scale civil war, with hundreds dead and hundreds of thousands more displaced as refugees. The United States, the Organisation for Security and Co-operation in Europe (OSCE) and NATO decided that it was time to intervene. A NATO-brokered ceasefire in October 1998 saw a large contingent of OSCE peace monitors move into Kosovo. The ceasefire broke down in December 1998, which led to many more deaths on both sides. Most notorious was in the village of Račak in central Kosovo where 45 Albanian villagers were killed in a supposed anti-KLA operation. This action has been interpreted in two very different ways, depending on viewpoint. From the Albanian perspective, the victims were unarmed villagers massacred by advancing Serb forces, whereas the Serb point of view maintains they were KLA fighters killed during anti-terrorist operations and that the 'massacre' had been staged later for the benefit of the Western media.

In February 1999, Serbia and the KLA representatives went to the negotiating table in Rambouillet, France. Here, the United States threatened air strikes against Serbia if Milošević continued to reject a NATO plan that wanted to station international troops in Kosovo to enforce a peace agreement.

The talks broke down on 19 March, when both the Serbs and the KLA rejected the terms of the agreement. The US had assumed that the KLA would sign and the Serbs would walk away, which would have paved the way for NATO air strikes on Serbia. But the KLA refused to sign unless the agreement promised them complete independence and not simply self-rule. Finally, on 18 March, after heavy pressure by US Secretary of State Madeleine Albright, the KLA signed while the Serbs continued to refuse because they objected to what they considered a NATO occupation.

After the withdrawal of OSCE monitors from Kosovo, the NATO bombing campaign began on 24 March 1999, an action still considered in some quarters to be of dubious legality. As well as the air attacks on Serbia, NATO flew 38,000 combat missions over Kosovo. Serbia claims that these caused the deaths of between 1,200 and 5,700 civilians, although NATO acknowledges 1,500 at most. Many Albanians fled the continuing inter-ethnic conflict to become refugees in Albania and Macedonia. On 7 April 1999, Serbia closed its borders to prevent ethnic Albanians from leaving but after protests from the West reopened them a few days later. More than 800,000 Kosovar Albanians are estimated to have left Kosovo at this time, mostly to refugee camps in Albania.

In July 1999, when the Serbian armed forces were finally ousted from Kosovo, some 40,000 NATO-organised Kosovo Force (KFOR) troops were sent in as peacekeepers. Ethnic Albanians started to return to the province from their refugee camps over the border, and embittered by what had gone on before, many felt urged to take revenge on what remained of the Serb population. Between July 1999, when KFOR troops first entered Kosovo, and November 1999, more than 80 Serbian churches were destroyed in the province.

Serious inter-ethnic violence took place in Kosovo in March 2004, when a story circulated that told of Albanian boys being pursued by Serbs with dogs, driving them into a river where three of them drowned. This prompted a sudden outbreak of violence in the province, especially in Kosovska Mitrovica, the only remaining town with a sizeable Serb population. Serb property was attacked across the province and 35 Serb Orthodox churches and monasteries burned and looted. In response, mosques were attacked in Serbia, with those in Belgrade and Niš being gutted by fire. During the unrest, eight ethnic Serbs and 11 ethnic Albanians were killed, and over 4,000 Serbs were forced to abandon their homes. This story was later proven to be wrong, the fabrication of the surviving boy of an accidental drowning.

GRAČANICA MONASTERY Ten kilometres south of Priština is the small Serbian enclave of Gračanica. It is little more than a village but has a remarkable Orthodox monastery that holds an important place in Serbian history. Many Serbs have left in recent years but a small community still hangs on doggedly.

The tall, gracious church at Gračanica was built between 1313 and 1321 by King Milutin Nemanja alongside a monastery that no longer exists. It was attacked several times by Turks between 1379 and 1383 when the dome was lost to fire, and damaged further during the Battle of Kosovo and when Novo Brdo was conquered in 1455. This was followed by a more peaceful period in the 16th century, during which a printing house, the first in Serbia, was set up here. Further Turkish attacks took place during the 18th century: in one incident the lead and tiles from the roof were removed and taken to Priština by an errant *paša*. This same tyrant was later to return them in a surprising display of repentance.

The church is a fine example of the Byzantine tradition in Serbian architecture – perhaps the finest – and is a graceful structure of brick and stone with four cupolas and a dome raised in pyramid form above arched gables. The brick is utilised in herringbone and cross-stitch patterns against the pale pink-coloured stone and the overall effect is that of a complex but meticulously balanced geometry. It is Gračanica that was the inspiration for the larger 20th-century St Mark's Church in Belgrade.

Inside the church, the walls are almost entirely covered with frescoes. The best of these are in the narthex and are contemporaneous with the original construction: portraits of King Milutin and his fourth wife Simonida, a Nemanjić family tree and *The Last Judgement*. The frescoes in the naos are later and include the *Dormition of the Virgin*, scenes from the life of Christ and various saints.

7

In 2006, the monastery church joined the UNESCO heritage list along with three other Kosovo Orthodox monuments: Visoki Dečani Monastery, the Peć Patriarchate and the Church of Bogorodica Ljeviška at Prizren.

THE CHURCH OF BOGORODICA LJEVIŠKA
The original part of this church at Prizren – a three-nave basilica – dates from the 11th century but much of it was added in 1307 by Milutin, who rebuilt the church, adding two more naves and a narthex with a bell tower. The church served as a mosque between 1455 and 1912 and its interior covered in plaster. Notwithstanding this many frescoes survived and there are examples of *The Last Judgement* in addition to portraits of the Nemanjić kings and Prizren bishops. Like all of the Orthodox monuments in Prizren this church came under serious attack during the disturbances of March 2004 when many of the remaining frescoes were badly damaged by fire. The church was adopted as one of four UNESCO heritage sites in Kosovo in 2006 but it continues to be looted.

THE MONASTERY OF VISOKI DEČANI
Located up a wooded valley 2km west of the village of the same name, and 10km south of Peć on the Prizren road, this monastery, now a UNESCO heritage site, was built by Stefan, son of King Milutin, between 1327 and 1335. Stefan went on to take his name from the project to become known later on as King Stefan Uroš Dečanski.

The monastery complex lies behind an imposing wall and is entered through a fortified gate. Few of the monastic buildings survive but the centrepiece is the **Church of Christ Pantokrator**, the work of a Franciscan monk from Kotor named Vid. The church, which combines an interesting mixture of Western and Byzantine traditions, is of pink, white and grey marble with a garbled façade and ornate carving around the Romanesque doors and windows. The central door has twin columns supported by lions, and in the tympanum above, the figure of Christ is flanked by two angels beneath an arch that has the 12 signs of the zodiac. The south door has a relief showing the *Baptism of Christ* and an inscription by the architect in Cyrillic. More lions bear columns at the mullioned window on the central apse and similar zoomorphic and anthropomorphic themes are repeated around the church.

The church's interior is rich with frescoes, all executed at the command of Dušan, Stefan's son, between 1335 and 1350. Many of these are considered to be masterpieces of medieval religious art. In the narthex are portraits of Dušan, his wife Jelena and their son Uroš, together with a family tree of the Nemanjić dynasty. The naos is entered through a Romanesque doorway that is also flanked by columns supported by lions. Here, there are paintings of saints, scenes from the life of Christ and the *Acts of the Apostles*. On the west wall, are stories from the Book of Genesis and the legend of Solomon; in the centre, *The Last Judgement* and the *Dormition of the Virgin*.

The tomb of Stefan Dečanski, which lies near the iconostasis, has long been considered to have magical healing properties by both Christians and Muslims alike. Dečani has held great sway with the Muslim community since the time, under the Turks, when it was planned to turn it into a mosque. An *imam* visiting the church was killed by a piece of falling masonry as he prayed outside the west door. This was taken as a sign that it was the will of Allah that it should not be altered and it was left well alone from then on.

THE PATRIARCHATE OF PEĆ (PEĆKA PATRIJARŠIJA)
This stands enclosed behind high stone walls close to the river in gorgeous mountain scenery just outside the town of Peć in western Kosovo. Entrance to the monastery is through a tall

gate in the walls. The immediate impression is one of peaceful isolation: the cars thundering towards Montenegro on the road above are just out of earshot and the predominant sound is that of bees buzzing around collecting nectar from the flowers of the monastery gardens (bee-keeping is an important activity both here and in other Serb Orthodox monasteries; it would seem that the collection and processing of honey has a strong spiritual dimension). To the left are the monastic living quarters – a wooden-framed *konak* – where a few nuns remain to pursue the contemplative life. In the far-right corner are the churches, the only remaining original buildings of the complex.

The three churches of the patriarchate sit side by side linked by a common 14th-century narthex. The oldest of the three, **Archbishop Arsenije I's Church of the Holy Apostles (Crkva Sveta Apostola)** is the central one of the group and contains frescoes modelled on the Church of Sion in Jerusalem, considered to be the true location of the Last Supper. The church was built in the 13th century and incorporates part of an earlier 12th-century building. The painting style of the frescoes inside is that of the Raška School – austere and monumental in scale. On the ceiling of the narthex are scenes from *The Passion* and portraits of Nemanjić kings. On either side of the west door are frescoes of *St Nicholas* and *The Virgin and Child*. The figure of Christ looks down from *The Ascension* in the cupola above, with the *Descent of the Holy Ghost, Doubting of Thomas, Mission of the Apostles, The Last Supper* and *Raising of Lazarus* adorning the arches beneath. All of these date from the mid 13th century, the work of an artist or artists of the same school that painted Studenica and Mileševa. Some of the frescoes were retouched in the 16th century.

The other two churches are later additions from the first half of the 14th century. **The Church of St Demetrius (Sv Dimitrije)** is slightly older and has a well-preserved fresco of *The Birth of the Virgin*, alongside frescoes showing scenes from the *Legend of St Demetrius* and a *Procession of Saints*. All of the frescoes here were painted at the time of building but were extensively retouched in the 17th century. **The Church of Our Lady of Hodegetria (Sv Bogorodica)**, completed around 1330, is lighter and has less atmosphere than the other two churches. It contains a large number of portraits of the Nemanjić dynasty in the narthex, all 14th-century works, alongside a later *Last Judgement*. In the naos are more 14th-century works: a portrait of founder Archbishop Danilo II offering his plan to the Prophet Daniel, above which is a *Dormition of the Virgin*.

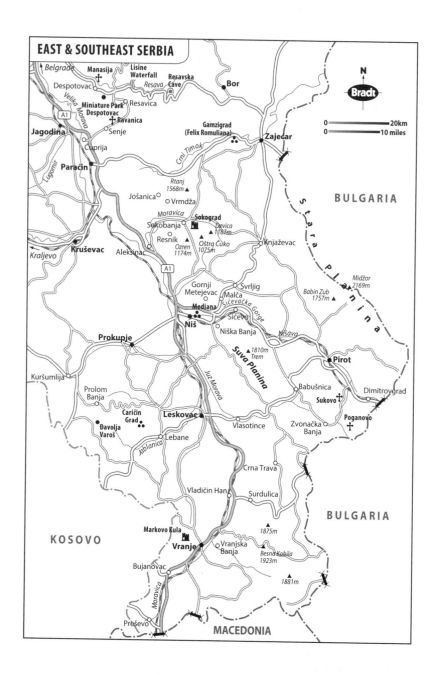

EAST & SOUTHEAST SERBIA

UPDATES WEBSITE

You can post your comments and recommendations, and read the latest feedback and updates from other readers, online at w bradtupdates.com/serbia.

8

East and Southeast Serbia

The Homolskje Mountain region, which runs parallel to and south of the Danube River, has been dealt with in *Chapter 4*. This chapter covers the area south of the Homolskje range and east of the Morava River, as well as the whole of the Niš hinterland as far as the borders with Bulgaria, Macedonia and Kosovo.

In many ways, this is one of the least-known parts of Serbia. Many travel through it – along the E-75 motorway that splits at Niš to lead east to Sofia and Bulgaria, and south to Macedonia and Greece – but few stop to see what the region has to offer. This is a pity, as there is plenty of interest in some of the towns of the region, and some fine countryside if you travel a short distance away from the motorway in either direction.

The highlights of the region are undoubtedly the monasteries of Manasija and Ravanica, hidden away in the hills just east of the E-75 motorway, and the city of Niš with its historic sites – the Turkish Fortress, the Skull Tower, and the Roman site at Mediana. Another interesting Roman site in the region is at Gamzigrad, close to Zaječar. Niš is also a good centre for outdoor pursuits: the Sokobanja region to the north of the city and the nearby Suva Planina (Dry Mountain) range both offer excellent hiking and cycling possibilities. Further east, flanking the Bulgarian border, the Stara Planina (Old Mountain) range and especially the rugged terrain around Babin Zub have spectacular scenery and plenty of hiking potential. West of Niš, close to the Kosovo border and town of Kuršumlija, are the fascinating and very distinctive rock formations known as Đavolja Varoš (Devil's Town).

ZAJEČAR (ЗАЈЕЧАР) *Telephone code 019*

An hour south of Negotin, and only 11km from the Bulgarian border, Zaječar is the cultural and geographic centre of the Timočka Krajina region. With a population of about 60,000, it is a quiet, self-contained sort of place: a middle-sized town without many specific sights of its own but a pleasant enough stop for the night, having some very reasonable hotel options.

Probably the best reason for being here is to visit the Roman ruins of Gamzigrad-Romuliana that lie 12km west of the town, but even without this intention there is a good museum and a few Turkish buildings to see, as well as the pleasure of simply absorbing the atmosphere of a relaxed provincial town. Foreign visitors are quite rare here and local people are warmly accommodating as a result. Admittedly, the same could be said for quite a lot of Serbia.

The centre of Zaječar is dominated by the tall edifice of the Hotel Srbije, which forms a centrepiece to the main square below, Trg Nikole Pašića, named after the founder and former leader of the Radical Party who was born in this town. The square is a light, airy place with a few outdoor cafés along its western edge, with popcorn

ZAJEČAR

Railway station,
Gamzigrad
(Felix Romuliana)

ŽELEZNICA

● Market

CRNOREČKA

KURSULINA

MOŠE PIJADE

PROTE MATEJE

GENERALA GAMBETE

Bradt

N

0 ————— 100m
0 ————— 100yds

Jugobank
Tržni Centar $

National
Museum

11   3   9

TRG NIKOLE PAŠIĆA

HAJDUK VELJKOVA

War
memorial

Town
Hall

10
i

DIMITRIJA POPOVIĆA

NJEGOŠEVA

LJUBE NEŠIĆA

DOSITEJEVA

4

7

SVETOZARA MARKOVIĆA

1

Radul begov
konak

8

6

5

Vila Tamaris

For listings, see pages 341–2

Where to stay
1 Garni Hotel Hamburg
2 Hotel Grinka M
3 Hotel Srbije – TIS
4 Vila Valentino
Off map
   Vila Tamaris

Where to eat and drink
5 Galerija
6 Kafana Hajduk
   Veljkov Konak
7 Kod mede
8 Mr Bean
9 Poslastičarnica Stella
10 Rivendell
   Srpska kuća (see 3)
11 Triton

sellers and toy electric cars for children in summer. On the square's northern side is the building that houses the town museum, unavoidably conspicuous with its peach and lemon paintwork. The street running left from the museum leads down to an interesting outdoor market area and the bus and train terminals.

Despite rampant modernisation, Zaječar still has a few traditional *konaks* scattered around the town. One that can be visited is **Radul begov konak** (⏲ *09.00–19.00 Mon–Fri, 09.00–15.00 Sat*), a late 18th-century Turkish house museum located at the end of Ljube Nešića, the main street that leads north from the central square. The *konak* was built for a local Turkish ruler between 1843 and 1856 and, as well as having period furniture and rooms laid out in the style of the period, there is a permanent exhibition dedicated to 'Old Zaječar' upstairs. Further down this street at number 37 is another *konak* that operates as a *kafana* – **Kafana Hajduk Veljkov Konak** – a place full of old-fashioned character, and a good choice for a meal or just a drink.

In late May and early June, the town hosts the **'Golden Hands of Zaječar'** festival, a series of events celebrating the food and culture of the region.

GETTING THERE AND AWAY Zaječar **bus station** (☎ 421 545), just north of the centre, has eight buses a day that run to Belgrade, and several to Bor, should you wish to go there. There is a daily bus to Donji Milanovac on the Danube (via Bor), eight to Kladovo, a dozen or so to Niš and four daily to Majdanpek. The six or so daily buses running west to Boljevac can drop you at the turning for the Gamzigrad ruins, although this is still 4km from the site. The village of the same name is also served by six buses a day, although Gamzigrad village is even further away from the site itself.

Train connections (📞 421 360) are slower and less frequent. Four trains a day leave for Niš via Knjaževac, four to Negotin, and three to Bor, although the same journey by bus is invariably quicker.

TOURIST INFORMATION Information can be had from **Cekit (Centar za Kultura i Turizam)** at Svetozara Markovića 2 (📞 421 521; e turizam@cekit.rs; w cekit.rs). The staff here are very helpful, speak good English and can help organise visits to Gamzigrad-Romuliana.

🏠 WHERE TO STAY *Map, opposite*

Zaječar has some decent accommodation options, all reasonably close to the town centre.

🏠 **Hotel Grinka M ***** (9 rooms, 3 apts) Prote Mateje 15; 📞 423 330. This hotel, signposted from the main square, in a white villa with wrought-iron balconies, can be found down a quiet side street a little way from the centre. Discount for stays over 4 days. €€€–€€

🏠 **Garni Hotel Hamburg **** (14 rooms, 2 apts) Svetozara Markovića 1; 📞 3100 136; e info@hotelhamburg.rs; w hotelhamburg.rs. Right in the heart of the town centre, this new hotel has rooms with free Wi-Fi, AC & cable TV. €€

🏠 **Hotel Srbije – TIS ***** (52 rooms, 10 suites) Trg Nikole Pašića 2; 📞 422 333; e mojatisekipa@gmail.com; w srbijatis.co.rs. This tall, formerly state-owned hotel is the centrepiece of the town's main square. The hotel was taken into private ownership in 2003 & refurbished. The hotel has a large restaurant, a fitness centre, barber, casino & currency exchange, & there is Wi-Fi access in the lobby. €€

🏠 **Vila Tamaris** (13 rooms) Ljube Nešića 58; 📞 428 781; e vilatamaris@nadlanu.com; w vilatamaris.co.rs. A small, modern hotel 500m from the centre. Rooms with TV, minibar & internet access. €€

🏠 **Vila Valentino ***** (12 rooms) Dimitrija Popovića 3; 📞 422 790, 424 687; e vilavelentinoplus@ptt.rs. A central pension with smallish rooms complete with cable TV, AC & bath. €€–€

✗ WHERE TO EAT AND DRINK *Map, opposite*

Apart from the hotel restaurants, most of the town's central restaurants seem to be pizzerias. There are several around the centre like **Triton** (📞 420 770; €€–€) at Nikole Pašića 4/9, and **Galerija** (📞 423 474; €€–€) at Svetozara Markovića 75. **Poslastičarnica Stella** (📞 426 409) on Trg oslobođenja opposite the museum has a good selection of ice creams and pastries as well as reliable Wi-Fi. For snacks, there are plenty of bakeries around town like **Mr Bean** on Ljube Nešića. For more traditional fare, the choice is limited: there is the **Srpska kuća** restaurant at Hotel Srbije – TIS (📞 422 333; €), which has an outdoor terrace, good-value daily menus and cheap draught beer, and the Kafana Hajduk Veljkov Konak detailed below. For grilled meat, a good *ćevapdžica* is **Kod mede** at Svetozara Markovića 56 (📞 425 311; €). **Rivendell** (📞 423 005; €) at Vojvode Mišića 10, just off Trg Nikole Pašića, operates as both an 'Irish pub' and a restaurant.

The **Kafana Hajduk Veljkov Konak** (*Ljube Nešića 37;* 📞 424 254; €€–€) is situated in an old Turkish *konak* with a wooden ceiling and chairs made out of barrels, and is rather like Zaječar's own version of the '?' café in Belgrade (page 125). Wrought-iron work with a *hajduk* theme decorates the walls. As well as a communal area, there are secluded cubicles available for dining parties. Prices are very reasonable, although it is unlikely that everything on the menu will be available. The portions are huge but it seems to be acceptable to ask for a half portion if you are dining on your own. As well as food, it is also a good place to try out some of the wines from the area. Zajačarska pivo – the local beer sold here – is pretty tasty too, and has a pleasant nutty flavour.

OTHER PRACTICALITIES There are plenty of banks with ATMs around Trg Nikole Pašića, and there is a branch of **Jugobank** with an ATM next door to the Tržni Centar. The **post office** is nearby, along Krfska, the next street heading towards the bus station from here, facing the other entrance to the Tržni Centar. There is a good outdoor market selling local fruit, vegetables and dairy produce next to the bus station.

WHAT TO SEE AND DO
National Museum (*Narodni musej Zaječar; Moše Pijade 2;* ✆ *422 930;* w *muzejzajecar.org;* ⏱ *08.00–16.00 Mon–Fri, 09.00–15.00 Sat; admission 300din, combined ticket for museum & Felix Romuliana 400din*) This museum has an interesting collection of archaeological, ethnological and historical exhibits from the region, with particular emphasis on the Roman site at nearby Gamzigrad. If you are planning to visit Felix Romuliana it is a good idea to come here first. That way, you will have a better idea of what to expect when you get there and it will help to set it all in context. The museum has some fine mosaics and Roman busts taken from the Felix Romuliana. Especially good are the mosaic that shows Dionysius nonchalantly quaffing from a goblet whilst seated on the back of a leopard, and the rather bulge-eyed head of Emperor Galerius in wine-coloured marble.

Gamzigrad (Felix Romuliana) The 3rd- and 4th-century ruins of the **Roman fortress** of Felix Romuliana at Gamzigrad are located a dozen kilometres west of Zaječar. Although the site was already well known, archaeologists digging here in 1984 unearthed the remains of an imperial palace within the ramparts of the fortress, finding especially fine mosaics, a vestibule, atria, marble floors, public baths and city gates. Felix Romuliana was listed as a UNESCO World Cultural and Natural Heritage Site in June 2007.

All of the evidence suggests that the palace at Romuliana was first built as the residence of Roman Imperator Galerius Valerius Maximillian and given the name of his mother, Romula. It appears to have been suddenly and mysteriously abandoned by its original creators, and then subsequently rebuilt by Justinian in Byzantine times, having been occupied and reinforced by Slavic tribes in the interim period, who named the place Gamzigrad (Slither Town) – probably a reference to the snakes they found there. The site was eventually abandoned altogether and totally forgotten for a thousand years before its rediscovery in the 19th century.

Although most of what remains is extensive foundations and grassed-over mounds, it is possible to get a good idea of its original plan from the ramparts. The ramparts, which originally had six towers on either side, form a trapezium measuring 300m by 230m. This, in turn is reinforced by an inner defensive system of 20 cylindrical towers with four gates. Some of the remaining pillars are in very good condition, as is some of the fine mosaic work found on the pavement, which has representations of the gods Dionysius, Heracles and Asklepios. Unfortunately, at the time of writing it was not possible to see these as they have been covered in sand as a protective measure. Part of the vestibule to the bath is intact, and consists of an octagonal chamber with a large room over the hypocaust and a larger room with an apse. The vestibule dates from the later Constantinian period but the mosaics, which show beasts fighting each other, and a hunter with his dog, are undoubtedly earlier, probably 3rd century. The remains of two temples have also been found, one of which was clearly dedicated to Jupiter.

Two burial mounds stand to the east of the site on Magura Hill and it is presumed that these represent the mausolea of Galerius and his mother. The outline of these can be seen clearly from the site itself.

There is a pleasant outdoor café on the site and a gallery of replica exhibits by the ticket office (⏰ *winter 08.00–16.00, summer 08.00–20.00 daily; admission 300din*). Combined tickets for both the Felix Romuliana and museum entrance can be bought for 400din at the National Museum in Zaječar. Buses to and from Boljevac pass within 4km of the site entrance but without private transport the best and easiest way to reach Felix Romuliana from Zaječar is by taxi. The fare should be around 500din each way.

ĆUPRIJA (ЋУПРИЈА) *Telephone code 035*

Ćuprija is a small but sprawling town just off the E-75 motorway on the Morava River. The only real point in coming here is to use it as a base for visiting the nearby Ravanica Monastery.

GETTING THERE AND AWAY Many of the buses that go north and south along the motorway do not stop here, although they may stop at Jagodina, the next town north. There are some direct buses to and from Belgrade, however, about 12 a day, in addition to three daily services from Kruševac and a dozen or so from Niš. There are also a couple of daily services to Despotovac that leave in the morning and early afternoon. This could be a useful way of getting to Manasija but confirm the time carefully at the bus station first.

The **bus station** is at the edge of town next to the *autoput*. To reach the centre of Ćuprija from the bus station, turn left (ie: in the *opposite* direction to the motorway) and follow the road into town. A 15-minute walk will bring you to a square and a T-junction – this is Cara Lazara, the town's high street. There are also a number of daily trains from the town's **railway station**, mostly to Niš but also to Belgrade and Kruševac.

 WHERE TO STAY AND EAT The **Hotel Ravno** (*Cara Lazara 2;* ☎ *8471 314*) was formerly the only place to stay in town but now there are a couple more to choose from. Dining options are fairly limited but there are a couple of pizza places in the town centre.

Hotel Plaza (20 rooms) Beogradska bb; ☎870 160. On the bank of the Morava River by the bridge & aimed at business & transit guests. Rooms with bath & TV. Restaurant with Serbian dishes. €€–€

La Luna (6 rooms) Moravski park; ☎476 140. A boat restaurant with rooms docked on the bank of the Morava River. Each dbl room with cable TV, AC & bath. The management can also organise excursions to Manasija Monastery & Resavska Cave. €

WHAT TO SEE AND DO

Ravanica Monastery This fine fortified monastery of the Morava School, the first to be built in this style, dates from around 1376. It was founded by Prince Lazar, whose body was brought here after his death at the Battle of Kosovo in 1389. It remains here today but only after having travelled a great deal around the Balkans in the interim period (see box, page 345). Lazar's well-travelled relics finally returned here in 1989, the 600th anniversary of his demise.

Ravanica lies just beyond the village of Senje, surrounded by green meadows beside a forested hillside. The monastery buildings are completely surrounded by a continuous fortified wall that previously had ramparts and towers like those of Manasija to the north. The church, with five cupolas, is built to a cruciform plan with apses on the north and south arms as well as on the more usual east. Alternate layers of brick and stone have been used for the walls and these are decorated with ornate bas-reliefs around the windows, doorways and cupolas.

The church was attacked several times by the Turks who destroyed most of the original frescoes. The narthex of the church is a later 18th-century addition, dating from a time when extensive restoration took place. The benefactor responsible for this work, the abbot Stefan, is portrayed on the west wall.

The older frescoes in the nave are in poor condition, partly because of Turkish mutilation and partly because of badly prepared plaster that faded the colours prematurely. The figure of Lazar with his wife Milica and their two sons Stefan and Vuk adorns the wall opposite the southern apse but this fresco is quite badly damaged. Better is the *Cycle of Miracles* on the south wall and the *Entry into Jerusalem* around the southern apse.

Getting there and away To reach **Senje**, the village next to Ravanica Monastery, there may be a local bus that picks up along Cara Lazara in Ćuprija before heading out to the village.

A more reliable way to visit the monastery is to take a taxi from the town centre or, better still, from outside the bus station. The price to Ravanica should be around 600din; if you add on a reasonable amount of waiting time at the monastery, and the fare back to Ćuprija, it will be something like 1,500din. The monastery lies to the east up a valley, about 10km from Ćuprija and a couple of kilometres beyond the attractive village of Senje. For those with their own transport, note that the road shown on some maps that connects Ravanica and Manasija by a direct route is mostly unsigned and in very poor condition – to reach Manasija from here, return to the main road at Ćuprija and then take the road to Despotovac.

JAGODINA (ЈАГОДИНА) *Telephone code 035*

Across the Morava River west of Ćuprija, Jagodina is another possible base in the region. As the stronghold of Kučuk Alija, a Turkish rebel, the town was burned to the ground in 1813 following the First National Uprising. The Turks left in 1830 and the town developed as an important staging point along the highway from Belgrade to the south. Until 1992, the town was formally known as Svetozarevo, in honour of Svetozar Marković, the famous Serbian socialist, who used to reside here. These days the town is better known for its naive art and, along with Kovačica in Vojvodina, it is one of the two main centres in the country for this. The town also has the third-largest zoo in Serbia with over 100 species of animals, which was opened in July 2006 along with an aqua park in the Đurđevo brdo town park.

The town's former mayor, Dragan Marković Palma, a member of the Serbian Parliament and founder and leader of the Serbia Unity Party, is quite a controversial figure in the Serbian media. Most notoriously, he raised a few eyebrows back in 2009 when he announced that: 'There are no gay people in Jagodina', asserting, 'In my town there are no guys who walk funny and pluck eyebrows.' So there you have it. In fairness, Jagodina's erstwhile mayor might perhaps be accused of being a little out of touch. He had also once said that Beethoven and Chopin had not played in Jagodina only because he hadn't been elected mayor at a younger age and so wasn't able to book them when they were popular. To his credit, Marković remains popular in the town itself thanks to his generous social welfare programmes. As well as building the zoo, the aqua park and a stadium in an effort to encourage domestic tourism to the town, he expanded social services enormously, paying for children to go on summer holidays and for the elderly to receive free medicine. The homophobe former mayor even arranged and paid for trips to take some of the town's pensioners to the Guča Trumpet Festival. Marković ceased his mayoral duties in 2012 when he became president of the city assembly. Jagodina was given city status in 2007.

GETTING THERE AND AWAY A number of buses travelling the Belgrade–Niš motorway route call in at Jagodina's **bus station** (✆ 220 205), which is right in the town centre. There are also local services to nearby towns like Ćuprija and Paraćin. Jagodina also sits on the main Belgrade to Niš railway line and there are fairly regular trains in both directions from the town's **railway station** (✆ 221 003), next door to the bus station.

TOURIST INFORMATION Found at Stevana Ivanovića 2 (✆ 252 983, 282 199; e togjagodina@gmail.com; w togjagodina.autentik.net; ⊕ 07.00–15.00 daily), at the tourist complex at Đurđevo brdo.

PRINCE LAZAR'S RESTLESS REMAINS

It remains uncertain whether Prince Lazar was killed during battle, or shortly after, in the hands of the Turks, who probably would have beheaded him. Whatever the cause of his death, his dead body would soon become an object of pilgrimage for many Serbs, who through the coming centuries would attribute great spiritual significance to his mortal remains.

After being first taken to the parish church at Priština in Kosovo, his body was transported to Ravanica Monastery in 1392, where it became the centre of a cult that drew pilgrims from all over Serbia. When the Ravanica monks were forced to flee from their monastery in 1690, they took the bones with them, settling first at Szentendre near Budapest, then at a monastery in Srem called Vrdnik that later became known as Sremska Ravanica. Rebecca West, during her pre-war travels in Serbia, tells of shaking the prince's hand whilst he was interned here. Lazar remained here until 1942, when he was moved, with German help, to Belgrade after Croatian Ustaša had stolen golden rings from his corpse. During his Belgrade years in the patriarchate, Lazar once again became the focus for pilgrimage, especially on 28 June, St Vitus's Day – Vidovdan – the date of the battle that brought his end. Lazar's body remained in Belgrade until 1987 when, as a precursor to the forthcoming 600th anniversary of the Battle of Kosovo, his well-travelled remains were taken on yet another tour of Serbian and Bosnian monasteries. With the festivities over, Lazar was returned once more to Ravanica, where he now receives visitors every Sunday, and where a plastic canopy prevents visitors from actually making physical contact à la Rebecca West. It is no exaggeration to say that Prince Lazar must have travelled a far greater distance in death than most of his contemporaries ever managed while they were alive. Hopefully, after 600 restless years of motion, his weary bones can remain at Ravanica for eternity now.

WHERE TO STAY AND EAT

Hill Hotel **** (20 rooms, 4 suites) Stevana Ivanovića 3; ☎252 202, 8100 181; e office@hill-hotel.com; w hill-hotel.com. A modern hotel situated in the green park surroundings of Đurđevo brdo close to the zoo. This has AC rooms with internet access & cable TV. Restaurant, bar, internet café & wellness centre. €€€

Hotel Jagodina ** (156 rooms) Slavke Đurđevića 3; m 062 1448 634; e hoteljagodina@yahoo.com. With coffee bar, restaurant, conference hall, swimming pool, pastry shop & disco. €€

Kafana Vitez (3 rooms) 7 Juli 29; ☎221 830. Close to the centre, a traditional *kafana* offering national dishes, a cheap fixed menu of the day & B&B in 3 rooms. €

Potok Aračlijski potok bb; ☎241 400. Located in a wooded area of Đurđevo brdo near to the zoo & aqua park. 2 terraces, local Serbian dishes & turkey, the house speciality. €€–€

WHAT TO SEE AND DO The town has two churches of note. The 'new' Church of St Peter and Paul, a five-domed neo-Byzantine structure with a separate bell tower that dates from 1899, and the smaller 'old' Church of Archangels Michael and Gabriel that was constructed in 1815. The tourist complex at Đurđevo brdo (George's Hill) has the town **zoo**, **aqua park** and **Museum of Wax Figures** (*Muzej voštanih figura; Stevana Ivanovića 2*; ☎252 983; e togjagodina@gmail.com; w muzejvostanihfigura. autentik.net; ⊕ summer 08.00–20.00, winter 10.00–17.00 daily; admission 150din), where you can see wax replicas of historic Serbian figures.

The **Museum of Naive and Marginal Art** (*Musej naivne i marginalne utmetnosti; Boška Đuričića 10*; ☎223 419; e info@naiveart.rs; w naiveart.rs; ⊕ 10.00–17.00 Tue–Fri, 11.00–15.00 Sat/Sun), housed in an elegant town villa, has around 2,500 works of naive art from all over Serbia, one of the biggest collections in the world. The museum was inaugurated in 1960 and the collection grew up around the work of local artist Janko Brašić.

DESPOTOVAC (ДЕСПОТОВАЦ) *Telephone code 035*

This small town to the east of the Morava Valley is the best place to aim for if you are visiting Manasija and want to spend the night in the vicinity of the monastery. It is a pleasant place in the middle of some beautiful countryside and so the lack of sophisticated facilities and night-time entertainment is hardly a hardship.

GETTING THERE AND AWAY Five direct buses run daily to Despotovac from Belgrade via Svilajnac at the entrance to the Resava Valley, and there is also an early morning and evening bus that originates in Svilajnac and travels on through to Ćuprija. Bus timetables are rarely carved in stone, so enquire at the **bus station** (☎611 162) for the exact times of this service.

Manasija Monastery is an easy walk from the town. From the town centre, walk towards the Hotel Resava and turn left along the road that crosses the river. After the bridge, the road curves around to the right in the direction of the river and leads to the gates of the monastery.

WHERE TO STAY AND EAT The restaurants in town serving standard Serbian food are listed below as well as a few accommodation options.

Motel Kruna (24 rooms) Rudnička bb; ☎611 659; e motelkruna@hotmail.com. 2km from the centre on the Despotovac to Svilajnac road.

Comfortable rooms & excellent food. €€–€

Hotel Resava (35 rooms) Despota Stefana Lazarevića 190; ☎611 963; e office@resava.info;

w resava.info. About 1km east of the bus station just past the junction for Manasija. The hotel, or rather, *konačište* ('inn' or 'lodgings'), has its own large restaurant but there are also a few grill restaurants & a pizzeria in the vicinity of the bus station. €

🏠 **Milenijum** (8 rooms) Rudnička 6; 📞611 263, 612 070. A restaurant serving national dishes & pizzas that also has a few rooms. €

✕ **Viking Pizza** Petra Drapšina; 📞612 839; w viking-passage.com. A pizza place that unusually combines elements of Swedish cuisine with Italian. Large terrace & live music in summer. €€–€

✕ **Fontana Plus** Vidovdanska 2; m 065 9875 000. €

✕ **Lavrint** Veliki Popović; 📞621 293. €

WHAT TO SEE AND DO

Manasija Monastery This Morava School monastery in the Resava Valley is so heavily fortified that it resembles a Byzantine castle. In all, there are 11 towers stretched along the high defensive walls. The fortifications were not just for dramatic effect; when this monastery was being constructed by Lazar's son Stefan in the early years of the 15th century (probably between 1408 and 1418), it was perfectly clear that it was only a matter of time before the Turks would move north to consolidate their earlier victory at Kosovo Polje. In the end it took them another half-century before they did this but there could have been no doubt in Stefan's mind that the fate was already sealed.

In the first half of the 15th century, under the patronage of Stefan Lazarević, Manasija became a haven for writers and artists from provinces that had already fallen under Turkish subjugation. The most illustrious of these was probably Konstantin Filozof (Constantine the Philosopher), Stefan's biographer. Had the Turks not interrupted these artistic endeavours when they attacked for the first time in 1439, it may also have become the focal point for the Serbian equivalent of the Italian Renaissance.

In many ways Manasija represents the final statement of a Serbian golden age that ended with the advent of almost half a millennium of Turkish domination.

The church within the walls is of marble, simple enough on the outside but decorated inside by frescoes that represent the pinnacle of the Morava School of painting. Many of the original frescoes have been destroyed, both by Turks during their occupation and later by Austrian troops in 1718, who inadvertently blew up the narthex when they were using the church as a gunpowder store. Out of those that remain, the gold-clad *Warrior Saints* on the north wall and the *Parable of the Wedding Feast* on the north apse are among the finest of their genre. It is thought that these frescoes are either the work of Greek masters or of local artists that had been trained in Salonica. Although the frescoes are partly ruined, it is easy to see that they represent the culmination of an artistic movement that had been developing and improving for decades. The colours used are bright and vivid, and the figures represented in the paintings seem cultured and worldly, fully engaged in the celebration of life.

The gift shop at the monastery is well worth a visit, with a wide variety of honey and herbal products on sale.

Resavska Cave (📞 611 110; e resavskapecina@yahoo.com; w resavskapecina.rs; ⏰ 1 Apr–31 Oct 08.00–18.30, 1 Nov–31 Mar 10.00–17.00 daily; admission 300din) This impressive cave system, discovered in 1962, is found 20km to the east of Despotovac. The total length of the galleries extends for 2,850m, although the tourist path itself is only 800m long. The system consists of three levels connected by artificial tunnels.

Parts of the upper and middle galleries may be visited, while an underground stream flows through the lowest gallery making it out of bounds for visitors. All of the galleries are rich in stalactites and stalagmites, and the rock itself is quite variable in colour. The underground temperature hovers around 14°C; humidity is 75–80%. Reasonably warm clothes are required.

There is a guide service and tours of the cave generally last around 40 minutes. There is no public transport to the cave but a return taxi from Despotovac should be in the order of 2,000din.

Miniature Park Despotovac (*Park minijatura Despotovac;* \ *612 101;* e *parkmaketa@gmail.com;* w *parkmaketa.com;* ⏲ *1 Apr–1 Nov 10.00–19.00 daily; admission 150din*) Well worth a stop if you have your own transport, this miniature park on the road between Despotovac and Resavska Cave has scale models of each and every Orthodox monastery in Serbia. All have been faithfully reproduced at 1:17 scale by the owner who has taken painstaking care with every detail. A path leads around the site and old Serbia hands can test their knowledge by ticking off those they have already seen full-size.

Lisine Waterfall This waterfall, which is said to be the highest in Serbia, lies east of Despotovac in the gorge formed by the River Resava. It is about a 30-minute walk from the Motel Lisine, an alpine lodge that lies at the head of the gorge at the end of the tarmac road beyond the village of Strmosten. There are several other restaurants here close to the waterfall, along with huts to rent and shady gardens. The waterfall can sometimes temporarily dry up in summer after hot, dry weather but it usually recovers to its usual abundance when rainfall normalises once more.

The track above the waterfall eventually leads back to the main Resava road and makes for good hiking or cycling.

 Where to stay

 Motel Lisine (approx 20 rooms, 3 suites) Savez Boraca 148, Despotovac; m 063 606 468. The motel has an eclectic collection of souvenirs from around the world & its own small hydro-electricity plant. The restaurant serves fresh trout from the motel's fish pond. €€

NIŠ (НИШ) *Telephone code 018*

Niš, with an estimated population of over 260,000, is Serbia's third-largest city. Authors of long-defunct guidebooks to the former Yugoslavia talk of a large 'dull and dirty town' and an air of 'grey, grim abandonment', but this is misleading as these days Niš is no longer an industrial wasteland but a lively university city with a handful of interesting sights. Its manufacturing pedigree has meant that it is not the prettiest of places but, then again, neither is Belgrade. In industrial terms, the city has certainly seen better days: its manufacturing base has largely been decimated over the past 20 years, thanks to economic sanctions, poor planning and NATO bombing.

Like Belgrade, Niš seems to make the most of what it does have – the Turkish fort by the river has been developed into a pleasant park, and some of the original buildings have been converted to galleries and smart café-restaurants; the main shopping street, Obrenovićeva, like its counterpart Kneza Mihaila in the capital, has been pedestrianised to become the route for a crowded *korso* every evening. At the end of this is Kopitareva (Kazandžijsko sokače – 'Tinkers' Alley'), a narrow alleyway filled with bars, cafés and restaurants. Aside from the Turkish fort, the city's number one tourist 'attraction' is probably the grisly Ćele kula (the Skull

Tower), which has been protected from the elements by having a small chapel built around it.

As well as a few interesting historical sites, the city has quite a lot else to offer: a number of excellent but inexpensive restaurants, a relaxed atmosphere, good places to stay and a nearby spa resort.

HISTORY The history of the city goes back to well before Roman times. Discoveries at Bubanj and Humska čuka, close to the city, suggest that the area was populated in the Neolithic and Bronze Age periods. The Celtic inhabitants of the region named the river that ran through it, Navissos, and a variation on this name was adopted by the Romans who eventually colonised the region.

As Naissus, Niš became an important city of the Roman Empire, and the emperor, Constantine the Great, was born here around AD274–80. Constantine was appointed emperor in 307 and in 313 he issued the Milan Edict in which Christianity, previously persecuted, was given equal status with all the other religions of the Roman Empire. He went on to move the seat of the emperor east to Constantinople and by doing this lay the foundations for the new Byzantine Empire. During this period, Niš became an important economic and artistic centre. Constantine returned to the city periodically, spending time at his summer residence of Mediana, the remains of which can still be seen just outside the city on the road to Niška Banja. Records testify that Constantine passed several more laws while he was resident here in Naissus – in 315, 319, 324 and 334.

The city was destroyed by Attila in 441, and later again by further Hun attacks in 448 and by Barbarians in 480. It was rebuilt in the 6th century by the Byzantine emperor Justinian only to be destroyed once more in 615 by marauding Avars. Around 987, the town was taken under the control of the Bulgarian emperor Simeon. Byzantium later regained control over Niš and the surrounding area in the early part of the 11th century but in 1072, the town was raided once more by Hungarians.

Slavs had been in the region since the 6th century but were a fairly disparate group until the organisational skills of the Nemanjić dynasty came to bear. Stefan Nemanja incorporated Niš as part of Serbia in 1183 with the intention of making it his capital. The city did not remain under Serbian control for long: in 1196, Stefan Nemanja was defeated by the Greek, Isak Angelos, and the city did not return to Serbian hands until 1241. The city slowly recovered and rebuilt itself under the leadership of the Nemanjić dynasty. After the years of uncertainty that followed the defeat at the Battle of Kosovo in 1389, the Turks finally wrested the city in 1448 and their rule lasted right up until 1877, apart from one brief period of Austrian rule.

As elsewhere in Serbia, there were revolts against Ottoman rule from time to time, most notably at the beginning of the 19th century, during the First National Uprising. These were brutally put down by the Turks. One particular incident of this kind in 1809, at the Battle of Čegar Hill, led to the construction of the city's famous Ćele kula (Skull Tower) as a deterrent to would-be insurrectionists. Finally, on 11 January 1878, Prince Milan Obrenović entered the gates of the fortress after a long and exhausting battle. After more than 400 years of Turkish rule, Niš was finally back in Serbian hands.

Niš became the Serbian wartime capital for a brief period during World War I, from July 1914 until October 1915, when it was occupied by the Bulgarian army until the end of the war. During World War II, the city suffered as much as, if not more than, most other Serbian towns. The Nazis built the concentration camp Crveni Krst in 1941 as an internment centre for the Jews, Roma and others they considered

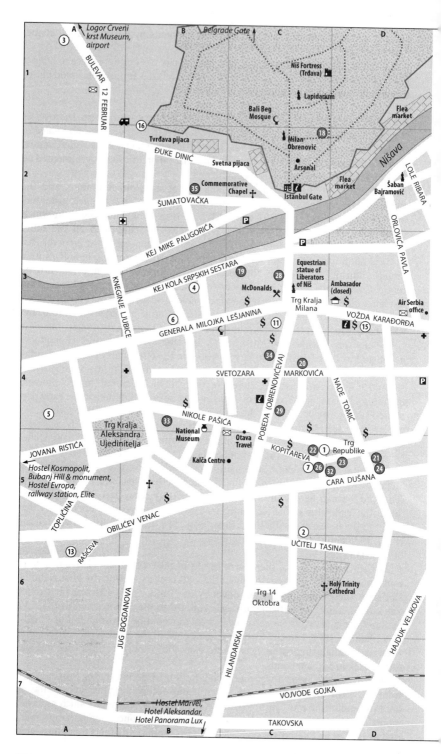

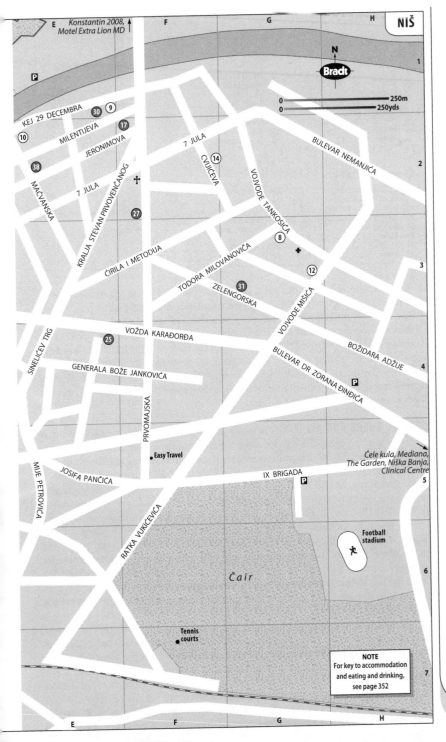

Konstantin 2008,
Motel Extra Lion MD

Bradt

N

250m
250yds

KEJ 29 DECEMBRA

MILENTIJEVA

JERONIMOVA

7 JULA

CVIJIĆEVA

7 JULA

MAĆVANSKA

KRALJA STEVAN PRVOVENČANOG

ĆIRILA I METODIJA

TODORA MILOVANOVIĆA

ZELENGORSKA

VOŽDA KARAĐORĐA

SINELĆEV TRG

GENERALA BOŽE JANKOVIĆA

PRVOMAJSKA

MIJE PETROVIĆA

JOSIFA PANČIĆA

RATKA VUKIĆEVĆA

Easy Travel

VOJVODE TANKOSIĆA

VOJVODE MIŠIĆA

BULEVAR NEMANJIĆA

BOŽIDARA ADŽIJE

BULEVAR DR ZORANA ĐINĐIĆA

IX BRIGADA

Ćele kula, Mediana,
The Garden, Niška Banja,
Clinical Centre

Football
stadium

Čair

Tennis
courts

NOTE
For key to accommodation
and eating and drinking,
see page 352

NIŠ

For listings, see pages 354–7

undesirable, and adopted Bubanj Hill just outside the town as the setting for many of their mass killings. Over 10,000 citizens were shot here during the war.

The most recent loss of life in the city as a result of armed conflict is still fresh in the city's memory. Niš was targeted quite extensively during the 1999 NATO air campaign. Bombs destroyed the airport, a tobacco factory and part of the industrial zone, as well as misfires that demolished civilian property. The worst 'misfire' was a missile that hit an ambulance by accident, killing several civilians and injuring dozens more. There is a small monument in a park close to the fortress and market that commemorates this event.

GETTING THERE AND AWAY Niš is easily reached from all directions. The main E-75 *autoput* bypasses the city *en route* for Macedonia and Bulgaria. Numerous daily buses link Niš with Belgrade; over 20 run south to Leskovac, the same number go southwest to Kuršumlija and southeast to Pirot. Five daily buses run as far as the Bulgarian border at Dimitrovgrad. Three buses cross the border into Bulgaria and on to Sofia, and a total of nine leave daily for Skopje in Macedonia. The **bus station** [350 A/B1] (*Bulevar 12 Februar bb;* ✆ *255 177;* w *nis-ekspres.rs*) is just around the corner from the fortress, beyond the market area to the left of the Istanbul Gate. There are comprehensive timetables showing departures and arrivals inside the ticket-office building. The bus station is run by Niš Ekspres but other bus companies such as Lasta and Simplon also run services from the station. To reach central Niš from the bus station, which is only a short walk, go out through the turnstiles, turn left past the market and then right over the bridge opposite Istanbul Gate to reach central Trg Kralja Milana.

Niš is also on an international railway line, although trains are not as frequent or as reliable as the buses. As well as going to Belgrade and Novi Sad to the north, there are train services east to Sofia and Istanbul, and south to Skopje, which continue to Thessaloniki and Athens in Greece. The **railway station** [350 A5] (✆ *264 625, 269 786;* w *zeleznicesrbije.com*) is some distance to the west of the city centre but the bus stop opposite on Dimitrija Tucovića provides a service to the city centre.

The city's **airport** [350 A1] (✆ *4583 003;* w *nis-airport.com*), now known as Konstantin Veliki (Constantine the Great) Airport, was reopened in the autumn of 2003, having been put out of action during the 1999 NATO air war. The airport currently offers flights to Berlin and other German cities as well as Bratislava, Milan, Eindhoven, Mälmo and Basel using Wizz Air and Ryanair. The airport lies close to the city, just 3.5km from the city centre.

GETTING AROUND The city centre is small enough to walk around but a useful local bus service is the number 1 that runs along Vožda Karađorđa, passing Ćele kula and Mediana on its way to Niška Banja. Other buses that run this route, as far as Ćele kula at least, are service numbers 3 and 10. Other useful routes are the number 6 bus that runs between the railway station and the centre of the city, the number 8 to Bubanj, and the circular 34A and 34B that connects the railway station with the centre, the bus station and the north side of the river. Tickets cost between 30din and 60din depending on the zone. Either pay the driver, or buy a ticket for slightly less from a Niš Ekspres stand. A one-day ticket can be bought, which will save you money if you make several trips. **Taxis** in Niš are easily found. Journeys out of the city tend to cost more per kilometre. Pre-booked taxis are invariably cheaper and more reliable. Some local firms are Banker Taxi (9707), Bingo Taxi (9704), Boom Taxi (9715) and Niš Taxi (244 144).

TOURIST INFORMATION [350 D3] (*Vožda Karađorđa 7;* 521 321; e *info@visitnis. com;* w *visitnis.com*) This sells maps, booklets and souvenirs and the staff can help with information on accommodation and sightseeing in the city. They also have another branch at the entrance to Tvrđava Fortress [350 C2] (250 222), one at Obrenovićeva 38 [350 C4] (520 207) and one in Niška Banja at Sinđelićeva 3b (4548 588). All branches can help book private accommodation in Niška Banja.

LOCAL TOUR OPERATORS

ACE Adventure Brace Ignjatović 17/37/1; 307 353; m 064 2476 311; e info@ace-adventurecentre.com; w ace-adventurecentre.com. This operator organises a variety of tours in the southeast Serbia region. They specialise in environment-friendly hiking & cycling w/ends in the region but can custom-design a tour according to specific requirements. ACE (Artists, Constructors, Engineers!), run by 2 Niš-based brothers, pride themselves on providing comfortable accommodation & gourmet meals as part of their package. They can provide a good selection of week-long escorted tours to various parts of Serbia, particularly the west & Vojvodina, & to Montenegro & other Balkan countries. Both guided & self-guided tours are available. The hiking or cycling involved in the tours can be tailored to personal levels of fitness ranging from easy to challenging. ACE will also happily design a private tour around any desired location for any number of people.

Easy Travel [351 F5] Prvomajska 4a; 292 555; e info@easytravel.rs; w easytravel.rs. City tours & guided walks as well as multi-day excursions in southeast Serbia.

Halo Travel [350 C5] Kalča Centre, Obrenovićeva 46; 240 700; e info@halotravel.rs; w halotravel.rs. Small company offering 'Ethno Niš' tours.

Nitravel [350 C5] Kalča Centre, Obrenovićeva 46; 511 002, 526 596; e nitravel@nitravel.rs; w nitravel.rs

Niturs [350 C2] Tvrđava, Stanbol kapija; 521 425, 511 985; e niturs.nis@gmail.com; w niturs.rs. With an office inside the fortress gate, this company mostly deals with travel to Bulgaria.

Otava Travel [350 C5] Kalča Centre, Obrenovićeva 46; 209 494, 209 490; e office@otavatravel.com; w otavatravel.com. Well-established company with tours to surrounding villages like Niška Banja & Sićevo.

 WHERE TO STAY Two of Niš's central hotels – the Hotel Park and the Hotel Niš – were closed down in 2004, meaning that there was a bit less competition for the other state-run hotels in town – the Ambasador and the Centroturist. However, the

Centroturist also closed for business in 2006, and the Ambasador more recently. To fill the void, a handful of new privately owned hotels have opened up and the accommodation situation has improved enormously in the city over the past few years. More than a dozen hostels have opened for business in recent years too, as well as convenient and well-priced accommodation in the form of *prenoćište* – city apartments, which do not as a rule provide breakfast. There are also a few more options out of the city in Niška Banja.

Upmarket

🏠 **Hotel My Place** **** [351 E1] (21 rooms, 9 suites) Kej 29 Decembra bb; ☎525 555, 293 600; e hotel@hotelmyplace.com; w hotelmyplace.com. The city's best hotel: a shiny, modern building, part of the Best Western group that has good service & comfortable rooms & suites. Fitness centre, sauna, 2 restaurants. €€€€–€€€

🏠 **Hotel Niški Cvet** **** [351 E2] (24 rooms) Kej 29 Decembra 2; ☎297 800; e office@niskicvet.com; w niskicvet.com. This modern well-appointed hotel is situated in a quiet cul-de-sac down by the river not far from the Turkish fort. All rooms have broadband internet. Conference room, nightclub, bar & restaurant. €€€€–€€€

🏠 **New City Hotel** **** [350 D3] (48 rooms) Vožda Karađorđa 12; ☎504 800; e info@newcityhotelnis.com; w newcityhotelnis.com. A slick new hotel in the city centre, with fully equipped, spacious rooms, conference centre & good restaurant. €€€€–€€€

Mid-range

🏠 **Eter Hotel** *** [350 C5] (19 rooms) Nikole Pašića 29; ☎3200 322; m 060 5557 777; e info@eterhotel.rs; w eterhotel.rs. Located in the heart of downtown Niš on the corner of Kopitareva with its restaurants & cafés, this recently opened boutique hotel has clean modern rooms & character aplenty. All rooms come with minibar, cable TV & work desk. €€€

🏠 **Hotel Aleksandar** *** [350 B7] (15 rooms, 9 apts) Njegoševa 81a; ☎562 333; e info@hotel-aleksandar.com; w hotel-aleksandar.com. Located high on a hillside above the city, this private hotel makes up for its awkward location with fine views – fine if you have a car. Each room or apartment has cable TV, AC & minibar. The spacious rooms are simply furnished but scrupulously clean & nicely decorated with modern abstract paintings. Wireless internet connection is available. The hotel has a smart restaurant with a terrace & snack bar, & an open-air swimming pool. €€€

🏠 **Hotel Duo D** *** [350 C5] (8 rooms, 4 suites) Kopitareva 7; ☎517 701, 517 702; e reception@hotel-duod.com; w hotel-duod.com. In the heart of Niš, this is a traditionally built *konak* tucked away in the bustling café street of Kopitareva. All rooms have handmade cherry-wood furniture, minibar, AC, internet connection & satellite TV. Restaurant & coffee bar. €€€

🏠 **Hotel Panorama Lux** *** [350 B7] (6 rooms, 2 suites) Svetolika Rankovića 51; ☎561 214; e info@panoramalux.co.rs; w panoramalux.co.rs. This modern purpose-built hotel, mostly aimed at business visitors, is quite close to the Hotel Aleksandar & shares the same advantages & drawbacks of an out-of-town location. The en-suite rooms come with satellite TV, minibar & AC. The restaurant is able to cater for vegetarian & diabetic diets. There is an outdoor swimming pool, an aperitif bar, 24hr room service & money exchange. Free shuttle service. €€€

🏠 **Hotel Regent Club** **** [350 C3] (20 rooms) Obrenovićeva 10, PC Gorča; ☎524 924; e recepcija@regentclub.com; w regentclub.com. Regency-style hotel in the pedestrian zone of the city centre, part of the Gorča shopping mall of Pobeda. Rooms & apartments with internet access, AC, cable TV & minibar. €€€

Budget

🏠 **Hotel Elegance** [351 G3] (9 rooms, 1 suite) Vojvoda Tankosića 28; ☎528 175; e info@elegance.rs; w elegance.rs. A new small hotel with comfortable modern rooms, some with balcony, with AC, cable TV, Wi-Fi. €€€–€€

🏠 **Hotel Rile Men** [351 G3] (24 rooms, 5 apts) Vojvode Mišića 111; ☎528 522; w rilemen.com. Modern, comfortable rooms & apartments. Popular with sports groups. €€€–€€

🏠 **Etno Konak Tašana** [350 C5] (6 rooms) Prijezdina 8a; ☎510 515; m 064 2023 200; e prenociste.tasana@gmail.com. Good-value modern lodgings in the city centre with rooms of different sizes & capacity. Shared kitchen, 1st-floor terrace & garden. €€

🏠 **Good Night Apartments** [350 A1] (12 rooms, 2 suites) Bulevar 12 Februar 69a; ☎250 250, 588 333; e info@goodnight.rs; w goodnight. rs. Just 300m north of the bus station, squeezed between the railway lines & the main road, this modern block has very comfortable, good-value rooms with TV, AC, internet access & modern bathroom. Quite luxurious for the price & quiet too, given the location. Friendly reception staff, coffee machine. €€

🏠 **Hotel Extra Lion MD** [350 F1] (17 rooms) Knjaževačka 28a; ☎570 010, 570 011; w hotelextralionmd.com. A comfortable motel with a restaurant, 4km from the city centre on the road to Knjaževac. €€

🏠 **Konstantin 2008** [351 F1] (12 rooms) Knjaževačka 15; ☎272 626; e prenociste_konstantin@yahoo.com. Apartment block some distance from the city centre providing accommodation in comfortable rooms with bathroom, balcony, cable TV, internet access & AC. B/fast provided. €€

🏠 **Laguna Lux** [350 A6] (7 rooms) Rašićeva 6; ☎4562 671; e office@lagunalux-prenociste. rs; w lagunalux-prenociste.rs. A modern building close to Trg Kralja Aleksandra Ujedinitelja & Kalča Centre. All rooms with TV, minibar, AC, cable TV & internet access. B/fast available on request, laundry service & parking. €€

🏠 **Majesty Apartments** [351 F2] (9 rooms, 3 apts) Cvijićeva 27; ☎519 755, 519 756; e info@ majestyapartments.com; w majestyapartments. com. Modern apartment-hotel with spacious comfortable rooms, all with AC, minibar, cable TV, internet access & balconies. Restaurant & café, b/fast is included in price. €€

🏠 **Royal Rooms** [350 B2] (5 rooms) Đuke Đinića 1; ☎292 960; e office@royalrooms.rs. Very close to the bus station & fortress, this has pleasant bright rooms with AC, satellite TV & internet access. Discounts for longer stays. €€

Hostels

🏠 **Happy Hostel** [350 B3] Kej kola srpskih sestara 17A/8; ☎252 839; m 063 8673 896; e info@happy-hostelnis.com. Close to the river & Turkish fortress, this small friendly hostel has a range of tidy sgl, 3- & 4-bed rooms. Discounts for groups & longer stays. €

🏠 **Hostel Aurora** [350 A4] Dr Petra Vučinića 16; ☎214 642; m 063 1095 820; e info@ aurorahostel.rs; w aurorahostel.rs. Opened in 2012, this has 8-bed dorms & trpl rooms in a converted building that was once the Turkish consulate. €

🏠 **Hostel Evropa** [350 A5] Leskovačka bb; ☎556 156; e hostel.evropa@gmail.com; w hostelevropa.rs. Several dorms, 4 dbl rooms & 2 apartments, all with AC & cable TV. €

🏠 **Hostel Kosmopolit** [350 A5] Anastasa Jovanovića 15; m 063 472 705; e hostelkosmopoli@hotmail.com; w hostelkosmopolit.com. West of the train station, with 8- & 3-bed dorms & private dbl room with AC & TV. €

🏠 **Hostel Marvel** [350 B7] 12 Srpske brigade 2; ☎265 674; e marvelnis@sezampro. rs, hostelmarvel@yahoo.com; w hostelmarvel. com. Some way south of the centre close to the Hotel Panorama. 5 rooms with 20 beds. Communal dining room & kitchen. €

🏠 **Hostel Sweet** [350 B3] Veljkovića Špaje 11/4; m 062 8942 085; e info@sweet-hostel. com; w sweet-hostel.com. Close to the centre, on the upper floor of an apartment block, this has 2-, 3- & 4-bed rooms with shared bathroom. Computer access, use of kitchen & living room. €

🏠 **The Garden** [351 H5] Vojislava Ilića 12; ☎236 165; m 062 9709 721. Situated east of the centre close to the Skull Tower, this has a quiet peaceful garden for relaxing as its name suggests. Rooms with 1, 2, 4 or 6 beds, all with cable TV, Wi-Fi & own bathroom. €

❌ **WHERE TO EAT AND DRINK** Although Niš is a city of café-bars more than anything else, it is well served by restaurants too, especially national restaurants and Italian pizza places. The area around Kopitareva (Kazandžijsko sokače – 'Tinkers' Alley') in particular has an eclectic mix of quite traditional national **restaurants** and modern, youth-oriented cafés. For cheap **fast food**, the neighbourhood north of the river close to the bus station is the place to look as numerous snack bars and bakeries are located in this area.

8

There are far too many cafés in the city to make many specific recommendations. The café-per-capita ratio here seems even higher than elsewhere in the country, but there tends to be concentrations of café-bars in certain locations around the city.

At Tvrđava, the Turkish fortress, there are several upmarket places close to the entrance gate. Across the river, around Trg Kralja Milana, are a few more, and the pedestrian street of Pobeda has **trendy cafés** with outdoor tables and cushioned seating all the way along it. Other café-bar enclaves include Kopitareva (also known as Kazandžijsko sokače – 'Tinkers' Alley'), a narrow pedestrian street that runs off the top of Obrenovićeva by the Kalča Centre, and also along IX Brigada next to the park. Many of the cafés at the Turkish fortress put on live music during the warmer months, usually a singer and a keyboard player, performing anything from Latin jazz to Beatles covers – or both. As well as plentiful cafés, Niš also has numerous **bakeries** and places to get take-away *pite* and *burek*. There are several around the bus station, and more along Vožda Karađorđa. Below are a few suggestions for good places to have a drink or a snack.

Restaurants

✗ Elite [350 A5] Prijezdina 3; ✆ 514 514; w eliterestoran.com; ◷ 08.00–midnight daily. As its name suggests, this is one of the best-regarded restaurants in the city. Top-notch Mediterranean & Serbian dishes served in elegant, atmospheric surroundings. Extensive wine list. €€€

✗ Casablanca [351 F2] Jeronimova 26; ✆ 523 353; ◷ 08.00–midnight daily. The emphasis here is on international dishes, with a few vegetarian choices. €€

✳✗ Meze [350 D5] Koste Stamenkovića 3; m 065 2280 333; w kafanamezenis.com; ◷ 08.00–midnight daily. Top-notch national restaurant serving delicious Serbian dishes in an airy dining room with modern furnishings & plenty of wood & wrought iron. The excellent food here is cooked with more flair & imagination than usual. €€

✗ Nišlijska Mehana [351 F2] Prvomajska 49; ✆ 511 111; w mehananis.com; ◷ 09.00–23.00 daily. This is a national restaurant that comes recommended by many. It is said to have the best *ćevapčići* in the city, although much fancier dishes are available too. The dining area has national costumes & musical instruments on display & there is live music at w/ends. €€

✗ Riva [351 E1] Kej 29 Decembar 18b; ✆ 523 200; w riva.rs; ◷ 08.30–midnight Mon–Sat, 12.30–midnight Sun. A smart pizza restaurant on the south bank of the Nišava River that also has steaks & salads on the menu & a lengthy wine list. €€

✗ Srbska Kuća [351 G3] Zelengorska 35; ✆ 242 097; ◷ 08.00–23.00 daily. As its name suggests, a homely national restaurant. €€

✗ Kafana Biser [350 D5] Koste Stamenkovića 1; ✆ 248 205; w kafana-biser.com; ◷ 07.00–midnight Mon–Fri. 07.00–02.00 Sat/Sun. Next door to Meze, this traditional Serbian restaurant has a few tables out on the pavement. Biser has good food, friendly English-speaking staff & low prices. Live music most evenings. €

✗ Kafana Kod Rajka [350 C5] Kopitareva 29; ✆ 241 721; ◷ 10.00–midnight daily. This is a friendly place for good-value, Serbian grill dishes that come in huge portions. It is 2nd from the end of the Kopitareva row, almost opposite Hotel Duo D. €

✗ Stara Srbija [350 D5] Trg Republike 12; ✆ 521 902; w starasrbija.com; ◷ 09.00–midnight Sun–Thu, 09.00–04.00 Fri/Sat. Located at the corner of Cara Dušana & Trg Republike, this old-fashioned place, close to Kopitareva, has good national food at very moderate prices. There is an outside terrace & a dark, rather musty dining room inside. Live music most nights. €

✗ Tri Fenjera [350 B2] Anete Andrejević 8a; ✆ 525 200; ◷ 08.00–23.00 daily. A family-run *kafana* close to the fortress with a charming, old-fashioned interior, delicious regional food & typically huge portions. €

Cafés, bars and snack bars

▣ Dom Planinara (Mountaineers' Club) [350 C2] Tvrđava; ✆ 525 254. Dom Planinara is a no-nonsense sort of place with tables spread out beneath the trees at the fortress. There is nothing fancy here, just good *Turska kafa* & cheap bottles of Jelen beer. To find it, walk through the entrance into the fortress, turn right up some steps after you have passed the Turkish arsenal-art gallery & the public toilets. The café is under the trees ahead. Watch out for mosquitoes after dusk.

🍺 **Irish Pub Crazy Horse** [350 C3] Davidova 8; **m** 062 780 574; **w** irishpubcrazyhorse.com; 🕙 08.00–02.00. A good choice of beers – not just Guinness – is available at this city-centre pub close to the river & Trg Kralja Milana. Live rock music, dartboard & football on TV. Light meals & b/fasts too. With seats & tables out on the street, it is also not a bad choice for a quiet drink.

🍺 **Jorgovan Mala** [350 C4] Svetozara Markovića 20; ✆ 514 288. Tucked away in a shady courtyard just off Pobeda, this café-bar is a peaceful city oasis in warm weather.

🍺 **Lagano** [350 D5] Trg Republike 3; **m** 064 8058 890. Close to the eastern end of Kopitareva, this has pancakes, cakes & sandwiches, & excellent coffee.

✴ 🍺 **Ministarstvo Beer Bar** [351 E4] Vojvode Vuka 12; **m** 063 460 350; 🕙 08.30–midnight. A small friendly bar with probably the best selection of foreign beers in the city. Very reasonable prices.

🍺 **Na Ćošku** [350 C5] Kopitareva 1; ✆ 294 660. One of many café-bars on this short busy street, this one is 'on the corner' (*na ćošku*). Mostly popular with young people, especially at night.

🍺 **Pekara Branković** [350 C3] Trg Kralja Milana bb. An excellent bakery with outside seats on the square & a delicious choice of *pite, burek* & pizza slices. There are several other branches around the city, including one on Nikola Pašića.

🍺 **Poslastičara Turist** [350 C4] Obrenovićeva 25; ✆ 511 700. This is nothing to do with tourists but a sit-down ice-cream place with a tempting variety of flavours.

🍺 **Stock Coffee** [350 B4] Trg Kralja Aleksandra Ujedinitelja 1a; **m** 069 4335 544. The go-to place for coffee in the city, this small hipster-style place has a good variety of blends as well as muffins & snacks.

🍺 **Tramvaj** [350 C4] Obrenovićeva 20; ✆ 257 909; **w** caffetramvaj.rs. A large café halfway along Obrenovićeva with extensive indoor & outdoor seating. Light snacks, juices & a huge selection of ice creams.

FESTIVALS AND EVENTS Niš is host to a number of festivals throughout the year. During July, an **International Choir Competition** is held at various locations in the city. This is followed, in August, by the **Niš Film Festival**. This makes way for the two summer music festivals described below.

Nišville Jazz Festival (✆ 533 022; **w** *nisville.com*) This festival takes place over three days each August, when a variety of international artists perform on three stages in the fortress complex. The headliners in 2017 were Candy Dulfer and Patti Austin. The price of a four-night ticket is in the order of €25; one-day tickets cost €10.

Nišomnia Held in late summer, this is a three-day music festival. It was inaugurated in 2002, and for the past few years has taken place around three stages in the fortress complex. Nišomnia (motto: 'Stay awake') is in the same vein as Novi Sad's EXIT, but much smaller, with a mixture of live acts and DJ stages. For the first few years the festival took place in mid-August but this was moved to early September in 2006. Past line-ups have included a variety of home-grown live artists, along with acts from Germany, USA and the UK. Information on future events and line-ups can be found at the visitnis.com website.

OTHER PRACTICALITIES There are plenty of **banks** with ATMs throughout the city: There are numerous exchange offices along Obrenovićeva. The **post office** [350 D3] on Vožda Karađorđa offers internet access as well as postal services. Opposite the post office on the corner of Vožda Karađorđa and Orlovića Pavla is the Air Serbia office [350 D3]. There is a state-of-the-art, well-equipped **Clinical Centre** [351 H5] (✆ 506 906; **w** kcnis.rs) at Bulevar Dr Zorana Đinđića 48, and a large number of **pharmacies** scattered around the city.

WHAT TO SEE AND DO
Niš Fortress (Tvrđava) [350 C1] The fortifications that exist today date only as
far back as the beginning of the 18th century, but the Turkish fortress on the north
bank of the river that survives was built on the same site as earlier fortifications
of Roman, Byzantine and medieval origin. The fortress, which was constructed
between 1719 and 1723, extends over an area of 22ha, with 2,100m of wall 8m high
that has an average thickness of 3m. Outside the walls is a moat, the northern part
of which still survives. Of the original gates, the southern **Istanbul Gate (Stambol
kapija)** [350 C2], the main entrance today, and the northern, **Belgrade Gate
(Beogradska kapija)** [350 C1] are the best preserved. There are plans afoot for the
Tourist Organisation of Niš to open another office in the walls of the Istanbul Gate
at some stage in the future. The **hammam** [350 C2] by the Istanbul Gate, which is
now a restaurant, dates from the 15th century and is the oldest Turkish building
in the city. Water would have been brought to the bath from the Nišava River by
means of underground wooden pipes.

Just beyond the smart cafés that extend along the walls to the left of Istanbul Gate
is a curious monument that looks like an extended lipstick and which is dedicated to
Milan Obrenović and the liberation from Turkish rule. A little further on, standing
alone at the centre of the fortress area, is the early 16th-century **Mosque of Bali Beg**
[350 C1], now an art gallery. A library once stood next to the mosque but only a ruin
remains today. Close to Bali Beg's mosque is the **lapidarium** [350 C1], a small display
of Roman gravestones and sculpture found within the fortress area and gathered
together here. The **arsenal** [350 C2] to the right of the Istanbul Gate, which dates
from 1857, is now an art pavilion while the adjoining guards' rooms have found new
usage as a souvenir shop. On the northern side of the fortress are the remains of a
Roman building with some mosaics.

The whole of the fortress area is a popular venue for the citizens of Niš, especially
on warm summer evenings when the city's more youthful element congregates at
its bars and cafés. The Tvrđava complex also serves as a park area where joggers,
cyclists and young families with toddlers all make the most of the shade and
greenery. It is possible to climb up on the walls to get a better look over the city and
the Nišava River – just climb up the steps immediately to the right of Istanbul Gate
on the inside of the fortress.

Skull Tower (Ćele kula) [351 H5] (*Bulevar Dr Zorana Đinđića bb;* ☏ *222 228;*
⊕ *09.00–19.00 Tue–Fri, 09.00–17.00 Sat/Sun; admission 150din; a combined ticket
for Ćele kula, Mediana & Logor Crveni krst can be bought for 200/170din adult/
child*) This grotesque memorial was erected by the Turks as an example to others
of the folly of opposition to their rule. Its construction followed the Battle of
Čegar Hill in 1809 at the time of the First National Uprising when the Serbian
General Stevan Sinđelić – 'The Falcon of Čegar' – fearing an ignominious defeat,
famously blew up himself and his outnumbered troops, along with a large number
of Turks, by igniting a gunpowder store. It is estimated that about 3,000 Serbian
soldiers were killed in the explosion, along with at least double the number of
their Turkish counterparts.

The tower was the Turkish response to this defiant yet suicidal act. On the order
of the Turkish *paša* Hurshid, the Turkish commander at the time, Serbian skulls
were gathered from the battlefield and skinned before being mounted in rows on a
specially built 3m-high tower.

Originally there were 952 skulls embedded in the tower and past visitors to the
monument have written of its eerie quality. In 1833, the French poet Alphonse de

Lamartine stopped in front of the tower and recorded what he saw in his book, *Journey to the East*. He commented that:

> The skulls, bleached by the sun and rain … completely covered the victory monument. Some of the skulls still had hair on them which fluttered in the wind like leaves on trees …

He went on to write:

> My eyes and my heart greeted the remains of those brave men whose cut off heads made the corner stone of the independence of their homeland. May the Serbs keep the monument! It will always teach their children the value of the independence of a people, showing them the real price their fathers had to pay for it.

Now only 58 skulls remain, the rest taken for a proper burial or presumably prised out by souvenir hunters in the interim period. In 1892, a chapel was built around the depleted column and, rather than fulfilling its original purpose as a totem of deterrence, it was reinvented as a monument to the spirit of Serbian courage.

To visit the Skull Tower take a number 1, 3 or 10 bus from the stop on Vožda Karađorđa close to Trg Kralja Milana. The tower is within a small chapel in a park. Just before this is a ticket office where someone will sell you an entrance ticket and unlock the door.

Another tower exists on **Čegar Hill** outside the city at the site where the battle took place. It was erected on the 50th anniversary of the liberation of Niš from the Turks on 1 June 1927. In 1938, this was supplemented by a bronze bust of the Serbian hero Stevan Sinđelić.

Pobeda [350 C4] This is the main café-lined pedestrian street, otherwise known as Obrenovićeva, which runs from Trg Kralja Milana, with the tall edifice of the (closed) Hotel Ambasador and an equestrian statue dedicated to the Liberators of Niš, south past the Kalča Centre to Cara Dušana. There are several wealthy merchants' houses along its course, like that of Andon Andonović at number 41 built in 1930 in a neo-Renaissance style. At the bottom end in the small plaza at the western end of Kopitareva is an interesting and photogenic bronze sculpture that depicts two traditionally dressed Serbian men sitting at a table. Kopitareva, also sometimes referred to as Kazandžijsko sokače ('Tinkers' Alley'), dates back to the early part of the 18th century and was originally a street of tinkers and copper craftsmen.

National Museum of Niš [350 B4] (*Narodni muzej Niš; Nikole Pašića 59;* ☏ *511 531;* ⊕ *12.00–18.00 Tue–Fri, 10.00–15.00 Sat/Sun; admission 130din*) This was built in 1894 as a bank and was used for this purpose for 70 years until it became a museum in 1963. It houses an archaeological exhibition with a range of sculpture from Roman times.

Mediana [351 H5] Emperor Constantine the Great, who was born in Niš, is said to have returned a few times in his life. At Mediana, alongside modern-day Bulevar Cara Konstantina, the Niš–Niška Banja road, a luxurious villa was built at his command in the early 4th century. What remains today are the foundations of several buildings spread over an area of 40ha: a villa, a baptistry, baths, lesser villas and a granary. Much of the site has now been covered by a roof to protect the remains and mosaics from the elements.

East and Southeast Serbia NIŠ (НИШ)

8

There is evidence of a street that ran in an east–west direction, connecting the various buildings. The central area was taken up by the palace, nymphaeum and baths, while to the west was the granary and to the north, a building with octagonal and circular rooms. Domestic buildings lay to the south of the complex.

The **museum** (✆ 550 433; ⏰ 10.00–18.00 Tue–Fri, 10.00–15.00 Sat/Sun; admission 150din) has mosaics and an exhibition of various Roman artefacts found on the site.

Mediana is to the left of the main road that runs past Ćele kula to Niška Banja, about halfway to the spa.

Holy Trinity Cathedral [350 C6] (Crkva svete Trojice; Prijezdina 7; ⏰ 08.00–19.00 daily)

Built in the second half of the 19th century when the region was still under Turkish rule, this is the second largest Orthodox church in Serbia. Allied bombing in 1944 badly damaged the building, and a devastating fire in 2001 destroyed much of the original interior, but the cathedral has since been thoroughly renovated. It was reconsecrated in 2006.

Logor Crveni krst (Red Cross Camp) Museum [350 A1] (12 Februar Bulevar bb; ✆ 588 889; ⏰ 09.00–16.00 Tue–Fri, 10.00–15.00 Sat/Sun; admission 150din)

The camp was first built as an army depot in 1930 but was adopted by the Germans during World War II as a transit camp for Roma, Jews, Partisans and communists who were thrown in here prior to torture and/or execution or their deportation to death camps. It is a grey, sombre place that seems full of ghosts, as well it might. Despite hopeless odds, a desperate escape bid was made on 12 February 1942 when an attempted breakout was made by scaling the walls. At least 50 prisoners were machine-gunned down immediately, while another 100 managed to escape to freedom.

The main building on the right shows the conditions under which the prisoners had to live – on concrete floors with straw for bedding. The solitary confinement cells in the attic are perhaps the most chilling. On the walls are numerous photos of the inmates taken in happier times, their smiling, handsome faces blissfully unaware of the fate that was to befall them, making them all the more poignant. Another photograph shows the leering face of the camp commander, Kommandant Schulz, nicknamed 'Stick' because of his taste for beating inmates to death with his cudgel. All the captioning is in Cyrillic but this hardly detracts from the sheer existential horror of the place.

There is also a room that has paintings done by children from a local school, which graphically depict the scenes of horror in the camp – attempts on the wire, beatings, rapes, torture – in the earnest, unflinching manner of children whose imagination has been painfully awakened.

The perimeter walls, the barbed wire and the watchtowers are all still in place. Visiting the camp is hardly a fun day out but it is a sombre reminder of the dangers of totalitarianism and the horrors of war, not that any citizen of Niš should need reminding, given their city's turbulent history.

To reach Logor Crvni krst walk past the bus station on Bulevar 12 Februar and keep going until you reach the Kafana 'Dve Lipe'. Turn right here across an area of wasteland to enter through the camp gates. Tickets are sold at the gatehouse to the left of the entrance. At the time of writing the camp was closed because of reconstruction.

The city's ghoulish memories do not end at Ćele kula and Crveni krst. Southwest of the city, on top of Bubanj Hill [350 A5], stands the **Bubanj Monument**. This monument, which resembles three giant clenched fists, commemorates the death of over 10,000 Niš inhabitants who were shot up here on the hill during World War II. The monument, the work of sculptor Ivan Sabolić, was erected in 1963 and symbolises the popular resistance to Nazi oppression.

In the same spirit, but much more recent, is the **Commemorative Chapel** [350 C2] (built in 2000) in the park by the main entrance to the fortress, which was constructed in memory of the civilians killed during the NATO bombardment of 1999.

The market area Just like a medieval city, the market area in Niš is clustered around the fortress, which is probably exactly where it was during Ottoman times.

To the left of Istanbul Gate, heading towards the bus station, is a small outdoor market, **Svetna pijaca** [350 C2], which sells mostly clothes and household items. A little further on is the much larger **Tvrđava pijaca** [350 B2], a vast indoor market with row upon row of stalls selling fresh vegetables, fruit, meat and fish. Around the entrance to these markets, and along the congested roadway of Đuke Dinić that links them, are dozens more vendors selling all manner of things: mushrooms, plums in buckets, sprigs of herbs and dried flowers. Most of the vendors are old, black-clad, country women or Roma of either sex, too marginalised by poverty and the limited goods they have for sale to afford a pitch inside. Indeed, it is in this part of Niš that the city's large Roma population becomes evident, their obvious poverty in stark contrast to those other citizens who frequent the fashionable cafés across the river in Pobeda. Also along the same street are several Chinese supermarkets – each one an Aladdin's cave of cheap imported goods. There is a sizeable Chinese community in Niš, although they tend to keep a low profile.

Walking in the opposite direction from the fortress gate, east along Jadranska next to the river, you pass through an area that at weekends is given over to a **flea market** [350 D1/2], with impromptu stalls with umbrellas on both sides of the road, and the pavement itself crowded with vendors. All manner of things are on sale: spare parts for cars, old clothes, medals, cutlery, pots and pans, tools and household goods – in fact, anything that people might conceivably want to buy at a bargain price. The market is on Saturdays and Sundays only and lasts from early morning until around 14.00.

Across the river from the fortress and weekend market, in a shady park next to Kej 29 Decembar, stands a statue dedicated to the memory of the Roma singer **Šaban Bajramović** [350 D2], the 'King of the Gypsies', who was a citizen of Niš. Despite enormous musical success and acclaim during the course of his colourful life, Bajramović died in poverty in the city in 2008 (pages 52–3).

AROUND NIŠ
Niška Banja (Нишка Бања) A health resort, Niška Banja is built around a natural hot mineral spring on a hillside 10km east of the city. The mildly radioactive waters are said to help rheumatic and cardiovascular complaints. Naturally, it was the spa-loving Romans who first discovered the spring. Following the Ottoman colonisation the Turks built *hammams* to take advantage of the natural source. The water is used for bathing, drinking and steam inhalation. Mud packs are also prepared, using a combination of the water from the spring and peat. There are eight indoor swimming pools filled with naturally heated water, as well as special treatment rooms for specific complaints. Scattered around the resort are pools and channels of warm spring water where you can soak your feet to your heart's content. Bear in mind that the water is slightly radioactive and so it is wise not

to do this endlessly. Above the complex are steps that lead up into the fragrant woods beyond – a nice place for a leisurely walk and an escape from the noise and heat of the city in summer.

There is **tourist information** (✆ *4548 588*; w *visitnis.com*) at Sinđelićeva 3b, just above the defunct Hotel Srbija and bus terminus.

🏠 ***Where to stay and eat*** Niška Banja could serve as an alternative place to stay if all of the hotels in Niš turn out to be full (highly unlikely) or if you just prefer somewhere quieter. If you are looking for private accommodation the branch of the Tourist Organisation of Niš at Sinđelićeva 3b should be able to help. There also a few '*sobe*' signs scattered around. A large **communal restaurant** serves both of the main hotels, which are more used to guests taking full or half board, rather than just bed and breakfast. Other options for eating are the **Kafana Beli Dvor** (*Ruzveltova 81*; ✆ *4548 801*; €), **Kafana Brka** (*Jelašnica*; ✆ *4640 113*; €) and **Mitke** (*Železnička bb*; m *062 8690 826*; €).

🏠 **Hotel Ozren *** (143 rooms, 4 suites) Trg Republike bb; ✆ 4549 008. The hotel now consists of 2 separate wings, A & B, one of which was formerly the Hotel Partizan. €€

🏠 **Institute Niška Banja** Srpskih Junaka 2; ✆ 502 211; e marketing.sluzba@randonnb.co.rs; w radonnb.co.rs. The institute has 3 3-star hotels in the resort – Radon, Terme & Zelengora – with more than 500 beds between them. You could stay at any of these although visitors might be expected to sign up for some form of remedial medical treatment. €€

🏠 **Vila Priča** (6 rooms, 3 apts) Vidolja Jovanovića prilaz 1, 7; ✆ 4547 295; e vilaprica@ yahoo.com; w vilaprica.rs. In the centre close to the spa. Smart, modern rooms with cable TV, minibar, AC & internet access. €€

🏠 **Vila Zone** (15 apts) Petra Seratića 8; ✆ 4549 838; e zone@vagres.rs; w zone.vagres. rs. An attractive modern building in the centre of the spa. Dbl, trpl & 4-bed apartments, each with kitchen, bath, cable TV & internet access. Free parking. Very good value for money, especially for stays over 6 days, which receive a discount. €€–€

SOKOBANJA (СОКОБАЊА) *Telephone code 018*

Sokobanja is a pleasant resort town to the north of Niš on the banks of the Moravica River, roughly halfway along the main Aleksinac–Knjaževac road. It is set in a valley at an altitude of 400m surrounded by the mountains of Ozren (1,174m), Devica (1,187m) and Rtanj (1,568m). The town takes its name from Sokograd (Hawk's Town), a medieval 7th-century fortified complex 2km away that stands on top of a steep rocky outcrop.

Sokobanja's thermal springs have been known since Roman times. The Turks continued the tradition and built a *hammam* here in the 17th century and the town remains a popular destination for Serbian holidaymakers. Organised spa-tourism began here in 1837 when Prince Miloš sent one of his soldiers here for treatment. Already he had ordered the renovation of the *hammam*, following the departure of the Turks, and the spa became a popular summer holiday spot for Belgrade intellectuals throughout the 19th century. The *hammam* has been restored and reopened as a wellness centre (✆ *830 914*) in recent years. Miloš's residence in the town, **Milošev Konak**, is still standing and is now used as a café.

Sokobanja has the distinct advantage of being close to excellent walking country and so a stay here does not necessarily have to mean days of languid inactivity, although that is perfectly feasible too should you so wish. The town itself is quite pleasant, with more character than most spa resorts and it is an ideal base for cycling or fine walks in the nearby hills.

TOURIST INFORMATION Information on local walks, accommodation and events in the town can be had from the helpful tourist information centre in the town centre (*Trg oslobođenja 2;* \ *833 988;* e *tic@otks.org.rs;* w *otks.org.rs;* ⏲ *07.00–15.00 Mon–Fri*).

The following local tourist agencies can assist in organising excursions:

Mogi-turs Omladinski 1; \ 830 247
Ozren Turist 27 mart 31; \ 880 088

Sokotours Čair bb; \ 880 100

🏠 **WHERE TO STAY AND EAT** There are plenty of places to stay in the town, most of which offer full board. There are a number of large, state-owned hotels like the hotels Moravica, Sunce and Zdravljak, as well as more recently opened private pensions that tend to be smaller and intimate, and generally cheaper.

Of the pensions, both **Pansion Restaurant Aleksandar** (\ *830 153;* €) and **Pansion Splendid** (\ *830 634;* €) on Kralja Petra I, around the corner from Hotel Turist, offer good value. Renting an apartment or taking comfortable homestay accommodation with a local family are further options that can be booked through the tourist office. All of the hotels and pensions have their own restaurants and provide full board should you require it. Like most spa resorts, eating out often means pizzas.

Sokobanja is also a centre for **rural tourism**, which is developing in the surrounding countryside in villages like Vrmdza, Resnik, Trubarevac and Jošanica. Details of rooms in private homes (€) may be had at the town's tourist office or by looking at the website w sokobanja.rs.

Other places to eat in the town besides the listings below include **Hajduk Veljko** (\ *834 329;* €€), in the centre. The **Milošev Konak** at the end of the pedestrian zone has the Irish pub '**Dublin**' (m *063 429 923;* €).

🏠 **Hotel Banjica** ** (108 rooms) Milutina Pejovića 40; \ 830 224, 830 204. Typical spa-style hotel. €€

🏠 **Hotel Moravica** *** (95 rooms, 6 apts) Timočke bune 4; \ 830 622, 830 602; e director@ hotelmoravica.rs; w hotelmoravica.rs. A modern tourist hotel with comfortable rooms. Writer Ivo Andrić used to stay here & the hotel has a memorial room devoted to him. Conference hall, national restaurant, sports facilities. €€

🏠 **Hotel Sunce** ** (100 rooms, 3 apts) Radnička 2; \ 830 047. Slightly less well appointed than the Moravica. Conference hall, swimming pool, sauna & discotheque. €€

🏠 **Hotel Turist** *** (43 rooms) Kralja Petra I bb; \ 833 232. A central hotel with terrace & garden. €€

🏠 **Hotel Zdravljak** *** (236 rooms, 6 apts) Miladina Živanovića 40; \ 830 722, 830 702; e hotelzdravljak@gmail.com. A very large hotel complex with tennis courts & sports facilities close to the bus station. €€

🍽 **Caffe Pizzeria Amam** Svetog Save bb (opposite the Turkish *hammam*); \ 830 687. Terrace & garden café with coffee, pizzas & draught beers, & occasional live music. €€

✖ **Čikago** Ljube Didića 2; \ 884 400. €

✖ **Kaskade** Ozrenska 13; \ 837 719. €

✖ **Župan** Jabukar 1; m 064 1115 837. A central restaurant that offers a range of typical Serbian dishes at good prices. Has an excellent 'special offers' menu available each day. €

WHAT TO SEE AND DO
Sokograd (Сокоград) This was first occupied in Roman times and the foundations date from that period. The fortress was constructed in the 7th century in two parts: a lower fort with a cistern that served as its water supply, and a smaller upper fort with seven towers that would have been used as living quarters. The fortress was destroyed by Turks in 1413.

Although Sokograd lies in ruins it is still well worth a visit, if only for the view of the surrounding countryside.

The best way to reach Sokograd from the town is to cross the sports fields north of the Hotel Moravica, then head through the woods to reach a picnic spot from where a steep path climbs up to the ruins. This can be slippery in wet weather, so take care. An alternative route coming back is to retrace your steps to the picnic place then follow the tarmac road downhill for a while before taking a footpath to the right that leads through woodland to the river. This will lead you to a cave that sometimes operates as a restaurant – **Restoran Pećina** (✆ *830 678*). The restaurant is not always open; it seems to depend on the weather. From here, follow the river south for a short way before taking the upper of two paths that leads over rocks and fields and then through woodland to emerge on the south side of the Hotel Moravica.

Sokobanja environs and the Moravica Valley (Моравица Долина) There

is a variety of walks and cycle rides that can be made in the Moravica Valley using Sokobanja as a base. To the south of the river, a gentle climb 8km to the west takes you to the tiny village of **Resnik** where there is a working water-powered flour mill, the project of a retired librarian from Sokobanja. It is hoped that government money will be forthcoming to fully restore the mill in the future. On the other side of the valley **Jošanica** is another village renowned for its restorative and healing waters. There are four varieties of mineral water here, two of which contain iron in varying concentrations (for treating anaemia), one that is very sulphurous and another that is categorised as an 'everyday' type of mineral water. This is supposed to be the only place in Serbia that has water capable of treating thrombosis. Jošanica's village church is relatively modern but next door is a tiny chapel, Crkva Velika Gospodina, which has an interior covered in intact frescoes. Local legend tells that bones and broken skulls were found beneath the exonarthex here (now missing), the handiwork of occupying Turks who caved in the heads of their victims.

Five kilometres east of Jošanica lies **Vrmdža**, a lovely, peaceful village with plenty of old wooden houses and a backdrop of sheer, rocky outcrops. It is certainly a beautiful village but life is undoubtedly hard for those – mostly elderly – villagers who scratch a living here. The village has a small shop, which also serves as a *kafana*, but nothing more.

There are two mountains that can be climbed in the Sokobanja region: 1,568m-high **Rtanj** to the north and **Oštra Čuko**, at 1,075m, the third-highest summit of the Devica massif to the south. Rtanj is a near-perfect V-shape, almost like a volcano, and is said to be the best place in Serbia for gathering a special herb that is used for making 'Rtanj tea'. The best approach is probably from the village of the same name that lies immediately north of Sokobanja. Oštra Čuko can be reached by a lengthy road walk to the south followed by a steep climb through meadows replete with all manner of wild flowers in spring and summer – geraniums, peonies and orchids. Oštra Čuko means 'sharp peak' and the name becomes clear during the last 200m of the climb: a scramble up jagged limestone to the summit.

EAST OF NIŠ

Beyond Niška Banja the road east follows the Nišava River to reach the **Sićevačka Gorge** (Sićevačka Klisura). The two-lane E-80 is often busy and congested here, especially with trucks, as this is the main road that leads to Sofia, Istanbul and the Middle East beyond. All road freight coming from or going in that direction needs to take this route. Just as in Ottoman times there is still a major trade of goods between eastern Europe and the Near East, but these days the caravans consist mostly of heavy goods vehicles. All of this will change in the near future when the new Niš to Sofia motorway via Jelašnica opens for traffic, making the Sićevačka Gorge an altogether more peaceful place.

The sheer cliffs of the Sićevačka Gorge rise high above the road to the south here, with the occasional bird of prey circling above the rumbling procession of trucks.

SIĆEVO (СИЋЕВО) The small village of Sićevo stands high above the road to the north. It is worth driving up here if you have your own car, as the view over the gorge from the village is stunning. Sićevo is a wine-growing centre, and there are vineyards stretching up the hillside all around the village. The vines, the rustic quietness and the stone houses of the village, all give the impression that you have momentarily been transported to Provence. Next to the village car park is the building of the local wine-growers' co-operative, and across from this is the household of the Vidanović family who will be happy to sell you the fruit of their vines. They have red and white wines made from their own grapes, as well as *šljivovica*, *vinjak* and other spirits that they sell straight from the barrel.

There is another interesting and historic vineyard in the area at the village of **Malča** west of Sićevo, where the Vinski Podrum Malča (m *062 8015 745*; w *podrummalca. com*) produces some of its wine by using the old Roman method of fermenting in amphorae. There is a shop here selling the whole range of wines produced by the vineyard as well as a museum and an excellent restaurant (€€).

GORNJI METEJEVAC (ГОРЊИ МЕТЕЈЕВАЦ) This village, 8km northeast of Niš and part of the Pantelej municipality of the city, is home to the small Byzantine church **Latinska Crkva** – the oldest church in the region. The church, of brick and stone with a Byzantine dome, was probably constructed in the late 11th or early 12th century during the reign of Emperor Manuel Comninos. It served as a Catholic church in the 16th century for the Ragusa colony but fell out of use in the 19th century when a new place of worship was erected in the village.

KNJAŽEVAC (КЊАЖЕВАЦ) *Telephone code 019*

Leaving Niš in the direction of Pirot, a minor road leads off north from the city outskirts towards Svrljig and Knjaževac. This is a highly scenic route that follows a minor river valley as far as Svrljig with the wooded slopes of the Svrljig Hills (Svrljiške planina) rising to the east. The oak forest along this route is a sight to behold late in the year around October, when the leaves turn to fiery red and yellow. The rest of the year is a pastoral delight too, with golden corn in the fields and colourful wild flowers on the grassy verges.

Svrljig is a typical small country town with little to distinguish it other than a name that manages to stack five consonants in a row – the sort of thing that Serbs delight in hearing foreigners struggle with (they enjoy foreign attempts at 'vrh' (peak) too; but that is easy, just pronounce it 'vrrkh' like a Scot might). At the entrance to town on the Niš side is the **Kamiondžija Kvalitet** restaurant (*Dušana Trivunća 35*; \ *821 268*; w *restorankamiondzije.com*; ⊕ *08.00–midnight*; €€), which is well known throughout all of southeast Serbia and highly popular because of its enormous helpings (see box, page 369).

The origins of Knjaževac date back to the time of the Romans when there was the settlement of **Timacum Minus** in the area. The modern town stands close to the Roman site. The town that developed became known by the name of Gurgosovac

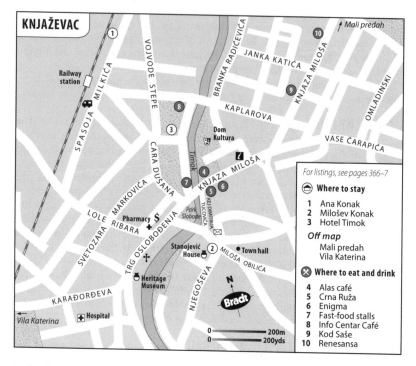

KNJAŽEVAC

Railway station

Mali predah

Dom Kultura

Pharmacy
Park Slobode
Kej Dimitrija Tucovića

Stanojević House

Town hall

Heritage Museum

Hospital

Vila Katerina

0	200m
0	200yds

Bradt

For listings, see pages 366–7

🏠 **Where to stay**

1 Ana Konak
2 Milošev Konak
3 Hotel Timok

Off map

Mali predah
Vila Katerina

✖ **Where to eat and drink**

4 Alas café
5 Crna Ruža
6 Enigma
7 Fast-food stalls
8 Info Centar Café
9 Kod Saše
10 Renesansa

in the Ottoman period but, in 1859, after liberation from Turkish rule, this changed to become Knjaževac. Today, the town is a peaceful, relaxing sort of place, with a pleasantly green riverbank area and some attractive 19th-century buildings along the stretch of the Timok River that flows through the town centre.

GETTING THERE AND AWAY Knjaževac's bus and railway stations sit side by side just to the west of the town centre. The town's **bus station** (☎ 733 027) might appear dilapidated and dysfunctional but it seems to work well enough, with regular services north to Zaječar and south to Niš, and less frequent services west to Sokobanja. Some of the services to Zaječar continue to Bor, or to Negotin and Kladovo. The **railway station** (☎ 731 147) has five services a day to Niš and Zaječar, and a morning train to Bor.

 WHERE TO STAY AND EAT *Map, page 366*

The Hotel Timok, the large state-owned hotel in the town centre, has been renovated in recent years, but there are a couple more options in and around town.

For eating and drinking, as well as the choices below there are **fast-food stalls** by the river at the bridge that leads to Knjaza Miloša, the **Alas café** opposite at Knjaza Miloša 1, and plenty of café-bars like **Enigma** along Knjaza Miloša itself. The **Crna Ruža** café around the corner on Kej Dimitrija Tucovića next to the river is another good place to watch the world go by.

🏠 **Hotel Timok** (40 rooms) Stevana Mokranjca 2; ☎ 731 122, 731 102. This state-owned hotel in a central park has been partially renovated. All rooms have AC, Wi-Fi & cable TV. Favoured largely by sports teams, its 200-seat restaurant is often hired for large private functions. **€€€–€€**

🏠 **Vila Katerina** (20 rooms, 4 suites) Karađorđeva bb; ☎ 733 379, 733 479. 4km from the town centre on the Sokobanja road. All rooms with AC, minibar, satellite TV & internet connection. This also has a restaurant. €€

🏠 **Mali predah** *** (22 rooms, 4 apts) Mile Julinog 4; ☎739 100, 739 200; e mali.predah@ mts.rs; w malipredah.com. A large restaurant with rooms at the junction of the Knjaževac–Pirot & Niš–Zaječar roads (go north along Knjaza Miloša from the centre, over the bridge then right). Clean rooms & helpful staff. €€

🏠 **Milošev Konak** (5 rooms) Njegoševa 4; ☎732 103. A cosy national restaurant (€) with rooms that have AC, Wi-Fi & modern bathroom. €€

🏠 **Ana Konak** (8 rooms) Spasoja Milkića 1; ☎730 185. Also referred to as 'Bela Sala', this white-brick building is close to the railway station with a 'ПРЕНОЋИШТЕ' (Prenoćište – 'lodging') sign. The reception is up the flight of stairs. Good clean rooms with bath & TV. €

🖳 **Info Centar Café** Kej V Vlahovića bb; m 063 826 318. A pleasant coffee-bar with a terrace facing the park. €

🍴 **Kod Saše** Knjaza Miloša 131a; ☎732 446. A very friendly ćevapdžinica with a cosy dining room. €

🍴 **Renesansa** Knjaza Miloša 163; ☎731 999. A spacious ćevapdžinica with standard Serbian fare. €

OTHER PRACTICALITIES

$ **Bank** Unicredit banka: Trg oslobođenja 12; ☎730 129

➕ **Hospital** Karađorđeva; ☎731 526

➕ **Pharmacy** Gradski pharmacy: Lole Ribara 2; ☎731 603

✉ **Post office** Kej Dimitrija Tucovića 1; ☎735 166

ℹ **Tourist information** Knjaza Miloša 37; ☎735 230; e toknjazevac@open.telekom.rs; w toknjazevac.org.rs

WHAT TO SEE AND DO Knjaževac has few specific sights and is more a place for gentle strolls along the riverbank. The **Stari čarsija** quarter alongside the river between the footbridges consists of a short row of colourfully painted 19th-century buildings that mostly serve as old-fashioned shops. There is a viewpoint directly above these that gives a good view of the town. This can be reached by taking the road that runs parallel behind past the police station. Opposite the 19th-century houses is the shady **Park Slobode** and a road, Karađorđeva, which curves uphill past a church.

It is possible to follow the bank of the **Timok River** through the town and some way out into the surrounding countryside by taking the path that leads from the post office. This eventually crosses another bridge from where it passes through grassy meadows to reach open fields.

More specific sights in the town include the **Heritage Museum (Zavičajni musej)** (*Karađorđeva 15;* ☎*731 407*), which was built in 1906 and has displays documenting the history of the town from the Roman period to the present day. It also has a collection of woollen socks from the region. The **Stanojević House (Musej Kuća Bore Stanojevića)** (*Njegoševa 6;* ☎*732 228*) is the house museum of a local artist.

STARA PLANINA (СТАРА ПЛАНИНА) *Telephone code 019*

The Stara Planina (Old Mountain) range straddles the border between Serbia and Bulgaria southwest of Knjaževac. The whole range falls within the confines of the **Stara Planina Nature Park**, the largest protected area in Serbia. **Midžor**, Serbia's highest peak at 2,169m, is the tallest summit here but more impressive, at least in terms of rugged scenery, is **Babin Zub**, a peak composed of a group of jagged rocks found to the southwest of Midžor. The name Babin Zub translates as 'Grandma's Tooth', a name that makes more sense after a glimpse at the near-vertical precipitous rocks on display here that do look just a little like worn-out canines. The summit is at an altitude of 1,757m, a few hundred metres short of Serbia's highest point.

8

Formerly there was just a small ski resort here along with a couple of places to stay. This has changed dramatically in recent years with the controversial development of a large-scale resort with numerous ski runs and attendant infrastructure. Naturally, this has had considerable effect on the local environment and, in addition to ecological concerns, there remain serious doubts as to whether there is a market for such capacity and whether global warming will inevitably reduce the amount of snow available for prospective skiers.

PIROT (ПИРОТ) *Telephone code 010*

Pirot lies 70km east of Niš, about 1½ to 2 hours by bus, depending on the traffic. This sleepy town on the Nišava River has little for sightseers but it still has some repute as a centre for *čilim* (Turkish: *kilim*) weaving (see box, page 371). If you are passing through to Bulgaria, it is well worth a stop, and it also serves as a good base from which to explore the surrounding countryside, in particular the Jerma Valley. Pirot can also be visited as a longish day trip from Niš.

These days the town is somewhat in decline. Its economy is centred upon the rubber industry, and factories at the edge of town still produce rubber goods like wellington boots and tractor tyres. Pirot's other industry used to be the mass production of textiles (factory-made carpets, not *čilims*), but that has completely collapsed in recent years.

The town is actually older than you might think. It was marked on Roman maps from the 2nd century AD as Mutatio Tures. Later on, Greeks would call the town Pirgos, which Serbs changed to Pirot in the 14th century. Turks took control of the town in 1415, renaming it Šahir kej, which roughly means 'town-village'. It remained in Turkish hands until 1878 and was later occupied by Bulgarians during both World War I and II. Pirot currently has a population of around 40,000. It was awarded city status in 2016.

GETTING THERE AND AWAY Pirot can be reached by train or bus by direct services from Belgrade, and 11 buses a day run to and from Niš. Both the **railway station** (☏ 322 528) and the town's small **bus station** (☏ 320 758) are on the north side of the town, east of the Nišava River.

TOURIST INFORMATION

🛈 Srpskih vladara 77; ☏ 320 838; w topirot. com; ◷ 07.30–17.00 w/days, 09.00–13.00 Sat.

The office can be a little hard to find, tucked away beside the theatre on the main square.

WHERE TO STAY AND EAT

The hotels below have their own restaurants, but a few additional dining options are listed. A culinary speciality of the region is *peglane kobasice* ('flattened sausage'). There are more traditional restaurants to be found in the centre around Srpskih vladara. Otherwise, there are a few fast-food places by the bridge like the **Čevapnička Šeki** and **Lion Roštilj**. The **Caffe Diavolo** (*Dragoševa 125;* ☏ *310 807;* €) and the central **Caffe Lisa** (*Srpskih vladara 20;* ☏ *341 750;* €) are both reasonable places to have a drink. There is also a parade of cafés that serve snacks and light meals along Dobrice Milutinovića, a pedestrian street behind the main square between Hotel Pirot and Dom Kulture. This area stands at the centre of Pirot's nightlife scene, such as it is.

🏠 **Hotel Analux ★★★★** (55 rooms, 5 suites) Srpskih vladara bb; ☏ 500 200; e office@hotel-

anakux.rs; w hotel-analux.rs. Brand-new (2016) 4-star hotel in the city centre with pleasant bright rooms, with minibar, cable TV, Wi-Fi & AC. Also rooms adapted for those with disabilities. Suites have kitchen & spacious living room. Spa, conference hall, restaurant, mezzanine café & banqueting hall. €€€

🏠 **Hotel Gali **** (25 rooms, 2 apts) Srpskih vladara 179; ☏ 324 324; e galidoo.pirot@open. telekom.rs; w hotelgali-serbia.com. Convenient & comfortable hotel in the centre of town, south of the central square. Separate restaurant for b/fast; free secure parking & internet access, TV & AC in rooms. €€

🏠 **Crystal Lights** (15 rooms, 1 apt) Nikole Pašića 184; ☏ 2100 147, 2100 148; e prenocistecrystal@gmail.com; w crystallights. rs. A small hotel with simple but clean dbl & trpl rooms. Discounts for groups. €€

🏠 **Hotel Sin-Kom ***** (19 rooms) Nikole Pašića bb; ☏ 322 505, 322 510; e hotelsinkom@ gmail.com; w hotel-sinkom.com. Modern hotel across the river on the northern side of town beyond the bus station. Cosy rooms with AC, TV & internet access. €€

✗ **Boem** Lava Tolstoja 15; m 064 1151 278. A cosy *kafana* with the usual grilled meat selection. €€–€

✗ **Dukat** Vuka Pantelića 55; ☏ 310 510; ⏰ Mon–Sat. A traditional *taverna* with good grill dishes & live music some nights. €€–€

✗ **Kraljev Čardak** Nikole Pašića 35; ☏ 346 737. Another traditional-style restaurant with good food & ambience. €€–€

WHAT TO SEE AND DO Walking south from the bus station and past a market area you soon reach a bridge that crosses the Nišava River. There are nice shady walks along the river if you follow the bank to the left here. In summer, local children swim from some of the river beaches. Continuing across the bridge, you soon come to the town's central square, **Srpskih vladara**. Turning right at the main street here leads back to the river and the site of **Momčilov grad**, a Turkish fort – or *kale* – of Byzantine origin that has quite well-preserved remains. Most of the fortifications

East and Southeast Serbia PIROT (ПИРОТ)

8

date from the 14th century. Occasional theatrical and musical performances take place here in the summer months. There is a bus stop and a ticket kiosk outside the *kale* where all buses to and from the town will stop.

Another place of interest in the town is the **Ponišavlje Museum** (*Nikole Pašića 49;* ℡ *313 850, 313 851;* ⊕ *08.00–15.00 Mon–Fri, 10.00–14.30 Sat; admission 100din*), which is located in one of the town's few remaining 19th-century *konaks*. The house museum, which is the former residence of local merchant Hristic Jovanović and his family, is lavishly furnished with carpets, fine furniture and carvings, and houses an interesting collection of folk costumes, pottery and, of course, *čilims*.

AROUND PIROT

THE JERMA VALLEY (ЈЕРМА ДОЛИНА) From Pirot, the E-80 continues to the Bulgarian border along a narrow canyon where the road and railway line are squeezed in next to each other. Just beyond Dimitrograd lies the frontier with Bulgaria. This is a wild region and one that requires private transport to explore properly. For the intrepid, there is the **Monastery of Poganovo** to visit along a quiet, country back road southwest of Dimitrograd in the **Jerma Valley**. This beautiful valley follows the course of the River Jerma, close to and more or less parallel to the Bulgarian frontier. As well as the Poganovo Monastery, which stands about halfway along it, there is another, less ancient monastery at **Sukovo** that is currently under restoration by a dedicated priest. The whole valley is a peaceful, bucolic sort of place, with neat haystacks in fields and rambling farmsteads with wooden corn granaries and neat piles of firewood stacked for winter. It is also a rather depopulated area; farming is not very profitable here and most young people leave for the towns as soon as they are able.

The scenery is quite gorgeous here and the village of Poganovo, set off from the road a few kilometres south of the monastery, has a particularly beautiful setting, sitting in the shadow of a large rocky outcrop. Heading west from Poganovo Monastery the valley narrows to a gorge where the road is tightly squeezed in between high rocky cliffs and the river in places. At the sleepy, half-deserted village of Zvonce, near the resort of Zvonačka Banja, another road climbs northwest towards Babušnica and then drops down into the valley east of the Suva Planina (Dry Mountain) range to rejoin the E-80 highway at Bela Palanka.

What to see and do The Jerma Valley provides ideal terrain for cycling: the road is good; the scenery, wonderful; the traffic, very light. It is also an excellent region for hiking. Without your own transport it is difficult to reach this area but it can be done by public transport ... just. Two daily buses leave Pirot for Zvonačka Banja, one in the morning and the other in the early afternoon. Both go via Sukovo, and drive the length of the Jerma Valley, passing Poganovo Monastery *en route*. Unfortunately, there is nowhere to stay along the valley as the Hotel Mir at Zvonačka Banja appeared to be closed on last inspection. Check whether it has reopened with tourist information at Pirot or Niš. They might also be able to advise on private accommodation in villages along the valley. Camping might be an option too.

POGANOVO MONASTERY This monastery, 25km south of Pirot, close to the Bulgarian border, was built at the end of the 14th century by the endowment of Serbian nobleman Konstantin Dejanović and his daughter Jelena. Jelena would go on to marry the Byzantine emperor Manojlo II but Konstantin died shortly after founding the monastery in 1395, fighting at the Battle of the Ravine. As a result, the

THE *ČILIM* WEAVERS OF PIROT

The carpet-making tradition in the southeast Serbian town of Pirot goes back at least seven centuries, a skill first introduced by the Turks and one that was continued after their eventual departure. Part of the reason for the tradition to establish itself here, rather than anywhere else, is the surrounding countryside. To the east of Pirot, and reaching up to the Bulgarian frontier, is a region of parched craggy hills and arid mountains where villagers eke out a living by rearing sheep. Having a ready source of raw material so close to hand helped to maintain the tradition in the town. Nowadays, many of the mountain villages are severely depopulated, with only the older villagers remaining – sheep-farming with its hard life and low profits is something that rural youth does not wish to pursue – and this has had its effect on wool production in the region.

Čilim production is a cottage industry, done solely by women, with the carpets being made on looms that are kept in the weavers' homes. The carpets are woven, not knotted – exactly the same technique used to make *kilims* in Turkey and central Asia – and because of this flat weave they are reversible, unlike a knotted carpet. *Čilims* can be made in any size required and are used for a variety of purposes: as floor covering, wall hangings, throws for furniture, even for cushion covers and bags.

Čilim manufacture in Pirot is not quite yet in its death throes but it has declined steeply in recent years. As recently as 1965, there were up to 1,800 townswomen involved in *čilim* production; now there are only 15 who still weave. Those few who keep up the tradition would like to encourage others to train in the art but learning the necessary skills is time-consuming (on average, training to a reasonable standard, at 4 hours a day, three days a week, takes around six months).

There are currently two state-run workshops in Pirot but they are a little run-down and only function periodically. There is vague talk of setting up a *čilim* museum, something that Pirot's women weavers would dearly love to see, but without government funding it is unlikely that this will become a reality in the near future.

Weaving *čilim* is hard work: to produce about one-quarter of a metre of carpet takes about a month, working part-time. Traditionally, only natural dyes were used, although chemical dyes are easier and are sometimes used these days, instantly recognisable for their brighter, more garish colours. The designs of the carpets utilise a range of fairly standardised motifs, many of which reflect their Turkish origin and incorporate Islamic patterns like that of a stylised *mihrab* (originally used in prayer rugs) and the universal 'Tree of Life' design. With the development of *čilim*-weaving in Orthodox Serbia, these historic patterns have become Christianised, with the inclusion of Orthodox symbols like fish and incense-holder motifs into the pattern. Certainly, the (Orthodox Serb) women who weave these carpets today are blissfully unaware of any remaining Islamic elements in their work.

interior of the church remained bare for over 100 years until frescoes were finally added at the turn of the 16th century. The frescoes, probably the work of Greek artists, are well preserved and display images of St Simeon, St Sava and St John as well as depictions of Christ's washing of the feet and scenes of Calvary. Some of the saints' eyes have been scratched away, either by Muslims incensed at the portrayal of the human form or, more likely, by pious worshippers who believed the pigment could cure failing eyesight.

The church, dedicated to St John the Divine, is an example of the Morava School, shaped like a clover leaf with three semicircular apses and an octagonal dome above the naos. A large bell tower stands above the narthex. The airy, pantiled porch is a far more recent, 19th-century, addition, as are the living quarters.

The monastery lies just across a wooden bridge from the road. Opposite, on the road itself, is the **Kafana Poganovo**, a suitable place for a drink or a bite to eat.

LESKOVAC (ЛЕСКОВАЦ) *Telephone code 016*

The E-75 dual carriageway degrades into a two-lane road just south of the city. It continues through a wide flat plain to reach Leskovac, 40km south.

Leskovac used to be known as the 'Serbian Manchester' because it once had a thriving cotton industry, which, as with its northern England counterpart, is now much in decline. Leskovac is probably better known these days for its spicy barbecued meat dishes – many towns throughout the country have restaurants that claim to serve genuine *Leskovačka roštilje* (Leskovac grill) dishes. The town has made the most of this foody connection by promoting a week-long annual event known as '**Roštiljijada**' in late August and early September – an event in which the eating of an inordinate amount of grilled meat is accompanied by fireworks, concerts and cookery competitions. The organisers of *Roštiljijada 2009* claim to have attracted 500,000 visitors to the town for the event.

Much of old Leskovac was destroyed during World War II by Anglo-American bombing and so most of the town centre is of a modern build. A few older buildings have survived along Bulevar oslobođenja and there is an early 19th-century church just off this thoroughfare next to a five-domed modern (1931) equivalent. The **town museum** (*Stojana Ljubića 2; ☎ 212 975; ⏰ 08.00–16.00 Tue–Sat; admission 100din*) is nearby in another 19th-century house.

 WHERE TO STAY AND EAT There is a reasonable choice of places to stay. For eating, given the town's reputation for grilled meat excellence, any of the central restaurants should be able to offer decent food.

ABC Hotel ★★★ (15 rooms, 3 apts) Južnomoravskih brigade 210; ☎ 234 040; e office@hotelhajats.com; w abcleskovac.com. Built in 2012, this is probably the best hotel in town, with smart modern rooms all having AC, minibar, satellite TV & Wi-Fi. Parking, terrace restaurant. €€€

Stojanović Hajat S ★★★ (50 rooms, 6 apts) Južnomoravskih brigade 210; ☎ 222 511; e office@hotelhajats.com; w hotelhajats.com. Business hotel, all rooms having AC, minibar, satellite TV & internet connection. €€€

Garni Hotel Đermanović (8 rooms, 5 apts) Učitelja Josifa 19; ☎ 242 456, 237 731; e info@djermanovic.co.rs; w djermanovic.co.rs. Centrally located boutique hotel. Nicely furnished rooms with satellite TV, internet, minibar & AC. €€

Hotel Groš ★★ (13 rooms) Svetozara Miletića bb; ☎ 220 900, 244 905; e bokigros@sbb.rs; w restorangros.com. A combined hotel & 'etno' restaurant with some rooms in a large annex. €

WHAT TO SEE AND DO

Caričin Grad (Царичин Град) West of Leskovac, 32km away, are the remains of the fortified 6th-century Byzantine town of Caričin Grad. Some think that Caričin Grad may have been Justinian's capital in this part of the Balkans. Whatever the truth of this, the extent of the remains suggests that it was certainly a very important centre; the fact that a 20km aqueduct was built to supply the town with water reinforces this. It is thought that the settlement was relatively short-lived and most likely was abandoned by the beginning of the 7th century, probably as a result of Slav attacks.

Outside the town's walls, which still have the remnants of towers and five remaining gates, are the remains of a basilica and some baths. Well-preserved portions of mosaic flooring survive in the narthex and nave of the basilica. The entrance to the town is through the south gate, from where a wide street leads past the foundations of a cruciform church that was most probably a private chapel. On the other side of the street is another basilica with three aisles. The town's forum is 50m further on, a large circular space, around which are the remains of public buildings and another large basilica. The acropolis, at the highest point of the town, is enclosed within a second set of ramparts. On the left of this is the cathedral, a large basilica with a baptistry, and on the right is the Bishop's Palace. At some distance away to the east is another basilica that has a large crypt beneath it where important clerics and local dignitaries would have been buried.

Unfortunately, there is no easy way to reach the site without your own car. If you have transport, you should drive first to Lebane, southwest of Leskovac along the Priština road. From here, you take a right turn and follow the road to the village of Prekopčelica. The ruins lie 8km beyond the village, on a hillside a 15-minute walk from the main road.

Vladičin Han (Владичин Хан)
Continuing south from Leskovac, the valley narrows dramatically as the road enters the canyon of the Grdelička Klisura alongside the Južna Morava River and the railway line. The small town of Vladičin Han is reached 43km from Leskovac. It is probably not worth stopping in the town as there is nothing really to see. However, it is worth noting that you are in the heart of brass-band country and that musical traditions are particularly strong here. All of the villages in this region have their own brass bands, mostly Roma – some have several – and the players around here are considered to be among the best in the country. The much-fêted Guča champion, Boban Marković, hails from Vladičin Han.

After Vladičin Han the valley widens once more and, after a further 25km, the largish town of Vranje is reached.

VRANJE (ВРАЊЕ) *Telephone code 017*

Vranje is an unremarkable agricultural centre and army garrison town that serves as the administrative headquarters for the Pčinja district of southern Serbia. In contrast to its quiet demeanour today, it was an important town in Ottoman times. There is still enough evidence of this – a Turkish quarter with a small Ottoman bridge, a *hammam*, a *paša's* residence – to make an overnight stay here worthwhile. There is also **Markova Kula**, an atmospheric medieval fortress high above the town, a few kilometres to the north, which serves as an excellent focus for country walks in spectacular countryside.

GETTING THERE AND AROUND Vranje is well served by buses from Leskovac and Niš to the north, although few of the buses that serve Skopje stop here. A dozen or so buses a day leave for Surdulica, east of Vladičin Han. The **bus station** (\ 421 201) is at the south end of town, and it is a fairly stiff, uphill walk to the centre and Hotel Vranje. Vranje is on the main Belgrade–Niš–Skopje railway line and there is a

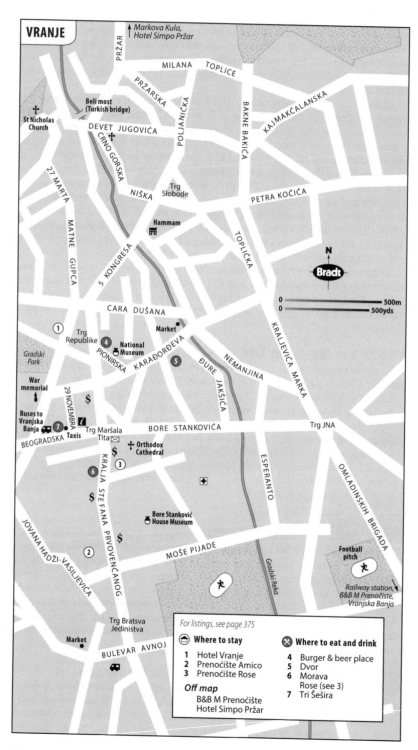

VRANJE

↑ *Markova Kula,*
Hotel Simpo Pržar

PRŽAR

MILANA   TOPLICE

PRŽARSKA

Beli most
(Turkish bridge)

St Nicholas
Church

DEVET JUGOVIĆA

CRNO GORSKA

POLJANIČKA

BAKNE BAKIĆA

KAJMAKČALANSKA

27 MARTA

MATNE GUPCA

NIŠKA

Trg
Slobode

PETRA KOČIĆA

5 KONGRESA

Hammam

TOPLIČKA

N

Bradt

0 ——————————— 500m
0 ——————————— 500yds

CARA DUŠANA

KRALJEVIĆA MARKA

Gradski
Park

① Trg
Republike

④ National
Museum

PIONIRSKA   KARAĐORĐEVA

Market ●

⑤

ĐURE JAKŠIĆA

NEMANJINA

War
memorial

29 NOVEMBRA

$

Buses to
Vranjska
Banja ⑦

Taxis

Trg Maršala
Tita ✉

BORE STANKOVIĆA

Trg JNA

BEOGRADSKA

$

③

✝ Orthodox
Cathedral

ESPERANTO

OMLADINSKIH BRIGADA

KRALJA STEFANA PRVOVENČANOG

⑥

$

⊞

$

Bore Stanković
House Museum

JOVANA HADŽI-VASILJEVIĆA

②

$

MOŠE PIJADE

Gradski Reka

Football
pitch

🏃

Railway station,
B&B M Prenoćište,
Vranjska Banja

🏃

Trg Bratsva
Jedinistva

Market ●

BULEVAR AVNOJ

For listings, see page 375

🛏 **Where to stay**

1 Hotel Vranje
2 Prenoćište Amico
3 Prenoćište Rose

Off map
B&B M Prenoćište
Hotel Simpo Pržar

❌ **Where to eat and drink**

4 Burger & beer place
5 Dvor
6 Morava
   Rose (see 3)
7 Tri Šešira

limited number of daily services north and south. The **railway station** (📞 *421 714*) is even further from the centre than the bus station, on the far side of the *autoput*, close to the Južna Morava River. A taxi is definitely recommended if you are arriving or leaving by train.

Taxis can be found outside both stations and in the town centre close to Trg Maršala Tita. Buses to the nearby spa of Vranjska Banja can be caught at the stop next to the taxi rank.

🏠 **WHERE TO STAY** *Map, page 374*

🏠 **Hotel Simpo Pržar ***** (18 rooms, 2 suites) Pržarska bb; 📞 423 900; e simpo.przar@simpo. This small hotel, just outside Vranje, passed into private ownership a few years ago. Located high on a hill to the north of the town, it is really too far out of town to consider staying here unless you have a car. €€€

🏠 **B&B M Prenoćište** (14 rooms) Radnička bb. A smart, modern hotel that is slightly inconveniently situated 2km from the town centre close to the highway & railway station. All rooms with AC, cable TV, minibar & Wi-Fi. Non-smoking & family rooms are available. Restaurant. €€

🏠 **Hotel Vranje ***** (68 rooms) Trg Republike 4; 📞 422 366, 421 776. This large hotel in the town centre is getting a little run-down these days. It has spacious rooms with TV & phone, & there is an attached restaurant & terrace bar. €€

🏠 **Prenoćište Amico** (11 rooms) Svetozara Markovića 2a; 📞 416 857; e amicovranje@yahoo. com; w amico.co.rs. Pleasant rooms, some with balconies, just off Kralja Stefana Prvovenčanog between the centre & the bus station. AC, cable TV, Wi-Fi & minibar. €€

🏠 **Prenoćište Rose** (15 rooms) Kralja Stefana Prvovenčanog 73; 📞 420 874; e rouzrestoran@ gmail.com; w restoranrose.com. Nice clean rooms of various sizes attached to a stylish modern Italian restaurant. €€

✖️ **WHERE TO EAT AND DRINK** *Map, page 374*

Apart from pizza and take-away fast food, there are limited dining options in Vranje. **Rose** (📞 *421 444*; €€) is a decent Italian restaurant, while **Dvor** (📞 *420 505*; €) at Save Kovačevića 46 is a national restaurant with a good range of Serbian food. The **Tri Šešira** at Beogradska 18 also has a good choice on its menu. **Morava** (*Kralja Stefana Prvovenčanog 166*; 📞 *414 444*; w *restoranmorava.rs*; €€) is another long-established Serbian restaurant with a pleasant summer garden. There are plenty of cafés with outdoor terraces along the pedestrian café-bar street that leads down from Gradski Park to Kralja Stefana Prvovenčanog, and some fast-food places by the park. One of the cheapest and least pretentious cafés in this area is the small **burger and beer place** immediately in front of the museum that does good *pljeskavica*. There are a handful of smart café-bars along the northern side of the park, although some of them tend to play music at deafening levels of volume. Further downhill, clustered around the central square of Trg Maršala Tita, are a few simple grill restaurants.

OTHER PRACTICALITIES

$ **Bank** Unicredit banka: Stefana Prvovenčanog 61; 📞 401 042

✚ **Hospital** City Hospital: Jovan Jovanovića Lunge 1; 📞 421 550

✉️ **Post office** Stefana Prvovenčanog 49; 📞 407 015

ℹ️ **Tourist information** 29 Novembra 2; 📞 417 545; e tovvranje@yahoo.com; w tovranje.rs

WHAT TO SEE AND DO

National Museum (*Narodni muzej Vranje; Pionirska 1*; 📞 *424 018*; w *muzejvranje. rs*; ⏱ *08.00–15.00 Mon, 08.00–20.00 Tue–Fri, 10.00–14.00 Sat/Sun; admission 100din*) The museum is in a *konak* built in 1765 by the *paša* Rajif Beg Džinić. It was sold by the daughter of the last *paša* to rule here and became Vranje's first high

8

school in 1881. It is an elegant airy building on two floors, which now houses a small ethnographic collection of costumes and period furniture alongside a few prehistoric finds from the region. The large house next door to the main museum building is another *konak* that is contemporaneous with the *paša's* residence. This building, the *haremluk*, was where his harem used to reside. Formerly, there would have been a 'bridge' connecting the two dwellings – the female *haremluk* and the all-male *selamluk* belonging to the *paša* – so that all movement between the two houses went unseen by the town's population. The **Bore Stanković House Museum** (*Kuća Bore Stankovića; Baba Zlatina 9;* \ *423 073* ☉ *08.00–15.00 Mon, 08.00–20.00 Tue–Fri, 09.00–13.00 Sat/Sun; admission 100din*) is another interesting house museum built around 1850. Formerly belonging to the Serbian writer Bore Stanković, it was turned into a museum in 1967.

The *hammam*, Roma quarter and Turkish bridge The *hammam* is reached

by walking north along 5 Kongresa from Trg Republike, then crossing the bridge across the river. The building is on the first corner to the right. The brick-built *hammam* originates from around 1690 and has three hexagonal domes. It has been restored and partly modernised but no longer serves its original purpose.

Continuing up here, you soon reach Trg Slobode, the heart of the **Roma quarter** of the town. Poljanička, the street that leads north off the square, is pure Roma, with women in long dresses sitting on their haunches smoking, violin music blaring from cassette players, and groups of burly men in singlets playing cards on the pavement. You may notice that most of the houses are built according to Roma tastes, opening straight on to the street, with external steps leading down from the upper floors. It is an intimate scene: poor but with a satisfied, self-contained air, a completely different atmosphere from a few hundred metres away where life is lived much more behind closed doors. There is no problem walking through the area as long as you don't appear to take too much interest in what you see. Roma, understandably, do not take kindly to outsiders nosing in on their affairs. Stopping to take photographs uninvited is probably ill-advised too.

At the top of Poljanička, turning left along Devet Jugovića will bring you to **Beli most**, the 'white' (or Turkish) bridge. The bridge is nice enough but it is hardly Mostar – just a small footbridge over the town's river, which here is barely a trickling stream. Some of the stone blocks are damaged but the inscription plaque in the Arabic script of Ottoman Turkish is in good condition. The bridge, dating from 1844, is known locally as *most ljubavi* – 'lovers bridge' – because of a story that tells of a Muslim girl Ajša and an Orthodox boy Stojan who became lovers. The girl's father was incensed by their liaison and shot at the pair of them, mistakenly killing his daughter rather than her lover, much to his distress. The bridge was built by the repentant, trigger-happy father to commemorate this act and the inscription on the tablet relates to this. This seems to be an almost universal folk tale: one that relates to forbidden love between those belonging to opposite sides of a divided community.

Just back along the riverbank from the east side of the bridge is a tiny chapel that has a bell tower that is a simple structure of wooden logs. Take the road running alongside this to return to Devet Jugovića and the top of Poljanička.

From here, you can continue uphill along Pržar, a road that eventually leads to the ruined fortress of Markova Kula. The streets are steep in this part of town and the houses are a mixture of old and new. The older houses all have red pantile roofs and whitewashed walls with enormous stacks of firewood piled against them. Many have their own wells. Although this is still effectively a northern suburb of Vranje the sense of rural tranquillity here is quite palpable. The garden plots are full of plum trees and small stands of maize. The only sounds are children's laughter, a distant radio playing folk tunes and sporadic hammering from one of the new building plots – a delightful place to live if you can put up with a stiff uphill walk back from the town centre every day.

Markova Kula The ruined fortress of Markova Kula was originally built by Serbs in medieval times, probably the 11th century. After the Ottoman invasion of the mid 15th century, it was taken by the Turks who expanded and fortified it further. It is said to have later become a *hajduk*'s stronghold, although the evidence for this is uncertain.

Markova Kula is reached by following Pržar out of town to the north. The road continues climbing and winds around several spurs of the valley, offering an ever-improving view of Vranje and the plain of the Južna Morava River far below. After a few kilometres, there is a signposted turn-off to the right to reach the Hotel Pržar. The traffic on the road towards the fortress is almost entirely that of heavily loaded lumber trucks coming downhill with brakes screaming, laboriously negotiating the sharp bends down into Vranje.

The fortress is located high above a bend in the road, 6–7km from Vranje. The remains of Markova Kula sit precipitously astride a steep ridge. A track leads off the road and swings around to the right to reach the ruins. There is not much to see of the fortress today, just some fortified walls and unidentifiable foundations, but the views south to Vranje and north and west to Kosovo are wholly magnificent.

To reach the fortress you can walk if you are feeling energetic – it is quite a steep climb all the way. An alternative is to take a taxi one-way and then walk the 7km back to town. This offers the best of both worlds as it is downhill all the way. A taxi taken from Beogradska in the town centre to Markova Kula should cost around 600din one-way, perhaps 1,000din if you get them to wait for you to bring you back.

Vranjska Banja (Врањска Бања) Vranje's outlying spa lies just a dozen kilometres east of the town across the Morava River and the E-75 main road. With the sole exception of Iceland, the spa boasts the warmest spa water (92°C) in the whole of Europe and the waters here are considered to be excellent for the treatment of rheumatism. There is the two-star **Hotel Železničar** (*Kralja Petra I;* \ *546 432;* e *vranjska.banja@zelturist.rs;* €€) for those wishing to stay.

SOUTH OF VRANJE From Vranje, it is less than 40km to the Macedonian border. The only towns south of here, Bujanovac and Preševo, have sizeable Albanian minorities and the region was the scene of sporadic disturbances a few years ago, with Albanian KLA-inspired factions caught up in small-scale conflict with the Serbian army. The situation appears to have settled and the British FCO no longer advises avoidance of this border area.

KURŠUMLIJA (КУРШУМЛИЈА) *Telephone code 027*

With the exception of those heading towards Kopaonik, few visitors travel this road beyond Prokupje, west of Niš. It is an attractive rural region close to the border with Kosovo that is worthy of a visit in its own right, although the undoubted stars here are the rock formations at Đavolja Varoš (**Devil's Town**). Kuršumlija is the largest town in the region and serves as a decent base for a night or two.

Ad Fines, a Roman military base, stood in the same location as the modern town of Kuršumlija in the 3rd century AD. In the Byzantine period, the settlement was known as Toplice and became the seat of a bishopric. The town became increasingly important during the medieval period when Stefan Nemanja built a residence and established his first capital here. Two monasteries were established close to the town in the early years of the Serbian state: St Nicholas, endowed by Stefan Nemanja, and the Mother of God nunnery endowed by his wife Ana. Subsequently, the place became known as Bele Crkve (White Churches), a reference to the shiny white lead that covered the roofs of the monastery churches. The Turkish invasion brought about its current name, which is a contraction of Kuršumlu-Kilise and roughly means 'leaded churches'. Three spas – Prolom Spa, Kuršumlija Spa and Lukovo Spa – all lie close to the town.

GETTING THERE AND AWAY Kuršumlija has more or less hourly buses each day to and from Niš. Other services from the **bus station** (*381 645, 381 038*) include two services a day to Priština in Kosovo, one of which goes on to Kosovska Mitrovica and Novi Pazar, and others to the surrounding spas like Prolom Banja.

TOURIST INFORMATION
*Palih Boraca 15; *380 963; e to.kusumlija027@gmail.com; w tokursumlija.rs

WHERE TO STAY
Hostel Franica * (18 rooms) 16 Februar 29; *389 088; e info@prolombanja.com; w hotelfranica.com. More a small hotel than a hostel. Plain dbl, trpl & 4-bed rooms with bath, cable TV, AC & Wi-Fi. €€

Hotel Radan * (212 rooms) Prolom Banja; *88 111, 88 092; e info@prolombanja. com; w prolombanja.com. In the spa of Prolom Banja, southeast of Kuršumlija & 28km from Đavolja Varoš. €€

WHAT TO SEE AND DO
Church of St Nicholas This squat Byzantine-style church (Crkva Svetog Nikole) lies north of the town centre across the River Toplica. This monastery church dates from the mid 12th century and became the seat of a bishopric in 1219. The narthex with its two towers is a later edition of the 14th century.

Đavolja Varoš (w *djavoljavaros.com*; admission 350din) Đavolja Varoš (Devil's Town) is the name given to a **strange and surreal collection of rocks** 28km from Kuršumlija that constitute what is perhaps Serbia's most intriguing natural landmark. Those who have seen Turkey's Cappadoccia region will have some idea as to what to expect, although the rocks here are smaller and cover a far less extensive geographical area than their Turkish counterparts. They are, nevertheless, highly impressive and well worth the effort it takes to reach them.

The rocks that constitute the 'Devil's Town' are actually a tightly packed group of over 200 unusual stone formations created by the dual processes of weathering and erosion. Individual stone formations range from between 2m and 15m in height and each is capped by a flat stone of a different colour to create a spindly mushroom effect.

The geomorphological conditions that create formations such as these are extremely rare, hence the relatively small number of similar sites throughout the world. Put simply, they are the result of the action of very acidic water with high mineralisation on easily eroded soft rock that has a harder layer on top. Naturally enough, these unusual formations have given rise to various legends and folk myths that range from God petrifying guests at an incestuous wedding to the rocks being devils that have been turned to stone.

The protected 67ha site was developed and upgraded by the Serbian government in 2008 and now has a large car park, restaurants, public toilets and gift shops in addition to a raised walkway that leads around the site to provide a variety of viewpoints. There are also some interesting wooden sculptures to examine along the tourist route and other features such as medieval iron mining pits to contemplate.

Other practicalities Đavolja Varoš is reached by driving 3km up a narrow twisting road from a turn-off on the main Kuršumlija to Priština highway – it is clearly signed. The site is difficult to reach without your own transport, although there may be occasional buses from Kuršumlija. Several travel agencies run tours here.

There is a café and restaurant at the site itself and another place to eat, **Etno krčma Božiji Raj**, nearby by the river. Also, on the approach to Đavolja Varoš, about 2km away, is **Dva Ambara** (m *064 8006 969*; €), a rustic wooden restaurant with a roaring fire, curios like pots, pans and gusles on the wall, and excellent traditional food – *kajmak*, *pršut*, *ajvar* and roast lamb.

Appendix 1

LANGUAGE

PRONUNCIATION AND TRANSLITERATION In Serbian, every word is pronounced exactly as it is written. Stress is usually on the first syllable but in some cases, as in words that have a prefix, stress is on the middle syllable. Stress never falls on the last syllable of a word.

There are 30 letters in the Serbian alphabet, which is written in both Cyrillic and Latin forms. The order of letters of the alphabet is different for Latin and Cyrillic script. The alphabet below is given in the Latin order.

Latin		Cyrillic		Pronunciation
A	a	А	а	'a' as in ask
B	b	Б	б	'b' as in boy
C	c	Ц	ц	'c' as 'ts' in flotsam
Č	č	Ч	ч	'ch' as in church
Ć	ć	Ћ	ћ	'tch' like the 't' in future
D	d	Д	д	'd' as in dog
Dž	dž	Џ	џ	'j' as in just
Đ	đ	Ђ	ђ	'dj' as in endure
E	e	Е	е	'e' as in egg
F	f	Ф	ф	'f' as in father
G	g	Г	г	'g' as in girl
H	h	Х	х	'h' as in hot; as 'ch' in loch before a consonant
I	i	И	и	'i' as in machine
J	j	Ј	j	'y' as in young
K	k	К	к	'k' as in king
L	l	Л	л	'l' as in like
Lj	lj	Љ	љ	'ly' like the 'lli' in million
M	m	М	м	'm' as in man
N	n	Н	н	'n' as in nest
Nj	nj	Њ	њ	'nj' like the 'ny' in canyon
O	o	О	о	'o' between the 'o' in bone and the 'aw' in shawl
P	p	П	п	'p' as in perfect
R	r	Р	р	'r' as in rough
S	s	С	с	's' as in Serbia
Š	š	Ш	ш	'sh' as in lush
T	t	Т	т	't' as in test
U	u	У	у	'oo' as in boot
V	v	В	в	'v' as in victory
Z	z	З	з	'z' as in zebra
Ž	ž	Ж	ж	'zh' like the 's' in pleasure

The table above does not show lower-case handwritten Cyrillic, which can be confusing as some letters change shape completely.

BASIC GRAMMAR Serbian is not an easy language to master for the non-Slavic speaker as it is grammatically complex, having eight cases to decline and three genders, which are distinct even in the plural (unlike Russian). There is no definite article in Serbian. Nouns may be masculine, feminine or neuter and are declined according to their function in a sentence. In their singular form, masculine nouns end with a consonant and generally end with an '-i' in the plural. Most feminine nouns end in '-a' in the singular and '-e' in the plural. Neuter nouns end in either '-e' or '-o' in the singular; generally, the plural form ends in '-a'.

An excellent free online tutorial is available at **w** serbianschool.com, which also has a grammatical dictionary.

ESSENTIALS

Good morning	*Dobro jutro*	May I?	*Da li mogu?*
Good day/afternoon	*Dobar dan*	Please give me …	*Dajte mi …*
Good evening	*Dobro veče*	That's fine	*U redu je*
Good night	*Laku noć*	Maybe	*Možda*
Hello	*Zdravo*	Well, thank you	*Dobro, hvala*
Goodbye	*Do viđenja/čiao*	Don't mention it	*Nema na čemu*
Have a good trip!	*Srećan put!*	Cheers!	*Živeli!*
My name is …	*Ja se zovem …*	Yes	*Da*
What's your name?	*Kako se zovete?*	No	*Ne*
I am from …	*Ja sam iz …*	Mr	*Gospodin*
England/America/	*Engleske/Amerike/*	Mrs	*Gospođa*
Australia	*Australije*	Miss	*Gospođica*
How are you?	*Kako si?*	I don't understand	*Ja ne razumem*
Pleased to meet you	*Drago mi je*	Please speak more	*Govorite polako*
Thank you	*Hvala*	slowly	*molim*
Please	*Molim*	Do you speak	*Govorite li engleski?*
Sorry	*Pardon*	English?	
No problem	*Nema problema*	Where are you from?	*Odakle ste?*
Excuse me	*Izvinite*		

QUESTIONS

How?	*Kako?*	When?	*Kada?*
What?	*Šta?*	Why?	*Zašto?*
Where?	*Gde?*	Who?	*Ko?*
Which?	*Koji?*	How much?	*Koliko?*

NUMBERS

0	*nula*	9	*devet*	18	*osamnaest*		
1	*jedan*	10	*deset*	19	*devetnaest*		
2	*dva*	11	*jedanaest*	20	*dvadeset*		
3	*tri*	12	*dvanaest*	21	*dvadeset i jedan*		
4	*četiri*	13	*trinaest*	100	*sto*		
5	*pet*	14	*četrnaest*	200	*dvesta or dve*		
6	*šest*	15	*petnaest*		*stotine*		
7	*sedam*	16	*šesnaest*	1,000	*hiljada*		
8	*osam*	17	*sedamnaest*				

TIME

What time is it?	*Koliko je sati?*	evening	*veče*
today	*danas*	hour	*sat*
tonight	*večeras, noćas*	minute	*minut*
tomorrow	*sutra*	month	*mesec*
yesterday	*juče*	night	*noć*
morning	*jutro*	now	*sada*
afternoon	*popodne, posle podne*	week	*nedelje*
day	*dan*	year	*godina*

Days (Days of the week and months do not require capital letters in Serbian.)

Monday	*ponedeljak*	Friday	*petak*
Tuesday	*utorak*	Saturday	*subota*
Wednesday	*sreda*	Sunday	*nedelja*
Thursday	*četvrtak*		

Months

January	*januar*	July	*juli*
February	*februar*	August	*avgust*
March	*mart*	September	*septembar*
April	*april*	October	*oktobar*
May	*maj*	November	*novembar*
June	*juni*	December	*decembar*

Seasons

spring	*proleće*	autumn	*jesen*
summer	*leto*	winter	*zima*

GETTING AROUND
Public transport

I would like …	*Želim …*	How far is it to … ?	*Koliko daleko do … ?*
… a one-way ticket	*… kartu u jednom pravcu*	What time's the next bus?	*Kada polazi sledeći autobus?*
… a return ticket	*… povratnu kartu*	What time does the	*Kada …*
… two tickets	*… dve karte*	… leave/arrive?	*polazi/dolazi?*
1st class	*prvu klasu*	bus	*autobus*
2nd class	*drugu klasu*	train	*voz*
I want to go to …	*Želim da odem u …*	tram	*tramvaj*
How much is it?	*Koliko košta?*	aeroplane	*avion*
Where is the …	*Gde je …*	boat	*brod*
… bus station?	*… autobuska stanica?*	taxi	*taxi*
… railway station?	*… železnička stanica?*	I want to get off!	*Želim da sidem!*
… airport?	*… aerodrom?*		

Private transport

car	*auto*	petrol (gas) station	*benzinska pumpa*
garage	*garaža*		

Directions

How do I get to … ?	*Kako mogu da dodgem do … ?*	left	*levo*
		right	*desno*

straight on	pravo	here/there	ovde/tamo
ahead/behind	napred/iza	road/street	put/ulica
up/down	gore/dole	bridge/river	most/reka
under/over	ispod/iznad	waterfall	vodopad
north/south	sever/jug	hill/mountain/peak	brdo/planina/vrh
east/west	istok/zapad	village/town	selo/grad
Is it near/far?	Da li je blizu/dalek?		

Signs

entrance/exit	ulaz/izlaz	УЛАЗ/ИЗЛАЗ
open/closed	otvoreno/zatvoreno	ОТВОРЕНО/ЗАТВОРЕНО
Information	informacije	ИНФОРМАЦИ Е
Prohibited	zabranjeno	ЗАБРАЊЕНО
Toilets	toaleti	ТОАЛЕТИ
Men	muški	МУШКИ
Women	ženski	ЖЕНСКИ
Danger	opasnost	ОПАСНОСТ
Arrival	dolazak	ДОЛАЗАК
Departure	polazak	ПОЛАЗАК
No smoking	zabranjeno pušenje	ЗАБРАЊЕНО ПУШЕЊЕ
No entry	ulaz zabranjen	УЛАЗ ЗАБРАЊЕН

ACCOMMODATION

Where is a cheap/good hotel?	Gde ima jeftin/dobar hotel?
Could you write the address please?	Molim vas, napišite mi adresu?
Do you have any rooms available?	Da li imate slobodnih soba?
I'd like …	Želim …
… a single room	… sobu sa jednim krevetom
… a double room	… sobu sa duplim krevetom
… a room with two beds	… sobu sa dve kreveti
… a room with a bathroom	… sobu sa kupatilom
… to share a dorm	… krevet u studentskom domu
How much is it per night/person?	Koliko košta za jednu noć/po osobi?
Where is the toilet?	Gde je toalet?
Where is the bathroom?	Gde je kupatilom?
I'll be staying …	Ostacu …
… one night	… jednu noć
… a week	… jednu nedelju
I'd like to pay the bill	Želim da platim račun

FOOD

We'd like a table for two	Želeli bismo sto za dve osobe
I'm a vegetarian	Ja sam vegetarijanac/vegetarijanka (m/f)
Do you have vegetarian dishes?	Imate li vegetarijanska jela?
May I have the menu please?	Mogu li da dobiem jelovnik?
Please could you bring me the bill?	Možete li mi doneti račun?

Basics

baked	pečeno	breakfast	doručak
bill	račun	butter	puter
bread	hleb	cake	kolač, torta

cheese	*sir*	pancake	*palačinka*
chips	*pomfrit*	pasta	*testenine*
cup	*šoljica*	pepper	*biber*
dinner	*večera*	plate	*tanjir*
eggs	*jaja*	restaurant	*restoran*
fork	*viljuška*	rice	*pirinač*
glass	*staklo*	salad	*salata*
grilled	*sa roštilj*	salt	*so*
homemade	*domaće*	soup	*supa, čorba*
honey	*med*	spoon	*kašika*
ice cream	*sladoled*	sugar	*šećer*
knife	*nož*	tavern	*konak, konoba*
lunch	*ručak*	yoghurt	*yogurt*
oil	*ulje*		

Fruit

apple	*jabuka*	pear	*kruška*
orange	*pomorandža*	plum	*šljiva*
peach	*breskva*	strawberry	*jagoda*

Vegetables

bean	*pasulja*	onion	*crni luk*
cabbage	*kupus*	potato	*krompir*
carrot	*šargarepa*	tomato	*paradajz*
garlic	*beli luk*	vegetables	*povrće*
mushrooms	*pečurke*		

Fish

fish	*riba*	fish soup	*riblja čorba*

Meat

beef	*govedina*	pork	*svinjetina*
beefsteak	*biftek*	roasted meat	*pečeno meso*
chicken	*piletina*	roast pork	*svinjsko pečenje*
chicken soup	*pileća supa*	roast chicken	*pečena piletina*
ham	*šunka*	sausage	*kobasica*
lamb	*jagne*	veal	*teletina*
meat	*meso*	veal soup	*teleca čorba*

Drinks

beer	*pivo*	drink (noun)	*piće*
brandy	*rakija*	juice	*sok*
coffee	*kafa*	milk	*mleko*
Turkish coffee	*Turska kafa*	plum brandy	*šljivovica*
black/white	*crna/bela*	tea	*čaj*
cappuccino	*kapućino*	(mineral) water	*(mineralna) voda*
cognac	*konjak*	(white/red) wine	*(belo/crno) vino*

SHOPPING

I'm just looking around	*Samo razgledam*	Have you got … ?	*Imate li … ?*
		How much is this?	*Koliko košta ovo?*

EMERGENCY

Help!	*Upomoć!*	accident	*nesreća*
Call a doctor!	*Pozovite lekara!*	ambulance	*ambulanta*
There's been an accident!	*Dogodila se nesreća!*	emergency	*nužda*
		fire brigade	*vatrogasna brigada*
I'm lost	*Izgubio/Izgubila sam se* (m/f)	hospital	*bolnica*
I am ill	*Bolestan/ Bolesna sam* (m/f)	police	*miliciju*
		thief	*lopov*
Go away!	*Bežite!*		

I'll take it	*Uzeću to*	newspaper	*novine*
Do you accept credit cards?	*Da li mogu da platim kredit kartom?*	postage stamp	*poštanska marka*
		postcard	*raglednica*
discount	*popust*	shop	*radnja*
market	*pijaca*	souvenir	*suvenir*
money	*novac*		

PRACTICALITIES

I'm looking for …	*Treba mi …*	church	*crkva*
bank	*banka*	exchange office	*menjačnica*
bookshop	*knjižjara*	post office	*pošta*
bus station	*autobuska stanica*	railway station	*železnička stanica*
chemist (pharmacy)	*poteka*	tourist information	*turističke informacije*

HEALTH

back	*leđa*	I have …	*Bolime …*
chest	*grudi*	… an allergy	*… alergija*
dentist	*zubar*	… anaemia	*… anemija*
doctor	*lekar*	… a cold	*… nazeb/prehlada*
ear	*uvo*	… a cough	*… kašalj*
eye	*oko*	… diarrhoea	*… proliv*
head	*glava*	… a fever	*… groznica*
heart	*srce*	… a headache	*… glavobolja*
medicine	*lek*	… indigestion	*… loše varenje*
		… an infection	*… infekcija*
		… a pain	*… bol*
		… a stomach ache	*… bolovi u stomaku*

OTHER

good/bad	*dobro/loše*	early/late	*rano/kasno*
small/big	*malo/veliko*	before/after	*pre/kasnije*
heavy/light	*těsko/lagano*	here/there	*ovde/tamo*
more/less	*više/manje*	old/new	*stao/novo*
hot/cold	*vruće/hladno*		

Appendix 2

GLOSSARY OF SERBIAN TERMS

Četnik	Chetnik: member of royalist resistance, now more widely used to describe an extreme nationalist
čoček	fast dance popular with brass bands
dahi	Janissary commander
Đurđevdan	St George's Day celebrated on 6 May
frula	small, recorder-like instrument
grad	town
gusle	stringed instrument used in performance of epic poems
hajduk	brigand or outlaw who fought against the Turkish occupation
Janissaries	elite Ottoman troops recruited from Christian subject families
jezero	lake
kafana	traditional tavern or café
kajmak	Serbian cream cheese-like product
knez	originally a Serbian local leader; later, a prince
koljivo	ground, cooked wheat used in a *slava* celebration
kolo	circle dance
konak	house in Serbian–Turkish style
konoba	traditional tavern
košava	dry wind from the southeast that sometimes blows in autumn
kula	tower
openac	traditional shoes with turned-up toes
Partisans	World War II anti-Nazi resistance movement led by Tito
paša	Turkish commander in Ottoman period
pašalik	division of Ottoman Serbia
pećina	cave
planina	mountain range
polje	field
put	road
rakija	alcoholic drink, usually made from grapes
rayah	Serbian serfs under Ottoman control
reka	river
šajkača	traditional Serbian cap
sandžak	administrative district of the Ottoman Empire, now a term used to describe the predominantly Muslim region of southwest Serbia
slava	ceremony devoted to commemorating the patron saint of a family, town or village
šljivovica	alcoholic drink made from plums

sloboda	freedom
spaji	Turkish cavalry unit
Šumadija	the 'wooded country', a term used to describe central Serbia
sveti	saint
trg	town square
turbo-folk	modern musical genre that is a fusion of traditional folk tunes, sentimental lyrics and electronic dance rhythms
ulica	street
Ustaša	Croatian Nazi movement in World War II
Vidovdan	St Vitus's Day on 28 June, which commemorates defeat at Battle of Kosovo on this date in 1389
vrh	mountain peak
zadruge	loose family groups living together as clans in medieval Serbia
župan	patriarch from around the time of the first Serbian colonisation

ARCHITECTURAL AND RELIGIOUS TERMS

apse	projected semicircular part of a church by the altar
Baroque	style of architecture with elaborate ornamentation
basilica	a Roman-style aisled church with a nave, apse but no transepts
exonarthex	porch before the narthex of a church
fresco	painting on freshly spread moist lime plaster
Gothic	style characterised by slender vertical piers, pointed arches and vaults
hammam	public bath in a Turkish/Muslim town
icon	religious image painted on to a small wooden panel
iconostasis	screen or partition with icons that separates the nave from the sanctuary of an Orthodox church
kula	tower
mihrab	niche showing the direction of prayer in a mosque
minaret	slender pointed tower attached to a mosque from which the summon to prayer is made
minbar	pulpit of a mosque
naos	innermost part of an Orthodox church beneath the central cupola
narthex	entrance hall of an Orthodox church, often decorated with frescoes
nave	main part of the interior of a church, especially the narrow central hall in a cruciform church that rises higher than the aisles
patriarchate	seat of Orthodox bishop or patriarch
pietà	depiction of the Virgin mourning the dead Christ
Renaissance	Neoclassical style in western Europe from 14th–17th century
Romanesque	style between Roman and Gothic characterised by the use of round arches and vaults and decorative arcades
transept	the part of a church that crosses the nave at right angles
türbe	small Turkish mausoleum

Appendix 3

MAGAZINES AND NEWSPAPERS
Entertainment
BelGuest (**w** belguest.rs) is a quarterly magazine with listings and articles about Belgrade in English and Serbian

Britić (**w** ebritic.com) is an English-language publication that looks at British Serb interests

Yellow Cab (**w** yc.rs) is a monthly magazine, a bit like a Belgrade version of *Time Out*, which is mostly in Serbian, but has very useful listings of forthcoming cultural events, restaurants, galleries and concerts

Politics
Belgrade Insight (**w** belgradeinsight.com) is a free fortnightly newspaper

BOOKS
History, politics and culture
Ali, Tariq (ed) *Masters of the Universe: NATO's Balkan Crusade* Verso, 2000. An anthology of writing concerning NATO's role in Kosovo.

Barnett, Neil *Tito (Life & Times)* Haus Publishing, 2006. A short, readable biography.

Benson, Leslie *Yugoslavia: A Concise History* Palgrave Macmillan, 2003. The most up-to-date book about the history of the federation that is currently available.

Bideleux, Robert and Jeffries, Ian *The Balkans: A Post-Communist History* Routledge, 2007. Weighty, post-communist history of the region.

Cartwright, Garth *Princes amongst Men: Journeys with Gypsy Musicians* Serpent's Tail, 2011. An excellent survey of the lives of Roma musicians in the Balkans, which includes profiles of Serbian artists like Šaban Bajramović.

Chomsky, Noam *The New Military Humanism: Lessons from Kosovo* Pluto Press, 1999. Written immediately after the Kosovo crisis, this is a harsh critique of the NATO campaign that has serious doubts about the wisdom of 'humanitarian intervention'.

Cirković, Sima *The Serbs (Peoples of Europe)* Blackwell, 2004

Cohen, Lenard J *Serpent in the Bosom: The Rise and Fall of Slobodan Milošević* Basic Books, 2001. Not that Leonard Cohen! The title says it all really – a very readable study of the man. The book has been revised with new material on Milošević's indictment at the International Tribunal at The Hague but does not quite go up to the time of his death.

Collin, Matthew *This is Serbia Calling: Rock 'n' Roll Radio and Belgrade's Underground Resistance* Serpent's Tail, 2004. A fascinating account of the history of radio (and now television) station B92 and its role in Milošević's downfall.

Deliso, Christopher *Culture and Customs of Serbia* Greenwood Press, 2008

Drakulić, Slavenka *They Would Never Hurt a Fly* Abacus, 2004. An emotional account of the war crimes tribunal in The Hague and an examination of how ordinary people can do dreadful things in times of war. Perhaps rather biased against the Serbs while more forgiving of the Croats (the author is a Croat) but fascinating reading nevertheless.

Đokić, Dejan *Yugoslavism: Histories of a Failed Idea* C Hurst & Co, 2003

Glenny, Misha *The Balkans, 1804–2012 Nationalism, War and the Great Powers* Granta, 2012

Glenny, Misha *The Fall of Yugoslavia* Penguin, 1999. Two books by Misha Glenny, a BBC correspondent and renowned expert on Balkan history and politics. The new edition of *The Balkans* is updated up until 2012.

Goldsworthy, Vesna *Chernobyl Strawberries: A Memoir* Atlantic Books, 2015. A beautifully written, moving autobiography of a writer growing up in a Belgrade middle-class family in 1970s Yugoslavia.

Goldsworthy, Vesna *Inventing Ruritania: The Imperialism of the Imagination* Yale University Press, 1998. An earlier, more academic, work by the same writer in which she examines the cultural background to the West's obsession with the 'Balkan' archetype.

Gordy, Eric D *The Culture of Power in Serbia (Post-Communist Cultural Studies)* Penn State University Press, 1999

Hammond, Philip and Herman, Edward S (eds) *Degraded Capability: The Media and the Kosovo Crisis* Pluto Press, 2000. An examination of the partisan role played by the Western media during the Kosovo war.

Johnstone, Diana *Fool's Crusade: Yugoslavia, NATO and Western Delusions* Pluto Press, 2002

Judah, Tim *Kosovo: War and Revenge* Yale Nota Bene, 2002

Judah, Tim *The Serbs: History, Myth and the Destruction of Yugoslavia*, Yale University Press, 2009. An in-depth history of the Serbs from the Battle of Kosovo to the break-up of Yugoslavia.

King, Iain and Mason, Whit *Peace at Any Price: How the World Failed Kosovo (Crisis in World Politics)* C Hurst & Co, 2006. An examination of the international community's failure at nation-building in Kosovo.

Lazić, Mladen (ed) *Protest in Belgrade: Winter of Discontent* Central European University Press, 1999. This is a hard-to-find study of the widespread protests in the city during the winter of 1996–97 seen from a sociological perspective.

LeBor, Adam *Milošević: A Biography* Bloomsbury, 2003. A balanced biography, written before his death, that gives a three-dimensional account of Milošević's complex, but deeply unpleasant, character.

Levinsohn, Florence Hamlish *Belgrade: Among the Serbs* Ivan R Dee Inc, 1994. This book helps redress the customary anti-Serb stance of the Western media. The author questions the way Serbs have been demonised through various conversations with intellectuals in the capital.

Little, Allan and Silber, Laura *The Death of Yugoslavia* Penguin, 1996. This is the book of the highly lauded BBC television series on Yugoslavia's break-up.

Lomas, Robert *The Man Who Invented the Twentieth Century: Nikola Tesla, Forgotten Genius of Electricity* Headline, 2013. A biography of Nikola Tesla, the highly eccentric scientific genius who never quite achieved the recognition he deserved.

Macdonald, David Bruce *Balkan Holocausts? Serbian and Croatian Victim-Centred Propaganda and the War in Yugoslavia (New Approaches to Conflict Management)* Manchester University Press, 2003. Despite the long, off-putting title this is a fascinating account of how both Serbs and Croats have exploited Holocaust imagery to help claim historical victimisation and the way propaganda was used as a weapon in Yugoslavia's secessionist wars.

Malcolm, Noel *Kosovo: A Short History* Harper Perennial, 2002

Mazower, Mark *The Balkans (Universal History)* Weidenfeld & Nicolson History, 2002. A short history of the entire region.

Mertus, Julie *Kosovo: How Myths and Truths Started a War* University of California Press, 1999

Parenti, Michael *To Kill a Nation* Verso Books, 2001. This book painstakingly examines the details hidden from us during the wars in Yugoslavia showing that, in Parenti's opinion at least, the Croatian and Bosnian leaders were just as manipulative and bloodthirsty as the Serbs and even more nationalist. Very critical of US and NATO policy, it could be argued that the book goes too far in invoking conspiracy theories that the West was engaged in a premeditated dismantling of Serbia as a nation.

Pavković, Aleksandar *The Fragmentation of Yugoslavia: Nationalism and War in the Balkans* Palgrave Macmillan, 2000

Pavlowitch, Stevan K *Tito: Yugoslavia's Great Dictator – A Reassessment* C Hurst & Co, 1993

Ramet, Sabrina Petra and Pavlaković, Vieran (eds) *Serbia Since 1999: Politics and Society under Milošević and after* University of Washington Press, 2007

Seierstad, Åsne *With Their Backs to the World* Virago Press, 2005. An intimate portrait by a young Norwegian journalist of the personal and political lives of a number of Serbs between 1999 and 2004.

Stephen, Chris *Judgement Day: The Trial of Slobodan Milošević* Atlantic Books, 2005. Of interest to those who missed following the slow turn of events at The Hague.

Stojanović, Svetozar *Serbia: The Democratic Revolution* Prometheus, 2003

Tesanović, Jasmina *The Diary of a Political Idiot* Midnight Editions, 2002. A first-hand account of life in Belgrade in 1999 by a dissident journalist who was against the war in Kosovo.

Thomas, Robert *Serbia under Milošević: Politics in the 1990s* C Hurst & Co, 2001. A rather scholarly account of how Milošević was able to exploit national and constitutional tensions to maintain his power base.

Todorova, Maria N *Imagining the Balkans* Oxford University Press USA, 2009. A post-structuralist analysis of the stigmatisation of the region and how 'Balkanisation' became a pejorative appellation.

West, Richard *Tito and the Rise and Fall of Yugoslavia* Faber and Faber, 2009

Zograf, Aleksandar *Bulletins from Serbia: E-mails and Cartoon Strips from Behind the Front Line* Slab-O-Concrete Publications, 1999

Zograf, Aleksandar *Regards from Serbia* Top Shelf Productions, 2007

Art and architecture

Blagojević, Ljiljana *Modernism in Serbia: The Elusive Margins of Belgrade Architecture, 1919–1941* MIT Press, 2003. An illustrated account of the city's modernist architectural movement between the wars.

Rice, David Talbot *Art of the Byzantine Era* Thames & Hudson, 1986

Language

Davidović, Mladen (ed) *Serbian–English English–Serbian Concise Dictionary* Hippocrene Books, 1997. A good, up-to-date dictionary but the Serbian component uses Cyrillic only.

Đukanović, Vlado *Around the World with Serbian* Agencija Matić, Belgrade, 2004. A useful Serbian language primer and phrasebook, available from bookshops in Serbia.

Hawkesworth, Celia *Colloquial Serbian: The Complete Course for Beginners* Routledge, 2005. A colloquial primer.

Javarek, V and Sudjić, M *Teach Yourself Serbo-Croat* Hodder and Stoughton, 1986. An out-of-print primer for a language that technically no longer exists.

Norris, David and Ribnikar, Vladislava *Serbian (Teach Yourself Languages series)* Teach Yourself Books, 2003. An excellent book if you are keen to learn the language.

Guidebooks *(See also, page 392)*

Blanchard, Paul *Blue Guide Yugoslavia* A&C Black, 1989 (out of print). Published just before the Yugoslav break-up, this is still useful on things like monasteries and architecture.

Ćorović, Ljubica *Belgrade Tourist Guide* Kreativni centar, Belgrade, 2003. This is an extremely detailed guide to Belgrade's sights and monuments, organised by way of walking tours through the city. Apart from public transport routes, it contains little practical advice. It is available in English translation at some Belgrade bookshops.

Cuddon, J A *The Companion Guide to Jugoslavia* Prentice-Hall, 1984 (out of print). Written in the 1960s, this is a very out-of-date but still interesting and opinionated guide to the former Yugoslavia.

Travel writing

Aldiss, Brian W *Cities and Stones* Faber, London, 1966 (out of print)

Bouvier, Nicolas *The Way of the World* Eland Publishing, 2007. An excellent Swiss travelogue from the 1950s with a fascinating account of life in post-war Belgrade.

Durrell, Lawrence *White Eagles over Serbia* Faber and Faber, 1993. Based on the author's experiences of working for the Foreign Office in Yugoslavia during the Cold War years of the 1950s.

Kaplan, Robert *Balkan Ghosts* Picador USA, 2005. A travelogue and sweeping *tour de force* of the whole region, first published in 1993. Very readable, but over-simplistic and sometimes rather one-sided. This, apparently, is the book that influenced President Clinton's policy in the Balkans.

Kindersley, Anne *The Mountains of Serbia, Travels through Inland Yugoslavia* Readers Union Book Club, London, 1977 (out of print)

MacCurrach, Robert *In the Bend of the River: Finding Vojvodina* Book Stream, 2011. This is a captivating account of the experiences of a British couple who settle in an ethnic Hungarian village in Vojvodina. Contains plenty of insight into Serbian culture and customs.

Maclean, Fitzroy *Eastern Approaches* Penguin Press, 2009

Murphy, Dervla *Through the Embers of Chaos: Balkan Journeys* John Murray, 2003. This is a superb and moving account of this stoic Irishwoman's journey through a deeply troubled political landscape in 1999 and 2000. Even more remarkable is that she travelled by bicycle at the age of 70. Full of perceptive insights and informed political analysis.

Newman, Bernard *Tito's Yugoslavia* The Travel Book Club, London, 1952 (out of print)

West, Rebecca *Black Lamb and Grey Falcon: A Journey through Yugoslavia* Canongate, 2006. A classic – the classic – this weighty tome with nearly 1,200 pages chronicles the pre-war Balkan peregrinations of this socialist aristocrat and her husband. Highly opinionated and generally rather pro-Serb, her prose, which can meander as much as her journeys do, infuriates and charms in equal measure. Not a light read in any sense of the word but highly recommended.

White, Tony *Another Fool in the Balkans: In the Footsteps of Rebecca West* Cadogan Guides, 2006. An interesting account of several journeys to the countries of the former Yugoslavia where the author meets up with a variety of artists, writers and politicians. However, not necessarily in Rebecca West's footsteps.

Serbian literature

Andrić, Ivo *Bridge over the Drina* Harvill Press, 1994

Kiš, Danilo *A Tomb for Boris Davidovich* Dalkey Archive Press, 2001

Kiš, Danilo *Encyclopedia of the Dead* Northwestern University Press, USA, 1998

Kiš, Danilo *Garden, Ashes* Dalkey WW Norton & Co, 2009

Kiš, Danilo *The Hourglass* Northwestern University Press, USA, 1998

Pavić, Milorad *Dictionary of the Khazars* Vintage International, 1996

Pavić, Milorad and Pribčević-Zorić, Christina *Last Love in Constantinople: A Tarot Novel for Divination* Dufour Editions, 1998

Selenić, Slobodan *Fathers and Forefathers* Harvill Press, 2003

Selenić, Slobodan *Premeditated Murder* Harvill Press, 1996. Two novels set in Belgrade that span the period from World War II to the present day.

Tišma, Aleksandar *The Book of Blam* Harcourt, 2000. Describes Novi Sad in the 1940s.

Natural history

Gorman, Gerard *Central and Eastern European Wildlife*, Bradt Travel Guides, 2008

Heinzel, H, Fitter, R and Parslow, J *The Birds of Britain and Europe with North Africa and the Middle East* Collins Pocket Guides, 1995

Raine, Pete *Mediterranean Wildlife: The Rough Guide*, Harrap Columbus, 1990

Polunin, Oleg *Flowers of Greece and the Balkans: A Field Guide* Oxford University Press, 1987

Other Eastern European guides For a full list of Bradt titles, see w bradtguides.com/shop.

Clancy, Tim *Bosnia & Herzegovina* Bradt Travel Guides, 2017

Evans, Thammy *Macedonia* Bradt Travel Guides, 2015

Kay, Annie *Bulgaria* Bradt Travel Guides, 2015

Knaus, Verena and Warrander, Gail *Kosovo* Bradt Travel Guides, 2017

Letcher, Piers and Abraham, Rudolf *Croatia* Bradt Travel Guides, 2016

Mallows, Lucy *Romania: Transylvania* Bradt Travel Guides, 2017

Phillips, Adrian and Scotchmer, Jo *Hungary* Bradt Travel Guides, 2010

Rellie, Annalisa *Montenegro* Bradt Travel Guides, 2015

WEBSITES Below are just a few of the many websites devoted to Serbia or the wider Balkan region. This selection gives a fairly good cross-section of cultural and historical information, together with a variety of news sources.

w **b92.net/english** Daily news in English

w **balkanalysis.com** Independent news and analysis of the region

w **balkanist.net** News, politics and travel features from the Balkan region

w **balkanology.com/serbia** Helpful information on travel to Serbia

w **iwpr.net** Institute for War and Peace Reporting with coverage of the Balkans

w **mfa.gov.rs** The website of Serbia's Ministry of Foreign Affairs

w **serbia.travel** National Tourist Organisation of Serbia website

w **srbija.gov.rs** Official Serbian Government website

w **stillinbelgrade.com** Belgrade arts, culture and fashion webzine

w **tob.rs** The website of the Tourist Organisation of Belgrade

w **visitvojvodina.com** Information on Vojvodina province

Index

Uroš, King *see* Nemanja, Stefan (Uroš I)
Ušće 316
Ustaša 21–2, 23, 25, 28, 38, 154, 225, 231, 251, 256, 261–2, 345, 387
Uvac and Mileševka Griffon Vulture Sanctuary 10, 330–1
Užice 57, **293–300**, *297*

Valjevo **222–6**, *223*
Velika Remeta Monastery 261–2
Veliko Gradište 187–8
Vienna 24, 47–8, 66, 184, 231, 235, 291
village tourism 81, 305, 309
Viminacium 11, 184, **187**
Vinča 180
vineyards 7, 159, 257, 276, 287, 365
visas 64–5
Visoki Dečani Monastery (Kosovo) 14, 42, 46, 160, 336
Vlachs 2, 12, **40**, 60, 152, 163, 190, 199, 201
Vladičin Han 302, 373
VMRO 21
Vojvodina **227–92**, *228–9*
Vranje **373–7**, *374*
Vranjska Banja 377
Vrdnik Monastery *see* Ravanica Monastery
Vrnjačka Banja 215–16
Vršac 84, **286–91**, *288*
Vučić, Aleksandar 34–5, 151

waterfalls 191, 299, 309, 348
watermills 226, 309
websites 392
west and southwest Serbia 63, **293–337**, *294*
West, Rebecca 38, 123, 149, 345
White Angel of Mileševa 197, 332
wildlife 4–10, 60, 179, 257, 278, 286
wine 82, 84–5, 86, 110, 141, 186, 197, 199, 201, 213, 241, 256–7, 272, 276, 287, 289, 291, 342, 365

cellars 84–5, 160, 201, 257, 276
routes 84–5
wolves 292, 308, 319
World War I 21–2, 47–8, 50, 100, 146, 150, 156, 164, 178, 180, 200, 204, 208, 221, 230–1, 269, 281, 291, 295, 313, 320, 349, 368
World War II 22–6, 38, 48–50, 56, 100, 142, 148, 150, 152, 154–6, 160, 166–7, 174, 178, 180, 184, 198, 200, 203–4, 208–9, 220, 225, 230–1, 248, 250–2, 256, 261–2, 269, 274, 279, 295, 300, 304–5, 313, 315, 320, 333, 349, 360–1, 368, 372

Yugoslav People's Army (JNA) 28
Yugoslavia 1, 3, 17, 21–30, 32–3, 37–8, 41, 47–52, 54–5, 74, 100, 113, 140, 148, 155–6, 159, 164–5, 167–8, 172, 185, 198, 206, 225, 230–1, 269, 299, 305, 313, 320, 323, 333–4, 348

zadruge (extended family groups) 16, 37, 387
Zagreb (Croatia) 21–2, 67, 105, 234, 262–4, 266, 269
Zaječar **339–43**, *340*
Zapadna Morava River 3, 216, 296, 300
Zasavica Special Nature Reserve 5, 10, 265
Zastava car factory 206, 208
Zemun 99, 100, **161–5**, *162*, 175 *see also* Belgrade
accommodation 120–3
eating and drinking 128–33
what to see and do 162–5
Zeta 12
Žiča Monastery 209, **212–13**
Zlatar Mountain 330–1
Zlatibor (Kraljeve Vode) **304–8**, 308–12
Zrenjanin 10, 285–6
župan (patriarchs) 16, 37, 387
Zvonačka Banja 370

INDEX OF ADVERTISERS

Travel the Unknown 1st colour section